FLORIDA STATE
UNIVERSITY LIBRARIES

APR 0 5 2001

TALLAHASSEE, FLORIDA

PROTECTIONISM TO LIBERALISATION

Protectionism to Liberalisation

Ireland and the EEC, 1957 to 1966

MAURICE FITZGERALD
Loughborough University

Ashgate

Aldershot • Burlington USA • Singapore • Sydney

© Maurice FitzGerald 2000

All rights reserved. No part of this publication may be reproduced, stored in a retrieval system, or transmitted in any form or by any means, electronic, mechanical, photocopying, recording or otherwise without the prior permission of the publisher.

Published by
Ashgate Publishing Ltd
Gower House
Croft Road
Aldershot
Hants GU11 3HR
England

DA
964
.E85
F57
2000

Ashgate Publishing Company
131 Main Street
Burlington, VT 05401-5600 USA

Ashgate website: http://www.ashgate.com

British Library Cataloguing in Publication Data
FitzGerald, Maurice
 Protectionism to liberalisation : Ireland and the EEC, 1957 to 1966
 1.European Economic Community - History 2.Ireland - Foreign relations - Europe 3.Europe - Foreign relations - Ireland
 I.Title
 327.4'15'04

Library of Congress Control Number: 00-110602

ISBN 0 7546 1456 5

Printed in Great Britain by
Antony Rowe Ltd, Chippenham, Wiltshire

Contents

List of abbreviations   vi
Acknowledgements   viii

    Introduction   ix

1   Small power and peripheral: Ireland in the 1950s   1

2   From the OEEC to EFTA, 1957 to 1959   31

3   Ireland's first EEC application, 31 July 1961   103

4   De Gaulle's refusal of the UK, 14 January 1963   171

5   The 1965 Anglo-Irish FTA agreement   237

6   Ireland's European integration, 1957 to 1966   291

    Conclusions   327

Bibliography   *335*
Notes   *361*

List of abbreviations

Please note that the abbreviations presented here are used extensively throughout both the text and footnotes; the first time that any one is used, it is also given in its full form.

ACE	European Community Archives, Villa Il Poggiolo, Florence
AIFTA	Anglo-Irish Free Trade Area
AnCO	An Chomhairle Oiliúna
BBC	British Broadcasting Corporation
B/T	(UK) Board of Trade
CAB	Cabinet Minutes (in both Irish and UK archives)
CAP	Common Agricultural Policy
CIO	Committee on Industrial Organisation
CRO	(UK) Commonwealth Relations Office
D/A	Department of Agriculture
D/EA	Department of External Affairs
D/F	Department of Finance
D/I&C	Department of Industry & Commerce
D/J	Department of Justice
D/T	Department of the Taoiseach
D/T&P	Department of Transport & Power
D/UhÉ	Office of Uachtarán na hÉireann
DDE	Dwight D. Eisenhower Library, Abilene, Kansas
EC	European Communities
ECA	Economic Cooperation Administration
ECSC	European Coal and Steel Community
EDC	European Defence Community
EEC	European Economic Community
EFTA	European Free Trade Association
EPC	European Political Community
EPU	European Payments Union
ERP	European Recovery Programme
ESB	Electricity Supply Board
ETA	European Trading Association (FO terminology)

Euratom	European Atomic Energy Community
EU	European Union
FO	(UK) Foreign Office
FRG	Federal Republic of Germany (West Germany)
FTA	Free Trade Area
GATT	General Agreement on Tariffs and Trade
GC	Government Cabinet Minutes (often abbreviated as G)
GDP	Gross Domestic Product
GIS	Government Information Services
GNP	Gross National Product
HST	Harry S. Truman Library, Independence, Missouri
ICTU	Irish Congress of Trade Unions
IDA	Industrial Development Authority
IMF	International Monetary Fund
IRA	Irish Republican Army
IUE	European University Institute, Badia Fiesolana, Florence
JFK	John F. Kennedy Library, Boston, Massachusetts
LBJ	Lyndon B. Johnson Library, Austin, Texas
NA	National Archives, Bishop Street, Dublin
NATO	North Atlantic Treaty Organisation
NFA	National Farmer's Association
NIEC	National Industrial Economic Council
OECD	Organisation for Economic Cooperation and Development
OEEC	Organisation for European Economic Cooperation
PE	European Parliament, Bâtiment Robert Schuman, Luxembourg
PRO	Public Record Office, Kew Gardens, London
RTÉ	Radio Telefís Éireann
Treasury	(UK) Department of the Treasury
UCC	University College Cork
UK	United Kingdom of Great Britain and Northern Ireland
UN	United Nations
UNESCO	UN Educational, Scientific and Cultural Organisation
US	United States of America
USSR	Union of Soviet Socialist Republics
WEU	Western European Union
WP#23	OEEC Working Party Number 23 (similar abbreviations are used for other OEEC Working Parties)

Acknowledgements

I would like to take this opportunity to express my gratitude to the many people who have helped me to realise my goal of completing this piece of research and seeing it in print.

Firstly, I want to thank Professor Richard Griffiths for offering me the chance to work on this subject, for putting his faith in my ability, and for his guidance. I am particularly indebted to Professor Dermot Keogh for acting as my academic mentor, for initially putting the idea of this text into my head, and for supporting me through to its conclusion. Indeed, special thanks are due to both Professor Brigid Laffan and Professor Alan Milward for their courtesy, incise promptings, and intellectual stimulation at a crucial stage of its gestation.

Additionally, I want to thank everyone in the Department of History & Civilisation at the European University Institute, Florence, and at Ashgate for their considerable assistance. It would also be most remiss of me not to mention the generous financial support of the European University Institute and Ireland's Department of Education, as their assistance allowed me to write the PhD that forms the basis of the findings presented here.

In relation to my research, I would like to thank the staff at the following: European University Institute, Florence; European Community Archives, Florence; University College, Cork; University College, Dublin; National Archives, Dublin; University of Leicester; De Montfort University, Leicester; Loughborough University; Public Record Office, London; European Parliament, Luxembourg; Harry S. Truman Library, Independence, Missouri; Dwight D. Eisenhower Library, Abilene, Kansas; John F. Kennedy Library, Boston, Massachusetts; Lyndon B. Johnson Library, Austin, Texas.

Finally, I want to thank both my family and friends for their encouragement and support. I am indebted to my parents – Tom and Jo FitzGerald, to whom this book is dedicated – as well as to Siobhán and Jill, for their unending confidence, faith and love; to them all I wish to redouble my thanks from the bottom of my heart. Ultimately though, I now look to Mark Bell, crediting him for giving my life fulfilment, reason and hope.

Introduction

Ireland and the EEC: past, present and future[1]

In an address he delivered on 15 October 1963 from the White House lawn, on a theme he regularly targeted at Irish people whether in Ireland or the United States of America (US), US president John F.Kennedy told his gathered guests that 'you are building a vigorous, new country which looks to the past with pride and the future with hope'.[2] The point was simple enough: in living for the present and looking to the future, Ireland must not be dominated by its past; the government and nation would need to be farsighted if this was to be achieved. This text focuses on *Protectionism to Liberalisation: Ireland and the EEC, 1957 to 1966*. Thus, the purpose of this introduction is simply to present a coherent and cohesive framework in which Ireland's historic relationship with the European Economic Community (EEC), specifically in the decade after the latter's foundation and initial entrenchment, is keenly examined. This presentation endeavours to fulfil that task in a thoroughly straightforward manner, with the function of this first section being to introduce the analytical and contextual approach within which this text operates, primarily in an effort to establish why this particular subject was chosen, but also in order to explain how this piece of research has been explored. It assesses the means that were employed in this text under four distinct headed sections:

- making some opening remarks about the delineation of this analysis;
- prior to demonstrating the validity of choosing Ireland as an individual case study, while defining the specific timeframe;
- before evaluating the methodological approach employed;
- then explaining the structur, while raising obvious and not so obvious questions, pinpointing specific problems, defining several intermediate conclusions, and generally outlining the direction taken by this exploration into Ireland's earliest links with the EEC.

These elements become more apparent as this introduction itself progresses.

It is the Irish government's own official up-to-date view of why the country originally applied to enter the EEC as a full member, however, which serves as the ideal prelude to this study. Prepared on the topic of 'The European Union and the new Europe' as a component of its formal contribution to the 1996 Intergovernmental Conference, this recent document stated that two fundamental considerations underlay the momentous decision, taken in the summer of 1961 by the taoiseach (Irish prime minister) and his cabinet, for Ireland to attempt – vainly, as it happens – to join the EEC. This assessment asserts that:

- 'it was believed that membership would provide the conditions in which Ireland could best pursue its economic and social development and would offer the best prospect for the protection and promotion of living standards in this country';
- 'it was felt that membership would enable us to participate fully with other democratic and like-minded countries in the movement towards European unity, based on the ideals and objectives to which Ireland as a nation could readily subscribe'.[3]

This text proves that, throughout the 1960s, there was much more to Ireland's proclivity for full membership than this bland modern assessment might at first imply. Indeed, the research presented here firmly places this analysis regarding relations with the EEC between the years 1957 and 1966 into the broader context of the country's experience of European integration in the decades following the Second World War, as successive Irish governments decisively moved away from a political to an economic basis when formulating foreign policy.[4]

Of course, bilateral Anglo-Irish relations have remained of paramount importance to Ireland in the latter half of the twentieth-century. Although not very original, this statement does recognise that this crucial relationship must be constantly borne fully in mind, as it is rather central to a deeper understanding of Ireland's ties with the EEC, whether that question is explored in economic or in political terms. As one celebrated Irish historian, J.J.Lee, has succinctly stated, the potential for the evolution of a patron-client relationship, or even for an inferiority complex to develop, between the United Kingdom (UK) and Ireland has never been beyond the realms of possibility.[5] Concurrently, the *Economist* has made a particularly pertinent point which should not be ignored; it states that:

For centuries, Ireland defined itself in relation to Britain, as a victim. If its much larger neighbour was not subjecting it to physical oppression, then it was wounding its pride with arrogance and condescension. This strain of thinking has by no means disappeared ... but it is far less prominent than before. These days, Ireland has bigger concerns. It defines itself in relation to Europe: an association of nations in which it is recognised as an equal.[6]

Thus, the UK has become a partner for Ireland, if undoubtedly still its foremost; nonetheless, it is only one concern amongst many, no longer necessarily defining Irish identity.

However, despite the relative merits of evaluations and interpretations past and present of Ireland's position within the European setting, it was found in the course of this research that one of the key issues boiled down to answering a relatively simple inquiry:

- Why should Ireland's relationship with the EEC in the period 1957 to 1966 be considered as an appropriate case study for further analysis within the context of European integration history?

In giving an answer to this specific proposition, this introduction was not necessarily intended as some sort of justification for making this particular subject choice. Indeed, illustrating the aptness of choosing Irish-EEC relations, as a matter worthy of inquiry in their own right, has its innate origins more in the realm of presenting an apropos explanation, regarding where this piece of history fits into the current state of the historical literature and research on the issue of Ireland and Europe, rather than acting as an apologia. Consequently, the question became: what is the validity of choosing Ireland as a case study? It is not difficult to explain logically or, if compelled, to defend vigorously the reasons why it proved to be a particularly suitable subject to select in furthering a better awareness of integration history or to demonstrate how it turned out to be as atypical as, though no more so than, any other case study. The fact is that there has been an ever-growing need in Irish history for cabinet, departmental and inter-governmental debates on its European integration experience to be thoroughly analysed.[7]

The essential theoretical point to be kept in mind during the course of this analysis is that Ireland revealed itself to be an excellent example of a semi-peripheral, underdeveloped and dependent state in the second post-war decade, subsisting within a regional/continental economic structure on the one hand, while, moreover, obviously existing within the broader global economy on the other. It went from a position of not being able to take on the full obligations of burgeoning continental free trade in 1957 to being in a Free Trade Area (FTA) with its main market less than a decade later.[8] Within this relatively short space of time, an innovative government jettisoned accepted economic and political dogma to embark upon a fundamentally new foreign policy direction; this was partly because of national preferences being exercised in the face of continental and global economic change, partly as a result of Ireland's ability or inability to negotiate better trading conditions with its neighbours, near and far.[9] The speed of this reorientation and the arguments which advanced or took away from its cause are wholly investigated as this text unfolds, so that the principal supposition – as outlined above – is comprehensively tested.

In this context, the value of any one theorist's work is obviously onerous for historians to determine until it is actually applied; this is attempted in the opening chapter, before being pursued thereafter in the main body of the text.[10] Even then, although it was found that certain parts of a political science theory might apply when others did not, the possibility of using such theories, which in themselves are often more generalised than specific in form, was not excluded. Thus, this text has not slavishly attempted to fit an Irish case study into any one single hypothesis. Nonetheless, even if this examination does not allude to being entirely aware, for example, of all the finer points of past or current debates on core/periphery or dependency theories, their use has still had some benefit. Indeed, in spite of that inherently problematic consideration, this investigation into the history of Irish relations with the EEC in the early years of the latter's development accordingly connoted an ideal opportunity to try to apply such theories. The technique employed consequently does two different things, presenting a Marxist paradigm within which this analysis is placed and, to a lesser extent, utilising a more liberal vein in its evaluation; this is not necessarily a revisionist argument, as the release of archival material has also allowed a certain degree of primary vision that was previously lacking. In doing so, it coincidentally confirms how and why Ireland had made for a good case study within which European integration history may be examined. With theoretical considerations such as those cited perpetually in mind, coming as they do from quite opposite perspectives, perhaps it is more profitable at an early stage in this investigation to deal in a categorical fashion with the great difficulties intrinsic in employing a comparative case study, thus leaving more theoretical issues to the first chapter.

A 'singular' case study and its timeframe[11]

It is imperative to explain why a comparative case study was not extensively employed in the course of this research without any further procrastination, as it might well be argued that one would readily have placed into a more comprehensive context the specific situation pertaining to Ireland. Therefore, prior to delineating the timeframe of this analysis, this portion of the introduction presents a brief dismissal of the merits of a comparative study in this particular instance. In revealing why no definitive comparison was undertaken, this explanation actually helps to solve one of the many problems that faced this research at its outset, as it included making a choice, if any, between a variety of possible comparative case studies. Indeed, an assortment of alternatives were suggested as parallel analyses, but each of these suggestions invariably revealed similar complications; basically, none of the recommendations proffered for this task were found to be practical in fully appraising Ireland's integration experience on the national front or on the international stage, with each presenting impediments that would evidently have limited the ultimate scope of this investigation in utilising the relevant material that was more widely accessible.[12] Yet, this decision to concentrate on Ireland has presented both clear advantages and obvious disadvantages.

With these obstacles firmly in mind, Denmark was seriously considered as a distinctly promising option, but ultimately it was determined that an exhaustive examination was not appropriate; Denmark therefore only acts as a sort of 'shadow comparison', that is a reference point to which Ireland is compared and contrasted.[13] Another nation – New Zealand – is also utilised in this regard, but mostly as a means of contrasting its experience with that of Ireland rather than acting strictly as a comparison.[14] Thus, neither instance detracts from the central focus of this analysis, Ireland's relations with the EEC. This investigation has concentrated precisely on that relationship mainly because an academic analysis of this nature has not been carried out in this way before now. Indeed, it is set in a more international dimension than might be implied by the title and thereby concerns domestic and external aspects regarding relations with the EEC, helping to put Ireland's world position into a clearer context.[15] It is not limited to a national framework, but concentrates on broader international aspects instead, specifically at the European level. Although this research is based on Irish archives and Ireland, it still provides a study that, in many ways, mirrors the experiences of other states on the economic, political and geographic periphery of Europe, some of whom joined these continental organisations in time, others which did not. Consequently, the archival work focused its attention on materials directly related to the subject at hand; this very point is explained in some depth in the next section after some remarks regarding the timeframe.

The period covered by this text encompasses the premierships of Éamon de Valera and Seán Lemass in the years between 1957 and 1966.

Without going into terrible detail, this section briefly now explains why certain subjects were chosen within the context of Ireland's EEC relations in the second post-war decade. It is immediately apparent, however, that they concentrate on specific crisis periods in Dublin's experience of the integration process. Each turning-point subsequently constitutes the basis for a different episode, its causes and effects, to be explored. These crises range from Ireland's participation in the negotiations for a wider FTA in Europe – sponsored by the Organisation for European Economic Cooperation (OEEC) from 1956 – and the subsequent creation of the European Free Trade Association (EFTA) in 1959, to the Irish government's application for full EEC membership in 1961, before extending to the French president's refusal in 1963 of the UK government's bid to participate in the EEC; it then moves from the signing of the Anglo-Irish FTA agreement in 1965 through to the eve of the second application in 1967. This chronological approach, centred as it is on particular crises, is best illustrated in the chapters themselves, the structures of which are explained in the last section of this introduction. Implications resulting from Ireland's experiences of these events are therefore pursued in some detail – relations with the EEC, the effects on trade, Irish neutrality – themes that are elaborated upon more precisely as the research itself progresses and which thus reoccur throughout the central text.

A concise explanation of the general timeframe involved is useful at this juncture as it also helps to explain further what is significant about Ireland as a case study in the context of European integration. This examination covers a decade which specifically encompasses the work of two taoisigh (Irish prime ministers) because this provides a convenient period for analysis, taking in as it does the terms of three governments. An assessment of the influence of these two men on Ireland's European policy has proven profitable as it goes to the heart of this investigation, although historians always have to be careful to make sure that research such as this does not become solely person-orientated, a trap of reification into which it is all too easy to fall. At the same time, however, the perceptions of informed historians regarding central personalities who played exceptionally significant roles in the course of Irish-European affairs still have to be borne in mind; admittedly, this line of investigation has considerable benefits therefore. As was previously noted, the more significant events in the time period around which this text has been constructed include the following:

- the formation of the EEC, plus the aforementioned FTA negotiations, ultimately concluding in EFTA's creation;
- Ireland's first bid to participate fully in the EEC;

- the refusal of the UK application for membership and, by extension, that of the Irish as well;
- the signing of an Anglo-Irish FTA agreement.

Around these landmark events, the central chapters are forged. No single development turned out to be more symbolic though than the opening of Ireland's diplomatic mission to the EEC; it was originally combined with its Belgian mission at Brussels in 1959, but seven years later finally became a separate diplomatic entity.[16] The representational advantages deriving from this initiative should not be underrated in the context of European integration because, in turn, any accruing benefits became much more substantive. The issue of diplomatic relations appropriately emerges as a theme which recurs throughout this analysis.

Of course, this history has previously been recounted in an authoritative analysis by D.J.Maher entitled *The tortuous path: the course of Ireland's entry into the EEC, 1948-73*, which has since proved to be a seminal text for students of Ireland's European integration.[17] There have been other important publications on this subject – including Miriam Hederman's detailed account of *The road to Europe: Irish attitudes, 1948-61*, and Dermot Keogh's indepth examination of *Ireland and Europe, 1919-1989: a diplomatic history* – critical appraisals of which are presented in more detail in a subsequent literature survey.[18] However, it is worth noting that, in his excellent *Irish foreign policy and the European Community: a study of the impact of interdependence in the foreign policy of a small state*, Paul Sharp has put forward the particularly germane theory regarding Ireland's position that:

> ... [the] Irish government pursue[d] a policy of international role-playing after Ireland became a member of the UN in 1956; and ... this policy continued after Ireland became a member of the European Economic Community.[19]

This statement has to be put into the context of Europe's view of Ireland because it is quite clear that economics soon became a more important basis for making decisions. For example, as stated in *La construction de l'Europe*, Pierre Gerbet's opinion – that Ireland was effectively in an economic union with the UK from which it could not disentangle itself – gives added credence to the economic reality of Anglo-Irish relations, while at the same time suggesting the gravity of French president Charles de Gaulle's decision to veto the UK's application for full EEC membership in January 1963.[20] Opinions on the subject abound.

If a considerable amount of information is readily available, an obvious question must thus be posed and answered: how innovative or relevant can this particular piece of research on Irish relations with the EEC between 1957 and 1966 actually be? A considered response to this inquiry is partially to be found in the ensuing section on methodological techniques, as well as through an archival appraisal.[21] Indeed, a rebuttal of this question's validity is followed in the final segment of this introduction by a detailed structural breakdown, along with the submission of some intermediate remarks; it then proceeds onto the opening chapter, essentially an examination of Ireland as a small power and peripheral detailing the theoretical context within which this case study fits. First things first, however, as this next section boils down to answering a central question: what methodological approach is taken to confirm the originality of this material?

Methodological approach

This text explains Irish government attitudes towards European integration in the second post-war decade by concentrating on crisis points or flashpoints; it does so in a fairly subject-oriented manner concerning Dublin's decision-making processes. By necessity, the central themes of this study are concentrated on economic matters, but they deal with other tenets when relevant too, be they of a cultural, diplomatic, ideological, military, political, or social nature. Changes in foreign policy as a corollary of economic realities or political exigencies thus became the 'dependent variable' upon which the rest of this investigation hangs. In the mid-1950s, the reserved views held by de Valera – then in opposition as leader of Fianna Fáil, Ireland's largest political party – on the value of European integration were subsequently even more notable for having been in such marked contrast to the dynamically evolving and, with time, very favourable attitude of his replacement. Speaking in 1955, the former firmly held to his belief that it would be:

> ... unwise for our people to enter into a political federation which would mean that you had a European Parliament deciding the economic circumstances ... of our life here.[22]

His successor was better able to adapt his political views to changing economic circumstances and, indeed, to the grim realities which faced the country, the latter's realism contrasting with the former's parochialism. In

1961, Lemass rather convincingly declared that:

> ... if all the countries of Europe with which we are trading, Britain and the Six, join together in an economic union, we cannot be outside it.[23]

Miscellaneous 'independent variables' – including factors both external and internal, such as diplomatic relations, emigration, domestic politics, trade with the UK – provided the scope within which to realise the aim of concentrating on certain major developments.

The pursuit of these goals was based on an assessment of readily available archives, which was coupled with a comprehensive assessment of influential secondary source material. The primary sources used during this research were based on four main sets of archives, each one fulfilling a certain defined purpose. The reasoning behind these sources reads as follows:

- domestic political considerations and Irish foreign policy – the National Archives at Bishop Street in Dublin (NA);
- various features of Anglo-Irish bilateral relations – the Public Record Office at Kew Gardens in London (PRO);
- the wider Irish diaspora – the presidential libraries of Harry S.Truman at Independence in Missouri (HST), Dwight D.Eisenhower at Abilene in Kansas (DDE), John F.Kennedy at Boston in Massachusetts (JFK), and Lyndon B.Johnson at Austin in Texas (LBJ);
- Ireland's process of European integration – the European Community Archives at the Villa Il Poggiolo in Florence (ACE) and the European Parliament at the Bâtiment Robert Schuman in Luxembourg (PE).

This approach was adopted because it was found that Ireland's relationship with the EEC was influenced by four chief factors, each of which is discussed by means of liberally employing information that came from these sets of complementary sources; it might be noted that the Irish records turned out to be the most useful, not surprising given the subject matter. Each investigative angle is comprehensively dealt with in the bibliography and in turn coupled with an indication of its relative merits regarding Ireland's process of European policy-making; as stated, an in-depth assessment of the current state of the literature regarding this subject was also established as being helpful in putting this research into its proper perspective.[24]

The employment of archival material has obviously helped to negate the dangers of viewing history in hindsight because, in contemplating day-today governmental concerns, the *ad hoc* character of much of the decision-making process was clearly shown. This method had more to do with chronicling daily concerns at certain moments rather than trying to put Ireland into a larger context which it did not necessarily occupy. In addition, this approach prevented value judgements from being made, providing a superior perspective and rational explanation of actions taken, as well as the viewpoints conceived, in this period. Of course, a full awareness had to be maintained that this material was often penned with other purposes in mind. The documentation analysed thus includes speeches written for public consumption and, understandably in that respect, frequently found that these documents were essentially justificatory. This study concentrates on private memoranda from ministers to civil servants and *vice versa*, communications that might alternatively be viewed as cajoling or informing, persuading or even vaguely threatening, in nature and tone. The wealth of recently released resources – not always written with self-justifying motives in mind, but with the development of policy – were supplemented by informal interviews with protagonists, though only to clarify points rather than to construct oral memoirs. The rationale in utilising these specific materials has therefore been worked out in detail and with some care.

The introduction opened with a relatively short section which posed a central question asking why did Ireland attempt to participate in the EEC and why this question is important. It moved on to explore the benefits of choosing this country as a case study by advancing a loose theoretical framework within which this examination operates before then surveying the timeframe within which it sits. Subsequently, in appraising the value of the primary source materials utilised and explaining how this research compliments and consequently extends the current state of secondary literature on the subject of *Ireland and the EEC, 1957 to 1966*, the methodological approach that was adopted has also been briefly analysed. It now concludes with a detailed structural overview of this text's central chapters; although they are in no way definitive, some intermediate concluding remarks are also made before these observations then run into the text. Additionally, this initial synopsis concludes with an attempt to trace the evolving nature of this study; six years of research have culminated in the presentation of these arguments, but doing justice to that is the purpose of the main body of this text.

Structural overview: the major issues at a glance

The purpose of this structural outline is to give some idea as to how this text operates. There are more questions than answers at this stage of the introduction; however, it is crucial to leave anything more than intermediate conclusions to the central text. Of course, it would be a mistake to have had any pre-conceived notions about where Ireland's relations with the EEC fitted into the European integration context. Nevertheless, the questions that must be answered are still fairly obvious; for instance, with regard to Ireland's exclusion from EFTA, the need to analyse in more detail why the UK government was intent on freezing Ireland out was a major issue and one that proved to be particularly arduous to answer. In turn, other more general questions which were raised during this research have included: what did Ireland feel that the EEC could help it to achieve and what could Ireland offer in return? In addition, how did Ireland prepare for this dramatic economic change and how did it view its future prospects within that organisation? Also, what economic and political paths did the Dublin government take after its initial EEC membership bid was refused? In truth, these questions multiplied as the research began to make more progress; their answers become more apparent as the chapters themselves open up, as the archives are fully assessed, and as the documentary evidence is itself presented.

Within this short explanation of how the text works, one central point needs to be repeated: Ireland's relative position in Europe and the world in general needs to be considered with its nearest neighbour constantly in mind. This introduction next blends into a relatively concise first chapter – *Small power and peripheral: Ireland in the 1950s* – the objective of which is fairly self-explanatory from its title. In fact, it is primarily employed as a means of placing Ireland in a proper historical context – both in domestic economic and political terms, but also regarding how it related to the UK, within and without a European framework, as well as its actual position in Europe and in relation to the world at large, including the two post-war superpowers, the US and the Union of Soviet Socialist Republics (USSR). Thus, by reinforcing an essential idea that has already been raised – during the late 1950s and early to mid-1960s, Ireland's remodelled foreign policy accommodated changes in Europe so that it had an economically, rather than a politically, oriented outlook which took account of the Six and the UK – it gives a greater sense of theoretical perspective to the subject here.

The second chapter – *From the OEEC to EFTA, 1957 to 1959* – follows up on this review of the mid-1950s by concentrating upon one particular crisis point, Ireland's exclusion from EFTA as principally effected by the UK government. In describing some of the implications of the creation of EFTA for Irish policies towards European integration, this chapter goes further into the realm of theorising rather than just stating facts. Heretofore, in terms of historical research on Ireland's experience of integration, little emphasis has been placed on the late 1950s; this chapter does something to alleviate that position. Indeed, this text argues that the full implications of EFTA's creation for Ireland have not been properly investigated before; as a direct consequence, many of its effects have thus far been largely ignored. Additionally, this chapter is also a particularly fine example of a crisis point in the history of Ireland's integration into the EEC and for that reason alone – due in part to the fact that such instances are usually considerably revealing, thereby giving a certain focus to what might otherwise have been a sprawling narrative – demonstrates itself to be a practical starting point for this research. Furthermore, within this chapter is an assessment of the significance of the UK's markets as the main conduit for Irish exports and, conversely and intriguingly, Ireland's importance as a market for goods originating in the UK.

At this stage, a third chapter – *Ireland's first EEC application, 31 July 1961* – deals principally with the lead-up to the decision by the Irish government to apply for membership of the EEC in the summer of 1961. This chapter concentrates on the determining processes which led to that decision and analyses two documents in detail, a government White Paper entitled *European Economic Community* and a subsequent *aide-mémoire* that was distributed to the six EEC member states. However, it extends beyond the request itself to the decision taken by the EEC Council in October 1962 to accept the Irish application to negotiate entry, even if only provisionally, thus exploring the paranoia felt at Irish government level regarding the relative lack of progress in the intervening eighteen months before this decision. In turn, it traces how Ireland viewed the UK and the Six, as well as how they saw the former.

Meanwhile, the next chapter – *De Gaulle's refusal of the UK, 14 January 1963* – carries on from there to explore the period prior to and implications of the French president's decision to veto the UK government's application for full EEC membership in the early days of 1963. Once again, Ireland's application to enter the EEC and de Gaulle's refusal can be termed flashpoints for the Dublin government, providing an excellent opportunity to assess its crisis management capabilities, that is how it coped with difficult situations. This fourth chapter subsequently offers an extremely valuable opportunity to explore why, out of the three European Communities (EC), Ireland was really only interested in the EEC; it is immediately apparent that for Dublin neither the European Coal and Steel Community (ECSC) nor the European Atomic Energy Community (Euratom) held any real attraction. Therefore, it leads into an exploration of what course of action was decided upon as the prospect of a return to the 'wilderness' years of the 1950s loomed.

The fifth chapter – *The 1965 Anglo-Irish FTA agreement* –

concentrates on the lead-up to the signing of this bilateral FTA agreement rather than dealing comprehensively with its implications and aftermath, because it is the earlier period which is most revealing in the context of Ireland's European integration. A lack of alternative economic options for Dublin, coupled with the beneficial economic development opportunities offered and, indeed, restraints imposed by this new agreement, make for an especially interesting analysis when Ireland's ongoing preparations for EEC entry are considered. The options from which it could choose are evaluated, as well as the actions taken. This harsh grounding in international economic reality continued for some time after Lemass's resignation in November 1966, ultimately only bearing fruit in January 1973 with Ireland's eventual accession to the EEC.

Finally, in the main body of the text, there is a further review chapter which is more abstract in form – *Ireland's European integration, 1957 to 1966*. This essay is combined and interweaved with the conclusions, before a series of useful appendices holding central documents and statistical tables are presented. The sixth chapter attempts to assess the progress made in Ireland's European integration policy during this decade, comparing and contrasting advances made in politics and economics with detailed interpretations linked to a series of illustrative graphs charting changes in the country's orientation. In this context, bilateral relations with Northern Ireland, the state of the Irish nation, and the personalities intimately involved in this continuously evolving reality are all thoroughly analysed; the sixth chapter draws to a close by looking to the future, a theme reinforced via brief conclusions on the question: why did Ireland's first application fail? Although necessarily a detailed list, the ensuing sections of the text present an extensive bibliography of relevant archival materials and secondary sources, even if the main matter used in the course of this research has already been briefly appraised during this introduction. Other subjects have understandably been dealt with in the course of this research and these have been intertwined with the text.[25]

Clearly, in order to put Ireland into its proper context, its internal economic, political and social workings, as well as relations with its neighbours far and wide, must be outlined. Central to the 'tortuous' course that Dublin followed throughout this era was the fact that its path ran for the most part parallel to – even if it sometimes went counter to or was hidden and meandered from – that of London. Certain decisions and developments outside of its control meant that it had to put its national position into an international perspective. Just like the UK once it decided that it would try to enter the EEC, it became more apparent over time that, if Ireland was ever going to join the Western European mainstream, it must:

> ... follow an extremely straight and narrow path, maintaining the true objective, overcoming disappointments, above all resisting the temptations of plausible but inadequate alternatives.[26]

This history retraces that process in Ireland's case, specifically for the decade that stretched from 1957 to 1966, but obviously it is necessary to begin with something of more immediate import. Therefore, the first chapter on *Small power and peripheral: Ireland in the 1950s* goes much more deeply into the theoretical aspects of this text, as well as providing detailed background to the subject of Ireland's relations with the rest of Europe, and raises the kind of issues that continually recur through the central chapters which then follow.

1 Small power and peripheral: Ireland in the 1950s

An introduction to the island

The island of Ireland is a mass of contradictions.[1] The identities divergently championed in its distinct administrative halves – Ireland and Northern Ireland – only demonstrate the extremely complex nature of the relationships that exist in both countries, between culture and politics, economy and society, as well as the numerous nefarious associations that are perpetuated by linking the past to the present. This chapter concentrates on the singularity of just one of those states in the first two decades following the conclusion of the Second World War, by exploring its experiences as an island-nation and examining an enduring relationship with its UK neighbour, by investigating the economic attractions Europe held and surveying its connections with the wider world. Much of the information that is presented here, however, is only a mirror-image of that which pertains to the aforementioned north-eastern section of the island. Thus, Ireland has to be investigated at a number of different levels – its politics, its inconsistencies, its nationalism, its geography – in order to understand the idiosyncratic disposition which it brought to bear upon its relations with the EEC in the years between 1957 and 1966. Essentially, this short first chapter therefore acts as a passage into the heart of this text.

In her account of *The road to Europe: Irish attitudes, 1948-61*, Miriam Hederman has discerned four features which, in the context of its European neighbours, distinguished Ireland in the immediate post-war period, even if it shared attributes too. She lists them as follows:

- neutrality – although it was able to maintain this stance in the face of considerable intimidation during war-time, pressure to conform did not abate in peace-time, as Ireland self-consciously and proudly remained a case apart from the European norm;
- partition – especially when linked with military developments,

Ireland's position on Northern Ireland's existence within the UK only tended to complicate its subsequent relations with Europe and the wider world;
- emigration – continuing to drain the Irish economy and society of its main resource, the cultural and psychological effects of this process were disastrous, negating most attempts to make economic progress and differentiating itself from the European 'mainland';
- nationalism – Ireland's views of itself and the outside world were both fashioned by its innate need to maintain a distinct cultural identity and through its continuing search for validation.[2]

That clearly leaves room for the question: what did it share with Europe and the UK? Indeed, to these features, additional assertions can be added. Post-war Ireland displayed, perhaps even enshrined, characteristics such as the absence of real reform or modernising processes, as well as a lack of dynamism regarding government-inspired programmes and the frailty of those in existence; to this list can be added a church-state relationship which all too often revealed that the former was at best 'interested' in state affairs, if not also an obstruction to real change, and the fragmentation of Irish politics with its endemic in-fighting, as well as the clientelistic nature and structure of its economics, politics and society.[3] The dangers inherent in utilising umbrella terms or categorisations are of course considerable, but via the use of prisms such as economics and politics, diplomacy and personality, colonialism, religion and nationalism, a clearer pattern emerges. However, theory must not be allowed to dominate at the cost of factual content; 'labels and packaging' of any kind are best avoided if at all possible, even if the application of theory is a very interesting and rewarding means through which to view Ireland's experience of integration.[4] How did it operate in Andrew Moravcsik's model, for example, as an outsider which, with its own national preferences, ultimately tried to negotiate EEC entry as it became more realistic about its position in the world?[5]

Continental Europe knew little of Ireland's political or cultural history, confusing the country with 'England', in much the same way as it still does Scotland and Wales. Its own views of Europe were equally suspect, although it did not necessarily consider the UK or the USSR to be in this politico-geographical category because of an intertwining history with the former and through pure ignorance regarding the latter.[6] Ireland did maintain a significant global presence in political and ecclesiastical circles, but the country was more likely to be known and represented in the Anglicised world of the UK, the US, Australia, New Zealand, Canada, or

South Africa, than anywhere else. Its position on the edge of the 'Great Europe of the geographers – the Europe which stretches from the west coast of Ireland to the Urals, and from the North Cape to the south coast of Sicily' – meant that relations with its European neighbours were always going to be somewhat complicated.[7] A legitimate basic question can therefore be posed straight off: what could Ireland and Europe have had in common with each other? Miriam Hederman has revealed three basic similarities:

- post-war economic crisis – disproportionately sharing the exigencies of the Second World War did not mean that Ireland could continue to remain impervious to world developments in its aftermath;
- changes in domestic politics – Ireland may not exactly have had the same political experiences as its continental brethren, indeed one foreign minister boasted that an indigenous communist party could not exist, but the country was ripe for radical political change;
- relations with the US and USSR – two superpowers now existed, with spheres of influence enveloping the whole globe, so that the world of 1945 was completely different to that of 1939.[8]

Each of these points is dealt with in the course of this chapter as the perception of Ireland as a small power and peripheral is introduced in some detail. Beginning with a review of this classification as a theoretical concept, this first chapter then examines Ireland in the context of developments in European integration in the years leading up to the particular period under review. A survey of the Irish political landscape within this European framework follows, before the concept of nationalism is explored. This chapter concludes with an investigation into the dramatic and dynamic changes in the orientation of Irish foreign policy at this time as economic considerations began to become more important than political ones.

So, what in brief can be said of Ireland in the post-war era by way of introduction? Covering an area of around 70,000 square kilometres, with a population of about 2.8 million inhabitants, Ireland was a relatively small and insignificant country in this post-war period.[9] This state of affairs was even more the case in the context of a Cold War that was dominating Western thoughts and actions, following on from a worldwide conflict which had only just previously devastated Europe, but which had largely bypassed the country. Its geographical position in the shadow of the UK and as an island on the fringes of the European mainland, with a poor transport infrastructure and a lack of good communications links, contributed to a sense of inversion and isolation which permeated to the core of a conservative and fairly undynamic political structure. Its insularity regarding the continent of Europe was not a new phenomenon or the wish to expand its influence there a new desire; only by combining both of these would Ireland maintain its individuality. This was projected on the European stage through its diplomats who, ever since the early 1920s, apart from being 'highly educated' and in the possession of 'sound judgment', were expected:

> ... [to] possess a European culture ... We cannot force our narrow farouche insularity on Continentals ... At least two Continental languages besides Irish and English should be laid down as fundamental condition.

The capacity of Irish representatives to do their jobs was not always beyond question, partly because of the fact that their instructions were sometimes not of the highest quality.[10]

Socially, Ireland was haemorrhaging: 'More than half of those who left school in the early 1950s had emigrated by 1961'.[11] For the most part, they went to high-wage economies in the Anglicised world; indeed, even when its status as a *de jure* 'republic' was established in 1948, Ireland's UK emigrants still enjoyed an unusually 'privileged citizenship status'.[12] At least this emigration process meant that unemployment stayed manageable – around 6.2% of the total active population in 1957 – but, as Kieran Kennedy has pointed out, this meant that, 'uniquely among European countries, the level of total employment was less (by about 17 per cent) than in the 1920s'.[13] That year, Gross National Product (GNP) was US$550 per head, which might have compared well to Greece, Spain, Portugal and Southern Italy, but bore no relation to any of the rest of the Six, or to Denmark and the UK for that matter; Irish *per capita* income that year was 46.3% of the latter's total, a figure which promised little sign of improvement.[14] The situation was becoming drastic; the continued economic viability of the state itself was seriously at issue, as solutions other than emigration were needed. Indeed, a radical economic and social overhaul of the country was required, even if the politicians did not themselves appear to be up to the task; it was a slow process facing up to the fact that this could only be done in the realm of Anglo-Irish relations working within the context of Europe. Only with the emergence of a vibrant new administrative elite, especially after 1959, was the government's economic direction transformed; the problems were monumental, but not necessarily insurmountable or in any way unparalleled. More detail on their extent in the post-war years is needed before explaining how the government went about solving them.

Ireland's world position[15]

Immanuel Wallerstein, author of *The capitalist world-economy*, uses the term 'semiperipheral' to describe countries positioned on the 'outer ring of Europe', the economies of which can neither be described accurately as core or peripheral; in turn, his definition is partly based on what he terms as the 'productive activities' of semiperipheral countries. Indeed, he says that: 'In part they act as a peripheral zone for core countries and in part they act as a core country for some peripheral areas'. In addition, he expounds upon this assertion by stating that:

> ... the mark of a 'non-socialist' semiperipheral country in comparison to a core country is: a larger external and a weaker internal property-owning bourgeoisie; a better-paid professional sector and a more poorly paid sector of fully proletarianized workers, but a far larger (and probably worse off) sector of semiproletarianized workers.

Notwithstanding this author's obvious political leanings – a Marxist view of history in itself being of no more or less value than any other validly arguable perspective – this designation as a semiperipheral can be applied to Ireland with some degree of success. Martin Mansergh, Fianna Fáil's official historian, has graciously conceded that some of the best books on the history of his party 'are written from an intelligent Marxist historical perspective'.[16] It is reasonable to argue, for instance, that extranational economic interests – such as absentee landlords and multinational companies – can be identified as the external bourgeoisie using this terminology, just as domestic business interests and larger farmers might be seen as the internal bourgeoisie. In this regard, it is worth noting that, in *Rethinking development: modernization, dependency and postmodern politics*, David Apter feels that:

> Radical dependency theory, like the marxist critique of capitalism from which it derives, focuses on relations between center and periphery. It shifts the focus away from endogenous to exogenous causes of class polarization, a process universalized by such instrumentalities as multinational corporations and compradore classes. Dependency theory thus attacks liberal modernization theory at the point of discrepancies

between its theory and practice, and, systematically, as a discourse.[17]

The value of this approach becomes more apparent as the chapters themselves progress, but is obviously only taken in conjunction with the facts that present themselves.

Dependency is actually a form of neocolonialism, applied and enforced through the use of economics – as opposed to military or political means – in order to retain control over former colonies. Westminster may not have exercised *de jure* control over Ireland's economy for the major part of this century, but the decisions it took in regard to European economic integration indicate that it exercised an influence which suggests *de facto* dominance or at the very least an overbearing influence. Of course, this can hardly be said to have been the fault of the UK governments concerned. However, it still remains difficult to classify Ireland in this period as either a dependent or as an interdependent country; neither category is totally satisfactory. Barbara Stallings, author of *Economic dependency in Africa and Latin America*, has explained the difference that exists between dependence and interdependence through the utilisation of export and import figures. Using this classification with regard to dependence, for instance, she states that:

> ... most of the underdeveloped countries depend for a majority of their exports and imports on one single advanced nation, while that nation, in turn, does only a small amount of its trade with the underdeveloped country ...

On the other hand, again using these same sets of criteria, she then goes on to add that:

> Interdependency ... might be exemplified by an industrialized country which trades with many countries (in that respect, it is not totally independent), but only a small portion of its trade is carried on with any one nation.

Obviously, Ireland does not fit easily or exactly into either classification as it was somewhere in between the two. Although this exercise demonstrates the relative needlessness of trying to pigeonhole Ireland into any one category ahead of another – indeed, into any one theory ahead of another – it proves to be a useful prism through which to view its experiences.[18]

In addition, by way of illustration of the uses of available political science theories, it might be pointed out that Immanuel Wallerstein perceives that there are two main sets of semiperipheral government policies which are utilised in times of global economic downturn that often lead to a worsening of a particular economic situation rather than to its intended alleviation. First of all, he offers the logical view that: '"Protectionist" measures can turn out to be merely obstacles whose very existence encourages the multinationals to determine new ways of hurdling them'. Significantly for this case study, Fianna Fáil, on resuming power in 1957, endeavoured upon a rather dramatic turn-around in its policy towards multinationals, reversing its position from opposition to support. This policy switch was a strong indication that economic reality was beginning to bite into Irish nationalist dogma.

Secondly, Immanuel Wallerstein has also stated that: '"Import substitution" may simply involve substituting one kind of import dependence for another, thereby creating an even worse "technological dependence"'. In truth, this consideration – which is evidenced by an investigation into the composition of imports in the next chapter *From the OEEC to EFTA, 1957 to 1959* – clearly applies in the Irish case. Notably, this statement can also be extended to discussing Ireland's peculiar export dependency, in turn leading this analysis to question profoundly the perspicacity of the economic choices pursued, as this policy continues beyond the period of this study. What were the benefits of swopping economic reliance from any one area to another, that is from the UK to Europe? Thus, the concept of Ireland's dependency upon the UK is a theme which understandably recurs throughout this research.

In applying a more liberal model to this Irish case study, a political scientist such as Peter Dicken, author of *Global shift: the internationalization of economic activity*, would feel more inclined to point out that what he terms as the 'relatively simple pattern' of core and periphery trade structuralisation no longer applies today because, as he says, in the past few decades trade flows have become far more complex than that. However, this model still describes a basic reality, even if it is through an over-simplified process, especially when he talks of this view of the world being divided into a '*tripartite* geographical structure of core, semi-periphery and periphery'. Indeed, Peter Dicken also takes an interesting instance which demonstrates why Ireland is in many ways a good case study to select. When the opportunity arose in 1948, Ireland did not in fact join one of the leading post-war mechanisms – that is the General Agreement on Tariffs and Trade (GATT) – used to stop the protectionist policies of the 1930s enduring. Irish governments did not appear to be terribly interested in reducing tariff barriers in particular or, subsequently, in prohibiting trade discrimination in general. Ireland eventually only joined the GATT in 1967. By then it had already been adhered to the International Monetary Fund (IMF) and the World Bank for over a decade, when the country was in fact led by John A.Costello governing a coalition of the main parties in Dáil Éireann (lower house of parliament) other than Fianna Fáil. Thus, Ireland was not necessarily totally outside of the economic and financial mainstream, but, when compared to more established Western norms and structures, it was frequently found to be operating quite differently. It was treading its own peculiar 'tortuous' path; the significance of this statement only becomes readily apparent as the central chapters progress, but it can also be partially explained in the context of other countries experiences.[19]

Undoubtedly, especially in agricultural terms, it might well have proven possible to compare the relationship between Ireland and the UK with that of Denmark and the UK or New Zealand and the UK. However, a factor which would have had to be taken into account is that these countries related completely differently to the global economy. Indeed, they had divergent political formations and social experiences. Not unlike Ireland though, the Danish economy, while largely dependent upon the UK, was rather underdeveloped and too based on agriculture in the early 1950s. The increasing importance of Sweden and West Germany to Denmark could hardly have been ignored in such a context, however, analogous relations such as Irish ties to the US notwithstanding. Simultaneously, of course, both Ireland and Denmark prospered and suffered from their proximities to more powerful and precocious neighbours, so much so that even if it was not an ideal comparative, there was invariably the point that Denmark did not necessarily need to be. Regardless of arguments for or against comparisons being made between these two countries, it is clear that Denmark was still developing and adapting faster than Ireland to the new world trading conditions; the bald fact that, in the early stages of the period 1957 to 1966, the latter's Gross Domestic Product (GDP) *per capita* was just under twice that of Ireland could hardly be disregarded. Indeed, by the end of that ten year period, the true extent of the discrepancy between the two countries economies was evidenced by the fact that the new figure was over twice that original amount. Denmark was quickly becoming integrated economically with other European economies, while Ireland's comparative process of adaptation was much slower; the Danish economy was obviously taking off at a far faster pace. Of course, the different outcomes for the two economies have had various external and internal factors, some shared, but many differing.[20]

What about Ireland and New Zealand? To paraphrase a recent assertion regarding the latter's relations with the UK: it is scarcely possible on this globe to be closer to the influence of Britain or the pull of its open markets than Ireland, indeed the pattern of production and trade in this neighbouring country was shaped almost entirely by Britain's own history and development.[21] An interesting aside, of course, is to place where Ireland came on the UK's list of priorities; in the context of the difficulties that the UK prime minister faced in winning the argument that they should enter the EEC it can be argued that, firstly, he had to convince a sceptical cabinet, closely followed by the Conservative party themselves, then he would also have to persuade the Commonwealth and, in turn, EFTA; Ireland would be very low on that list.[22] New Zealand contrasts with Ireland as much as, if not more so than, it may be said to have been in common. Its provision of wool, lamb and mutton, as well as butter, to UK markets meant that it actually had a GDP *per capita* at the end of the 1950s which was higher than that of the UK; even if it was not developed industrially, it was quite the opposite of poor, having 'one of the world's most comprehensive and lavish welfare states', as well as a population two-thirds the size of Ireland's.[23] Oriented somewhat similarly, New Zealand's economy concentrated on agriculture and was dependent upon the UK; however, it also had considerations such as maintaining its economic position within the framework of the British Commonwealth firmly in mind. Ireland was searching for another solution altogether.

Rather than choosing Denmark or New Zealand as a comparative case study, it has proven to be more relevant to note that Faysal Yachir – author of an interesting article entitled 'The future of Southern Europe: Canada or Puerto Rico?' – posed a question in relation to the Mediterranean countries that can as easily be applied to Ireland in the present as in the past. It further demonstrates that including a detailed comparative case study was of little relevance in an investigation centred on Ireland's own peculiar historical situation. The use of numerous reference points to various countries – different or similar to Ireland – was more profitable than comparing it to just one country and, in the end, threw added light onto the central study. What Faysal Yachir's examination actually does is to make the point that the EEC offered Southern European nations, and by extension countries like Ireland, the chance:

> ... to be part, even be it as a poor relative, of a metropole of the world economy. Between dependence alone and dependence as part of a dynamic and powerful grouping, the choice has certainly been made easier by the desire to strengthen the newly acquired democracy and by the cultural proximity to northern Europe ... [and has] perhaps also been guided by the hope of a greater prosperity.[24]

This prospect of economic betterment is literally what guided Ireland; it has not historically had the same type of relationship with the UK that either of the polar opposites Canada or Puerto Rico have had with the US, its own peculiar experiences putting it somewhere between the two. What is clear is that modern Irish industrialisation only really dates from the 1960s. 'The Republic of Ireland ranks', according to Liam Kennedy, 'among the late industrialising countries of the European periphery and the Third World'; what is important about it is that Ireland is a 'particular instance of economic transformation in a peripheral region'.[25]

Irish fealty for the concept of European integration?[26]

Ireland's commitment to the European concept is well known, but the path which the country took in the years after the Second World War has been too well trodden by previous analyses for it to be taken up again in any depth here. Nonetheless, a brief assessment of the principal developments serves as an introduction to the substantive issue at hand. Just how enthusiastic was Ireland for European integration? Although it was not allowed to join the United Nations (UN) immediately after the war's conclusion – indeed, it only eventually entered towards the end of 1955 – Ireland took part in the Economic Commission for Europe which was based at Geneva in Switzerland, although only in a non-voting capacity. This was the first step that it would take on the road to European unity, a concept which was new for Ireland and one which fell on 'virgin soil' that was waiting to be cultivated. As Miriam Hederman says:

> It would not have the historical pull such ideas exercised on the 'mainland', neither would it appear as a particular threat. Its appeal ... was as a means of getting out of the straight-jacket of British-Irish preoccupations ... [from] a relationship which ... had become stifling.[27]

Set up as a regional commission of the UN Economic and Social Council on 28 March 1947, this initial grouping was intended:

> ... [to] initiate and participate in measures for facilitating concerted action for the economic reconstruction of Europe, for raising the level of European countries, both among themselves and with other countries of the world.[28]

As a pan-European institution, its regular meetings offered Ireland an additional 'escape-route' away from post-war isolationism, just as the wider world had traditionally offered Ireland an avenue away from religious intolerance or economic strife.[29]

Over the next number of years, the 'road to Europe' would, starting with the European Congress of The Hague attended by Irish delegates in 1948, see the creation of a variety of European institutions such as the Council of Europe, the European Court of Human Rights, the ECSC, Euratom, and the EEC. As John A.Murphy has written:

> In these post-war years, the country was beginning to learn the first faint lesson that her destiny might have to be worked out in a European context as well as in an Anglo-Irish one.[30]

A haphazard pattern of representation, both at the European and at a global level, continued to symbolise Ireland's attempts at broadening its international outlook.[31] Domestic political parties would leave their own individual imprint on how the country was perceived abroad. Beginning with the Fianna Fáil government in 1947, via a policy subsequently carried through by the Inter-Party coalition government of 1948 to 1951, the country also participated fairly enthusiastically in the European Recovery Programme (ERP) – more commonly known as the Marshall Plan – sponsored by the US government. The European participants in ERP initially met in Paris on 12 July 1947 and set up the Committee for European Economic Cooperation. The then Irish industry & commerce minister, Lemass, 'remarked that Ireland would be very glad to participate in the work of the conference, which was seen as "essential" to improving the economies of Europe'. At a later meeting in Paris on 22 September 1947, de Valera:

> ... warmly welcomed the initiative of a 'friend', the US, in instigating this European self-help programme, enabling all the participants to 'provide for their own needs and preserve their traditional civilisation'.[32]

Ireland, in cohorts with its fellow Europeans in the OEEC, had the opportunity 'to organise and to develop their recovery together'.[33] It remained to be seen if the government could avoid controversy and get on with the task at hand, while edging closer to Europe; at any rate, the receipt of $150 million in grants and loans by 1950 facilitated Irish adherence.[34]

The funds received were administered by the OEEC of which Ireland was a founder member. In brief, the ERP advocated European cooperation on three different levels:

- economic – the OEEC was principally charged with implementing the financial aspects of the Marshall Plan;
- political – the Council of Europe was organised to provide an official forum where European integration could be promoted;
- military – NATO guaranteed the security of countries that were situated on the North Atlantic seaboard.[35]

It can be argued that the ERP had a beneficial and long-lasting effect upon Western Europe, especially as it appears to have profoundly affected Ireland in the process essentially as it 'indicated a shift in emphasis away from the diaspora to Europe ... a triumph of geography over history'.[36] Washington's foreign policy promoted this change, feeling that the 'future of the country was clearly going to be within the framework of closer European integration, rather than in some kind of undefined Anglo-centric or Catholic-oriented world'.[37] Although its precipitous parting from the British Commonwealth on 1 September 1948 may not have been interpreted subsequently as the most clever of economic or political moves, it did mean that Ireland was going to have to look elsewhere for inspiration and sustenance; thus, Europe's pull-factor was growing, as much out of necessity as out of desire.

On 5 May 1949, Ireland became a Council of Europe founder member, a political arena which allowed for open debate and the exchange of ideas by bringing 'together all European parliamentary democracies'.[38] With European unity as its goal and the protection of human rights a priority, the Council of Europe subsequently acted as a direct link to later institutional developments such as the European Parliament through its embodiment and promotion of democratic European unity. Ireland – its foreign minister, Seán MacBride, in particular – had 'seized on the opportunity afforded by membership of the OEEC and the Council of Europe to establish links outside the English-speaking and Irish ethnic world'.[39] In Dáil Éireann, soon after the formation of the Inter-Party government, MacBride was moved to say:

> I referred to it ['United States of Europe'] not to suggest that it was a practical possibility at the moment, but to convey to the House that it was one of the plans that are being discussed in Europe at present, not by Governments but by Parliaments in Europe independently of Governments. We here should try to keep abreast of political developments in the international sphere ... we should know what things are being discussed by them and ... think out our attitude in advance. We should not wait until a *fait accompli* is presented to us.[40]

He reaffirmed that Irish 'sympathies' were with Western Europe because of the country's belief in democracy and its firm attachment to the 'principles of Christianity'. Ireland could not remain insulated from global affairs – 'isolationism' had indeed become 'impossible' – so it was better to work within the context of this new reality.[41]

One year later, on 13 July 1949, MacBride again spoke in Dáil Éireann about these new advances in Western Europe politics, although he noted the 'number and multiplicity of international organisations'. The issue of Irish delegates in the Council of Europe's Assembly in Strasbourg was divided according to their representation in the national parliament, even if the foreign minister stressed the importance of these representatives then working together and appearing to work together. MacBride was pleased to announce that Ireland's financial contribution to this organisation was based upon population, while the number of delegates was weighted in such a way that small countries were over-represented.[42] As the Minister for External Affairs, he was not averse to making more sensible statements as well regarding the European developments which would impinge upon Ireland. Indeed, he even encouraged the new parliamentarians at the Council of Europe to empower themselves; he said:

> ... the members of the Assembly themselves will take things into their own hands ... That may be bad for the Foreign Ministers concerned, but it may be quite good for the development of the idea of European federation.[43]

Other than MacBride, who served as an OEEC vice-president from February 1950, however, there did not appear to be much enthusiasm for the work of the Council of Europe amongst Irish political leaders, especially when the partition issue did not attract the kind of attention in that forum which they felt that it deserved.[44]

Several interventions from Irish delegates – such as de Valera, the Fianna Fáil deputy Seán MacEntee, or the Labour party leader William Norton – degenerated into acrimonious denunciations of partition no matter what the subject was at hand. If Ireland was not going to receive satisfactory European support for ending partition, it was not going to pay anything more than lip-service to an idealised vision of a federal European superstate which they did not necessarily support. Irish politicians, particularly crucial figures such as de Valera, did not consider European unity to be an end in itself, but only as a means to an end. Indeed, his own views on integration were gradualist, if not minimalist. As Miriam Hederman has said: 'the end he [de Valera] envisaged was the cultural, social and economic progress, in a gradual way, of all the peoples of Europe'.[45] Conor Cruise O'Brien has been scathing of contributions such as these emanating from Irish politicians; he has written:

> Our Parliamentary delegates to the Council of Europe seemed to devote their time to making speeches about partition; speeches which were designed to be read at home, but which unfortunately had to be listened to abroad.[46]

More progressive views emanated from Ireland too, but they tended to be in the minority.

In a meeting on 11 April 1949 with Dean Acheson, the US secretary of state, the Irish foreign minister encouraged the US to bolster European economic and political integration. As far as the latter was concerned: 'Europe would thus need even more support, with the promulgation of shared political ideals, as well as demonstrable and demonstrative actions, to counteract the threat of communism'.[47] Two years later, on 14 March 1951, he addressed a gathering of American journalists on a wide variety of subjects including the Council of Europe and the OEEC, stating 'that Ireland continued to endorse the wider concept of a united Europe, both through greater trade liberalisation and through the establishment of a European parliamentary system'.[48] On 1 October 1953, this theme was expanded on when Lemass addressed a similar audience; he said that 'far from wanting to exclude itself, Ireland had been actively seeking to play a role in the international arena ... He stated that Ireland's participation in the Council of Europe and the OEEC was further evidence of this desire'.[49] However, Ireland's innate enthusiasm for the economic, social and political aspects of the ERP was not mirrored by a similar attitude to military matters.

Just as it was positing itself firmly into the Western world, Ireland, although fervently anti-communist, decided not to participate in any European defence mechanisms. The stated view of the Dublin government was that it could not participate in military alliances, firstly because of Ireland's inherent attachment to a policy of neutrality and, secondly, as a result of the more practical matter that resulting military cooperation with Great Britain would entail a full political recognition of its territorial integrity thus contradicting *Bunreacht na hÉireann* (Irish constitution of 1937).[50] Therefore, Ireland's partitioning would have been cemented. The fact that moves towards European integration were aimed at the rebuilding of war-torn economies and the avoidance of future conflict does not appear to have been motive enough for the Irish government to change its policies.

Ireland did not sign the Brussels Treaty of 17 March 1948, in which five European powers – Belgium, France, Great Britain, Luxembourg, and the Netherlands – together 'agreed to establish a common defense system and to consult on economic and cultural matters', in what was essentially a cooperative agreement, or the Western European Union (WEU) which was later to devolve from it following an abortive attempt at a European Defence Community (EDC).[51] Indeed, four Irish members of the Consultative Assembly of the Council of Europe had voted against the 'Schuman Plan' of August 1950 which 'recommended the creation of a single, integrated European Army', despite the EDC idea having the considerable support of the Irish foreign minister. MacBride, then President of the Council of Foreign Ministers, was not at one with his fellow countrymen, even those belonging to parties which were in the coalition government of which he was a senior member. In truth, the EDC did not even attract serious debate in Ireland, which partly explains why the government was making such a mess of its participation in a much more serious military proposition.[52]

Ireland did not choose to participate in the North Atlantic Treaty Organisation (NATO) of 4 April 1949 either, an expanded military alliance which also included the US and Canada, as it guaranteed to protect its members sovereignty from outside military aggression. The government was not prepared to accept the inviolability of the border with Northern Ireland, but in so doing was not part of the European mainstream, in the process eschewing the geographical, ideological and political reasons that said Ireland should be in NATO.[53] The feeling that partition was a serious anomaly within Western Europe was not one which was shared by many people outside of Ireland's borders; observers of Irish politics had moved on and had become bored with the question. Indeed, when Marshall Aid was politicised by the US government to take in a security dimension in the early 1950s, 'Ireland was the only ERP country which was unwilling to heed this remodelling and, therefore, was suspended from the programme'.[54] Despite taking some positive steps on emerging from its war-time isolationism – such as the fact that it was the first country to accept the jurisdiction of the European Court of Human Rights by signing the convention on 4 February 1950, though this move was partly undertaken 'to press for changes in the conditions of the Catholic minority in Northern Ireland' – more substantial integration developments began to pass Ireland by.[55]

Just as the government was able to sign up immediately to the European Payments Union (EPU) – an organisation established by the OEEC and the US wing of the ERP, the Economic Cooperation

Administration (ECA), in 1950 – the ECSC was instituted without its participation and indeed with little interest shown by Ireland; as Peter Sutherland has written:

> From the outset there was less than adequate interest in European integration in Irish political circles. Thus the reaction to the Coal and Steel Community, the Treaty for which was signed in April 1951, was one of almost total lack of interest, and such interest as there was seems often to have missed the point ... After all the fundamental intent as expressed in the Preamble was 'to lay foundations for institutions which would give direction to a destiny henceforth to be shared'. Notwithstanding the fact that coal and steel were of limited direct economic interest here a greater concern might have been expected for an event which presaged a developing European Union.[56]

Ireland had missed the larger political picture, the reasons for and implications of European integration. Similarly, a European Defence Community (EDC) was debated – and rejected by the French National Assembly in August 1954 – without attracting much Irish interest; the same would happen when the ECSC Six met at Messina to consider the future of integration in June 1955. Although the UK followed those proceedings and the work of the subsequent committee headed by the Belgian federalist, Paul-Henri Spaak, they were only interested in trying to channel the discussions along 'lines amenable to themselves'. The recommendation of the Spaak committee that a common market was the next logical step thus proved to be anathema to London.[57]

Ireland did not appear to have readily understood the implications either, even when substantial progress was made by the Spaak committee by the time that the Six met less than a year later at Venice. A distinctive pattern had been set, Irish politicians generally exhibiting certain limitations in looking beyond the opinions of their UK counterparts; they really did not show an understanding of what was happening in European economic or political terms. This might not have mattered so much except that Europe looked beyond Ireland's ability to read London's intentions and thought processes to its own capacity to be an integral part of the European experiment; it may have had a 'much closer historical experience of the British' than most other European states, but this could just as easily be interpreted as a disadvantage as much as it was an advantage.[58]

De Valera's considerable shadow

Irish governments did not show any signs of real enthusiasm for European integration in the early 1950s beyond the usual platitudes. Even in rhetoric, the substance of national interest weighed heavily. Thus, the Council of Europe was acceptable only because it was no more than an 'instrument of co-operation'. The May 1951 general election saw de Valera back at the helm, this time at the head of a weak minority government. Unable as a consequence to pursue anything resembling adventurous policies, Irish politics began to fester. Mediocrity was the order of the day, innovation in domestic or foreign affairs appeared to be unofficially discouraged as nationalism was preserved from any further dilution. Ireland had earned its individual place on the world stage and the taoiseach was not prepared to sacrifice something so substantial for anything ethereal. Indeed, his role in foreign affairs, even after appointing a separate foreign minister to himself in the post-war years, did not lessen. His views should not be looked at in isolation though, as they were generally shared by those around him.

De Valera did not support the previous government's – read MacBride's – efforts to forge a European party political approach, a position espoused by Ireland's fellow 'continental representatives' in the Council of Europe Assembly. Indeed, he regularly said so; in his view:

> They thought they had a Parliament of Europe and that they could immediately divide themselves up into political Parties with the Committee of Ministers acting as a kind of Cabinet of Europe. I felt that was a line upon which we could not proceed, certainly not for a very long time to come.

De Valera reinforced Ireland's categorical position in 1952: 'Membership of the Council of Europe imposes on us no obligation which is inconsistent with our national rights'.[59] The pooling of sovereignty was viewed with suspicion, basically because it was felt that it would bear 'particularly heavily on the small States and to the advantage of the large'.[60] Another thing which was vital to him was the financial cost involved in belonging to such groups; on more than one occasion he held that 'it is important that our means should be strictly taken into account in these international organisation'.[61] Thus, he was not prepared to give up any substantial sovereign control having fought so hard to realise independence in the first place; he was not inclined to be caught for the bill either. Two years later, his opposition went a step further when he dismissed the prospect of Ireland being in any way heavily involved in a 'European Federation'. His fear was that the larger states would protect their own interests and overlook those of the small powers, even if he also stated that:

> Close co-operation for specific purposes, such as the ... 'European Coal and Steel Community' ... was quite a different matter ... he believed, in present circumstances, that that was the most fruitful line to pursue.[62]

However, the point was that Ireland had not joined the ECSC. Thus, there was no substance to the taoiseach's claims beyond grandiloquent attachment to a European success story. The formation of the ECSC in 1951 did not attract much publicity in Ireland, because the truth of the matter basically boiled down to the fact that 'neither coal nor steel played any major role in the Irish economy (other than as imports)'.[63]

De Valera's foreign minister, Frank Aiken, was hardly any better. Out of government in 1949, he felt compelled to say that: 'The proposal of a customs union, as I see it ... means in practice the most wholesale and the most rapid uprooting and re-deployment of working populations and capital equipment ever effected'. Indeed, he deplored its possible short and long-term economic and social consequences.[64] This scarcely suggested the vision needed to realise close economic cooperation with Europe, never mind anything mildly approaching economic unity. In government, Fianna Fáil was hardly any better, developments in Europe were 'going a bit too fast for comfort'. A wait-and-see policy was the preferred option, but this only succeeded in instituting inertia. Ireland had two main difficulties with participation in any grouping resembling an FTA. Miriam Hederman has written that:

- '... first was the severe economic hardship already being endured and the danger of adding dramatically to it before there was some specific aid to cushion the blow';
- '... second was the fear of losing the British market before Irish industry and agriculture had managed to secure a firm footing in European alternatives'.

Ireland was obviously moved by the same selfish motives of national self-interest as any other country. One government official said:

> ... we are very much interested indeed in the European movement; we wish it well, and anything that will not directly interfere with the progress of our own country we shall be most happy to support.

European politicians, however, viewed Irish reservations – for example, about lower tariffs in a customs union – with scepticism. The potential for Irish agriculture was vast, they insisted. Rather than seeing European integration as a threat, they were advocating the concept as a real and necessary challenge. The Dublin government was not convinced, but in doing so was demonstrating its lack of vision beyond the UK for its economic needs.[65]

Ireland was thus involved, though not particularly enthusiastically, in the opening of OEEC negotiations for the setting up of a pan-European FTA in the mid-1950s. Even so, this organisation was having a 'chastening and exhilarating' influence upon the Irish economy. F.S.L.Lyons, writing in his *Ireland since the Famine*, has explained:

> Chastening because, as the early OEEC reports on Ireland made icily clear, standards of productivity and efficiency were among the lowest in Europe, but exhilarating ... because the links with Europe, and even the opprobrious reports themselves, brought with them the possibility of change and improvement, opening the way for the genuine and sustained advance that came at the end of the 1950s.[66]

Notwithstanding the various conflicting attitudes prevailing within each of the participating countries, the Irish government was itself riven by polarised viewpoints – limited not only to the cabinet – which emerged within the individual government departments themselves. The bizarre situation existed in 1957 and thereafter in which, on the one hand, the Irish industry & commerce minister, Seán Lemass, found himself in general agreement with T.K.Whitaker, the Department of Finance secretary, regarding the future direction of the economy; because, on the other hand, these views were in direct opposition to those held by J.C.B.MacCarthy, the Department of Industry & Commerce secretary, and Seán MacEntee and then James Ryan, successive Irish finance ministers. These conflicting and ultimately damaging departmental divisions were only symptomatic of wider deficiencies in the government's economic policy. Indeed, as a direct consequence, Ireland's approach to the whole FTA issue was permanently confused and lacking in coherence throughout this early period.

In truth, the unhelpful identification at the outset of the negotiations process of Ireland as a peripheral nation needing special treatment gave the country a tag that it was not to lose easily and helps to explain why certain countries were, as a result, adamant in not wanting its participation in such an organisation, especially until an initial agreement had been reached by the more enthusiastic or, at least, less-demanding nations. Therefore, after the OEEC negotiations for an FTA themselves collapsed towards the end of 1958, the Seven got on with the process of forming a smaller FTA of their own for the freer flow of industrial products. Ireland – which had been more interested in the question of agriculture anyway by favouring a single European market for farming produce that dated as far back as the 'Mansholt Plan' of November 1950 – was thus excluded.[67] F.S.L.Lyons has shown that agriculture was the key for the Irish economy in stating that:

> Because of her small internal market and her lack of fuels and raw materials, Ireland could not achieve Western European living standards without selling abroad. For her, to sell abroad meant in effect to sell her agricultural produce. In the last resort everything depended upon that. And it was in this sector that the government made its most determined efforts at stimulation.[68]

Dublin did not learn the important lesson proffered on this occasion regarding the setting up and running of international trade organisations; it would continue not to do so for some time. An analysis of Ireland's role in the FTA negotiations, dealt with in the second chapter of this text, moves on to detail the other preoccupations of the government in the summer of 1959 which, pivotally for politicians of all hues, always seems to take precedence ahead of all else, domestic politics and the possibilities of exercising power. Even if at first it appears to be a paradoxical argument, a presidential election, a referendum on proportional representation and a change of taoiseach only combined to distract attention away from the actual governing of the country, with repercussions both at home and abroad.

As the Irish government readily admits today, the attractions of a 'large economic area in which goods, services, people and capital can move freely', as established through the EEC, was a different proposition altogether to the ECSC.[69] Problems would arise though, of course, when Ireland's commitment to European integration was tested more thoroughly by its counterparts. Dublin did not yet appear to appreciate that the EEC was not just an economic development. The German chancellor, Konrad Adenauer, agreed with the French government's view that there was a vast potential for political development as well, especially efforts aimed at consolidating Europe's prevailing peace.[70] In recalling the achievements of European integration on the fortieth anniversary of the Treaties of Rome, the Economist stated that it was important to do so 'because they are too often taken for granted'. It added:

> The European Economic Community ... helped to keep the peace in Europe, by making it even more unthinkable that Germany and France, the adversaries of 1870, 1914 and 1939, would ever go to war again ... tying West Germany firmly to a liberal, westward-looking European block ... it was invaluable in encouraging democracy ...[71]

For politicians in the late 1950s and early 1960s, the political dimensions of European integration would have to be kept in mind. They could not leave the economic benefits of membership blind them to the wider implications of this development or they would be rudely awakened. Ireland was always going to profit handsomely from Europe in comparative terms as it was 'both very poor and very agricultural';[72] but, was it prepared to pay the price?

The political landscape and how it pertained to Europe: Part I[73]

Ireland, the US State Department recently declared, is a 'parliamentary democracy with a long tradition of orderly transfer of power'.[74] In the first decade and a half after the end of the Second World War, this was evidenced by successive changes in government, in 1948 and every three years thereafter until 1957. As the US State Department has pointed out: 'Irish politics remain dominated by the two political parties that grew out of Ireland's bitter 1922-23 civil war'.[75] Having been in power for sixteen years, de Valera lost Dáil Éireann's support following the general election of 1948 and was replaced as taoiseach by Costello, heading up a Fine Gael led Inter-Party coalition government. A decade of relative political instability ensued as governments came and went with alarming regularity. This situation was reflected in the economic inertia which prevailed, as short-term expediency took the place of long-term planning. In 1957, this situation changed when Fianna Fáil won a stable workable majority for the first time since 1944.[76] It was completely aware of how Europe pertained to Ireland because the Irish civil service had produced a memorandum – subsequently approved by the previous government on 18 January 1957 – which, as Peter Sutherland has stated, 'commented prophetically that if Ireland should decide to remain outside the free trade area she would be outside the mainstream of Western European development'.[77] It was from this point in time that Fianna Fáil was able to reestablish the kind of hegemony that it had enjoyed in the pre-war and wartime periods; in addition, however, European integration was now a very serious factor.[78] Nevertheless, a lack of voter confidence in the ability of all the political parties to carry out their wishes for an economic upturn meant that the turnout in the 1957 and 1961 Irish general elections was well below the average turnout for the rest of the first two post-war decades, with average figures of 70.3% and 74.5% respectively.[79]

In turning to the electoral performances of the various constitutional parties in Ireland in the period under review, it is interesting to note their positions briefly on the integration issue, even if it was Fianna Fáil which exercised power throughout this period and well beyond.[80] European economic developments did not have a significant impact upon Irish election campaigns or results; as always, these were determined by more provincial considerations. Fine Gael and the Labour party, the two most important opposition parties, together comprised between one third and a half of the available parliamentary seats at this point in time. However, diverging views on Ireland's role in the integration process only led to a confusion in the opposition's overall tactics; the smaller parties were either too narrowly focused or internally split to cause Fianna Fáil overly-significant electoral problems or to pose difficulties for them with regard to European integration. Thus, in the period 1957 to 1961, Fianna Fáil maximised the use of their absolute majority in the Dáil, easily facing down any opposition that was mustered.

It was thus left to Fianna Fáil on its own to determine the direction that Ireland took throughout this period and the policies that the country would pursue. Fianna Fáil's position as the 'country's largest and most successful political party' was achieved by de Valera, its founder, in the process quickly creating a mass party akin to, what it would like to see itself as, a national movement. Its core support, which transcends the classical left/right divide, has been based on the participation and voting power of small farmers, businessmen and the urban working class, the 'plain people' of Ireland. From 1957 onwards, Lemass embarked upon an economic odyssey in order to modernise the country and to adapt it to the new economic realities, a total contradiction to the enduring protectionist policies of high tariff walls and the exclusion of foreign capital, while supporting state backing of small-scale agriculture, that he had himself enshrined and masterminded in the 1930s. As one commentary puts it:

> The great turning-point of the past half-century of Irish history came at the end of the 1950s. That was when the country abandoned the autarchic social conservatism of Eamon De Valera (who had led the country's struggle for independence) and, under its new leader, Sean Lemass, opened its economy, its society and its politics to the modern world.

Inward investment backing the new industrial development strategy was rapidly followed by foreign funding as the economy began to take off quite quickly. The choices for economic reformation were taken by Dublin, with a shift to outward-oriented economic policies and the establishment of subsidiaries by foreign multinationals from Europe, the UK and the US.[81] Nevertheless, Fianna Fáil would have to go through an awful amount of internal party soul searching before the benefits of European integration were seen to outweigh the drawbacks. It would also do so in the context of failing to reach an appropriate economic settlement with the UK in its 1960 Anglo-Irish trade agreement, finally realising that it would have to look beyond the UK, while never forgetting its importance, in constructing an economic future.

Economic nationalism in a small European state

In 1910, long before Ireland became an independent state, Tom Kettle, the poet and economist who later died on the battlefields that rent Europe apart – not once but twice in a generation – realised the potential that the European continent held for a nascent nation:

> ... if this generation has, for its first task, the recovery of the old Ireland, it has, for its second, the discovery of the new Europe ... My only counsel to Ireland is that in order to become deeply Irish, she must become European.[82]

When Lemass took over as taoiseach half a century later, the inherent contradiction between his party's economic nationalism and the fact that he was governing a small European state at the end of the 1950s could no longer be dismissed away. Certain choices might be made, but others were going to be forced upon them; it was a case of making the best of the given economic situation or remaining implacable until defeated. Ireland had to look to the future, while building upon its past; but, what did this tradition and heritage it had mean?

Writing in *The politics of European integration in the twentieth century*, David Arter refers to three main elements that were present in economic nationalism during the inter-war years. He lists these components, each of which will be dealt with in turn, as follows:

- 'the subordination of the economy and its deployment in the realization of nationalist political goals';

- 'the propensity (rhetorically at least) to seek to organize the economy around the economic heart of the nation, in most cases meaning the peasants';
- that it 'was characterized by an insular and introverted orientation which was essentially antithetical to regional integration'.[83]

Of course, there is the issue of the part played by economic nationalism in larger European nations – such as France under Charles de Gaulle – as well, but this emerges later when the European motives regarding the UK are referred to in some detail; just for now, however, the question becomes: how can each of these elements be applied to Ireland's position within the context of Europe and be of use as historical background?

Firstly, when the author speaks of economic nationalism making the economy and its categorisation a secondary consideration in the pursuit of 'nationalist political goals', what he actually suggests is that this 'meant the zealous protection of any newly-won independence and sovereignty and the related concern to avoid economic dependence on the former Imperial power'. With specific regard to the Irish case, he is thus able to declare that:

> ... a fundamental premise of economic nationalism was the aim of self-sufficiency or autarky ... at its inception in 1926, one of the basic objectives of Fianna Fáil's *coru* (constitution) was to make Ireland ... economically self-sufficient, consonant indeed with ... Eamon De Valera's vision of 'a frugal Gaelic Ireland, gnawed at as little as possible by the worm of civilization, especially the British, and in which there were to be no rich and no poor, but many small farmers and small industries scattered over the country'.[84]

Thus, an argument can be made in support of the idea that subsistence was a good thing and that it was deeply ingrained in the Irish psyche. Indeed, the protectionist policies that were being pursued by the government were viewed as positive factors in the economy, as it was felt that they only brought the realisation of this goal of self-sufficiency closer.

Secondly, David Arter moves on to state that there was a penchant, real and rhetorical, to try to order the financial workings of the state around the 'economic heart of the nation', in Ireland's case meaning those living in rural areas, especially small farmers. Although it was delivered during the course of the 'Emergency' – the government's innocuous looking terminology for the Second World War – one oration in particular by de Valera presented his indefatigable vision of a Gaelic Ireland for a Gaelic people, in the process revealing where he felt the future lay. In his radio broadcast of 17 March 1943, the taoiseach expounded upon his dream of an 'ideal Ireland', addressing the country with a proclamation. He said:

> That Ireland which we dreamed of would be the home of a people who valued material wealth only as a basis of right living, of a people who were satisfied with frugal comfort and devoted their leisure to the things of the spirit – a land whose countryside would be bright with cosy homesteads, whose fields and villages would be joyous with the sounds of industry, with the romping of sturdy children, the contests of athletic youths and the laughter of comely maidens, whose firesides would be forums for the wisdom of serene old age. It would, in a word, be the home of a people living the life that God desires that man should live.

De Valera's vision contrasted with the reality, one in which poverty was widespread, disease such as tuberculosis rampant, and despair enshrined.[85] However, it was also the dogma that dominated the Irish political landscape well into the late 1950s and cannot just be dismissed in the light of subsequent developments and difficulties.

Thirdly, the author asserts that economic nationalism was distinguished by an 'insular and introverted orientation' which was basically antagonistic towards the concept of regional integration, agreeing with the view that it was not until 1960, after years of recession, that:

> ... Fianna Fail 'finally lifted the "green curtain" in favour of greater economic links with the outside world' and, by extension, recognized the failure of its blueprint for autarky.[86]

In the meantime, however, over a decade had been lost, time in which countries like Denmark had made remarkable progress. Ireland's idiosyncratic economic nationalism helped to shape a distinctive foreign economic outlook for fifty years after its formation, years in which other states had initially pursued similar protectionist policies, although afterwards they learnt the valuable lesson that cooperation was more beneficial and thus introduced dynamic changes. Ireland still looked at itself in the context of the UK. Irish nationalism had not allowed it to develop beyond that, but Europe would offer it that opportunity.

As Irish 'ambivalence and ambiguity' endured for some time to come; perpetuated in everything associated with it, it also became characteristic and self-defining – in diplomatic relations, economics, military neutrality, politics, society and, indeed, in its very peculiarity. In supporting this viewpoint, Nina Witoszek cites a convincing argument regarding Ireland's recent history which actually holds that 'Irish nationalism has failed and, indeed, has been long relinquished at an official level'. As evidence of this conviction, she has written that:

> As early as 1966 Conor Cruise O'Brien charged that there was 'no cause for self-congratulation' since the two major national objectives – reintegration of the national territory and restoration of the Irish language – had been quietly abandoned.[87]

The government's endorsement of a European integration policy from the early 1960s was a vital part of that process, even if this decision had as much to do with the failure of Fianna Fáil's economic nationalism as much as anything else. In taking an economic rather than a political course, many fundamentals in Ireland shifted, but many things also stayed the same. Nonetheless, there was no denying the speed of accepted change when the end of Lemass's premiership was compared to the beginning of de Valera's final turn at the helm.

A process that began in part with Ireland's application to join the EEC in July 1961 resulted in the 'tiger economy' of more contemporary times. Indeed, it has been argued that Ireland's newly assimilated identity from this period 'had to resonate with the assumptions, needs, longings and interests of ordinary people', which is what the government banked upon. In fact, through the utilisation of the Irish people in what has been identified as a 'community mobilized in the pursuit of a collective interest', supporting the modernisation of the economy by joining the European integration process, the Irish government continued to use nationalist rhetoric in order to embolden the country's sense of identity. Nevertheless, in comparing the present to the past, Nina Witoszek goes on to say in further commentary that:

> The reality of the contemporary situation in Ireland is one of economic and ideological crisis as socio-economic disparities widen, emigration persists, and unemployment seems as intractable as ever. Nationalist ideology in the North and its relics in the South are seen, at official level, as an embarrassment to the modernizing project. The history taught in schools, official ideology, and the discourse of the media have in the past thirty years promoted a liberal, secular humanism as opposed to the parochial and conservative values of traditional Irish society.[88]

Ireland has been transformed as a result of the modernising process that was exemplified by its official approval of European integration and by its earliest and persistent endeavours to participate in the EEC, but only in certain instances for the better.

In truth, the annual jingoistic celebration of the 1916 Easter Rising against the British forces, which should have reached its climax upon its 50th anniversary, was allowed to tail away instead, embarrassedly marked in a false and fabricated manner that was meant to pass off as unassuming. Writing in 1916, V.I.Lenin hoped that the Irish rebellion, which signified an enlightened attempt by a band of revolutionaries of all hues to attain self-determination, was 'more significant politically' because it took place in Europe; half a century later, the Irish government was doing its best to engender a domestic boom to take advantage of the corresponding economic revitalisation of the Western world, reflecting a revolution in the creation of Irish foreign policy and its enactment.[89] No political doctrine or dogma was going to get in the way of transforming the country, although this did not mean that such changes could not be couched in the language of progressive nationalism. Dating from the late 1950s and early 1960s, Ireland's economic rebirth has obviously had its 'disablements and defects', but these negative considerations are far outweighed by its benefits.[90] The foreign policy orientation of the Irish government changed from being fixated with political purposes to one that was in future going to be dominated by economic dimensions.

It was only during the mid-1950s that services began to overtake agriculture as the nation's most important sectoral employer; indeed, there were still difficulties to come when, for instance, the significance of the industrial sector dipped in 1960.[91] The policies being adopted soon began to realise beneficial effects though. Thus, Ireland was a totally different country back in March 1957 to the one that it was to become by November 1966. Economic nationalism no longer reigned supreme as a stimulus, realism and a degree of imagination had taken its place. It remained to be seen whether that which had been given up would outweigh that which might be gained. However, one thing was clear; the role of Irish representatives abroad had changed unambiguously, with 'an increased involvement in diplomacy of home departments in addition to foreign ministries', leading to some interesting power struggles, which only went to prove that 'economic diplomacy' had become the order of the day.[92]

Irish foreign policy: from the political to the economic

Although not a participant itself, Ireland had been substantially damaged by the effects of the Second World War, both in economic and political terms. That it was psychologically scarred more than the combatants themselves is not open to debate because unquestionably it was not. Nevertheless, something more substantial than blind neutrality, unfettered nationalism or even economic dependence, was responsible for Ireland's introversion continuing into peacetime. Using Stanley Hoffmann's thesis, Alan Milward unambiguously asserts in The European rescue of the nation-state that:

> ... the evolution of the European Community since 1945 has been an integral part of the reassertion of the nation-state as an organizational concept ... The European Community has been ... an indispensable part of the nation-state's post-war construction.[93]

Was Ireland any less of a nation state than its European neighbours? An argument such as this would be spurious to make because Irish history made it different to, but no more unique than, any other country; nonetheless, pervasive retardation continued well into the late 1950s, a period historians and political commentators commonly refer to as the 'lost decade'.

At this time, it was very much an underdeveloped nation, with an extremely backward economy which was nearly totally dependent upon agriculture. The predominant market for this produce was, indeed remains, the UK. Although Ireland's relationship with its powerful neighbour was by no stretch of the imagination as dependent as, for example, that of Lesotho upon South Africa, the importance of Anglo-Irish links should not be underestimated. These close bilateral ties, especially in economics terms for Ireland, did not demonstrate a healthy relationship based upon interdependence, but were an example of acute dependence. As has been underscored by Susan Baker in her PhD thesis, *Dependency, ideology and the industrial policy of Fianna Fáil in Ireland, 1958-1972*, Ireland was a 'peripheral economy tied into a relationship of dependence with Great Britain'.[94] Additionally, a fundamental part of this attraction to the European integration process was, as Stanley Hoffmann and Robert Keohane have shown, based solely on the EEC's 'initial period of success in lowering trade barriers and establishing common policies for agriculture and a number of other sectors'.[95] This development in Irish foreign policy came as no surprise though to any informed or perceptive commentator at that time. It was both an informed and a logical development.

The economic figures for Irish imports and exports between 1946 and 1969 bear this argument out, while also marking a definitive change of tack by the government. In the ten years following the end of World War Two, Ireland exported 89.2% of its goods to the UK, on average; the corresponding figures for the original six EEC members totalled only 5.5%, however. During the years in which Lemass was in power, these numbers became 72.8% and 8.4% on average respectively and, indeed, reached 69.6% and 11.1% by 1966. Alan Milward has remarked that one of the new markets which opened up to Ireland was West Germany and has written that: 'The Irish government in a series of annual trade agreements with the Federal Republic sought to weaken the monopsonistic position of British official and private purchasers'.[96] Indeed, in an extension of this change in Irish foreign policy orientation away from a political to an economic emphasis – as the search for new markets continued and as the government displayed admirable initiative in directing the economy away from traditional means and methods – Susan Baker remarks upon the economic policy changes of 1958. The publication of *Economic development* and the subsequent introduction of the *Programme for economic expansion* together constituted a radical transformation in the Irish government's economic approach.[97] Ireland had finally embarked upon its own post-war construction.

In point of fact, the logic favouring this argument becomes even more apparent when the percentages of Irish imports from both the UK and the Six are considered as well. From 1954 to 1959, the average figure for imports from the former was 55.9%, though this figure actually dropped to 50.4% in the next five years. It is the statistics from the Six, however, which are the most impressive aspect of such figures. In the five years which followed the Second World War, Ireland imported 6.0% of its needs from the Six; during the 1950s, this percentage averaged 10.4% and had become 14.8% by the 1960s. Furthermore, when one considers that concurrently the volume of trade was increasing rapidly, these simple findings alone go a long way towards explaining the EEC's attraction and economic significance for Ireland and, indeed, the compelling nature of the policy decisions that were obviously being taken in Dublin. Nevertheless, all of this still meant that Ireland was tied to the UK, to its economic vicissitudes and, indirectly, to the political options it chose. London's failure to exercise economic control over the Six – its determination to implement an FTA in Europe as outlined in its 'Plan G' – or political power in the wider world – exemplified by the Anglo-French debacle at Suez – meant that Ireland was outside the European mainstream, not only through its own mistakes, but also by association.[98] Under Éamon de Valera's conservative leadership, progress was slow and change slower still.

In truth, Lemass's own pragmatism on the European integration issue as Irish industry & commerce minister was really only accentuated on his becoming taoiseach in June 1959, in the process taking a new policy direction that was in marked contrast to his predecessor's unyielding parochialism. This change in the country's economic direction, confirmed by the trade figures, is even more impressive when Ireland's evident intention to ready itself for a rapid lowering of tariff barriers and a freer exchange of goods is considered. Its traditional protectionist policy had not succeeded; Lemass himself finally realised that Ireland could not be 'outside' if all of the European countries with which it was trading were to come together as an economic unit.[99] The nation was still at a crossroads in the late 1950s, its future path had not yet been worked out. However, it was becoming obvious that there was a need to do something radical and to do it fast; innovation in agriculture and industry were particularly needed, as well as recognition of other economic possibilities such as tourism. Ireland was proving to be very slow in learning new lessons and suffered the consequences as a result; what was most wanting in 1957, however, was an overarching plan or process.

2 From the OEEC to EFTA, 1957 to 1959

Ireland's position on the FTA debate: an introduction

Western Europe, which for some years had tried to engender economic integration under the auspices of the OEEC, suddenly splintered into three separate, and highly disparate, economic camps of the Six, the Seven and the peripherals by 1959. The latter grouping was astutely termed the 'Forgotten Five' by Miriam Camps in her authoritative *Britain and the European Communities*.[1] As May 1959 came to a close, the predicament in which Ireland found itself in relation to the newly-proposed EFTA was a rather straightforward, albeit highly perturbing, one. Indeed, at that particular stage, it was publicly declared that Ireland would not be invited or be permitted to be present at the forthcoming meeting of the Seven in Stockholm, not even as an observer. The EFTA negotiators – prime amongst them the governments of Sweden and the UK – were exceedingly adamant about this point, in fact, basically because they felt that 'no good purpose would be served at present by having observers in the attendance'.[2] Thus, Ireland had essentially been fobbed off by the Seven, but it was not alone in that. In reality, what was then being made crystal clear was the fact that the negotiation proceedings behind EFTA's formation, which had secretly been going on in Geneva since November 1958, would be continuing without the participation of any of the peripherals.

In the meantime, of course, the archetypal establishment of the EEC, a development closely followed by the inception of EFTA, had also made the need for Ireland to consolidate and expand its domestic agriculture and industry – while increasing the value and volume of exports to keep up with a commensurate demand for imported manufactured goods – a virtual economic necessity. Otherwise, it was becoming patently obvious that the country's future prospects for economic survival were not at all healthy. The previous attitude of the Dublin government to European integration, however, that is of participating in trade liberalisation negotiations for the 'sake of international appearance', had long since passed away. In reality, partially as a result of the intrinsic dynamism of the post-war integration process and partly because the government recognised the necessity of such changes, Ireland was finally being forcibly dragged into the modern era and, indeed, into the European economic and political mainstream that these changes represented.

As was previously stated, this second chapter centres on the period *From the OEEC to EFTA, 1957 to 1959*; thus, it mainly deals with the Dublin government's participation in the negotiations process for an OEEC-sponsored FTA. Indeed, it examines the 'crisis' aspect of the EFTA announcement for Ireland and, at the same time, presents an initial assessment of its ensuing role within the much larger context of European integration. It analyses this process in a chronological order and in so doing specifically attempts to answer one of the questions of primary importance to this research, thus asking: why was the UK so intent on freezing Ireland out of EFTA? In fact, all considerations on the subject of Irish-European integration policy in this period come back to determining the significance of the answer to this crucial question. There were hints however from the fact that London expressly wanted any resulting FTA to exclude agriculture, thereby continuing Anglo-Irish and Commonwealth preferences, while at the same time including industry, thus eliminating certain trade barriers. Certainly, from the start of the OEEC-sponsored FTA negotiations right through to EFTA's creation, London saw a European FTA as a trade grouping which would probably not include Ireland due to the latter's own economic deficiencies and choice. A very significant reference in the UK government's famous 'Plan G' of 14 September 1956 read: 'The United Kingdom should enter a partial free trade area with the Customs Union of the Messina Six (Benelux, France, Germany, Italy) and all other OEEC countries that wished to join (probably Norway, Sweden, Denmark, Switzerland, Austria)'.[3] Ireland was not mentioned or considered.

This extended introduction to the subject of Ireland and the FTA negotiations broaches the main issues that come up in this chapter, beginning with an in-depth examination of the OEEC report on Ireland in 1956, before moving onto a detailed evaluation of the stops and starts of Ireland's original FTA negotiations in the section subsequent to that. This important appraisal then leads to a deeper consideration of this chapter's opening remarks, that is the shock value to the Irish government of the announcement of FTA negotiations being launched by a group comprised only of the Seven, thus excluding the other members of the OEEC. Obviously enough, it then moves on to explore in more specific terms the position of the UK government towards Ireland and *vice versa*, in addition to an assessment of both countries respective attitudes towards the excluded OEEC members. In the meantime, this chapter also evaluates the significance of Ireland being classed amongst the lesser developed nations in the OEEC, that is the group which was disparagingly termed in the UK and elsewhere as the peripherals; essentially, it was felt that these countries would not have been able to take on the full burdens of an FTA and were thus excluded.[4] Indeed, at this point, a general analysis is presented on the reactions and implications of the formation of EFTA on Ireland in political terms, as well as upon the general Irish economic situation, and this section then brings the second chapter to a close save for some concluding remarks. These intermediate conclusions serve as an appraisal of the impact of the FTA negotiations on Anglo-Irish economic relations as well as introducing Ireland's relationship with the EEC. In an effort not to restrict the dimensions of this chapter, it also concludes by referring to Ireland's position regarding the GATT and introduces its relationship with the US as well.

One theme which remains of decisive importance throughout this investigation is to determine whether the publication of *Economic development* and the consequent government enactment of its *Programme for economic expansion* were the primary causes of a remarkable indigenous economic recovery that began in these years or whether these policy innovations coincided fortuitously with a general global economic upswing.[5] A repeated feature of these central chapters is also to include a detailed, though unobtrusive, appraisal of the political situation in Ireland and in related international affairs throughout this period.[6] It is necessary to begin these highly-descriptive and narrative-based chapters on the subject of *Ireland and the EEC, 1957 to 1966*, with something of more import however. Consequently, a fascinating OEEC report on Ireland's peculiar economic circumstances in 1956 is a logical starting point.

The OEEC's 1956 annual report

The annual report in 1956 from OEEC WP#13 – that is the economic committee – has a precis providing a useful introduction to the subject of Ireland and European integration by giving detailed and practical information on the state of the Irish economy as seen through European eyes.[7] As background data, the report points out that, after being stable for some years, its economic situation had begun to deteriorate rather badly and rapidly the previous year in 1955. With imports rising fast – because of domestic industry's failure to keep up with the demands of a burgeoning consumer economy – and exports falling nearly as quickly – due to Ireland's failure to compete in both traditional and potential new markets – the country was facing a financial crisis. In fact, there was a growth in the volume of national consumption of some 6% between 1953 and 1954, with an extraordinary increase of nearly 23½% in the following year. Although these sharp rises were said to owe much to increasing availability of bank credit and to a decrease in the willingness of the general populace to save, this period also saw a reduction in the country's monetary reserves, which, coupled with a rise in wages in real terms and the resultant increases in inflation, finally spurred the Irish government into action in an attempt to avert an economic crisis.

The main aims of the then coalition government, led by Costello of Fine Gael, were two-fold and may be listed as follows:

- to curb the inflationary tendencies of the Irish economy which stood at 4% *per annum* in the mid-1950s;
- to alleviate the increasingly negative balance of payments situation.

Noticeably, the diverse and remedial economic actions introduced by the Irish government – which have been inimitably described by J.H.Whyte in *Church and state in modern Ireland, 1923-1979*, as 'ferocious fiscal measures' – included a new tax on the importation of non-essential items.[8] This particular economic prescription was introduced in March 1956 and was subsequently reinforced that July by Gerald Sweetman, the Irish finance minister. The obvious purpose of this new policy direction was to combat what appeared to be a growing and insatiable domestic demand for foreign goods. The 1956 OEEC report still felt that the general Irish economic situation would in time improve, despite a peculiar lack of investment and the haemorrhaging effects of rising emigration, both of which were seen as culturally-based phenomena. Indeed, this report also remarked positively upon further Irish government measures that were introduced in October 1956 to facilitate the country's agricultural and industrial development. In fact, these economic conditions operated in conjunction with an innovative and newly-enshrined policy that positively encouraged private investment in the economy; in this regard, the report noted that the establishment of Córas Tráchtála Teoranta in 1951, which had the goal of developing industrial products and promoting them abroad, had proved to be relatively successful. Nevertheless, the coalition government was beginning to realise that a basic need was developing to attract foreign investment into the economy, as the narrow and singular promotion of domestically owned and based exports would no longer suffice as an economic panacea for Ireland, especially without working in concert with a wider, coherent and planned set of policies.

As a result, direct foreign investment quickly became the corner-stone of Irish economic policy.

Nonetheless, the OEEC report on the economic situation that was prevailing in Ireland remained very critical in tone. Evidently, the chief implication of the report was that the Irish government would have to fundamentally change its economic attitudes and, in addition, that it would have to redirect the economy away from protectionism if it was to remain viable and if it was to emerge from the severe economic crisis that it was both experiencing and facing. As is seen in a subsequent chapter – *De Gaulle's refusal of the UK, 14 January 1963* – this advance in economic thinking did not actually take place in any substantial terms, that is in terms of direct implementation, until the early 1960s. Nevertheless, it was clear that an economic corner had to be turned, because otherwise Ireland was threatened with becoming an economic, political and social desert-like landscape, a nation from which the young and the educated would have to continue to emigrate in order to advance themselves.

The 1956 census demonstrated that, in the previous five years, the Irish population had fallen by over 2%, a trend which would continue well into the next decade. Indeed, even from these figures, it can be ascertained that the prospects for the future of the Irish economy were very bleak. In that year, however, a significant development had taken place in the Irish power apparatus when T.K.Whitaker was appointed as the Department of Finance secretary, an appointment which Tim Pat Coogan, author of *Ireland since the rising*, describes as 'one of the most fortunate decisions of Irish politics'.[9] Within twelve months of taking up his post, the new departmental secretary had the full backing of a new administration in order to pursue his economic ideas, a government headed by de Valera, the leader of Fianna Fáil, but which was effectively directed by his tánaiste (deputy prime minister), Lemass. It is at this point in the early stages of this chapter that it turns specifically to the OEEC negotiations for an FTA, keeping in mind the political and social, as well as the economic, changes that were beginning to characterise a new Irish outlook on the world.

Background to the OEEC-sponsored FTA negotiations

As J.H.Whyte has stated, 'it is generally agreed that, towards the end of the nineteen-fifties, Ireland as a whole ... passed some kind of turning-point'. Irish historians have not actually been able to agree fully upon the exact timing of this reformation; in relation to its intrinsic nature, however, there is at least a consensus that the change was a 'psychological one' and as a result that 'the Irish people have become more optimistic, more adventurous, more self-confident and more ready to accept criticism from themselves and from others'. J.H.Whyte has identified five factors which help to explain the chief causes of Ireland's psychological transformation during the late 1950s and well into the 1960s; he specifically points to:

- an economic amelioration generally, coupled with political and social innovation, creating both confidence and new demands;
- a shift from an inherent national policy of isolationism to a much more outward-looking view, as seen variously in the increasingly progressive attitude of the Irish delegation at the UN to the communist world, its application to join the EEC, Dublin's rapprochement with Belfast;
- the introduction of diverse foreign cultural and economic influences, as defined by an expansion in the number of foreign-owned factories, an increase in tourism, a loosening of the censor's grip on literature/film, and evidence of greater professionalism in native journalism;
- the setting-up of Radio Telefís Éireann (RTÉ – the national television broadcaster) and its first transmission in December 1961;
- the drive for liberalisation in the Catholic Church as initiated by Pope John XXIII and continued through the Second Vatican Council.[10]

With this context firmly in mind – that there was some sort of psychological metamorphosis going on in Ireland – it is also possible to examine the relevance and significance of the FTA negotiations within the wider question of European integration.

D.J.Maher has shown that the original suggestion within the OEEC to consider the formation of 'free trade zone arrangements' was strongly supported by the UK government. Indeed, in July 1956, the UK also favoured the decision to form OEEC WP#17, which had the task of investigating all the means and ways of associating the Six – which as a specific grouping was due to come into effect the following year – with the other OEEC members. One of the methods that was to come under serious consideration was the creation of an FTA, which can be defined as 'an area in which countries undertake to abolish progressively their customs duties and quantitative restrictions *vis-à-vis* each other while maintaining their individual tariffs, etc., with respect to the outside world'. Of course, there were categoric and inherent differences between an FTA and a customs union such as the EEC, primarily because it can also be said that a 'customs union requires the adoption by member countries of a common tariff with respect to all other countries'.[11] In truth, the institution of an FTA actually suited the purposes of the UK government and obviously – just as one of the primary considerations in this discourse on Ireland's experience of European integration was the whole tangled issue of Anglo-Irish relations – the UK began to play a rather pivotal role in respect to it. This situation was reflected politically in Ireland, despite the fact that the economic realities facing the nation were both inescapable and unpalatable.

In January 1957, for instance, it was encapsulated in the views of the tánaiste and Irish industry & commerce minister, William Norton, who held the strong belief that the constant and innate concern of the Irish economy, even within an OEEC-sponsored FTA, remained Ireland's 'vital trade interest' in the UK. He said that:

> The pattern of our trade down the centuries has been with Great Britain, and there is probably nowhere else in the world a condition of trading relations paralleled by the relations we have with Britain. We are Britain's second best customer. Britain is our best customer and it does not need very much emphasis for me to get you to realise what a change in that relationship would mean for a small country like ours with an economy which has not yet reached its optimum limits and where in fact, it can be said that our economy is still developing. The whole question requires clear and careful analysis ... no sense of sentimentality or illusory oneness, no sense of a situation in which we got the crumbs and others got the cake ought to induce us to take a step which could set back overnight all we have striven for in the past 30 years.[12]

An important point has to be made at the outset of this section because, in dealing with any aspect of Irish history, one has to be very careful of the Anglo-Irish dimension. Indeed, as is pointed out in Roy Foster's *Paddy and Mr Punch: connections in Irish and English history*, there are dangers inherent in the 'disingenuous ... notion that "we Irish" are more influenced by Europe than by Britain', holding that this has never in fact been true; he actually extends his strongly-held contention by calling such an idea 'grandiose self-delusion'.[13] Therefore, this particular argument becomes a vital consideration about which one has to be extremely aware when appraising any aspect of Irish history and, most especially, when specifically dealing with Anglo-Irish relations.

It should be emphasised that Ireland had many of the same economic interests as the UK government. However, when the OEEC actively began to consider the establishment of an FTA in 1956, the UK immediately and understandably concentrated on prioritising the place of industry in any negotiations. Indeed, it felt that any other economic concerns, which essentially meant agriculture, would be best considered at a more advanced stage in the whole FTA process. At this point in time, the UK government's position on the European free trade issue was assessed by the Department of External Affairs in Dublin as being influenced by three main considerations, which meant that:

- any FTA scheme would have to leave the UK free to retain the existing British Commonwealth preference arrangements;
- the exclusion of agricultural products from an FTA would make UK participation very possible and even attractive, as such a development would not seriously affect British Commonwealth imports which were of course mainly agricultural;
- a serious threat was posed for UK exports to continental Europe if the UK remained outside an FTA in which it was quite conceivable that West Germany might become dominant.

Nonetheless, despite the seriousness of these developments and the positions being taken by the UK government, even the question surrounding the degree of Irish participation in the FTA process was fundamentally at risk because, as late as October 1956, Dublin had not made a final decision about whether or not it should be fully represented in OEEC WP#17. The issue was still being debated in fact.[14] It is important to emphasise this specific point as an illustration of the endemic lack of vision and parsimonious nature of Irish bureaucracy and government in their views on the possibilities and requirements of integration.

More generally, the Department of External Affairs felt that participation in an FTA would fundamentally question two issues of integral importance to the Irish economy, namely:

- the ingrained and institutionalised protection of domestic industry;
- the maintenance of Ireland's 'special position' for its produce in the UK marketplace.

Firstly, with regard to the problem of protectionism, it was fully recognised that participation in an FTA would entail the 'progressive reduction' of Irish customs duties *vis-à-vis* the other FTA members. However, a question of even greater significance was posed by the second issue: would Ireland be able to maintain existing preference rights and entry into UK markets if it remained outside an FTA? Clearly, the Department of External Affairs felt that Ireland's full participation in OEEC WP#17 would be vital if the nation was to keep entirely abreast of any developments in that direction: 'We ... cannot afford to ignore the Working Party'. Additionally, as has been explained, it was also felt that UK attitudes made it 'essential that Ireland should be fully represented in the Working Party so that our interests may at all stages be fully safeguarded'. Thus, one of the earliest conclusions of substance reached was that, notwithstanding the outcome of OEEC WP#17's deliberations, 'serious problems' would be created for the Irish economy whether or not the government finally decided to accept or to reject its recommendations. Thus, the point made regarding Ireland's full representation on OEEC WP#17 comes even more sharply into focus and can be best explained as this section progresses. The Department of External Affairs recognised that Ireland would, by necessity, have to participate wholeheartedly in any discussions and negotiations from their very outset, so that the government could be kept fully informed and, more importantly, so that it could participate in the actual shaping of an FTA itself.[15]

D.J.Maher has also pointedly remarked that the prospect of an FTA was not viewed very enthusiastically by the Irish government, again for the two principal reasons referred to previously, that is that:

- the necessity of dismantling Ireland's industrial protection policy was seen as a serious threat to domestic industry;
- the subsequent removal of import barriers into the UK would result in the elimination of the Irish preferential position in that market *vis-à-vis* the other OEEC FTA countries.[16]

Right from the beginning of the whole FTA process, it was patently obvious to all concerned that agriculture would be a central debating issue; indeed, its inclusion or exclusion would determine the whole complexion of an FTA. Nonetheless, the UK government's deliberate insistence that products including raw and processed foodstuffs, drink and tobacco, should be excluded – so that British Commonwealth preferences could be maintained – did not soften or sway, despite Danish and Dutch opposition. On this particular issue, as with the entire concept of European trade liberalisation, the Irish government stayed relatively quiet and sat on the fence for as long as was conceivably possible, thus avoiding having to take any concrete position. For example, at the first meeting of OEEC WP#22 – which dealt with the special position of agriculture – the Irish contingent felt that it would probably become necessary for Ireland to state its official position on agriculture rather quickly, a stance which had not of course yet been finalised by the government. A compromise, the usual procedure in such a situation, was put forward when it was suggested that a 'non-committal statement' could be prepared, referring to Ireland's 'general interest in expansion of agriculture, trade and our special position as the only member of the OEEC in the Commonwealth preferences system'.[17] Nevertheless, it was becoming evident to the other OEEC members that the Irish government was not particularly enraptured at the prospect of an FTA, either for agricultural or industrial products, an attitude which reflected rather badly on its declarations about it having the required European integration credentials.

The internal debate that went on within Irish government circles was evidently much more vociferous. In fact, in October 1956, the Department of Agriculture stated its view that 'we should use our influence to secure the exclusion of agriculture' from an FTA. However, it must be said that attitudes were not all negative. Indeed, they perceived the prospect of an industrial FTA, offering improved sales opportunities in the UK market, fairly positively. Nonetheless, they felt that an all-encompassing FTA would not offer the 'essential safeguards' — that is in relation to agricultural policy harmonisation or market organisation — that for instance a common market would. In truth, D.J.Maher feels this conclusion to have been 'realistic' at that stage in the OEEC consultations process. Significantly, he also points out that there was little prospect of the UK being prepared to accept either the loss of British Commonwealth preferences or the dilution of sovereignty that would ensue from the creation of a common agricultural market organisation — as was envisaged by the Six — superseding individual national controls. From this point in time, therefore, the Dublin government only envisaged the possibility of an industrial FTA being established and, thus, began to prepare itself accordingly.[18]

Understandably, UK government attitudes and changes in opinion towards European integration tended to have dramatic effects upon the Irish position throughout these years. For example, also in October 1956, the Irish embassy in London dispatched a memorandum to the Department of External Affairs in which the essential point made was that economic thinking there was undergoing 'rapid change'. Indeed, it was stated that for the UK to remain outside of the European integration process — even if this was only to lead to the signing of an associative arrangement with a common market — had become quite 'unthinkable'. London could not stand 'aloof' any longer, though the report readily admitted:

> ... that any British decision to become associated with the Common Market will have been motivated not so much by enthusiasm for it as by a realisation of the disastrous consequences for British industry — and British

political prestige – of remaining outside it.

No real need exists for this analysis to go into the pros and cons of such a policy for the UK right here, as in many ways they emerge once the Irish position is examined in more detail. Nevertheless, it should be emphasised that the economic and political freedom and power to have self-imposed tariffs with countries outside the ambit of an FTA was what particularly appealed to the UK government about the free trade form of European integration, because this course of action would clearly not have been possible within the confines of a common market. Thus, the UK's subscription to the concept of a 'partial' FTA – that is one excluding raw and manufactured foodstuffs, drink and tobacco – was due in no small part to the 'special position' of agriculture and horticulture to the UK at home and in its wider global economy, as well as within the economies of other Western European countries. In fact, this situation suited Ireland perfectly and coincided with Dublin's thinking at that point in time.[19]

Of course, the large-scale agricultural benefits accorded by the British Commonwealth preference system still existed and operated; indeed, Ireland was included *de facto* within this economic structure even though it had declared itself a republic in 1948 and had *de jure* 'left' the British Commonwealth at that juncture. In truth, agriculture was seen as the 'basis of the whole preferential system'; industry would, however, have to compete on the same terms for all members of an FTA. Nonetheless, while it appeared to be of the utmost importance to the UK, the British Commonwealth was being slowly replaced the whole time by the growing significance of Europe. Indeed, the Irish embassy report also noted that UK industry 'seemed to stress the challenge and opportunity [of an FTA] for British industry rather that the threat which the scheme undoubtedly represented'. The threat of agriculture also being included in a common market of the Six was seen as being some way off just yet and, apart from that consideration, was recognised as a stumbling block to the hopes of any FTA agreement being completed. This possible solution to additional European trade, that is excluding agriculture, appealed to the London government for the two-pronged reason of British Commonwealth preferences and the UK's indigenous and vastly protected agriculture industry. In reality, in the context of the British Commonwealth, an FTA for manufacturing industry posed less of a threat because the volume of trade was not substantial. Indeed, 87% of the UK's imports from the British Commonwealth would remain unaffected if agriculture was excluded from an FTA and industry in the UK would, over time, still have freer access to a potential market of up to 300 million people as recompense. This Irish embassy report thus concluded that 'it is abundantly clear that a bold break with past British policy may be close at hand'.[20] The pressure on the Irish government to prepare properly and thoroughly its own definitive position had for quite a time impelled a decision yet to be made.

As the UK government's crucial, indeed intrinsic, role in Ireland's process of European integration has been identified, perhaps a more detailed look at the various standpoints of the relevant Irish government departments would be of interest in developing this argument. A report from the Department of Industry & Commerce from October 1956, on the proposal for an FTA of OEEC countries, makes the existence of divergent Irish bureaucratic positions all too apparent. Notwithstanding this point, the fact that the distinctive views of this particular department did not alter in any fundamental way in subsequent years is testament to its own idiosyncratic and inherent conservatism. One of the central aims of the Messina resolution, for example, dating from when the Six had initially met in June 1955, was 'the creation of a common European market, excluding all customs duties and all quantitative restrictions'. This move was generally envisaged as necessitating the removal of all tariffs and quantitative restrictions within a set timeframe, coupled with the institution of a common external tariff. The initial fear that the OEEC would break-up as a result into 'two rival trading groups' was obliquely confronted by the UK through the setting up of a working party to investigate what form the OEEC countries trading links should consequently take, with one of the main proposals put forward being the initiation of a wider-FTA to include the Six and the other remaining OEEC members. The role of the UK aroused surprise in the OEEC because it had commonly been expected to oppose an FTA due to British Commonwealth preferences, but, as has already been explained, the UK government's position in this period was very fluid and even more difficult to interpret. Indeed, the UK was apparently now 'genuinely in favour of the idea of a free trade area'. Nevertheless, it was made clear by the UK Chancellor of the Exchequer that the agricultural sector – the area in which the British Commonwealth countries had the greatest interest – would have to be excluded from an FTA before the UK could:

> ... become a party and that if there is any question of choosing between Europe and the Commonwealth, the Commonwealth must be Britain's choice ... [with] agriculture, horticulture, food, drink tobacco and feeding stuffs ... excluded from the free trading arrangements.

The Department of Industry & Commerce remarked quixotically upon the sudden enthusiasm exhibited by the UK for an FTA. Still more importantly, the report also commented on the implications for Ireland if this turned out to be the true direction of UK government policy.²¹ If this was how the Westminster government's position was being interpreted, the question remained: what were the ramifications for Ireland?

It was felt by this Irish government department that one of the principal implications would be to challenge Ireland's 'traditional attitude' to the OEEC, as well as to question the measures it had taken for the liberalisation of trade which was 'to regard these measures as being something in which we had to acquiesce for the sake of international appearance but which the country would be better off without'. This Department of Industry & Commerce report continued its summary of the Irish position in much the same vein by declaring that the government had felt that it was much more important to have the 'maximum freedom to develop and protect our own industries [rather] than to obtain tariff or quota concessions in O.E.E.C. countries outside Britain'. This was Dublin's policy mainly because Ireland's tariff preference position in the UK was safeguarded under the various pre-war Anglo-Irish trading agreements. Notably, it was also stated that 'insofar as we had duty-free entry to Britain guaranteed on most goods, while other European countries were subject to duties, it was against our selfish interests that Britain should reduce the latter duties'. Thus, faced with the possibility of the UK being prepared to abolish duties *vis-à-vis* the OEEC countries, Ireland's interest in the matter of an FTA had suddenly become a very 'live' and serious one.

In reality, because the UK government was proposing to exclude agriculture, Ireland's future economic prospects were actually much improved, because it would as a consequence be able to hold onto its agricultural preferences in the UK market; if Ireland was to join the FTA that the UK envisaged, it would not necessarily have to remove agricultural protection. At this point, it remained to be seen whether an FTA would be formed at all; it was still very much in the balance. However, the Department of Industry & Commerce felt that if the FTA became a reality, with the UK and other Western European countries joining together for the:

> ... abolition of tariffs and quotas and for close co-operation in the other fields envisaged for European development, Ireland could be in a difficult position if she remained isolated between the U.S.A. on the one hand, and what, in effect, would be a United States of Europe on the other.

Of course, these implications equally applied to the UK government's own position regarding its participation in an FTA. Critically, the report then went on to suggest:

> ... that it might be to our advantage to agree to certain limitations on our right to maintain tariffs and quotas in return for some of the other benefits which might accrue from membership of the free trade area such as, for example, capital and technical assistance for development purposes.[22]

One of the reasons behind its ultimate exclusion from this development of European trading blocs – that Dublin was looking to extract an economic price for its participation – was born at this point. Indeed, this argument ties in with a widely-held belief about Ireland's process of integration, that it was not a question of the country's continuing peripheralisation, with its inherent and very real economic dangers, but the government's reluctance to confront it.

On 11 October 1956, a meeting of departmental secretaries was called to consider the economic and political situation confronting the country.[23] It must be said that this initiative to establish a committee of departmental secretaries under the control of the taoiseach, mainly in order to discuss developments relating to the OEEC proposals, was a major step forward in terms of a more positive outlook on Europe being demonstrated by the Irish government. However, in summarising the diplomatic report received from the Irish embassy in London on the subject of UK government attitudes to an FTA, J.C.B.MacCarthy, the Department of Industry & Commerce secretary, presented a rather negative analysis of Ireland's relative position. In doing so, he outlined four possible outcomes facing Ireland; he concluded that:

- the UK might only participate in a partial FTA – that is one in which raw and manufactured foodstuffs, drink and tobacco, were excluded – and that Ireland might then decide to stay out;
- the UK might only participate in a partial FTA and that Ireland might also decide to take part;
- the UK might participate in an all-embracing FTA – that is one in which agriculture and industry were included – and that Ireland might then decide to stay out;
- the UK might participate in an all-embracing FTA and that Ireland might also decide to take part.

Illustrating exactly where his department stood on the issue, MacCarthy explicitly envisaged the first of these four possibilities as the best option for which the government could hope, even though it was one in which 'Ireland would lose preferential treatment in Britain for its industrial exports and the equality of status with Britain and other European countries for industrial exports to Europe'.[24]

Although there would be no direct 'counterbalancing gain' for Ireland in this instance, he felt that this was a distinctly more suitable outcome than that envisaged by the fourth of the four possibilities, wherein:

> Ireland would stand to lose preferential treatment in Britain for its agricultural and industrial exports and protection in the home market from British and European competition in industry and agriculture ... [the] only gain would be the rather doubtful one, in such circumstances, of duty-free access to European markets for Ireland's industrial and agricultural exports.

MacCarthy continued in this fashion, according to the report from the departmental secretaries meeting, 'taking the narrow view, [that] the best that we could hope for under any of the possibilities envisaged was the loss of the greater part of our British export trade in industrial products'. However, he also stressed that the 'worst we might expect was the loss of this export trade and of a great part of our industrial output for the home market, together with whatever loss to our agriculture might be caused by the withdrawal of British preferences'. Conspicuously running throughout each of the possibilities outlined by MacCarthy was the underlying promise of a transition period for Ireland's economy being granted in order for it to adjust to the new economic conditions prevalent in Europe. In effect, the setting up of any kind of FTA was considered as having by necessity to be a gradual process, one which had to be accompanied by 'saving clauses' for the weaker countries of the OEEC.[25]

In summary, what MacCarthy in fact pointed out was that Ireland's participation in an industrial FTA would lead to a serious decline in Irish exports to its UK markets because of the loss of tariff preferences and, in addition, that the possibility of an FTA making up for these losses was at best problematic, if not improbable. There was another consideration, especially within the Department of Industry & Commerce, of a commensurate loss of jobs occurring through the establishment of an industrial FTA with clear subsequent ill-effects on the Irish economy. Opposition to this negative attitude was mainly found in the Department of Finance, most specifically with the departmental secretary.[26]

Indeed, Whitaker was not particularly impressed with this 'narrow view' as it did not take any future Irish economic developments or evidence of expansion into account. He did not go on to question the idea of protectionist policies *per se*, however, but asked whether in the long term it might not be better for the protection of Irish industry to be lessened and gradually eliminated after, for instance, a period of twenty-five years. At the meeting, he then raised another possibility because, in recognising that the cattle export business was arguably the only export industry of particular importance to Ireland and indeed that this product was competitive throughout Europe, he questioned whether Irish people would not be better off within an FTA that 'accepted freedom of trade, mobility of labour and capital'.[27] Whitaker was manifestly on the opposite spectrum of the European integration argument to MacCarthy, reflecting the contradictory emphases of the two departments on this issue. The Department of Finance secretary argued that the economy was more dynamic than the image portrayed by MacCarthy and suggested that it was actually capable of radical expansion. Indeed, for the first time, an Irish government official openly 'questioned the wisdom of backing a policy of sheltering permanently behind a protectionist blockade', according to D.J.Maher.[28] There were, of course, other voices in this departmental secretaries debate.

Meanwhile, Maurice Moynihan, the Department of the Taoiseach secretary, had the more practical view 'that the most likely eventuality was that a partial Free Trade Area would be set up with British participation' and that the Irish government should, therefore, operate under this assumption whilst not ignoring the existence of other possibilities. In short, he felt that the government should ardently consider what 'direct effects' on the Irish economy could result from the setting up of an FTA. Although 'it seemed reasonably clear that the scheme that would emerge would not seriously affect agriculture', Moynihan understood that there would be important repercussions for Ireland.[29] What was really needed was for the Dublin government to formulate a coherent set of policies to prepare for any such eventualities. Ultimately, the departmental secretaries felt the need to urge the taoiseach that Ireland should have the option of escape clauses being built into the FTA negotiations process, particularly before it made any decision or commitment to join such an FTA; this recommendation was subsequently to have highly significant consequences in relation to Ireland's links with EFTA. The departmental secretaries also made an important suggestion with regard to the UK's role in an industrial FTA by declaring that the UK government's final decision on participation should not be seen as a determinant of Ireland's own position within the FTA process.[30]

The meeting of departmental secretaries then went on to discuss whether or not Ireland should have a representative seated on OEEC WP#17, an issue raised previously and one which was critically important to their wider investigation into European integration. In the early stages of this working group's existence, Ireland was only represented by an observer and consequently lacked the influence to dictate the direction or speed of deliberations. In fact, despite the obvious and desirous need for delegate representation, unanimous agreement on this move was not immediately forthcoming from within the Irish government. The departmental secretaries were all in favour of making this appointment, although Whitaker personally felt that the Irish embassy in Paris should have been able to fulfil this role from within its own ranks. Seán Murphy, the Department of External Affairs secretary, replied at the time that it was not possible to supply someone of the 'requisite rank and experience' from the embassy staff and that Conor Cruise O'Brien, who had attended the first meeting of OEEC WP#17, was no longer in a position to continue to do so. Thus, dissension on the representation issue remained and, while all of the departmental secretaries felt that a senior officer was required for this position, Moynihan and Whitaker felt inclined to stress the need for an experienced, independent and unbiased officer to take up the post. Therefore, though not able to make a final decision on Ireland's future representation at OEEC WP#17 there and then, the departmental secretaries did at least agree that the Irish ambassador in Paris should attend the second meeting of the working group as Ireland's representative.[31] However, the Irish government eventually only took the step of changing its representation from observer to delegate status on 12 November 1956. According to D.J.Maher, the Irish delegate would:

- study any FTA schemes proposed at first hand;
- keep the Irish government fully informed of any developments;
- try to influence the deliberations of the OEEC;
- advise the Irish government on what steps it should be taking.[32]

The question has to be asked: if this post was so important, why was the decision about the representative's status not taken at an earlier stage? It may be said that the prevailing attitude to this appointment was totally symptomatic of Ireland's entire attitude towards European integration and particularly of its imbued position on agricultural and industrial protection.[33]

In early November 1956, the departmental secretaries held a second meeting which merely confirmed the various stances that had already been taken within the administration. Indeed, Whitaker again decried the 'policy of sheltering permanently behind a protectionist blockade', whilst Moynihan was less enthusiastic about substituting this course of action for something untried and untested. Division over the future direction of Irish policy remained. Ultimately, this meeting was more significant because of the decision taken regarding the necessity of introducing 'saving clauses' for the lesser-developed members of the OEEC. This new approach centred on initiating a thorough investigation into possible escape clauses that the Dublin government could call for in the FTA negotiations. Indeed, consideration of these escape clauses appears to have been the single-most important issue up for discussion at this time by the Irish government. A basic, but absolutely critical, stance of incalculable significance for Ireland's future policy direction in the FTA negotiations had been adopted, even if neither the government nor the various government departments appeared to be any clearer about how they should proceed.[34] However, once Harold Macmillan, UK Chancellor of the Exchequer, confirmed on 26 November 1956 that the UK government was in favour of negotiating an FTA, Irish minds were soon concentrated on the subject of European trade and European integration, perhaps for the first real time since Marshall Aid.[35]

1957: Ireland and the European integration question

In giving this background information to the decision by the Seven to exclude Ireland from EFTA membership in the summer of 1959, these opening sections to the chapter have tried to distinguish trends that subsequently continued or halted during the whole FTA process. It is interesting to note that some of the earliest Irish newspaper speculation centred on the probability of an FTA being formed comprising the Six, along with the addition of Austria, Denmark, Norway, Sweden, Switzerland and the UK. The question being asked was: where was Ireland going to fit into this 'revolutionary' and 'fabulous' idea? [36] Still, the *Irish Press* could not resist saying that: 'Part of our country, the Six Counties, will have no option but to follow Britain into the Free Trade Area'. Nonetheless, this otherwise well-informed and unbiased report from the beginning of 1957 continued to hold that: 'Irrespective of whether we join the proposed Free Trade area or not our agricultural products will continue to enter the British market on preferential terms'. Misgivings remained about whether, apart from the UK, other FTA members would seek free trade for agricultural produce in addition to the proposals for an industrial FTA. Thus, the vital point at issue here was that Ireland could not afford to ignore economic developments in Europe, especially as they might result in the eventual disappearance of its agricultural access to the critically important UK markets, the possible development of which would spell economic disaster.[37]

In the meantime, the general media perception was that the government had a decision of fundamental importance to make regarding whether or not to join an FTA. However, the perceived wisdom was that it would not because of two main reasons, which can be listed as:

- the UK government's insistence that raw and manufactured foodstuffs, drink and tobacco, must be excluded from the plan;
- Ireland's own peculiar need to protect its under-developed and weak manufacturing industry.[38]

Both of these points were to prove fundamental in how Ireland viewed Europe and how it was in turn seen, directly and indirectly; firstly, it was identified – no matter how much it insisted to the contrary – with the UK economy, while having to consider its own retarded economic position as well. Of course, domestic politicking continued in this background, as did a rather revolutionary government policy of informing the nation about European integration issues. A substantial amount of time and consideration was being given by the cabinet to determining the country's position on the FTA proposals throughout the period between 1956 and 1959. However, the government had, at least, made sure to make their decisions as informed as possible; at this stage, an extensive examination of the views held by Costello's government is thus useful in further understanding the immediate background to the FTA negotiations. The Fine Gael led coalition of 1954 to 1957 had not, for instance, hesitated in continuously consulting with the principal groups that would be affected by the projected abolition of tariff barriers – farmers' organisations, trade unions, bodies connected with commerce, foreign trade and industry – as well as with other groupings of economic and political import that would be affected by additional changes resulting from Ireland's European integration.

In a speech delivered in the middle of January 1957, the taoiseach thus had the ideal opportunity with which to air unambiguously the government's views on the economic and political situation that was developing. It is worth quoting extensively because he said:

> As a member of that Organisation [the OEEC], we will very shortly have to decide whether we should participate in the formation of the Free Trade Area, and if so on what conditions. In our present stage of development a proposal to participate ... raises grave and serious problems which have been, and are, receiving urgent consideration by the Government. Since the decision we take is bound to have a fundamental and lasting effect on our economy, it is essential that interested bodies and the public generally should be given an opportunity of appreciating the problem and of expressing their views. It is intended that the public shall be kept fully informed on this subject. Whether we join or not, it is certain that we cannot hope to remain unaffected by the establishment of the Area. The future prosperity of Ireland will depend on whether we meet successfully, by increased and more efficient production, the challenge presented by the

proposal to establish a unified free trade market in Western Europe, comprising up to 250 million people. In facing that challenge and the more immediate difficulties which lie ahead, we are fortified by the fundamental economic and financial strength of the country, based on the extensive economic and social investment of the past thirty-five years. Our aim must be to build on that strength, and our faith and confidence in the future, which are our most precious assets.[39]

In fact, the Irish cabinet decided to make it absolutely clear to the other OEEC nations that Ireland had finally determined upon its position towards the whole concept of an FTA and, indeed, that it had resolved its position on the question of European integration. As a direct consequence, it was minuted in cabinet that:

> In accordance with her general attitude to movements by European countries towards closer economic association, Ireland welcomes the proposal to form a European Free Trade Area. While her attitude to the question of participating in the Area will, as in the case of other countries, be determined in the light of considerations of her own national interests, Ireland views with sympathy this latest movement towards closer association among European countries and wishes the proposal every success.[40]

The Irish government had made a very important statement of intent which, nonetheless, was surpassed by its own propensity to except itself from the FTA process, an action which had become a regular occurrence in its dealings on the wider European integration question.

During both the build-up and subsequent OEEC-sponsored FTA negotiations, it soon became apparent that Ireland was most concerned with the protection of the lesser developed OEEC countries like itself. This was despite the fact that each of these peripherals were, to all intents and purposes, ostensibly different from one another; Ireland's economic dependence on UK markets for its agricultural products, for example, put it into a totally unique position within the OEEC when compared to Iceland's dependence upon fish. Indeed, for the lesser developed countries, one of the few basic shared characteristics put forward by this unlikely grouping was their geographical peripheralisation and their heterogenous nature. Therefore, this course of action by the peripherals – for them to have grouped themselves together – was a fundamental mistake, affirming their exclusivity, rather than their inclusiveness, within the OEEC system, whether as separate nations or even as a distinctive grouping.

This position was not tackled by Liam Cosgrave, the Irish foreign minister, who tried to further the European integration debate when he said later that month, January 1957, that though the government had not yet made a final choice on whether or not to join an FTA the issue was under detailed study. He added that any important decisions on the matter would only be taken when the views of interested bodies and the general public were ascertained and taken on board. Cosgrave continued by saying that Ireland was confronted with the joint probability of an industrial FTA of 250 million people being formed and, additionally, by a group of Six operating a fully functioning agricultural FTA. Accordingly, any meaningful economic decisions which had to be taken by the Dublin government, notwithstanding the anticipated existence of an FTA in some shape or form, would by definition have to have a 'far-reaching impact' upon the Irish economy.[41] Thus, the stimulus of European integration for Dublin was predominantly economic rather than political.

Nevertheless, the Irish government was evidently unable to make a fully informed choice at this stage and was thus consulting enlightened – as well as public – opinion before coming to any decision. The UK government's determination to pursue the matter of an FTA was obviously going to force Ireland into making a decision one way or another; however, the former's reticence to include agriculture in such a trading bloc gave the latter some much appreciated room for manoeuvre. There remained a huge risk to the Irish economy though, with a very real fear existing that Ireland's 'protected industries might shrivel up before the blast of unaccustomed competition from every part of Western Europe'. The difficulty facing Ireland's entry into an FTA was therefore balanced in a complex and delicate consideration between enhanced opportunities for agriculture and extensive difficulties for industry. There was still a limited amount of time in which to decide about how to proceed, but the initial reaction of Irish manufacturing industry was that even more time was needed to study the proposals and that the advantages of joining an FTA were, apparently, not 'very great'.[42]

An important point regarding secondary sources arises here, because Miriam Hederman holds that the Irish application to join the EEC was:

> ... the first time ... [that] the government began to consult with producers' organisations, professions and trade unions during an international negotiation. This practice was quite new in 1961, and arose from the pressures built up by the government's non-committal handling of the European issue.[43]

Of course, this view is a patent misreading of the public and private debate that was being conducted in Ireland before and during the FTA negotiations.

One of many examples one could use to contradict Miriam Hederman's statement includes a Department of Agriculture progress report on the FTA negotiations from early 1957 which directly refers to the Dublin government's process of consultations with public and private bodies interested in determining and understanding the position faced as a result of the OEEC-sponsored FTA negotiations.[44] European integration was an inclusive debating issue in Ireland even though the arguments deliberated did not confront the essential concerns of the wider OEEC membership.

One of the fundamental problems that was undoubtedly facing Ireland with regard to European integration was the fact that the country was disproportionately reliant upon the UK economy. Indeed, 79% of all Irish exports went to this one market in the year that Fianna Fáil came back into power.[45] Even if the UK market was diminishing in relative importance year by year – in 1954, for instance, at the beginning of the Costello administration, the figure had been just under 90% – and although the total export share of manufacturing goods from Ireland was rising and that of live animals falling, its economy remained remarkably immature and closed by most contemporary European standards in 1957. Indeed, in that year, 43% of total exports still consisted of live animals, while the totals for food, drink & tobacco on one side and manufactured goods on the other were 31% against 21% respectively. Such analogous sets of data illustrate graphically Ireland's dependence for exports on a single underdeveloped market, as well the immaturity of its economy.

Equally, this contention is self-evident from Irish import figures, demonstrating that Ireland had fallen well behind its European counterparts in what should have been a decade of impressive post-war development. 57% of all Irish imports in 1957 were sourced directly from the UK, with the combined figure for European nations hardly reaching 16½% of the total. This sort of economic dependence is even more evident when one considers that 74% of all Irish imports at that time consisted of manufactured goods, a staggering total suggesting a highly undeveloped domestic manufacturing industry in Ireland. With their numbers combined, the various European trading blocs only managed to absorb 9% of Irish exports in that year, a remarkably small figure given the Irish government's repeated statement about its growing commitment to the opening up of access to heretofore virtually untapped markets. Even from such relatively uncomplicated sets of figures, it is not difficult to grasp the enormity of the problem that was facing the country as a whole, because the threat being posed by the UK's participation in a wider European trading bloc was a very real one, especially when, in the case of Ireland, membership of such a grouping was being flagrantly excluded.

By early February 1957, the Fine Gael led government was still publicly unsure of which economic avenue to take, with Costello stating that:

> ... [although the] attitude that this country should adopt towards the proposals for a European Free Trade Area is at present being considered ... a final decision will be taken only after full consideration of those opinions [from the organisations directly concerned] and of the best advise that is available to the Government.

In other words, they did not possess any concrete ideas regarding how to proceed in the more immediate future.[46] Nonetheless, the *Irish Times* still managed to put Ireland's true trading position into some sort of perspective by questioning 'whether ... the risks of abstention [from the integration process] are not enormously greater than those of participation'.[47] Evidently, the choices that the government felt it faced did not appear to be so straightforward.

Costello's government may not have failed to intimate that they found the concept of an FTA appealing, but they also publicly insisted that every OEEC country would have to be fully protected from untoward circumstances causing any 'serious damage to its economic fabric'.[48] The Irish delegate at an OEEC meeting on 12 February 1957 'made it clear that Ireland's decision on the question of joining or not joining the area would, of course, depend on our assessment of how our national interests would be affected'.[49] The next day, formal negotiations for an OEEC-sponsored FTA were initiated.[50] Additionally, emanating directly from the cabinet itself, there was publicly declared enthusiasm for the country to cooperate fully in the European economic integration process. The reality of Ireland's position on an FTA remained remarkably fluid, however, with the prospect of remaining disengaged from such an economic bloc even being considered as an option if the UK government decided to table an 'offer to make it worth our while to stay out'.[51] As with the other members of the OEEC, national interest came before any conviction among the Irish government in favour of some undefined European ideal regarding integration. In spite of such doubts, the truth of the matter was that Ireland was at the same time manoeuvring itself into a corner through its espousal of FTA membership preconditions, a position that would ultimately prove to have far-reaching negative consequences, economic and political, right through to its application to join the EEC and beyond that point as well.

Even with a change in administration – from a Fine Gael coalition to the formation of a Fianna Fáil minority – following the March 1957 general election, immediate attitudes in official circles to European integration did not vary significantly. It should be borne in mind that this election greatly distracted public debate away from the FTA issue altogether to the most important political consideration of all, that is local rather than national, never mind international, politics. Even the signing of the Treaties of Rome on 25 March 1957 – thereby creating the EEC and Euratom – appears to have attracted little attention. Paradoxically, the man who in succeeding years would come to epitomise Ireland's more open trade policy was the new tánaiste and industry & commerce minister, later viewed as some kind of visionary on the implications of European affairs and developments. Lemass took over the crucial role as the Fianna Fáil government's principal spokesman on this issue, while assuming virtual prime ministerial powers in lieu of the taoiseach, de Valera, who in turn exercised less and less influence over the day-to-day direction of policy or the running of government.[52]

From the beginning, it was clear that the new government was not about to enact any radical policy departures without thinking them through. Responding to questions regarding the propriety of maintaining its protectionist policies, Lemass declared that a comprehensive and continuing review was taking place, but he was not prepared to go much beyond that.[53] All that he would emphasise was that Irish industry had to be clear that certain practices must change and that it had to become more efficient. He stated:

> ... I think everybody has now come to realise that, in the new circumstances which may develop in the next year or so, efficiency in all phases of manufacturing activity is the only possible basis for survival. I hope that that is now being very widely appreciated and that there will be a coming together of parties engaged in industry to ensure how that efficiency which means survival can be realised ...[54]

The pace of that change was another matter altogether. Thus, despite the new domestic *status quo* resulting from the election, it came as no surprise that the Fianna Fáil led government initially decided that it was only prepared to assume FTA membership obligations when it had been established beyond reasonable doubt that the Irish economy had achieved ameliorated relations with the economies of those FTA members more highly industrialised than itself.[55] In so doing, the government explicitly categorised Ireland as an underdeveloped country within the context of the OEEC.[56] As a result, this signalled to the UK government that it was not particularly interested in putting Anglo-Irish trade at risk through its engagement in the uncertain process of European integration. The Irish agenda for the FTA negotiations had been unequivocally set, much to its own detriment. However much

Dublin made clear its intentions to move away from a policy of wholesale protection, to depart from the imposition of customs duties and qualitative restrictions, it was going to prove more difficult to convince prospective European partners of its good faith.

The FTA negotiations

On 11 May 1957, Ireland submitted a detailed document to OEEC WP#23, the grouping that had ostensibly been set up to deal with the positions and needs of the peripherals, that is the industrially underdeveloped countries in any FTA. The government argued that Ireland could not expect to share in the benefits of such an arrangement unless its special economic position was fully taken on board by the other FTA members. In fact, this memorandum pointed to various problems facing Ireland's economy, including those cited as follows:

- an unbalanced employment situation in which agriculture was a bigger employer than manufacturing industry;
- the existing high levels of unemployment and underemployment;
- the historically based retardation of the indigenous industrial sector;
- the disastrous past and continuing effects of emigration;
- an isolated geographical location on the European periphery.

The main derogation to the general conditions sought by the Dublin government was for the intermediate maintenance of protective economic measures to be guaranteed until Ireland's assumption of FTA membership obligations became a more 'practical proposition'. Their finely documented case centred on the reality of the Irish economic situation, that the country could not immediately face up to full-scale competition without suffering dire consequences as a result. Consequently, a twenty-five year timeframe was put forward in which to remove all quota and tariff restrictions. This proposal was envisaged as a necessary practical and desirable interim step leading to Ireland's full participation in an FTA. Obviously, there was an additional proviso in which the Irish government declared itself prepared to assume FTA membership responsibilities at a proportionally faster rate if the national economic situation improved more rapidly. Initially, this presentation was viewed in a fairly positive light by the other OEEC countries, even if these views tended upon more mature reflection to be of a more pessimistic and negative nature.[57]

An OEEC delegation subsequently visited Dublin the following month, primarily in an effort to flesh out more detailed, relative positions on an FTA. However, the government's presentation to the delegation was rather meagre, restricting itself to proposing that Ireland:

- be exempted from automatic tariff reductions for at least ten years after the first general set of OEEC tariff reductions were introduced;
- should have the freedom to impose new tariffs or to increase existing tariffs by up to 50% *ad valorem*;
- would reduce its tariff rates by 5% annually once the exemption period concluded, until their eventual elimination;
- would reduce all tariffs of 50% or over – a commitment which actually represented half of all Irish tariffs – by 5% upon the first general set of OEEC tariff reductions.

Of course, other significant economic questions were raised, the most important of which directly concerned the UK's position. Indeed, the government made it categorically clear that it was not prepared to commit itself to giving anything away in relation to the mutually beneficial Anglo-Irish trade agreements of 1938 and 1948. The Department of Agriculture had stressed to the government the need to maintain Ireland's 'special advantages' in the UK market, emphasising that this requisite should not be ignored in the heat of the negotiations for an OEEC-sponsored FTA. Thus, on the critical question of agriculture, the government informed the OEEC delegation that they expected opportunities to be given for the export of agricultural, as well as industrial, products to all OEEC member countries in an FTA. In fact, they added that they expected that any impediments to this policy – such as domestic support policies established to shut out imports, high and/or frequently changing tariffs, obstructive administrative regulations – would not be tolerated. It is abundantly clear from these negotiating positions that, as D.J.Maher puts it, the Dublin government was looking for special treatment in specific economic areas. Critically, it was also the first official indication that the government would want agriculture to be an integral part in any FTA resulting from the OEEC negotiations.[58]

In particular, the Department of Finance argued that the impetus on the question of industrial protection had to come from central government, contending unsuccessfully at the time that the primary stimulus for change needed to come directly from that source because otherwise native industry would not react positively to the process of European integration but would continue to shelter behind institutionalised protectionism.[59] Indeed, the position regarding Ireland and the proposed FTA was beginning to appear rather more static. It was becoming clearer that Dublin would be ready to join such a grouping if it was economically possible to do so, but it was also signalled that it still had to consider how Anglo-Irish trade relations and other such considerations would be affected first.[60] The unyielding nature of Irish politics did not help the situation and was instanced by an opposition motion put forward in Dáil Éireann in June 1957 when the suggestion of forming a bipartisan committee – with the intention of examining the whole question of an OEEC-sponsored FTA and the EEC – was flatly rejected by the government. However, for two central reasons this simple episode still proved to be a significant development when placed in the context of Ireland's experience of European integration; importantly, this was the first parliamentary debate in Ireland on Irish participation in Western European economic groupings and, secondly, the government was from then on at pains to point out that Ireland could not accept EEC membership obligations if the UK remained outside the Six.[61] The Irish position was crystallising.

Meanwhile, OEEC WP#23 was able to report on a set of positions then being taken by the group of less developed OEEC countries, that is Greece, Iceland, Ireland and Turkey. The most significant and universally-held stance being forwarded by these countries was that certain special provisions would have to be made for them; these included stipulations that:

- appropriate means would have to be found generally to enable their chiefly agricultural exports to benefit from the creation of an FTA;
- during the much needed transitional period, conditions would have to be provided within which they could then be permitted to maintain a greater degree of tariff protection than that generally allowed in the rest of the FTA;
- within the institutional framework of an FTA, financial resources would have to be made available to assist their economic development so that they would be able to attain a position enabling them to undertake the full obligations of the FTA more rapidly.

In specific terms, Greece and Turkey were strongly seeking the inclusion of agriculture in any FTA, for example, and wanted institutions to be developed to provide financial assistance to the less developed countries; indeed, generally speaking, they sought better treatment than that with which Ireland would have been well satisfied. Thus, although this statement by OEEC WP#23 should be viewed as one of a more generalised nature, it had the negative effect of clustering these four nations together, so much so that they were unequivocally seen by the other OEEC members as a coherent, special-case grouping.[62] Indeed, one of the implications of this opinion was that Ireland was seen as being outside the mainstream FTA process.

A full appreciation of the implications of this stance are central to this study, both in understanding the background to London's subsequent attitude to Ireland's proposed EFTA membership in 1959 and in the Irish government's ensuing dealings with the EEC. Indeed, this highly symbolic stance on derogations was to have major implications for Ireland's whole experience of European integration in this second post-war decade. The Irish government was expecting OEEC WP#23 to recommend derogations for Ireland and for the other peripherals from otherwise accepted FTA obligations. The OEEC partners did not view demands such as these with equanimity. At the same time, Dublin also wanted to solidify already existing Anglo-Irish trade agreements.[63] However, even at this relatively early stage, the Irish were under the distinct impression that the UK did not visualise Ireland actually joining an FTA.[64] Decisions about the conditions and the future conduct of Irish foreign economic policy were continually having to be faced and made. Nevertheless, at this point, there was little room for doubt amongst informed observers about the economic import and magnitude Anglo-Irish relations played for Ireland, even within the context of its expanding integration policy.

At a crucial Irish cabinet meeting held at the beginning of November 1957, exchanges centred on the upcoming bilateral consultations planned with the UK authorities. In fact, it was decided that Dublin would be represented at these Anglo-Irish discussions at the highest possible practicable level so that the UK government would be left under no illusions about the sincerity of Ireland's future intentions. In the process, it was decided to inform London:

> ... that the Government are proceeding on the assumption that, in the event of the Organization for European Economic Co-operation granting the waiver on agricultural tariffs for which the British have asked, the benefit of such waiver will apply automatically to imports of agricultural products from this country.

With this supposition in mind and assuming that this would indeed be the UK government's position, the cabinet decided that the Irish representatives at these forthcoming Anglo-Irish talks would have to draw attention to Ireland's deteriorating position regarding industrial exports to the UK, mainly in an effort to obtain some sort of 'compensation', that is improved terms for Irish agricultural exports.[65]

These concessions, which in truth amounted to a rather parochial set of demands from the Irish government, were listed as:

> ... the removal of the possibility of quantitative restrictions on our agricultural products on entry into Britain, the abolition of the differential in cattle prices, coupled with an arrangement for the indefinite maintenance of the store-cattle and sheep price-links, and provision for consultation on a bilateral basis with a view to securing balanced agricultural development in both countries ... the admission of duty free fish caught by Irish boats and landed direct from the fishing grounds in Britain or the Six Counties ... clarification of the position in regard to fish and fishery products and also in regard to manufactures of food, drink and tobacco.

Furthermore, it was also proposed that London should be asked to support the proposition that the FTA recognise the 'special' Anglo-Irish economic relationship, especially with regard to agricultural products. If it supported this idea, the government was prepared to propose at once to the OEEC that Ireland maintain the 'system of preferential tariffs in favour of Britain for as long as tariffs are in operation, on the grounds that these preferences are necessary to the satisfactory operation of the special relationship'. In turn, as some sort of *quid pro quo*, Ireland would agree to support the UK's stated desire for an agricultural tariff waiver.[66]

In addition to the specific Anglo-Irish dimension, an attempt was also to be made by the representatives at this bilateral meeting to secure a general statement in support of special provisions being made for the less developed OEEC countries.[67] This move emphasised that the Anglo-Irish relationship within an FTA was not to be linked to Ireland's ambition to be treated as an underdeveloped country through OEEC WP#23. Indeed, it also accorded with two of the main holdings of *Economic development*, which were that Ireland would:

- have to broaden the destination of its agricultural exports;
- ensure that Anglo-Irish trading relations did not disimprove.[68]

In fact, this was to shadow Ireland's basic attitude to agricultural and industrial sectors within a European FTA, exposing the fact that in its list of foreign economic and political priorities Anglo-Irish considerations came well before any stated concerns about integration. Of course, it has to be said that Anglo-Irish talks such as these were always going to be of paramount importance to the future shaping of bilateral trade relations, especially as far as Ireland was concerned, but at this time they assumed an even greater significance. Indeed, these particular discussions dealt comprehensively with the most important aspects of this vital and reciprocal economic relationship. The crucial consideration for Ireland was that strong Anglo-Irish trade relations should actually be maintained within the context of an FTA.

At the talks themselves, Reginald Maudling, the UK Paymaster General, restated that the UK government was seeking a waiver for agricultural produce in the FTA and that as a consequence this would duly apply to Anglo-Irish commitments. Nonetheless, he also said that the UK was not in a position to go any further on this particular issue at that time and, in addition, it would not be able to preserve Anglo-Irish industrial preferences. In particular, Maudling was at pains to stress to the Irish delegation that they should do nothing rash at the OEEC WP#23 and strongly advised that Ireland should not take up positions that could be termed as being prejudicial to the accepted and enduring *status quo*.[69] Evidently, right from the beginning of the talks, all was not going according to plan for the Irish delegation.

The position of the UK's agricultural sector within this European integration context was much more straightforward because, according to Heathcoat Amory, the UK agriculture minister, speaking in the second series of Anglo-Irish trade discussions, London's basic stance *vis-à-vis* an FTA remained the same. He said that it was:

- to protect British Commonwealth preferences;
- not to surrender control over UK agricultural policies.

Once again, as with Maudling, the UK agriculture minister was not prepared to entertain any suggestion that Irish agriculture imports into the UK could replace any Irish losses that were suffered on industrial preferences. In fact, Amory was much less prepared to give future commitments to Ireland at all in regard to agriculture. Indeed, he even asked his visitors whether they were considering the possibility of staying out of an FTA altogether, to which the tánaiste felt obliged to reply that Dublin would act purely out of national self-interest. As a matter of fact, the Irish delegation at these bilateral talks stated that their government was actively contemplating joining an agricultural FTA, news which was evidently much to the UK deputation's chagrin, but it agreed that any undertaking of this nature would obviously depend both upon OEEC attitudes to agriculture and, ultimately and more importantly, those of the UK. Indeed, such a decision would, the Irish delegation reassured their hosts, show full consideration to London's own attitude on the issue.[70]

In the third of these series of bilateral meetings, David Eccles, the UK President of the Board of Trade, was also of the opinion that nothing could be promised to Ireland until more detailed positions regarding an FTA were forthcoming. Again, according to Eccles, the UK government clearly did not envisage agriculture being allowed to become some sort of economic 'headache' within a future FTA, thus assuaging Ireland's main fear, that is the possible imposition of tariffs on Irish agricultural produce. It was undoubtedly going to be difficult for the UK to preserve the historical and special agricultural arrangements in the case of a European nation – Ireland – as distinct from those of a British Commonwealth country, due in no small part to the anticipated loss of tariff and/or trade reciprocity rights regarding agricultural and/or industrial products. The Irish delegation was soothed somewhat though by the promise of future close consultations on the subject of Anglo-Irish trade questions that were being raised through the FTA process.[71] In short, although not all the positions being taken by the UK government were in accord with Irish predilections, at least these bilateral talks presented the Irish with a clearer picture of where Anglo-Irish relations stood within the wider framework of European integration.

Accordingly, the UK Paymaster General paid a visit to Dublin in January 1958. In preparation for this event, the Department of Industry & Commerce duly made its concerns regarding Anglo-Irish trading relations apparent to the Irish government, listing five central objectives that it wanted to see achieved. Their memorandum recommended that:

- the Anglo-Irish 'special trading relationship' continue in an FTA;
- any FTA proposals should not affect the place of agriculture within this 'special arrangement';
- bilateral arrangements should be rebalanced in the light of changes in the preferential position of Irish industrial products in the UK;
- the UK should openly declare its interest in preserving its preferences in the Irish market;
- London support Ireland's call for 'special treatment as a country in the process of development', including the possibility of the setting up of an OEEC investment bank and/or readaption fund for members, though this was not to be considered a development fund.[72]

A major preoccupation of the Irish government was connected with how native industry could best be protected within the European integration process, including ascertaining the lengths to which the OEEC countries would be prepared to go to help; Ireland's insistence on support for the readaption of industry was a noteworthy and significant position to take.[73]

One of the government's more specific preoccupations remained over the question of its freedom of movement within an FTA, on the right to take unilateral action on an issue such as dumping for instance. Generally speaking, the main economic and political desire, indeed preoccupation, it had at the time was to preserve the Anglo-Irish 'special relationship', including all the benefits and drawbacks that this position actually implied. Another concern, however, was the perceptible equivocation felt to be present in UK government statements and positions.[74] Nonetheless, it did not yet seem as if London was prepared to take any major specific positions until the FTA process itself had been further clarified; as one UK official said: 'let us catch the hare before we decide how much pepper and salt it needs'.[75] The Irish government had to accept this as the official UK attitude even though it continued to try to temper its implications through its bilateral links. In public, Lemass continued to remind the country of what was at stake, telling one employer's organisation that:

> The implications of such a decision [the pursuit of economic isolation in the face of a European FTA] would be political as well as economic. It is right, therefore, for us to decide even now that if and when a European economic arrangement, embracing all the countries of Western Europe, including Britain, comes into being, it is more likely than not that we will elect to go into it, and to begin now the reconsideration of economic aims and policies which such a decision would force on us.[76]

However, although the future was not necessarily beyond the government's control, sometimes any decision was not better than none at all.

Of course, throughout this period of intense Anglo-Irish consultations, the peripherals continued to work upon a common negotiating formula in the FTA talks, despite the fact that all of their deliberations were totally dependent upon the major powers, France and the UK, being able to iron out their own differences, which they were not. In early January 1958, the Greek, Irish and Turkish delegations submitted a position paper to OEEC WP#23. In this presentation, each country demonstrated that they had come independently to the same final opinion that they could not accept the full obligations of an FTA until they had each reached a higher level of economic development. Their main concerns remained threefold: firstly, in relation to agriculture and fisheries; secondly, concerning the development of a triumvirate of support agencies – a European Development Authority, a European Investment Bank and a European Readaption Fund; lastly, a sincere undertaking throughout the OEEC to promote investments needed to stimulate their respective economies. If the OEEC was able to address positively these immediate concerns, the peripherals proposed:

- to introduce unilaterally a 5% reduction on all tariffs over 50% in the first year;
- to seek an exemption from further tariff reductions until the tenth year at the very least;
- to maintain the freedom to impose limited tariffs, particularly in the case of perceived product 'dumping', if the need arose.[77]

The scale of existing trade barriers was not endearing to outsiders, nor were intervening steps to shore up some of the gaps created by new demands or new product lines.[78]

Ireland had just cause for complaint and worry, real concerns that could not be evaded because of the potential damage that they could cause; as the industry & commerce minister informed the Seanad:

> ... any agreement for the establishment of a Free Trade Area in Europe will not merely involve arrangements for the gradual removal of tariffs but also for the removal of unfair trade practices. The agreement will certainly provide that action can be taken by any country against dumping, as it will be defined in the agreement ... It will provide, I hope, for the elimination of cartels, which distort trade, and thus give full play to competition and give access on equal terms to raw materials for the industries of all countries.[79]

Most of the positions addressed by the three countries did not alter significantly throughout the first half of 1958, although each of the considerations were fleshed out somewhat.

Therefore, by the autumn of that year, the position of the peripherals on the question of their participation and role within an FTA had developed to read as follows:

- the transitional period for the dismantling of protectionist policies for the peripherals should be set at a minimum of thirty years;
- there should be an initial exemption period of at least ten years for the peripherals on the first stage of reductions;
- during this initial exemption period, reductions on tariffs exceeding 50% would be made at the rate of 5% in the first and sixth years;
- the principle of review by authorised institutions was accepted by the peripherals but only on the express understanding that any resultant recommendations would not in fact be binding, though they would be considered by the country concerned with the 'utmost attention';
- proceedings against 'abnormal imports' would only be dealt with under the conditions of an FTA convention dealing with dumping.

In public, however, the government's stated position did not totally accord with its private efforts to be treated differently within an OEEC-sponsored FTA. For instance, in reply to a question in Dáil Éireann on whether Ireland had been declared an underdeveloped country by the OEEC, Frank Aiken, the Irish foreign minister, had a reply drafted to say:

> This country has not been decreed an underdeveloped nation by the O.E.E.C. or any other international organisation. The Deputy may, however, have in mind that the O.E.E.C., in the discussions on the proposed Free Trade Area in Europe, has recognised the need to grant special treatment in such a scheme to some Member countries, of which Ireland is one, which are considered to be in process of economic development and which could not, therefore, be expected to assume from the outset all the obligations involved in membership of a Free Trade Area.[80]

Nevertheless, despite its best efforts to disguise the truth, the Irish government had in reality placed itself in the invidious position of being perceived as less developed and peripheral by the other OEEC members than it necessarily was, even if regular public utterances were made to express the contrary position for domestic consumption.

Notwithstanding such efforts, the truth of the matter emerged in mid-November 1958 when Jacques Soustelle, the French information minister, announced that the differences at the FTA talks in the French and UK positions were intractable. An official communiqué from the former stated that 'it is not possible to create a Free Trade Area as wished by the British'. As a consequence, the OEEC FTA negotiations came to an abrupt halt; the UK government accused the French of obduracy, but this feeling was only reciprocated.[81] Having come to power that summer, Charles de Gaulle reinvigorated France's confidence in its own capacity, including a commanding position within the Six via a rapid improvement in Franco-German relations, and in its own ability to engender unanimous EEC support against any European FTA. Paris had effectively vetoed the whole idea. The *Irish Press* duly ran the headline 'Deadlock over free trade' just as the secret talks between the Seven were opening.[82] Irish deliberations within OEEC WP#23 were thus in vain even if, within the context of the OEEC-sponsored FTA negotiations, the degree to which Ireland was prepared to move on the subject of tariff reductions has itself to be questioned anyway.[83]

Amidst these developments in the realities of the European integration process, the Irish government had not noticed that the rules of the game had changed. Indeed, Lemass clung to the view that Ireland's request for a 'dispensation' from obligations for the reduction of protective measures was still valid, going so far as to declare that the country needed a decent interval in which to achieve such a development.[84] In truth, this belief ultimately helped to exclude Ireland from the subsequent EFTA negotiations process. Publicly, however, the tánaiste had managed to betray the lack of choice facing Ireland, as well as the lack of influence the country could exercise through the course of its European integration generally and more specifically regarding the institution of an FTA. The choice facing the country was bleak. If the UK finally decided to enter into a wider European agreement on agriculture, with even the limited possibility of Anglo-Irish agricultural trading agreements having to be modified as a result, Ireland 'could not stay out'; if on the other hand the UK decided to stay outside of such an arrangement, the immediacy for Ireland to determine its relative position would be lessened. Nonetheless, Lemass fully expected the UK to join an FTA and thus the spectre of an agricultural settlement being incorporated into such an agreement remained a very real economic threat to Ireland.[85] Even worse news was yet to come.

EFTA's creation: the 1959 announcement

The sudden announcement in May 1959 of a decision by the Seven to form an FTA caused shock-waves to run through the Irish economic and political establishment. Along with the other OEEC peripheral nations, Ireland was pointedly not invited to the trade discussions that were then taking place. The primary reason for this snub was plain for all to see. The Seven did not want to get bogged down with the problems of the peripherals, instead they wanted to form an FTA to complement and/or even to rival the Six. Once again, severe economic isolation loomed as a consequence, though this time as a result of Ireland's position outside of the integration process. As was explained in the introductory section to this chapter, the comprehensive examination of a 'crisis' issue – such as its exclusion from EFTA – helps to make the wider assessment of Ireland's experience of economic and political relationships within the broader question of European integration, specifically with the EEC between 1957 and 1966, much more logical and substantial.

The announcement of the formation of EFTA in 1959 was just such a moment and, indeed, played what can be considered a defining role in Ireland's subsequent attitudes and history. If it did nothing else, the public proclamation of the impending formation of EFTA caused the Irish government to confront seriously the question of European integration once and for all. In reply to the expected ensuing barrage of questions in parliament – including one, for example, which asked what was Ireland's attitude to the Swedish proposals for a smaller FTA and another which asked if the government was aware that 'fresh discussions relative to the free trade area have been initiated ... and whether Ireland is privy to such consultations so that no agreement may be reached by this block of seven nations without our interests being considered' – the tánaiste answered at some length. Lemass explained to the Dáil that the OEEC-sponsored FTA discussions had originally been intended as a means to secure a multilateral agreement associating the EEC with the other OEEC countries, Ireland included. Indeed, he added that Ireland had participated fully in these discussions for two main reasons; firstly, because it was a member of the OEEC; and secondly:

> ... because we considered that Ireland should support the efforts being made to prevent the trade divisions which threatened to arise in Europe if the European Economic Community were not associated with the other OEEC countries on a basis acceptable to all seventeen members.

It should be pointed out that this was a rather disingenuous and highly misleading argument, mainly because Ireland could hardly have stayed in the OEEC and persisted in implementing its protectionist policies, without at the same time joining the other members in making some efforts towards negotiating for the creation of an FTA.[86]

During the course of his remarks on 20 May 1959, the tánaiste stated that although the FTA negotiations had been suspended, it could not be said that the idea of a multilateral arrangement between the various countries concerned had actually been abandoned. Indeed, Lemass stated that a seventeen-nation FTA was ultimately what Ireland in fact favoured, a statement which was manifestly an erroneous analysis of the actual situation as it did not take stock of the realities that had led to the creation of separate Western Europe economic blocs. He continued his statement to Dáil Éireann by saying:

> Accordingly, our attitude since the suspension of the Paris negotiations has been governed by a desire not to engage in any action which might prejudice work towards the eventual conclusion of a multilateral agreement between all OEEC countries. Among developments which have taken place since the suspension of the Free Trade Area negotiations last December are the discussions between a number of other countries (including Britain) outside the European Economic Community on the possibility of establishing a free trade area comprising certain countries outside the Community. These discussions were not carried out under the auspices of OEEC and the Government have insufficient information on the progress of the discussions on the proposals reported to have been put forward by

Swedish interests and on the attitude of Governments towards them.

Indeed, this was stated as being one of the main reasons behind his upcoming meeting with the UK Paymaster General, that is 'to clarify the status of these proposals and to discuss their possible effects on future trading relationships between the two countries'.[87] Undoubtedly, the UK's stance remained the Irish government's pivotal consideration. The parliamentary debate continued, so it is worth going into these questions and answers in some detail.

In reply to a further enquiry – which asked if Ireland had been invited to participate in the discussions, which were said to have been 'apparently initiated' by Sweden, or whether the Irish government had intimated to the convenors of the negotiations that it did not want to participate – Lemass said that the government had concluded that the 'best interests' for Ireland would be served by an OEEC 'multilateral agreement' and that it had not prejudiced or delayed the emergence of any such agreement. He had not answered the question asked. Continuing upon this line of questioning, the tánaiste was asked by his interlocutors if Ireland had received an invitation to participate in the negotiations as it was plain to see that the other nations 'did not just all arrive there out of some feeling that they would all meet'. Lemass replied that he did not know if invitations had been issued but maintained that 'certainly, we received no invitation'. He was then asked whether the OEEC-sponsored FTA talks had been suspended indefinitely or if there was some arrangement to reconvene them. The tánaiste said in reply that the arrangement agreed upon at the breakdown of those talks was to recall the participants in January 1959; this meeting had not taken place, leaving the negotiations issue up in the air somewhat. The volley of questions in Dáil Éireann continued unabated.[88]

Lemass was asked if possible future links for Ireland with the EEC could arise out of an amalgamation of smaller agreements, so that those outside the Six might join just such a multilateral arrangement at a later stage; he was obviously not prepared to comment and was not really in a position to do so. Finally, an insightful inquiry was made querying if he had any more information about whether the talks were 'confined to free trade in the industrial field and whether they include free trade arrangements in which agriculture will be included'. Thus, Lemass finished his inquisition by stating that: 'No definite statement on the proposals has been published, so far as I know, but the information available to us suggests they relate only to the industrial field'. In fact, throughout this parliamentary question and answer session, he was not able to impart much in the way of new information at all. Certainly, the Irish government was in some disarray concerning the affair, but the tánaiste was not in a strong enough position to influence matters to any large degree. It should be remarked that this relatively adroit domestic handling of the predicament in which the government now found itself was commendable, especially considering the relatively poor position it actually faced.[89] In spite of such verbal dexterity, however, it did not hide the truth of the matter or take away from the fact that Ireland had been totally excluded from the EFTA process.

The Anglo-Irish meeting that was held on 26 May 1959 was an ideal opportunity for the Irish and UK governments to exchange views on the creation of the Seven. On behalf of the latter, Maudling tried to explain the formation of EFTA as only the first step towards a wider seventeen-nation OEEC FTA for industrial products; the possibility of agriculture becoming involved however, as a *quid pro quo* for Danish involvement, was nonetheless a distinct one. The central advice of the UK Paymaster General to the Irish was to disassociate themselves from the peripheral grouping, an intention that Lemass was able to confirm as being on his government's immediate agenda. Nevertheless, the Irish were not particularly interested in joining an industrial FTA anyway because Ireland stood to lose its Anglo-Irish preferences either way. There was a problem though, because the UK team felt that the Irish were exaggerating their losses on this particular account. In any event, the tánaiste was concerned with agriculture most and thus was not really impressed with Maudling's view that everything would somehow come out well in the end. With their inherent potential to deal comprehensively with agriculture, the main Irish worry was that economic isolation would result from the regressive development of Europe divided into separate economic blocs. The UK delegation did nothing to alleviate that fear.[90]

On 29 May 1959, the Irish minister in Stockholm informed the Department of External Affairs that he had met with Hubert de Besche of the Swedish foreign office, a meeting in which he obtained a press release announcing a meeting involving the Seven that was to be held some days later. This press release declared that the Seven had already met on three previous occasions, expressly to discuss the economic integration question in Europe; these meetings had been convened at Geneva on 30 November 1958, at Oslo on 21 February 1959, and at Stockholm on 17 March 1959.[91] Of course, there was an interesting footnote to the first of these meetings because William P.Fay, the Irish chairman of OEEC WP#23, had also been invited to represent the interests of the peripherals. As Richard Griffiths has said:

> It is difficult to talk about solidarity in the OEEC, to keep a common front against the Six if you are going to have a set of negotiations that are going to exclude four of the members with whom you are being solid in the

context of the OEEC. The presence of Fay doesn't particularly help the negotiations to go with a swing.

Ireland was not a party to any further discussions of this nature and, although they were told that they would be kept informed about any developments, an important decision was taken at this early stage. Indeed, Richard Griffiths has also pointed out that:

> One thing that Geneva meeting does is to insist that the Seven have a right to continue meeting separately, in other words, even while the Irish representative is there, the future members of EFTA actually confirm their own right to go on meeting not having to have representatives from the peripherals there in the future.[92]

In addition, it should be added that the Seven understandably convened as a group – although not in such a formalised manner – independently of these meetings. It all just meant however that Ireland was going to be excluded from the new smaller-scale negotiations.

Another crucial point is that the communique from Ireland's Stockholm ministry also stated that, with the suspension of the original FTA negotiations on 15 December 1958, the governments of the Seven felt that there had been little substantial movement in rectifying or reviving the negotiations process. Therefore, the press release now announced that the Seven were going to restart the OEEC negotiations on a smaller scale, with the forthcoming meeting planned for 1 June 1959 thus being seen as a further promotion of this cause. Significantly, the statement then specifically addressed the situation of the peripherals stating that:

> It was recognized ... during the negotiations in Paris, that some of these countries are in a special position and that they have problems which, not being alike to those of the other member countries, call for special treatment. In the preliminary work which has taken place so far within the seven it has not been possible yet to approach those questions, which however are acknowledged to constitute an important part of the problem of economic cooperation in Europe.

The meeting held in Stockholm on 17 March 1959, de Besche informed the Irish diplomat, had engendered various ideas from the Seven participants and these were now the subject of the impending meeting. The Swedish foreign office official told him 'that the British were in general in agreement with the Swedes on the proposals made', at which point the Irish minister was formally notified that: 'Attendance at the meeting will be confined to the seven countries'. Effectively, Ireland had been excluded from EFTA.[93]

The diplomatic report from the Irish minister to his superiors in Dublin continued by saying that de Besche had already been asked:

> ... whether or not the four countries, including Ireland, which had claimed special treatment should be represented by observers, but the feeling of the Seven was that no good purpose would be served at present by having observers in the attendance. The aim of these negotiations amongst the Seven is to formulate a scheme for free trade amongst themselves, which would enable them to present the six Common Market countries with proposals for a co-operation which would be satisfactory to both groups. While that was the aim, at the same time the Seven's plans will, it is hoped, be a practical alternative to the Common Market, should the negotiations between the Seven and the Six not meet with the success desired.

De Besche felt the need to stress that, in the view of the EFTA countries, the creation of the Seven 'was not a move of discrimination against the Common Market, though the Common Market had discriminated against the seven countries'. Indeed, in specific regard to Ireland, de Besche said that it would not be adversely affected by any likely outcome because it had already agreed, in general, with the plan for the abolition of tariffs at the OEEC-sponsored FTA negotiations. Unquestionably, this was not what the Irish government itself supposed. Regardless of what the Irish diplomat was being told, the fact of the matter was that the talks themselves between the Seven were due to begin within days. In fact, in this regard, the Irish minister was able to report that de Besche was 'reasonably hopeful' but, at the same time, 'cautious in his prognosis' regarding the outcome that could emerge from that meeting. Of small comfort to the Irish government was the news that de Besche personally agreed to keep Ireland informed on the progress of the EFTA discussions.[94]

The offhand and matter-of-fact way in which this information was conveyed must have come as a hammer-blow to the Irish government. After all, the basic message conferred was that Ireland had been well and truly excluded from the EFTA process and, for the immediate future, from the process of European integration. It may have reacted with caution as a result of this development, but the Dublin government was clearly frustrated at this turn of events. Indeed, aside from the public statements of the tánaiste, there was to be an immense degree of furtive diplomatic activity in the months that lay ahead; rather understandably, this chiefly concerned Anglo-Irish trading relations. The wider ramifications of EFTA's inception have to be evaluated at this point, especially when considering the question of its implications for Ireland's future integration policies. These two subjects form the basis of the next section of this analysis regarding the negotiating period stretching from the OEEC to EFTA.

Immediate reactions to a new economic development

The blackballing of Ireland from EFTA was one of the more serious matters with which the Irish government had to contend in the post-war period. Indisputably, it was a situation that merited deep-seated concern. However, it still had to be determined by the Irish whether their barring from EFTA was a problem which required immediate explanation and/or redress. Of course, the fundamental impact of EFTA exclusion upon Irish government thinking was that it was now glaringly obvious that the country would have to make the transition from being a less-developed economy to a modern industrial one very quickly or else Ireland would risk becoming a European economic backwater. Certainly, the economic outlook appeared to be rather barren as the summer of 1959 approached.

As with the failure of the OEEC-sponsored FTA negotiations the previous winter, the creation of EFTA in mid-1959 potentially had major implications for Ireland. Indeed, it was immediately obvious that one crucially important repercussion was that the UK would have to begin to dismantle its industrial tariffs with its EFTA partners as a result, in the process eliminating Irish industrial preferences. However, there was also an even more significant danger of EFTA extending its remit to include agricultural produce, for which strong support could already be found from some of its projected members, including Denmark and Norway, both of which were major competitors of Ireland's in the export of agricultural produce. The government was left with the stark choice of either seeking EFTA membership or else risk engendering even closer and possibly spiralling dependence on the UK. In reality, all other economic options open to the new taoiseach, Seán Lemass, elevated to the post in late June 1959, had either become untenable or unthinkable. Therefore, the Irish government chose the second option, primarily because of the significance of UK markets to Ireland. Thus, as an immediate economic priority, it set about building on existing Anglo-Irish trade agreements, before thinking of, or indeed implementing, other ways to develop the domestic economy and/or to expand Irish exports. The government had unremittingly felt that, even without an FTA, bilateral trading agreements might very well suffice for Ireland's immediate economic needs. Nevertheless, the opening of the Seven's intensive negotiations to create EFTA had made improvements in this regard an absolute necessity.[95]

An Irish Department of Finance memorandum on Anglo-Irish

economic matters that dates from July 1959 gives a summary of bilateral discussions up to that point. It began with an apocalyptical announcement, coupled with a recommendation; it said that:

> ... a Free Trade Area of the Seven ... will cause us to lose, eventually, our industrial preferences in the British market over Britain's partners in the Area and may lead to an immediate reduction in our agricultural exports to Britain if, as appears likely, Britain grants concessions in the agricultural sphere to Denmark as a quid pro quo for Denmark's joining the proposed grouping. These losses would upset the balance of advantage of the Anglo-Irish Trade Agreements as to warrant our seeking a revision of the Agreements which would secure for us compensating advantage from the British.

The report specifically recounted an Anglo-Irish meeting from 26 May 1959, when Lemass had called upon the UK Paymaster General to give Ireland more up-to-date information on FTA developments in general and upon the reported proposals for an FTA of the Seven in particular. Lemass, still tánaiste at that stage, told Maudling that, whether it joined the Seven or not, Ireland would lose its advantages in the UK market's industrial sector as a direct result, specifically in relation to timber products such as paper. More importantly still, because of the possibility of concessions being made to Denmark, Ireland stood to lose out on the agricultural side as well, especially in relation to bacon and dairy products.[96] In bilateral economic exchanges, the Irish were never averse to getting down to minutiae.

Lemass was primarily interested in preparing the way for a 'joint look' at the existing Anglo-Irish trade agreements, with a view to seeing what were the prospects for increasing bilateral trade. The tánaiste expressed his anxieties to Maudling, stating that he foresaw the disappearance of smaller economic entities in Europe as a consequence of the creation of blocs. The main hope for the small economies, therefore, was for economic association with these large groups. However, if Ireland was to enter any such group, it would understandably have to be an arrangement that included the UK. At this meeting, Lemass made it clear that he was not inimical to recognising the basic need for Ireland 'to maintain and develop our economic relations with Britain since we might undergo appreciable losses as a result of the formation of the Seven and might also lose trade in the Common Market'. Thus, before the UK government committed itself to the new *status quo* in Europe, Lemass remarked that he wanted both nations to look at the Anglo-Irish trade arrangements already in existence and, if the need arose, to adapt them accordingly to these new developments. However, the UK Paymaster General was not particularly enthusiastic about the Irish proposal for these trade agreements to be jointly examined, even if he did not have much to offer in return by way of recompense. In fact, regarding the Irish delegation's views on the formation of European trading blocs and the relative positions of small nations, all he had to tender was the opinion that there was bound to an OEEC solution sooner or later, that 'all would come right in the end'. Obviously, this belief was never going to be a satisfactory enough guarantee for the Dublin government and, understandably, they set about looking for something more concrete and substantial straightaway.[97]

On 10 July 1959, the cabinet met to consider the various problems faced as a result of this new set of economic circumstances. What they decided to do was to put their case forward to the UK during the bilateral discussions on future trade relations that were due to commence within the following few days. At these meetings, the UK delegation made it clear that they understood the problems that would be created for Ireland by the proposals to form an FTA of Seven. Indeed, the new taoiseach was summarised as having said that:

> We see two large trading groups preparing to dismantle their tariffs and to enter into closer trading relationship within each group. We can see no advantage to ourselves in entering either of these trading groups. In fact with the new developments we see the markets of Europe beginning to close to us. Simultaneously with this development trade prospects for Ireland in this market are likely to contract because of Britain's proposed entry into a Free Trade Area of the Seven.

In trying to put the Irish argument across, Lemass recalled that 'special consideration' had been given to Ireland's position during the earlier OEEC talks on the creation of an FTA and that the 'possibility had been discussed of regarding the trading relations between our two countries as being in a special category'.[98] As elucidated by the UK President of the Board of Trade, London's reply was that by staying out of both the Six and the Seven the Irish were putting themselves in a very awkward position; they added that it was difficult for the UK to see what they could do for Ireland in such a situation.[99] Ireland was evidently in danger of not only isolating itself, but of bogging itself down in the morass of continued negotiations, with all hopes of a positive outcome resting upon the UK government.

At the same time, the determining factor in Ireland's relationship with EFTA, through its formation and its ensuant economic consequences, was the attitude of the UK government, to which it is necessary to give some brief background information. Interestingly, at rather an early stage, the UK Department of the Treasury noted that, upon the formation of an FTA, that is one excluding the Six and the peripherals, the major task faced would be the mediation of a wider European FTA to be carried out through two separate processes:

- negotiations between the Six and the Seven;
- the resultant negotiations with the peripherals.[100]

It was quite clear that the Treasury's positing of any negotiations with the peripherals, to take place only after the mediations between the smaller FTA and the EEC had concluded, was not accidental or just some UK government oversight. It felt that:

> It will be wholly advantageous if 'The Hague' Treaty [between the Six and the Seven] can be negotiated first and the position of the peripherals dealt with subsequently ... It seems inevitable that ... additional protocols or treaty [sic] should grant rights to and impose obligations on Greece, Turkey, Ireland and Iceland separately, not to them as a group. Their needs are dissimilar, and there is no reasonable basis on which they could constitute themselves as a group.

Indeed, within the UK government it was felt that, once the smaller FTA had been formed, this new grouping would firstly wish to negotiate with the Six – mainly in order to remove trade barriers and to secure effective arrangements for future economic cooperation – and only then would they deal with the other outlying members of the OEEC; it was acknowledged that some of these peripherals would have 'special problems requiring special treatment'.[101]

According to the UK Department of the Treasury, however, it was recognised that Ireland would 'be adversely affected by these proposals [for an industrial FTA] rather more than most members of the Commonwealth'. It also gave a warning because, as Ireland was a member of the OEEC, it was fully capable of causing 'unnecessary difficulty' for the UK government if it was to line up with Greece and Turkey. Therefore, it was recommended by the Treasury that the Irish should be kept informed of UK government thinking, in much the same way as the members of the British Commonwealth would.[102] Nevertheless, the whole emphasis of this line of argument with Ireland was that all future considerations such as bilateral trade relations, should be in the 'broad political setting'. Furthermore, the Treasury went on to say that, apart from the proposals to explain the UK's situation to the Irish, the government should not feel the need to explain to the other peripherals what it was doing.[103] Therefore, Ireland was being treated as an exceptional case and, for all practical purposes, as a member of the British Commonwealth, albeit one that was also a member of the OEEC.

Various meetings, which do not have to be listed here, between representatives of the UK and Swedish governments took place around this time in order to discuss the Swedish draft proposals for an EFTA. At these gatherings, the specific question surrounding the future role of the peripherals arose more than once. When the existence of the new EFTA project became public knowledge, both sets of participants clearly felt that they would have to reassure the peripherals of their continued role within the European economic framework. However, a decision as to whether a statement should be issued holding open the prospect of the peripherals being welcomed into the EFTA grouping or whether EFTA should offer to bring the peripherals into a wider FTA with the Six was not easily taken.[104] Nonetheless, with regard to the actual EFTA membership question, it can be asserted that the Swedish proposals adamantly stated that it would 'be open to any country willing to undertake in full the obligations of the Area'.[105] Of course, there was also a vigorous debate within the UK government about the future role of the OEEC peripherals, with particular attention being paid to Ireland. However, the Irish government was not willing to enter an FTA without certain derogations being made, so, in effect, this economic avenue was in fact closed off to them. EFTA membership was not a serious option for Ireland. Nevertheless, its very existence posed a grave threat to the future well-being of the Irish economy.

The UK Foreign Office also referred to the problem of members of the OEEC who were set to be non-members of both the EEC and EFTA. Indeed, they placed Ireland in a category containing the 'old' peripherals – that is Greece, Turkey, Iceland and, by definition, Spain – before going on to say that the prospective problems presented in this regard would be very different in two major respects from those faced previously. Firstly, because the earlier FTA negotiations had been on the basis of a seventeen-nation OEEC, the course of those discussions had attempted to associate all members 'in a movement to free trade and cooperate in economic matters on a multilateral, seventeen-country basis'. In 1959, however, the negotiations for an FTA were now going to be between two separate groups of countries, in addition to a number of individual countries which would be, it was presumed, 'unlikely' to result in a seventeen-nation organisation of the 'old pattern'. Secondly, because of their 'form and purpose', the OEEC-sponsored FTA negotiations had placed the peripherals in a powerful position to block or veto wider progress if their individual demands were not met. The peripherals would not enjoy such a position in the new negotiations that were now to follow, as they would not take place under OEEC auspices and because the peripherals would have no direct role to play in them anyway.[106]

This assessment of the difficulties created by the presence of non-members of both the EEC and the EFTA within any negotiations scenario contended that the peripherals problems would, in fact, now be three-fold. The reasons for this situation were listed as follows:

- the existence of two European economic groupings 'each engaged in reducing tariff and quota barriers within the group, but neither extending benefits of these reductions to outsiders';
- 'the expectation which Greece and Turkey had formed during the former F.T.A. negotiations (and will have retained) that the new organisation would supply them with financial assistance to develop their economies. Ireland and Iceland are to a lesser extent interested in development capital, but if Spain joined this group she would be a candidate on par with Greece and Turkey';
- 'their desire to be associated as equals with the other members of any all-European economic association ... associated with the institutions of neither the E.E.C. nor the F.T.A., they would fear that they would be increasingly excluded from the machinery of European cooperation.'

Thus, the actual distance between the peripherals and the two blocs was, according to the UK Foreign Office, rather a large one in negotiating terms, even if it was not felt to be especially or necessarily insurmountable.[107]

In the same report from May 1959, the UK Foreign Office then raised certain basic questions with which the UK government would thus have to deal. Firstly, should all or any of the peripherals be allowed to take part, fully or as observers, in the negotiations for EFTA and should they be consulted or kept informed about progress? Secondly, should any account be taken of the likely requirements of the peripherals in drafting a convention for EFTA? Finally, should any of the advantages of EFTA then be extended to the peripherals? Although of a rudimentary nature, these considerations addressed Ireland's central integration concerns. At this point, with possible solutions for the dilemma presented in mind, the Foreign Office paper stated that:

> Our main long term objective is to restore and strengthen European cooperation through measures to free trade carried out by common institutions. In negotiating an E.T.A., we shall make it clear at all stages that we consider E.T.A. the surest means of achieving the long term objective, which will itself be in the interests of the peripheral countries. Our immediate objective would therefore rightly be to secure maximum

freedom of action so that agreement on E.T.A. may be reached in the shortest possible time and with the minimum of complication. The fewer the countries involved, the easier the negotiation may be expected to be.

Furthermore, it declared that none of the peripherals would be in a position to accept the obligations of the proposed EFTA and, therefore, that their presence at the EFTA negotiations would only 'complicate and delay matters'. Indeed, the Foreign Office wanted 'to resist any claim by them to take part, fully or as observers, or to be consulted', unless of course the Seven actually found it 'opportune' to do so.[108]

In any event, chiefly in order to avoid any resentment resulting from their exclusion, this UK Foreign Office memorandum proposed that a general statement on EFTA's basic aims and obligations should include a reference to the needs of peripherals. In fact, an example of such a statement was given; it read:

> When we have formed the association we shall wish to negotiate with the Six members of the E.E,[sic]C. and the other members of O.E.E.C. (some of whom, we recognise, may have special problems, requiring special treatment) in order to remove trade barriers and to secure effective arrangements for economic cooperation.

In this regard, the Foreign Office analysis went on to assert that, provided the intention of the EFTA negotiators to proceed to wider negotiations with the other OEEC members was 'categorically and publicly stated', there was no necessity to 'complicate the task of drafting by trying to take account ... [of] the needs of individual peripherals'. An understanding that Portugal's position within the EFTA negotiations could be construed as anomalous by the other peripherals was explicitly recognised, because if it was allowed to have special terms the report stated that 'difficulties in dealing with the peripherals would be greatly increased'. Indeed, this was seen within the Foreign Office as a 'strong argument' for not making any concessions at all.[109] The Portugal issue – how its proposed membership of EFTA reflected on Ireland – is dealt with later in this section, as is an assessment of the type of EFTA that was actually negotiated. However, the peripherals, determined not to be forgotten, posed other pressing problems.

The peripherals were manifestly not going to be happy with only the airing of their long term aspirations, as it was clearly expected that they would seek watertight guarantees on their relative positions. This UK Foreign Office paper recognised, for example, that the make-up of any subsequently expanded FTA would have to include quota and tariff provision for the peripherals 'not less favourable' than those mutually accorded by the EEC and the EFTA. In addition, it went on to say that it must also be recognised that:

> ... consideration will sooner or later have to be given to the case which Greece and Turkey and perhaps others of the peripheral countries may be expected to make out for their being given special financial assistance from other members to enable them to play a full part in a wider European association ...

Additionally, the Foreign Office argued that it would 'not be in our interests to encourage the peripherals to form anything like a "third college"'. Indeed, such a pressure group was to be expressly avoided, it felt. The express feeling was that directly effected countries outside the OEEC, such as those in the British Commonwealth, were 'less likely' to be 'troublesome' to the UK government during such negotiations than the peripherals.[110]

In a separate report that outlined a brief history of European economic cooperation and integration from the viewpoint of the UK government, it was stated that the formation of the Seven was foreseen as a means of putting pressure on the Six through the resulting reduction in trade, that the ultimate prospects of negotiating a wider FTA agreement would therefore only be enhanced. In direct relation to the peripherals, this UK departmental secretaries note from June 1959 asserted that the express intention of the UK was to find a way of bringing the peripherals into such a wider European FTA. The report went on to point out that this preliminary procedure of setting up EFTA was chosen only because such 'great difficulties' had been experienced in attempting to negotiate a seventeen-nation FTA in 1958 that it had now been decided that a much wider association would pose 'almost insuperable problems of negotiation' unless it was accomplished piecemeal.[111]

Ireland, however, remained a case apart and would have to be treated accordingly. It is readily apparent that within the UK government there were differing attitudes concerning the position of the peripherals relative to the new economic blocs. The UK Board of Trade, for instance, held that although the 'Stockholm undertaking' was made amongst the Seven – meaning that 'there was an understanding that the Seven should not treat one another worse that they treated the Six and that they should treat one another better where possible' – it would doubtlessly be difficult for them to justify discrimination against the peripherals.[112] Equally, it would be very difficult and probably undesirable to have to vindicate prejudicial behaviour against the Irish. A different briefing from the UK Department of the Treasury made further reference to the peripherals and stated that, although press interest in the UK on the subject of the peripherals was not to be expected, it was still recommended that the UK 'make it clear that it would be our intention to find some way of bringing the peripherals into a wider European association with the two main groups'.[113] At the same time, the Irish situation would undoubtedly receive significantly more media attention and would have to be somewhat more influential on the direction taken by London as a direct consequence. Ireland was a separate consideration for the UK government and one that could not be ignored.

Related to this consideration of Ireland as a distinct case and in direct relation to the process of the Stockholm EFTA negotiations, there was also the heated question of the part to be played by the British Commonwealth countries – to which Ireland belonged in various respects – not only in terms of trade. Therefore, the Commonwealth governments, including Ireland, were usually kept fully informed about the EFTA discussions. Indeed, they were told that the Seven were making 'rapid' progress in their negotiations because of the 'general desire' to reach a widely acceptable agreement. Apart from the general reassurance given to these nations that on the industrial side they had nothing to worry about – that the 'Stockholm discussions are proceeding in accordance with the principles which we indicated as being desirable' – other interesting observations and remarks were made available for the general consumption of all the Commonwealth countries, Ireland included. London prefaced this particular information by saying that, within the EFTA group, there appeared to be universal support for the principle that it was not the intention either to form some kind of free market to modify existing international obligations of the EFTA members in any way or to use the quantitative restrictions issue to create some new type of preferential system. In fact, this UK departmental secretaries note continued by reassuring the Commonwealth that it appeared to be the 'clear intention' of all the EFTA governments that any free market amongst the Seven would only be designed to provide the bridge to an ultimate agreement with the Six. Importantly for Ireland, however, the UK also said that some:

> ... agricultural provisions will be necessary to complement industrial Free Trade Area. Our aim in this context has been to avoid a comprehensive agricultural agreement similar to that discussed in relation to the seventeen country Free Trade Area.[114]

Nevertheless, the notion of an agricultural side to EFTA being born was obviously much more complicated and heated than that. Indeed, it had much more serious implications for Ireland, as well as for the Commonwealth as a whole, than this report implied.

As far as the UK government was concerned, the main problem was the 'disposition' that the Danes had towards concluding some 'far-reaching agricultural agreement'. According to information supplied by the UK to the members of the British Commonwealth, this idea did not actually receive wide support. However, such circumstances did not stop the Danish government from stating that it was ready and willing to consider an FTA agreement on agriculture among the Seven, for a limited number of years, even if only based on a few general principles. As the London government noted in its telegram to the Commonwealth members and Ireland, ultimately there would have to be Anglo-Danish bilateral discussions to consider what would be the resulting arrangements for those agricultural commodities in which Denmark had an export interest. Indeed, this UK departmental secretaries report to the Commonwealth governments then said that the UK government had considered the Danish statement and had decided to agree to bilateral talks, which were envisaged to take place soon thereafter. It was appreciated that it was impossible for the Danish government to decide on its attitude towards EFTA until it had some idea of the treatment that would be accorded to its agricultural exports. As a result, the UK government regarded the procedure of Anglo-Danish bilateral discussions as the most practical way of handling the complicated agricultural situation.[115] Understandably, the Dublin government was particularly concerned about the efficacy and suitability of this strategy.

There was, however, an additional telegram for the 'Old Commonwealth' nations – that is Australia, Canada, New Zealand, Rhodesia (later Zimbabwe), South Africa, and Ireland – from the UK government which had important implications for the latter. This addendum pointed out that one of the main fears of the UK government was that a delay in discussing agriculture with the Danes would have a resultant delay upon the EFTA discussions as a whole. It was clarified in this second exchange that the Danish commodities that were to be discussed at this bilateral meeting included bacon and pig meat, beef and other meat products, dairy produce and eggs. Indeed, as the telegram actually remarked, this represented the 'whole range of Danish agricultural exports to us', but at this delicate stage in the EFTA negotiations the UK felt that it was not in a position to argue against it too vigorously if it was to receive its industrial FTA. As a result, the telegram tried its best to be reassuring; it pointed out:

> Fact that discussions may cover all important items in Danish agricultural exports to this country does not of course mean that we contemplate making concessions to the Danes over the entire field.

The UK government was nevertheless looking to achieve a balance between EFTA goods and British Commonwealth considerations. For example, one central idea that was put forward as a compromise was to give tariff concessions on bacon to Denmark – which in fact covered around 50% of total Danish agricultural exports to the UK – as it considered that: 'Imports of bacon from the Commonwealth countries ... are very small'.[116] Obviously, however, this was not what the Irish government itself felt regarding the matter of UK bacon imports.

Another important consideration, of course, was dairy produce. In this case, the UK government was not as inclined to yield to Danish insistence, but still felt that it might be necessary, in resisting this pressure from the Danes on the general question of dairy produce, to make a concession in a more limited sphere, such as the tariff on imports of blue veined cheese for instance. The thinking behind this approach was very simple:

> It is ... our hope that if in the course of the negotiations it seems to us necessary to make this concession in order to avert pressure for concessions on other dairy products of greater interest to Commonwealth countries, the latter will agree to waive the preference binding in the wider general interest of securing a Free Trade Area of the Seven, with the advantages to the Commonwealth as a whole which as [previously] explained ... will it is expected go with it in the long term.[117]

Nonetheless, Denmark's inclusion in EFTA was already proving to be a very demanding and most inconvenient consideration with which the Irish government had to deal, because not only was Ireland now in danger of losing its industrial preferences into the UK market, but its agricultural preferences were now under serious threat too.

The implications of EFTA's conception

In the meantime, some very important decisions had already been taken regarding EFTA's composition. As a result of its exclusion, the question of new members in this grouping was now a significant consideration in Ireland's case. Therefore, it is worth noting that in relation to the accession of other countries, it was agreed by the Seven that this must only be by 'unanimous agreement'. However, while some of them expressed a preference for confining EFTA accession to countries drawn from the OEEC, it was clear from an early point in time that the Scandinavian members were in 'some difficulty' over Finland's position.[118] In fact, a draft plan on the question of further EFTA membership remarked that it would only be open to countries 'ready to assume the obligations', while also reinforcing the view that there would have to be unanimous consent to any such decision.[119] Therefore, Ireland had been excluded not only because the Irish government was not ready to assume all the obligations necessary and was not in a position to negotiate concessions or derogations, but because it was not receiving the support of the UK government to further its candidature. As has been noted previously, one of the pivotal determining factors in Ireland's relationship with EFTA was the attitude of the UK government, not only to the fundamental make-up of EFTA, but also both to the Irish role with EFTA and to the Anglo-Irish trading relationship. Thus, this brief background information that has been presented on the part played by the UK serves as a significant introduction to the actual reactions of, and implications for, the Irish government to its exclusion from the new European grouping of Seven.

At a meeting of the UK cabinet steering committee on EFTA held on 25 June 1959, one of the main items reviewed were the discussions held with representatives of the Irish government from the previous day. In this regard, one of the UK officials present said that the Irish delegation had evidently been extremely concerned at the prospect of UK tariffs on bacon and cheese actually being removed within EFTA. Indeed, this report continued by stating that the Irish representatives were:

> ... also perturbed by the political, as well as the economic damage which they might suffer as a result of their being exluded [sic] both from the Six and from the Seven, and were sending a note to all the countries concerned proposing that, pending negotiations for a seventeen-country free trade arrangement, the members of the Six and of the Seven should extend to the Irish Republic the tariff and quota adjustments which they were making among themselves.

The Irish delegation had then asked for UK government support for this proposal and urged that they ought to be allowed to attend the forthcoming EFTA meeting in Stockholm to argue their case. Quite understandably, the UK representatives informed their Irish counterparts that this would be 'impracticable'. Needless to say, the Irish deputation felt that it was imperative that another Anglo-Irish meeting be convened without delay to discuss the whole trade issue, but the UK was not immediately clear whether the Irish envisaged such an encounter as a repetition of the meeting held the previous day or as a meeting to review the 1938 Anglo-Irish trade agreement. In either case, the UK steering committee on EFTA felt, that from the Irish viewpoint, the purpose of such a bilateral meeting was 'likely to be one of presentation rather than one of substance'. However, according to the steering committee, such a dialogue would 'serve little useful purpose if it were devoted to a review of the Trade Agreement'. Indeed, it is instantly discernible from this report that consideration of the Irish, though a burden, was not going to influence radically the course of action taken by the UK government in the EFTA negotiations or in further Anglo-Irish meetings.[120]

Critically, the UK Department of the Treasury again remarked that there was a special problem regarding Ireland's non-participation in EFTA that was thus raised by the inclusion of Portugal amongst the Seven. In fact, it was felt that:

> The Portuguese need for special terms faces us with an awkward problem. We have said that membership of the Group will be open to other countries ready to assume the full obligations. We cannot create a special position for Portugal in the Stockholm Group without laying ourselves open to strong pressures from the Peripherals – Ireland, Iceland, Greece and Turkey – to participate also, on the same or even laxer terms. (Ireland is already much concerned about participation, not because she has any economic interest in doing so, but for political reasons, i.e. explaining at home why she is out if Portugal is in.) Whilst these pressures might not be impossible to manage if it were a question of permitting or refusing accession or association after the Stockholm Convention had been signed, to admit any one of the Peripherals to the negotiations would be a serious handicap and to admit all of them, including Greece and Turkey, would be intolerable.

Accordingly, in coming up with a general escape clause from this 'intolerable' position, one formulated to pacify Portugal, the Treasury noted that it was most unlikely that, with the possible exception of Ireland, other peripherals could actually take up these terms. As this escape clause was only being couched in sweeping terms, it would thus be possible to resist pressure for any laxer interpretation to be conceived. Of course, it was fully realised that:

> If Ireland applied for association [with EFTA] on these terms after signature of the Convention, we should have no reason to refuse.

The idea behind this formulation, however, was to keep all the peripherals out of EFTA.[121]

The one exception to this rule was, perhaps, going to be Portugal, which alone was to have a special position devised for it. In this case, although it would clearly prove to be difficult to implement, it was felt that it should be made harder for the 'infection of Portugal' to spread towards facilitating other OEEC members to join EFTA. Obviously, there was always the option of Portugal signing a separate treaty, in which case there would be 'little difficulty' in accepting Ireland on the same terms. Nevertheless, the UK Treasury clearly felt that the government could drop Portugal from the EFTA picture altogether, a choice which presented no difficulty at all *vis-à-vis* the peripherals and which, at the same time, had the added bonus of instantly removing any political difficulties that might potentially be created by the Irish.[122] It was quite clear that Dublin would take some convincing on the matter.

The UK Department of the Treasury followed up this assessment with other specific references to the Portuguese problem which continued to have a crucial bearing on Ireland's position. One report, further indicating the relative importance of the Portuguese question in the wider concept of EFTA, stated that:

> ... the membership of the Group so far has been described as being limited to countries which were willing to accept the full obligations from the beginning. This has been the basis on which the peripherals have been excluded. Had either the Greeks or the Turks been allowed to come in ... there can be no doubt that the work would have been less far advanced and a great deal of time would have been wasted ... It is almost certain that ... Ireland could not accept the obligations which it is likely Portugal will accept ... Ireland has really no economic interest in being a member of the Stockholm Group; she already has free access to the main market, the United Kingdom, and membership of the Group would oblige her in time to take down her own tariff against U.K. goods ... But the problem ... is at the moment not primarily economic; it is political ...[123]

The basic hub of the matter was evidently understood by the UK. For the Irish government, exclusion from EFTA had become a political, rather than an economic, problem.

Therefore, despite the debate that was going on within the UK government, the Irish obviously felt that the time had come to move things along. As a result, Hugh McCann, the Irish ambassador in London, delivered an Irish government *aide-mémoire* dated 26 June 1959 to the UK Commonwealth Relations Office; the latter, it has to be remembered, still dealt with Ireland rather than the UK Foreign Office. In fact, Dublin handed similar documents over to the other members of the Six and the Seven. London's immediate reaction was that most of the Irish proposals outlined in the *aide-mémoire* would actually make 'no practical difference' in the treatment accorded by the UK to imports from Ireland and that, as far as it was concerned, only one part of the *aide-mémoire* really 'bites' and that this would have to be actively considered. The paragraph of the document in question read:

> As an interim measure and pending the negotiations of a multilateral association comprising all member countries of the OEEC, which would precisely define Ireland's obligations concerning the reduction and eventual elimination of trade barriers vis-a-vis other OEEC countries, the members of the European Economic Community and the members of any other grouping which may be formed by other OEEC countries should, without obligation of reciprocity, extend to Ireland the benefit of tariff reductions and quota enlargements made in favour of one another.

The Commonwealth Relations Office reported that the Irish ambassador had explained that the philosophy behind this initiative was simple. Indeed, it was the intention, in principle, of the Irish government to join any FTA of the Seventeen which might be negotiated and, therefore, that this desire, as stated in the *aide-mémoire*, might provide a basis for acceptance of what they considered to be a genuine proposal.[124]

The Irish ambassador was reported as saying that it was his belief that Irish goods were in fact receiving the benefit of tariff cuts made by the Six on 1 January 1959 that had been extended to other members of the GATT, although, as he pointed out, Ireland was not a member of either organisation. The UK government had, at this point, given no particularly deep thought to the question of extending the benefit of tariff reductions due to be introduced from 1 July 1960 to other OEEC or GATT members, primarily because it would only weaken the bargaining position of the Seven in relation to the Six. Indeed, it was stated in the UK departmental secretaries report that it could be 'difficult' to reconcile any extension of these tariff cuts to Ireland considering not only the GATT position, but knowing that Ireland would have 'difficulty ... in declaring any intention of joining the Seven'. Nonetheless, McCann concluded by saying that the Irish government was still owed a reply to its proposal that a trade delegation might come over to London for talks during the course of July 1959. Indeed, the Irish were treating the situation so seriously that it was said to be wholly conceivable that the taoiseach himself might possibly be able to participate at the meetings.[125]

In the days ahead, a flurry of urgent Anglo-Irish communications on Ireland's trade with Europe followed and the meeting between their bilateral representatives duly took place on 13 July 1959, giving both sides the opportunity to detail their relative positions.[126] At the meeting, those present included the taoiseach, Seán Lemass, the Irish agriculture minister, Patrick

Smith, and the Irish industry & commerce minister, Jack Lynch, as well as diplomats and departmental secretaries that consisted of Hugh McCann, J.C.B.MacCarthy, J.C.Nagle and T.K.Whitaker. Rather a high-powered Irish delegation it must be said for a simple and hastily arranged bilateral meeting. It is worth exploring this encounter in some detail, however, as it demonstrated both the progression of Dublin's thinking on European integration and the role that the UK government was playing in that context.[127]

In opening the exchanges, Lemass let it be known that there was a lot of 'anxiety' in Ireland about the division of Europe into two distinct trading groups, neither of which the Irish government expected to be able to enter 'with advantage'. Indeed, the Irish delegation made it clear that they feared that they might subsequently find not only some European markets closed off to Ireland but also their main market in the UK restricted. This would be especially painful at a time when expansion of Irish agricultural and industrial production and trade was becoming increasingly vital if Ireland was ever going to see its standard of living raised so that it could come more closely into line with that of the rest of Western Europe. The new taoiseach held that the expansion of trade that was necessary for Ireland could only come from trade with the UK, as continental Europe was not as yet an important Irish export market. In this regard, the Anglo-Irish trade agreement of 1938, which had essentially been based on the principle of mutual preferences being exchanged, had lost much of its value to Ireland because of the twin reasons of a 'fall in the value of the preferences expressed in cash terms' and because of the UK's agricultural support policy. The obvious implication was that the UK's proposed agreement with Denmark threatened only to reduce the value of this trade agreement even further. Lemass duly went on to suggest a solution to this problem. Indeed, he was paraphrased as saying that what Ireland really want was:

> ... to explore, in informal discussions, the possibility of putting trade between the two countries on a new basis that would offer the Irish Republic an assured market and reasonable price stability for their exports, especially of agricultural products, in return for concessions in favour of the United Kingdom manufacturers.

What this actually boiled down to was the suggestion that a new price for Irish agricultural products should be set somewhere between the UK domestic price and the contemporary Irish export price. In return, as a kind of economic *quid pro quo* for the UK, the Irish delegation offered increased preferences. At that moment in time, however, the Irish were particularly concerned that the question of further bilateral discussions should be agreed to in principle. Meanwhile, Lemass indicated that he would request that the UK government should avoid any general or specific commitments being made to EFTA that would preclude recognition of the existing and future 'special Anglo-Irish relationship'.[128]

In reply to the Irish delegation, the UK President of the Board of Trade, David Eccles, went on the offensive. He said that he understood the Irish position perfectly and, in fact, fully appreciating their difficulties, but stated that the UK already gave British Commonwealth treatment to Irish goods, as well as giving subsidised prices for Irish store cattle and sheep. Indeed, he felt compelled to ask: 'What more did Mr.Lemass think we could do?' It was becoming evident that the Irish government seemed to be asking the UK either 'to subsidise their domestic price level or perhaps to join them in some form of bilateral Free Trade Area'. However, the Irish continued to impose high tariffs against UK goods and, therefore, one of the questions that the UK was asking was: 'Would they be able to reduce them?'[129]

In turn, the taoiseach replied by saying that the Irish government was not seeking any advantages for which it was not prepared to pay, but that as Ireland was not a member of GATT it was able to think much more in terms of a bilateral solution to its trading problems. In this context, C.J.M.Alport, minister of state at the UK Board of Trade, said that:

> ... he recognised and sympathised with the difficulties which the present situation held for the Republic but Mr.Lemass seemed to have proposed something wider than a renegotiation of the existing Agreements. While we must recognise our long standing special arrangements with the Republic of Ireland we also had to take into account how any wider arrangement would affect our commitments to Commonwealth countries.

To this intimation, which took place at a momentous meeting in which the taoiseach flew many economic and political 'kites' containing radical new ideas for further consideration by the UK, Lemass made an historic statement when declaring that he was indeed thinking of something more far-reaching than a new, enhanced Anglo-Irish trade agreement. In reality, what he actually had in mind was the 'movement towards the integration of the Irish and United Kingdom economies'. Not entirely surprisingly, Eccles replied that this suggestion raised 'great difficulties'. Indeed, he stated that, although the British Commonwealth could not expect the UK to reduce its own food production, they had a reasonable expectation that it would stay at its then level and added that there was not much room for any increase in consumption. The President of the Board of Trade then stated that, if the UK government was to offer any further advantages to anyone in its market, the question immediately arose as to whose expense such a new arrangement would be.[130]

Lemass admitted that the Irish government had not as yet attempted to formulate its ideas on an Anglo-Irish FTA in detail, but that they would be prepared to do so if there was some willingness from London to accept the principle which had just been put forward. He tried to make it clear to the UK delegation that the Irish government did not, in fact, desire an arrangement which would give Irish farmers access to the UK market at UK prices, indeed this would not suit Irish subsidy arrangements. What he did want from London though was something more along the lines of an intermediate price being set up with a greater degree of stability tied into it. The Irish ambassador added the view that any change in the Anglo-Irish trading situation was, of course, bound to be at the expense of somebody, just as the projected EFTA arrangements would indisputably be for Ireland. Lemass then continued with his original line of argument by saying that Ireland had considered some means of diverting trade to the UK at the expense of others, that some Irish industries were 'feather bedded' and that the Irish government would consider dismantling some of its complex set of protective tariffs, but that any arrangement such as an FTA would have be a 'very long term affair'. Indeed, the taoiseach said that he hoped that the Irish market for UK goods would actually expand with a growth in Irish prosperity.[131]

Alport then asked him about the agricultural goods in question that were of particular interest to Ireland, to which Lemass replied store cattle and sheep, milk and eggs. The taoiseach then came back to the heart of the matter by requesting that London secure a general clause within EFTA to make it possible for the UK to join, subject to a special arrangement also being constructed with Ireland. Not unexpectedly and rather understandably, the UK deputation replied that its government 'could not keep open a position in which we were committed to give any other country better treatment than we were offering to members of the Group'.[132] Dublin had received its answer; EFTA was going to become a reality, but a crucial question was still left hanging: what would become of bilateral trade?

During the course of the meeting, Lemass had changed the subject to Northern Ireland and had unequivocally stated that he was ready to consider any new Anglo-Irish arrangements which would help Northern Ireland. To this statement, Eccles replied that there clearly were 'special problems' for the Westminster government in relation to Northern Ireland. However, the taoiseach said that the Irish government 'was not averse in principle from a special regime for Northern Ireland products being arranged, possibly in separate talks'.[133] This issue was only skirted over though and was separate to the central message from the Irish deputation. Eccles, in concluding the morning meeting with his Irish counterparts, said that he felt that further consideration of all the various ideas put forward was needed, a sentiment to which Lemass acquiesced. The taoiseach felt though that the two sets of officials should be given an overriding directive, one enabling them to think in wider terms than just considering an adjustment to existing Anglo-Irish trade agreements.[134]

When the Anglo-Irish meeting reconvened, Eccles said that after subsequent talks with the UK Chancellor of the Exchequer, the UK contingent now felt that it should be quite clear that if asked publicly whether the possibility of extending the benefit of UK agricultural subsidies to Ireland had been discussed in these bilateral trade meetings that he would have to say that it had not. Lemass concurred. Nevertheless, the taoiseach also agreed that the Irish side would prepare detailed proposals for their UK counterparts to consider at a later meeting and that in the meantime there would be further high level meetings of officials to examine trade and economic problems of mutual interest. The whole question of Anglo-Irish trade was becoming inextricably entangled up with European integration, tying in with the central argument regarding the crucial importance of bilateral relations in particular, as well as economics in general, to Irish attitudes towards Europe.[135]

At a meeting of the UK cabinet steering committee on EFTA, held the following day 14 July 1959, the central item reviewed was a progress report on the Stockholm negotiations; however, the talks with the Irish deputation were also raised. It was duly stated that, in his discussions with the UK President of the Board of Trade, Lemass had confirmed the previous day that Ireland was 'distressed' at the prospect of two trading groups in Europe being formed, to neither of which Ireland belonged. Furthermore, it was reported that:

> [The Irish] were not anxious to join the Seven and did not press to be allowed to take part in the forthcoming discussions at Stockholm, but the establishment of the Stockholm Group would mean a serious loss of preferences on their exports of industrial products to this country while they believed that their agricultural exports had been endangered by the Anglo/Danish agreement. The Irish Ministers had talked in terms of economic integration with this country, and were prepared to offer us substantial concessions on industrial trade; but since we already gave the Republic of Ireland free entry both for agricultural and industrial products there was little that we could offer them. In discussion, reference was made to the Anglo-Irish Economic Committee which was being set up as a result of the recent discussions – albeit with little Irish support – and the Irish Ministers had undertaken to produce a paper within a fortnight setting out

their proposals. It appeared that they wanted to receive the benefit of the agricultural prices given to our home producers and they might suggest that in return they should give us preferences in their market and instruct their state undertakings to buy British products, but these suggestions would be embarrassing in view of our relations with other countries. They might also suggest the establishment of a free trade area covering Northern Ireland and the Irish Republic.

In addition, the *aide-mémoire*, which the Irish government had previously sent to the Six and the Seven, was first reported by the Irish to have been received 'not unfavourably' by some countries. Nonetheless, the basic UK government view was that it had explained to Ireland that the UK was already giving it free entry for its produce and that the UK could not then press other countries within or without the Seven to make the concessions for which they now asked.[136] Indeed, J.C.B.MacCarthy, Department of Agriculture secretary, was correct when he wrote that no OEEC country had given the Irish government 'any real grounds for hope' with regard to its request in the *aide-mémoire* for FTA concessions. In fact, he admitted that there was actually 'no prospect that the principle of our request will be conceded'.[137] The Irish government was understandably in a distinct quandary as to how to proceed.

The critical point that this chapter reveals was the UK government's determination to keep Ireland outside of EFTA. Indeed, the fact that the Irish were themselves extremely hesitant about joining this European trading bloc remains relatively irrelevant. Ireland was expressly excluded from the EFTA negotiations for two not unrelated reasons: firstly, because the UK government wanted to protect its Anglo-Irish agricultural preferences and did not want an agricultural FTA anyway; and secondly, because the UK did not want Ireland or any of the other peripherals to delay the negotiations process for an industrial FTA through the utilisation of tactics aimed at achieving economic concessions. Ireland was not even allowed to observe the EFTA negotiations at first-hand and thus had to rely primarily upon the UK government for information on the progress and substance of the discussions.

It is interesting to note that by the end of July 1959, the UK Foreign Office recognised that the decisions that were being taken at the EFTA negotiations raised three separate, but immediate, problems in relation to the peripherals and Finland, which were in assessing:

- what information was to be given to the peripherals and Finland about the outcome of the EFTA meeting then taking place;
- what arrangements were to be made to afford facilities to the Finns to follow further discussions on EFTA more closely;

- what arrangements would have to be made to enable the peripherals to follow the forthcoming EFTA negotiations.

Of these difficulties, only the first and the last obviously applied to Ireland. However, it can also be deduced from this analysis that Ireland was not being seriously considered within the EFTA context by the UK government or by any of the other EFTA members. Therefore, the question facing the Irish was: where did it go from here in terms of European integration and what did the future hold for the economy in a Europe at 'Sixes and Sevens'?

Ireland in a Europe at 'Sixes and Sevens'

Ireland had suddenly entered into a period of dramatic change, both in the internal and the external arena. In the realm of domestic politics, the summer of 1959 is viewed as a critical turning point in the political development of the country. The decision by Éamon de Valera to resign from 'active party politics' in June 1959, with Lemass subsequently taking over as taoiseach, is rightly regarded as having released a governmental log-jam that had heretofore clogged up Irish political life and had kept it enclosed in some form of national economic, political and social time-capsule. Even though Lemass was from the same political epoch as de Valera – that is Irish civil war politics of the early 1920s – and although he came from the same political party, the former immediately appeared to belong to a different generation in terms of political outlook; this became especially apparent once he came to power.

De Valera himself went from the post of taoiseach to the Irish presidency in a matter of two days, in turn replacing Seán T.O'Kelly, after being inaugurated on 25 June 1959; he had beaten the opposition candidate, Seán MacEoin, by 538,003 votes to 417,536 in the Irish presidential election which had been held a week previously. As Uachtarán na hÉireann (the Irish president), de Valera played a more minor role in Irish political affairs during the next decade and beyond. Significantly, however, the day of the presidential election was also the date set for a referendum on the future of the electoral system of proportional representation. Previously, in March 1959, Seanad Éireann (the upper parliamentary chamber) had for the first time in its history rejected an Irish government bill, because the government wanted to abolish proportional representation in favour of a first-past-the-post electoral system. After the bill became law three months later, in accordance with Irish legislative procedure, the referendum that had to be held to change Article 23.1.2° of *Bunreacht na hÉireann* was set for 17 June 1957 in order to coincide with the Irish presidential election. Although de Valera was elected as Irish president for a term of seven years, the Fianna Fáil sponsored referendum failed. The majority of the voting population had seen through the electoral ruse and as a result forced the political establishment to take direct, but accountable, responsibility for the future of their nation. So, if this was what was happening on the domestic front, what was happening to Ireland on the political level in the context of the wider world?

J.H.Whyte has said of Lemass that he possessed a 'critical, questing mind, continually re-examining old assumptions and looking for better ways to do things'.[138] Indeed, under the new taoiseach, an inventive and vibrant political elite emerged in Ireland, comprised of young, energetic and ambitious politicians who brought a sense of innovation to Irish life and politics. At the end of the 1950s, a long overdue generational take-over of politics had taken place. Nevertheless, this does not suggest that Ireland's exclusion from EFTA membership was a precipitating factor in this development. However, Ireland's continued growth in the international sphere is indicative of the different direction being taken and nature of politics, both at home and abroad, from this point in time.

The changing realities of a new European military and trading situation that faced the country were mounting.[139] As the 1960s dawned, there were two main sets – one political, the other economic – that demanded consideration: (i) NATO, depicting security; and (ii) the OEEC, representing trade.[140] If it was going to survive as a dynamic and legitimate political entity, Ireland was going to have to escape from its position of economic dependence on the UK and, at the same time, reverse its peripheralisation from the European economic mainstream. With these twin impressions of Ireland firmly in mind, it seems more than an accident that, just after it had been left outside of EFTA, the government made strong moves towards the establishment of diplomatic relations with the EEC. Indeed, one of the more important results to emerge from its exclusion from EFTA was the fact that, on the question of European integration, Ireland was then forced to turn to the EEC as a consequence and to effect beneficial and constructive relations at a bilateral level. Therefore, one of the first real moves in this innovative external economic reorientation was – as Patrick Keatinge has pointed out in *The formulation of Irish foreign policy* – the formal opening of Ireland's diplomatic mission to the EEC in December 1959, a development which was in fact originally combined with its mission to Belgium in Brussels.[141] Once again, an advance in foreign policy could only take place after an intense period of internal Irish government consideration and debate; angst regarding the implications, mainly pecuniary, was eventually overcome.

On 2 July 1959, the Department of External Affairs was informed by the UK embassy in Dublin that the UK government had decided to establish formal diplomatic relations with the EEC. Up to this point, the UK had only had a diplomatic representative accredited to the ECSC and to Euratom, with a member of that particular diplomat's staff then informally responsible for keeping in close contact with the EEC. The Irish government was thus told that an informal approach was being made by the UK to see whether the Six would actually be 'favourably disposed' to the establishment of formal relations between the UK and the EEC.[142] Fully briefed on this matter by his departmental secretary, Maurice Moynihan, the prime minister therefore 'raised the question whether we should approach the E.E.C. Council of Ministers with a view to the establishment of diplomatic relations between this country and the Community'. Obviously, the new taoiseach was particularly interested in having other views such as those of his foreign minister, Frank Aiken, on the issue, but this was to be one of the last instances in which the latter played any significant role in the course of Ireland's European integration. From that point onwards, Lemass began to take this responsibility more fully upon himself rather than depending on Aiken.[143]

The UK government duly made its approach to the EEC Council of Ministers to find out whether there would be any objection from the Six to full UK diplomatic accreditation. Indeed, the Irish embassy in Brussels was able to inform the Department of External Affairs that this matter would probably be decided upon by the end of July 1959. In fact, it was also reported that the Austrian government would probably accredit a representative to the EEC in the near future and, furthermore, that although a final decision on the subject had not yet been taken by the Swiss authorities, it was understood that a similar appointment would also be made by them within a fortnight.[144] Knowledge of this state of affairs followed a series of reports from Irish diplomatic missions abroad regarding representation to the EEC. One stated that there was every indication that, with Denmark – though one of the Seven – already having accorded a representative to the Six, 'all seven may soon agree to have representation [in Brussels]'.[145] As a result of this information, Lemass became ever more anxious to hear the views of his foreign minister as to whether Ireland should establish diplomatic relations with the EEC or not. Indeed, he considered having this decision announced in the course of a debate in Dáil Éireann that was due to begin on 21 July 1959, as it gave the his government the ideal opportunity to signal its 'intention to take the necessary steps with a view to the accreditation [sic] of a representative to the Community'.[146]

After an interminable two week wait, Lemass was finally told that Aiken could see 'no objection' to the taoiseach announcing that it was the intention of the Irish government to take such steps. The Irish foreign minister informed Lemass that four states had already accredited diplomats to the EEC, that is Denmark, Greece, Israel and the US; at this point, the UK decision to accredit a representative to the EEC had only reached a preliminary stage. Moreover, Aiken stated in his memorandum that the remaining members of the Seven would quickly follow suit and that a definite decision was due. Of course, this would leave Iceland, Ireland and Turkey as the only OEEC countries without diplomatic representation to the EEC; but, why should the government have been so intent on considering the question of whether to have a representative accredited to the EEC? Importantly, Aiken considered that:

> ... particularly from the point of view of the desirability of being kept informed about the policy of and developments in the Community, e.g. on agriculture, it would be advisable for us to approach the Council of the E.E.C. with a view to the establishment of diplomatic relations.

His memorandum continued by reporting that Ireland's ambassador in Brussels had already established informal links with the EEC, but that it was considered by his superiors that the 'necessary steps should be taken with a view to the accreditation of the Ambassador as our representative to the Community'.[147] However, it was decided to raise the matter informally in cabinet before finally deciding whether or not to go ahead with the idea.[148]

On 21 July 1959, the Irish cabinet duly met to discuss the issue of diplomatic relations being formally opened with the EEC. The decision was made for the foreign minister to take the necessary preliminary steps to establish ties.[149] Thus, Lemass delivered a statement in Dáil Éireann to the effect that while the establishment and the gradual growth of the EEC, together with the emergence of a plan for the initiation of a smaller seven-nation FTA, had created problems for Ireland, he thought that it was desirable that the seriousness of the situation should not be exaggerated. In truth, he said that it was a situation over which the nation as a whole needed to ponder calmly and objectively. The taoiseach went on to state unequivocally that the evolution of the economic situation in Europe 'may well offer us new opportunities as well as new problems'.[150] Optimism was tempered with realism.

Indeed, Lemass generally kept his remarks upbeat and positive by commenting that Ireland still had recourse to bilateral trade agreements with EEC member countries; in fact, the only country with which bilateral negotiations had actually failed that year was France and even this anomaly, he said, would possibly be rectified by 'further diplomatic approaches'.

Pivotally, he added that the Irish government's policy in relation to negotiating bilateral trade agreements with EEC member states was essentially driven by 'opportunity', that is when it was considered that such agreements would serve Ireland's essential interests by assisting in the expansion of its total agricultural and industrial exports.[151] According to the taoiseach, the economic outlook might not be so bleak after all. In fact, on another occasion, Lemass stated with regard to Ireland's economic situation with the Six that, as far as the government understood the position, the EEC would not begin to undertake formal trade negotiations on behalf of the Six for some time to come.[152]

Privately, however, the Department of External Affairs foreign trade committee viewed the government's bargaining power with respect to the negotiation of trade agreements as 'virtually a farce' because Ireland had, for the most part, globalised quotas and thus had little room for manoeuvre economically. Indeed, in relation to the rest of Europe, Ireland was, with the exception of its trade with Spain, already in a negative trading position. In 1958, for instance, its trade deficit with West Germany was at a ratio of nearly 3:1, France and Italy at over 3:1, Belgium and the Netherlands more than 3:1 and 4:1 respectively, Sweden at over 5:1, Denmark at 21:1, and Finland at 33:1.[153] Additionally, it was known that, in the very near future, there was the virtually assured prospect that there would be collective negotiations with the Six through the EEC, a revolution in European trade practices.

With all these considerations in mind, it comes as no surprise that the government proposed to open discussions with the EEC Council of Ministers with a view to establishing formal diplomatic relations just as other countries had done or were about to do.[154] It had become imperative to avoid isolation, although that does not mean that it was not considered. An indication of the striking consequences of the division of Europe into separate economic blocs was that serious consideration was given to the idea of Ireland actually leaving the OEEC if the Irish government chose to continue to pursue a foreign policy of bilateral trade agreements and OEEC obligations prevented it from doing so. The government was in a peculiar dilemma as to how to proceed.[155]

On 31 July 1959, the Irish ambassador at Brussels finally made the necessary approach to the EEC Commission president to seek the establishment of diplomatic relations.[156] It was only in early October 1959 though that the EEC agreed to the opening of formal relations with Ireland. In fact, as this arrangement involved the designation of an Irish representative to the EEC – indeed, because no reciprocal provisions were established when dealing with other similar organisations such as the UN, the OEEC, or the

Council of Europe – it was proposed that the task of taking on the job should fall to Denis MacDonald, the Irish ambassador to Belgium.[157] The issue of appointing a representative to the EEC finally came to the Irish cabinet for a decision on 13 October 1959 and, as a result, MacDonald became Ireland's first ambassador-designate to the EEC.[158]

Thus, on 3 December 1959, Con Cremin, the Department of External Affairs secretary, confirmed that MacDonald's appointment had been accepted by the EEC. In informing the government about this decision, Cremin also included a statement on the appointment for release to the press, because the taoiseach had indicated that 'he would like a certain amount of publicity to be given to the appointment'. The proposed statement said that MacDonald had been appointed to the EEC while retaining his duties as Irish ambassador to Belgium, a post to which he had been attached since the beginning of the year. It also stated that:

> Ireland has important trade connections with these six countries. In 1958 exports to them were valued at £6.1m. (or approximately 5% of total exports), and imports at £22.1m. (or approximately 12% of the total). It is, therefore, desirable that this country should be in a position to obtain information about the policies adopted by the Community towards outside countries. The existence of formal relations should, furthermore, enable the Government to be kept informed of the trend of thought within the Community in regard to a wider trade association of members of O.E.E.C. Other countries which have established diplomatic relations with the European Economic Community are Austria, Denmark, Great Britain, Greece, Israel, Japan, Norway, Portugal, Sweden, Switzerland and U.S.A.

It was noted that MacDonald was due to present his diplomatic letters of credence to the EEC Commission president, along with five other new diplomatic representatives to the EEC, on 15 December 1959.[159] Ireland now had direct access to the EEC and, from this point, could only be limited by the imagination of the government and its representatives.

It must be said that the appointment of an Irish ambassador to the EEC was one of the most significant developments in the history of Ireland's integration into European affairs. It may not have been one of the most spectacular events, but it was a move that was highly charged with symbolism and one which eventually had important consequences. For instance, Dublin was henceforth kept fully informed of developments in the EEC on subjects such as the Common Agricultural Policy (CAP). In addition, as a result of the constant stream of information emanating from the Irish embassy in Brussels, the government was also fully alert to the evolution of the EEC membership process, so that by 1961 Ireland was in an informed position to decide on whether or not to apply. Indeed, the promise of constant interaction at this diplomatic level thus had a constituent part to play in the government's ultimate decision to seek full EEC accession.

In the meantime, the official position regarding EFTA hardened somewhat. While the Dublin government was in fact prepared to consider participating in an OEEC-wide trading agreement, it was made abundantly clear to Western Europe that Ireland would only be able to do so if the 'special circumstances' of its economy were taken into account. Otherwise, the government did not feel called upon to take any steps designed to encourage renewed FTA negotiations. Indeed, as a result of the FTA negotiations process, the Irish government realised that when it came to applying to join the EEC it would not be able to maintain the high-powered negotiating position that it had previously held with any conviction, especially regarding the propensity of this tactic to garner results. At least there was also the realisation that Ireland would actively have to pursue a policy in the future of reducing tariffs if it was going to be in a position to join.[160] This view was endorsed by officials at the Department of Industry & Commerce, who for their part perceived 'little case for contemplating joining the Outer Seven', even if the latter did announce its determination to establish a multilateral association between OEEC countries which would remove trade barriers and promote closer economic cooperation.[161] Full EEC membership for Ireland was another matter altogether.

Intermediate conclusions

One of the principal purposes of this chapter has been to act as a comprehensive introduction to the heart of Ireland's EEC relations in these early formative years of European integration; as was already outlined, the next chapter – entitled *Ireland's first EEC application, 31 July 1961* – concentrates on the Dublin government's decision to apply to join the EEC for the first time. In doing so, it argues that the realities of the economic situation facing the government forced certain economic and political consequences to be accepted and sanctioned at this point in time, that this is what European integration really meant for Ireland.

The stark choices facing the Irish government regarding the country's future policy towards the EEC and EFTA, that is the pros and cons of membership in either or both groups, were succinctly put by Garret FitzGerald, one of the more informed commentators on Ireland and the question of European integration, in March 1960. He felt that Dublin obviously had to reckon the economic and political balance between staying out of EFTA or had to make a serious and concerted effort to join. There were two considerable arguments against the idea of accession, with FitzGerald noting that:

- in reality, EFTA membership for Ireland would bring 'few tangible trade advantages', firstly because of the various Anglo-Irish agreements that continued to protect Ireland economically and secondly because of the relative lack of importance of the other EFTA members to Ireland in terms of foreign trade;
- there was also the fact that EFTA was already being dwarfed by the EEC, both in economic and political terms, with the latter's attempt at integration enjoying the considerable support of the US government.

There were, of course, other arguments which did the opposite and favoured membership of EFTA; according to FitzGerald, the most important of these were based on the belief that:

- otherwise it would isolate itself from one of the foremost economic developments in European history and risked the prospect of its non-participation in any future EFTA negotiations with the EEC;
- EFTA membership would actually force Ireland to reduce its tariffs, which would be quite painful in the short term but would be extremely beneficial in the long run, especially as tariffs would have to go at some stage anyway if it was to move towards full membership of the EEC.

As a matter of fact, government policy was slowly coming to view participation in a regional economic grouping as a necessity, but it was equally obvious that such a move would have to be coupled or tied in with improving Anglo-Irish trade relations.[162]

A relatively dispassionate assessment of the destination and origin of Irish exports and imports, as well as their composition, has proven to be a very useful tool for inquiring into whether there was a changing pattern in Irish attitudes towards Europe at the earliest stage of this analysis. New export markets were continually being sought by the government in Dublin – primarily in Europe and the US – but, because the UK has always been Ireland's most important market, accounting for what can only be described as a disproportionate and economically unhealthy dependency, previous Irish governments which had tried to wean exporters off the UK market had done so with varying degrees of success and sometimes none at all. Indeed, the process of redirecting Irish exporters attention towards these new trading destinations was taking a considerable period of time to impact. All the same, Ireland was at least exercising its right to, and furthermore recognising the power of, importing goods from further afield than the UK, particularly as the need to import foreign technology gained increasing importance both in terms of percentage and volume of product. The relative imbalance between Irish exports to, and imports from, the EFTA countries – 1% and 5% of its respective totals – thus became a major concern in relation to the FTA negotiations. The lack of any real opportunity for trade reciprocity with EFTA's members essentially made the UK's position the main concern for the Irish government.[163] The fact remained that the UK market was by far and away Ireland's most important economic consideration in any terms, including European integration. Ireland remained a peripheral European economy tied into a relationship of dependence with the UK.[164] Of course, this does not suggest that Ireland was an underdeveloped country, but it is difficult to argue that it did not display the classic characteristics indicating a highly dangerous lack of diversity and an exuberant propensity towards reliance on one predominant economic outlet and source.

In truth, the central argument in this chapter gives further credence to the view that Ireland was inextricably influenced by the economic and political actions and activities of the UK government, indeed by similar pressures – from the EEC for instance – on the UK. When the option of joining EFTA was denied to Ireland by London in May 1959 – albeit for its own reasons, such as its desire to protect the free-flow of cheap agricultural imports and a lucrative export market, as well as its wish to confront the EEC with a coherent alternative organisation – the Irish government, though initially infuriated and alarmed about its future prospects, was also given an opportunity, that is the freedom to act upon its own economy, not as it saw fit, but as economic survival dictated. The need to diversify markets was plain to see, as was the need to improve and vary domestic produce. What had been lacking more than anything in Ireland was the imagination, coupled with the impetus, for change. The creation of the EEC and then EFTA proffered the necessary stimulus to the Dublin government for the ready and serious enactment of an economic reformation.

A notable exception to those historians who have examined this period and ignored the importance of EFTA to Ireland is J.J.Lee; in his *Ireland, 1912-1985: politics and society*, he has viewed the formation and development of both the EEC and EFTA as having offered both opportunities and having posed threats to the Irish economy. Indeed, he has written:

The scant sympathy shown by members of EFTA towards Irish demands for 'special treatment' carried the warning that a supplicant posture was unlikely to win concessions. Lemass held that once Britain applied for membership of the EEC, Ireland's dependency left her with little option but to follow suit, whether she liked it or not ... Lemass ... though as ignorant of European cultures as the majority of his countrymen, came to increasingly convey the impression that he relished the prospect of EEC membership.[165]

As has been suggested, EFTA, while not giving Ireland the opportunity to join, did not meet its specific needs anyway. The government wanted a loosely organised free trade area which took special regard for Irish agricultural produce, while enshrining a transitional period for industrially retarded countries to catch up. EFTA was not the organisation that Ireland needed or wanted to join. Indeed, this was the most significant difference between EFTA and EEC membership because it is true to say, as Brian Girvin has, that 'in the former agriculture was not in question for Ireland and therefore it had been government policy to pursue the effective protection of existing Irish industry'.[166]

However, when it came to the EEC, the only valid conclusion that can be drawn from Irish policy is that this possibility entailed taking the economy as a whole into account and not just one sector; both agriculture and industry had to be taken into full consideration. The point being made is that Ireland had not just been given the incentive for economic change by the various developments in Europe; in fact, it had also been shown the virtual necessity of doing so. Any country with exports equivalent to *circa* 36½% of its GDP, as Ireland had at this time, places itself in a dangerous economic position, allowing an invidious dependence on the whims of the international marketplace, with the domestic economy often suffering accordingly as a result.[167] The direction and composition of Irish trade, as well as its overly protective nature, had to be transformed as an economic prerequisite if Ireland was going to reorganise itself economically. European integration offered Ireland this possibility.

In February 1960, the taoiseach travelled to London in order to seek an adjustment to Anglo-Irish trade so as to gain recognition from the UK of the invidious position in which Ireland was finding itself. The subsequent signing of a new bilateral trade agreement two months later – after a lengthy and strained period of negotiations in which Dublin failed to make the kind of economic progress that it really desired – at least gave the Irish government some respite from having to make far-reaching or fundamental decisions about its future role in Europe.[168] Indeed, Ireland's relations with the GATT and with the US are evidence of this economic phenomenon. The government had not been prepared to take part in the GATT negotiations of the mid-1950s, mainly because it was felt that its participation in any OEEC developments that took place would ultimately fulfil any necessity to eliminate undesirable or incidental trade barriers.[169] As a consequence, it managed to bypass the whole issue of GATT participation until its inscription to this global trade organisation began to become unavoidable. As a future GATT member – although that was not for some years to come – it was felt by J.C.B.MacCarthy, secretary at the Department of Industry & Commerce, that at least 'Ireland could be selective about the concessions we would negotiate on a reciprocal basis'. In his opinion, EFTA was offering less and less to the country; indeed, he felt that membership would mean 'throwing away tariff and quota concessions for nothing to the British'.[170] As was the case with the EEC and EFTA, Ireland was prepared to explore the possibility of its accession to GATT, but also wanted to keep its Anglo-Irish trade preferences alive.[171] Equally, the US was not only becoming a more important market destination, but it was also becoming a major source of technological and manufactured goods for the country. However, Ireland was dwarfed by the US and was not in a position, it was felt, to expand this bilateral economic relationship in any meaningful way. Overall, therefore, the economic route that was beginning to look most promising, outside of the ever-present system of Anglo-Irish trade arrangements, was the EEC.

At the very least, it can be said that the changing orientation of the Irish economy was becoming rather evident; the establishment in 1959 of the Shannon Free Airport Development Company was an example of that.[172] What needs to be explored in more detail at this point are the hows and the whys – the purpose of the opening parts of the next chapter – especially when political questions such as neutrality began to play a secondary role to economics in the foreign policy emphasis of the Irish government. In this period, it becomes clearer that, in regard to foreign economic questions, Lemass exercised the real control over policy direction. Indeed, on becoming taoiseach, he was slowly, but purposefully, able to redirect government policy on an issue such as neutrality, basically by making it 'negotiable'. In fact, his publicly stated opinions quickly moved beyond this position, actually in a direction whereby he was prepared to set neutrality aside as soon as was necessitated by developments within Europe. In reality, Ireland was beginning to place a certain emphasis on economic development ahead of political considerations and, by implication, upon European integration.

3 Ireland's first EEC application, 31 July 1961

The decision to join the EEC

On 26 July 1961, Harold Macmillan, the UK prime minister, informally told the taoiseach, Seán Lemass, that his government had finally come to a decision to join the EEC as a full member. With respect to this hotly-debated issue, Macmillan wrote that: 'after weighing all the considerations we have reached the conclusion that the right course for us is to seek to enter into negotiations with the Six'.[1] This move, hardly unexpected, consigned to the past what had been an uncertain period of hypothesising and speculation regarding Ireland's own future role within Europe's integration process. Indeed, as a direct result of this entreaty by London, one of Dublin's central foreign policy dilemmas – over whether or not to establish an explicit relationship with the EEC – suddenly gained the sense of definition that it had heretofore been lacking. As a consequence, the taoiseach formally initiated what has become the single-most important policy development in the Irish state's post Second World War history, forming part of the first concerted attempt by the countries of Europe to build upon the sense of community awakened by the Six some years previously. Unquestionably, the essential ingredient in Dublin's decision was the fact that London had decided to do the same; additionally, it also marked the definitive transition of Irish foreign policy from being decided by political considerations to being determined by economic factors.

Within a week of this remarkable development, Lemass wrote to the EEC Council president, Ludwig Erhard, to relate that Ireland wanted to become a full member of the EEC. Accordingly, the government presented its application to join under the relevant provision in the *Treaty establishing the European Economic Community*. The article specifically dealing with the application of a state for full membership of the EEC (Article 237) read:

> Any European State may apply to become a member of the Community. It shall address its application to the Council, which shall act unanimously after obtaining the opinion of the Commission. The conditions of admission and the adjustments to this Treaty necessitated thereby shall be the subject of an agreement between the Member States and the applicant State. This agreement shall be submitted for ratification by all the Contracting States in accordance with their respective constitutional requirements.[2]

This formal request, unlike the *aide-mémoire* circulated to the Six by the Irish government at the beginning of July 1961, made no reference to positions that Ireland would subsequently wish to take in any admission negotiations, even though the state obviously continued to have two principal economic interests at heart. These preoccupations concerned:

- the whole question of agriculture;
- the fact that many indigenous Irish industries were not only relatively weak, but that they would also be severely at risk once tariff and trade barriers were eliminated.

As a Council of Europe report from 1961 pointed out, agriculture was the leading determinant in the Irish economy. In fact, as an economic sector, it came well ahead of any industrial concerns.[3] Therefore, Ireland's application was kept deliberately brief and was also couched in essentially vague terms, stating that the government 'fully share the ideals which inspired the parties to the Treaty and accept the aims of the Community as set out therein, as well as the action proposed to achieve those aims'. Essentially, Lemass petitioned the EEC Council to facilitate Ireland in its quest for full membership of the EEC.[4]

In an effort to preempt Macmillan, this Irish government overture thus came ten days before London made a similar request and commitment. The regular bilateral and high-level exchange of economic and political communications had, however, left Dublin confident in the knowledge that, in taking such a momentous decision, they would not find themselves out of step with the former.[5] Ireland's application for full membership was being openly made in the context of an expected corresponding move from the UK government, but was actually received much earlier than envisioned by the EEC Council.[6] Notwithstanding this particular point, the decision to apply was merely announced to the general public on 1 August 1961, but even this disclosure nearly caused a 'breach of courtesy' as Ireland's application to join the EEC was only read into the records of Dáil Éireann upon confirmation of its receipt by Erhard. In spite of this break with protocol, the taoiseach went on to explain in parliament the wider significance of the move, essentially that it would have been economic suicide to have stayed apart from the momentous developments in European integration.[7] Importantly, though this move was overshadowed by similar decisions being anticipated from the Danes and the UK – both of which followed on 10 August 1961 – it was noted in Brussels that, apart from it being dependent upon a UK bid, the Irish application differed significantly from their earlier *aide-mémoire* by not mentioning any exemptions that Ireland might wish to receive during accession negotiations.[8] No definite reply from the various EEC institutions or the Six regarding this process was expected until the following September, but at least its desire to join was now official and public.

The magnitude, indeed, the momentous nature of this move by the Irish government is difficult to over-emphasise. This formal application for full EEC membership heralded Ireland's reorientation away from economic dependence on the UK and, at the same time, its realignment away from the radical politics it had pursued at the UN. As Dermot Keogh has shown, however, even this move was not allowed to escape from Ireland's perceived need to steal a march on its neighbour, by applying for full membership before the UK.[9] Obviously, this decision was taken as much for public consumption and gratification as for anything else, mainly in order to demonstrate that it was not as a consequence of a similar move being taken by the UK government, but that it was taken independently. Nevertheless, this new Irish government foreign policy process, the progenitors of which had actually been domestic in form – T.K.Whitaker's *Economic development* and the subsequent *Programme for economic expansion* – had the sound belief at its core, that as a small peripheral economy, Ireland had to become less dependent upon its larger neighbour if it was ever going to thrive. Although tentative moves were made towards GATT membership, for instance, in order to realise its economic independence, Ireland would do so through aligning itself with Europe, deemed to be its 'most realistic alternative' to continuing dependence upon the UK.[10]

At the same time, political considerations such as the island's political partitioning and its military neutrality were swept aside, ignored or just paid lip-service as Lemass adopted, what Ronan Fanning terms, a 'more pragmatic approach' to such questions.[11] Constitutional objections to EEC membership, though valid, were not initially admitted to publicly, as the Irish government went through its usual practice of expressing information in 'general, vague and even ambiguous terms' and even then only doing so quite grudgingly. A prime example of the government's rather blasé handling of the political implications of Ireland joining the EEC was the taoiseach's stated view that:

The factors which arise in connection with possible membership on our part of the European Economic Community are primarily of an economic nature. There are, as well, certain political implications which, in my opinion, are not such as to make it undesirable for this country to join the Community on the hypothesis mentioned [the political desirability of membership] ...[12]

Throughout this period, Lemass did not elaborate any further on the implications of European integration, prompting Patrick Keatinge to remark that, for the taoiseach, 'vagueness was his most effective weapon'.[13] By definition, economics were beginning to come out way ahead of political considerations when related to the question of Ireland's European integration, a theme which would develop throughout the 1960s.[14]

Nonetheless, the government decision to apply to join the EEC must be viewed primarily as a pragmatic one. Indeed, Miriam Hederman has pointed to three leading factors that determined, and equally were determined by, the development of a credible and sincere policy towards the EEC, suggesting:

- the relative position of the UK government;
- the influence of domestic interest groups;
- the decision itself to go for full membership.

With all of these considerations in mind, it is firstly possible to say that there was an explicit government policy, based upon the realities of Anglo-Irish trade, which determined that the UK's actual status for Ireland would not be supplanted, but augmented, by the EEC in an effort to see that a better economic balance could be struck. Secondly, it has been noted that groups representing farmers, federalists and industrialists which, when added to the existing domestic power structures such as the civil service and Dáil Éireann, increased the pressure on the Irish government to act on European integration and, in so doing, helped to empower themselves. Thirdly, the conclusion that full membership was the only real and valid policy option open to the Irish government initially became a self-perpetuating notion, before finally becoming irrefutable dogma.[15] When considered together, these three key components give a clearer picture of the economic and political realities that were facing Ireland, while at the same time constraining the government's *bona fide* room for manoeuvre.

After the UK indicated its intention to adhere to the EEC in July 1961, it should be highlighted that Ireland was left in a relatively unenviable quandary. Indeed, as it had been given no choice about EFTA membership, a position previously clarified in *From the OEEC to EFTA, 1957 to 1959*, it should also be reasserted that this particular European trading alliance did not meet Ireland's needs anyway. However, the EEC's potential to cater for the agricultural question – aside from industrial issues – put it into a totally different category altogether. It was quickly determined that Ireland could not afford to be outside a powerful integrated economic bloc such as this, especially if it was going to include its most important trading partner as well. Its total national income had been in the order of IR£491 million in 1959; 75% (IR£96½m) of its entire exports, worth IR£131m, went to the UK, while under 6% (just over IR£6m) went to the EEC; furthermore, it also imported IR£110m worth of UK goods, fulfilling 52% of its total needs. Can statistics cloud opinions or enhance them?

A more explicit idea as to how these Anglo-Irish trading arrangements both contained and safeguarded the Irish economic position is depicted in the figures.[16] Barriers to trade were overcome by complex systems of preferences. This obviously worked in reverse as well, with imports from outside the UK subject to harsh measures which did not endear Ireland to the OEEC in the 1950s and did not help to distinguish it to the EEC either. In purely monetary terms, the UK was so much more important to it than the EEC that it fairly beggars belief that successive Irish governments had allowed such a position to endure, that is until the level of Irish tariff preferences in the UK, as compared to the level of the common EEC external tariff, are examined. Ireland's external economic ties thus displayed two dominant traits:

- an extreme concentration and reliance on one market, the UK;
- a system of trading preferences that was, for all practical purposes, the same as, if not better than, that governing the British Commonwealth.

In brief, Ireland exported agricultural products to the UK without restrictions and exported industrial products under a preferential arrangement; in turn, the UK had recourse to cheap agricultural goods and a market for its industrial goods. Of course, if such an agreement was to continue indefinitely, Ireland would have been economically protected, though at the same time, it would also still be in a position of acute, even reinforced, dependence. However, the prospect of losing these arrangements, first to EFTA and now to the EEC, had a remarkably sobering effect upon Irish policy-makers.

Obviously, the Irish government was loath to give up such an arrangement, even if just for an intermediate period – that is while Ireland's trading status came into line with any new UK arrangement with the EEC – as it not only conferred incredible trade benefits to the Irish economy, but it also gave it a high degree of security. Thus, in July 1961, the taoiseach was able to state conclusively in Dáil Éireann, without the fear of opposition antagonism, that:

> ... if all the countries of Europe with which we are trading, Britain and the Six, join together in an economic union, we cannot be outside it. That clear simple proposition can hardly be seriously contested. Whatever might be the problems for us of entering into such a union – and there is not doubt these problems would be very considerable – to stay out in these circumstances would be disastrous. We can see no economic future for this country if it were to be cut off by a uniform tariff applying to both agricultural and industrial projects from all our European Markets.[17]

In truth, the EEC was literally seen as some sort of economic panacea for all of Ireland's ills, an outlandish feeling which was especially heightened with the prospect of the UK becoming a member. Thus, to state that the 'decision to apply for membership was unwelcome to the Irish government' as Brian Girvin does, indeed that the UK government's decision in 1961 to join 'undermined Ireland's capacity to make policy in an independent fashion, challenging the traditional certainties on which policy had been based', is to miss the point of the matter. In truth, to contend that it was the view of Lemass that it was not to Ireland's advantage to join either major European bloc, that its economic development would not be improved by doing so, is to raise a spurious argument. Ireland had never exercised such independence and, apart from working within the realities of world economics, was always going to be at the whims and mercies of the international economic system, just like nearly every other nation. The application from the Irish government may indeed have been an 'emergency response to external changes over which the state had no control', but it was one for which much in the way of preparation had already been made and it was also part of a 'development strategy' which had been envisioned for some time.[18]

The government was not committed to the concept of European integration *per se*, as can quite clearly be seen from the lack of enthusiasm shown by Ireland towards the other two European Communities – the ECSC and Euratom of course – but it was prepared to go to any legitimate lengths to try to solve the country's economic problems. However, within this begrudging attitude lay the seeds of Ireland's subsequent rebuff by the EEC and the Six. The taoiseach repeatedly undermined and, indeed, contradicted the reality of Ireland's explicitly stated desire to join the EEC when he observed that: 'Our accession to the Rome Treaty would involve us in no specific commitments other than those set out in the Treaty'.[19] The Irish government had equated that the cost of EEC membership, between obligations and opportunities, would ultimately bring a favourable balance to the country. As John A. Murphy has written in his *Ireland in the twentieth century*, Dublin had turned its 'eyes towards the European fleshpots' when it decided to adhere.[20] This lack of real enthusiasm for European integration would later make it difficult for Ireland to convince the EEC and the Six that it was indeed applying ready to accept the full implications of the Treaty of Rome, rather than just going through the motions in becoming a member of this trading bloc, one with potential for a myriad of developments, in order to reap its inherent economic benefits.

This chapter – *Ireland's first EEC application, 31 July 1961* – thus aims to consider the lead-up to Dublin's decision to apply for membership of the EEC in the summer of 1961 and to introduce subsequent developments. It achieves this by linking with the previous chapter and by extending some of the questions and themes raised there so that there is a greater sense of continuity. This third chapter does not aim to eulogise the role played by Lemass in this process, but to analyse it. Therefore, it does not necessarily agree with Brian Lenihan, a junior minister in the early 1960s, who has commented that:

> Lemass in my view is best described as a pragmatic visionary. I saw this demonstrated during the General Election of 1961, when he made speeches up and down the country explaining our early application for membership of the European Community, and the benefits that would accrue from it. All this was done 12 years before we actually joined. He predicted that the Community would evolve a political character, and that Ireland would develop more fully, when its people worked within a European dimension, free from the psychological malaise of living in the shadow of Britain. This is as relevant [today] ... as it was when Lemass pioneered the nation towards Europe ...[21]

Of course, this particular point of view is highly misleading and terribly simplistic. In 1961, the taoiseach was paying tacit lip-service to political issues such as partition and neutrality, when what he was really endeavouring for was the economic transformation of the country at any reasonable price. Lemass was by no means a European prophet. This chapter presents a far less fatuous view of Ireland's integration process; instead, it appraises and chronicles the whole experience, extending beyond the particular subject at hand – the first application and historic decision in July 1961 to try and join the EEC – to the decision taken in October 1961 by the EEC Council to seek more information from Dublin regarding its application and to when the government was offered the chance to state its case in Brussels in January 1962. It begins, however, by outlining the various external and internal forces that contributed to the decision to apply before moving on to the substance of the application itself.

Determining factors – Part I: external forces

In coming to their decision to apply to join with the Six, the Irish government went through a complicated and in-depth analysis of what the EEC actually had to offer Ireland and, more importantly, how it would affect and be affected by Anglo-Irish relations. Evidence for the critical nature of this last point is substantial, but it is sufficient at this stage to note one of Lemass's earliest remarks on how the UK government's position regarding the EEC would impact upon Ireland. In March 1961, the taoiseach declared in Dáil Éireann that:

> The question of the British position in relation to the Common Market and the possible repercussions of that position on this country has been the subject of frequent exchanges with the British authorities, and we shall continue to follow these matters with the closest possible attention, bearing carefully in mind our very material interest in any arrangements affecting British relations with the European Economic Community and our own situation in regard both to the British market and to the Community.[22]

Indeed, the taoiseach repeated this message many times. In May 1961, he stated in a foreign newspaper interview that 'a decision by Britain to join the European Economic Community would immediately raise the question of Irish membership of the Community also'.[23] The importance of UK opinions and deeds upon Ireland's determining process is self-evident. Nevertheless, the primary purpose of this particular section is to bring to light the influential nature of views and positions taken by other external parties – the Six and the institutions of the EEC – and to assess their impact upon the decision-making process. Thus, it evaluates the extent to which each of these European players impacted upon the Irish government and, in doing so, leads into a detailed appraisal of the pertinence of Anglo-Irish relations, but only after domestic considerations are dealt with in an intermediate section.

As early as July 1959, a conference held in Dublin attended by distinguished European federalists outlined the choices that Europe – and Ireland – faced. The political implications of joining the EEC were laid out in full. Indeed, Walter Hallstein began by stating that:

> ... the reasons for establishing the Common Market are largely political. We are seeking to develop a new strength, a new political factor in the free world, which will, by its very existence, strengthen the camp of freedom. We want to make our contribution to the cause of the free world in the great struggle, which is dividing East from West. For our part, we intend to take up a position of our own choice, not merely to stand somewhere between the camps. No responsible person in our Community has ever toyed with the idea of our being a 'third force'. Our idea is to strengthen the defence of liberty. We can best help here through the new strength we produce in Europe and by at last creating genuine peace for all time between European States in the Community of the Six.

This assertion was next followed by Maurice Fauré, the former French foreign minister, who reiterated these words by stating that the latter:

> ... has already stressed the living reality of the European Community. He emphasised the first steps that have been taken towards achieving a common social policy and a common agricultural policy, as well as a common transport policy. We are not purely concerned with economic policies; our interests are wider and deeper ... Thus the Community is not only a living reality as an economic organisation; it is also a psychological and political reality. Those of us who are concerned with political life in our different countries realise how true this is: we realise that this new driving force, the psychological and political concept of a united Europe, has changed the thinking of our peoples, and has brought them to think in terms of working in the interest of the European community and not purely in the interest of their own nation.

Thus, from these speeches alone, it is clear that it is not as if Ireland was so out of touch or so peripheral that it should not have known exactly what was happening in Europe.[24]

With direct reference to these pressures on the Irish government, it is crucial to note what Ireland was actually telling its European neighbours. Irish diplomats abroad constantly communicated the view that, to all extents and purposes, Ireland's membership of the EEC was dependent upon the direction taken by the London government; they stated that:

> ... if Britain joined or became associated with it, we should in all probability have to follow suit ... having regard to the overwhelming importance of the British market for our products, we had really no alternative to basing our action on the British.

Of course, the EEC was basically of 'great interest' for Ireland because it offered to it a vast potential outlet for Irish goods, specifically agricultural produce.[25] In return, considerable dangers were posed to native Irish industries, especially those which were not economically viable, even if there were substantial rewards in store for those which were. However, if that is what the Irish government felt and was saying, the question must be asked: in what way did the Six actually interpret Ireland's posturing on European integration?

The Dutch government, for instance, thought that the general impression of the Six was that there existed a 'lack of any very great interest' on the subject of Ireland's views upon or intentions regarding the EEC. Obviously, it is possible to deduce from this opinion that Ireland's wish to establish a more intimate relationship with the EEC was evidently not being communicated properly. Although it was felt that there was an 'obvious Dutch desire to get us in', it was clearly going to be up to the government to make its wishes both more compatible with the general trends inherent in European integration and also better known to the constituent members of the Six and to the EEC's apparatus. Indeed, the Irish ambassador to London, Hugh McCann, reported that Ireland faced two major problems in this regard:

- he held that newspapers on the European mainland were giving a lot of prominence to pronouncements on the EEC by countries such as Austria, Denmark, and Norway, but not to Ireland;
- McCann added that reports from the various diplomatic missions of the Six in Dublin to their superiors were comprised of information that was either of 'no help at all or contradictory'.[26]

This report from London actually prompted the taoiseach into arranging what subsequently turned out to be a critically important meeting with the ministers and secretaries from all the major government departments on 8 June 1961. Crucially, this meeting was convened in an effort to determine what action Ireland must take regarding the EEC.[27] Ireland's ambassador to the Netherlands, B.Gallagher, meanwhile added that, although the Dutch government was rather anxious to expand the EEC so as to have the widest possible membership, Ireland's candidature had not been examined by them in any great detail. Nevertheless, it is possible to remark that the Dutch did not view Ireland's non-participation in NATO as an obstacle to participation at this early stage and that EEC membership would not be denied because of neutrality.[28] A similar situation existed with regard to Belgium, but this was not, however, necessarily the same case with the West German government.

The Irish ambassador to Belgium, Frank Biggar, revealed that, as far as the Belgian government was concerned, an Irish application for membership of the EEC would be judged under two principal criteria; the Belgians would ask:

- whether Ireland would be able to fulfil European commitments from the economic point of view;
- if Irish participation in the EEC would 'help or hinder' the Six to attain their ultimate aspiration of European unity.

An interview with Paul-Henri Spaak, the Belgian deputy prime minister and foreign minister, had revealed Belgian government surprise at a report – Biggar presumed that it had emanated from the Belgian embassy in Dublin – that Ireland's intention to join the EEC had the solution of the partition question as one of its foremost aims.[29] The Irish ambassador told Spaak that there was no formal connection between the two issues as such, but that while Ireland was considering EEC membership very carefully it was at the same time 'by no means indifferent to the possibilities of solving Partition which the E.E.C. offered'. However, Biggar stressed that Ireland's position *vis-à-vis* the EEC was ultimately dependent anyway upon what London decided to do. Indeed, he stated that, while he saw obvious difficulties confronting the UK government over whether or not to join up with the Six, he did not see the UK as having any other choice, especially in the long-run, a point with which Spaak readily concurred. The Irish ambassador tried to emphasise during their meeting that, economically-speaking and especially in the context of EEC membership, Ireland felt itself to be competitive with regard to agriculture, but that the Irish government believed that domestic industry posed a problem. Biggar also stated that Ireland was not necessarily an underdeveloped country – especially in comparison to Greece or Portugal – but that it would want a voice in the formulation of EEC agricultural policy particularly and that it would also need help in bringing industry into line with the other Six. Therefore, he said that Ireland would seriously have to consider applying for full membership on these terms only.[30]

However, as a former secretary-general at NATO, Spaak was clearly more interested in an issue such as Ireland's neutrality and how it might impinge upon the ultimate political direction that the EEC was taking. Biggar was thus at pains to point out that Ireland was not neutral in the same sense as Austria, Sweden or Switzerland were, for example. It was not, he said, a member of any military alliance, as all the members of the EEC were, and only held onto this position of neutrality for reasons related to partition.

Indeed, it was his view that Ireland remained 'profoundly European and perhaps the most anti-Communist country in Europe'. The Dublin government's foreign policy position was still independent, he held, and, furthermore, it had been able to utilise this stance in helping to foster world peace at the UN. The Irish ambassador told Spaak that he knew that the Treaty of Rome imposed no political obligations upon its members, but he also emphasised that the Irish government fully realised what the ultimate objectives of the EEC literally were. Indeed, these are implied in the preamble to the Treaty of Rome which states that members are: 'Determined to lay the foundations of an ever closer union among the peoples of Europe'.[31] Therefore, he accepted that these aspirations would, in time, have defence and foreign policy implications. However, while Spaak agreed that NATO membership was not *sine qua non* for participation in the EEC, Biggar 'could detect no signs of enthusiasm for a new member who did not conform to the existing pattern'. Nonetheless, as with the Dutch, the Belgians were not felt to have given any profound consideration to the Irish position regarding the EEC anyway and, thus, that they were not necessarily prejudiced against its membership.[32] On the other hand, the West German's actual attitude towards Irish membership was, nevertheless, far more complex and entangled.

While serving as West German deputy prime minister, Ludwig Erhard had seemingly made an emphatic statement that only those members of EFTA which were also members of NATO could join the EEC. Consequently, on 25 May 1961, Lemass proceeded to speak on this subject in the Irish parliament. In the process, the taoiseach repudiated Erhard's reported remarks by saying that there was nothing specific or substantial in the Treaty of Rome which was expressly related to the question of defence. As a result, he believed that there could be no good reason why membership of NATO would be a determinant in Ireland's ability to subscribe to the EEC.[33] On a subsequent visit to Ireland, the West German foreign minister, Heinrich von Brentano, pointed out that what Erhard had said should not in fact be taken literally, because he had probably meant to say that only NATO members were likely at that juncture to want to join the Six. Nevertheless, the whole issue of neutrality was becoming entangled in the general question of whether Ireland should apply for full or associate EEC membership. Indeed, a subsequent report from the UK Foreign Office on the West German foreign minister's placatory statement further maintained that, in the context of the possible UK accession to the EEC, the Irish government had 'more or less implored' von Brentano:

> ... to see that their interests should be safeguarded ... that while they were most anxious to maintain their neutrality and did not want to march in line

with the U.K., in view of the great consequences to their economy they might have to consider any step that might be necessary.[34]

There were, of course, conflicting views within the UK government structure about the Irish position. On the one hand, the Irish government was seen as being 'typically remiss' in its efforts to try to make its position clear and stated that it was not by 'whining to the Germans' that they were ever going to safeguard their economic interests.[35] On the other hand, a more considered view held that the Irish government had in fact stayed in close contact with the UK and that they would ultimately have much less difficulty than, for example, Portugal in accepting the obligations of full EEC membership.[36] Indeed, Ireland would not necessarily have to be another 'millstone' – certainly not a solicited one – around the neck of the UK in entry negotiations, even if that was one of the fears held by those in London.[37]

However, a report on a conversation with a senior West German official from the UK ambassador to West Germany, E.M.Rose, gives the most balanced and unbiased view of the Irish government's position by being able to report more precisely upon the discussions held between Lemass and von Brentano during the latter's Irish trip. On the question of Erhard's comments on Ireland and the EEC, the UK ambassador recounted that the Irish leadership had told von Brentano that they wanted to join the EEC, but that they had been 'disturbed' by the statement attributed to Erhard that membership of NATO was a necessary qualification. The taoiseach was reported to have told von Brentano that it was impossible for Ireland to join NATO because of partition, but the West German foreign minister was able in turn to tell Lemass that membership of NATO was not necessarily a condition for EEC membership. More importantly perhaps, Rose also recounted that, on the question of the UK's entry into the EEC and its impact on Ireland, Lemass had told von Brentano that his government could not take any decision regarding EEC entry until they knew what the UK government intended to do. Obviously, von Brentano could not shed any real light on how London proposed to act, but he stated that he hoped that they would join even though it would be at least a year before the UK could formally accede. Finally, on the question of agriculture, it was disclosed that Lemass had told West Germany's foreign minister about Ireland's special interest in a Common Agricultural Policy (CAP) of the Six and about the Irish fear that such a CAP might already be in place before Ireland had time to accede and to incorporate its own point of view into the process. However, von Brentano went on to assure the taoiseach that his government intended to keep 'potential' members of the Six informed about any progress on the CAP negotiations and to discuss the issue continually and fully with them.[38]

The NATO matter did not rest there in the Irish media, though, with one *Irish Times* article in particular inducing the Department of External Affairs secretary to say that:

> I am afraid that this is one of these 'canards' which Muray [the journalist involved] has been trying to keep alive, despite the very definite statement of the Taoiseach in the Dáil on the 25th May ... It is a pity that he should show such irresponsibility on a matter of such current importance, and that the Irish Times should continue to publish his remarks. Dr.von Brentano was, of course, very categoric in denying Muray's thesis at his press conference on the afternoon of 31st May – even more categoric, I gather, than the newspaper reports on the interview.[39]

In point of fact, the *Irish Press* reported the West German foreign minister as stating that:

> Economic and political cooperation within the European Economic Community has nothing whatever to do with the North Atlantic Treaty Organisation, and I am convinced that a number of countries which pursue a neutralist policy today can participate in the Common Market, and that this would have no effect on membership of NATO either directly or indirectly.[40]

Indeed, upon von Brentano's return to West Germany, the *Irish Times* itself hinted at Irish membership of the Six and made no mention of any NATO dimension within the equation.[41] This implies that European politicians did not view Irish neutrality as being an obstacle to its membership of the Six necessarily, though it remained problematic. However, EEC officials would prove to be more pedantic upon this issue. In the meantime, though, what about the views of the other members of the Six and their influence upon the determining process for Ireland regarding the choice to be made between full or associate EEC membership, indeed, in relation to participation at all?

The French government's position on the issue was much more 'enigmatic' than the West Germans were. In fact, it was much more a question of the continuous 'uncertainty' of France's attitude towards the idea of the UK and EEC membership, thus leaving Ireland in the unenviable position of remaining only a secondary consideration within the process.[42] Anyway, the French were not particularly interested in having the UK as a member of the EEC, certainly not on the UK government's own economic or political terms.[43] In truth, its whole attitude to the admission of new members was possibly best put by the French foreign minister, Maurice Couve de Murville, who said: 'we do not think about it'.[44] The French government did not view

Ireland's case for membership in an antagonistic way but, because of its dependence upon the UK, it was always going to be a rather minor factor in the wider process of European integration, as well as in the more specific context of Anglo-French rivalry. In July 1961, for instance, the Irish ambassador to France, D.R.McDonald, reported on a meeting that he had with a French foreign office official. This source indicated that:

> Ireland's position relative to the E.E.C. seems to be well understood ... it was felt here, generally speaking, that Ireland's attitude was more favourable to the E.E.C., especially in the setting of European unity, than that of the Commonwealth countries. He said this with an expression of satisfaction and said our position seemed most like that of Denmark.[45]

Nevertheless, the reality of the Irish situation was that the UK was still a decisive factor in its relative position on EEC membership, but that France also had an ardent role to play.

Additionally, although there is strong evidence to suggest that the Italian government understood the Irish situation, Italy was no more central to Ireland's situation than Belgium or the Netherlands. The Irish ambassador in Rome, Thomas V.Commins, was informed that the Italians 'fully appreciated' Ireland's position regarding both the EEC and the UK, and that they were determined to see that a 'fair deal' was sorted out, whether this was taken in the context of either full or, interestingly, associate membership of the EEC.[46] Moreover, the position of Luxembourg on the Irish question also appears to have been similar to that of the Belgian and the Dutch governments. However, the respective positions of the French and West German governments remained crucial, because as long as they were unclear, either regarding Ireland or the UK, obviously enough the wider question of EEC membership also remained in the balance. Ireland's position was beginning to appear invidious.

The outlook of the EEC institutions was not as positive in relation to Ireland, but has to be seen in the light of the Irish government *aide-mémoire* of 5 July 1961 and the actual application to join itself to be fully appreciated. Considering that these were the general and pertinent views of the Six in the first half of 1961, it would be more beneficial at this stage, however, to ask what sort of questions and pressures were being brought to bear on the Irish government in more domestic terms and to see whether and how government decisions and actions were influenced as a result. The next section on domestic considerations in the determining process thus proposes answers to such queries, before moving on to assess the role played by London in Dublin's decision-making process.

Determining factors – Part II: domestic considerations[47]

There were, obviously enough, some serious indigenous concerns for the Irish government to take into account in the determining process over whether or not to join up with the Six. Lemass had frequently made clear what he expected from EEC entry negotiations and from the resulting trade arrangements, but he did not hide legitimate Irish fears. He said that:

> In all negotiations and discussions on the future trade arrangements of Europe and the world in which we have taken part we have been drawing attention to the unfairness of a situation which, while helping to widen the market for industrial goods, does not at the same time provide a corresponding improvement for countries who rely largely on agriculture.[48]

However, an opinion poll for the *Irish Press*, taken around this time, found that 65% of those polled considered that the UK was the single-most important foreign consideration for Ireland, whilst 29% replied that it was the US and only 1% that it was Europe. In addition, 95% of those sampled attached significance to continued close international relations with the UK, with 89% assigning similar prominence to the US, but only 62% giving such value to Europe. Of the people that were tested, 76% of those surveyed still said that they approved of Irish entry into the EEC; the corresponding figure was only 44% in the UK. Interestingly, if the London government decided not to join up with the Six, it was shown that such a decision would have a major impact on Irish public opinion regarding membership, with 38% of those polled against entry as a result and only 36% still in favour. In any event, the fact that only 10% of Irish people were worried about any loss of sovereignty resulting from membership demonstrates that economic priorities overrode any other consideration.[49]

It was clearly evident, both from what the taoiseach said and from the views of the general public, that even if opinion over Europe was divided, other factors had to be taken into account by the Irish government, especially emanating from those most intimately and vocally involved in lobbying for or against EEC membership. This begs the understandable question: which sectors of Irish life were putting pressure on the government over whether or not to join? In fact, these representative sections of the community can be divided into three main categories, the first of which will be dealt with in detail here because the other two groups are continuously analysed throughout the central chapters. The groupings were:

- native Irish federalists versus those hostile to the EEC;

- backbenchers and the opposition in the Dáil and Seanad;
- indigenous farmers and industrialists.

It is also possible, within the context of evaluating the role played in the determining process by Irish federalists and those skeptical of European integration, to assess the sort of feedback that the government was receiving from the various institutions and members of the EEC and how they in turn affected Irish foreign policy.

The federalist Irish Council of the European Movement played what was considered by T.K.Whitaker, Department of Finance secretary, to be a 'valuable' role in informing the government about European integration in the run-up to Ireland's decision to apply for EEC membership. For instance, this lobby group's chairman, Garret FitzGerald, reported to the Irish government on a visit paid by an Irish Council of the European Movement delegation to the EEC Commission in the middle of April 1961. Indeed, in expressing their views on the question of whether or not the government should apply for full or associate membership, this account also detailed various meetings with a diverse and informed group of European officials, a comprehensive appraisal of which is necessary to determine its role in impacting upon domestic considerations in the determining process. FitzGerald's central advice to the Irish government was that the advantages and disadvantages of associate and full membership would obviously need to be fully assessed and considered, certainly before any informed action could be taken. Earlier that month in Dáil Éireann, Lemass had already said: 'The best situation possible for us would be association with the Common Market, if Britain were also a member of it, on a basis which satisfactorily took account of our economic circumstances'. In a relatively short space of time, this position advanced rather rapidly, indeed quixotically, so that, when Ireland finally applied, Lemass chose to request full membership. Questions that were being asked included: why had the government's position changed, indeed had its membership status changed? Therefore, in the context of the lobbying pressures put on the government by domestic interest groups, such as the federalists, each of the choices facing Ireland in the summer of 1961 have to be reviewed in turn.

Although not explored thus far, the government could have chosen a different sort of relationship with the EEC, one which was also provided for in the Treaty of Rome. Indeed, the article specifically dealing with the application of a state for associate membership of the EEC (Article 238) read as follows:

> The Community may conclude with a third State, a union of States or an

international organisation agreements establishing an association involving reciprocal rights and obligations, common action and special procedures.[50]

The problem with associate EEC membership as a policy option for Ireland was in relation to the place of agriculture and the question of assessing what benefits the country could hope to accrue as a result. Free access for agricultural products to the EEC was, of course, viewed as problematic at the very least. Indeed, this measure was possibly only going to be extended to existing member states, despite the fact that the EEC Commission officials insisted that associate membership would open up many possibilities for Ireland, while full membership of the EEC would require an as yet uncertain, but probably stringent, compliance with the Treaty of Rome. As an associate member, the Irish government would have been looking for a transitional period to be in place for tariff reductions on industrial products, just as Greece had received in its arrangement for associate membership.[51]

According to the Irish Council of the European Movement assessment, Ireland was should be prepared to harmonise its agricultural policies with those of the EEC, but would obviously want to balance allowing the free access of EEC agricultural produce into Ireland in return for its own free access to the Common Market. As an associate member, however, the EEC Commission could not guarantee that Ireland would be able to participate fully in any agricultural arrangements while it was at the same time negotiating temporary derogations in relation to industrial trade. Although FitzGerald felt that detailed negotiations would have to be undertaken before further clarification could be received, it was becoming obvious what choice he advocated most. The disadvantages of being accepted as an associate member were considerable and varied. Indeed, these handicaps, according to the report, included:

- the uncertainty related to agricultural product concessions;
- the fact that Ireland would have no direct control or influence over the policies that were to be adopted and, thus, it would be committing itself 'blindfold' to the EEC;
- Ireland would not have free access to the European Social Fund;
- unlike Greece, Ireland was also unlikely to be in a position to receive any European Investment Bank money if not a full member.

Therefore, the relative advantages of associate membership appeared to figure rather poorly in comparison to the disadvantages. The question FitzGerald thus asked was: what were the corresponding benefits and drawbacks then of full EEC membership for Ireland?

As was previously explained, Ireland had the further possibility of applying for full membership of the EEC, also provided for under the Treaty of Rome (Article 237). However, FitzGerald reported that the EEC Commission was loath to give any significant concessions away to Ireland on this provision, primarily because it would create an 'undesirable' precedent which could lead, in effect, to the watering down of the original treaty. Nevertheless, it was apparent that if Ireland was prepared to accept the whole treaty in principle, it was assured of 'sympathetic treatment', as was instanced by the case with the protocol accorded to Italy in relation to the underdevelopment of its Mezzogiorno region. Additionally, full membership would clearly entail accepting the transitional period for the dismantlement of tariff and quota restrictions – 1970 was the stipulated date, perhaps even earlier if unilaterally agreed – as the Commission was clearly looking to strengthen posthaste the whole idea of a common market. FitzGerald recognised that, despite some possible transitional derogations, in addition to more definite benefits such as access to the European Social Fund and European Investment Bank, full membership would still 'impose a considerable strain on the Irish economy'. In fact, there was little room for doubt about its obligations; any concessions granted would remain limited and temporary only. However, the agriculture situation was very uncertain, basically because the Commission had not fully thought through this particular problem. Nonetheless, it had to be weighed against the fact that the terms related to agriculture would be extremely important in the case of associate membership, because Ireland might find itself with limited policy-making influence if it only had a confined role. Associate status paled in comparison to the prospect of full membership in terms of possible benefits and drawbacks.

The Irish Council of the European Movement document reported that the general drift of views in Brussels was that Ireland should ultimately apply for associate EEC status, essentially because they considered that Ireland would not be able to undertake the rigours required by full EEC membership. Furthermore, FitzGerald had the feeling that the EEC Commission did not actually want another country complicating the decision-making process at that stage. Thus, their report recommended that the Irish government should be looking:

> ... to adopt in full the common agricultural policy with its advantages and corresponding obligations, while at the same time having a limited participation in industrial trade with significant concessions along the same lines as those accorded to Greece.

Their key finding and subsequent main advice was that the associate versus full membership debate should be entered into as fully as possible. Indeed, FitzGerald noted that this avenue might potentially offer the opportunity for the status issue to be used by the Irish government as a bargaining chip in return for concessions being granted as an associate member.

The opinions of the various EEC functionaries interviewed by FitzGerald are worth exploring in the context of the membership debate, as well as on the classification that was being accorded to Ireland and the standing that was being given to agriculture. Together, they offer an insight into the lack of cohesion with which the Irish position was actually viewed. Much of the meeting conducted with Richard Mayne, a member of the official spokesman's group representing the EEC Commission, was limited to the subject of the UK government's relationship with the EEC, reflecting the actuality of Ireland's relative lack of importance. However, on the subject of agriculture, this spokesman said that he felt that Ireland would be 'more complementary than competitive' in the EEC framework, mainly because the effects of the agricultural production of beef and dairy products, though they would affect the EEC countries as a whole, would be spread out amongst all the members. Indeed, on the formal attitude of the Commission towards Irish membership as a whole, this particular official was able to inform the Irish federalist delegation that:

> Any application from Ireland would of course be seriously considered and when association was being negotiated every effort would be made to take into account the special needs of the potential associate.

Of course, this statement clearly shows that it was felt in Brussels that the Irish government would be applying for associate membership, as it was thought possible for Ireland – as was the situation with Greece – 'to negotiate much more flexible and wide-ranging concessions' within this scenario. Ireland's relative status had already been formulated in Brussels.

Nevertheless, a later meeting with an EEC Commission official from the directorate-general dealing with agriculture was particularly illuminating because this functionary was, in reality, firmly opposed to the opinion which classified Ireland as an 'undeveloped country'; however, this particular official also recognised that this was not necessarily the view of the EEC Commission itself. Notwithstanding personal beliefs, it was apparent to FitzGerald that the division between Commission officials on issues such as agriculture did not auger well for the completion of any subsequent membership negotiations for Ireland, whether it was for full or even for associate membership status. Obviously, there were other views emanating from the Commission regarding European integration which this delegation of Irish federalists was able to bring to bear upon the Dublin government.

The report from the Irish Council of the European Movement also detailed a meeting with Jean Deniau, who was officially Director for Association of Non-Member Countries in the Directorate-General for External Relations at the EEC Commission. Deniau showed that he was firmly of the opinion that associate status was the answer for Ireland with regard to the EEC, with the possibility of full membership being accorded to it only being considered apt at some later undefined stage. In truth, though he did actually perceive Ireland to be an 'undeveloped country' in the European context, Deniau could not envisage how the country would be able to adhere fully to the Treaty of Rome, something which he was not prepared to see watered down. As far as he was concerned, any concessions granted in the Irish case would have to be limited and specific, as was the position with Italy. Of course, the Greek government had been able to gain considerable concessions as an associate member, according to Deniau, which was regarded as demonstrating the 'suppleness of the Association formula'. However, the Treaty of Rome was clearly going to be interpreted in a very strict manner, as the Commission wanted to maintain the treaty totally intact and did not want to create any 'dangerous precedents'. The fact was that full EEC membership was considered to be very difficult, if not impossible, for Ireland to undertake at that time, because it would have had major difficulties, for example, in keeping pace with the required tariff reduction levels. Nonetheless, although unable to satisfy the Irish deputation fully on the specific issue of agriculture, Deniau did think that a position could ultimately be negotiated. What about other views within the Commission?

It is true to say, however, that the discussion conducted with Columb de Daumont, who was the Head of the Division for West European Countries in the Directorate-General for External Relations at the Commission, did not give the Irish delegation much grounds for optimism either. Other than conveying the view that negotiations with the EEC would have been simplified by Ireland's adherence to the GATT – it only joined at the end of 1967 – de Daumont did not have much to offer by way of compensation and, in particular, he was not prepared to see any negotiations for full membership taking a more flexible turn. The Irish argument that the country had an adverse trade balance with the EEC did not, for instance, cut any ice. Indeed, as far as these officials at the Commission were concerned, although the issue of Ireland's economic status was up for in-depth discussion – indeed, the very nature of any future relationship that it might conclude with the EEC – the Treaty of Rome was very definitely not on any negotiations agenda. Ireland could adhere completely as a full member or not at all.

FitzGerald followed up this report for the government, on behalf of the Irish Council of the European Movement, by outlining the difficulties that Ireland would encounter either way. A letter to the taoiseach stated that it was the unanimous view of his organisation that Ireland should approach the EEC Commission with the objective of achieving some form of participation with the EEC. He restated his organisation's view that the establishment of Irish membership should coincide with or follow a similar move when it was made by the London government. Indeed, he also declared the hope that his group's point of view would help the taoiseach 'in formulating policies consonant with the evolution of public opinion'.[52] But, of course, the pressure being applied to the government regarding the formation of its foreign economic policies and its role in the process of European integration was also considerable from other native sources, most notably from those voices in Dáil Éireann both dissenting and in favour, as well as from economic sectors, which basically meant farmers and industrialists. The federalists were thus only one branch in a tripartite series of pressure groups trying to influence the Irish government's ultimate decision. Thus, there were other eminent domestic voices, other than the federalists, for Lemass to have to consider as well.

In Dáil Éireann, for example, the opposition continually sought information about the government's position on European integration, eventually forcing out of it the publication of a White Paper entitled *European Economic Community* on 30 June 1961.[53] It has to be said that the government was finally pressurised into taking this affirmative action despite its general unwillingness to be open about foreign policy issues and only came about as a result of its propensity to take such decisions for political gain. Dating from the establishment of EFTA, there was a 'steady stream' of questions in Dáil Éireann regarding the government's actual policy towards European integration, in reply to which the taoiseach continuously gave limited answers, lacking in any meaningful detail. On 2 March 1960, for example, in reply to a question specifically asking for some elaboration on the type of alignment that Ireland could be expected to have with the EEC, Lemass said:

> Among the questions at present under examination by the Government in connection with our external trade policy is that of our future relations with the European Economic Community. I am not in a position to say anything more on the subject at the present time.[54]

Indeed, this was to be the usual form of reply given to such questions during this period in time. Once the UK government began to indicate that it was considering joining the EEC, Lemass was able to expound upon the issue a little further. One year later, he stated:

> It is the Government's view that, if Britain should take this step, we should consider establishing a link with the Common Market and endeavour to secure terms of membership or association which would satisfactorily take account of our economic circumstances.[55]

However, the usual lack of lucidity in Irish government statements on official policy towards European integration resumed soon after this atypical relapse; explicit answers on issues such as this were a relatively rare occurrence.

Due though to the increasing preponderance of questions being posed in the Dáil and Seanad regarding the government's policy, Lemass was eventually forced to announce that a White Paper was being issued forthwith on the subject. J.J.Lee's comment in relation to the government's continuous reticence, indeed opprobrium, to giving out useful information is particularly appropriate here; it was, he maintains:

> ... merely a species of the wider genus of the furtiveness that often seemed to characterise the official mind in Ireland, where 'the general lack of openness in public administration' remains striking.[56]

This analysis of the lack of interaction between the government and the general public on any issue, including European integration, is especially appropriate when the resulting White Paper on the *European Economic Community*, in itself rather disappointing because of the lack of analysis and content presented, is considered and especially as it might otherwise have offered a valuable opportunity for debate. In truth, the government, although regularly pressurised by various members of the Dáil and Seanad to outline its policy and to indicate clearly its intentions, acted in a peculiarly furtive fashion on the EEC membership question, despite the varied informed inputs from groups and individuals concerned by the whole issue. Indeed, even with secret confirmation of the fact that the UK had decided to attempt to join the EEC, the Irish finance minister categorically declared in the Seanad that Ireland had not ruled out seeking entry into the EEC if the UK elected not to apply; this was a clear misrepresentation of the facts of the situation.[57]

Irish farmers and indigenous industrialists, represented by a myriad of groups such as the National Farmers' Association (NFA) or the Irish Congress of Trade Unions (ICTU), were also applying considerable pressure on the Irish government regarding its integration policy. Indeed, throughout this time, they continually tried to influence policy in an effort to protect their own interests, but the fact remained that the future course of Irish policy was more or less known and understood if the UK joined the EEC. However, despite efforts by the NFA to suggest that Ireland should join the EEC before the UK and, in fact, that it should pursue its application whether the UK joined or not, Lemass, in assessing the wider Irish economic situation as well as the real position of Irish agriculture, asked: 'If Britain finally decides not to join, or if her application is repulsed because her conditions are unacceptable, what then?' The starkness of such an eventuality would obviously leave his government with no other reasonable option but to try to enhance existing Anglo-Irish trade relations in the realisation that associate or full EEC membership for Ireland would not then be practical.

In truth, the Department of Agriculture was able to argue cohesively that there were major disadvantages as well as advantages to the EEC for Irish agriculture, that it would be 'unrealistic' to suppose that there would be the 'necessary degree of support and stability ... in the absence of some special economic understanding with Britain, whatever solution may ultimately be found' within the European context.[58] In his correspondence with the NFA, the taoiseach still remained hopeful though that this would not have to happen and that both countries would be admitted without exigencies arising.[59] It should also be noted that over-riding this debate was the knowledge that the previous Anglo-Irish trade agreement dating from 1960 had not exactly been what Dublin had wanted or hoped for, even if they had been 'glad to conclude' it at the time of asking because the agreement at least reaffirmed bilateral trade links.[60] It was Lemass's considered view that the UK remained an essential economic concern for Ireland within any future economic integration scenario.

At the heart of the problem facing the Irish government regarding domestic lobbying groups was the fact that Irish farmers and industrialists were not in agreement about what to do if the UK decided not to join the EEC. The former grouping was strongly pro-European even if the UK did not become a member of the EEC. Indeed, the farmers had been openly calling for membership for Ireland since the middle of 1960 because they felt that – within the EEC – the 'CAP offered guaranteed high prices, access to an expanding consumer market and new trading opportunities'.[61] Although there were exceptions, usually depending on the industry concerned, Irish industrialists were, generally speaking, not so enthusiastic. It was certainly felt that the free trade blocs were starting to cause job losses, but there was also a fear that, even in joining, even more redundancies would be incurred. What was most clear were the implications and 'effects of the higher rates of duty Irish goods have to bear to enter EFTA countries' and, by extension, the EEC as well.[62]

Nevertheless, the continual flow of information between the Irish government and the various farming and industrial organisations, especially the various meetings held before any decisions were taken, did at least give the impression that the government had the country's fate in its own hands. Indeed, the fact remained that, even though London had not taken a final decision regarding the EEC, Ireland was proceeding on that assumption that it would apply to enter.[63] The truth of the situation was never far away, however. In reality, in what was interpreted as a major speech on the industrial implications of EEC membership, Lemass definitively stated that:

> ... [if the UK joins] then this country will go along with that Community and we will have to accept with membership a dismantling of our industrial tariffs and quotas over a period of years.[64]

By definition, Dublin's priority was to ready the economy for the tremendous implications that these changes in European trading circumstances were incurring, departures which would soon be intensified. How it would actually deal with this situation was another issue entirely.

Each of these domestic considerations – native Irish federalists, the backbenchers and opposition in the Dáil, indigenous farmers and industrialists – had an important input into the final government decision, even though none of them would be the primary influencing factor in the act itself of applying for full EEC membership. That would be done by the UK. At this stage, therefore, the unique role played by the London government within Ireland's European integration process has to be considered more fully, before completing this introduction into the determining process and analysing exactly how the country's definitive position in relation to the EEC was finally formulated.

Determining factors – Part III: the UK

Generally speaking, the available archival material shows that Ireland's position was not of fundamental concern to the UK in its own EEC negotiations, certainly little regard was paid to its needs for economic advancement in the formulation of EFTA in 1959 or in the signing of the Anglo-Irish trade agreement the following year. Notwithstanding this, the UK still had an enormous impact in determining Ireland's EEC membership application. This section of *Ireland's first EEC application, 31 July 1961*, concentrates on the contrasting importance of the UK to Ireland when compared to the relationship that applied *vice versa*. It is divided chronologically and encompasses various germane aspects of Anglo-Irish relations relative to the subject of European integration, including an initial assessment of the detailed and regular correspondence that went on between the taoiseach and Macmillan at this time. It leads into an analysis of the Irish government's White Paper on the *European Economic Community* and subsequently analyses the government *aide-mémoire* issued on 5 July 1961. In point of fact, later sections also make a detailed review of the bilateral meetings held on 18-19 July 1961 and then look at the immediate lead-up to, as well as the announcement and aftermath of, the Irish application to join the EEC. All of these points are actually introduced throughout this brief analysis of the role of the UK government in Ireland's decision-making process, but are intended to lead to just one main conclusion. Dublin could not act on the EEC issue without a deep awareness and appreciation of what London was going to do.

In this context, it is therefore particularly interesting to note what the UK thought of the taoiseach, before moving on to give more detail about its views on the Irish government's position on European integration. In fact, Lemass was seen as being untypically Irish; he was described as being 'sensible, courageous and cool-headed'. He had been, it was said, the 'apostle' of the policy that led to the establishment and continued protection of indigenous Irish industries. Indeed, when this assessment was presented in July 1961, the view was put forward that the taoiseach's opinions on economic self-sufficiency appeared to have become considerably modified. In point of fact, Lemass was seen as being 'more progressive than the majority of his colleagues and fellow countrymen', but that as an adept politician he was 'too shrewd to try to force the pace'. Importantly, however, he was perceived to be fully 'alive to the need for changes in the economic policies which he had himself forsaken'.[65] Although at most only a pen-picture of private UK government views on the taoiseach, these opinions have a credibility which has to be kept in mind when the part played by London in the formation of Ireland's European policy is taken into consideration.

Of course, the Irish government was well informed about the public and private UK position on the EEC throughout the period in question, knowing about most of its motives and reservations. Indeed, in turn, the London government rightly felt that it had kept the Irish 'in touch on pretty much the same basis as Commonwealth countries'.[66] Such communications were carried out through formal private means – by way of the various sets of Anglo-Irish talks, as well as through the continuous exchange of correspondence between Lemass and the UK prime minister – and through more public methods – via statements issued by the UK government, as well as through newspaper reports. These formal private means included, for instance, remarks made by A.H.Tandy, the UK chef de mission to the EEC in Brussels, in May 1961, that in his opinion his government had:

> ... gone too far to withdraw ... MacMillan [sic] had already made up his mind on the subject and he fully expected to receive an instruction within the next three or four months to submit a formal application for British membership.

Tandy expected this announcement to come before Westminster adjourned for the summer recess, even if it was still recognised that this would 'only be the beginning' of the process and that the resulting negotiations would be 'long and tedious'. Most importantly, however, he felt that the London government had now gone 'beyond the point of no return'.[67]

On the other hand, various high profile statements by prominent UK politicians gives credence to the view that, in addition, the Irish received much of their information on the UK government's position through more public means. This source would have included, for example, the important speech made by Edward Heath, then UK Lord Privy Seal (effectively a junior foreign ministerial post), to the House of Commons in mid-May 1961, when he gave what was then described as the 'fullest public exposé to date of Britain's attitude to Europe'. With the accumulation of such evidence, the Irish ambassador in London felt that the UK would yet 'take the plunge' and try to join the EEC, though he had to report at the time that a final decision had obviously not as yet been taken.[68] Nonetheless, it becomes clear from this line of argument that the government was receiving its information on the position of the UK regarding its integration from a wide variety of sources. The relatively simple question that therefore must be asked remains: if an application to join the EEC was so expected from the UK, why is it worth investigating the decision-making process in such detail?

The simple answer to that query is that the UK government's standpoint on European integration impinged upon Dublin's thinking to such a degree that it is only by tracing the development of positions taken by both sides that the degree of Anglo-Irish interdependence and, more specifically, the extent of Ireland's dependence upon the UK can be appreciated. Right from the beginning of the process, it was obvious to the UK that, because of Europe's trading divisions into groupings of the Six and of the Seven, Ireland was going to have to 'consider carefully the question of associating herself with one or other of the two groups'.[69] The fact that the general UK announcement to join the EEC could still come as some sort of a 'surprise' to the Irish government – to the extent that, when London's position was finally and publicly formalised, it still precipitated a 'crisis-point' – is reason enough to investigate the issue. Nonetheless, it was also obvious to all concerned that the time for decision-making was close at hand. Indeed, Lemass said as much in a speech he delivered in early June 1961. His statement is worth quoting fairly extensively because he asked:

> If this Western European Community should extend its membership to include most of the States of Western Europe – not only the present Six but also Britain, Denmark, Norway, Portugal and possibly Spain – with Sweden, Austria, Switzerland and Finland linked with it – could we, in any circumstances, contemplate remaining outside it? The consequences arising from such a position of isolation must also be visualised. We would be cut off from European markets by the imposition against our products of the permanent common tariff of the whole Community, and left in an economic back-water, unable to participate in the economic expansion which the creation of the Community is designed to generate. The prospects for Irish agriculture in that situation would be very depressing, and for Irish industrial expansion practically non-existent.

As Lemass concluded: 'The alternative to accession to the European Community, if all our European neighbours join it, does not seem very attractive'. Therefore, it was not only the case that Ireland's decision to accede to the Treaty of Rome would cause 'many and serious problems', but that the flip-side to this argument provided no relief either as there would also be considerable problems in remaining 'aloof'. In fact, a resolution was considered to be the stark choice of deciding between two sets of complex problems and, thus, for Ireland, there was to be no easy or readily apparent solution.[70]

In expressing its opinion on the Irish situation, the UK Foreign Office remarked that the Irish ambassador in London had a 'good understanding' of the UK government's position on European integration and of the particular difficulties that the EEC posed to it. In that context, McCann had in fact informed the UK that he personally felt that, if the UK decided to go ahead and accede to the EEC with 'whatever reservations might be necessary', the Irish government would not be able to stay outside. Indeed, although his government had not yet reached any firm conclusions about the relative merits of full membership or association, the Irish ambassador also told the UK that he felt that full membership was the better option.[71] Opinion regarding the rectitude of Ireland's EEC membership was quite divided within the Foreign Office, with one viewpoint raising doubts about 'whether the Six would greet an Irish application for membership with much enthusiasm'. Meanwhile, another opinion that was expressed stated that, for

Dublin, it would be of 'critical importance' that they be allowed to join the EEC if they so desired.[72] Significantly, in direct conjunction with these views, the UK Commonwealth Relations Office summed up its view of the Irish position on adhesion by saying that:

> ... while the Republican Government do not rule out the possibility of trying to obtain an association with the Community, they would, if possible, prefer to go for full membership so as to have a better chance of influencing its agricultural and economic policies in the way that they would like to see them develop.[73]

Thus, despite appreciating the reality of the situation that there was a limited list of options available to Ireland regarding its process of European integration, the London government was obviously determined to go its own way on the issue. Undoubtedly, the same criteria did not operate the other way round. However, this only leads to the question: what exactly was the Irish government prepared to do about this situation and how was it to proceed?

With the UK's role foremost in the Irish government's mind, a critically important meeting of departmental secretaries and ambassadors was convened on 6 June 1961. At this gathering, a consensus of opinion emerged that it was becoming more and more obvious that there was a vital need for Anglo-Irish talks to be called to discuss the matter. As a result, it was recommended that the taoiseach should write to the UK prime minister so as to give 'greater emphasis' to the impression of seriousness with which the subject was being treated in Ireland.[74] Dispatched some days later, Lemass pointed out in his letter to Macmillan that he had personally made repeated statements to the effect that, should the UK decide to join the EEC, the Irish 'Government would consider applying for membership also, endeavouring to secure such terms as would satisfactorily take account of our economic circumstances'. Of course, the taoiseach's principal intention throughout was to procure private advance notice if such a decision was going to be taken by London and, thus, he sought an early opportunity for bilateral consultations.[75]

Meanwhile, a meeting of government ministers and departmental secretaries that was held on 8 June 1961 did not alter the general direction of the earlier recommendations, except that it was decided that the Irish government should no longer make references to associate membership of the EEC as an Irish foreign policy option. This was another critical moment in the history of Ireland's experience of European integration because, from this point, it was made clear that full membership, rather than association, was the government's primary and sole objective in relation to the EEC. In this regard, Ireland would, however, push for special economic treatment from the Six by arguing that:

- the country had a lower living standard when compared to the various members of the EEC;
- it carried a high level of unemployment and was also demographically hindered;
- compared to the Six, it had a slower rate of economic progress;
- the government wanted its *Programme for economic expansion* to be taken into consideration.

In the meantime, other significant decisions regarding European integration were also taken. For example, the government wanted observer status to be granted at the CAP discussions if such a facility was accorded to other non-members or prospective members of the EEC. It was also decided that all of these points would be conveyed by means of an Irish government *aide-mémoire*, which was to be made available not only to the Six but also to the UK and US governments; in addition, this move would coincide with an announcement in Dáil Éireann. At the same time, the Irish government went about preparing the groundwork that would be needed for the opening of membership negotiations – by intensifying the consultation process with interest groups and by determining the various positions that required to be taken within the different government departments – within the framework of the envisaged turn of events, that is a formal UK government application for full EEC membership.[76]

Notwithstanding this consideration, it was obvious from the outset that the slated tour by UK government ministers to sound out British Commonwealth views in relation to its role with the EEC was going to be part of a dynamic over which the Dublin government could exercise very little control. Nonetheless, their chief hope remained to influence and, indeed, to participate in the UK's decision-making process, an ambition which they aimed to fulfil through their own full bilateral discussions. At least, the Irish government had the power to influence the Six and the UK government in other ways. However, its White Paper entitled the *European Economic Community* and the issuing of an *aide-mémoire* entirely failed in this regard. The government *aide-mémoire* of 5 July 1961 is fully assessed later in this chapter, but only after an in-depth investigation of its White Paper is presented. Nonetheless, it is still possible to contend, even at the beginning of this analysis, that both of these documents must be evaluated as valuable missed opportunities by the Dublin government. In fact, its efforts at convincing its European neighbours of its perspicacity for membership failed miserably, perhaps even having the opposite effect to the one intended; instead of persuading Europe that Ireland was primed for full membership, these documents only confirmed that it was anything but ready. The damage caused would have serious repercussions.

European Economic Community: the White Paper[77]

With the continued growth of external and internal pressures on the government in the early 1960s to articulate its position on the EEC, it was decided that the 'unexpected announcement of the imminence of a White Paper' – that is by publishing a document on the issue – would meet what seemed an insatiable appetite for information. The Department of Finance secretary was particularly concerned that the Irish government should not be distracted from taking this course of action, as he was inclined to see the 'merit of presenting information in a co-ordinated, comprehensive manner' in the form of a government White Paper, rather than issuing the facts on an *ad hoc* basis. The opposition in Dáil Éireann had by this stage been swamping the government with incessant questions, at the same time accusing it of lacking direction. Whitaker felt that it would be 'good administration' therefore for the government to make its position clear through the publication of a White Paper; he thought that 'criticism is unlikely to be stilled by a willingness to answer questions which is more apparent than real'.[78] Assessing the genuine value of the White Paper is an important aspect of this text's argument, mainly because the publication of *European Economic Community* was one of the few extensive public statements of intent by the government regarding the EEC at this point in time. There had, of course, been many speeches on the subject of European integration by Irish politicians and there had also been a vast amount of newspaper coverage. However, this White Paper was to become the first formal indication of the Irish government's views on the issue that was made widely available to the general public.

In fact, the necessity of preparing and publishing a White Paper on the issue had been agreed at the various meetings held between government ministers, departmental secretaries and ambassadors in early June 1961. It was decided that the publication would come in two separate parts, only the second of which would deal with the implications of EEC membership for Ireland. According to the government, however, this second part could only conceivably be prepared when the actual membership negotiations themselves had gotten underway and a clearer picture of the resulting agreements had emerged, before it could be ascertained what they would entail for Ireland. In spite of such logic, it soon became apparent that what was inherently correct in this supposition was also going to be the major failing of the document *European Economic Community*, because it was precisely this argument which was used to prevent a fuller examination of the political dimensions of EEC membership being generated. The White Paper was envisaged as a means of detailing the contemporary history of European integration, as well as assessing how Ireland had fared throughout the OEEC-sponsored FTA negotiations and the instigation of the Treaty of Rome, and what the effects of the proposals for a CAP would be. Indeed, it was felt that this document would also explain what positions the taoiseach and the government had taken and, in the process, furnish 'useful statistics and factual material' such as those related to bilateral Anglo-Irish trade, as well as Irish trade with the Six.[79] It was decided that the White Paper would be published as soon as it was practicable to do so, but that there would be no attempt as yet to go into detail about the wider implications of EEC membership for Ireland. There was 'no point ... at present' in doing so, it was felt, because of course there was the ever-present danger of prejudicing any forthcoming membership negotiations.[80] The various recommendations that arose from the meetings on a White Paper being published were forwarded to Lemass.

As the summer months of 1961 quickly progressed, there was a public air of pace and immediacy about the whole subject of Ireland's possible membership of the EEC. To a large extent, the Irish government either did not have control over many of the events that affected it or precipitated new crises by its actions. All of these background European events occurred with other less unusual developments such as the setting-up of the Anglo-Irish meetings to be held from 18-19 July 1961 in these critical, indeed crucial, initial stages. However, the explicit need in Ireland to have a definitive statement on European integration available for the general populous – although clearly recognised by the opposition parties in Dáil Éireann and by informed public opinion – was only recognised by the Lemass administration after much hesitation. The taoiseach was particularly adamant that his government's announcement regarding Ireland's desire to have consultations with London should not be misinterpreted. For the duration of the protracted build-up to Ireland's application for EEC membership, there appeared to be a domestic political need for Lemass and Fianna Fáil that their decision should not be seen as consequential on the forthcoming bilateral talks.[81] The need not to fall into the trap of being perceived to be dependent upon the UK – the reality of the situation – was tempered by political necessity to appear to be taking the decision independently.

The questioning of the government within Dáil Éireann continued on various topics concerned with the EEC, adding to the pressure on it to act. For example, Brendan Corish, the Labour party leader, thoroughly quizzed Lemass on the related issue of neutrality; in three separate, though interlinked, instances, the latter replied in the negative each time. Indeed, the taoiseach stated that:

- Ireland had not consulted the Austrian, Swedish or Swiss governments regarding the obvious problems involved in entering the EEC without already being a member of NATO;
- the US government had not in any way tried to influence Ireland upon the desirability or otherwise of joining NATO, even if Ireland decided to join the EEC or not;
- on the direct question of whether EEC membership would in fact affect Ireland's position on neutrality, he declared unequivocally that the 'Rome Treaty does not bear directly on the policy of a member State in the matter of neutrality or otherwise'.

When all was said and done, Irish neutrality was not a serious consideration for Lemass in the context of European integration.[82] Eventually, on 30 June 1961, the Irish government's White Paper was laid before the Oireachtas.[83] One of the major stated aspirations given for going ahead with the publication of *European Economic Community* was to explain and list the numerous postwar developments that had then led to the establishment of the various Western European trading groups. This was an aim because, as Con Cremin, the Department of External Affairs secretary, informed the US ambassador to Ireland, Edward G.Stockdale, the document was chiefly intended as 'an effort ... to bring out the political aspirations behind the establishment of the Community'. Nevertheless, the White Paper did not do so explicitly. At this meeting, Cremin also drew particular attention to the official Irish view of the major developments which had led to the establishment of closer European integration in those two decades.[84] The principal historical importance of the government's publication of its White Paper *European Economic Community* was that it finally introduced its position with respect to the EEC into the public sphere. Although there is no particular need to go into any great detail in describing this document here, some interesting and relevant points do still emerge from this manuscript as they illuminate government thinking.

As described in *European Economic Community*, the creation of the EEC in 1957 was viewed by the Dublin government as 'an event of the utmost significance affecting not only future economic and political developments in the member countries, but also their trade and economic relations with other countries of Western Europe and the world at large'. Lemass had made it obvious in Dáil Éireann on 16 May 1961 that, in direct contrast to the EEC, EFTA did not offer Ireland any 'substantial advantages'. He explained that this was because the existing Anglo-Irish trade agreements – economic arrangements which helped to govern trade within this bilateral relationship – were recognised as already giving 'mutual advantages' which could not have been substantively added to within EFTA. Nevertheless, despite the vast size and opportunities offered by the EEC, it was still held by this document that in any:

> ... consideration of Ireland's position *vis-à-vis* the EEC a major factor must be the large proportion of Ireland's external trade which is with the United Kingdom ... In any assessment of the economic effects of a link between Ireland and the EEC it would be necessary to take account of the extent to which such a link might affect Ireland's trade with the United Kingdom ... Ireland's ... national interest ... would, in certain circumstances, be served by our joining a grouping of which the United Kingdom was a member, it would not be served by joining the EEC if the United Kingdom remained outside and we had to forgo our preferential advantages in that market.

The taoiseach had previously said as much in parliament on 26 April 1960 and, indeed, further reiterated the substance of this position a year later when he said:

> ... the best situation possibly for us would be association with the Common Market, if Britain were also a member of it, on a basis which satisfactorily took account of our economic circumstances.

Ireland was therefore faced with two principal choices regarding the form of its participation in the EEC, either full membership or associate membership. Even still, both of these options remained totally dependent on the direction taken by the UK government. In actual fact, the Irish government wavered dramatically between both of these alternatives, each of which need to be assessed in the light of what the White Paper actually said.

As was stated previously, it was evident that Ireland would be applying for full EEC membership under the relevant provision in the Treaty of Rome (Article 237). However, as no other country had as yet applied for membership under this provision, there was no prior experience from which the government could work. Notwithstanding this fact, it was under no illusions regarding the substance of what this particular stipulation entailed. Indeed, it was fully recognised in *European Economic Community* that:

> ... possible adaptions to the Treaty on accession of a new member would not be such as to modify in any important respect the basic provisions of the Treaty ... Membership would entail acceptance of the principles and obligations of the Treaty.

Nevertheless, although this statement formalised the limits within which the Irish government could operate, full membership was additionally deemed to proffer many opportunities. As a full member of the EEC, for instance, Ireland was assured that it would have an equal:

> ... voice in the formulation of policies and ensure access on a footing of equality to a large and growing market with the prospect of sharing in the benefits which would flow from the progressive achievement of the aims of the Community ...

Of equal importance to Ireland, of course, was the fact that full membership would open up access to the various sources of financial assistance that were on offer, such as access to the European Investment Bank, to the European Social Fund and to the European Fund for Structural Improvements in Agriculture. Thus, according to *European Economic Community*, there were distinct benefits to be garnered from Ireland's full adhesion to the EEC, advantages that weighed up rather favourably when stacked against the disadvantages.

Of course, as was explained earlier as well, Ireland also had recourse to another form of relationship with the Six, that is associate membership, an alternative arrangement which was also governed by the Treaty of Rome (Article 238). However, as only one other country – Greece – had by this stage negotiated an associate membership agreement with the EEC, once again there was little previous experience from which the Irish government could work. It was recognised that the Treaty of Rome was quite capable of supporting a variety of forms of association with the EEC and, therefore, that it was within this context that the individual needs of certain countries might be catered. In spite of this explicit undertaking in the Treaty of Rome, the exact manner in which such a relationship might affect, for example, agricultural trade was not as yet clear. Thus, there was no formal indication, for instance, as to how a CAP within the EEC might apply to an associate member. Indeed, this was also the case regarding the various sources of financial assistance that were actually available for associate members. Therefore, the real set of choices facing the Irish government was relatively stark because, in addition to the limitations of full membership, *European Economic Community* made it clear that the possibilities inherent in associate membership were also circumscribed. Nonetheless, at least it was clearly seen that:

> The influence which an associate would be able to exert on the formulation and modification of Community policies would of course be determined by the provisions of the relevant agreement of association. It could not be expected to be as significant as that of a member.

Consequently, the Irish government did not have a blinkered view of the possibilities intrinsic to associate membership. The arguments for and against full membership as opposed to the more limited associate status were out in the open at last. Perhaps, however, it is better to finish this examination of *European Economic Community* with a brief investigation of the one aspect which clearly demonstrates Ireland's true orientation, that is trade, before moving onto an analysis of the Irish government's *aide-mémoire* of 5 July 1961.

By choosing a category such as trade, it is immediately apparent that Ireland did not, in fact, have much room for manoeuvre on the question of European integration. Indeed, it could not be said that the government was operating within a scenario over which it extended much freedom of control. The truth of the situation was that Ireland was completely limited by how the UK government intended to proceed on membership. The Irish government could not act, it could only react. This conviction can clearly be seen from the statistics.[85] There is no real need to go into too much detail about such figures, except to say that the volume of Irish exports was obviously increasing rapidly, while the importance of the UK market was decreasing, however slightly; in turn, Ireland was importing more goods, while determinedly sourcing them from further afield than previously.

When this limited data is added to the evidence presented that Ireland was orienting itself towards markets different to that of its mainstay – the UK – there is no question but that it was totally reliant upon Anglo-Irish trade and that, until this situation of dependence was finally rectified, this bilateral consideration would be the sole significant determinant in any major foreign economic activity undertaken by Dublin. While it can be legitimately argued from the trade figures that this bilateral trade relationship was mutually beneficial, Ireland had hit upon a situation over which it could exercise very little control, the process of European integration. Ireland's relative position in any trade talks could only suffer as a result. This was the unenviable situation in which Dublin now found itself. EFTA may not have turned out to be the immediate potentially devastating threat to the Irish economy that had initially been envisaged, although the soundings that were coming from it were not too helpful to the Irish cause either.[86] However, it was undeniable that the EEC could pose such a threat, if only because of the agriculture question; this was excluded for the most part by EFTA, but it was very firmly on the former's agenda. Dublin thus had to act both quickly and rationally. Notwithstanding these considerations, the *aide-mémoire* issued by the government on 5 July 1961 was certainly not the right answer.

The *aide-mémoire* of 5 July 1961[87]

For the purposes of this special analysis, it is the various European and UK reactions to the Irish government's *aide-mémoire* which was issued on 5 July 1961 that are actually more interesting rather than the substance of the document itself. Of course, it is still necessary to reveal how the government was thinking, how its views developed and what it expected the *aide-mémoire* to achieve. Nonetheless, this can best be done in many ways by integrating the different sets of reactions to the text of the document and to its nuances into this appraisal here. It is possible to divide the responses upon receipt of the *aide-mémoire* into two main categories; each was foreboding and may be listed as follows:

- the UK government's veritable lack of enthusiasm for the actions that Ireland prescribed;
- mixed reactions from the Six and from the institutions of the European Communities, though on balance they looked upon it unfavourably.

Both sets of responses are dealt with in turn, while also being interspersed with an analysis of Irish thinking behind, and reactions to, the manuscript itself.

The EEC was well aware already through informal means that the Irish government would make its proposed application for membership contingent upon the UK's own decision. Thus, the UK government's attitude to Ireland's proposed *aide-mémoire* was most revealing within this context. Indeed, the Irish ambassador in London, Hugh McCann, was reported by the UK as having tried to explain that the *aide-mémoire* to be issued by his government:

> ... was intended to serve much the same purpose so far as the Irish Republic is concerned as our own informal talks with certain of the Governments of the Six and that his Government wished us to know of it in advance. They

hoped that it might elicit information which would be helpful to us as well as to themselves.[88]

UK Foreign Office officials privately admitted that an Irish approach to the Six at that time had 'obvious disadvantages'. Indeed, they were actually opposed to the idea. However, it was asserted within UK government circles that 'it is difficult to see that we can do anything at this late stage effectively to delay the proposed Irish action', partly as it was pointed out that Ireland's diplomatic representatives to the Six and the EEC would already have received their instructions. Thus, it was decided that, even if London was able to persuade Dublin to delay this course of action – and presumably then only momentarily – Ireland's intention to convey the *aide-mémoire* to the Six would quickly become known and, more importantly, it would then come out 'together with the fact that we had been against their execution'. It was felt that such an initiative would ultimately only rebound on London, damaging the way it was perceived and disadvantaging its own position in relation to the EEC even further.[89]

Indeed, two supplementary arguments were also put forward by the UK Foreign Office against taking any action to dissuade the Irish from making its move. These contended that:

- the proposed Irish *aide-mémoire* was intended to find out whether the Six would be prepared to envisage special provisions being made to enable Ireland to become a full member of the EEC and that the Irish government had made it clear that it did not propose to join the EEC unless, and until, the UK did so as well. Additionally, it was pointed out that 'they are not proposing to try to get in first';
- the *aide-mémoire* was also seen as only the formalisation of what was already known to have been previously said between the West German foreign minister and Lemass. In fact, it was thus argued that the Irish government initiative might not be 'wholly disadvantageous' to the UK, especially in regard to lessons that could be learned from how the Irish presentation was received.[90]

In turn, the UK Commonwealth Relations Office also felt 'that it would be extremely difficult for us to object to the proposed action of the Irish Republican Government'. In truth, it was recognised that the taoiseach was committed to saying something substantial on the subject of European integration in Dáil Éireann on 5 July 1961 and that what he really wanted was to be in a position to announce that his government had taken some 'exploratory action' with the Six.[91] Thus, the UK did not find itself in a position to object strongly to the issuing of this document, though Dublin was certainly aware of their reservations.

It is with this background in mind that, in addition to its publication of *European Economic Community*, the *aide-mémoire* distributed by the Irish government on 5 July 1961 should also be considered as a major step in the history of Ireland's European integration. Announcing the decision that 'in the event of the United Kingdom applying for membership of the EEC, we will also apply', the taoiseach declared that Ireland did not have any:

> ... obligations under international agreements or arising out of traditional national policies, such as appear to arise in the case of Switzerland, Austria and Sweden, which need cause us to hesitate in accepting the authority of the institutions of the European Economic Community. If we can be satisfied that it will promote this country's economic welfare and progress we can welcome the prospect of European integration, even those of us who are not prepared yet to look further than the obligations which are specified in the Rome Treaty.

The UK would, of course, remain integral to Ireland in economic terms. Indeed, Lemass held that the 'facts of geography cannot be changed by either the institutions or the rules of the European Community and it is certain that the proximity of the two countries will retain a situation in which the great bulk of our exports to and imports from Europe will be consigned to and from Great Britain'.[92] In this way, Dublin once again made its intentions regarding the EEC and the role that the UK would play public knowledge; simultaneously, it tendered its *aide-mémoire* to the members of the EEC.

The *aide-mémoire* itself marked the first formal occasion in which Ireland unveiled its foreign policy intentions in relation to European integration unequivocally to the members of the Six and to the institutions of the EEC. However, the Irish government made a grievous error by giving too much information away, that is by not keeping the *aide-mémoire* simple and to the point. All that was required from this document was an uncomplicated statement of intent. In spite of this, the government submitted a detailed memorandum. D.J.Maher has remarked that the Irish government's declaration was instead comprised of three major policy components which it wished to impart. Indeed, the *aide-mémoire* maintained that:

- Ireland favoured attaining full membership of the EEC;
- it wanted to convey the impression of a 'dynamic and rapidly growing economy';
- it invited consideration of Ireland as a developing economy in the

same light as that previously accorded to Italy during the negotiations for the Treaty of Rome.⁹³

As the nation was admitted to be economically dependent upon its neighbour, understandably enough the *aide-mémoire* opened up with a statement which basically declared that Ireland's possible candidature of the EEC would depend upon the UK's decision on whether or not to join.⁹⁴ Thus, despite the fact that the government stated that it had followed the EEC's birth and evolution with interest and that it was in accord with its aims and plans, the *aide-mémoire* then made the mistake of going on to impart much more information than was required.

Indeed, the Irish government's *aide-mémoire* stated that, although it was prepared to accept the Treaty of Rome in principal, it had not developed its economy enough to undergo the full adaptive rigours, within the envisaged timescale, necessitated by membership.⁹⁵ A more explicit declaration of support for the political concept outlined in the preamble to the Treaty of Rome was obviously necessary from Ireland. As a result, the Irish government's statement was found wanting, the consequences of which soon became readily apparent. The *aide-mémoire* also made strong references to the *Programme for economic expansion* being an integral part of its envisaged future economic policy and, indeed, expressed the desire that it wanted the EEC to facilitate Ireland in accomplishing this ambition. This document insisted that not only did the goals of its economic initiative conform to those of the EEC, but that their realisation was in the interests of the common good.⁹⁶ In addition, the *aide-mémoire* also demonstrated Ireland's special interest in using the EEC's economic facilities, such as the International Bank for Reconstruction and Development, an assertion which obviously did not prove to be particularly endearing in Brussels or elsewhere. It was no wonder that, from the outset, the EEC suspected Ireland's real motives in applying as a full member. After all, the *aide-mémoire* did not exactly display wholehearted enthusiasm for membership, certainly not for participation without some sort of a price or even without preconditions.

Before moving onto to give the views of the Six, it is perhaps beneficial to deal briefly with the sort of information that the Department of External Affairs was issuing to the Irish representatives abroad to use in conjunction with this *aide-mémoire*. Six principal arguments were being issued in fact, each of which related to Dublin's stated desire for special economic treatment from the EEC. Each of these requirements needs to be dealt with in turn. Firstly, the Irish government particularly wanted Ireland to be recognised as a country in the process of economic development and, at the same time, to be seen as one requiring special measures to raise *per capita* incomes so that they could come closer to the average of the Six. To put this statement into context, it was estimated in the data supplied that the *per capita* income in Ireland in 1959 was 60% that of the Western European average with, for example, the Swedes earning nearly three times as much as their Irish counterparts, the UK's workers over twice as much, and the Danes just less than that again. Indeed, by this scale of reckoning, Ireland was only ahead of Italy, Greece and Portugal in economic terms; it was shown that its GNP had only increased by 10% during the 1950s, in marked contrast to the OEEC's average of a 45% increment. The only saving factor, according to this analysis, was that the *Programme for economic expansion* was gradually reversing this economic anomaly.

Secondly, it was also declared in this Department of External Affairs review that the government wanted to increase the contribution of industry to the economy, both in terms of the relative percentage of the Irish workforce employed in this sector and, additionally, in order to speed up an increase in national industrial production. In 1959, it was asserted that 28.6% of Irish GDP came from industry, in contrast to, for example, a figure of 54.9% for Austria, 47.9% for the UK and 42.3% for Denmark. Indeed, even Portugal had 38.2% of its GDP coming from industry, with only Greece and Turkey trailing after Ireland when this method of gauging the health of the economy was used and then, in the case of Greece, only just. Once again, the memorandum held firmly to the view that progress was being reflected through the impetus of the *Programme for economic expansion*. However, the Department of External Affairs brief did state that 'Ireland cannot yet be regarded as an industrialised or advanced economy'. Indeed, according to the information that was imparted to the Irish representatives in the capitals of the Six, Ireland, although still encumbered with the tag of 'less developed status', was merely a country in the 'process of development'.

A third desire that was to be communicated to the Six, as outlined in this Department of External Affairs memorandum, was the need for recognition at European level of Ireland's various demographic, social and economic difficulties, especially those directly related to the critical problems of emigration, underemployment and unemployment. Irish unemployment was considered to be 'very high by European standards' with a figure of 6.7% given, which compared rather badly to corresponding figures of 4.3% for Denmark, 1.8% for the UK and 1.2% for West Germany. Indeed, when these statistics were then added to the considerable problems of emigration, a declining population and underemployment, the Irish government was keen to stress the country's real need for special treatment from the EEC. In fact, this argument led to a fourth requirement being proclaimed, which appertained to how dependent Ireland had actually become on its foreign trade. In 1960, Irish imports amounted to 35% and its exports to 23% of GNP. Indeed, these sets of data ably demonstrated that Ireland's finances were utterly dependent upon the fortunes and intentions of the UK, indeed that in real terms increased trade with the EEC bore at best secondary, if nonetheless highly symbolic, consequences for the realities which distinguished the economic situation that the Irish faced.

The penultimate Irish government request slated to be communicated by its diplomatic representatives was that it specifically wanted the *Programme for economic expansion* to be given full consideration, not least because it was supported by various organisations which favoured international cooperation, but furthermore because it was in harmony, rather than in conflict, with the economic aims of the EEC. However, the main point to be made in this regard by the various diplomats was that Ireland was 'not at present in a position to undertake all the obligations of full membership', in particular the accelerated programme of tariff and quota dismantlement. Thus, it was recommended that it would need a 'reasonable period' to adjust its economy to the new realities and that the *Programme for economic expansion* must be protected within this wider framework. It was considered that a 'prosperous Ireland, with a balanced economy and a high standard of living, would be of benefit to Europe generally', and that this message should be imparted to the Six. Indeed, this request led onto a last point listed to be relayed to the EEC institutions and members.

The final stipulation in this document called for a general provision to be afforded to facilitate the country's requirements within the context of EEC membership. After all, the government had a very difficult decision to make between two highly problematic and not particularly welcome positions – whether or not to enter the EEC – which were, in any case, dependent upon London's attitude. However, if Ireland's 'developing' status was accepted as a reality by the EEC, it was felt that such difficulties as those which existed could be more easily overcome. Nonetheless, this series of demands issued by the Department of External Affairs only aroused connotations and feelings at home and abroad of 'an béal bocht', the traditional Gaelic saying parodied in a novel by Flann O'Brien of the same name; these indicated that Dublin's *aide-mémoire* and its subsequent diplomatic instructions simply meant that Ireland was once more 'putting on the poor mouth'.[97]

Indeed, entreaties such as these, intended to be appealing and endearing, at eliciting sympathy, were not very positively received by the EEC, especially in the long run. As was stated at the beginning of this segment, the reaction of the Six to the *aide-mémoire* and to the logic of the argument presented by the various Irish diplomats was for the most part fairly mixed, although there were some positive responses initially. Frank Biggar, the ambassador in Brussels, informed his superiors that in the course of various conversations with EEC and Belgian officials he had received general support for Ireland's action. Walter Hallstein was noted as being 'fairly non-committal, but sympathetic', and was said to have felt that Ireland was doing the right thing in seeking membership of the EEC. Interestingly, Hallstein also mentioned that, when he was in Dublin in 1959, the taoiseach had consulted him about the possibility of Ireland joining EFTA, but that he had advised against it at the time. Indeed, according to Biggar, Hallstein regarded subsequent developments in the intervening period as having justified his advice then.[98] Meanwhile, in direct relation to the wider economic implications of membership, Paul-Henri Spaak told Biggar that if the UK joined the EEC, then Ireland would have to do so as well.[99] Additionally, a senior Belgian civil servant was quoted as being generally in favour of Ireland's stated desire to join the EEC, although he did point out that the Belgian government would have to 'fight' the Irish position on agriculture. Nonetheless, Biggar still felt this attitude to be 'not unencouraging'.[100]

The immediate response of the Dutch government appeared even more favourable. The Irish ambassador in the Hague, B.Gallagher, stated that he had given the *aide-mémoire* to the Dutch prime minister. He assessed his government's move as follows to the Dutch:

> ... [the] *aide-mémoire* might virtually be regarded as a conditional intimation of our intention to seek membership ... conditional on Britain applying to become a member of the Community, because it would be impossible for us to join without Britain ... However it now looked as if Britain was going to apply. The Prime Minister said he realised that it would not be possible for us to apply for membership unless Great Britain did.

With regard to Ireland's retarded economic development, it was further noted that the Dutch government would consider this approach in a 'sympathetic spirit'.[101] The same can be said for the initial, unofficial West German government reaction to the *aide-mémoire*, which was stated as being 'very warmly welcomed'; indeed, it was added by Ireland's representative in Bonn, Brian Ó Ceallaigh, that 'Germany would be happy if Ireland could join'.[102] Equally, this position applied to the Italian government's intermediate reply, according to the Irish ambassador in Rome, Thomas V.Commins, which viewed the initiative positively as well; the ability to take the full commitments of the Treaty of Rome on board was another matter.[103]

In fact, it was universally noted in diplomatic reports that, when the *aide-mémoire* was presented, none of the Six raised any problems, not even in relation to defence or neutrality, for instance, issues which later became of prime importance.[104] Notwithstanding such signs, these instantaneous reactions do not underline the general perception of wariness displayed towards Ireland or towards the Irish government's motives in applying. The *aide-mémoire* was interpreted in Brussels as meaning that the EEC would, despite the fact that Ireland was prepared to accept all the inherent rules in the Treaty of Rome, have to acknowledge both its weak economic situation and Irish efforts to improve it. If the EEC accepted this line of argument, even if only on a temporary basis, it would also have to admit that Ireland would thus require 'special time limits and even special clauses' for it to adapt fully.[105] It was no wonder that the institutions of the EEC and the Six subsequently became more skeptical about the government's reasoning once further appraisal was made of Dublin's position.

Before moving on to analyse the UK government's view of the Irish initiative and the issue of Anglo-Irish relations within the context of this development, it is worth looking at the attitude of the US government towards the question of Ireland and European integration too. For the US, the Treaty of Rome had very definite political goals and was 'considered ... to constitute a most significant step in the direction of European unification ... [which] is the reason why Washington has always supported it'. It was also clear that the US supported the UK's bid to join the EEC and, in turn, that it was in favour of the ensuing candidature of Ireland being proposed. The US ambassador to Ireland even went on to suggest to the government that the Kennedy administration was prepared to come out publicly in support of Lemass's integration policy, though this initiative was politely turned down.[106] Crucially, what this particular perspective ignores, however, is that the US did not influence European integration policy to such a degree that the Irish government could put any faith in it as a mechanism through which to attain full EEC membership. Such a desire would have to take London's position into consideration and, even more importantly, the attitudes and opinions of the Six and the institutions of the EEC. The French government's antipathy towards the US was even more pronounced than their attitudes towards the UK.

Despite all of this initial support, the majority of the departmental secretaries seemed to be in accord about not wanting to risk giving the governments of the Six the impression that the government in Dublin was lukewarm towards the concept of the EEC, in the process 'compromising the prospects of our securing satisfactory conditions for entry to the Common Market within the framework of the Treaty'. In fact, it was Cremin, Whitaker and J.C.Nagle, the Department of Agriculture secretary, who were of this view, while J.C.B.MacCarthy, the Department of Industry & Commerce secretary, was understandably enough more ambivalent about the whole situation considering the department he ran.[107] It is with this complicated picture in mind that the next section makes a detailed review of the weeks leading up to the Irish government's decision to apply for full EEC membership on 31 July 1961. In truth, the part played by the UK government proved to be singularly influential in the development of Ireland's policies on European integration in this period. Obviously, the Dublin government was finding it particularly difficult to escape from the economic and political realities of its foremost bilateral relationship, a feature inherent in Irish-European relations which cannot fail to have gone unnoticed in Brussels and the other capitals of the Six.

The 'appropriate moment': Anglo-Irish relations and integration

It has been thoroughly illustrated throughout this investigation that the single-most important consideration for Ireland in relation to the EEC was the UK's standpoint on membership. The UK government had assured Dublin that, although it had formed a *prima facie* view of the question, it would not make a final decision regarding membership until it had ascertained the views of the members of the British Commonwealth and, at the 'appropriate moment', had also exchanged opinions with the Irish government. The Irish ambassador in London was told that an unspecified date in July 1961 would probably present a timely opportunity. McCann was subsequently reported to have replied that:

> ... his Government would welcome this, because they are under pressure from their public opinion and would be sensitive to any charge that events in Europe are moving on without their participating in their development and that they may be presented with a package all sewn up to take or leave.

However, the Irish ambassador also informed the UK government that before joining the EEC Ireland would need indepth bilateral discussions to be held to consider two main problems. He said that these would require:

- deliberations on the possibility of securing a longer transitional period for Ireland to dismantle its tariffs against Europe and the UK;
- an investigation into Ireland's participation in the CAP negotiations.

The 'appropriate moment' to hold these Anglo-Irish consultations was eventually considered by London to be between 18-19 July 1961. Despite the evident reluctance of the latter to hold such talks, these were still seen by the Irish as proffering the ideal opportunity for full bilateral trade discussions in the framework of European integration.[108]

The UK prime minister had replied to Lemass's initial overture of 10 June 1961 for bilateral discussions in a positive and open manner. Indeed, he remarked to the taoiseach that the EEC was a 'subject on which we must keep in close touch with each other'. This contact was scrupulously maintained. The UK government had already been maintaining close links with Ireland through the Irish ambassador, but Macmillan was also said to be encouraged by the suggestion of Lemass to have a series of Anglo-Irish consultations on the issue, preferably from the UK's perspective, during the impending British Commonwealth tour by its ministers. Apparently, Ireland would therefore have significant access to London's thinking.[109] The advice from McCann to his superiors in Dublin was that such a set of meetings were not only 'important', but opportune. Indeed, he reported that:

> British thinking is now moving around to the point of view that it will be impossible to get a clear impression as to the likely terms on which Britain can join the Common Market until actual negotiations are entered into.

Thus, high-level Anglo-Irish consultations presented the ideal chance to deal decisively with the broader issue of whether Ireland should stay in or out of these European developments. At the same time, however, diplomatic reports that were being relayed to the Department of External Affairs continued to emphasise that the UK government was definitely heading in the direction of filing an application for full EEC membership.[110] Indeed, this was also the case with Irish newspaper reports, which subsequently showed that other European countries were in the same position as Ireland. The Danish prime minister was paraphrased as having said, for instance, that he 'could not find a more satisfactory solution to Denmark's marketing problem than British membership of the Common Market, but there was no possibility of Denmark joining alone if Britain did not'.[111] Thus, although it can be argued that Lemass was rather fawning in so readily agreeing to Macmillan's suggestion regarding the timing of these bilateral Anglo-Irish meetings, it was not as if Ireland's position in regard to integration was very strong; a reliance upon trade relations with the UK saw to that.[112]

The main motivation behind the Irish government seeking consultations with their UK counterparts was, according to a draft agenda prepared for the meetings, to enable them to discover their 'present mind' with respect to fields of specific interest, areas which were also directly related to European integration. These necessitated up-to-date information on the positions of the EEC and the UK on a wide variety of considerations – the future status within this context of the British Commonwealth, the CAP difficulty, and future role of EFTA.[113] Paramount in Irish government minds was, of course, the wish to protect their own respective economic position. Obviously, self-interest was the leading consideration for London as well, particularly in the light of the fact that Anglo-Irish relations appeared to be 'one of those illogical arrangements which worked so well', even if Ireland was presumably not a crucial factor in the UK's decision-making process.[114] Consequently, before it came to the time to make determined decisions, one of Dublin's principal aims in these bilateral consultations was to make sure that in any 'negotiations with the Common Market Britain would have as much regard to our position as to that of her EFTA partners'.[115]

Understandably, Ireland still wanted to negotiate entry into the EEC on its own account, independently of the UK government's own negotiations with the Six. Nevertheless, it was interesting that, according to Whitaker, if it was felt that the UK was indeed prepared in such negotiations 'to take account of our interests, to the same extent as those of EFTA members', that a decision had already been made within the Irish government that it should be indicated to the UK delegation in the talks that such a stratagem would very obviously be 'welcome'.[116] Ireland wanted and needed to have the appearance – at least – of independence of action although, in truth, its position would be severely compromised in the eyes of those who knew the reality of its situation.

At the same time, the Irish government recognised that there were some extremely serious problems confronting the UK regarding the issue of full economic union with the Six. These difficulties were ascertained as:

- the resulting status of the British Commonwealth in the EEC;
- the subsequent position of EFTA within that same context;
- the question of where UK agriculture would stand;
- the requirement that the UK would also observe a common commercial policy towards third countries;
- the sovereignty issue, as related to the subordination of Westminster to European institutions.[117]

Although, each of these complications are fairly self-explanatory, they need to be dealt with in some detail. It is interesting to note regarding the British Commonwealth, for instance, that as far as London was concerned, the views of Reginald Maudling, the UK Board of Trade president, went straight to the heart of the matter especially when he asked rhetorically:

> Would you be enthusiastic to give away something which you had which you valued, in return for something unspecified which you are not yet sure you will receive?[118]

Of course, it was also noted by the Irish government that its own individual interests might end up running contrary to those of the UK as, for example, with the position of agricultural products within the whole integration process. Thus, the question of Anglo-Irish talks being held was considered to be all the more relevant and timely as a result.[119]

The belief that these bilateral consultations were of fundamental significance to the Irish government can be gleaned from the taoiseach's presence alone. Indeed, because of this decision, Heath was chosen to head up the UK's delegation; it was thus readily apparent from the outset that these Anglo-Irish talks were going to be of considerable importance. However, this did not stop the negotiations from having their teething problems. It should be noted that through an accident of history, it was the UK Commonwealth Relations Office which usually dealt with Ireland rather than the UK Foreign Office; surely, London's attitudes to Ireland were complicated enough regarding European integration without them being kept within the remit of the Commonwealth Relations Office rather than the Foreign Office. As a result of this state of affairs, there was an odd dispatch from the latter during deliberations about who exactly should be chosen to head up the UK deputation which reads:

> Why doesn't the Commonwealth Sec deal with him? We don't want to get mixed up with S.Ireland do we?

In point of fact, there was a instant reply to these queries to the effect that the Commonwealth Relations Office secretary was not going to be in the country at the time and clearly therefore would not then be able to attend the meetings. Additionally, the Foreign Office was told that these bilateral discussions would 'deal only with the Common Market business not anything else!'[120] Evidently, neither UK government department was in a particular rush to take on the responsibility of dealing with the Irish delegation.

As a consequence, Heath was specifically chosen to meet the taoiseach, partly because it was felt that no other UK government minister would be able to deal effectively with him, but also, it should be noted, because it had already been decided by the UK government that any decision regarding the EEC would 'not be affected by the discussions with the Irish'.[121] Of course, throughout this time, London did not want to give the impression that, because of the Commonwealth tour by its ministers, it would by that stage have already reached a final decision before talking to the Irish. Macmillan had other things to consider:

- a House of Commons question had been tabled on the issue;
- there was EFTA to think of as well and whether the other members of the Seven 'might well feel that they had a right to know as soon as the Irish what we were going to do'.

In any case, the point for the UK government of the bilateral Anglo-Irish discussions was 'to take them [the Irish deputation] over the ground rather than to let them know what we intend to do'.[122] Evidently, London did not recognise Ireland as an important consideration in the determination of its policy towards the EEC, but clearly realised that Dublin could never be allowed to know that this was its private position.

As was generally known, both at home and abroad, it was basically agriculture which was at the heart of the EEC's appeal to Ireland, as industrial considerations posed a much greater problem. Upon his departure for the Anglo-Irish talks to be held in London between 18-19 July 1961, the taoiseach declared that the political implications of the Treaty of Rome did not necessitate partnership in a military alliance. Noticeably, right from the beginning of the membership negotiations process, it was economics, rather than any other consideration, which mattered most for Ireland in the context of European integration. During his airport press conference, in remarks that were expressly meant for domestic consumption, Lemass said that he personally felt that the linkage at European level between economics and politics would eventually result in the unification of Ireland. However, despite paying homage to this ritualistic rhetoric, at least he appreciated that any notions such as these were all in the long-term, because even negotiations for entry into the EEC would take a year to complete at the earliest. Thus, the taoiseach concentrated on the vitally important task at hand, even if it was crucial that the domestic audience's appetite for reassurance remain satisfied.[123]

The Anglo-Irish talks themselves saw considerable progress being made and were in fact based on the assumption that both countries would manage to enter the EEC. Therefore, the bilateral discussions were focused on two central integration issues, which were:

- the arrangements that needed to be made for Anglo-Irish trade in the transitional period before both countries could join the EEC;
- ascertaining what the UK government eventually hoped to secure

from the Six regarding agriculture.

During the meetings held on 18 July 1961, the Irish delegation insisted that it would negotiate with the EEC independently from the UK, but made it clear that it would want to attain entry simultaneously.[124] Replying to a comment during a British Broadcasting Corporation (BBC) interview conducted between the two sets of meetings, that of all the UK's trading partners Ireland seemed to be the least concerned about the prospects of UK membership in the EEC, Lemass baldly stated that:

> The bulk of our exports go to the British market, and a very high proportion of imports are consigned from Britain. It's therefore obvious that the facts of that trade situations make it necessary for us to base our decision upon the decision of Great Britain. If Britain goes into the Common Market we could not contemplate a situation in which the common external tariff of the European Community would be interposed between ourselves and Great Britain. Therefore we have to apply for membership also, and have in fact announced our decision to do so.[125]

Ireland's actual situation regarding membership was not, however, as simple as that; it would not just be determined by what happened to the UK.

It was unquestionably recognised from the outset that there would be both advantages and disadvantages to entry, sometimes with these pros and cons intertwined. For instance, industry would need time to adapt to this change in circumstances but, at the same time, the two countries sharing the island of Ireland would experience similar economic phenomena concurrently and thus would come closer together as a result, economically and otherwise. Dublin was prepared to accept all of the obligations implicit in the Treaty of Rome, economic and political, with the taoiseach even going so far as to say that, for Ireland, the supranational elements of membership were not considered to be a barrier to its entry.[126] In spite of this position, Ireland would essentially be able to do very little about events which were outside of its control. Similarly, however, it would be found that it also failed to deal properly with many of the events that it could have influenced.

The Anglo-Irish meetings of 18-19 July 1961 only confirmed the Irish government's innate feeling that, although the EEC was very appealing on the agricultural question, it posed quite obvious problems regarding industry. The *Irish Press* reported that the talks with the UK government had 'not displeased or disappointed' Lemass. At least, he now had a better appreciation of where the UK actually stood. Indeed, the taoiseach publicly declared that he expected Ireland to receive modifications or at the very least a postponement in implementing the Treaty of Rome. Furthermore, he expected that there would not be problems regarding Anglo-Irish trade arrangements during the membership negotiations process.[127] At the same time, Lemass continued to emphasise the pragmatism of Ireland's relationship with the UK in the context of the EEC. He stated that:

> ... [Ireland] could not permit a situation to develop in which the right of free entry now enjoyed in respect of our exports in our principal market, would be replaced by tariffs against them. There would be no sense in giving ourselves a hard kick in the pants just to show that we could do it, or to prove that nobody would be interested in stopping us from trying.[128]

Every consideration for Ireland in relation to European integration was ultimately dependent upon the UK government's final decision on EEC membership and the subsequent timing of any future application that it would tender. Everything else was secondary.

Critically, however, the two sides attending these consultations were either oblivious or failed to appreciate fully the significance of a statement that was made by the leaders of the Six during the course of these talks. The substance of the Bonn Declaration delivered on 18 July 1961 – which Patrick Keatinge neatly analyses as having 'clearly envisaged a form of eventual political union of Europe' in *A singular stance* – impacted severely upon Ireland's position relative to EEC membership.[129] This was primarily because the preamble to the Bonn Declaration expressly stated that there was a desire within the Six:

> ... to strengthen the political, economic, social and cultural ties which exist between their peoples, especially in the framework of the European Communities, and to advance towards the union of Europe.[130]

Ireland would find it difficult in such circumstances to convince the members of the EEC that it in fact accepted unequivocally and unreservedly the political aspirations outlined in the Treaties of Rome and, indeed, in the Bonn Declaration despite warnings on the matter in the Seanad, amongst other fora.[131] Regardless of this consideration, the government had another more immediate concern to face before all the implications of this development had been fully assimilated. Thus, Irish government members were finally starting to ask the most pertinent question of all: where exactly did Ireland actually fit in the UK's EEC membership equation and what implications would that position have *vis-à-vis* Ireland's prospective application?

Pulling the rug out or paranoia?

An ever-present Irish government worry in the days that followed the Anglo-Irish meetings of 18-19 July 1961 was centred on the uncertainty over whether something substantial would happen concerning London's negotiations with the EEC over which it had neither control nor prior notice. Indeed, throughout this time, Dublin continuously emphasised to the UK that it needed to be kept informed about any analogous move in its European integration policy or even changes in its commercial arrangements which would have any direct effect upon the Anglo-Irish trading position. Moreover, it is possible to contend that, in basic terms, what Dublin was really worried about were London's true feelings emerging regarding the prospect of an Irish application being tabled.[132] The UK government knew that it could not object to such an initiative *per se*, but there was very definitely a move afoot in the Foreign Office to discourage Ireland from doing so, because of what were vaguely termed as potentially 'serious political difficulties'.[133] The truth of the matter was that London really wanted the inherent advantages in full EEC membership all for itself, while simultaneously retaining the privileges in existing Anglo-Irish trading arrangements; it certainly did not want it somehow to make the likelihood of that happening more distant or unnecessarily complex.[134]

The UK ambassador to Ireland, Ian Maclennan, called on the Department of External Affairs secretary, Con Cremin, to show him an important UK Foreign Office minute that had previously been shown to the Irish ambassador in London on 19 July 1961. In this note, a senior West German foreign ministry official – heretofore considered to be sympathetic to the position of the Dublin government – was paraphrased as having said that he 'thought it very unlikely that the Six would be prepared to accept the Irish Republic as a full member'.[135] At the same time, the UK ambassador was under strict orders to go on the 'attack' in an active effort to dissuade the Irish from applying to join. Privately, the Foreign Office did not feel particularly happy to leave Ireland to 'run head on into trouble on this' if this was in fact the line that was going to be taken by the Six. Indeed, it was felt that: 'The effect on the Irish themselves might be unfortunate; even worse might be the strengthening of the fears held by some members of the Commonwealth ... that the E.E.C. is a kind of economic arm of NATO'.[136] The Foreign Office minute shown to Cremin expressed the opinion that West Germany was actually airing the view that:

> ... while NATO members of EFTA might become members of the Community, he doubted whether we could do so by reason of the political

factors and that this view was strengthened by the fact that we had intimated that we could not comply fully with some of the provisions of the Rome Treaty within the time appointed.

Therefore, this was the first really substantial indication that there were political, as well as economic, grounds for Ireland to worry regarding full membership. In reply, the senior Irish official pointed out to Maclennan that, when the German foreign minister, von Brentano, was in Dublin, he had made categoric statements to the effect that NATO membership was not in any way some sort of precondition for membership of the EEC, however, a view which had been echoed subsequently by Spaak, the Belgian foreign minister.[137]

Another UK Foreign Office minute gave further information, reputedly from the same senior West German foreign ministry official, which said though that while his superior's remarks were formally correct, that it was 'doubtful whether they reflect the realities of the situation entirely accurately'. Of course, what this whole anecdote boiled down to was an informal UK attempt to block full Irish membership by making the suggestion that Ireland's application should be worded so as to leave all options regarding a formal relationship with the EEC open, thus including full or associate membership. This second Foreign Office minute actually remarked that the UK had already warned the Irish that full membership of the EEC should not be taken for granted and that the 'appropriate relationship for them was association'. This was not a feeling which dulled over time. Indeed, not too long afterwards, it was noted in one publication that: 'Associate membership would be the best solution ... for Eire'. The West German official, meanwhile, had actually advised that:

> ... the Irish might be wise not to commit themselves too far to any particular form of relationship. If they were thinking in terms of a communication to the Six they might leave the question open and apply for membership or association, or use some vague phrase like 'a close relationship'.[138]

London was being underhand in its communications with the Irish who, not surprisingly in turn, were entirely suspicious of the former's real motives.

At their meeting, Cremin informed the UK ambassador in Dublin that Ireland had already announced that it would be seeking full membership of the EEC if the UK did so as well. Indeed, he added that the declaration by the Six desiring 'the accession to the European Communities of other European States which are ready to assume in all fields the same responsibilities and the same obligations' was totally acceptable to the Irish government and therefore was not necessarily interpreted as a stumbling-block at all.[139] Maclennan thus reported that the Department of External Affairs secretary 'did not seem particularly disturbed by its implication of difficulties arising over forms of association' with the EEC. In fact, the UK ambassador attributed this to being the reality of a situation in which the Irish had already committed themselves to applying for full membership of the EEC in the event of the UK doing so: 'It may be that the Government here have been unwisely sticking their necks out, but I do not see that there is much that they can do about it now and they seem content to await developments'.[140] In truth, what Dublin was actually more worried about were the real motives of the UK, not the views of the Six or the EEC.

The presentation of these two UK Foreign Office minutes was obviously viewed in Dublin as a 'somewhat unusual step' and was being interpreted in one of two ways. On the one hand, it appeared as if the UK was being very frank with Ireland, even to the extent of passing on the doubts – on grounds other than economic ones – of at least one member of the Six over its proposed candidature; on the other, London evidently might have a more self-interested motive in mind and was thus engaging in efforts to discourage Ireland from seeking membership. If it was thought that the latter tactic indeed reflected the real UK position, the Irish government could clearly no longer accept London's views without qualification, either on EEC membership or on other aspects of the Treaties of Rome. Certainly, Cremin was able put two principal political reasons forward as to why the UK government might not want Ireland to join as a full member of the EEC. These arguments he listed as follows:

- Ireland would not only continue to enjoy advantageous access to its UK markets, but it would now also have access to the EEC, two privileges which would probably be denied in fact to the members of the British Commonwealth;
- the Stormont government in Northern Ireland was against Ireland's membership, essentially because the EEC was all about breaking down economic barriers and, thus, membership would further diminish the significance of the border dividing the island into two jurisdictions.

Cremin advised the government that Ireland needed to clarify the NATO position in relation to the EEC, regardless of the fact that he did not personally think that the UK government was deliberately using these unofficial West German foreign ministry views to discourage the Irish from applying for membership. Clarification of the views of the Six and indeed of the UK's true position had become of the utmost importance, however, before he felt that Ireland could proceed in its quest without further vacillating.[141] Nevertheless, it has to be conceded that a decision of the magnitude and resoluteness of Ireland's official application for full membership of the EEC on 31 July 1961 was not the most subtle of strategies that might have been pursued in order to achieve this clarification. Nonetheless, this was the actual strategy that ultimately was chosen by the Dublin government.

In the meantime, there were conflicting reports emanating from Brussels in the lead-up to the application which, while noting Ireland's 'positive attitude' towards the EEC – partially interpreted as a vindication of the route taken by the Six towards integration – were literally suggesting that any substantive membership overtures which were emanating from Ireland were actually 'premature'.[142] Thus, receipt of the application did not alleviate the confusion that was being felt in Brussels. Indeed, it only served to exacerbate it. For better or worse, Ireland had taken a position. It is by addressing the reactions of the Six and the EEC to the government's decisive move of 31 July 1961 that this investigation next proceeds.

Reactions to the Irish application for full membership

As with the Irish government *aide-mémoire* of 5 July 1961, arrangements were made for the application for full EEC membership to be made available to all the members of the Six, as well as to the governments of the UK and the US, while being formally directed towards the EEC. Of the various immediate reactions given to this application, the general feeling was either one of ambiguity – regarding the implications and real meaning of this decision by the Irish government to apply – or surprise – as the view existed that Ireland's move in requesting membership negotiations had been untimely because its entry was so dependent in real terms anyway upon consequent UK government negotiations.

In relation to Ireland's application, any positive feelings on it emanating from those actors most intimately involved were limited to the fact that the Irish government had at least given away as little information as possible about its economic situation and its views upon European integration through the wording of its communication. Indeed, the letter's brevity and terseness was held to be one of its more positive aspects. It might be worth remarking that a more detailed enunciation on its position would probably have prejudiced, rather than aided, Ireland's application to the EEC for membership negotiations to open. In addition, however, the UK chef de mission in Brussels, A.H.Tandy, in analysing this formal application for his superiors, noted that Ireland was applying for full EEC membership and not for association. In fact, a subsequent meeting with his Irish counterpart elucidated the heretofore unexpected response that Ireland's application had become quite literally a 'brief request for negotiations expressing adherence to the general objectives of the treaty and making no mention of special problems'.[143] It has to be said that Dublin appeared to have learned a valuable lesson from the cool reception accorded to its earlier *aide-mémoire*.

Upon reading the official Irish application for membership negotiations to begin, one senior EEC civil servant in Brussels responded by declaring: 'I see that the Government of Ireland understand perfectly the Treaty of Rome'. The fact that the said letter contained no expressions about conditions for membership, as the *aide-mémoire* had previously done, did not mean that the Irish government would not have liked to have made its economic worries and political position on European integration clear at this point in time. However, as the Irish ambassador in The Hague, B.Gallagher, pointed out regarding this reaction, he did not think that it was 'opportune ... to dampen in any way' what he felt to be 'the excellent effect created by the form of application made by the Taoiseach'. In truth, Gallagher did not find himself in a comfortable position – when presenting the Irish application during the series of meetings that he held with a myriad of responsible EEC officials and representatives of the various governments that were present in Brussels – to draw attention simultaneously to the problems that Ireland would possibly have to face in regard to its European integration. His final word was that these difficulties would have to be left to the membership negotiations themselves or, at least, to more formal meetings with EEC officials.[144]

It is interesting to note that Spaak was more circumspect in his response to Dublin's initiative, seeing Ireland's application as being totally contingent upon the success of a similar UK government move. Indeed, he contented himself to speak of the difficulties involved in arranging the actual form of membership negotiations, a ploy which was obviously meant to stall Irish aspirations of instantly entering the EEC. With regard to the UK's role, Gallagher informed the Belgian foreign minister that, although Ireland's desire to adhere to the EEC was independent of any consideration outside of the Six, the country's ability to accede was also obviously affected by the realities of its economic relations. In addition, Ireland was stated to have no fundamental political reservations on European integration. Overall, however, the Irish ambassador thought that Spaak was 'restrained' in his general reaction.[145] In point of fact, he was not in the least bit enthusiastic about the prospect of this application for full membership being deliberated.

This position was reflected throughout the EEC Commission as informal talks regarding adhesion negotiations progressed; Ireland's application at this time was proving to be rather less than constructive in its opinion.[146]

There were, of course, varying reactions from the member states, even if reports from the Netherlands appear to have been more helpful than was the norm. Indeed, those accounts appear to have been fairly positive initially, with the Irish chargé d'affaires in The Hague, Florence O'Riordan, reporting that the Dutch government was actually pleased with Ireland's initiative. In point of fact, the Dutch foreign minister, Joseph Luns, complemented the Irish government on its 'excellent letter' by saying that their 'manner of doing it is excellent ... you have been very quick, indeed, very quick'. Somewhat surprisingly, he also reportedly felt that the decision of the EEC Council on the advisability of opening negotiations would only be a 'formality' in Ireland's case.[147] The reality was very different indeed; any initial Dutch enthusiasm for the Irish decision to apply for full membership soon waned.

The Irish chargé d'affaires was subsequently summoned for a *tête-à-tête* at the Dutch foreign ministry to discuss some aspects of the Irish application which the Dutch government said 'intrigued' them. In delivering his report on this encounter, the Irish diplomat concerned actually had to plead for more instructions from the Department of External Affairs because his lack of knowledge on Irish government motives for applying had been so exposed at this meeting.[148] It has to be said that this particular report was itself damning, revealing the lack of preparation and coordination in government circles. It seems absurd that a diplomat could be embarrassed in this way. O'Riordan summarised one Dutch foreign ministry official who frankly stated the Dutch government's position on Ireland by recounting that:

> ... at the discussions in Brussels ... and elsewhere, following our application for membership of the E.E.C. 'some countries' had asked whether it was worth having Ireland ... in view of the fact that she was an underdeveloped country with apparently many difficulties, who would be looking for assistance, would be asking for so many concessions, all of which would make it impossible to accept her without breaches of the Treaty which could not be considered.

Quite obviously, what the Dutch government was in fact looking for was more information from Ireland about the precise meaning of the earlier *aide-mémoire*, precisely what were the concessions that the Irish envisaged as being necessary at the adhesion negotiations. As a result, the Irish were advised to apply pressure on both the Six and the UK for support of its candidature, without which Ireland's weak position would be exposed. Indeed, they were forcefully cautioned to downplay any talk of economic underdevelopment and were told that the time for further elaboration regarding entry issues would best be left to the membership negotiations themselves. O'Riordan felt that, although the Dutch government official with whom he had conversed was 'embarrassed by the fact that these difficulties were being raised now in our case (and not in that of the British) ... he was certainly giving the impression that the Dutch were more anxious to help than other Governments who should be pressurised'.[149] Clearly, the Dutch attitude to Ireland's application was as yet 'less explicitly formulated' than its opinions on the UK's position. It was concluded by the Dutch that the prospect of Irish membership should be met officially with a positive response, that this bid should be 'applauded'. This opinion was expressed despite the fact that there were various good reasons why the Netherlands should have insisted that it would be more appropriate for Ireland to seek an association agreement rather than full membership, reasons such as 'neutrality or relative economic backwardness'.[150]

Nevertheless, the central advice from the Dutch, which appeared to be that Ireland should bide its time, was expressly ignored in Dublin. Throughout this period, in fact, the Irish government was not just waiting to receive the various reactions from the Six or the EEC, but it was actively engaged in taking new and at times unsuitable initiatives of its own, notably in relation to the agriculture question and particularly with regard to the possibility of a CAP being formed by the EEC. However, before considering such a specific aspect in this analysis of the different reactions to Ireland's first EEC application, it is more relevant at this stage to investigate the official EEC responses to the Irish initiative. It appeared as if Ireland wanted to run before it was up and walking.

The UK government, which had applied for membership of the EEC ten days after the Irish government had done so, was generally expected to receive an intermediate reply from the EEC Council before Dublin did. It is interesting to note, therefore, the petty nature of the latter's thinking. Even within the Department of External Affairs it was advised that:

> ... there would be no point in our trying to get a reply before the British, even though *we applied first*; the E.E.C. reaction would probably be that our application was contingent on the British one, and therefore that it should take second place.[151]

The fact that such an gesture was even contemplated exposes the complete lack of acumen or insight being displayed on the Irish side. There was something that the Irish government appeared to be forgetting. Richard Vaughan has written in his *Twentieth-century Europe* that:

> Although the Irish had been careful to apply separately from and in advance of Britain, membership of the EEC was economically unthinkable for them without British Membership ... the EEC could not undertake to negotiate with several different countries at once. Inevitably, then, the decision was to negotiate first and foremost with Britain.[152]

Ireland was not expecting to receive a definitive reply concerning the opening of membership negotiations until September 1961, although Gallagher was still able to inform his superiors that the EEC Council president, Ludwig Erhard, was going to answer the Irish government's request forthwith, even if it was only an intermediate reaction.[153]

Before responding officially, however, the Irish government was informally sounded out by the EEC as to whether the *aide-mémoire* of 5 July 1961 was to be regarded as part of its official application. Of course, panic ensued in Dublin. A UK Foreign Office report from this time remarked that Ireland's application was actually causing extreme embarrassment in Brussels and smugly added the view that this was 'no more than we expected'.[154] The Irish diplomatic representative was ordered to inform the EEC that the government *aide-mémoire* was not to be considered part of Ireland's official application for full membership and tried to explain that it had only been intended as an indication of its views regarding the agenda and content of subsequent negotiations. The damage had been done though. So worried was the Irish government about the implications of this earlier submission that Gallagher was told to make 'every effort' to avoid reference being made to the *aide-mémoire* in Erhard's formal reply to Ireland's request for membership negotiations. Lemass clearly did not want the *aide-mémoire* to become either public knowledge or even more widely known than it already was in official EEC circles, presumably because it now only compromised Ireland's negotiating position.[155] However, it was becoming increasingly apparent that it was already too late to retract the statement. Ireland's *aide-mémoire* had developed into a *bête-noire*.

On 14 August 1961, Erhard's official reply to the taoiseach's request for membership negotiations to open began by expressing general satisfaction with Ireland's stated desire to be associated with the future development of the EEC and, furthermore, he remarked that the EEC Council was pleased that the Irish government shared the ideals which had originally motivated the Six in its formation. To this end, he added that Ireland's application would be processed through the EEC Council. Erhard was also moved to ask for more information, however, specifically in relation to a previous communication from the Irish government, the curious *aide-mémoire*. Indeed, it should be pointed out that, as a result, even this interim reply from the EEC differed significantly from those which had been accorded to Denmark and to the UK, both in its content and form.[156] It was a taste of things to come.

Thus, to his obvious embarrassment, the taoiseach had to respond on 18 August 1961 with a statement to the effect that the Irish government only wanted its formal application of 31 July 1961 – as well as this subsequent further elaboration – to be considered by the EEC Council. The *aide-mémoire* of 5 July 1961 was deemed to be no longer valid. This new Irish government position came about, Lemass declared to Erhard, 'after full consideration'. It was now felt that any problems and obligations arising out of EEC membership would best be resolved by Ireland going through with the negotiations procedure that was outlined in the Treaty of Rome (Article 237). Dublin continued to insist, all the same, that they wanted these discussions to run concurrently with, although independently of, the UK's own negotiations for entry. In the process, of course, Ireland only created another unnecessary precondition to talks before they had even begun, further alienating goodwill towards their application.[157] Unknown to the Irish government, it was strongly felt within the Foreign Office that the task facing the UK was whether it 'should now consider seriously how much importance we attach to Irish membership of the Community: and if we do think it important, what – if anything – we can do to help Ireland to get in as a full member'. As a consequence, both of previous positions taken and events outside of its control, Ireland was in serious danger on two counts of being left out in the cold regarding European integration, in relation to how the EEC Council acted towards its prospective candidature and how the London government proceeded in either promoting or hindering that status.[158]

At the same time as this procedural mechanism was operating, the Irish government was giving different explanations to different audiences regarding the probity of its move, mainly in an effort to justify its membership application. For instance, the taoiseach was keen to tell the nationalist audience in Northern Ireland that the political implications of the border dividing the two countries would in fact 'diminish very considerably' once Ireland and the UK were operating in harmony within some form of European FTA. Indeed, he stated that he personally believed that the problems of economic development were rather similar north and south of the border, that European integration would benefit the island as a whole.[159] Such an outlook could only lead to a serious question being put forward: what was Ireland hoping to receive exactly from EEC membership? After all, as Bill McSweeney has written in his study 'Out of the ghetto: Irish foreign policy since the fifties', despite what the Irish federalists may have felt regarding European integration, no country was actually trying to join the Six 'for the good of mankind or [for] any other predominantly altruistic reason'.[160] Therefore, it could reasonably be asked: why should the Irish government have had different motivations? Ireland was clearly attempting to adhere because of economic considerations. However, the fact that Dublin was at the same time ignoring the political consequences of membership was not being lost on the EEC; it still appears to have been blissfully unaware of the trouble into which it was at that point proceeding headlong.

Of course, the main beneficiary of EEC membership in Ireland's case, especially in the short-term, was seen to be agriculture, mainly because of the potential it offered if the negotiations for a CAP proved to be successful. In this regard, the Anglo-Irish talks that were held in the middle of July 1961 had somehow raised Irish government hopes about being able to influence the whole procedure. The UK Lord Privy Seal had already declared that he did not foresee any difficulty about securing observer status at the CAP talks; indeed, he stated that London expected this facility to be offered.[161] As a direct consequence, J.C.Nagle, the Department of Agriculture secretary, actually suggested that Ireland should enquire informally of the EEC whether or not this facility would be granted. Indeed, Nagle also noted that, because his department was in fact having some difficulty in following the rapid and rather complex evolution of the EEC's agriculture proposals, Ireland needed to have more regular contacts with European agriculture officials.[162] This move was subsequently approved and an appropriate official was accredited to the EEC.[163] The government also decided that, if the UK and Denmark obtained observer status at the CAP negotiations, they too should insist on receiving similar treatment. Indeed, an approach on this matter to Sicco Mansholt, the EEC agriculture commissioner, was approved by the cabinet as well, as was a explicit appeal to the Six for equal treatment.[164]

In spite of perceptible progress being made, the immediate sense that was emanating from Brussels on these various ideas was not a positive one; the suggestion of observers at the CAP, for example, was envisaged as a non-starter from the outset.[165] Indeed, it has to be said that the Irish government's basic lack of sensitivity regarding the circumstances and context of European integration – that, while Ireland was earnestly looking towards something as specific as observer status at the CAP, the EEC was questioning the whole rectitude of its application for full membership at all – leads this analysis to question the standard of policy procedures that Ireland was following in its attempted economic integration. Dublin was about to find out much more

Ireland: left out in the cold

In truth, the country was to come in for quite a shock. There were two fundamental sets of difficulties confronting the Irish government in the wake of the series of delays that began to affect its application for membership of the EEC. The Council of Europe, a relatively dispassionate viewer of the process, summed up the intricacies of the situation facing Ireland, stating that they could be divided into two distinct categories:

- the complexity of the country's economic difficulties;
- the equally demanding question posed by political problems.

In fact, it was in relation to economic factors that the main difficulties arose, although the government would ignore the political issues involved in European integration at its peril. Of course, as has been repeatedly stated, Ireland was economically dependent upon the UK and the quasi-British Commonwealth preference arrangements which were still then in force, a relationship which had been reinforced by the various Anglo-Irish trade agreements dating from 1938, 1948, and 1960. However, the Council of Europe report felt that Ireland's tariffs were at such a high level that it was quite probable that it would not only experience grave difficulties in adopting the common EEC external tariff that was required by full EEC membership, but that it would also encounter serious problems in deconstructing the customs barriers that it had raised against the import of goods from its possible future partners. The adoption of the common external tariff and the deconstruction of internal trade barriers were part of a foreign economic policy envisaged by the Six as being commonly enforceable within an accepted and restricted timeframe.[166]

According to this Council of Europe publication from 1961, the political problems that were facing Ireland in relation to its full adhesion to the EEC, albeit not as important as the economic considerations, were nevertheless rather significant in terms of European integration. These political difficulties included the fact that Ireland observed a policy of neutrality, which the government said it wanted to maintain as long as partition remained in place, an obvious contravention in itself of the political desires inherent in European integration. In addition, there was also the problem that Ireland shared many institutional forms and traditions with the

UK, many of which differed considerably when compared to those which were operating on the European continent, the sum of these views not being particularly helpful to the Irish cause.[167] Indeed, the Six and the institutions of the EEC both remained totally unconvinced about Ireland's economic and political propensity for full membership and did not hesitate in enunciating their considerable reservations.

Of course, many of the doubts regarding Ireland's suitability for full EEC membership dated back to the demands that it had made for economic concessions to be allowed for the peripherals during the OEEC-sponsored FTA negotiations. However, as has been pointed out, there were also serious political reservations too. The fact that Ireland was not a member of a security alliance was the most obvious explanation being put forward to justify this reserve and was partly the reason why the government found that its EEC application soon stalled. Indeed, the *aide-mémoire* issued on 5 July 1961, which had concentrated upon elucidating various envisaged economic difficulties that accession would doubtlessly bring, did not sit well with the Bonn Declaration of the Six that followed a fortnight later, an announcement which itself was concerned with investigating how European foreign policy cooperation could be further developed. Ireland was thus pointedly excluded from the positive interim replies that were issued to the other prospective applicants by the EEC Council.

Indeed, EEC membership negotiations actually opened with the UK government on 8 November 1961 and with the Danish government on 30 November 1961, even though the UK and Denmark had both applied to join the EEC after the Irish government had done so. It should also be noted that the Norwegian government, which only applied to join the EEC on 30 April 1962, was also able to open its EEC negotiations on 12 November 1962, leading to D.J.Maher's biblical reference to the procedure followed in Brussels as being 'decidedly a case of the first being last'.[168] Undoubtedly, the question that the Six were in fact asking themselves was whether Ireland would actually be ready or not to follow through with the ideals envisaged, though not manifestly stated, by the Treaty of Rome. The Irish government, however, concluded that the problem with the membership negotiations not opening was more to do with the general perception of Ireland rather than with the reality of the situation. Thus, it began to tackle those perceived problems one by one.

As a result, two senior Irish civil servants, T.K.Whitaker, the Department of Finance secretary, and Con Cremin, the Department of External Affairs secretary, were sent to the capitals of the Six in September 1961. This endeavour was primarily attempted in an effort to explain Ireland's own peculiar economic and political position within the wider context of European integration. Once there, these officials were typically confronted with the argument that Ireland would not in fact be a suitable candidate for full EEC membership, substantially because of economic, rather than political, misgivings on behalf of the Six. Indeed, there was a strong body of opinion within the Six and the EEC which viewed associate, rather than full, membership as the most 'appropriate link' for the Irish.[169] The UK Lord Privy Seal did of course state on 10 October 1961 that Ireland was also a consideration for the UK in its own application for membership. In his statement, Heath said:

> There is one other European country I should like to mention, namely the Irish Republic. We have special trading arrangements with the Irish, deriving from the days when they were part of the United Kingdom. I do not think it necessary to describe these in detail. I will limit myself to saying that we in the United Kingdom were pleased to see that the Republic had applied for membership of the Community. If their application succeeds – as we hope it will – out trading arrangements with them will be subsumed in the wider arrangements of the enlarged Community, and no special problems need arise.

Heath had won the UK cabinet over to his point of view regarding Europe and had managed to carry Irish interests along with him as well.[170]

The EEC Council met to discuss the issue at the end of that month but, unlike the UK and Danish cases, decided to postpone an examination of the Irish government's application until a later date. In actual fact, the EEC Council eventually only examined Ireland's request on 24 October 1961 and, once again, decided that still further information was needed from Dublin before they could proceed. Erhard informed the taoiseach that the EEC Council had unanimously decided to suggest that the Irish should present their case for membership to the Six in Brussels at the beginning of January 1962. Ireland would therefore be accorded the opportunity to discuss its own particular problems and, at the same time, begin to address the question of how its European integration process should proceed. Within this proposal, there was the intrinsic promise that, once the wider implications of this proposed meeting between the Six and the Irish government had been fully examined, membership negotiations proper would begin in earnest for Ireland's entry into the EEC.[171] Dublin was not yet placated.

The Irish government, which had also received electoral reconfirmation of its mandate in October 1961, immediately set about clarifying its integration position even further still. Indeed, running through his speeches on the subject of Ireland's aspirant status, the taoiseach constantly reiterated that the EEC was a 'development in which we want to participate', both economically and politically. On the economic side of the equation, he summarised the Irish position by stating that once 'granted reasonable temporary arrangements in the industrial field, we can face up to the obligations of the Treaty'. Obviously, agriculture within the EEC presented a much greater opportunity for the country than did industrial considerations and, indeed, did not pose anything like the kind of problems that industry did. Meanwhile, on the question of the political implications inherent in European integration, the fact which was constantly reiterated was that Ireland was neutral in practice, although not constitutionally. It was clearly seen by Lemass as a highly significant, if not vitally important, complication. As a direct result, therefore, the demystification and devaluation of neutrality as an absolute and accepted government policy option quickly gathered pace.[172] In fact, by this process, it can be said that the taoiseach was quite prepared to sacrifice the 'political' for the 'economic', even confirming upon re-election to office that:

> ... there is the consideration that it will, in my view, be necessary at some stage, arising out of our relations with the European Economic Community, to set up a new Ministry to deal with European Community affairs and with foreign trade generally.[173]

It was becoming more readily apparent in government circles that the positive economic aspects that European integration held for the country were quite easily prevailing over all other – thereby including political – considerations. Clearly, however, they did not exercise control over the situation prevailing in Europe.

Intermediate conclusions

Writing to Friedrich Engels on 2 November 1867, Karl Marx equanimously declared that:

> Formerly I considered the separation of Ireland from England impossible ... I now consider it inevitable, although after the separation may come federation.

Essentially, what Marx foretold actually came true.[174] In the first place, Ireland did indeed become an independent and integrated nation, considerations such as the partitioning of the island aside; and, secondly,

Lemass, while espousing and initiating the country's European integration, in the meantime also forged a situation whereby Ireland was treated as part of the UK for trading purposes. In order to become more 'deeply Irish', it would have to utilise its links with the UK more positively and concurrently become more European. Consequently, the reasoning behind and real value of the constant flow of anti-partition propaganda that was emanating – even if it was to a lesser degree – from Dublin throughout this period has to be questioned. It is true that economics were coming out ahead of political considerations in the determination of foreign policy. Thus, a central issue has to be more fully explored: what was the taoiseach's real agenda in saying that European integration would bring about an end to partition? Indeed, another question might be raised: what about the role of Irish neutrality in the particular context of partition, never mind its wider implications in an EEC which only had members of NATO and no other neutrals? The answers to these reveal that economics was gradually overtaking politics.

The reality of the situation was that, to all extents and purposes, Ireland became part of an economic federation, initially through the Anglo-Irish FTA agreement – a subject that is investigated in the penultimate chapter entitled *The 1965 Anglo-Irish FTA agreement* – and subsequently through to its final accession to the EEC in 1973. However, this does not answer the immediate question about what the Irish government was prepared to sacrifice in a decisive effort to further its chances of fully taking part in the European integration process. Perhaps some intermediate conclusions on this issue are appropriate here, before moving on to a much more extensive elucidation of these issues, dealt with in the next chapter centred on *De Gaulle's refusal of the UK, 14 January 1963*. It comes as no great surprise that the role played by the UK remained absolutely integral throughout.

Of course, the implications of Ireland's application for EEC membership and, indeed, the various reactions to it were diverse. Economically, it was felt that Ireland might only end up impeding the process of European integration because its needs were so vast. This did not apply so much in relation to agriculture because, after all, this economic sector was also in need of special care and attention for each of the Six; the Irish government's main worry was that a CAP would be developed without its input. Industrially, other than fears of dumping and increased compatibility difficulties, Ireland clearly did not have that much to offer and would suffer initially from the removal of industrial tariffs. Dublin's position on other issues such as, for instance, the EEC's external tariff policy and transport policy, what it thought of European institutions, as well as UK membership, would also need to be defined. However, Ireland had political problems with which to contend, even if the government quickly went about allaying the fears of the Six with regard to foreign policy cooperation. For example, although partition might have been a little more exacting to explain, Dublin made sure that neutrality consequently became, by definition, 'negotiable'. Indeed, it was quickly guaranteed that this subject would not be allowed to encroach on a concerted campaign for participation in the process of integration. In fact, it was ignored domestically or just glossed over when it suited the government. Neutrality was viewed by Lemass as a policy of expedience and was never seen as something 'traditional'.

Indeed, in the spring of 1960, the government had even seriously examined a proposal for the establishment of a factory to produce 200,000 hand grenades – detonators and die-cast metal casings – for sale to Venezuela. The Department of Justice informed the government that it could do so with a 'clear conscience' – Washington and London having intimated that they were not opposed to this economic initiative – but realised that it could 'not divorce itself from the responsibility for the end-use of the weapons sold'.[175] The Department of External Affairs was worried about them falling into the wrong hands though; Cuba and Algeria were mentioned specifically.[176] It is not clear if the arms were sent, they probably were not, but that is not the point. In time, the focus of foreign affairs would change from a political to an economic outlook, but Lemass was not ready just yet. Dublin's approach to the issue of neutrality was always a cautious one, chiefly because of the Irish people's inherent fealty to the concept; they had not reached a stage where they were ready to sanction the manufacture of grenades for the Venezuelan government. Instead, in the course of a decade, successive governments embarked on a policy that was specifically designed to erode, quite gradually, the country's allegiance to the idea of neutrality and, therefore, benevolently and consistently consented to its gradual desanctification and ultimate cheapening.[177]

Under Lemass, the government had not implicitly accepted the political ramifications inherent in the Treaties of Rome because, of course, they were not explicitly stated. By its very nature, however, Ireland's membership application represented tacit approval of its indisputable aspirations. Throughout this period, as Trevor Salmon has critically concluded in *Unneutral Ireland: an ambivalent and unique security policy*, it appears that:

> When it was expedient to stress commitment to the European cause, or even to European defence, then this was done [but, at other times, such commitment became conditional and was expressly muted] ... Although there certainly was ambiguity in the Irish position, one is left with the

impression that they would have been prepared to do virtually all that was necessary on the political side, because of the perceived economic case for membership.[178]

Economics and, by some sort of instinctive extension in the 1960s, European integration thus began to come before political considerations – such as partition or neutrality – for Ireland, as the Irish government enthusiastically and willingly sought to enter the EEC. Sometimes, what it appears to have been oblivious to was that there were other considerations over which it has no control. As with the state of its economy, Irish political views and affiliations were very important. Anglo-French relations were to prove even more fundamental however to the successful conclusion of Ireland's aspirant status.

4 De Gaulle's refusal of the UK, 14 January 1963

France's rejection of UK membership: an introduction

Ireland failed to gain admission to the EEC at the first time of asking, following a relatively brief negotiations period between July 1961 and January 1963 in which it did not participate to any great degree; indeed, there was no real progress on its application until October 1962. This disappointing outcome was on the surface primarily due to the intransigence invariably exhibited towards the UK's application by the French president. Dublin's distinctive bid was still entirely contingent upon the success or otherwise of its neighbours negotiations, a factor over which it patently exercised no substantive control. Indeed, once France acted negatively and decisively towards this one applicant, it effectively did so for all the prospective members – Denmark, Ireland, Norway, and the UK. History has shown, however, that Ireland's request for full membership was not refused *per se*; its application had, in point of fact, been almost entirely ignored. That is why the Irish bid for membership, essentially a reaction to London's decision to negotiate entry, failed in the early 1960s.[1] The reasons why it was overlooked go way beyond its links to the UK or the latter's application; Ireland failed to join the EEC for reasons all of its own, essentially because it was economically unable to do so by itself.

It has proven possible to view Seán Lemass's European adventure – as William Nicoll and Trevor C.Salmon have done in *Understanding the new European Community* – as having been 'stillborn' basically because, following de Gaulle's veto, Ireland's attempt to join the EEC had no alternative but to fall into a limbo-like state or be withdrawn completely.[2] For the time being, there was absolutely no prospect of Ireland's application making any progress. As a result, the taoiseach's vision of the EEC as an economic vehicle through which Ireland could break away from its suffocating commercial reliance upon the UK had to be postponed, with the country once again facing an uncertain economic future. Ireland, which had already been relatively isolated economically during the late 1950s, especially in the context of the principal developments in European integration, had nowhere else to turn except back to the UK. The EEC had long been envisaged in bureaucratic and government circles as being the indispensable component needed to facilitate Ireland's escape from this economic quarantine. However, following the French president's decision, it was clear that the state's endeavours to attain 'economic independence' would have to be postponed for now.[3] The collapse of the UK's negotiations for EEC membership may not – as Brian Girvin has suggested – have been unwelcome to the Dublin government; indeed, it may just have provided Lemass with the necessary motivation required to prepare Ireland for eventual accession.[4] In the meantime there were more immediate concerns with which the Lemass government had to contend now that its chosen path had been cut off to it.

As has been indisputably pointed out by a series of historical commentators, the Irish were fully aware that the 'Treaty of Rome ... created an enticement to a journey into the blue and demanded an act of faith'.[5] The irreversible decision that was made on 31 July 1961 to apply for full EEC membership was not lightly taken. Nevertheless, as Eoin O'Malley, the author of *Industry and economic development: the challenge for the latecomer*, has written, for all the economic policy influences on the Irish government of *Economic development* and the *Programme for economic expansion*, 'no steps had yet been taken to dismantle protection and to influence freer trade', even by the beginning of the 1960s.[6] In addition, this writer has elsewhere declared that, although general incentives were introduced in the 1950s into Ireland in order to promote export industries and attract foreign investment, the removal of protectionism did not begin in earnest until the mid-1960s.[7] It can still be said in reply that although the dismantlement of tariff barriers may not have begun until a relatively late stage, momentous decisions regarding freer trade had nonetheless already been taken well before then by the Dublin government. Ireland's foreign economic policy was indeed based on full EEC membership and it was in this regard that the disassembly of protectionist measures was being undertaken; political considerations were not necessarily a part of this equation.

At this point in time, another major aspect of development that was being highlighted by the government as the future for the economy was the adoption of a foreign-owned export-orientated investment policy. In fact, this concerted series of attempts to attract investment into the economy from outside sources was particularly concentrated in the manufacturing sector, with most of this new investment being export-driven. This official government policy contributed to a rapid expansion in the sheer number of plants alone established in the country.[8] Indeed, this exponential growth came far ahead of similar investment in Northern Ireland or in other UK 'development areas', never mind in the UK as a whole. In fact, as a direct result of this Irish economic policy, a total of sixty-two new foreign firms opened up in the country through the period 1960 to 1963; this figure was over six times the comparable aggregate for Northern Ireland, even if it was opening up to investment from foreign capital, and actually corresponded more than favourably with the total amount for the UK as a whole.[9] Prior to the introduction of this innovative policy, the number of foreign firms opening up in Ireland was minuscule; indeed, the figure for the period between 1952 and 1959 was only eleven new foreign firms opening up. From that time onwards, however, this impulse burgeoned to such a tremendous degree that the establishment of foreign-owned businesses in Ireland quickly became a veritable explosion; for instance, 188 firms were established in the corresponding interval between 1964 and 1971. If numerical evidence of a changing orientation in the economy was needed, this data regarding the establishment of foreign-owned firms would be more than sufficient evidence to argue a strong case.

Tellingly, James Wickham has pointed out in his excellent article 'Dependence and state structure' that, while foreign-owned firms which initially emanated from the UK were the 'single most important group in terms of national origin, many of these companies were in fact established before the end of protectionism as subsidiaries serving the domestic Irish market'. Indeed, this commentary serves as a rigorous policy critique because, in addition, the author has added that it was 'astounding' how little attention was devoted by successive Irish governments, through their economic policies, to the relative increase in foreign-owned manufacturing plants, despite the unremitting rise in their significance within the economy. In fact, he has discerned the various economic programmes enacted by the governments of this period to have only been 'indicative plans' rather than possessing the required hands-on approach.[10] In the taoiseach's defence, it might be asserted that intensive intervention was no longer his intention with regard to the economy; indeed, Lemass's economic thinking had undergone a major u-turn from his prewar period as Irish industry & commerce minister. In his opinion, post-war governments could only indicate what they wanted and then facilitate that development, but they could no longer try to control the industry sector *per se*. At the same time, however, it has to be said that this policy did not necessarily ameliorate the true economic situation in Ireland all by itself. Something more substantial than pontification was needed from central government.

The economic trend towards the end and subsequent to the period of protectionism in Ireland was for US-owned, export-orientated firms to set up, taking advantage of a generous Irish government incentives package. This set of inducements included the granting of export profits tax relief, the creation of new infrastructural networks for specific projects, and access to capital grants for plants and machinery, as well as making full use of relatively low cost, available and educated labour. Therefore, during the period 1961 to 1966, it comes as no big surprise to learn that there were, on average, seventeen new foreign firms established in Ireland *per annum*. Although a detailed analysis and breakdown of the monetary incentives package that was made available to foreign firms is not necessary here, it has proven to be a rather rewarding way of tracking the development of initiatives enshrined in practice by the Irish government, especially in the context of their resulting economic, political and social effects. These consequences have been felt right up to the present day.

The export profits tax relief procedure, for example, was first introduced in 1956, but was initially limited because it was applied to only 50% of the profits earned on increases in export sales over and above the previous year's level. Ostensibly, this was not a crucial or even decisive government initiative except, of course, for the fact that it set a significant precedent. Indeed, the actual extent of export profits tax relief was substantially strengthened two years later, when this proportion of tax relief was raised to 100% with a similar proviso; in addition, the initial period for which full tax relief was to be extended to a new foreign firm setting up in Ireland was extended from five to ten years. This initial period for full tax relief was actually extended from ten to fifteen years in 1960, yet another fiscal enticement for foreign investors. Furthermore, while writing in an article entitled 'Industrial policy and economic development', Barry Moore adds his voice to the view that 'there is clear evidence that the policy package in the Republic was particularly successful in encouraging foreign-owned firms, and there must be a presumption that the export profits tax relief was effective in this respect'. Certainly, the government's practice of encouraging export profits tax relief as official policy was very 'effective' when considered in these terms, even if the implications of this strategy in later years may not have been so readily apparent.[11]

Although the government's Industrial Development (Encouragement of External Investment) Act of 1958 had removed many of the restrictions on foreign ownership, it was not until the Control of Manufactures Act – which dated from the first Fianna Fáil government of 1932 and which restricted foreign ownership and board membership of Irish manufacturing industries to a minority position – was fully revoked in 1964 that this process of reforming the issue of alien proprietorship was finally completed. Obviously, the development of the Industrial Development Authority (IDA), through the IDA Act of 1950, was an integral step in this effort to attract foreign investment; indeed, this initiative was in itself further supplemented by the Adaption and Re-equipment Programme that was introduced in 1963, a new initiative over which the IDA exercised its control. Accordingly, the fundamentally important economic developments of 1958 – the publication of T.K.Whitaker's *Economic development* and enactment of the Irish government's *Programme for economic expansion* – led directly, according to James Wickham, to the removal of 'many traditional aspects of dependency'. Certainly, while the increased role of foreign-owned manufacturing industry in Ireland obviously 'involved new forms of dependency', new economic growth and fewer economic ties with the UK came about as a immediate and welcome consequence.[12]

At the same time, of course, there were other important domestic economic initiatives being taken by the Irish government. The Committee on Industrial Organisation (CIO) was, for instance, set up in 1961 by the Irish Department of Industry & Commerce in a concerted attempt to effect two interlinked enterprises. These were:

- the CIO was going to facilitate the adaptation of existing Irish firms for the impending onslaught of free trade;
- it had to report to the government on their progress in that endeavour.

Meanwhile, there was also the National Industrial Economic Council (NIEC), initiated two years later. The NIEC was itself perceived as a broad forum for discussion – representing the government, employers and trade unions – through which future economic developments could be better coordinated.[13] Obviously, this examination must still come back to asking the question: where did these economic innovations fit in the wider integration process?

Ireland's application to join the EEC may have remained the first absolute step in the country's journey towards freer trade, but it was not the only one. Indeed, this development was quickly followed by other initiatives, especially once the EEC Council agreed to open membership negotiations. On 13 October 1962, in anticipation of it having to fulfil EEC requirements, the Irish government formally announced that it was introducing a unilateral, if highly symbolic, 10% cut in its tariffs to come into effect from 1 January 1963. Indeed, at the same time, it also announced that it wanted to proceed thereafter on the basis of regular, if gradual, reductions in relation to preferential arrangements and industrial tariffs. This move led one UK official to remark, somewhat condescendingly, that this Irish tariff cut created 'some sort of precedent (although not a very strong one)'.[14] Notwithstanding such negative points of view, it was a step upon which the Irish government felt that it could build. However, its act of faith in the EEC was not reciprocated because, within a fortnight of the implementation of this tariff cut, it found itself peripheralised once again, this time by de Gaulle's decision. In the meantime, in the expectation of being a member of the EEC by 1 January 1964, Ireland had committed itself to observing an economic transitional period in which tariff reductions would finally be completed by the end of the decade. In themselves, unilateral tariff cuts were a worthwhile addition to an open economic policy. In spite of these efforts, Ireland was left down by circumstances that were outside of its control.

Ultimately, however, the economic developments of the Six and the Seven meant that the *status quo* enshrined by previous European trading arrangements had changed forever. Through necessity, the taoiseach had engendered an outward-looking economic orientation for Ireland, primarily in an effort to diversify its foreign markets and also to continue to attract foreign multinational investment into its economy. John Bradley *et al* have clearly shown that Ireland revolutionised, rather quickly at that, its manufacturing employment base, which from the 1920s had been one dependent upon 'traditional' industry – such as 'food, drink, tobacco, textiles, clothing, footwear, wood and paper' – to an economy that was soon attracting much more 'modern industry' – such as 'chemicals, minerals and metal products', before the subsequent advent of computer technology – as the 1960s progressed.[15]

Protectionism – the progenitor of which had been Lemass himself – was no longer a viable economic policy alternative. Therefore, almost immediately after the French president vetoed the UK's application for full EEC membership, Ireland had to look elsewhere to safeguard its immediate agricultural and industrial future, while keeping an eye open as to when European integration would be a viable proposition. Indeed, Dublin's resulting bid for short-term economic preservation and the stability of its export markets quickly resulted in the seemingly incongruous move of signing *The 1965 Anglo-Irish FTA agreement*, subject of a subsequent chapter. Although launched in an effort to enhance future Irish economic competitiveness in what was rapidly becoming an ever-changing and highly unpredictable European economic environment, this apparently contradictory manoeuvre demonstrated that there sometimes is truth to the dictum that there exists 'the need to go one step backwards', in terms of economic dependence, 'before then going two steps forward', towards economic diversification. Invariably, the ultimate goal remained the same. Although impeded for now, Ireland continued to prepare itself for full EEC entry and for its economic integration into a larger, more reliable, trading entity.

Expounding upon the Dublin government's presentation in Brussels in January 1962 of its case for full EEC membership, this fourth chapter – *De Gaulle's refusal of the UK, 14 January 1963* – winds its way through the positive reaction to the provisional opening of negotiations with the EEC in October 1962. It then traces the pivotal developments in the history of European integration that ran through the first months of 1963 before introducing the Anglo-Irish FTA agreement of December 1965, when Ireland secured even closer bilateral economic ties than it already had with the UK. Perhaps, it is Pierre Gerbet's belief, opined in *La construction de l'Europe* which best sums up the true economic situation facing Ireland, when he states that it found itself in an economic union with the UK from which it was not able to find a means of disengaging. This view not only gives added credence to the conventionally held impression of economic dependence that was the reality of Anglo-Irish relations, but it also suggests some of the implications for Ireland that were innate in the French government's rejection of the UK's membership application.[16]

The Irish government confronted what was, in effect, another 'crisis point' following de Gaulle's press conference of 14 January 1963. Ireland's plans for entry negotiations with the EEC were rendered nugatory as a result of this episode. However, before moving on to explore the main features of this press conference and to an investigation of its ramifications, it is important to trace the development of the Irish case for full EEC membership, how it was presented and viewed. Indeed, it is imperative to detail its preparations for entry negotiations, as well as describing its outlook towards membership of the other European Communities, the ECSC and Euratom. Therefore, the meeting that was scheduled for mid-January 1962 in Brussels presented the ideal opportunity in which the Irish government could explain, once and for all, its attitude to the process of European integration. Nevertheless, in spite of this genuine attempt to inform the Six and the institutions of the EEC regarding its capacity to undertake full membership, Lemass found that it would take the better part of a year to explain the position properly and facilitate the opening of the admission's procedure.

The Dublin government presents its case in Brussels[17]

In the previous chapter on *Ireland's first EEC application, 31 July 1961*, it was shown that, following a brief examination of its request for membership three months after the original bid had been made, the EEC Council had asked the Irish government to provide even more clarification regarding the reasoning behind its contemplated participation. An explanatory meeting to be held in Brussels was consequently set for a date which only came six months after Ireland's formal application had been delivered, arriving long after negotiations with the UK and the Danes had already begun. This delay did not auger well. Ireland would get an opportunity to plead its case in the heart of Europe; the danger was that its candidacy was not only being viewed as unimportant by the Six or the institutions, but that it was also seen as being intrinsically flawed.

Indeed, the enormity of the situation was not lost on those most intimately involved in the process in Dublin. As the Department of Finance secretary reminded his minister:

> We have applied for membership of the EEC because it would be economic disaster for us to be outside the community if Britain is in it. We cannot afford to have our advantageous position in the British market turned into one of exclusion by a tariff wall, particularly as our chief competitors would be inside this wall.[18]

It was implicitly understood that the Irish delegation dispatched to Brussels and charged with this responsibility would have to use the opportunity to make an extremely good impression upon the Six and on the EEC, a factor emphasised by the Irish ambassador in Brussels. As Brian Girvin has explained, however, Biggar had warned his government against appearing 'lukewarm' on the issue of membership. In fact, this Irish diplomat said that Ireland would have to demonstrate convincingly that it was applying to the EEC without reservations if it was ever going to make its case both attractive and persuasive. He wrote:

> ... the EEC, despite its title, is first and foremost a political concept and not merely an economic organisation with a few political ideas added as an afterthought.[19]

At this stage, it appears that common sense – in the form of similar advice from Whitaker to the Irish finance minister, Jack Lynch, and from Biggar to his superiors at the Department of External Affairs in Iveagh House – began to prevail within Irish government circles. Indeed, it was eventually reflected in the taoiseach's address to the EEC Council on 18 January 1962. So, what was the actual substance of what Lemass said in Brussels?

Throughout the Irish government's development of a European integration policy, the Department of Finance played a pivotal role, directing and shaping its inexorable progress. As Brian Girvin has stated so unequivocally: 'Finance insisted that joining the Community was an imperative if Ireland was to survive economically'. Nothing should be allowed to get in the way of this, the departmental secretary felt; but, as Ireland had made a commitment to seek full membership of the EEC in good faith, it was equally not in a position 'to pick or choose the circumstances under which it would join'. Indeed, Whitaker personally considered that it would be 'extremely unfortunate' if Ireland's application was subsequently withdrawn on grounds such as the efficacy of its foreign policy; clearly, he had partition, neutrality and NATO membership in mind. He noted:

> Nobody has yet told us that this is a condition of membership of the EEC. On the other hand, nobody so loves us as to want us in the EEC on our own terms. The Community have difficulties enough without adding those introduced by a 'contrary' new member who will bring the Community no particular benefits but will inflict on it additional problems including (as they might well view it) this tiresome 40-year old squabble with Britain.

Ireland's case for membership was in a precarious enough position already and would not be helped by any attempts to link partition to NATO membership or to full EEC accession; as far as Whitaker was concerned, it was more important for Ireland to play down the whole neutrality issue lest it be confused with the Irish government's attempt to negotiate full EEC entry.[20] This eminently sensible piece of advice was duly taken by Lemass.

Obviously, although attention was thus being paid to the political aspects of full EEC membership, it was the economic aspects of Ireland's participation which were always going to dominate the taoiseach's thinking. Just as well really, because it was these aspects which most troubled the Six and the EEC. Of course, agriculture was a prime concern within these circumstances, but it was always going to be difficult to deal with this subject as long as it remained undefined in the context of European integration. However, it was becoming clear that Irish industry was ill-prepared for the onset of European integration and in reality the fear persisted that up to 100,000 industrial jobs were at risk from the dismantlement of protection. Therefore, what Lemass was invariably seeking for the future balanced development of both Irish agriculture and industry was the awareness and help of these prospective new economic partners.[21] It is true to say that the main aim of the government's foreign economic policy at the beginning of 1962 was to secure entry into the EEC on as favourable a set of terms as was possible. Thus, part of this process entailed meetings with various concerned groups in domestic agriculture and industry, representative organisations such as the NFA and ICTU.[22] Nevertheless, it was clear from the outset that no single sector of the economy was going to be allowed to dictate or to mitigate against the perceived general economic good.

In the days which immediately preceded the presentation of Ireland's case to the EEC Council, Lemass delivered his address to the Árd-Fheis (party conference) of Fianna Fáil with a number of objectives securely in mind. Brian Girvin has listed these as follows:

- reassurance of the party faithful with regard to the propensity of a new economic policy, moving Ireland from a protectionist era to one of free trade and, in so doing, 'dismantling ... the entire economic nationalist superstructure which had been established over the previous 30 years';
- helping to develop the necessary momentum for adhesion;
- guaranteeing foreign observers that the Irish government was indeed totally committed to entry.

It was a difficult mélange of items over which to exercise control in a speech and at the same time to appear comfortable, but the taoiseach was in no doubt about the economic legitimacy of the direction in which Ireland was heading. Lemass declared that:

> Membership of the Common Market is open to those nations which accept the political aims which inspired it. A movement to political confederation in some form ... is ... a natural and logical development of economic integration ... our national aims must conform to the emergence, in a political as well as in an economic sense, of a union of Western European States, not as a vague prospect of the distant future but as a living reality of our own times.

In economic and political terms, European integration was not just held to be the only real option available to Ireland, but it was now felt to be apt as well. Multilateral arrangements in the European context would replace bilateral agreements, especially with the UK; indeed, confederation would overtake partition as a government policy determinant.[23]

Finally, on 18 January 1962, the taoiseach went on record, proclaiming at length to the EEC Council that Ireland not only agreed with the ideals behind European integration and even the general aims of NATO, but that it was also prepared to fulfil the 'duties, obligations and responsibilities' that full EEC membership would bring. It must be said that, although Lemass was fairly persuasive in his line of argument regarding the political considerations of membership, he found himself betraying the relative weakness of Ireland's position in relation to native agriculture and industry by having to expound upon the true needs of the economy. Obviously, it is worth going into the particulars of this speech, not only as it was the most precise affirmation regarding Ireland's relationship with the EEC delivered at this time, but also because, through this statement, the Six were made totally aware of the realities of the domestic economic and political situation, the Irish government's hopes and fears, its opinions and views, as well as a categoric understanding of the degree to which this prospective new member needed full membership.

The taoiseach's statement to the EEC Council can be divided into two main sections because, once he had introduced his government's application with the general assertion that 'Ireland belongs to Europe by history, tradition and sentiment no less than by geography', he primarily spoke upon the political and economic implications of membership. Specifically on the political aims of the EEC, Lemass stated that the Irish government and people were not only ready to subscribe to these goals, but that they were also eager to play an active part in achieving them for the benefit of all. Indeed, this had been a constituent facet in the reasoning behind Ireland's 'deliberate decision' to apply for membership. The country was, the taoiseach said, in full agreement with the general purposes of the EEC, as defined by the *Treaty establishing the European Economic Community* (Article 2), and sincerely wanted to work in harmony with the other six members in the 'accomplishment of these purposes by the methods prescribed' (Article 3); in addition, the government agreed that the various EEC institutions should ensure that the tasks of the EEC would in fact be achieved (Article 4). In truth, however, what were essentially mediocre assertions – statements to the effect that the Irish 'people have always tended to look to Europe for inspiration, guidance and encouragement', for example, or that the government's membership application of 31 July 1961 'declared that we share the ideals which inspired the parties to the Treaty and accept the aims of the Community ... as well as the action proposed to achieve those aims' – would clearly need more substantiation if they were to convince the EEC Council about the Irish propensity for full membership. Indeed, in concluding his presentation, Lemass said that:

> ... the Irish Government feel that the problems involved in accepting Ireland as a member ... will not prove to be greater and may, indeed, be less than those which were originally overcome by the member States in accordance

> with the spirit expressed in the preamble to the Treaty ... As a country small in extent, population and production, Ireland would not represent, in terms of statistics, any considerable addition to the Community. We do feel, however, that we have a contribution to make to the accomplishment of the Community's design for a new European society and would wish to be given an opportunity of bringing our national qualities and potentialities to the service of this ideal in a spirit of loyal and constructive cooperation.

Nevertheless, it was in regard to the economic aspects of EEC membership that Ireland was undoubtedly most interested and, indeed, vulnerable. It was also the subject area it was felt with which the EEC Council was most unclear, even more so it should be said after the taoiseach had delivered his statement to them.

Speaking on economics, the second part of his address, Lemass further divided his remarks into two sections dealing expressly with Irish agriculture and industry, before moving on to make some general remarks about Ireland's position on European integration. There was, of course, no real point in the taoiseach understating the importance of agriculture, it was patently clear to the EEC Council how vital this sector really was to the economy. Therefore, he readily acknowledged that:

> It generates about one-quarter of the national income, employs over one-third of the gainfully-occupied population, and is responsible, directly or indirectly, for three-quarters of our exports.

Obviously, there is no point in going into tremendous detail regarding the Irish agricultural situation, except to say that the government was undeniably interested in the proposals for a CAP and that Ireland's 'principal concern' in the sphere of agriculture and the EEC was in relation to the relative position of the UK and its trading arrangements within that context. Indeed, the taoiseach made specific reference to the relative implications of UK membership for Ireland and stated that his government hoped that the discussions for Irish admission to the EEC would be 'brought to completion at the same time as those for the United Kingdom', although, as Lemass pointed out, Ireland also had important bilateral trade agreements with individual members of the Six as well. Overall, however, in relation to agriculture, he made it readily apparent that the Dublin government would particularly 'look forward to active and constructive collaboration with the other members in their efforts to overcome the problems arising in putting into effect a common agricultural policy in accordance with the objectives of the Treaty'. It was clear where Ireland's chief interest, indeed preoccupation, lay. Despite his best efforts, mistakes in presentation were being made.

The taoiseach then moved on to consider at length the position of industry within the general economic framework of full Irish adherence to the EEC. Speaking on progress made in the economy ever since the era of protectionism began to draw to a close and furthermore in the light of the *Programme for economic expansion*, Lemass made direct reference to the role of the industrial sector in Ireland's economic renaissance. He declared:

> The volume increase in gross national product, which averaged only 1 per cent per annum in the preceding decade, amounted to 4½ per cent in 1959, 5 per cent in 1960 and not less than 5 per cent, it is estimated, in 1961. The greater part of this expansion is attributable to the industrial sector. For manufacturing industry rates of growth of 6 per cent and 7 per cent were achieved in 1959 and 1960, respectively, and the estimate for 1961 is almost 9 per cent, a rate of expansion amongst the highest in Western Europe.

Indeed, the taoiseach continued his address in much the same upbeat vein, with special regard being paid to these positive economic indicators. He added that:

> ... results confirm not only the considerable scope for economic development in Ireland but the capacity of Irish initiative and effort, augmented by Western European enterprise, to exploit the existing potentialities. We have an economic and social infrastructure capable of supporting a much greater degree of industrial development. We also enjoy conditions of political and social stability conducive to maintenance of the higher rate of economic growth achieved in recent years. There is, therefore, good ground for the belief that a total increase in production of 50 per cent by 1970 is within the capacity of the Irish economy ...

However, obvious difficulties would also have to be faced by the Irish economy within a free trade environment and it was within this context that the Six had most worries about Ireland's capacity for full EEC membership. Indeed, very little of what the taoiseach actually said did much to allay these fears and the Irish government subsequently encountered an extremely difficult, though not impossible, task in persuading the EEC Council otherwise.

Of course, once Lemass began to explain the more precise implications of Ireland's economic situation to the EEC, *vis-à-vis* its relations with the UK, no generalised entreaties about how the country had the ability to accept the obligations of the Treaty of Rome in the industrial field were going to suffice. This would especially be the case when Dublin began to look for special economic treatment of its case under existing provisions (Article 226) or, indeed, under any separate 'protocol dealing generally with the subject of tariff reductions'. The taoiseach went into some detail regarding the subject of tariffs – that is Ireland's need for an 'appropriate rhythm of tariff reductions' – and specifically mentioned the fears that the government had in regard to 'dumping'. It was becoming rather an extensive list.

In addition, though, it should also be said that Lemass made reference to the various sections of the Treaty of Rome with which Ireland was ready and willing to comply forthwith. However, some aspects of his statement to the EEC Council were bound to attract the wrong sort of attention. For instance, the taoiseach said:

> Detailed negotiations will provide an opportunity for discussing questions of interpretation of particular Treaty provisions and of the implications of the regulations, decisions, directives and recommendations issued by the Council and the Commission.

Such a generalised statement about difficulties that the Irish government had with the Treaty of Rome was never going to be regarded with anything other than trepidation and derision. Obvious questions were begging to be asked: did Ireland perhaps feel that it had views on the Treaty of Rome – the provisions and realities of which it had conspicuously not actually been operating with the six other states – upon which it felt accomplished and worthy to extrapolate or, more pointedly, did it expect that the Treaty of Rome should be interpreted or, indeed, revised on its account? It appears that Lemass did not fully appreciate or even realise the precariously weak position of his government's application for full membership. In reality, his statement of 18 January 1962, delivered to the EEC Council in Brussels, did little to assuage the anxieties of the Six. Indeed, it probably exacerbated them.

D.J.Maher has subsequently written that, at this presentation, the taoiseach set out the Irish 'Government's understanding of the political and economic aims of the Treaty of Rome and declared the Government's willingness to accept the obligations of membership of the Community under both these heads'.[24] However, the actual situation was not as simple as that, because not only did this meeting present Ireland with its first major chance to elucidate and explain its position on full EEC membership, but it also introduced the Irish government into the complex political arena that encompassed the whole issue of European integration. The fact that Maurice Couve de Murville, the French foreign minister, who was chairing this particular meeting, limited himself to saying that the Six needed more time in which to study the taoiseach's statement before responding to it, undoubtedly meant that the Irish application to begin accession negotiations had been delayed further still. Indeed, this limited response should have been evidence enough that Ireland would in fact be playing a fairly minor role within the whole membership negotiations process. This interpretation of events and their implications was reflected in a journal article, based on French government sources, which claimed that the Irish application had received a 'frigid reception'.[25] The Irish government actually had rather a lot of work to do yet to convince the Six and the EEC of its suitability. Indeed, as was previously noted, the EEC Commission had already ascertained that the Irish government would have rather obvious special problems with respect to full EEC membership and, thus, had decided that those would have to be given very careful consideration prior to the opening of any formal and substantive accession negotiations. Ireland would have a long wait for its case to be heard with the attention and care that it felt was warranted.

Second time around[26]

At this point in time, there was no definitive immediate reaction from the Six in relation to the taoiseach's statement of 18 January 1962 that was delivered in Brussels, except to assert that Ireland's case would come under still further consideration at the EEC Council meeting that March. However, it was blatantly obvious that they were not particularly impressed and were not at all convinced that Ireland could fulfil the inherent obligations. In the meantime, there were other ongoing developments originating from the Irish side regarding its candidacy for full EEC membership. Indeed, Lemass continued to speak openly and publicly about the government's acceptance of the political implications inherent in Ireland's full participation, although he made sure to do so in strict accordance with a warning from Whitaker that any hint of dissent on the issue within the Irish domestic or international political arena would convey the wrong sort of message to Europe.[27] Thus, for instance, the taoiseach frankly declared on 14 February 1962 that Ireland acknowledged and agreed 'that membership of EEC is open only to states which accept the Bonn Declaration'.[28]

Obviously, it was becoming as important to consider the political questions that were being raised by Ireland's membership application as it was to present an explanation of the economic direction in which Irish relations with the EEC were moving. Therefore, political and economic considerations have to be appraised in conjunction with one another. This was not unlike the approach adopted by the Irish government, especially when soundings from the continent continued to stress that no state would be permitted into the EEC unless it accepted both economic and political integration.[29] In fact, Lemass took every available opportunity to reiterate that Ireland had no political reservations about joining the EEC or to participating in it fully.[30] As a result of the government's efforts to deal with political problems raised by its aspirant status, the foreign minister, Frank Aiken, stated in Dáil Éireann that it was not, for instance, in touch with other European neutrals about a common foreign policy approach to the EEC, but that Ireland's approach to the issue of neutrality was actually totally different. Dublin was not about to jeopardise the EEC's political orientation through its policies, he argued; equally, Aiken held that the EEC would not be forcing Ireland into compromising its international political outlook, because their views were in fact complementary.[31]

There was some data to back up the foreign minister's claim. At the UN, for example, although regarded by the US as a 'maverick', Ireland was not particularly close to any of the members of the 'non-aligned' movement. In fact, even in the 'heyday' of Ireland's promotion of independence at the UN – *circa* 1957 to 1961 – its voting record on all Cold War issues showed that it was in accord with the US three times as often as against her.[32] Thereafter, Ireland's voting pattern was 'solidly riveted' to that of the West except on issues such as arms control and self-determination.[33] It generally agreed with US positions, but that is not a big surprise; thus, its policy can still be seen as 'independent' in such circumstances but it was also pragmatic, realistic and Western-orientated. This was not even unusual for the other European neutrals, it has to be said. Figures available on UN votes cast on Cold War issues in the period 1955 to 1959, show that, in a voting index ranking the degree of support for US positions ranging from -1 to +1, Ireland read +0.739; for the other European neutrals in the UN, this read: Austria +0.783; Finland +0.174; and Sweden +0.607. This shows that the degree of Irish support for US positions was therefore not 'remarkable' as Dennis Driscoll holds, but quite the opposite, that is completely expected. In relation to the EEC, the latter does make the fair point that its attempted – and ultimately successful – admission to an 'organisation which anticipates the ultimate political union of most of the European members of NATO seems somewhat incompatible with the independence suggested by the concept of "neutrality"/"non-alignment"'. Nevertheless, he is clearly mistaken in using such data to argue that as 'Ireland distances herself even from those European states which regard themselves as non-participants in either the Eastern or Western blocs ... it is clear that Ireland cannot be regarded as a "neutral"'.[34] Indeed, this is exactly what the EEC held in the early 1960s because that is what Ireland had been telling the world ever since the outbreak of the Second World War.

As time passed, however, although the EEC Council became more convinced about it on the political level, doubts still remained about its economic ability to accede fully to the EEC. Indeed, as D.J.Maher has said, from this point onwards there was an absence of any substantial indication of concern by the Six towards Ireland's political suitability for full EEC membership.[35] However, it should be pointed out that Brian Girvin has been able to detail the main developments in the first half of 1962 regarding Ireland's relationship with the EEC in a much more systematic way, undermining this very argument. He contradicts D.J.Maher's view when he states that EEC unease about Ireland's political credentials for entry actually continued for some considerable time to come. The fact that the UK government had no such qualms about Ireland's candidacy suggests that they were much more in tune with the realities of the Irish political situation. Indeed, Heath was able to reassure the taoiseach on this very point by stating that NATO membership was not very important in the EEC context. Indeed, with regard to a meeting between them, it was reported by the Irish embassy in London that:

> In an effort to combat the idea that Ireland joining NATO was a prerequisite for EEC membership, Lemass, of course, replied that the Irish government fully recognised the validity of the argument in favour of a common defence policy evolving.[36]

In time, this attitude appears to have been accepted in the wider world as well; for instance, Washington obviously never looked upon Ireland's candidacy for full membership in the same negative way that it viewed the efforts of the other European neutrals, especially as they were seeking associate membership and thus were not prepared to pool allegiances in a Western European economic and political organisation.[37] However, efforts by Ireland to convince the EEC regarding its political suitability for full membership were another issue altogether. Indeed, uneasiness was still being felt by the Six regarding the propriety of such a relationship with the Dublin government, particularly when the EEC itself had so many integral questions regarding European integration still left almost completely unanswered.

On 15 February 1962, the Irish ambassador in Brussels met with Walter Hallstein, the President of the EEC Commission, to discuss Ireland's position. Although favourably inclined towards their argument for membership, Hallstein raised the issue of their continued non-participation of NATO as a lingering factor. This opinion was reflected in a subsequent meeting between Irish embassy officials in Brussels and Sicco Mansholt, the Vice-President of the EEC Commission, when the issue was brought up once more. Indeed, Mansholt held that France was against Ireland's entry into the EEC on these defence grounds, but also added that an indication from the Irish government that it would be prepared to join NATO would 'virtually assure our admission to the Community and would put us in a very strong position to negotiate favourable terms'. As Brian Girvin has since highlighted, the fact that the EEC Commission's president and the vice-president were prepared to raise the subject of defence and, in addition, to report upon French government opposition to Ireland's application must have created uncertainty, perhaps even a degree of worry, in Irish minds.[38]

It was soon noted that the Dublin government's application for full EEC membership was not going to be considered however at the next meeting of the EEC Council scheduled for March 1962. Nevertheless, Whitaker advised that only the most measured response of disappointment should be conveyed to the Six at this turn of events, coupled with inquiries for further clarification. Of the dangers inherent in pushing the Six into making a decision, he wisely cautioned:

> ... it is impolitic to rush them when they have other and more pressing preoccupations. If rushed, they may take up the position suggested by the most negatively minded member, this being the line of least resistance.[39]

Indeed, when it came to a meeting of departmental secretaries on 1 March 1962, he was even more insistent in stressing the political issues that were involved. The Department of Finance secretary was summarised as having said that:

> ... while membership of NATO may not be a *sine qua non* for entry into the EEC, we would be committed to participation in the common defence arrangements and foreign policy of the Community. While European Ministers would, no doubt, understand political difficulties presented by a name or by certain formalities, he thought there was considerable danger that our present attitude would be understood in community circles to mean that we could not join in any defence system with Britain.

Opinion was divided about how to proceed, with the Department of External Affairs secretary, Con Cremin, advocating a cautious approach; this was rather a propitious warning, it has been remarked, considering that the political debate in Europe was still scarcely evolving.[40]

In public, Lemass was much more assertive about his government's commitment to all aspects of the EEC. In an RTÉ interview broadcast on 15 March 1962, he said that Ireland accepted its obligations and recognised where it was leading. He declared:

> Economic integration is not regarded as an end in itself but as a step towards political union, and is, of course, in itself a political development of major significance.⁴¹

However, it was always going to be in private that the most realistic assessments of Ireland's relative position were being made. Cremin made it quite clear, for instance, that Ireland was in a situation at total polar opposites to that of the UK, which was after all a 'major European power, if at times a disinterested one'; the London government was much more advanced in the negotiations process than Ireland it was noted. In contrast, therefore, the Irish position appeared to be rather 'precarious'. The Department of External Affairs secretary wrote:

> Our position is radically different. We have not been, except perhaps spasmodically, active protagonists of European political union, nor have we been actively associated with any of the major movements to this end, apart from such organisational instances as the Council of Europe ... we are not yet formally at the stage of negotiation for membership of the E.E.C. or, in other words, we are not yet a potential member of the Community in the same sense as Britain.⁴²

Dublin was going to have to try harder to persuade the Six and the EEC institutions that Ireland merited attention in its own right. Heath's support was strong – in his statement to the WEU Council on 10 April 1962 he said that the UK recognised the political and economic objectives of the Treaties of Paris and Rome in the future context of an 'enlarged community including not only the United Kingdom, but also other European States who will be joining the European Economic Community' – but not sufficient for Irish purposes.⁴³

Therefore, as if in a further effort still to convince the EEC about Ireland's suitability in political terms, Lemass made his clearest statement yet on the position of neutrality relative to Irish foreign policy in an interview given to the *New York Times*, subsequently published on 18 July 1962. Through this medium, the taoiseach said:

> We recognise that a military commitment will be an inevitable consequence of our joining the Common Market and ultimately we would be prepared to yield even the technical label of neutrality. We are prepared to go into this integrated Europe without any reservations as to how far this will take us in the field of foreign policy and defence.⁴⁴

In truth, a portentous evolution in Irish foreign policy was taking place, a strategic rethink on security procedures that continued to develop throughout the whole application process. The Irish government was making it crystally clear to the EEC that it would not have balked at indicating its lack of attachment to neutrality – by dropping this defence stance altogether if it was to be replaced by an EEC sponsored military structure – if this was deemed contingent for membership. Indeed, Trevor Salmon has since written that:

> Adherence to neutrality had become conditional and transient, depending upon how the Community developed; any lingering long-term aspiration to it was yielded in the commitment to the future development of the Community.[45]

If participation in NATO had been made a prerequisite to EEC membership, Lemass had left no lingering doubts regarding his government's readiness to accept such a repercussion, if not welcome it. In his opinion, the political price of membership was worth paying in return for the substantial economic benefits that Ireland would subsequently accrue.

The emphasis of its diplomacy turned from being dedicated to political action within the UN, that is 'active neutrality', to being focused economically on Europe, that is 'military neutrality'.[46] Irish political strategy fell in behind new developments at the EEC rather than those at the UN as the consideration of EEC membership began to play a continuously larger role in the actual shaping of government policy.[47] At the same time, neutrality was undergoing a process of dilution through the European integration policy it was pursuing. In the context of integration, the early 1960s thus marked a subtle shift in emphasis; Ireland's orientation towards the EEC was increasingly being viewed as an economic necessity with Lemass seeing membership as something that might be partly exchanged for its independent foreign policy, though obviously only if need be.

Despite the taoiseach's speech in Brussels at the beginning of 1962, the EEC Council stated that it needed still more clarification from the government, specifically regarding economic concerns appertaining to Ireland's candidacy. However, the EEC Council subsequently delayed forwarding the questions that it felt needed answering for no apparent reason other than to stall its application. In time, a list of fifteen questions was finally submitted by the EEC on aspects of Ireland's position over which it needed further elucidation. However, no commitment was made by the EEC regarding the opening of negotiations, nor was there any indication that the Dublin government could directly influence any such decision by its actions.[48] In most respects, Ireland's aspirant status was actually out of its own hands and dependent on much wider European integration considerations and developments.

Ireland's detailed reply to the questions posed by the EEC Council was delivered at a meeting held in Brussels on 11 May 1962 between senior Irish government officials and the permanent representatives of the Six. It is worth analysing this second major presentation of the Irish government's case for membership in a matter of months and examining the issues raised at this meeting. The questionnaire, although concerned with Irish agriculture, was most interested with the problem of indigenous Irish industry adapting to the rigours of full EEC membership; indeed, in this regard, it was actually the suggested timetable for the elimination of quotas and tariffs which troubled the Six most. Although the Irish attitude to this issue is dealt with in considerably more detail in a subsequent section centred on the government's preparations for negotiations to begin, at this early stage it is interesting to note the position of the EEC towards the Irish application bid because, rather suddenly, the political aspects of Ireland's candidacy were apparently being skipped over, thus legitimising the timeframe proposed by Brian Girvin rather than that put forward by D.J.Maher.[49] Nonetheless, the fact of the matter is that the Irish government was still finding it difficult to make itself clearly heard and understood. The negotiations were not going too slowly; indeed, in any accepted sense, they were hardly happening at all.

In fact, it was the taoiseach's pointed reference during his address to the EEC Council in Brussels regarding Ireland's desire that possible relief be administrated to 'basically sound industries', either under the Treaty of Rome (Article 226) or a new and quite separate protocol, which attracted particular attention. As D.J.Maher has stated, further information was sought on:

- specific details on the industries which would be affected;
- the Irish government's opinion as to whether the difficulties envisaged could not be solved through existing procedures;
- if this could not be done, a more detailed breakdown of the industrial products that would necessitate the insertion of a separate protocol.

At this meeting with the permanent representatives on 11 May 1962, questions such as these went unsatisfactorily answered as far as the EEC was concerned. For instance, when senior Irish civil servants present replied that, pending the results of industrial surveys being carried out and following an analysis of the actual effects of tariff reductions, it was not possible at that stage to identify the industries that would be affected. However, the Irish government's 'double-barrelled' approach to the question of relief on tariffs was justified at this meeting, it felt, on the rather precarious grounds that it was 'not sufficiently familiar' with the EEC's own interpretation of the safeguards provided for in the Treaty of Rome.

Overall, it has to be said that the permanent representatives of the Six did not furnish much of a reaction to the Irish government's second presentation except to seek even further clarification on technical details such as the 'dumping' provision (Article 91).[50] Indeed, as D.J.Maher has correctly stated, although Ireland's status as a prospective member of the EEC was not being examined any longer in direct regard to its political suitability for membership, the Six were evidently still very worried about its relative acceptability and viability on purely economic grounds.[51] By the middle of 1962, it was economics, not so much politics, which was the vital consideration for the Irish government. It was finally being realised in Dublin that Ireland would have to assist more readily in promoting its own case for membership if it was going to be successful in its endeavours, as the EEC and the Six obviously remained rather unconvinced. So, how did the Lemass government decide to proceed and what impact did their policies have on Ireland's candidature?

Ireland finally forces the pace

Despite not receiving any real encouragement to do so, the Irish government began to make serious preparations for membership negotiations to begin. Efforts by the Irish delegation at the meeting with the Six permanent representatives in Brussels held on 11 May 1962 to fix a date to hold a ministerial-level meeting in the near future – the main item on such an agenda being to mark the official opening of Ireland's negotiations with the EEC – failed. Each of the major Irish government departments were, nevertheless, duly handed the responsibility of compiling and coordinating negotiating briefs. At the same time, preparations began for the publication of a follow-up White Paper to *European Economic Community*, which was primed with the main objective of summarising the latest developments in the EEC. As a result, this up-dated document subsequently appeared on 28 June 1962.[52] At last, the government had decided to take the initiative, no matter how inconvenient that was for the EEC or for the Six. It was finally beginning to force the pace of events rather than reacting to them.

Most significantly, perhaps, the newly revised White Paper detailed the advances made by the Six regarding the CAP, once again signalling one of the government's main concerns in relation to the EEC; this document dealt with other major developments by the Six in the previous twelve months as well. However, because there was no move from the EEC on the opening of membership negotiations throughout the summer of 1962 – in fact, it was felt that Ireland's candidacy was being postponed rather too easily and regularly – Dublin discerned the danger of falling even further behind the UK – as well as Denmark and Norway – in the negotiations stakes. The fact that this substantial delay was creating 'unease' in government circles and was not particularly remarked upon by the Six, led to further feelings of anguish and disquiet. Indeed, according to D.J.Maher, such emotions were felt despite the fact that:

> Inquiries through diplomatic channels produced soothing assurances that little or no progress had been made with the Danish and Norwegian applications, which must necessarily wait on the processing of the British application, and that the Irish application presented so few problems that it could be dealt with very quickly.

As a result, the government decided to go on a propaganda offensive in an effort to quicken the tempo further still.[53] Even though no assurances regarding its candidacy had been received by that stage – indeed, reports to the contrary suggest that relations between the Irish embassy in Brussels and the EEC Council were at an unusually low ebb – therefore, it could only be deduced that the 'status of our application is as yet undetermined'.[54]

Consequently, Lemass decided upon a two pronged approach to be personally enacted throughout Europe, firstly, in a concerted bid to promote a more favourable view of the Irish government's application for full membership and, secondly, in an intensified effort to hasten a more promising decision from the EEC Council. His strategy combined two strands:

- the issuing of an invitation to prominent European and UK journalists, through the Irish Council of the European Movement, to visit Ireland in the first week of September 1962;
- a tour by the taoiseach of the main European capitals in October 1962.

The journalists involved were thus given wide-ranging access to leading Irish economic and political figures, as well as being given the chance to view Ireland for themselves. At the most important organised event, a press conference held on 5 September 1962, the taoiseach used the opportunity to consider the main reservations of the Six regarding Irish membership. Indeed, he meticulously crafted even further placatory remarks regarding Ireland's political convictions and the appropriate nature of its candidacy. Ireland, he said, had no reservations regarding European defence and, indeed, 'accepted the political aims of the Community and their proposed method for realising them'. What the taoiseach was worried about throughout his presentation was perpetuating any myth or misunderstanding that NATO and the EEC were linked in some way, formally or otherwise. In concluding his analysis of the Irish political situation and in explicit reference to the Irish people, Lemass said that the EEC would still find:

> ... strong adherents of the principles of parliamentary democracy and strongly opposed to communism and everything that communism represents. We do not wish, in the conflict between the free democracies and the communist empires, to be thought of as neutral. We are not neutral and do not wish to be regarded as such, even though we have not got specific commitments of a military kind under any international agreements.

With regard to economics, the taoiseach was obviously not in as strong a position to advance his view of the situation as Ireland could not be so easily defined that it would comfortably fit into the existing European context.[55]

Nonetheless, Lemass boldly stated that Ireland was a 'European country, historically and geographically, and in our view fully qualified for membership'. Indeed, he said that Ireland must participate in the EEC 'not in any qualified way, not as a reluctant partner, not as a poor relation and not with any inferiority of status'. The government's acceptance of associate membership status was out of the question as it expected the country to be able to adapt fully economically to meet the requirements of the EEC, especially if it received the consideration and help of the Six. Therefore, Ireland only felt itself to be in a position to accept full membership status. Indeed, Lemass claimed that his government saw a net gain for the country on the industrial side through such membership, stating that it would 'assist and accelerate our economic development'. At the same time, it should be remarked that the taoiseach's press conference of 5 September 1962 marked a subtle departure from previous policy positions regarding Ireland's unstated, but understood, dependence on the success of the UK application for the effective conclusion of its own aspirant status. Lemass held that:

> If the negotiations with Britain should fail, we would, nevertheless wish to pursue our application provided it was economically possible for us to do so.

In fact, he adamantly insisted that Ireland's status as a candidate existed in its own right and that – unlike the other aspirants Denmark or Norway – it was not conditional upon the success or otherwise of the UK's application. In truth, of course, Ireland was in no position to enter the EEC as a fully fledged member if the UK did not do so as well.[56] However, the noises emanating from Dublin were beginning to sound better to European ears.

A report from the American ambassador in Dublin to his superiors in the US State Department provides adequate proof regarding the importance of this press conference as the 'most complete analysis of [Irish] Government policy toward the question of membership in the EEC that has yet appeared'. Additionally, Matthew McCloskey informed Washington that there was full cross-party support in the Dáil for the taoiseach's position from James Dillon and Brendan Corish, the leaders of Fine Gael and Labour respectively. In his summary of these frank views, this senior US diplomat reported that Lemass had been 'clear and forceful' in the answers which he had given. McCloskey then outlined the situation regarding Ireland's applicant status as follows:

- the attitude taken thus far by the EEC towards Ireland's application was seen as encouraging;
- Ireland would continue to seek Common Market membership – if it was economically possible to do so – even if the UK did not succeed in its own application;
- the Irish government was at that time considering the practicability of unilateral tariff dismantlement;
- associate EEC status was strongly rejected;
- the gains to Irish industry from full EEC membership would outweigh the losses, while indigenous agriculture should greatly benefit;
- Ireland had made known its agreement with the aims of NATO, despite the special circumstances which had resulted in its non-membership of the latter, while Lemass noted that it had not recently been invited to join nor had there been any discussion of such an invitation. Indeed, he then added: 'nor would we wish to receive and invitation at this time, because it would, I think, create misunderstanding in the mind of the Irish public as to the aims and purposes of the European Economic Community and be a further complication for us in the consideration of the problems which membership of the Community must necessarily involve for us'.[57]

There was little room for any misreading of Irish incentives for membership or its intentions.

The press conference in Dublin was followed by a more meaningful tour of European capitals conducted by the taoiseach himself during October

1962. Lemass immediately set about convincing the leaders of the Six that Ireland wanted to participate fully in the process of European integration. Indeed, what he most definitely needed to hear was some news or even an indication regarding the opening of negotiations at some suitable, though unspecified, time. The Irish delegation duly met with senior elected representatives of the Belgian, Dutch, French, Italian and Luxembourg governments during the second week of October, as well as meeting with senior officials at the EEC, including Hallstein. It was, emphasised Lemass to his hosts, the uncertainty regarding the outcome of Ireland's application for full membership which was creating the most serious difficulties for his government, especially with regard to its rationalisation and reorganisation programme for the economy. What Ireland wanted most, the taoiseach stressed, was some concrete reassurance from the EEC Council regarding the continued validity of its candidature. In fact, the Irish government was quite prepared to consider announcing an early unilateral tariff cut if such encouragement was received.

As D.J.Maher has since stated, it was subsequently noted that: 'Without exception all the host Governments showed sympathy with, and understanding of, the Irish Government's position'.[58] However, it was obvious from the deputation's meetings with representatives from the various member states and from the institutions of the EEC that not only had the UK government's negotiations reached a critical stage, but that they were also still concerned about certain economic and political aspects of Ireland's candidacy. Of course, Lemass could only respond by reconfirming in the strongest terms that his government was committed to the wider process of European integration, both economically and politically speaking. For the moment, however, Ireland did not yet appear to be doing enough to persuade its detractors and repudiators. The government's stated desire to play a full role in the EEC remained unrequited. Indeed, it did not appear to be in a position to do anything other than to wait for an undefined amount of time to come. Ireland was running out of ideas as to how to promote its candidacy any further and the frustration was beginning to show.

In this regard, it is interesting to note that the UK government was fully aware of what Lemass told the French president during their meeting of 13 October 1962. The taoiseach had said that, because of its strong ties to the UK, it would suit Ireland if the UK government negotiations with the EEC came to a successful conclusion. However, during this encounter he did not dismiss the possibility of Ireland continuing its candidacy for EEC membership even if those negotiations failed, declaring that the Irish government would have to investigate the prevailing circumstances. Indeed, the taoiseach told de Gaulle that Ireland's application was not dependent upon, or subordinate to, that of the UK, a point of view which apparently appealed to the French president's sensibilities. In Lemass's view, the EEC was 'vital' to the future of the Irish economy. Therefore, he informed de Gaulle that Ireland wanted to join the EEC whether or not the UK itself ultimately adhered.[59] This has led one historian to state that the Irish government's continued emphasis of this position was an integral part of the strategy it employed to unblock French opposition to its proposed candidacy.[60] Another commentator has proffered the view that in the end the taoiseach 'gave de Gaulle all the assurances he was seeking about his commitment on both economic and political levels'. In fact, the prognosis from France might have been interpreted as very good at this point in time, with the French prime minister, Georges Pompidou, able to tell the taoiseach that: 'One could consider the entry of Great Britain as probable, even if the outcome is still uncertain'; however, this was not de Gaulle speaking of course, even if one might have expected the French prime minister to be able to echo his president.[61] There was an additional footnote to Lemass's tour of the European capitals which cannot be ignored, but which throws light on the realities of French and European politics. The taoiseach actually had it on good authority – he had been made aware of this opinion by Amintore Fanfani, the Italian prime minister, amongst others – that the French government's fundamental strategy, which meant de Gaulle's policy, was to delay the UK's accession to the EEC for as long as possible, perhaps even until the end of 1965, a position which obviously had crucial implications for the future of the Dublin government's bid.[62] Thus, the Irish application was doomed to failure right from the beginning.

Meanwhile, while the taoiseach was in Bonn, the Irish government received the news for which it had been waiting on 22 October 1962. Ireland was finally invited to participate in membership negotiations by the EEC Council at a mutually acceptable date to be agreed. At last, Dublin's concerted efforts to obtain a 'firm commitment' from the EEC Council on the opening of negotiations had borne fruit.[63] Through this decision, the Six thus committed themselves to inaugurating membership negotiations with Ireland. Indeed, the very next day, 23 October 1962, an official communication followed from Emilio Colombo, the EEC Council president, to inform the taoiseach that, in responding to the call from the government for the EEC Council to open negotiations with Ireland, so that it might adhere to the Treaty of Rome, the Six had decided unanimously to accede to its entreaty.[64] Having patiently waited in the wings for fifteen months, the Irish application was up and running.

Understandably enough, on 9 November 1962, Lemass replied to the EEC Council by saying that this news had been received with 'much satisfaction' by his government.⁶⁵ As a direct consequence, the closing months of 1962 thus saw the country propel itself into an upbeat pre-accession mode, as it enthusiastically prepared for the successful outcome of its talks, with specific attention being paid to those discussions which would be most intimately involved in considering the benefits and problems that faced Irish agriculture and industry. The prospect of a 'Europe of the Ten' – consisting of the Six, Denmark, Ireland, Norway, and the UK – was becoming a distinct and exciting reality; of course, this also made its failure to accede all the more disappointing.⁶⁶ At the same time, the state of Irish negotiations meant that the UK's discussions were beginning to come to their conclusion before its own efforts had barely begun. The inherent dangers in such a situation were readily apparent.

In fact, the government's working assumption was that its membership negotiations would be completed by the middle of 1963 and that Ireland would be a member of the EEC by the beginning of the following year. Obviously enough, de Gaulle saw to it that this could not happen, even if there were more reasons to Ireland's ultimate failure to accede other than this decision taken by the French president. It should be reasserted that, all the while, Dublin was under no illusions about where it ultimately stood in relation to the Treaty of Rome or how it was viewed by the Six or the institutions. Indeed, according to the UK's negotiating team in Brussels, Ireland was always only going to be offered full membership of the EEC 'on a more or less take it or leave it basis'; in their opinion, Lemass was fully aware of this situation. Not unlike Denmark and Norway, Ireland would ultimately have had no choice but to sign up completely to the EEC if a 'Europe of the Ten' was to come about or else to stay outside; as one informed view put it, 'the alternative to taking the Treaty as it stood would be consignment to outer darkness'.⁶⁷ The Dublin government was not about to lose out on the opportunity to accede now that it had become a distinct possibility.

Of course, in the interval between the EEC Council giving Ireland the 'green light' for negotiations to commence and de Gaulle 'pulling the plug', there were some interesting developments in the Irish government's position on various economic and political matters related to its aspirant status. At the end of October 1962, for instance, the taoiseach declared that Ireland had notified the Six that it was quite prepared to participate in whatever form of European political union developed and, in this regard, that it was not making any sort of reservation, including those matters which were directly related to defence considerations.⁶⁸ Lemass reiterated the fact that:

> ... 99 per cent. of the people agree with my view that this country is anti-

Communist and will remain anti-Communist ... There is no doubt that this Christian country is and will remain to be completely antagonistic to the Communist concept ...[69]

The EEC Council's promise to open negotiations may, as it turned out, have given the Irish government false hopes, but at least this decision had invigorated the country's preparations for membership, especially corrections in the economy that were much needed anyway. The inherent promise from Lemass to reform Ireland's status as a military neutral, if and when the need arose to do so, also exploded the quasi-mythical nature of Irish neutrality; it would be surrendered as soon as it could be bargained away at a profit.

On 22 November 1962 in Dáil Éireann, Lemass went so far as to pronounce that the application to accede to the Treaty of Rome would present no difficulty.[70] In direct relation to Ireland's economic restructuring, his government also made a unilateral, if highly symbolic, 10% tariff cut as a sign of its faith in the whole integration process. This new position was to take effect from 1 January 1963. On the one hand, the Irish were creating the impression that they were prepared to pay any price in order to gain full accession to the EEC but, on the other, obviously realised the value of both independent negotiation and, indeed, the ability to put forward their own suggestions, positions that might not necessarily be in the UK's best interests.[71] A good illustration of this approach was the fact that the government was quite ready to submit an *aide-mémoire* to the EEC on the importance of mutton and lamb in the Irish agricultural sector, a move which did not please the UK government. However, as the departmental secretaries said: 'There was no good reason why we should not protect our own interests in an important matter such as this'.[72] Nevertheless, speaking generally, Ireland and Norway never got much beyond the initial stages of beginning their negotiations with the EEC – limited to putting out 'feelers' – a crucial factor which distinguished their efforts from the proceedings engaged in by the Danish and UK governments.[73] Ireland would not feel as reproachful towards the EEC or the Six, especially France, as the UK would; when it came to the next time to apply, the Irish government would fell chastened, but would also have to have learned a very valuable lesson if it was going to be successful.

The EEC Council's decision to open negotiations with Ireland was, of course, soon overtaken by events which are described in a series of sections later in this chapter that also analyse how and why Ireland's application had not failed, but that it had in fact been ignored. In the meantime, however, it has proven necessary to investigate in some detail the substance of the Irish government's preparations for entry negotiations to begin with the EEC and to explore its relations with the other two European Communities, the ECSC and Euratom, up to the beginning of 1963.[74] Furthermore, it should be remembered that the government was also committed to preparing a follow-up plan to the *Programme for economic expansion* at this time. However, notwithstanding this particular consideration, the Irish government concentrated its attention upon preparing for the forthcoming EEC negotiations to begin as it considered that all future developments depended on adhesion. Sadly, its faith in the good intentions of the French government was wholly misplaced.

Lemass prepares for EEC entry negotiations to begin[75]

The EEC was, of course, generally well aware of the positions that Ireland would wish to take in its membership negotiations. Lemass's statement to the EEC Council on 18 January 1962 and the meeting on 11 May 1962 of senior Irish officials with the permanent representatives had actually left little of substance unsaid, even if clarification had been sought each time. There are no tangible grounds to go into immense detail regarding negotiation positions taken prior to Ireland's proposed accession. Nevertheless, some observations that come from a draft brief prepared by the Department of the Taoiseach with the onset of Irish-EEC negotiations in mind can be highlighted and, in turn, related to the relevant articles of the Treaty of Rome. This analysis by the most important government department in terms of European integration is of consequence mainly because is provides a priceless picture of positions being taken on the EEC membership question at the end of 1962, on the eve of negotiations beginning.

Ever since the inception of its application on 31 July 1961, the Irish government had gone out of its way to convince the EEC that Ireland accepted its vision of Europe, as set out in the preamble to the Treaty of Rome, without diminution. Additionally, it was well aware that there was no room for manoeuvre regarding the 'Principles' that continued to guide the foundation and further establishment of the EEC (Articles 1-8). Ireland was happy to signal its agreement with these principles. Indeed, as was outlined at the beginning of the part of the Treaty of Rome headed 'Foundations of the Community', there was a further aspiration which was clearly in favour of the free movement of goods (Articles 9-11); Ireland was also happily in favour of that. Certainly, another accepted assumption was the section of the treaty on the elimination of duties between member states within the customs union (Articles 12-17). So far, so good. The Irish government would be able to send all the right signals to the Six on the preamble and the initial articles of the

Treaty of Rome.

However, regarding the section on the setting up of the common customs tariff within the customs union (Articles 18-29), the taoiseach had said that Ireland was prepared to accept such a tariff, but subject to negotiations for the revision of some items, 'mostly downwards'. Indeed, at the meeting with the permanent representatives of the Six, it had been added that the government was 'prepared to make an initial approximation towards the common external tariff on the date of Ireland's accession to the Community'. Regardless of this stance, a position of more fundamental importance to Ireland *vis-à-vis* its proposed membership of the EEC – regarding the free movement of goods – had already been demonstrated on both formal occasions in Brussels. As the Irish government had insisted at these meetings, it intended to 'replace industrial quantitative restrictions as soon as possible by tariffs of no greater and probably less restrictive effect'. Therefore, by the end of 1962, this standpoint had in fact become Ireland's official negotiating position in relation to the elimination of quantitative restrictions between member states (Articles 30-37). In the process, it also signalled what would have become a major issue of contention with its prospective new economic partners if negotiations had actually gone ahead as planned. The accession process would have started to become a little more awkward at that stage, explaining why the Six had been so reluctant to introduce Ireland into negotiations before the UK's adhesion had been solved.

In relation to the free movement of persons, services and capital, however, the Irish government's stance was relatively straightforward. Indeed, as regards the free movement of workers (Articles 48-51), 'no derogations or special arrangements' were being sought at the negotiations, as was the case with the right of establishment (Articles 52-58) and the freedom to provide services (Articles 59-66). Of course, the free movement of capital (Articles 67-73) was complicated by Ireland's strong ties to the UK, specifically to the 'Sterling Area', and to a neighbouring economy which had weak and fitful growth. The government's negotiating position therefore depended on arrangements that the UK would make through its own EEC accession negotiations. It is interesting, in this regard, to note T.K.Whitaker's remark on the 'Sterling Area' to the effect that 'when we were getting on well in the world, England was going backwards'.[76] Ireland had its eyes elsewhere for markets.

In actual fact, it was West Germany and the US which were being foreseen by Ireland as two of its most important future economic partners, conclusions understandably discernible from the figures. As a potential market for goods and services, Ireland's attitude towards West Germany transformed rather quickly from the relatively contemporary times of

Heinrich Böll's travelogue *Irisches Tagesbuch*, only published in 1957, when Irish bankers had difficulty in recognising, never mind changing, a West German bank-note.[77] Indeed, by the early 1960s, the FRG was fast becoming the most important economy in Europe, as well as a very significant new trading partner for Ireland. In the period 1957 to 1966, its average export to import ratio with Germany was well under 3:1 – itself a very big improvement on the rest of the 1950s when it was well over 4:1 – but there was still some way to go. By 1962, over 6½% of its total imports came from the FRG, with most of these – 90% or more – being manufactured goods demanding high capital and technological input. Meanwhile, West Germany was also quickly becoming an important market for Irish goods, especially for agricultural products demanding less input, with over 3% of its total exports going there; regularly during the 1960s, live animals still accounted for around 30% of these goods however, even if Irish manufactured products were slowly becoming more significant. It was obviously growing in terms of trade for Ireland's rapidly developing economy, as was the rest of the European mainland, but there were clearly other alternatives to the UK as well.

It is a very interesting exercise therefore to put these German figures into the context of a comparable destination for Irish goods, as well as a source for its growing needs at home. Concurrently, over 7½% of its total imports came from the US, with 8¼% of its total exports going in the opposite direction. There was not much of a basis for getting too excited by these sets of figures however, as Ireland had a significant negative trade balance with both countries. In 1962, Ireland imported over 3½ times the value of goods from West Germany as it exported; with the US, it amounted to 1½ times as much. These statistics only provided evidence of serious, habitually negative trade deficits. Of course, the continued growth of foreign investment in Ireland from the end of the 1950s onwards also meant that both West Germany and the US had quickly developed into highly significant factors in the continued development of the Irish economy. However, a truthful assessment of the position meant that the country's definitive economic dependence upon the UK would not have given Ireland's negotiators with the EEC much room for instigating major new initiatives. Bilateral Anglo-Irish economic relations would remain of paramount importance to the Irish economy in the short and medium term, no matter how much Ireland searched for new markets.[78]

The question mark that was surrounding the institution of a common transport policy in the EEC (Articles 74-84) was another area within the context of European integration in which the Irish government had decided rather early on that it was not going to look for a 'derogation or any special arrangements' at the membership negotiations stage. Nonetheless, the Irish Department of Transport & Power hoped that, once in the EEC, Ireland would of course be able to influence the formulation of the as yet undefined common transport policy, thus enabling it to draw particular attention to the country's peripheral nature. At the same time, of much more specific interest to the Irish government was the wish that the 'removal of the existing restrictions on the licensing of the entry of road transport vehicles should be gradual'. Notwithstanding this consideration, the establishment of a common transport policy within the EEC was still a relatively long term goal at which to aim. Indeed, according to this draft brief for Ireland's talks with the EEC dating from December 1962, there were even more pressing matters in relation to the Treaty of Rome still to which the government would seriously have to attend at its forthcoming accession negotiations.

One of the areas that undoubtedly worried the Irish government was in relation to the part of the Treaty of Rome headed 'Policy of the Community', more specifically in relation to the rules that governed competition and, in particular, to those provisions that dealt with dumping (Article 91). Indeed, these fears had been explicitly acknowledged on both of the two previous occasions at which the government had presented its case for membership to the Six in Brussels, the taoiseach's statement to the EEC Council and the meeting of senior Irish officials with the permanent representatives.[79] The provision against dumping stated:

> If, during the transitional period, the Commission, on application by a Member State or by any other interested party, finds that dumping is being practised within the common market, it shall address recommendations to the person or persons with whom such practices originate for the purpose of putting an end to them. Should the practices continue, the Commission shall authorise the injured Member State to take protective measures, the conditions and details of which the Commission shall determine.

This provision was inadequate as far as the Irish were concerned because of a fundamental flaw. On 18 January 1962, Lemass had been moved to declare that:

> Because of the small home market and the size of Irish industrial units, Irish industry is particularly vulnerable to dumping, and the Irish Government would hope that an arrangement could be made under which it would be possible for them to take effective counter measures against any dumping or threat of dumping in good time.

In addition, on 11 May 1962, the reply that was given to the permanent representatives of the Six further aired government fears about the effectiveness of this provision, because in reality they doubted its actual applicability. In the opinion of senior government officials, this provision 'would not provide sufficient protection against the dumping of goods'. Indeed, the government stated that the Treaty of Rome in fact only provided for remedial measures to be taken after dumping had taken place and also after it had then been investigated by the EEC Commission. It was pointed out by the Irish delegation that this retort might come too late for an Irish industry, because the saturation resulting from dumping could have caused 'serious disruption of production and employment' in the meantime. The government felt that Ireland was especially vulnerable to dumping because of factors such as the limited size of its market, and therefore suggested that it be allowed to take immediate, albeit temporary, action if there was evidence that dumping was actually already occurring or that it was about to occur. Of course, the government made it clear that the EEC Commission would then be called in to deal with the matter, but only *post factum*. This view on dumping was explicitly held in the draft brief for negotiations with the EEC and would obviously have been reflected in the Irish government's subsequent efforts at arbitration.

Another question related to the rules on competition which was dealt with at this time by the government in its preparations for full membership negotiations to begin was on the rules regarding aids granted by states (Articles 92-94) but, once again, it was felt that this subject did not arise at this early stage. The remaining aspects of the Treaty of Rome which were reviewed in this draft brief for Ireland's negotiations with the EEC were equally lacking in difficulty. In regard to economics, it was noted that the Dublin government accepted the objectives outlined in the section dealing with commercial policy (Articles 110-116) and that it would not be seeking any derogations here. Indeed, the provisions that were laid down in the area of social policy (Articles 117-122) were viewed similarly.[80] Actually, Lemass had already specifically spoken in Brussels regarding the other area of social policy – that is the European Social Fund (Articles 123-128), and, in addition, on the European Investment Bank (Articles 129-130) – envisaging no genuine difficulties there either. Certainly, the taoiseach appeared not to feel that Ireland would need any 'special financial assistance', because he assumed that the country would have the same access to the European Social Fund and to the European Investment Bank as the other member states. So far so good.

There were some major lacunae in this draft Irish government brief for negotiations with the EEC, noticeably with regard to the whole question of agriculture (Articles 38-47), an area which was at the heart of the part of the Treaty of Rome which was labelled as the 'Foundations of the

Community'. Indeed, there were also large gaps with regard to the part denoted as the 'Policy of the Community'; more precisely, these areas dealt with the rules on competition, specifically in relation to the rules applying to undertakings (Articles 85-90), as well as tax provisions (Articles 95-99) and with the approximation of laws (Articles 100-102). Furthermore, in relation to economics, there were also some significant gaps, expressly on conjunctural policy (Article 103) and on the issue of balance of payments (Articles 104-109). Nonetheless, this document remains extremely valuable as a snapshot of what were in fact the vast majority of considered Irish government positions regarding the Treaty of Rome at the end of 1962. Obviously, agriculture was still the most important consideration for Ireland in any negotiations with the EEC and, indeed, remained highly problematic. Notwithstanding the lack of analysis of this integral component, amongst many other gaps, this Department of the Taoiseach survey merited investigation here. Indeed, although this short review of the negotiating positions that the Irish government was taking regarding the Treaty of Rome may have gone into some detail, it does at least give a strong indication of the extent to which the Irish were preparing themselves for the accession process to start.

It is also worth pointing out that plans were made at this time for the publication of a brochure containing the most important speeches that had been delivered by the taoiseach in connection with Ireland's application, because it adds a public dimension to the private Irish government preparations that were being made for membership negotiations to begin. Indeed, Lemass stated that the main intention behind such a brochure was that it would prove to be primarily useful for 'Dáil Deputies and public commentators, and ... representatives of other Governments and press representatives from abroad'. In fact, totally ignoring the facts of the matter, he also added, one suspects more in hope than with much conviction, that it would demonstrate the 'consistency of our policy from the start' with regard to the EEC.[81] Of course, this claim was rightly castigated by the *Irish Independent*, because, for example, there had undoubtedly been a complete turn-about by the Lemass government in relation to defence, noticeably on neutrality. Indeed, it quoted him as having said two years previously that: 'We do not accept that it is only through a regional military alliance that this country can make a useful contribution to the defence of these principles'. At the end of 1962, the Irish government's position was that it was now willing, in principle, to enter into a European defence alliance if compelled by the process of integration. As the *Irish Independent* stated: 'Surely this is a clear change of emphasis and there is no point in cloaking it'.[82]

In connection with this issue, it is thus also interesting to note that there was a debate between the departmental secretaries over whether or not to include in the proposed brochure the speech made by Lemass, dating from 1 December 1960, on Ireland's position relative to neutrality. It was only latterly, therefore, that he felt compelled to think the implications of its inclusion through. The taoiseach sought advice from his departmental secretary, explaining the two sides of the argument, as much to himself as to Nolan. Lemass wrote:

> While not related to our EEC application, its inclusion would help to emphasise that our position in this regard was taken before our EEC application was possible. On the other hand, its inclusion may over-emphasise the neutrality issue.

The editors of this brochure of speeches made in connection with Ireland's application were faced with a difficult conundrum. Interestingly, they decided in the end that this speech on neutrality should not be included, partially as a result of the newspaper's intervention it must be said, even if the evidence in surmising such a conclusion is at best circumstantial.[83] However, it does appear that the taoiseach was prepared to dissemble the realities of his government's position on neutrality for the benefit of its endeavours in joining the EEC; the pamphlet itself was not in fact published anyway, events overtaking its usefulness.

Publicly, the taoiseach had been very upbeat ever since the EEC Council had made its historic decision to open negotiations in October 1962 and, although he now saw that the timetable for adhesion had been put back somewhat – even at a very optimistic estimate to the beginning of 1964 – he did not appear to be unduly worried at this point in time about the ultimate outcome. Indeed, although the Danish and Norwegian applications were themselves contingent upon the UK government's success, Lemass emphasised that Ireland's request was not. This assertion did, of course, carry a crucial proviso:

> ... a failure of the British negotiations would require us to reconsider our position in the light of the circumstances which may then prevail.

The worry foremost in Irish government minds was that there might be a substantial 'hiatus' between the UK's adhesion to the EEC and Ireland's accession. However, notwithstanding this critical consideration, the country was still preparing itself for the full implementation of the Treaty of Rome by 31 December 1969. Therefore, the first unilateral tariff cut announced at the end of 1962 was part of this process. At the stage, Lemass actually declared that he found the 'prospect of intensive activity in preparing the national economy to meet the new circumstances not in the least distasteful'. Indeed, he added:

> The sense of the historical significance of what is happening, together with the understanding that everything which we do in preparation is worth doing for its own sake and will give us an economic organisation which will be permanently stronger and sounder, helps to generate the enthusiasm which will make the work seem lighter.

It was clearly recognised that every national plan for economic and social advancement must henceforth be based in the belief that free trade in Europe would continue to develop.[84]

The Irish government's painful conversion from the economic policy of protectionism to one accepting the exigencies of European integration may in truth have been based on the premise that there was no other 'practical alternative' available. However, in a crucial speech that he delivered to the Fianna Fáil Árd-Fheis in Dublin on 20 November 1962, the taoiseach publicly maintained that Ireland was particularly excited at the prospect of participating in 'one of the greatest and most imaginative developments in the history of mankind'.[85] This sudden conversion on European cooperation and integration still paled in comparison with that of London, but just like the latter, it was not 'merely due to a change of mind of the political leadership, but was the outcome of an agonising reappraisal involving policy-makers as well as the bureaucracy, the public as well as non-governmental élites'.[86] Major uncertainties remained about the timing and form of adhesion, but the readjustment of native agriculture and industry continued apace nevertheless.[87]

These aspirations for Ireland to participate in the wider integration process came to mean little however on 14 January 1963 when the French president finally made his feelings known and, thereafter, as the implications of his pronouncement began to be more thoroughly evaluated. Before dealing directly with this specific subject, there were also some important developments in this period with regard to Ireland's relations with the other two European Communities that need to be considered, as the government finally set about joining the ECSC and Euratom, European institutions which it had heretofore deemed to be so relatively insignificant that it could virtually ignore them. Paradoxically, this evolution in Ireland's integration policy has to be fully explored in order to understand more fully the importance that it was attaching to the EEC, proving that the latter was the only consideration.

Ireland and the other two European Communities[88]

Membership of the other two European Communities – the ECSC or Euratom – were never important considerations for the Irish government, basically because, in terms of European integration, the question of full EEC membership thoroughly dominated Ireland's thinking. Indeed, it can be argued that the final opening of diplomatic relations with the ECSC and Euratom by Ireland – in fact, the resulting applications to join them – therefore signified nothing more than a kind of afterthought. In truth, Ireland had opened diplomatic relations with the EEC in December 1959, but it did not subsequently accredit a representative to the ECSC until January 1963 and to Euratom until April 1963. Indeed, these three postings, along with the jobs of Irish ambassador to Belgium and Irish minister to Luxembourg, were all held by one person until October 1966. Thus, Patrick Keatinge is mistaken when he states in *The formulation of Irish foreign policy* that Ireland actually had diplomatic relations with the European Communities from the earlier date mentioned.[89] The general lack of available or relevant archive material strongly indicates that Dublin did not rally pay much attention to either the ECSC or to Euratom, although it has to be said that the question of steel was a relatively significant factor in the subsequent development of its strategy towards the ECSC. However, the importance of these other two European Communities paled in comparison with that of the EEC in the development of Ireland's foreign economic policy.

Overall, of course, the three European Communities were not at all averse to the idea of Ireland joining their organisations, but only so long as the Irish government was, in turn, prepared to accept and to fulfil the necessary economic and political conditions inherent in membership. In addition, there were obvious reasons for Ireland's slighting of the ECSC and Euratom at this time, with these grounds emerging as the relationship between Dublin and these two other European Communities, largely forgotten by historians and the general public alike, is chronicled. The purpose of this particular section is therefore to consider the Irish government's position in relation to nuclear power, coal and steel in this period, while also investigating how these concerns impacted on Ireland's general relationship with the Six. As these topics have not yet been dealt with in any great detail in these central chapters, the backgrounds to Ireland's relationship with both the ECSC and Euratom also have to be considered. Indeed, this section chronologically traces the various developments that were made in regard to both of these institutions, especially in the early 1960s, before making some remarks that lead into the next section which centres on de Gaulle's famous press conference and veto of the UK.

On 18 January 1962, in the course of his statement to the EEC Council in Brussels regarding Ireland's case for EEC membership, Lemass stated that:

> If Ireland's application for membership of the Community is accepted in principle, we shall apply for accession to the European Coal and Steel Community and Euratom.[90]

As was previously stated, Ireland had applied to join the EEC at the end of July 1961 and, while it was understood by the Irish government that there was 'no formal requirement' for EEC members to be members of the ECSC and Euratom as well, towards the end of 1962 it was also 'recognised that the three Communities are complementary to each other and that membership of one entails membership of all'.[91] Indeed, an Interdepartmental Committee report on Ireland's membership of the ECSC from that latter period had stated that:

> Membership of the European Coal and Steel Community is dependent on whether or not our application for membership of the European Economic Community is successful. If this country's application for membership of the EEC is accepted we are committed to becoming a member of the ECSC.

Equally, the same case applied to Ireland's membership of Euratom. In addition, however, it was noted that association with the EEC – unlike full membership – would not necessarily involve accession to either of these other organisations.[92] Thus, when the EEC Council agreed to open negotiations in October 1962, accepting in principle Ireland's application for EEC membership, the government was prompted for the first time into having to consider seriously opening membership negotiations with the ECSC and Euratom as well.

In point of fact, Ireland's continued anomalous position with regard to the ECSC and Euratom, having stated a desire to join both organisations at the beginning of 1962, had finally forced the UK to warn the Irish government that the continued absence of membership applications from both Ireland and Norway 'risked creating difficulties, especially in the matter of the timetable'; furthermore, it advised that Ireland's undefined position with regard to these two other European Communities also had much wider implications. Although the 'practical consequences' of joining either European Community would 'not for the moment be great', according to the Irish chef de mission to the EEC, Francis Biggar, he still advised the Irish government to open formal diplomatic relations with the ECSC and Euratom as soon as was practicably possible. It was pointed out that such amended circumstances would enable Ireland to be in a similar position to that of the UK government when it would come to negotiating actual EEC entry. In fact, Dublin retained the expectation that any negotiations with the European Communities would operate in tandem with those of the UK, but it was, of course, to be extremely disappointed on this score. At any rate, the adhesion process was going to be a protracted one and would thus necessitate immediate action if Ireland's actual accreditation to these two other European Communities was to be fulfilled by January 1963. Biggar noted that the EEC Council's decision of October 1962 had realised Lemass's own acknowledged conditions for entry into the ECSC and Euratom. Thus, the Irish diplomat 'suggest[ed] that the sooner the matter is put in hands the better'; indeed, he also advised his superiors to take the unusual short-cut of presenting the *agréments* for diplomatic relations simultaneously with the documents for accreditation.[93]

In mid-November 1962, Lemass asked the authoritative Committee of Departmental Secretaries for its 'views on the desirability of applying now for membership of Euratom and the Coal & Steel Community'.[94] The London government had already stated its desire to join the ECSC the previous July and thus was in a position to negotiate to join all three European Communities; indeed, Denmark had applied to join both organisations on 16 March 1962, but, at this point in time, Norway was still in a position similar to that of Ireland.[95] As a direct consequence of this situation, the departmental secretaries 'agreed that the time had come to present formal applications for membership of the two Communities' at their meeting in mid-November 1962.[96] Of course, this still leaves a very important question unanswered: what would the implications for Ireland be in joining these other two European Communities?

The ECSC – formed through the Treaty of Paris from 18 April 1951 – came into being on 1 July 1952 and had six participants – Belgium, France, West Germany, Italy, Luxembourg and the Netherlands. It had been established in order to form a common market in coal and steel (although these categories were still restricted in some ways) to ensure easily accessible and regular supplies of these products for its partners, obviously at the lowest prices possible. This development consequently led to the abolition of tariffs and quantitative restrictions on the import and export of coal and steel products between the members of the Six. Indeed, this agreement catered for problems like 'dumping' as well and made provisions to deal with the iron and steel scrap market. In the end, however, the UK decided to remain 'aloof' from the ECSC process for two principal reasons. The London government felt that:

- it did not receive the full support of the ECSC member countries to participate, because they in turn were worried about the structures and power of the coal and steel industries in the UK;
- the UK was already in a very strong position to maintain its policies in regard to both industries.

Ireland thus followed the UK's lead, but did not seriously have to consider the implications of this decision for some years to come.[97] Pointedly, this archetypal stance did not help to distinguish its application for EEC membership from that of the UK. In the meantime, the UK did of course sign an association agreement on 21 December 1954 with the ECSC; evidently Ireland was not interested.[98]

As Dermot Keogh has subsequently written in his *Twentieth-century Ireland*: 'Nothing was done to borrow from the approach in Europe which led to the creation of the European Coal and Steel Community. The idea of functional integration did not appeal to politicians on either side of the House [Dáil Éireann]'.[99] Notwithstanding this particular slant, in itself quite representative of the reality, it is worth noting that there is some evidence, albeit retrospective, to show that the Lemass government actually felt that:

> ... there were certain features which distinguished the ECSC from the other Communities ... The establishment of the ECSC was primarily a political development which arose in the context of German rearmament. The philosophy behind it was very different, therefore, from that of the EEC.[100]

Therefore, once the country began to move more in favour of integration, the ECSC suddenly became an ardent consideration. After applying to join the EEC in the middle of 1961, it was still many months, however, before the taoiseach in fact noted that the ECSC agreement was 'being scanned with a view to our accession'.[101] However, he was particularly concerned with the implications of initiating such a move for Irish Steel because, as he stated, the coal and steel 'agreement provides for something like a managed market for steel'.[102] Thus, the government set about assessing the implications of ECSC membership.

Coal was not particularly important in this context because Ireland's production was minimal – peat, an important domestic source of fuel, was actually outside the scope of the Treaty of Paris – and the country depended on imports. The only significant consideration for the government in regard to coal was therefore limited to sourcing. The Interdepartmental Committee report presented in December 1962 had said, in reference to the implications of ECSC membership for the Irish coal industry, such as it was, that: 'It is considered that the country's membership of the ECSC would not have any appreciable effect on the home industry'. This was, in fact, a belief to which the Department of Finance strongly concurred. Ireland was, after all, producing only 150,000 tons of anthracite *per annum* – most of which was said to be 'duff', that is poor quality – and 60,000 tons of semi-bituminous coal – the majority of which came in the form of 'slack' and which was used by the Electricity Supply Board (ESB) at its Arigna power plant. Irish production hardly rated more than a mention. On the other hand, it still proved necessary to import vast quantities of bituminous coal and 55,000 tons of anthracite for the home market. What did this imply?

As can be ascertained from this data, the UK remained the most important source of Irish bituminous coal imports and, for all practical purposes, accounted for all of Ireland's import needs with regard to anthracite as well. However, as the Department of Finance noted, the UK was losing its importance as a sourcing point for the Irish market, mainly due to the increased mechanisation of UK mines which did not in fact cater for Ireland's needs for large coal. Ireland had therefore begun to source elsewhere. Indeed, it began this change of tack by concentrating more on imports from countries within the ECSC, specifically from Belgium and West Germany. In addition, under ECSC regulations then in force, although of course always liable to change, Ireland was not required to impose a tariff on non-ECSC coal – that is coal which came to it from Poland or the US – and so was sourcing from further afield as well. At the same time, Ireland's coal industry was not protected, even though the various Anglo-Irish trade agreements put a tariff of 3 shillings per ton on non-UK coal, this sum had in fact been waived in relation to large coal for a number of years. Essentially, Ireland operated its own coal-mining industry under free trade conditions and, by that reckoning, had nothing to fear regarding any proposed membership of the ECSC.[103] Steel was an entirely different matter altogether, however. Firstly, though, it is interesting to note what the ECSC itself was thinking before detailing Irish considerations.

Archival sources amply show that Ireland was not particularly interested in moving too quickly on the subject of tariff reductions. An illustrative example of this is a handwritten note from within the ECSC headed 'Irlande 1958', which gruffly states that Irish tariff #58/3 essentially meant that Ireland's imports of coal, culm, shale, slack and coke from the ECSC totalled 'néant'. As was previously stated, the duty on these goods stood at three shillings a ton, even if that did not amount to very much, but the ECSC was determined upon receiving an exemption from this tariff. Other items which were dealt with in detail by this ECSC document included various iron and steel products covered by Irish tariffs #125/1 and #125/4. In this regard, the general demand of the ECSC countries was for a cut in the tariff rate down from 37½% to 25%. Indeed, the rest of the document, actually compiled in 1961, amounted to a detailed statement of Irish tariffs on all major related products, with a list of some of the concessions that the Six were demanding from Ireland. As all of these tariffs were within the parameters of ongoing negotiations with GATT, it was stated that the demands of the ECSC had not as yet been explicitly defined. Of course, Ireland was not a vitally important market but, nevertheless, the very fact that it was 'closed', that foreign produce was handicapped by duties upon entry into the Irish market, did not at this point in time predispose the Six to the government's case for membership.[104] In turn, how did Dublin view the idea of the country actually becoming a fully-fledged member of the ECSC?

Irish Steel, a state-owned company based in Cork and the only domestic steel producer that would be affected by Ireland's ECSC membership, had only been in production since 1947 and remained highly protected. Indeed, as previously stated, the full customs duty rate was 37½% and there was a preferential rate of 25%, with a minimum duty respectively of IR£30 and IR£20 per ton on imported iron and steel products other than galvanised steel.[105] As a result, the Interdepartmental Committee report of December 1962 subsequently stated that Irish entry into the ECSC in the near future would duly create a 'difficult situation' for that company, mainly due to the incurring of higher operational costs. In fact, these costs resulted from a redevelopment programme that was then being completed and which had been approved by the government in 1959 in an effort to reorganise fundamentally Irish Steel. It was also felt that ECSC membership would impact in a number of ways, including what was said to be a 'considerable increase' in imported steel prices, as steel from the Six was being imported at a price 'substantially lower' than prices operating within the ECSC. At that time, Ireland was importing its steel from the UK and the ECSC in more or less equal proportions. In addition, it was noted that this was all happening at a time when Irish Steel was meeting less than 25% of Irish domestic requirements, even if it was aiming to produce between 40% and 45% of the country's needs and was also aiming to employ around 700 people by some stage in 1964. The Irish market was consuming 130,000 to 140,000 tons of unfabricated steel a year, but Irish Steel was only producing 32,000 tons. It was also said that Irish Steel had a small, although not very significant, export trade averaging about 7,000 tons *per annum*. However, not only did home produced steel exceed the price of ECSC steel bought under export rules then in operation, but it was also stated in Irish government documents that it would be 'somewhat higher' in price than the fixed internal market prices operating within the ECSC.[106] What did this all mean in terms of Ireland and the ECSC?

While accepting the conditions of ECSC membership in principle, what Irish Steel in fact wanted were concessions, including continued protection for a specified amount of time, to help defend it from, as the company itself put it, the 'full rigours' of free trade. Indeed, Irish Steel had the departmental secretaries considerable support for 'special arrangements' to take this industry's recent reorganisation into account. After all, the company had initiated its development programme in the knowledge that the Irish steel industry would continue to be afforded protection and understandably felt that the government should not be allowed to renege on its agreement. It was further argued that Ireland would not be creating a precedent in regard to concessions, as Italy had already received 'substantial concessions' – essentially a transition period from the inauguration of the Treaty of Paris until February 1958 – through its membership negotiations. In this context, it was noted that the UK government was likely to seek 'some concessions' too.[107] However, the departmental secretaries were not particularly optimistic about what concessions Irish Steel would receive in the end and therefore recommended a conservative and conciliatory line of argument in any ensuing ECSC membership negotiations, primarily so that any fall-back position then adopted would still be broadly acceptable in the circumstances. As a result of this investigation into the implications of ECSC membership, the departmental secretaries stated that they wanted a 'greater degree of consistency' to be exhibited in the government's approach to the EEC and demonstrated that they were very sensitive to the accusation emanating from other Irish industries that it was displaying signs of favouritism towards a state-owned operation.[108]

At the same time, of course, Ireland was also considering entry into the second of the other two European Communities, Euratom, and it is with some background information on this development in mind that this section proceeds, before moving onto the actual events that unfolded in the course of Ireland's changing relations with both European organisations at the end of 1962. Euratom – established on 25 March 1957 through the second, less well-known, Treaty of Rome – came into being on 1 January 1958 and comprised the same six nations as the members of both the ECSC and EEC. Euratom had been formed with the central aim of creating the conditions that would be necessary for the expected rapid establishment and growth of nuclear powered industries in Europe. In preparation for this major evolution in European integration, the government quickly set up an Atomic Energy Committee in March 1956, which subsequently recommended in May 1958 that an Atomic Energy Board be founded. This development did not in fact happen, however, mainly because de Valera's government rejected the

Atomic Energy Committee's majority recommendation that Ireland should acquire a research reactor. It must be said from the outset that the whole question of nuclear energy was not very coordinated in Ireland's case, as it was dealt with by not one, but up to seven different government departments at this point in time. Ireland was therefore not in a particularly good position, not even a perfunctory one, to take any real advantage of Euratom's establishment and growth, certainly not without a nuclear reactor which it, rather evidently, was not particularly interested in acquiring, given the relative lack of government enthusiasm or organisation.[109]

One of Dublin's major concerns regarding membership of Euratom was related to the costs that it would obviously as a result incur for what it considered to be a minimal return. Indeed, it was calculated that Ireland would have to pay *circa* IR£335,000 annually towards the two Euratom budgets for operational costs and expenses relating to both research and development. As a consequence, the Department of Finance felt that Ireland should try:

> ... to obtain agreement to a reduced rate of contribution ... on the grounds that, as we are unlikely to be concerned in the use of atomic power for some years to come, the research and investment programme will not benefit us to any great extent for some time. A further consideration in this regard would be that, as we would merely be buyers of nuclear plant, we would not benefit from the research projects to the same extent as the member countries manufacturing this plant.

Of course, this really appears to have been a rather spurious argument for the Department of Finance to have put forward, because it undoubtedly realised that membership of Euratom offered Ireland many significant advantages as well, such as the use of its training facilities, access to its research and technical knowledge, the ensuing availability of the nuclear fuels themselves, and the utilisation of radioactive materials in agriculture, industry and medicine. At any rate, the ESB had informed the Irish government that it did not anticipate commissioning a nuclear power plant for ten years at least, as nuclear energy still remained commercially unviable.[110] Thus, the whole issue of Ireland's financial position as it related to Euratom membership is, if nothing else, an interesting further illustration of the Dublin government's generally penurious attitude towards European integration.

In his opening speech to Euratom delivered on 3 July 1962, Edward Heath, the UK Lord Privy Seal, had actually advocated the expansion of UK research programmes in relation to nuclear energy, a stance which of course proved to be anathema to the cash-conscious in Dublin.[111] As a consequence of taking its contentious position by raising the idea of Ireland 'seeking a reduced rate of contribution', at least the Irish government realised that:

> ... [it] may tend to strengthen any existing feeling that, generally, we are unwilling or unable to bear our share of the Community burdens ... [especially as Ireland was] not spending any appreciable amount of money ... on nuclear research and development.

At the same time, it was recognised that the advantage of Ireland actually joining Euratom was that it 'would be benefitting from advances in knowledge and techniques in the other countries of the Community'. Nonetheless, a strong suspicion remains that once the real goal of Ireland's relations with the European Communities had been achieved, EEC membership, other considerations, such as ECSC or Euratom membership, would essentially no longer be of any major interest. Therefore, in the eyes of the government, it was felt that it would not necessarily 'be good tactics to ask for a reduced contribution – unless, by the time such a request fell to be made, we were assured of membership of the EEC'.[112] Thus, a more considered appreciation of the ramifications of this attitude is fundamental to understanding Ireland's genuine, but otherwise not deeply-held, attraction to certain aspects of European integration and, accordingly, what they then meant for the country. So, with this background in mind, the issues raised become: what were the steps regarding entry into the ECSC and Euratom being taken by Ireland towards the end of 1962 and how did these tie in with its central criterion, the idea of gaining full EEC membership?

It was felt that a decision regarding membership of both European organisations had finally become 'imminent'.[113] Therefore, on 23 November 1962, at a crucial Irish cabinet meeting and on the advice of the Department of External Affairs, the Irish government decided to seek to establish diplomatic relations with the ECSC and Euratom. Meanwhile, it also sought to have Francis Biggar, the Irish chef de mission to the EEC, fully accredited to both of these European Communities, with the further view of entry negotiations to the two organisations beginning soon thereafter. In the process, a central promise made by the taoiseach during his tour of the EEC capitals in October 1962 would thus be fulfilled.[114] On 13 December 1962, a meeting of the departmental secretaries dealt with the linked considerations of ECSC and Euratom membership. On the ECSC question, for instance, it was clearly recognised that coal was not a very significant factor, but it was still felt that there would be difficulties for the steel industry. Meanwhile, on the Euratom question it was felt that 'no urgency arose' for Ireland on this point because, somewhat fortuitously, 'developments in the field of nuclear power were further away than was thought ... that it might be 1975 before a nuclear power station became a feasible proposition'. At the same time, however, pressure from the UK government for Ireland to apply to join both organisations was becoming particularly ardent, with the UK ambassador in Dublin, Ian Maclennan, a leading proponent of such an initiative coming.[115] The question remains: what did the Irish government decide to do?

A further meeting of the departmental secretaries on 10 January 1963 recognised that, even if Ireland formally submitted its application to join the ECSC at that stage, it would not be until some point in February before it could finally make its 'opening statement'.[116] In the meantime, agreement for the government to open diplomatic relations had arrived from the ECSC Council.[117] Thus, as the year drew to a close, the pressure started to build even further for the government to elucidate its position regarding the ECSC. Indeed, Ireland's ambassador in Brussels, due to present his diplomatic letters of credence for the ECSC post, requested more detailed information from his superiors at the Department of External Affairs regarding Ireland's exact relationship with this European Community; it does not appear that this diplomat was being furnished with the required materials.[118] The department's response was to issue him with what they considered to be an appropriate memorandum, but there was no mention as yet of any 'special arrangements' that the Irish government might necessarily request in subsequent membership negotiations.[119]

On the morning of 14 January 1963, Biggar duly presented his diplomatic credentials to the ECSC High Authority president, Piero Malvestiti, who expressed the ECSC's 'pleasure that Ireland had formally established relations with the Community'. That very same day, in fact, even though Ireland's accession was still expected to take some time, the new Irish representative took advantage of his journey to Luxembourg and also presented his country's application to join the ECSC; thus, through the appropriate provision in the Treaty of Paris, Christian Calmes, the ECSC Council secretary general, accepted the official Irish application to accede.[120] Article 98 of the *Treaty establishing the European Coal and Steel Community* deals specifically with a state's application for ECSC membership; the relevant section for adhesion reads:

> Any European State may apply to accede to this Treaty. It shall address its application to the Council, which shall act unanimously after obtaining the opinion of the High Authority; the Council shall also determine the terms of accession, likewise acting unanimously. Accession shall take effect on the day when the instrument of accession is received by the Government acting as depositary of this Treaty.[121]

In its application, the Irish government pointed out that, while it unreservedly accepted the aims of the Treaty of Paris and wanted them to be realised, it recognised that there existed the need to discuss 'problems'.[122] Of course, later the same day, 14 January 1963, in a striking coincidence, the French president gave the press conference which effectively rejected the UK's first attempt at membership of the EEC and rendered similar negotiations involving Ireland, Denmark and Norway pointless, if not null and void. As a result of this particular announcement, the Irish ambassador noted afterwards that it left those working at the ECSC High Authority 'profoundly depressed'. Obviously, de Gaulle's decision also consigned an ambiguous status to the Irish applications for Euratom and ECSC membership.[123]

Nonetheless, the ECSC membership process continued. Indeed, the Irish government was informed by a senior UK Commonwealth Relations Office official that, although the UK government was having to deal with a number of problems regarding the ECSC, it was felt that 'if they could do anything to hasten the admission of new applicants for membership such as Ireland, this might have the effect of making the obstacles to British membership a little less forbidding'. Indeed, Ireland's potential entry into the ECSC was interpreted as being of potential help to the UK in that context. Therefore, it was noted in Dublin that the UK government was prepared to 'put us in the picture' regarding its accession negotiations with the ECSC.[124] However, when the accession negotiations were subsequently suspended, the official in question quickly rescinded this suggestion of giving greater help to the Irish cause, confining this short, albeit illuminating, episode to history.[125] As a direct result of the particular situation affecting the UK, the Irish government's own position regarding ECSC membership also fell into what was described as 'suspended animation'. Indeed, in addition to the UK's own peculiar circumstances, the taoiseach had to question profoundly if Ireland could be expected to continue with its application to join the ECSC when its, quite separate, EEC application had already been deferred. As it turned out, events quickly overtook such worries and Ireland's ECSC application fell into a limbo-like state anyway.[126] What were the main implications of this affair therefore, if any, for Irish coal and steel?

Obviously, coal remained fairly unaffected as a result of the suspension of Ireland's ECSC candidature. At the same time, nevertheless, especially as other indigenous industries continued to remain unaffected by these events, it was felt that Irish Steel could hardly be expected to undergo the rigorous requirements that were necessitated by the dismantlement of protectionism all on its own. However, it was determined that the unilateral reduction in Irish tariffs of 10% obviously had to apply to Irish Steel in the same way as it applied to the rest of Irish industry.[127] Basically, the outcome of the French president's decision was that the Irish government thus determined upon a rather different, albeit complementary, course of action for Irish Steel when compared to the one originally envisaged if Ireland had taken up ECSC membership. In comparison to the ECSC, however, there was even less activity on the subject of Ireland's immediate future relationship with Euratom.

In fact, even the process of Ireland's accreditation to Euratom had originally been delayed because under the Treaties of Rome, unlike the Treaty of Paris, each of the member states had to agree separately to the opening of diplomatic relations. Subsequently, because Ireland would not then have been able to open accession negotiations simultaneously with the other applicants, it was a matter of relative concern both for the European Communities and for the UK, that is of course until de Gaulle's press conference.[128] Indeed, as Whitaker at the Department of Finance argued before this occurred, the 'important point' for Ireland in the wider context of European integration was that:

> ... [the government had] to so arrange our programme as to ensure that we will not be responsible for delaying any arrangements the Six may wish to make for the opening of talks on the institutional questions. Rather than risk that ... [it was suggested that it would have to] submit our applications even if the necessary preliminary investigations had not been completed ...[129]

Indeed, this is exactly what the Irish government set about to do and thus prepared to submit its application to Euratom under the appropriate article of the other Treaty of Rome. The *Treaty establishing the European Atomic Energy Community* (Article 205) deals specifically with the application of a state for membership. The relevant section for accession reads:

> Any European State may apply to become a member of the Community. It shall address its application to the Council, which shall act unanimously after obtaining the opinion of the Commission. The conditions of admission and the adjustments to the Treaty necessitated thereby shall be the subject of an agreement between the Member States and the applicant State. This agreement shall be submitted for ratification by all the Contracting States in accordance with their respective constitutional requirements.[130]

However, as was the case with Ireland's aspirations towards joining the ECSC, de Gaulle's veto of the UK government's application for membership of the EEC similarly left Ireland's position as regards its proposed candidacy for Euratom membership in a limbo-like state. Non-entry into the EEC meant non-entry into both Euratom and the ECSC.

Clearly, the successful nomination of the Irish ambassador to Belgium, Francis Biggar, as Ireland's Euratom chef de mission obviously did little to allay the disappointment that was being felt in failing to join the EEC; this newest appointment to the diplomatic corps was quickly and conclusively put into its proper perspective. Nonetheless, before his appointment, Biggar recommended that 'in present circumstances we may prefer to make no announcement in Dublin and to let the news come through to our newspapers from Brussels', apparently in an effort to placate public opinion over the Irish government's handling of its EEC accession. At least that way any disappointment might be tempered somewhat. This minor diplomatic triumph – in opening relations with Euratom – was duly set to be confirmed when Biggar presented his letters of credence.[131] On 2 April 1963, the Euratom Commission president, Pierre Chatenet, received the Irish representative for the diplomatic exchange to take place. It was a very minor positive note for Dublin at the beginning of a year in which dreams of EEC membership had, for the time being, to be shelved. Subsequently, Biggar reported on the 'cordial nature' of the reception he had received. Ireland's official new representative to Euratom recounted that:

> ... [the Euratom official] spoke of the Community's satisfaction at the opening of diplomatic relations with Ireland and looked forward to the time when we would become members, stressing that the Commission fully appreciated the sincerity of our desire to join the European Communities. He concluded by an assurance that, in the meantime, the Euratom Commission would be very pleased to assist the Irish Government in every way we could.

As it happened, the Euratom Commission's offer of assistance to Ireland in the field of nuclear power included access to documentation and to training facilities. It was obviously welcomed by the government and, indeed, was viewed as a valuable additional resource.[132] However, this section, which has concentrated on Ireland's true relationship in the early 1960s with these other two European Communities, still begs a basic question: what conclusions can be made about the ECSC and Euratom in relation to the much wider issue of Ireland and the concept of European integration?

It is, of course, possible to say that the ECSC and Euratom were not particularly predominant considerations for Ireland in this respect, mainly because the EEC remained of paramount importance. Indeed, in summarising the Irish government's considered views on these aforementioned organisations, the following can be stated with equanimity:

- in regard to the native Irish coal industry, it was considered that ECSC membership would not have had 'any appreciable effect' and that, as a result, the only significant factor for the government to consider was the 'sources of our coal imports';
- in relation to the indigenous Irish steel industry, the question of a steel capacity was the foremost consideration for Ireland with regard to the wider ECSC membership issue.[133]

In fact, the Committee of Departmental Secretaries supported Lemass quite strongly on the position ultimately adopted by his government on ECSC membership. It was stated that:

> ... our view is that it would not be in our interest to seek to maintain this application while our EEC application remains in suspense. The difficulties of adjustment which adherence to the ECSC would entail for the Irish steel industry are of the same order as those which adherence to the EEC would involve for Irish industry generally; it would be hazardous to believe that Irish Steel could take a greater strain of adaption than other industries. In any case, there has been a doctrine that membership of the ECSC and Euratom depends on membership of the EEC. It is noteworthy that the Euratom have already taken the initiative in suspending further negotiations with Britain, following on the break down of Britain's negotiations for entry to the EEC.[134]

Rather neatly, this leads to some remarks on the issue of nuclear energy.

As with the indigenous coal industry, the issue of an Irish nuclear power capacity was not a particularly serious consideration for the Dublin government in the context of European integration, as was made clear by the miserly manner in which Ireland considered the relative merits and value of Euratom membership. Indeed, it was noted that:

> ... membership would not appear to involve any immediate obligations ... [but, it] would enable us to participate in facilities for training of personnel in preparation for the time when we will have a nuclear power plant, and will give us access to the results of the Community's research programme and to its documentation service.

Notwithstanding the advantages of Euratom membership, when it came down to making a decision, the Irish government, which had a considerable amount to gain at a relatively low price, still prevaricated. Consequently, Ireland has never had a large-scale nuclear industry and has restricted its use of nuclear power to research purposes only. Initially, the US was also particularly keen to facilitate the Irish government with supplies of fuels and information, but no real interest was ever shown in return. Ireland's indigenous power resources had been reaching their known limits at this time but, although the production of electricity by atomic energy was of 'great interest' to the Dublin government, it was still deemed to be a very long-term consideration. It has to be said, understandably, that membership of neither the ECSC nor Euratom ever came close to attaining the significance that full EEC membership had for Ireland.[135]

Evidently, the various institutions of the European Communities and the Six were completely aware of this. The opening of diplomatic relations with the ECSC and Euratom, coupled with the ensuing applications to join these two organisations, signified a distinct lack of interest from the Irish government in these particular aspects of European integration. This attitude did not lessen in the years that followed, clearly because EEC membership was all that mattered. Indeed, this phenomenon was further illustrated by the fact that it was only in October 1966 when Ireland established a mission to the European Communities that was completely separate from its diplomatic mission in Belgium and Luxembourg. Thus, if the ECSC and Euratom were not considerations for Ireland in the integration process, this leads to a basic question central to this investigation: what were the repercussions of the French president's decision for Ireland's EEC membership application?

14 January 1963: the UK is refused entry into the EEC

At his dramatic press conference held on 14 January 1963 at the Élysée Palace in Paris, the French president, Charles de Gaulle, announced that he felt that the UK was not a suitable candidate yet for full EEC membership. This was due, he declared, to a number of factors all of which were based around the central question of whether or not the UK was able and ready to integrate itself into the EEC. Famously, de Gaulle rhetorically asked if London was prepared to accept the following conditions of entry:

- the adoption of the Common Customs Tariff;
- the yielding up of the British Commonwealth preference system;
- the modification of its agricultural system;
- the cancellation of the agreements which bound it to EFTA.

The French president thought not, mainly because the UK's position relative to the Six was very discordant. He maintained that the UK was both island-bound and maritime, insinuating that it had an enclosed mentality. Indeed, he argued that it was also tied to its markets and supply bases, sourcing in diverse countries which were often very far away. De Gaulle held that the UK employed predominantly commercial and industrial activities in its economy with very little emphasis on agriculture. Damning the UK's circumstances with faint praise, he held that its work habits and traditions were both distinctive and 'original' in the European context. In brief, de Gaulle concluded that, by its very beliefs, nature and structure, the UK was profoundly dissimilar to countries on the European continent. The French president did not actually say 'no' to the UK's application for EEC membership. Instead, he pointed out the disparities between the UK and the Six. By definition, the UK was totally different, it was 'insular and unique', while the Six were entirely complementary because, as he said, they were 'continental and economically one'.[136] Remarks such as these, coming from the mouth of the French president, were death by compliment.

It must be said that this attitude did not come as a shock to any observer. For quite some time, the signs in relation to the UK government's membership negotiations with the EEC had not been particularly good. Indeed, a few days before de Gaulle made his famous pronouncement upon the UK's candidature, the French information minister, Peyrefitte, had said that the French government was not pleased about the closeness of the ties that were operating between the UK and US governments. Meanwhile, the media and politicians in the UK had also appeared to be widely pessimistic about the prospects for a positive outcome to the talks. Of course, in Dublin, the government had already been seriously considering the possibility of such a scenario developing and, as a result, fully realised that no stronger links than some kind of bilateral trade agreement would probably be made with the EEC, chiefly due to the envisaged impact and repercussions of the various Anglo-Irish trade agreements. In these circumstances, it had been agreed within the government that, if the UK's accession talks with the EEC did not go according to plan, recourse would then have to be made as quickly as possible to its much maligned mainstay, Anglo-Irish trade relations, the perennial economic option in times of trouble.[137]

It has already been remarked that the UK government's original decision to join the EEC 'exemplified the primacy of politics over economics in Britain's post-war policy *vis-à-vis* European integration'.[138] Of course, this incentive was rather the opposite motivation to the one which propelled Ireland. In truth, the French president's main wish was to keep the EEC paralysed regarding any developments that did not fit in with his own designs for a Europe of the nation states, his *Europe des états*. Certainly, de Gaulle did not want to see economic integration leading to some type of political integration, especially one in which the 'Atlanticist' UK played a leading role and, by extension, one over which France could no longer exercise full control.[139] In March 1960, he specifically warned Harold Macmillan, the UK prime minister, that he would have to choose between the US on the one hand and Europe on the other.[140] The fact that London was not prepared to make this choice was thus the rationale for France's veto of its application. The reasons themselves were not terribly important for the Irish government, especially as it was not in a position to influence them greatly. What was going to be very significant, however, were the immediate and projected effects for Ireland of this decision by the French president.

Obviously, de Gaulle's announcement sent shockwaves through the Irish government, although there was no direct reference to Ireland's case at the press conference itself, except to say that, once the UK entered the EEC as a member, other countries in the free trade zone would wish to follow suit. Extended membership of the EEC would have changed absolutely the intrinsic nature of the Six, primarily because, in bringing their own peculiar needs to bear, a refreshed common market would by necessity have to be created to facilitate their demands. Nonetheless, although the French president's 'ambiguous' attitude towards Ireland can in part be gleaned from this episode, it must be said that it was only consistent with the attitude to the Irish quest for full membership that the French generally displayed, even if the UK's own application usually tended to overshadow all other considerations.[141] Indeed, France had made it very clear – in direct response to the EEC Council's reply of 23 October 1962 to the Irish initiative – that it did not consider the opening of negotiations as actual acknowledgement of Ireland's eligibility for membership.[142]

Although the UK government negotiations with the EEC did not break down at this specific stage, it was clearly only a matter of time before they would do so. Indeed, it was not until four days after his president's press conference that Maurice Couve de Murville, the French foreign minister, asked that the UK government's accession negotiations be suspended. As the French agriculture minister so succinctly put it:

> It is very simple. Now, with the Six, there are five hens and one cock. If you join (along with the other countries), there would perhaps be seven or eight hens. But there would be *two* cocks.[143]

By the end of the month, it was recognised that a deadlock in the negotiations process had been reached. Consequently, as with all the other applicants, those striving for either full or associate status, the door to the EEC had effectively been slammed in Ireland's face; it would have to await any new developments.[144]

The taoiseach's immediate public reaction was an interesting one and the significance of the platform that he used to deliver his response noticeably symbolic. Indeed, speaking on 16 January 1963 at the opening of a new foreign industrial plant in the west of Ireland, traditionally the country's most depressed region, Lemass declared that, while he felt that the immediate outcome of the UK government's negotiations with the EEC had now become 'doubtful' and that the ultimate form of trading arrangements in Europe was indeterminable, there was no doubting the continuing forward thrust of European states towards free trade. In his opinion, therefore, in the context of Ireland's economy, he could state that:

> Nothing has happened or is likely to happen which will alter in the least degree the urgency and scope of our preparations.

However, despite the promise of forthcoming government financial aid, the impetus was on old industries to adapt themselves to these new economic conditions, he said, as the country could not afford to carry 'passengers'. Meanwhile, new industries would have to be attracted at a rate which would continue to ensure industrial growth, both in terms of employment and output. The principal message that he was trying to deliver was centred on the fact that:

> ... whatever difficulties of adjustment we have now to resolve, the economic survival of our State would not be possible at all except within an arrangement which would facilitate the expansion of our exports. The great difference between the difficulties arising in the context of assumed E.E.C. membership, and those which we would face if we decided to remain outside, is that those we now face are capable of being removed if our efforts are adequate, while those we would face in the alternative circumstances – if we elected to remain cut-off from European markets – could not be solved at all by any means within our power.

Indeed, he maintained that – explicitly in regard to the preparations that were being made by the government for full EEC entry – nothing had fundamentally changed.[145]

In fact, perhaps as a result of the events that were unfolding in Paris, the taoiseach continued to instill a sense of optimism and urgency in Ireland. However, he also warned of the difficult period that lay ahead for Irish industry in the new conditions of free trade, but was confident that, generally speaking, indigenous industry would be able to reorganise itself and that it was thoroughly capable of diversifying and expanding to meet these new economic conditions.¹⁴⁶ Of course, the imposition of a universal 10% tariff cut on imports was meant to be part of this encouragement process, because it was realised that Irish industry would have to change in order for it to compete openly in this newly liberalised trading environment. Such a momentous development leads to a central consideration: what were the implications for Ireland of this new economic and political situation in Europe?

The wider implications of the French president's rebuff

On 24 January 1963, the taoiseach stressed that the 'tempo of events which has characterised the opening weeks of the year are merely a foretaste of what the coming months will bring'. Indeed, as far as he was concerned, Ireland was entering into 'a decisive period of human history in which the destiny of many nations will be determined for decades to come'.[147] By way of a series of speeches delivered in an effort to calm the sense of frustration and fear that was being felt around the country about Ireland's future economic position, it has to be said that Lemass appeared to be rather philosophical about the whole situation. Thus, while Joseph T. Carroll's thesis that it was capitous to protest – he holds that the government, 'although deeply disappointed at the French veto, refrained from any public criticism of the French President' – can be accepted, it is true to remark as well that the taoiseach spoke rather cautiously, although fairly unambiguously, about the Irish government's true assessment and interpretation of its relative position within the wider context of European integration. More importantly again, its understanding of the specific type of relationship that it would now have to fashion with the EEC had also been clarified.[148]

Some days later, in what can only be interpreted as a veiled censure of the position taken by the French government on the UK's bid for full EEC membership, Lemass said that:

> It may be that the original conception of the European Community, as a society of nations open to all the countries of Western Europe which accept the aims and obligations set out in the Rome Treaty, is now in question.

However, the taoiseach moderated that assertion when he went on to declare that:

> For our part we applied for membership of the E.E.C. on the basis of the Treaty of Rome and the Bonn Declaration, which we read – and which

were indeed so interpreted by the authors – as meaning that an invitation to membership of the Community was being held out, to us as to other democratic West European countries, subject only to unreserved acceptance of the political and economic aims of its founders and of the specific obligations involved.

Accordingly, while bemoaning the fact that Ireland was not in a position to 'shape or alter' the recent turn of events, Lemass also held that the 'complications' which had arisen in the negotiations process 'originated in stratospheric politics in which we play no part'. However, he continued to believe that the general atmosphere would, in all likelihood, be more positive sooner rather than later and, indeed, that progress on the EEC membership issue within the integration framework was still a strong motivating force for the Irish economy.[149]

Therefore, the taoiseach declared in a speech delivered on 29 January 1963 that it was in anticipation of this day arriving that the Irish government would continue with its policy of adjusting the economic direction of the nation away from protectionism towards freer trade. Of course, mindful of this, Ireland would have to take full account of what the UK now did as a result of its exclusion from the EEC, but at this early stage the situation remained so unclear that it was difficult for anyone to make any authoritative or clear-cut decisions as of yet. Indeed, there might have been seriously negative repercussions associated in doing so. Thus, Lemass was prepared to demonstrate that he remained upbeat about Ireland's economic future and felt that, despite the failure of the Irish government's membership negotiations with the EEC to open, the whole process had in itself been worthwhile, particularly as it was still ameliorating the redevelopment of the Irish economy. The taoiseach therefore stated that:

> It is a matter of satisfaction that nothing which we proposed to do in preparation for Common Market membership, in relation to any sector of the country's organisation, was not worth doing for its own sake and for the advantages it would confer in our economic development in any international circumstances.[150]

Protectionism had been a product of its time but had long outlived its usefulness. As a direct consequence, the government decided, according to T.K.Whitaker writing in 'From protection to free trade: the Irish experience', that it would continue to prepare for the day when free trade finally came into force and that it would endeavour to make 'the transition towards free trade in contemplation of EEC membership'.[151] Notwithstanding this stated desire, it was also true that the realities of the new trading situation were slowly emerging.

Speaking in Dáil Éireann at the beginning of February 1963, Lemass was moved to mention his government's 'deep disappointment' at the breakdown of accession negotiations and stated that he hoped that the 'deadlock' in the talks would soon be broken. Significantly, the Irish prime minister also used this occasion to proclaim that the government would continue to 'prepare and plan' for Ireland's entry into an enlarged EEC and that it was 'taking every step which will further this objective and avoiding any that might make it more difficult to attain'. Obviously, full EEC membership remained the primary objective for the Dublin government but, until that was in fact achieved, it was also indisputable that Anglo-Irish trading relations would in the meantime have to be enhanced. Indeed, Lemass said that:

> The concern of the Irish Government will be to explore the possibility of widening our export openings in Europe and elsewhere, while developing further our trade with Britain. We will be prepared to consider participating in any negotiations for collective arrangements for freer trade involving our principal trading partners. In any negotiation, whether multilateral or bilateral, it must be expected that better export opportunities for agricultural and industrial products will be obtainable only in consideration for continued reduction of protection.

Therefore, he took the opportunity to announce that, as and from 1 January 1964, there would be a further unilateral 10% tariff cut on imports and that his government's *Second programme for economic expansion* – a successor to the *Programme for economic expansion* – would have to be adapted to these changed circumstances. As a result of the French government's veto, Ireland was faced with many possible options, one more unappealing than the next, for its future foreign economic policy; entry into the EEC as a full member was no longer one of those. The remaining choices thus included associate EEC membership, participation in EFTA, and/or accession to the GATT. Ireland's actual room for manoeuvre was fairly limited however; as far as the Dublin government was concerned, upgraded bilateral trading relations with the UK remained the best – and perhaps also the only – available intermediate solution, especially until full EEC membership could be achieved, itself just a future possibility then. Thus, Lemass felt obliged to declare that:

> While we would much prefer to see our future trading arrangements with Britain as with other European countries conducted under the rules of an International Community such as EEC, if there is a need to re-negotiate our

> bilateral trading arrangements with Britain, either for a temporary period pending our common membership of EEC, or for an indefinite period, there is a possibility that it would take a different character to the present arrangement ... we must recognise that world trade is moving from the framework of bilateral agreements to that of multilateral arrangements and that the possibility of negotiating satisfactory arrangements on a purely bilateral basis with Britain or with the EEC, or any other country or any other group of countries is rapidly decreasing.

In the meantime, he stated that his government's preparations for entry into the EEC would of course continue and, indeed, that they would be intensified, primarily because it remained the principal long-term foreign economic and political option.[152]

Writing in *Seán Lemass and the making of modern Ireland*, the authors Paul Bew and Henry Patterson spoke of the 'reported ... deep pessimism in government circles' at that time. It has to be said though that Lemass was determined to continue upon this theme of tariff cuts as part of his government's wider economic strategy. Indeed, as early as one month after the infamous de Gaulle press conference, the taoiseach announced in Dáil Éireann that:

> We intend to base our policy on the assumption that circumstances will emerge which will permit the admission of the present applicant countries to the EEC. In such an event we would be faced with the obligation to eliminate tariffs on imports from the community by 1970 ... There may be a tendency for some sections of industry to adopt a 'wait-and-see' or even a complacent attitude. Some compelling discipline – some additional pressures – will be necessary.

The unilateral tariff reductions would continue until 1965, he declared, and although it was clearly foreseen that some indigenous industries would suffer harshly as a consequence, the general thread of Lemass's thinking was that Irish industry, as a whole, would be better off. The policy of trade liberalisation would continue, therefore, as indeed would preparations for Ireland's accession to the EEC by the end of the decade.[153] Meanwhile, what could Dublin do about the precarious economic situation that was facing the country?

An interesting footnote to France's exclusion of the UK as a candidate for full EEC membership was the fanciful, but briefly raised, possibility of adhesion being independently pursued by Ireland. In fact, at the beginning of February 1963, the Irish government was still officially undecided about the possibilities of it seeking full EEC membership, even though it was anticipated that the UK was going to remain outside for the immediate future. Indeed, independent Irish membership of the EEC had been seriously suggested as an option during the taoiseach's meeting with de Gaulle some time previously. Of course, as David Arter has recorded in *The politics of European integration in the twentieth century*, de Gaulle personally offered EEC membership – 'full or associate' – to the Danish prime minister, Jens-Otto Krag, in the summer of 1963. This move backfired on the French when the Danes made a 'strong declaration of solidarity' with the UK position. Notwithstanding this affirmation, the French president's real agenda was questioned, but as David Arter has added:

> Whether de Gaulle's offer was genuine or not or simply an attempt to split EFTA was ultimately less important than the fact that the Danish government's strategy was based on concurrent entry with Britain ...[154]

Obviously, more or less exactly the same considerations applied in Ireland's case. There were some encouraging signs for the government from the Commission and from five of the Six that, once the UK's impasse to membership was unblocked, other states – specifically EFTA countries – could quickly join up with it, which by implication also meant Ireland.[155]

Of course, London quickly realised that it was 'doubtful' whether Ireland would be able to get as much out of the EEC without the UK as it would stand to lose in terms of the economic advantages innate in bilateral Anglo-Irish trade. This was especially true when the CAP, which was still in the early stages of its development, was considered and also when the dismantlement of industrial tariffs was continuing apace. Therefore, separate adhesion was never a very serious prospect for the government. In truth, the likelihood of the situation was that Ireland would soon have to turn back to trade with the UK as a fundamental part of its foreign economic policy. In reality, this is exactly what happened.[156] At a meeting held between Hugh McCann, the ambassador in London, and his UK counterpart, it was pithily pointed out that although Ireland's application had not 'technically' been linked to that of the UK, it was plain to all the participants in the process that this was a 'technicality rather than any form of reality'. Therefore, despite some imprecise flirtations with the idea of associate EEC membership and even with the suggestion of Ireland joining EFTA, as well as various concrete advances that were made in relation to the question of its adhesion to the GATT, it must be said that the Irish government was much more eager to renew its bilateral discussions with its UK counterparts on their future relationship rather than going down any uncharted economic avenue.[157] So, what were the tasks that faced the Lemass government?

D.J.Maher has pointed out that the expression of economic realities took three distinct forms, which he listed as follows:

- concerns regarding the future implementation of the *Second programme for economic expansion*;
- problems in relation to Irish agriculture and industry;
- the forecasted difficulties involved in Ireland's tariff policies.

Firstly, the planned *Second programme for economic expansion* was clearly still in the early stages of its development, but it was noticeable that Lemass was eager to launch a modified version of this plan as quickly as possible, so that there would be a formal framework within which the economy could continue to grow. Indeed, a basic assumption in this belief was that Ireland would be a member of the EEC by 1970; a rather weak basis, although one which was very difficult to disavow, on which to underpin economic policy.[158]

Secondly, it was recognised that the adaption and reorganisation of Irish agriculture and industry would have to be reinforced. Once again, on the continued assumption that EEC membership could come at any time for Ireland, the Department of Agriculture had initiated its investigations into the future of this sector in August 1961, through the General Committee of Agricultural Producers mainly. In the meantime, operating on a similar basis to that of the Department of Agriculture, the Department of Industry & Commerce had been actively surveying industry in general and specific terms since the autumn of 1961, mainly through the Committee on Industrial Organisation. However, work on agricultural considerations in the context of European integration was significantly complicated by the fact that everything depended on the outcome of the CAP negotiations. Obviously, the Treaty of Rome had been much more specific in relation to the EEC's plans for industry than it had been in relation to agriculture. Regardless of what had just happened in the first weeks of 1963, the taoiseach revealed in Dáil Éireann that the surveys into agriculture and industry would continue and that the results would be acted upon immediately.[159]

Finally, there was the heated question of Ireland's future tariff policy. At this point, tariff reductions had not begun to take effect in any serious manner. It was announced that unilateral reductions, as with the further 10% reduction effective from 1 January 1964, would continue to be imposed. However, the government was in fact finding it virtually impossible to keep pace with similar efforts being orchestrated by the EEC and EFTA. Clearly, though, there was little alternative to this policy. As the taoiseach was quick to point out:

> In a world committed to the progressive lowering of barriers to international trade, there was no choice but to move in the same direction.

Thus, as time passed and as the immediate danger of the EEC imploding began to desist, the government's hopes were raised by the possibility that some interim arrangement could be worked out between Ireland and the EEC, with or without the UK's participation. It was with this in mind that an Anglo-Irish meeting was arranged for the middle of March 1963.

De Gaulle's 'no' not only ended the UK's short-term hopes of entering the EEC as a full member, but it also had a profound effect upon its domestic politics; Macmillan soon left Downing Street, to be replaced by the patrician, Alec Douglas-Home.[160] Throughout, the UK was evidently uninterested in some type of provisional agreement being concocted which would bring in association. Both sides in these bilateral talks agreed that there was little likelihood of any permanent arrangement being made as long as the French presidential incumbent remained in power or, at the very least, for some undefined years to come. Thus, instead of some sort of accommodation being reached with the EEC, it started to become progressively clearer that the immediate economic future for both countries best lay in the further strengthening of already existing bilateral relations. Obviously, although it suited the UK to do so, this policy option was becoming especially necessary for Ireland.[161]

The Irish application for full EEC membership was not suspended but it has to be said that, in the three and a half years between February 1963 and September 1966, the question went firmly onto the backburner. At one point, Lemass had to reply to the affirmative in Dáil Éireann that, indeed, Ireland still had an ambassador accredited to the EEC. In addition, it was repeated *ad nauseam* that the 'ultimate objective' of the Irish government remained full membership of the EEC.[162] Of course, that left a problem which forms the centrepiece of the next chapter: what, other than encouraging further dependence upon the UK, was Ireland supposed to do in economic terms until adhesion to the EEC was finally achieved? Indeed, did Europe have any hope of offering Ireland an escape from dependence on the UK?

Intermediate conclusions

When the Irish government had applied to join the EEC at the end of July 1961, it did so in the knowledge that it basically had a free trade relationship with the UK. In any subsequent negotiations, Ireland's continued aim would clearly be to find a way to protect the immensely important Anglo-Irish economic link, especially until both countries gained full membership. However, once the French president had firmly announced that the UK was not yet a suitable candidate, Ireland was thrown back onto dependence upon its immutable trading relationship. It had, of course, been assessed by the Irish government that there were more disadvantages than advantages in it trying to gain EEC membership independent to that of the UK. It is also fair to say that separate membership would probably not have been possible for Ireland to achieve anyway. Thus, the government had no other economic choice at this point but to turn back to the UK for economic inspiration. Indeed, de Gaulle's gesture in refuting the UK government can be perceived as the necessary prompting for the Anglo-Irish FTA agreement of December 1965, a trading arrangement which provided for the complete phasing out of Anglo-Irish industrial tariffs over a ten year period effective from July 1966. This, in turn, created the conditions demanded for Ireland's ultimate accession to the EEC. In addition, this new agreement also widened Ireland's economic horizons even further still, climaxing in the country's accession to the GATT in 1968. Of course, at the same time, Ireland's dependence upon the UK also spiralled to what in any other circumstances could very well have been seen as totally unacceptable levels.

It is possible to add, however, that the 1960s marked an enormous departure from the 1950s. In terms of industrial production, for example, there was a huge increase of over 85% in the volume of Irish industrial production in the latter period, compared to a figure of only just over 27% in the former. It has since been remarked that this 'acceleration in the growth of output ... would not have occurred in the absence of policy', adding credence to the view that it was Lemass and Whitaker who were ultimately responsible for showing the vision and for changing the direction of the national economy.[163] However, even though net industrial output in 1963 may have been 47% above its 1957 level, agriculture was still having major trouble in adapting to the new circumstances that it found were inherent in playing a full role in the process of European integration. F.S.L.Lyons, writing in *Ireland since the Famine*, has said that planning was 'evidently less effective' in relation to the former because, as he points out, net agricultural output was only 1% higher in 1963 in comparison to the corresponding figure given for 1957.[164] Adverse market conditions might not have helped the situation, a problem which the farmers felt could only be resolved by Ireland's membership of the EEC, because market size and stability would as a consequence increase.

Nevertheless, despite Ireland's growing reliance on footloose foreign-owned industries, Lemass was in a hurry to make the economy competitive in time for adhesion. As a result, although there is always a danger in looking at history in hindsight, it is also possible to say, as T.K.Whitaker has when assessing the implications of de Gaulle's veto of the UK, that this delay in Ireland's accession to the EEC was beneficial to the economy in the long run and, certainly, that it acted as a catalyst for later membership applications. He wrote:

> In retrospect, one can scarcely doubt the economic advantage to Ireland of the time gained through the reluctance of France (at least) to see Great Britain in the EEC, of the surveys and adaption measures taken in the nineteen sixties, and of the experience provided by the tariff reductions of 1963 and 1964 and under the AIFTA.[165]

The French president's decision was not a disaster for Ireland, certainly not in the respect that its exclusion and the UK's inclusion would have been. Efforts to change the economy were in the country's own best interests anyway; Ireland had moved from its position in the 1950s of 'restless discontent' to one where it was finally 'getting out of the desert'. EFTA, which did not appear to have tangible economic advantages for Ireland, was emphatically replaced by the EEC as its preferred economic option, the latter having the combined advantages of strong protective support for agriculture, a ready and challenging market for industry, and a greater feeling of exercising 'political independence'.[166] In real terms, EFTA possessed none of these qualities, but the EEC certainly did. The Irish government's aim of achieving 'economic independence' from the UK was made achievable by remarkable developments in its foreign economic policy, such as its reorientation towards and preparation for full membership of the EEC.

Although this is a relatively contemporary view of the motivations behind seeking EEC membership, it is also an opinion which is significantly close to the basic reality given in any assessment that is made on the value of its integration policy. Ireland's economic dependence upon the UK stopped it from having any independent chance of admission to the EEC in 1963; indeed, the 'Catch-22' position in which it found itself economically gave it no other intermediate alternative except to turn back to the UK. As a US journalist, who was not necessarily atypical of informed commentators, was inspired to write:

> Ireland has applied for membership in the Common Market but she is not pressing it. France's veto of England has complicated the Irish position. Great trading problems would be raised for Ireland if she were in the Common Market while England was denied equal membership. Until the

British relationship with the Common Market is settled, Ireland prefers to have her own application rest, without actually withdrawing it ... the government and people of Ireland are too acutely aware of their economic dependence on the British market to endanger this association by premature membership in the Common Market.[167]

While the situation may not have been so dramatic and even if little concept of the actual repercussions of this situation were as yet evident in Irish government thinking, the basic foundations of the Anglo-Irish FTA agreement had been laid. At the same time, integration was evolving as well, in areas other than economics or politics – such as social policy, for instance – which would profoundly affect Ireland in the future, once it became a member; the EEC that Ireland tried to join in 1961 was changing just as the latter was trying to adapt itself to the new economic conditions.[168]

5 The 1965 Anglo-Irish FTA agreement

Background to the AIFTA

Principally due to its failure to exact entry into the EEC in 1963, the Irish government quickly set about enhancing the country's trading position with its crucial UK markets, as well as its bilateral relations with other states. However, once Anglo-Irish discussions got under way, it was clear that Ireland favoured the idea of an FTA with the UK rather than just enhancing bilateral agreements of old. There was a simple interlinked set of motivations behind this decision. An FTA was chosen primarily because it was seen as a viable intermediate step in preparations for its ultimate aim, achieving a position of full European economic integration, but also because it would solve a more immediate economic problem as well, keeping Ireland a feasible trading entity. Apart from considerations about the future, an innovative free trade area arrangement solved an immediate problem, because of the UK's overwhelming importance to its economic position, providing a concrete and fresh impetus for plans held by Dublin. Additionally, it marked a tenable step in Ireland's actual – rather than heretofore provisional – course of European integration. The 1965 Anglo-Irish FTA (AIFTA) agreement was in fact a means to an end, not necessarily an end in itself, as was made readily apparent at the time of these bilateral talks. Thus, the main reason behind negotiating an AIFTA, as far as Dublin was concerned, was to facilitate Ireland's full membership of the EEC when that became possible, although these changes were worth implementing in their own right too. These new trading arrangements with the UK were in no way intended to impede that ambition; rather, they were wholly intended to expedite it.[1]

The creation of the AIFTA was 'indubitable and significant' evidence that the UK and Ireland had finally realised that they had 'common interests' which needed to be nurtured if they were to 'combine their efforts in entering Brussels'. As the ground-breaking historian T.D.Williams has written regarding Ireland in the mid-1960s, the 'EEC was beginning to play an ever increasing role in the actual shaping of policy'; in combining the prospects of

EEC membership to continually improving Anglo-Irish relations, whether in regard to agriculture or to Northern Ireland, mutual self-interest meant that the AIFTA was a logical step to take. It was clear that a 'new era of co-operation in economic and ... political collaboration' was at hand.[2] Nonetheless, some background information regarding the AIFTA agreement is also needed in order to put this bilateral development into its proper historical context and also to demonstrate how it related to Ireland's evolving European integration policy.

In the immediate aftermath of de Gaulle's rejection of the UK bid for full EEC membership, the Departments of Agriculture, Finance, and Industry & Commerce began receiving a flood of reports on the state of Irish agriculture and industry. Indeed, the CIO was able to furnish four interim papers, all of them accepted by the government, on the following:

- the rate of adaption of marketing;
- joint export marketing;
- the provision of adaption facilities;
- industrial grants.

Five other reports on separate industrial groups – 'the cotton, linen and rayon industry, the leather footwear industry, the paper and cardboard industry, the motor assemble industry, and the fertiliser industry' – had already been published and further papers – on industries including glassware, iron and steel, pottery, sugar, and wearing apparel – were expected. In parallel, other study groups – made up of government departments, processors, producers, and trade unions – were investigating agriculture, although it was rather difficult for them to proffer sound advice quickly because the CAP had not yet been clearly defined. These areas in Irish agriculture included:

- cereals and cereal products;
- milk and milk products;
- cattle and beef, sheep and mutton;
- pigs and pigmeat;
- poultry and eggs;
- fruit and vegetables.

The first four of these reports were being supplemented by separate surveys being carried out independently by the Department of Agriculture itself. Thus, with these reports and surveys starting to come on line, it is obvious that the Irish government was searching for ways to reorganise agricultural and industrial production so that Irish products might compete with foreign goods, both at home and abroad.[3]

It must be said that Dublin tried various means to improve external trade relations, not all of them restricted to deals made with London. In mid-1964, for instance, eighteen months after France's veto and humiliation of the UK, a serious attempt was launched to rehabilitate delicate Franco-Irish relations when Maurice Couve de Murville, the French foreign minister, paid a visit to Ireland. Frances Nicholson & Roger East, who have gone to some lengths to record the various developments which led from Ireland's application for EEC membership to its eventual accession, have recounted that, following the breakdown of the UK's entry negotiations, 'Ireland retained good relations with the EEC governments and, in particular, with France'. During his trip between 11-12 June 1964, de Murville met with de Valera and, more importantly of course, also had talks with Lemass and Aiken. A joint communiqué issued on 13 June 1964, marking the conclusion of the French foreign minister's visit, dealt with the 'close review' of bilateral economic relations that had just taken place. In their resulting declaration, Aiken and de Murville 'noted with satisfaction that trade had more than doubled since 1961 and that this growth was taking place in both directions'; indeed, they hoped that bilateral trade – 'balanced in so far as may be possible in the mutual interest of both countries' – would increase further still. Through this statement, evidence of deepening bilateral cooperation was afforded by the two foreign ministers, thus highlighting French participation – ongoing for nearly a decade – in Ireland's economic progress; indeed, the value of investment in the economy originating from France was underscored.[4]

Among the topics discussed by de Murville with his Irish counterparts were relations between the latter and the EEC, a fact that he reported some days later to his colleagues in the French cabinet. At this cabinet meeting, the French foreign minister 'noted that the Irish government wished to find a formula for rapprochement with the EEC', that he had 'verified the Irish government's interest in developing its ties with Europe in whatever form might be possible', and that he had himself 'given an assurance that France was favourable to such a rapprochement and to the development and forging of links between Ireland and the Common Market'. The other announcement of note from this visit was that bilateral trade talks would open in Dublin on 6 July 1964; these then continued for four days. This successful summit culminated in an official announcement which declared that an already existing Franco-Irish agreement would continue 'with provision for increased import facilities in respect of certain products'. It also stated that French investment in Irish industry would be increased and there was also the additional possibility that arrangements to stimulate the growing tourist traffic between the two countries would be discussed and increased.[5]

The previous month's joint communiqué had been a masterful example of diplomatic platitudes entwined with clichés, although at least it demonstrated that bilateral Franco-Irish relations were functioning again. Besides references to bilateral economic relations, however, the rest of the communiqué appears to have been rather banal, citing close historical ties while making reference to a future cultural agreement; still, these meetings also marked progress in relations that could do Ireland's chances of acceding to the EEC no harm in the long run. Although by no means a useless exercise, such diplomatic niceties essentially ignored the realities of Ireland's precarious economic position, however.[6] On more than one occasion, the Irish foreign minister emphasised the importance of export trade and tourism, especially the role that Irish diplomats had to play with regard to these activities.[7] It was obvious that, if Ireland was ever going to make any substantial progress in its external trading position, its biggest obstacle needed to be addressed first; this meant that Anglo-Irish relations came back onto the top of the Dublin government's negotiations agenda.

On 5 November 1964, the taoiseach, Seán Lemass, met Harold Wilson, the newly elected UK prime minister; the possibility of holding discussions which would centred on the prospects of improving the future permanent trading arrangements between the two countries began to be deliberated in earnest.[8] This rendezvous marked the first significant move in a rapid series of bilateral discussions, meetings and negotiations. Indeed, this process quickly led to the signing of an Anglo-Irish FTA agreement in December 1965 and to its enactment by the middle of the following year. Of course, this momentous bilateral trade development must be viewed here within the even wider context of Irish and UK relations with the EEC. Nevertheless, the fact that Ireland actually had no ministerial contact with Brussels throughout the whole of 1964 itself suggests that, apart from the internal problems within the EEC and between the Six themselves, the Irish government had gradually came to the conclusion that the only realistic way forward for Ireland in the realm of external economic growth was going to have to come from self-initiative. In conjunction with this bilateral economic innovation, Ireland would also have to make a determined effort to fashion its candidacy for the EEC as a feasible and attractive proposition, both at home and abroad, while making completely sure that its European ambitions were not subsumed by reinforced Anglo-Irish relations.

In fact, throughout this period in time, the Irish government consistently signalled its willingness to consider all of the various economic options open to it, both in regard to full EEC membership and to Anglo-Irish trade relations; one of the additional possibilities that was not ruled out was interim associate EEC membership. Indeed, every tenable relationship was thoroughly debated. On 11 November 1964, the taoiseach declared in Dáil Éireann that:

> Even if full membership of the Common Market is not immediately

practicable we would be very interested in any arrangement with [the] EEC which would reinforce our status as an applicant country and ... imply the willingness of the Community to complete the process of negotiation with us without delay when this course is desired by us.[9]

Thus, the question of association was finally introduced into the economic debate as a viable policy option, but only if it swiftly led to full EEC membership. However, in the aftermath of de Gaulle's refusal to consider seriously Ireland's application for full membership, it was becoming increasingly obvious in the eyes of the government that the first and most important intermediate step that would have to be taken to achieve this aim would be a consolidation of the existing Anglo-Irish economic relationship. Before moving on to analyse this bilateral renovation of Ireland's economy, it has also proven necessary to investigate the government's relationship with the EEC in the period which subsequently followed the French president's calamitous and categorical decision to exclude the UK.

Understandably, Ireland's official position on the European integration process is best summarised perhaps by the taoiseach himself. In early January 1965, he delivered an address to the NFA – the main agricultural lobbying group in Ireland – which specifically referred to the situation pertaining in Europe and encapsulated recent developments. Alluding to remarks made on behalf of this farming organisation in which Lemass's government was accused of 'vacillating' on the EEC membership question, the taoiseach replied to these accusations by stating that there had been very few advances in the previous year simply as a consequence of the uncertainty surrounding the new UK government's position. It may have appeared that Ireland was in a position to act alone on the European integration issue, without a complete knowledge of or full regard to the UK position, but this was positively not the case, according to Lemass. In his opinion, such well-meant sentiments did not in any way reflect the realities of the predicament in which the country found itself. The Irish prime minister then went on to reveal to the NFA that:

> We did not think of 1964 as the year for decision in these matters, and neither apparently did anyone else. We do not regard it as vacillating to decide not to run headlong into a fog.

He declared that it was only sensible for his government to take such an irrevocable decision when it knew exactly what the EEC and the UK were actually going to do. Thus, he felt able to insist: 'We took a very firm decision to this effect and there was no vacillation about it'. Indeed, Lemass added that Ireland would not itself be rushing – or would not be rushed – into coming to any conclusions just yet because, as the taoiseach warily pointed out, 'there should be no misunderstanding of how final a decision it would have to be'.[10]

At this stage in his speech to the NFA in January 1965, as he tended to do on all such public occasions, the taoiseach used the opportunity to state clearly his government's position on the European integration process. It is worth emphasising here because it acts as a fitting reintroduction to the continuing debate as to how the country must proceed. Indeed, fearing no contradiction, he asserted that:

> We are an applicant country for E.E.C. membership. There is nobody who can have any doubt about our desire to obtain membership or misunderstand our position in any serious degree. We will reactivate our application when, after a cold, calm and comprehensive calculation of all the facts and probabilities, we see that our national advantage will be served thereby. That calculation cannot yet be made with any confidence, and we have no intention of making it until that is possible.

As the taoiseach said himself, a restatement of the government's policy on EEC membership from time to time could do no 'national harm'.[11] Nevertheless, on the question of European integration, one critical consideration still played a pivotal role within any forecasted course of action; put simply, that factor was London's attitude and where, in turn, Ireland then stood on whatever matter was at hand.

The election of a new Labour government in the UK in October 1964 had complicated the membership issue though, while at the same time promising fresh possibilities. However, a major set-back for the Irish government occurred on 27 October 1964 with the subsequent adoption by London of what D.J.Maher terms a 'package of measures to correct the serious deterioration in the British balance of payments', before adding: 'Prominent among these measures was a temporary 15 per cent surcharge on the value of all imports of manufactured goods'. For the Dublin government, two concerns predominated as a consequence of these changes. These modifications in UK import policy had effects which can be listed as follows:

- previous bilateral trade arrangements were subsequently negated;
- Irish exports were being particularly badly hit because of the products which were being targeted by this policy revision.

These two changes had an instant adverse impact upon bilateral trade practices. Firstly, this tax was an infringement upon the Anglo-Irish trade agreement of 1938 because it put a price on the entry – heretofore guaranteed as duty-free – of Irish industrial goods, practically all of which went to the UK marketplace. This obviously came as a 'severe blow', knocking much of the recently acquired confidence out of the industrial sector for its future well-being. Such a reaction was understandable because this sector regarded Ireland's established free access to the UK market as the 'corner stone' of its present economic policies and, indeed, figured heavily in its plans for prospective development thereafter.[12]

As D.J.Maher explained, there was a second set of repercussions, the statistics for which represent the severe outlook facing Irish industry for as long as the UK surcharge on imports endured. He wrote that:

> ... while the surcharge was in principle non-discriminatory, it bore most heavily on Irish exports. Irish exports to the United Kingdom of the goods liable to surcharge (valued at £45 million in the year to August 1964) represented about 21 per cent of Ireland's total exports to all destinations. This percentage was by far the highest known for any country affected. The comparable figure for the EFTA was 5 per cent; for the EEC 5 per cent; for the British Commonwealth 2½ per cent; and for the USA 2½ per cent.[13]

The plans for remedying Ireland's economic position were, of course, thrown into complete disarray as a consequence of this UK initiative. If Ireland could not rely upon the UK, there was clearly no other country or organisation to which it could easily turn, precisely illustrating the reason why it was seeking an alternative economic orientation. It was another reason why Ireland was prepared to swop dependence on the UK for interdependence with the EEC.

It was with issues like these in mind that the taoiseach unambiguously stated that the ongoing Anglo-Irish trade talks had to be his government's single-most important foreign policy priority. In fact, this particular consideration came well ahead of any other, certainly before it could readily contemplate any alternative economic ventures, whether it be EFTA, the GATT or even the EEC, full or associate status. Regardless of this radical redirection in Ireland's orientation – temporary, it was hoped – and even though it could not be said that the new year promised that the economic impasse with the UK or in Europe could be cleared up to the satisfaction of any or all of those taking part – in fact, it was held that this eventuality did not appear to be very likely at all – it was still strongly felt that there was plenty that the Irish government could do in the meantime in order to ready agriculture and industry for the vagaries of the future, wherever that might lead.[14] In asking what could have led to such a situation in which the UK suddenly appeared at the only alternative, a stark prospect arose: what else was Ireland supposed to do next to alleviate its position?

The renewal of ministerial contacts with the EEC

The Irish agriculture minister, Charles Haughey, duly paid a visit to Brussels in January 1965, both in an effort to sell what were the beginnings of a new Anglo-Irish plan to the EEC and in order to consolidate Ireland's own relationship with the Six.[15] Of course, the importance of these contacts in the history of Irish relations with the EEC should not be underestimated. Indeed, it has to be pointed out that the series of meetings that followed – convened in an effort to exchange information on the latest Irish and European situations with the foreign relations commissioner, Jean Rey, and with Sicco Mansholt, the agriculture commissioner – were the first contacts at ministerial level between Ireland and the EEC since November 1963; well over a year had elapsed since then, 1964 having been totally lost.[16] That a deterioration in relations of this magnitude could have been allowed to occur was inexcusable, especially for a government which was apparently prioritising such links; at least it demonstrates the extent of the disappointment and malaise caused by de Gaulle's rejection of the UK.

The meeting between Haughey and Rey took place on 26 January 1965, opening with an articulate statement by the Irish agriculture minister in which he meticulously underlined Ireland's continued interest in obtaining full EEC membership as soon as it was practicable. In reply to Haughey, the EEC commissioner acknowledged the latter's position and remarked that its enterprise remained 'undamaged' by the events which had led to the suspension of its membership negotiations. The minister was at pains to point out that the *Second programme for economic expansion* envisaged full EEC membership by 1970 and thus enquired whether there had been any new thinking in Brussels regarding Ireland's application, indeed if there had been any developments since the negotiations were suspended which were relevant. Rey took this opportunity to allude gently to the ongoing associate membership negotiations with Austria as perhaps being of particular interest to Ireland – as a precedent, he maintained – but reiterated that it was worthless for the EEC to resume negotiations with the UK government as long as the political issues involved in their initial collapse – such as defence – endured as bitter points of disagreement. Yet, it was clearly recognised that, in the event of ameliorated circumstances encompassing such considerations, the extension of full EEC membership might become a much more reasonable expectation and that it could then take effect rather quickly.[17] It was quite appropriate in these circumstances for Haughey to ask: what could the Irish be expected to do economically or politically to help themselves?

The foreign affairs commissioner thus informed the Irish delegation that the foremost difficulties between the UK and the EEC remained political considerations and that there was very little that Ireland could actually do in this regard. Indeed, an Irish diplomatic report on this meeting summarised his view as having been that:

> If the Irish Government decided to approach the Community with a request

to re-open negotiations for membership, he thought that no one would take the responsibility of refusing to talk to us.

In spite of this apparent relaxation in the EEC position, Rey further added that, until the Six themselves were totally at one in relation to the future organisation of Europe, it would be rather premature and by implication quite damaging for Ireland to take concrete steps. He understood that the Irish government desired membership at as early a date as was feasibly possible and tried to be reassuring on the point that the EEC fully appreciated both Ireland's inherent interest in the UK market and its understandable pursuit of European integration.[18] This only raised another question: if this latter route was closed off to the Irish government, where could discussions on any future relationship with the EEC have been expected to have gone from there without the UK also taking part?

At this point, the Irish ambassador to the EEC, Francis Biggar, specifically referred to the Austrian government's argument for membership, an approach which was discerned as a 'test case' by all concerned. Despite having to face accusations from farmers organisations and federalists that the Dublin government was dragging its feet, in addition to claims from journalists that an interim arrangement with the EEC could actually be concluded without too much difficulty, Rey assured the Irish deputation that, although the EEC Commission was not awaiting a move from Ireland, equally it was not expected to have to wait for many years to elapse before joining. Indeed, according to the foreign affairs commissioner, its ultimate accession to the EEC by the end of the decade remained a reasonable working assumption. Nonetheless, as a member of the EEC's delegation pointed out during this ministerial meeting, it was actually with the 'harmonisation' aspects of European integration, economic rather than political, that Ireland's real difficulties lay. Thus, its problems were completely different to those of Austria. Two dominant reasons were cited:

- Ireland's abiding interest in the UK market;
- the supposition of its ability to become a full member.

The government was obviously looking for Ireland to become a full member of the EEC for economic reasons but, at the same time, it was restated that it was totally prepared to accept the concomitant political obligations by working towards European political unity. It was at this stage in the bilateral discussions between Haughey and Rey that the possibility of an 'interim status for an applicant country' was timidly broached by the agriculture minister.[19] Thus, the prospect of associate EEC membership being adopted as the means to another end – full membership – a policy championed by the EEC as being more appropriate for Ireland, had finally been raised by a senior Irish government official at the European level, even if only informally and tentatively.

As was pointed out at the time of this meeting, both Greece and Turkey had already concluded association agreements with the EEC. However, what the Irish delegation actually had in mind has not been so easy to discern subsequently. Indeed, it was even asked of the EEC Commission delegation at that stage what should Ireland in fact be doing 'to promote our case either for full membership, association or an item by item agreement'. Thus, the full extent of options was laid out for informal discussion. However, the possibility of the Irish government making special arrangements with the EEC for agreement on individual items – primarily agricultural, *à la* Denmark – was met with a meaningless answer from Rey, mainly because he does not seem to have been in a position to reply unequivocally without reference back to the EEC. Nonetheless, it does appear that the Irish delegation was only probing for reactions to these suggestions and that it certainly did not want such questions to be raised at EEC Council level just yet, fearing that they would be lent credibility and legitimised as equally favoured options. Of course, as Rey asserted, the conclusion of any new commercial agreement would need the go-ahead of the EEC and the Six. Indeed, in response to concerns expressed on the matter, the commissioner pointed out that the Danish government's existing cattle arrangements with West Germany – due to conclude by the end of 1965 but which were clearly of very great interest to the Irish deputation in general, principally J.C. Nagle, the Irish agriculture secretary – merely exemplified the EEC honouring existing agreements, nothing more.[20] Evidently, the Irish had good reason to doubt the verity of this argument, rightly fearing that such agreements might be reviewed or revamped to its disadvantage.

At this stage in the discussions, it was established by the Irish delegation that the EEC Commission was not making any link between the various proposed membership applications. Indeed, although there was no doubt but that the EEC would eventually be extended, it was still impossible to say exactly when. However, even if only from the practical point of view, it was clarified that it was not envisaged that Irish or Danish negotiations with the EEC could be resumed until a certain stage had been reached in any deliberations between the UK and the Six. European economic realities would obviously take precedence before less meaningful membership aspirations of the minor powers. In response to Haughey's contention that they might perhaps be able to do something in the meantime regarding membership – full, associate or commodity by commodity arrangements – Rey said that there was 'nothing specific' in his personal view at that point which Ireland should have then been doing to facilitate any or all of these developments. A 'wait-and-see' policy appears to have been the one which was most strongly being advocated. By Ireland taking an equivocal position, events in Europe would take their own course, the UK might decide to apply for membership at the appropriate time, and then the other states seeking to join could enter into the equation. However, forcing the issue would probably only lead to a negative and quite possibly retrogressive outcome. These discussions with Rey, remarked upon by the Irish as having been 'characterised by a note of cordial frankness', duly came to a conclusion with nothing innovative or tangible having been decided.[21] This was exactly what the Commission wanted most.

The very next evening, 27 January 1965, at a dinner given by Mansholt in honour of the Irish agriculture minister, direct reference was once again made to the potential form of a prospective link being made between Ireland and the EEC. Regardless of what Ireland did, it was felt that the collapse of the UK's own negotiations and the lack of any direction from the new Labour government meant that certain difficulties were created for all the applicants. However, according to the commissioner, who was said to be speculating out loud, there was no 'absolute barrier' to a resumption of negotiations between Ireland and the EEC, including the vague possibility of an interim arrangement being envisioned which would fully take the Anglo-Irish relationship into consideration.[22] Clarity regarding these proposals was notable though by its very absence. Ireland could not join as a full member without the UK; thus this alternative was a non-starter. Options were then limited because, on the one hand, the EEC did not want a line-by-line agreement and, on the other, Ireland was not keen at the thought of association even if that was being actively considered. Once more, the Irish were informed that the EEC Commission recognised that Ireland had been prevented from entering the EEC in 1963 by events which were outside of its control, which was somewhat reassuring. As a result, the minister categorically restated his government's desire to enter the EEC as a full member as soon as circumstances made that at all possible. In fact, Haughey quickly added that this ambition to join was not based solely on 'material grounds', but that Ireland wanted to become a member of the EEC because of what he indeterminately called the 'historical and sentimental associations that attached us to Europe'.[23] Undoubtedly, Dublin was not going to be found lacking in the political rhetoric stakes a second time around.

Of most obvious concern to the Irish delegation was the subject of EEC developments on the agriculture issue, in which it was noted by the commissioner that the main decisions in this area were then being taken on a day-to-day basis in Brussels rather than in the national capitals. This had major implications for future participants, as Mansholt held that the EEC could not be confined forever to the Six and that, when the economic realities of the situation were finally confronted, the UK government would sooner or later be forced to adhere. When this eventually happened, however, the agriculture commissioner held that the UK government would find itself in the position of gladly taking what would then be on offer by the EEC. Indeed, further indignity would be heaped on the UK because there would be no possibility of the issues which were then being decided in their absence being reopened at a later stage. Importantly in Ireland's case, the commissioner also let it be known that, for instance, with regard to agriculture, it was felt to be easier to negotiate full membership rather than associate status. As a consequence, Dublin was confronted with a dilemma of significant proportions with respect to the immediate future. Nevertheless, the fact of the matter was that the Labour government in the UK was not apparently troubled at that point in time over concerns such as its part in the European integration process. Therefore, the main implication for the Lemass government, as long as London remained disinterested, was that there was no possibility of an agreement of any substantive nature being accorded between Ireland and the EEC.[24] Dublin was constantly being confronted with having to find a different escape route away from its economic reliance problems. Even still, although this option now appeared to be closed, the question of a new relationship with the EEC being formed rumbled on into the spring of 1965. At least, the Irish government appeared to realise that continued contact with Brussels could only be beneficial in the long-run and so did not unconsciously ignore their European ambitions as they had done following France's veto two years previously. The EEC remained to be convinced of Ireland's merits but was open to persuasion.

The Irish agriculture minister continued his European tour, with West Germany his next port of call after Brussels. Obviously, this strategy of forging contacts with the EEC and with the Six was concurrently undertaken by other Irish government ministers; for instance, the Irish industry & commerce minister, Jack Lynch, met a senior West German government official who was reported to have given 'every assurance' of his country's continued goodwill towards Ireland's application for full EEC membership.[25] The agriculture minister's trip was still attracting the biggest headlines. In a meeting with his West German counterpart, Haughey made it 'clear that the German market for meat was, and would continue to be, of considerable importance to Ireland'. The bilateral agricultural trade deal still existing between Denmark and West Germany remained a sore point for the Dublin government, especially as the Irish were not themselves in a position to strike a similar deal on an item by item basis squarely because of the common external trade policy that was operated by the Six. Indeed, the Irish agriculture minister felt that all he could do in return was to reiterate to the West Germans his government's position, obviously that:

> ... Ireland's application for full membership still stood, and it was the desire of his Government and people that Ireland should become a member of the Community as soon as circumstances made it practicable to do so.

In reply, the West German agriculture, forestry & food minister articulated – in this meeting of 31 January 1965 which was not surprisingly reported as 'cordial' and 'friendly' – that his government was still endeavouring for an enlarged EEC, one which would include Denmark, Ireland and the UK.[26] In essence, the Irish application for full membership was clearly no further forward and concerns about the Danes receiving preferential treatment persisted.

It was only on the agriculture minister's return to Ireland though that some controversy arose, ironically because of a platitude that he delivered on a question relating to European integration in lieu of substantial analysis or comment. In fact, Haughey had only restated that the Irish government's 'position remains that we still desire full membership of the Common Market as soon as that is practicable'.[27] Notwithstanding this apparently reasonable stance, the *Irish Independent* accurately commented that, while this policy was unchanged, in line with other members of the government, the agriculture minister's glib answer on the European integration issue:

> ... is the cliché that we are interested in full membership. There has been too much of this stonewalling. It is an empty, meaningless answer. Most would agree that we cannot join the Common Market as a full member without Britain. The real point is whether we should move ahead and seek a form of association as an interim step.[28]

Several Irish newspapers had previously carried reports that, while in Brussels, Haughey had indicated that, if encouraged, Ireland might feel inclined to seek associate EEC membership pending full admission. In Dublin, however, Lemass decided not to contradict these rumours, primarily because they received so little attention at home and abroad, but also because they were not so out of line with a statement which had been delivered in Dáil Éireann only a few months previously by the taoiseach himself.[29] Although fully cognisant with the advantages and disadvantages of this lesser membership status, it is clear that the government was actively reconsidering its feasibility as an interim step towards full EEC membership, but was also weighing it up against another – this time hardly unsurprising – consideration.

Nonetheless, what was happening to the political debate in Ireland was very significant in the development of a coherent Irish government policy towards European integration. The principal implication of what Lemass and Haughey were saying, of course, was that full EEC membership was no longer seen as *sine qua non* and that Ireland might in fact be willing to accept a lesser status. In reality, associate EEC membership had furtively, albeit seriously, reentered the equation as a optional, if still intermediate, answer to Ireland's ever expanding economic needs. Nevertheless, this new relationship would have to be balanced against the considerable benefits of stronger bilateral links with the UK, which was viewed as the second plausible interim step for it to choose; the policy choice was clear, but it was no secret which one was favoured between associate EEC status and closer Anglo-Irish ties. The scene was still set for a serious debate to take place on the issues and implications involved in choosing between associate membership or augmented bilateral relations, even if these discussions were largely conducted within the confines of the Irish government.

Associate EEC membership versus enhanced Anglo-Irish links

Some days after his return from Europe, in a speech delivered in Dáil Éireann, the agriculture minister presented his report. Once more, Haughey restated that Ireland's application for full EEC membership still stood and that it was still the express intention of the Irish government to proceed with its candidacy at the earliest appropriate moment. Indeed, the minister made a particular point of adding the assertion that Ireland's desire was to achieve membership as soon as that was practicable.[30] The internal debate within the Irish government had by now moved on from there to include other possibilities, which basically amounted to ascertaining whether a formal link with Europe might be forged, the UK's participation withstanding or not, or if it might be better to concentrate mainly on enriching relations with the UK. Thus, the issue of obtaining associate EEC membership, as an interim step before full membership might be achieved, was being soberly considered for the first time. EFTA was always in the background as a further option, of course, as was the prospect of adhering to the GATT, but the argument usually just came back to deciding on how Anglo-Irish relations might work in the context of the EEC to Ireland' best advantage. Of course, the instinctive choice would have been to stick with the UK but, nevertheless, other possibilities for the way forward were also being mentioned by Lemass as the debate over Ireland's economic future gathered pace.

In an address delivered in early February 1965, he stated that, although it doubtlessly needed to reduce the scale of its dependence on the UK market for exports – indeed, that the country obviously had 'too many eggs in that basket' – the realities of the troubled economic situation that it was facing meant that a more innovative approach would have to be taken on the issue. Lemass decided therefore to outline categorically that:

> The facts of geography, and many other facts as well, determine that trade with Britain will always be of predominant interest to us, and for that reason we would wish to put our trade relations with Britain on a secure and permanent basis, preferably by reason of membership of E.E.C. by both

countries, but until that is practicable, by a revision and strengthening of our bilateral trade agreements.[31]

The direct implication of the taoiseach's speech was that Anglo-Irish ties might first have to be strengthened before they could be loosened; implicit, however, was his conviction that the search for new markets would have to be redoubled, that older links – especially with the likes of France and West Germany, as well as with the US – would have to be cultivated, and that the vaguely understood concept of 'innovative means' would have to be reconsidered afresh. The public and private debate on the future of the economy had dragged on, especially within the context of the EEC membership 'escape-route' having been cut off, and thus set the stage for a much needed rethink in the policy tack of the Irish government. The answer to a very elementary question needed to be determined: in which direction exactly would this shift in foreign economic strategy go and what was to be the substance of this change?

Throughout this period, full membership of what was considered both a 'great and historic' development remained the Irish government's foreign policy priority. Indeed, according to Lemass, although the impediments forcing Ireland's delayed EEC participation persisted and even if they were expected to continue to do so for another year at least, the Irish government would then proceed without delay to 'secure the advantages and accept the obligations of membership'. In fact, he proclaimed that there was no reason to modify his estimate that this full status would be achieved by the end of the decade.[32] According to reliable and regular diplomatic reports emanating from Europe, however, this evaluation of the situation was quickly becoming rather untenable. Accounts from the Netherlands stated, for instance, that its government thought that the UK and/or other countries entrance into the EEC – that is Denmark, Ireland and/or Norway – would still take several years with no date for accession specified, even if their full membership remained both 'desirable and envisaged' according to The Hague. The Dutch were concerned with the lack of movement from the UK government on the membership question, but it was not Dutch policy – or indeed that of the other member states – to try and persuade Ireland, Denmark and/or Norway to join the EEC without them.[33] Even if it complicated the associate membership issue, another option was always available to Ireland of course, that is stronger bilateral links with the UK.

Regardless of other considerations, desires or needs, the truth of the economic situation was that the UK remained of profound importance to Ireland, even with the 15% surcharge that had been introduced and which continued to be imposed on all products – including Irish goods – being sent there. Was there more to Irish foreign economic policy than better trade relations with the UK? As the taoiseach made readily apparent:

> Irrespective of how our present trade discussions with Britain may work out, the drive to open up new markets for our industrial and agricultural products in Europe, North America, and throughout the rest of the world is most important ... This drive to find alternative market outlets must not be thought of merely as a temporary necessity forced on us by the British surcharge, which will cease when the surcharge is removed. We must think of it as much more important and permanent. We must train ourselves to look around the whole world for possible outlets for our exports, and to neglect no possibilities of doing business in any part of it, understanding that in diversity there is safety, and with growing confidence in our capacity to design and produce goods which can be sold in most markets.

As he concluded, Ireland had a lot to learn from the new economic conditions with which it was being confronted, both from its mistakes as well as from its successes, but he emphasised that lasting benefits to the Irish economy would in fact accrue from such experiences.[34] This view might appear in some ways naive, especially when constituent sectors of the economy, including areas such as foreign-controlled export-oriented industries, were finding it harder to compete on the UK and international markets, but the country had to be able to operate in such difficult times if it was going to be competitive and if it wanted to make an acceptable impact when conditions were more suitable. Otherwise, how would these industries compete whenever the next negative cycle occurred, as it most certainly must.

At the same time, the Irish external affairs secretary, Hugh McCann, felt inclined to reappraise his counterpart, T.K.Whitaker, at the Department of Finance with a point of view to which they were both exceedingly familiar. He wrote declaring that:

> ... our objective was, and still is, full membership of the EEC with Britain also as a member. We appreciated the circumstances which had delayed this desired eventuality. In the meantime, we wish to push ahead with our plans for economic expansion. Economic growth requires increased outlets for our exports. We are anxious to explore all such possibilities, in the interim period, without departing from our ultimate objective of membership of the Common Market. We wish to know whether there is a possibility of any form of interim arrangement with the EEC which would meet with the approval of the EEC and still safeguard our important trading interests in the British market. We are also exploring the possibility of improving our trading arrangements with Britain.[35]

In brief, this was the situation which applied in early 1965. Ireland was going to explore the possibility of combining its two alternatives, closer ties with the UK and the EEC, as it did not just want to become even more dependent upon the former, but it was apparently not in a position to have more than an ambiguous relationship with the latter. The central question that should have remained uppermost was: where should Ireland proceed to next? Unsatisfactorily, this issue remained unresolved and, for some unbeknown reason, except perhaps to itself, the Irish government's answer apparently lay in the Vatican.

The taoiseach's visit to Rome for the papal consistory [36]

Throughout the first half of its existence as an independent state, Ireland often looked to the Catholic Church for guidance on matters upon which religion impinged.[37] De Valera was the personification of interactive church-state links, of course; indeed, he wrote a special place for it into *Bunreacht na hÉireann*.[38] In public, his successor gave the impression of being quite sympathetic to this view and was certainly not antagonistic, it would have been political suicide otherwise; in private, he held a different position to his predecessor, although all he really did was to keep religion expressly out of state affairs. J.H.Whyte has written that there did not appear to have been as a high frequency of interaction between Lemass and the Catholic hierarchy, unlike de Valera's relationship; it is quite clear that the former preferred to keep it that way.[39] All the more surprising, therefore, that when he was in Rome at the beginning of 1965, ostensibly for a church celebration, he was presented with the opportunity to meet up with the Italian prime minister, Aldo Moro, but appears to have been reluctant to utilise this opportunity to further bilateral relations. Indeed, returning from the Vatican at the end of February 1965, Lemass was more inclined it seems to speak of Ireland's relations with the Holy See rather than with Italy; he evidently rated his papal audience higher than forging links with the Palazzo Chigi, the offices of the Italy's prime minister.[40] Originally, Lemass had no plans therefore to meet any members of the Italian government during his brief stay, despite the precarious position of Ireland's candidacy for the EEC. In what should have been considered an ideal opportunity for him to discuss areas of specific interest to bilateral Irish-Italian relations with his counterpart in Rome, the taoiseach had other things in mind. He was evidently more preoccupied with the intricate processes involved in procuring his audience with the pontiff – with whom he eventually met on 27 February 1965 – than he was in furthering bilateral relations with a critically important European state.[41]

    Clearly, the trip was not left to go totally to waste because even the European question was raised. The taoiseach stated that Pope Paul VI had expressed appreciation and, indeed, had encouraged the influence that Ireland brought to bear on international bodies such as the UN and, by implication, in other areas such as European affairs.[42] However, it is obvious from this visit that, on a scale of importance for the government, the desire to procure an audience with the pope while in Rome came out way ahead of any urgency that might be expected to have been attached to efforts to procure substantive discussions and meetings with representatives of the Italian government.[43] Therefore, it is with Dublin's stated interest in the development of a coherent and progressive integration policy in mind that, it has to be said, this trip provided evidence of a missed opportunity by the taoiseach to advance Ireland's relations more than superficially with one of the Six. Lemass might have employed some of his time in Italy to better effect than just by concentrating on meeting the pontiff.

Obviously enough, with integration viewed as a response to the communist threat, the Vatican itself had played a role in the development of various government's foreign policies during these post-war years. Ever since the mid-1950s, when Pope Pius XII had delivered a Christmas message in which he urged the European integration process, although conveyed in general terms, Ireland had started to pay very close attention to the thoughts that emanated from the Vatican on this matter.[44] It can be surmised from the regular Irish embassy reports dating from this period – coming as they did from one of the countries with which it has held diplomatic relations the longest – that Ireland was well aware that the papacy was in favour of European union going beyond the bounds of the Treaty of Paris, both in spirit and in letter. However, it was also noted by the Irish ambassador at the Holy See that, although the Vatican was in favour of European unification, it was reticent about saying so too loudly.[45] In fact, it was only by the summer of 1962 that the Irish ambassador was apparently able to make it clear that the Vatican had substantially changed its mind on the issue; the Holy See was now 'officially and unreservedly on the side of advance towards European union'. Indeed, critical of the French president's displays of excessive nationalism, it was said of the members of the Vatican's administration – the Curia – that the various cardinals:

> ... strongly ... shared the opinion that European countries must, at the expense of whatever degree of individual national sovereignties which might be necessary, move towards political unification if European civilization and culture is to survive the threat from the East.[46]

The Dublin government thus acquired fresh inspiration and stimulus in favour of its European integration policy, especially coming as it did from a source other than those which were led purely by economics. Still, a natural question might be posed at the outset of this discussion: where exactly did the taoiseach's visit to the papacy fit in with Ireland's strong declaration of affinity for the concept of European integration?

The Irish prime minister was ostensibly visiting Rome in early 1965 in order to attend a religious ceremony – termed the papal consistory – an event at which William Conway, the Catholic Archbishop of Armagh, was being elevated to the position of cardinal. Ultimately, however, Irish-Italian relations were allowed to intervene on the hectic schedule of Ireland's visiting delegation in Rome, however slightly – in the end, Lemass accepted an invitation to lunch with the Italian prime minister – but they did not, of course, interfere with the main substance of the taoiseach's visit to Italy, attending the papal consistory and meeting with Paul VI.[47] Before moving on to deal with the substance of the bilateral meetings that did, in fact, eventually take place, some background information on the purport of Irish-Italian relations – as well as an analysis of the Italian government's opinions on Europe's political integration and the experience of its own 'economic miracle' – needs to be presented. Thus, questions which need to be asked at this point include: how important was Italy to Ireland in terms of actual trade, what view did it hold on the Irish application for full EEC membership, and what efforts did Ireland make to raise its standing with Italy? [48]

It was admitted by the Department of Foreign Affairs in a briefing for Lemass that a marked improvement in overall trade terms had been taking place between the two countries and that Ireland had recently achieved a 'better balance in our trade with Italy than with any other EEC country' – this belief is clearly borne out in the figures.[49] Up to 1962, Ireland was importing up to and over three times the value of goods from Italy that, in return, it was exporting to the latter. However, this situation was remedied somewhat in the ensuing years. By 1964, the balance of trade deficit that existed between the two countries, although still in Italy's favour, had been redressed, even if it was often destined to drift. Of course, in the general scheme of things, Irish-Italian trade was an infinitesimal part of Ireland's trade, accounting for only 1% of total exports and 1.2% of total imports, on average. Nevertheless, these figures are symptomatic of the government's efforts to expand the country's export base and to exercise the economic power that the procurement of foreign goods gave it. Indeed, unlike its economic relations with many other European countries, Ireland was making steady progress therefore on the question of bilateral Irish-Italian trade, a trend which needed further enhancing – based on the Dublin government's impetus – at every given opportunity.

Indeed, this report from mid-February 1965 regarding Ireland's trade and commercial relations with Italy particularly credited the large increase in exports there to the establishment and rapid development of a substantial market for fresh and chilled Irish beef – in the process quickly becoming the largest single export market on the European continent for this product – and also of course for live cattle. In addition, it was noted in this report that the burgeoning Italian market for frozen meat from Ireland had been facilitated by a veterinarian agreement which had only come into force the previous year. Nevertheless, although not unexpectedly, it was pointed out that the export of Irish industrial goods to Italy did not fare out so well in comparison to agricultural produce. Of course, what this implied was that value-added goods were not able to break into the sophisticated Italian market as easily as primary or basic food products. In turn, it comes as no surprise that Ireland's major imports from Italy listed in this report included agricultural produce – such as fruit, nuts and vegetables – and manufactured goods – including cars and scooters. Despite the uneven nature of the relationship inherent in the make-up of these exports and imports, however, this significantly healthier balance of economic activity singled Italy out as an important trading partner for Ireland.[50]

In reality, Ireland's trade relations with Italy were solely governed by an agreement which dated from 1953. Not unlike most economic arrangements from that era, it was only outlined in the broadest terms, along with an imprecise aspiration towards expanding bilateral trade. By the early 1960s, the Irish government had rather understandably been actively trying to copperfasten such accords for some time, primarily in an attempt to expand and to extend these agreements, especially in an effort to remedy the heavy imbalances that existed in trade terms, but also to guarantee continuity regarding access. This endeavour was guided by a Department of External Affairs recommendation that:

> ... [as] there is little scope for bilateral negotiations to serve improved import facilities for Irish industrial products in West European or North American markets, existing trade agreements should be reviewed to assess whether this country is still receiving benefits commensurate with the concessions given to other countries under these agreements.

As a matter of fact, the growth of Italian financial investment in Ireland was also a new factor in the bilateral trading situation – centring on footwear and textiles, as well as on car assembly with Fiat of Turin being one of only two car manufacturers to have an Irish assembly plant. Indeed, at that particular point in time, the IDA was concurrently dealing with twenty-eight separate industrial enquiries from Italy to set up investment projects in Ireland.[51]

This data presents only a fraction of the hard evidence backing up the opinion that the taoiseach's trip to Rome in the spring of 1965 offered Dublin an important economic opportunity to build upon bilateral trade relations, one which seems to have been almost totally missed in the practically frantic efforts to receive a papal audience. Obviously, there were other considerations for Lemass to ponder upon apart from those purely related to Irish-Italian trade interests – including, for example, the Italian government's proposals for the political future of the EEC or its perception of Ireland's readiness to participate fully in the European integration process – in the lead up to his trip to the Vatican for the consistory. One of the most meaningful implications and insights to emerge from this affair, one that is indubitably inferable from this series of diplomatic reports, was that Dublin did not consider that there was a strict dichotomy between politics and economics at this level of bilateral interaction; it did not appear to see that they were only opposite sides of the same coin. Simultaneously, however, it was at least discerned that the UK remained the key for Ireland's economic future as far as both countries were concerned. Indeed, it was widely accepted that, no matter what scenario developed in the meantime in Europe, Ireland 'apparently would not be able to join unless Britain did so at the same time'.[52] Thus, these bilateral discussions with the Italian government came at a very important stage in Ireland's process of European integration and clearly should have received more priority than they in fact did.

When it came to the substance of the bilateral meetings that were in the end held as planned on 26 February 1965, the taoiseach was able to talk with the Italian prime minister and, indeed, could also have met with some senior Italian foreign ministry officials as well. At the very least, these deliberations afforded a limited opportunity for the Irish delegation to discuss matters of mutual interest but it appears that, although some significant points were touched upon during these exchanges, nothing of real substance was discussed. There was, of course, a brief exchange of views between the two sides on Ireland's relationship with the EEC. It was made clear by the Irish delegation that the application for full membership was still on the agenda, indeed, that its preparations for accession were in full swing. As a result, it was declared that Dublin was taking every step to further its objective and that they were anxious to maintain the impetus and momentum achieved thus far. Thus, it was announced to the Italians that:

> Rather than risk the loss [of] this momentum in the present impasse we were considering the possibility of examining in the not too distant future the question of some form of interim economic association with the EEC pending ultimate membership, which would take into account our special trading relations with Britain which were basic to us.

Additionally, it was stated that, as Anglo-Irish discussions for the purpose of reviewing the existing trade agreements was becoming due, Ireland was considering the examination of a European dimension somewhat more closely. Subsequently, the Irish external affairs secretary then added for the benefit of the Italians that the prospects for finding a suitable formula – enshrining an interim arrangement such as association – might be enhanced if it was based on the hypothesis that full membership would ultimately follow.[53]

Later that day, at a further bilateral Irish-Italian meeting at which the taoiseach was not present, the prospect of some form of economic association being formed between Ireland and the Six, based on the premise that the country ultimately achieved full membership, was discussed once more, but again no conclusions were reached. However, the Italian deputation present at the meeting did advise that the Irish government could perhaps make a more fully developed appraisal of this idea available to the EEC Commission – as well as to the Six – for their perusal if it was indeed interested in pursuing the matter seriously.[54] It was readily apparent though that such an initiative would have to come from Ireland itself. Thus, the opportunity of meeting with the Italian government, almost spurned in the enthusiasm to meet the pope, garnered some important information and reaffirmed Ireland's standing as a prospective candidate with an integral member of the Six. An occasion which was very nearly missed consequently provided the government with some serious food for thought.

A provisional arrangement with both the EEC and the UK?

At the end of March 1965, the Departments of the Taoiseach and External Affairs seriously considered the possibility of Ireland seeking an interim arrangement with the EEC and the UK as its route out of the membership application impasse. However, it should be noted that the outlined proposals were viewed as dependent upon the Irish and UK governments not being able to formulate an improved economic relationship of their own instead; in other words, if an all-encompassing Anglo-Irish trade agreement emerged, it would automatically negate the necessity for an extensive alternative arrangement being proposed to the EEC.[55] Therefore, the UK alone remained the pivotal factor in Ireland's European integration policy.

During his meeting with Mansholt, the Irish agriculture minister was made aware that the EEC Commission would not discount out of hand the possibility of arriving at a mutually acceptable settlement, one whereby Ireland could link up with the EEC, with the UK formally situated outside although connected in some way through existing economic arrangements.[56] Under the taoiseach's subsequent plan for an interim agreement with both the EEC and UK, the proposals – if needed – that would be made to the former were envisaged as necessitating five separate interlinked steps. These stages were listed as follows:

- the Irish government would agree to eliminate, by a gradual process, all tariffs on EEC products *pari passu* with UK goods, in return for the EEC extending to Ireland the benefits of tariff reductions/removals that were already being enjoyed amongst themselves as full members;
- Ireland would agree to maintain the EEC Common External Tariff against all imports, except those originating from the UK of course;

- in addition, there was a recognition that special machinery would need to be established in order to provide safeguards against the diversion of UK exports through Ireland into the EEC;
- Ireland would participate in the EEC's agricultural arrangements;
- this joint agreement would be expressed as only temporary, pending the UK's admission into the EEC.

As this blueprint suggested, the elimination of Irish tariffs on UK goods would actually mean the *de facto* creation of an FTA between the two countries; this development would require this process to be explicitly enshrined – by making it *de jure* – offering Ireland a heightened sense of economic security. Evidently, this new arrangement would apply to the EEC as well, necessitating the renegotiation of existing Anglo-Irish trade agreements, mainly because the Commonwealth preference system would encroach upon this novel procedure.[57]

Obviously, it was not expected that London would necessarily agree to these proposed changes in its trade patterns, but the taoiseach felt that the submission of innovative ideas to the Six in an effort to subvert or, at least, to bypass the deadlock was far better than inaction, especially if Ireland's heretofore inchoate European integration process was ever going to make any substantial progress. At the same time, the Dublin government still recognised that it could not make any breakthrough in the form or the substance of its relationship with the EEC – that is in regard either to associate or full membership – without the consent and the support of the UK. As it was pointed out in the course of internal debate, failing the attainment of any additional advantages in the UK market through these proposals for an interim arrangement with the EEC and the UK, the attraction of this alternative project was that Ireland would still gain improved terms of access for its agricultural and industrial goods to the latent, though vast, EEC market. In addition, the potential beneficial effects of access for the Irish to internal EEC tariff reductions was very appealing.[58]

Other questions which the taoiseach's plan raised – such as recognition, for example, that special arrangements would be needed to guard against the diversion of UK goods into the EEC through Ireland and *vice versa* or, for instance, with regard to Ireland's precise status within the EEC because this could encroach upon economic areas *vis-à-vis* the CAP – would, it was felt, also prove to be significant hurdles however to a final agreement being reached. The balance in choosing between the pros and cons of associate and/or full membership had not yet been struck, basically on account of agriculture, and the idiosyncratic UK government always loomed large in economic considerations of any substance. Nonetheless, the Irish government was still resolved to searching for a solution, even if the EEC external relations commissioner had advised them to sit tight, await developments and do nothing radical. Ireland had other ideas. Indeed, it seriously considered what was in effect no more than a 'casual remark', exchanged between the EEC agriculture commissioner and the Irish agriculture minister, had:

> ... touched on the possibility of an arrangement that might be made to enable us to acquire membership of the Community and at the same time maintain our access to the British market.

While it was thought that an arrangement of the kind mentioned in passing by Mansholt had 'little prospect of materialising', at least it was determined that more information should be informally sought from the EEC Commission at the first suitable opportunity that presented itself before any formal move was made. Regardless of such considerations, the idea was still a rather academic one, mainly because understandable doubts and uncertainty lingered about the possibility of Ireland being capable of establishing any meaningful link in the short term with the EEC. In the meantime, the latter was faced with more immediate problems because, amongst other considerations, the UK's position remained unclear, the Austrian membership question lay unresolved, and the future political direction to be taken by the Six themselves was as yet undecided. The Department of the Taoiseach felt that the balance of probability meant that the EEC would not be prepared to enter into any serious negotiations with a view to admitting Ireland as either an associate or as a full member at that point in time.[59] All the signals from Brussels appeared to be saying the Dublin should bide its time.

It appears that the Department of External Affairs had other ideas though and it thus suggested another alternative arrangement. As a result, it was intimated that:

> This variant envisages a form of association with the EEC which would bring us within the customs union of the Community and would provide terms of access for our principal agricultural exports to the Six which, though falling short of full participation in the common agricultural policy, would help to guarantee a certain level of trade.

Once again it was felt, even by the proposers themselves, that there were certain obstacles in relation to the fruition of this plan which quite possibly made it unnegotiable. It has to be said that, by seeking special arrangements from the EEC at this stage in the development of European integration – especially for agricultural produce such as beef, mutton and lamb – it does not appear to have been a very imaginative or even worthwhile tactic for the government to have thought about pursuing. Essentially, what this addendum proposed was the creation of a new and unique FTA for Ireland within the

EEC, one with some agricultural concessions added; at the same time, this would be coupled with the separate but interlinked construction of an FTA between Ireland and the UK which would provide for their bilateral agricultural arrangements to continue. The conclusions drawn were, to say the least, fascinating. Indeed, they thoroughly question the validity of the whole exercise as they read:

> While the foregoing seems prima facie an attractive proposition from Ireland's point of view, there are serious doubts as to whether it would be negotiable.

Thus, the Department of External Affair's proposal does not appear to have taken the reality of the situation into consideration and did so on purpose. Indeed, the character and evolution of economic and political integration appears to have been ignored in the formulation of this alternative plan of action; this was subsequently proved by the more sensible assessments of the position in which Ireland found itself which later followed.[60]

In the middle of April 1965, the Department of Finance presented the Irish government with a pertinent assessment of the process of European political integration; this appraisal also dealt with its history and implications. This document was divided into six principal parts which, not altogether unlike the analysis presented here, dealt with the following subjects:

- efforts made at integration before the decision to establish the EEC;
- the establishment of the EEC and subsequent moves towards political integration up to 1962;
- renewed efforts in 1964 towards political integration;
- special aspects of European integration;
- statements by the taoiseach on political aspects of the EEC;
- issues raised by the proposals for political integration.

There is no particular need to go into this specific memorandum in too much detail because, after all, points such as these have been made before and have been explained in detail during the course of this investigation. Notwithstanding this fact, it is worth noting that, in reference to previous statements made by the taoiseach on the political aspects of the EEC, it at least becomes clearer from this assessment that the government knew from an early stage, even if not expressly, what EEC membership actually meant in practice; economic integration would indeed lead to political integration, it was a 'natural and logical development'.[61] However, the political aspects of full EEC membership clearly did not outweigh the economic.

Of course, although it was fairly easy to pay lip service to such platitudes, there were more substantive issues raised by the proposals for political integration in Europe which not only the Six, but also the Irish government, had to consider at length. The two main factors which were faced remained relatively simple and can be listed as:

- the nature and interlinking relationships of the institutions that would in the end be established as part of a political union;
- the subsequent policies to be followed by that political union.

Understandably, the decisive consideration for the government was that, not being an active or direct participant in the process, in essence Ireland could only watch from the sidelines and try to influence unfolding events from there; or else, of course, it could do something about them by embarking upon a riskier strategy. Ireland had much to gain, but it also had a lot to lose, from the developments which were then taking place. In fact, it was felt that it was in Ireland's interest, for example, to see a stronger supranational element entering into the proposals for political integration, indeed, that it was also necessary to see a more democratic European parliament elected, but that in return the question of Ireland's non-aligned status would need to be reassessed, for instance. Thus, there were many outstanding issues remaining to be decided but, if the government was seriously interested in joining the EEC, these considerations, both at home and abroad, would all have to be quickly, but sincerely, addressed. Otherwise, of course, it would run the perilous risk of not being allowed or able to participate in economic and political integration.[62] So, the next question being posed was quite simply: where should the government decide to go from here?

Throughout this period, Anglo-Irish discussions continued in earnest on the possibility of improving the permanent trading relations existing between the two countries.[63] Indeed, the necessity of putting bilateral economic relations on a sounder footing was self-evident to both parties. In the meantime, there were some very positive developments to recount. For example, on the larger economic scale, it was observed that the UK surcharge on imports was going to be reduced from 15% to 10% as and from 27 April 1965 – in fact it was not totally removed until 30 November 1966 – but, the government had obviously been objecting all that time to its use for various reasons, including its contention that the surcharge complicated Irish and UK relations with the EEC. There was a simple logic which necessitated change. Meanwhile, it was also noted that there had been advances on the smaller scale. For example, in the forthcoming financial year Irish exports of butter to the UK would total 18,905 tons, as compared to 17,405 tons for the previous year; while any increase was welcome, what the Irish government was really seeking, even beyond longer-term basic quota grants to be increased, was a comprehensive bilateral trade agreement between the two countries.[64] The government was starting to look at the bigger picture once more; it was also working within the confines of reality rather than the realms of fantasy.

There are clearly two issues which need to be analysed at this point. Apart from the central one of what the government was actually thinking and doing in relation to the EEC and the UK, it is easy to miss out on the second consideration regarding what Ireland was in fact telling them. On the one hand, the Irish ambassador in Brussels was able to express his government's attitude in numerous conversations with important EEC officials; for example, remarking on his country's candidacy, he regularly recounted that:

> ... it remained unchanged and that we were hoping for membership before the end of the transitional period. It was difficult, however, having regard to the overwhelming importance of our commercial relations ... to envisage a situation in which we might join while Britain remained outside ...[65]

It is plain that Ireland's attitude to full EEC membership, cognizant of the UK's position, was unchanged. With respect to the UK, the taoiseach's secretary, Nicholas Nolan, wrote on the other hand that, at its meeting on 27 April 1965 to discuss future bilateral economic relations, the Irish government had:

> ... approved the continuance of the trade discussions with Britain ... agreed, in principle to the adoption of a formula recording the willingness of the Government to consider, at the end of the five-year review period, the question of participation in the European Free Trade Association ... authorized the Minister for External Affairs, in consultation with other Ministers concerned, to agree to the issue of a communication by Britain to the other member-countries of the European Free Trade Association about the discussions when the appropriate stage therein has been reached, the substance of any such communication, and also of any associated public announcement, to be settled in consultation between the two Governments.[66]

There was clearly more fluidity on the Anglo-Irish question because EFTA was suddenly back on the agenda in the context of an FTA agreement with the UK. Nonetheless, all that these revelations – regarding what the Irish government was telling the EEC and the UK – do is to leave yet another question unanswered: what was the government saying to the general public at home regarding its prospective intentions?

Public preparations for the implications of integration

Through its use of a variety of means, the government made its position – at least, a version of its true status – on European integration policy relatively accessible to the general public and to Dáil Éireann. In a series of documents, interviews and speeches, Lemass and other government ministers regularly spoke on the subject of Ireland's candidacy for membership, although frequently employing an ingenuous manner to do so. Indeed, in answers prepared for an interview with a West German newspaper, which in the end did not in fact take place, it may be contended that the taoiseach's replies displayed a certain degree of calculation and reticence. Essentially, nothing new was going to be said, equivocation was generally the key on fresh ideas; Ireland still wanted to participate fully in every effort to achieve European integration, he would have stated, the application for full membership would be reactivated as soon as there was any development which made such a move feasible. The only initiative which was being taken in the early months of 1965 was on the question of seeking association with the EEC as an interim arrangement, but even in this area there existed major doubts as to whether such a plan was practicable.[67]

The interviews that were being published proved to be no more revealing with insipid replies regularly being employed to avoid giving candid answers to direct questions. This sort of attitude was all too characteristic of the government's conduct, its European perspective being portrayed as one distinguished by 'great friendship, interest and attraction' rather than the issues being openly debated. Indeed, according to Lemass, there was a 'very strong desire for us to be linked with the Continent, especially in this effort toward economic integration and, beyond that, toward some sort of political unification'; the taoiseach's promulgation of 'membership by 1970' was repeatedly utilised and viewed as eminently achievable.[68] The government's replies to questions regarding the future of Ireland's relationship with the EEC remained far from satisfactory however. As the agriculture minister maintained in parliament on 29 April 1965: 'With regard to the European Economic Community, our application for membership still stands and will be actively pursued when circumstances make this course desirable in the national interest'.[69] Nothing new was being given away, but the taoiseach himself realised, however, that he would have to give a fuller explanation of the European trade situation in Dáil Éireann and, indeed, that 'it would be desirable to do so'.[70]

When the opportunity immediately presented itself in early May 1965, Lemass bided his time in giving such information. Replying to a parliamentary question, he said that:

> There have been no developments regarding Ireland's application for membership of the European Economic Community since I replied to a similar Question on the 18th November last. We continue to maintain close touch with the Community but it is unlikely that negotiations on our application will be resumed in the near future.[71]

The signs regarding the UK's position were not proving good – there were reports from the Irish embassy in London maintaining that there was 'no immediate prospect' of a membership application being made and from the Irish embassy in Brussels suggesting that the UK was 'gravely mistaken' if it believed that time was working in its favour as regards its eventual accession – but, at least there were some positive whispers in relation to Ireland.[72] Indeed, there was an account of deep dissatisfaction radiating from influential Europeans about the EEC Commission's lack of substantive contact with Ireland and at the fact that 'satisfactory arrangements' had not yet been made to deal with the outstanding question of its accession negotiations.[73] It was a good opportunity for the government to restate its case, both to the country's elected representatives and to the leaders of agriculture and industry.

At the beginning of May 1965, Lemass delivered a significant speech on the question of Irish industry. As he said himself, the 'first and most obvious development in our national situation, so far as industry is concerned, is that the age of protection is coming to an end'. European integration was thus having a major impact on the most intimate workings of the economy without Ireland's express participation. Older indigenous industries were having to adapt to these new circumstances or else faced going to the wall, while modern enterprises which were being set up were specifically designed to meet this challenge in conditions. As the taoiseach said, the main aim of his government's external trade policy was to ensure rights of access to foreign markets for Irish exporters similar to those available to other European countries already operating under the aegis of a continental trade grouping. For this to work, however, certain facts could no longer be ignored. Lemass reasserted that:

> To make this policy practicable we must be sure that the efficiency of our industrial and commercial enterprises individually, and of our national economic organisation as a whole, are such that opportunities so won can be fully used, and that the reciprocal reduction of our own protective measures will be countered by the growing efficiency of Irish firms so as to enable them not only to win larger markets elsewhere, but hold their positions in the Irish home market as well.

It was obvious that the government's original plan for Ireland to be a constituent part of this drive towards European integration by the mid-1960s had been dashed by events outside of its control. This had in turn led to uncertainties being voiced about its economic future. As it could hardly affect outside events, it could at least effect changes at home. Regardless of the problems the country faced, in the taoiseach's view, there were grounds for hope.[74]

Lemass made it readily apparent that he believed that the deadlock would be broken given time, although he could not be expected to know when exactly. In not being a member of the EEC or EFTA, however, Ireland was in a position which was causing his government 'constant concern', but the historical weight of what had been a 'courageous decision' only four years earlier had been lifted.[75] The future was clear. As he said:

> We cannot remain aloof from these developments. There would be a very dim future for Ireland as an island of protection on the edge of a free-trade Europe and, whatever it may involve, we will have to find a means of getting into the main stream of events.

With this promise to industry regarding entry into Europe, the taoiseach declared that Ireland would have to be willing to tear down its own protective trade barriers if it wanted to take part fully in the economic integration process. He therefore added:

> We cannot expect to acquire the benefits of participation in these developments and arrangements to the extent that will secure for our exports assurance of tariff-free rights in export markets, without our being willing to share, equally with the other participants, in the obligations as well.

That being said, the constant and indeed urgent necessity to introduce and institute measures of industrial reorganisation and adaption at home, in order to make such policies practicable and also to guarantee Ireland's continued industrial growth in an era of free trade era, could not be 'over-stressed' the prime minister insisted. Indigenous and foreign-owned industries, just like agriculture, had a duty to ready themselves for the onset of freer trade.[76] Finally, Lemass appears to have felt that the time was right to take this debate to Dáil Éireann, a body which had essentially been excluded from such discussions for some time.

On 13 May 1965, the taoiseach spoke at length in parliament about the possibilities and problems facing the country, explaining his government's role in the light of prevailing economic circumstances. He stated that central to ongoing discussions were the workings of a bilateral Anglo-Irish economic committee that was meeting regularly to examine the possibility of improving the permanent trading relations between the two countries.[77] There were obvious reasons why the UK was given such coverage in this debate, especially in the context of this statement he was delivering on Ireland's external trading situation and the most up-to-date developments in European and world trade. As the taoiseach told Dáil Éireann: 'For the present ... it seems sensible to concentrate on our relations with our principal trading partner, Great Britain'. Running through the recent history of bilateral trade discussions – which in this case had been initiated the previous November having been in the pipeline since de Gaulle's veto – he said that the two governments had agreed to confer with each other regarding the possibilities of improving economic relations.[78] He was thus able to add that:

> Discussions have since been continuing at the level of officials and matters are now reaching a stage at which can be discerned the outline of possible improvement in our trade relations which, if agreement can be reached, would confer additional advantages on both sides and would ... be consistent with the eventual entry of both countries to an enlarged European community.

It was readily apparent that what he actually envisaged was an innovative Anglo-Irish trade agreement in which the basis for an even higher level of bilateral trade would be created in the short term as the means to achieving greater diversification in the future. Lemass held out the prospect of this revised Anglo-Irish relationship being achieved within the inclusive economic context of an even larger trading group, one in which it was realised that Ireland would face considerable competition. Evidently, the exact make-up of this new trading sphere had yet to be defined however. Nevertheless, the possibility of Ireland linking up with EFTA – more in conjunction with the UK than for any other reason – does not appear to have either been expressly raised or discounted. Although he only spoke in general terms, it did appear that a possible relationship with EFTA was right back on the agenda.[79]

During his statement to Dáil Éireann, the prime minister admitted that the idea of a European FTA did not appear to be 'capable of revival', but that it was also evident that, because of recent encouragement from the UK government, EFTA and the EEC were making overtures to one another. Once again, Lemass only gave a glimpse of what he was thinking, vaguely hinting at what he was driving. It is still possible to draw certain conclusions from his statement because, as he said:

> EFTA was never so far as we know envisaged heretofore as an end in itself but as a possible step to a wider European Common Market but it may last for some time and may even go on to the consideration of measures which will bring it closer to the concept of a common market including the extension of its scope to cover agricultural arrangements. The significance of these events, in my judgment, is that they show that some movement has been introduced again into this situation ... While it is impossible to say what may eventuate it is not unlikely that events may begin to move, if they move at all, rapidly enough.[80]

He left his remarks at that. Thus, a brief impression of the future for Ireland in Europe had been presented and then left hanging in the air. However, nothing concrete was decided and, within days, the taoiseach was again talking up the possibility of Irish EFTA membership; as with the other possibilities open to Ireland, Lemass said that it was being kept under constant examination by his government.[81] All the same, if there was going to be any development, it should be stressed that habit had shown Dáil Éireann to be one of the last bodies to know. Of course, the only real economic option open to the Irish government was to embark upon a deeper, and by now necessary, consideration of how to formulate an improved relationship with the UK, but that did not stop the other alternatives being considered.

EFTA, the GATT, and other considerations

Before dealing specifically with the reappearance of EFTA as an option for the government, which then leads into a detailed analysis of the emergence of the Anglo-Irish FTA agreement as its preferred intermediate foreign economic route, there were other aspects of the statement delivered to Dáil Éireann by Lemass in May 1965 which are worth deeper investigation, both in relation to European integration and to Irish trade considerations in the wider world. Indeed, it was within this tangled pronouncement by Lemass on Ireland's foreign economic position that the EFTA option suddenly rematerialised after a prolonged absence. In a cabinet meeting the previous month, the government had been persuaded by the argument to continue trade discussions with the UK, 'to consider, at the end of a five-year review period, the question of participation in the European Free Trade Association', and to communicate with the other EFTA countries regarding these Anglo-Irish negotiations when the appropriate time came.[82] How serious the government was about this issue is debatable; after all, the only attraction that EFTA really held was the fact that the UK was a member.

In the speech he made to parliament on 13 May 1965, the taoiseach stated that Ireland was operating in an external trading environment over which it exercised little or no control. It was divided into two principal Western European groupings, but the country had a vested interest in only one of the participants. As Lemass said:

> The implications of this situation for our export trade and for our whole future economic development are of such importance that we cannot afford to neglect any measures which will help to promote the internal strength of the national economy and offset the disadvantages inherent in this present situation.

The starkness and immediacy of the situation that the government faced became all the more readily apparent when he added, by way of illustration, that not only were internal tariffs on industrial products within EFTA due to be eliminated by the beginning of 1967, but that it was also highly probable that a single market for agricultural and industrial goods would be established within the EEC some six months later. As the taoiseach explained:

> It is in these areas we have to sell the bulk of our exports in competition with domestic producers who will in two years time have the advantage of tariff-free access to wider markets within their respective groups.

The enormity of the problem facing the country must have been particularly striking, but the options open to it were limited. However, the government knew that, as far as was possible, it would have to introduce freer trade and at the same time try to obtain 'equal treatment' for Irish exporters alongside their European competitors if sales were going to be maintained, never mind expanded. As was made manifestly clear on all such occasions, membership of an enlarged EEC, anticipated by 1970 as fully embracing Ireland's principal export markets, was seen as the 'trading arrangement best calculated to meet our needs'. Nevertheless, within this grand design lay grave problems. While the government continuously encouraged Irish agriculture and industry to prepare for the fateful day when they would have to compete on equal terms with the other members of this enlarged economic grouping, it was accepted that such an 'expectation ... does not in itself provide the answer to the trading problems arising in the years immediately ahead of us'. Thus, Ireland's difficult position begged the question: what was the government actually prepared to do in the interim period? [83]

One of the main developments in Ireland's external trading situation actually came at this time with the revelation – just announced by the finance minister – that the government had applied to join the GATT. The arguments for membership were not lost. This institution would entitle the country to two main benefits; it would allow:

- it 'to share in whatever trading concessions may be negotiated' through the Kennedy Round of the GATT negotiations;
- it to some extent to ease trading barriers with continental Europe and the US, facilitating the diversification of Irish export markets.

In spite of these welcome developments, it was noted that Ireland's relationship with the UK market would suffer as a result of membership; for instance, exporters would encounter more competition within this context because of the reduction in preference margins. Thus, even if GATT membership was desirable, Lemass stressed that it would not provide a substitute for Ireland's participation in a major European trade grouping such as the EEC or, indeed, EFTA.[84] Thus, by May 1965, the issue had become:

where did Ireland stand regarding membership of these organisations and which option was the most preferable?

It was in fact at this point in the parliamentary debate that the taoiseach made a very interesting assertion in relation to his government's European integration policy. He said that there were not the 'same obstacles' to joining EFTA as there existed to entering the EEC; on the other hand, Lemass added that there were not the same advantages. Of course, the fact that the UK was in the former and not the latter counted for everything. EFTA membership was, he maintained, a possibility which his government would 'keep under examination'. Indeed, the taoiseach went so far as to assert that:

> It might conceivably emerge at some future date that the national interest would be served by joining EFTA as an interim step towards participation in a wider European Community.[85]

In fact, wide-ranging efforts at this time to facilitate discussions for closer relations between EFTA and the EEC briefly raised hopes in Dublin; indeed, there were initial attempts to make sure that the country would be represented at any resulting talks.[86] However, prospects for this proposal to provide substantive contact between the two trade groupings soon floundered and, although the government was interested in participating in these discussions, there was little chance of them happening, partly due to the debates which were going on within those organisations themselves.[87] Europe was not providing the economic cure to Ireland's trading ills, but it had already been looking elsewhere.

Towards the end of the summer, Lemass again contended that entry into the EEC was only envisaged by the end of the decade. Indeed, he began to grow tired of being asked that same question every time there was some degree of controversy on the European continent.[88] At one point during a parliamentary debate, clearly irritated, the taoiseach said:

> The assumption we have made as to the date by which we may expect to be admitted to membership of the European Economic Community is a long-range one and I do not consider it necessary to revise it every time some difficulty arises in the Community.[89]

Obviously, unofficial discussions with the EEC were continuing, but there was nothing there which held out much promise for Ireland or encouraged unfounded hopes of accession. At any rate, bilateral Anglo-Irish trading relations had retained a certain amount of economic priority and were always going to be the most favoured government option once it became clear that full EEC membership was not possible without the UK's participation.[90]

Ireland therefore hurriedly turned back to its old reliable – the UK – and in the process readied itself for ultimate accession to the EEC by paving the way economically; as one commentator has noted, this move also had the rather more ambiguous and contradictory effect, especially in economic terms, of restoring the 'union' between Ireland and Great Britain.[91]

The 1965 Anglo-Irish FTA agreement

At the end of May 1965, there were newspaper reports that the UK prime minister felt there was no early prospect of his country being in a position to seek admission into the EEC.[92] Of course, remarks such as these did not endear the UK's plight to those in the EEC who were not looking for its inclusion; indeed, the comment that was being made fairly generally in Brussels was that: 'Wilson still does not understand what the EEC is all about'. However, as the taoiseach said, events did not in any way suggest a change in London's attitude to EEC entry. The taoiseach reiterated that his government was not expecting the UK to join in the 'near future' and that the UK prime minister's reported statement had not in fact altered that situation.[93] At the same time, however, this might also present previously uncountenanced opportunities for Ireland within the context of Anglo-Irish trade.

In Ireland's case, it does not appear as if it had many options open to it at that point in time as it searched for an improvement in its external trade position. Indeed, in reply to questioning in Dáil Éireann, Lemass was embarrassingly forced to restate that his government still had an ambassador accredited to the EEC; attitudes towards EFTA also remained exactly the same, he said, although Ireland was closely monitoring the situation.[94] It was not a very comfortable position in which the government found itself, especially when it was looking to Europe for direction and counsel. When statements such as these had to be made, resulting mainly from a lack of movement on its application, but also in an effort by the opposition to humiliate the government, it was clear that it was struggling. Any efforts which were made to normalise Ireland's relations with Europe – such as accepting changes from its own tariff system to the Brussels Nomenclature, being careful not to introduce sweeping new tariffs, or in streamlining and expediting the procedures for customs clearance – were only small parts of a much larger economic picture.[95] Understandably, there were good reasons for London not to be interested in embarrassing itself once again in front of their European neighbours; indeed, the UK government would not risk applying for EEC membership until it felt that such a move had a good chance of succeeding, which was unlikely as long as France wished to remain *prima inter pares*.[96] Thus, Ireland's only foreign economic option appeared to be to look to London for help; two decades after the Second World War, never mind a generation after gaining political autonomy, it was no closer to economic independence.

On 26 July 1965, the taoiseach led a delegation to London comprised of his finance, industry & commerce, and agriculture & fisheries ministers, a high-level trip obviously being conducted in order to discuss the possibility of improving permanent trading relations existing between the two countries.[97] In announcing his trip, Lemass was summarised as saying that:

> ... if a satisfactory permanent arrangement on the lines under discussion can be completed, it would have an important bearing on the country's economic situation and would contribute to its improvement both in the short and the long term.[98]

The government's hopes for the economic well-being of the country in the immediate future rested on one source and in that they were not disappointed; still, it seemed to many observers as if Ireland was going one step backwards in order to go two steps forward, as it pursued greater dependence on the UK in order to encourage interdependence with Europe.

At this meeting, the two sides evaluated the results of the bilateral trade review which had been conducted on an ongoing basis ever since the disclosure of this Anglo-Irish trade reevaluation process on 5 November 1964. The first examination had shown evidence which favoured the construction of an FTA between the two countries. Indeed, the bilateral talks had continued on the basis of seeing whether a 'mutually advantageous agreement' might be concluded. Therefore, with the successful conclusion of his summit meeting with Wilson, the taoiseach was undoubtedly very pleased to be in the position to make a somewhat surprising announcement; the Irish and UK governments had agreed to examine whether they could create an Anglo-Irish FTA.[99] In announcing this momentous initiative, Lemass stated that:

> The effect of today's meeting was a joint decision that the purpose of these negotiations is to develop eventually a free trade area between Britain and Ireland, a bi-lateral free trade area agreement.

At last, the government had achieved its foreign trade deal, although it was emphasised that a 'great deal of work' still needed to be done on a resultant FTA agreement. Notwithstanding this proviso, the important news was that the negotiations and talks between the governments would be on the basis of securing this agreed goal, raising Irish spirits considerably.[100]

As seven months of talks on this first step on the road to an FTA came to fruition, the Irish media greeted this announcement with due respect.

The *Cork Examiner*, referred to this agreement as the 'most important milestone' reached to that date in bilateral relations. Of course, there were many advantages to such an arrangement for both countries, although especially so for Ireland; on the one hand, it would open the way for its subsequent membership of the EEC and GATT, while on the other, it would see the harmonisation of Anglo-Irish agricultural and industrial trade. At the press conference – held at the Irish embassy in London and conducted by the taoiseach – following the conclusion of this series of trade talks, it was stressed that any new Anglo-Irish FTA agreement would not be instituted immediately, even after it was signed. Additionally, it was emphasised that the 'rhythm of elimination' for Irish tariffs on UK goods would extend over a number of years, though there would be the more of less immediate removal, with few exceptions, of all UK tariffs on Irish industrial goods.[101]

With respect to the European dimension of this Anglo-Irish initiative, the taoiseach ignored integration by drawing attention to the fact that:

> ... we contemplate in our arrangements with Great Britain for the elimination of our protective tariffs that we will have a longer period than we envisaged in our membership application to E.E.C.

It was always important to emphasise the positive gains in any agreement. The removal of tariffs would effectively mirror, of course, although it would not in itself institutionalise, the FTA conditions under which agricultural goods originating from Ireland were already treated in the UK marketplace. It was revealed that much of the time actually envisaged for further Anglo-Irish negotiations would concentrate on this very issue, an undertaking which the Irish government viewed as ultimately giving it a 'reasonable prospect' of increasing agricultural exports to the UK, thereby boosting its market share. Thus, it appears that the industrial side of this arrangement had already been sanctioned. Indeed, it was supposed that one of the immediate effects of a new bilateral agreement would be that UK restrictions on particular products such as Irish man-made fibres – generating in turn an improved share for exporters in that textile market by up to 20% a year – would be waived. What remained to be found, however, was an acceptable solution to the agricultural aspects of an FTA. Once a settlement to that question had been reached, Lemass stated that a new comprehensive agreement would 'cover every aspect of trade between the two countries' and, as a result, would consequently 'replace the three earlier agreements'.[102]

In fact, there was still a lot of work to be done by both sides because, for instance, it was noted that this proposed bilateral trade agreement would be 'quite independent' of the import surcharge which the UK wished to continue to impose. As the taoiseach said:

> There is no prospect of that surcharge being repealed in respect of Ireland alone in advance of its general repeal, and ... this is not likely to happen before the middle of next year.

Another important factor for the government, although this time in the political sphere, was the position of Northern Ireland within this new arrangement. As is clearly demonstrated by the figures, the northern part of the island already played a very significant part in Ireland's economy and, in reality, this applied the other way round as well. Indeed, around 17% of its exports to the UK in 1965 – circa 12% of total exports – went directly to Northern Ireland; additionally, nearly 8% of its imports from the UK – almost 4% of total imports – also originated there.

A more detailed evaluation of north-south trade – again using the figures – is necessary, however, in order to give even further credence to this view and also to demonstrate how the breakdown of trade figures revealed the evolving nature of Irish exports, as well as changes in the import needs of the country. At the same time, it also gives an idea of how quickly Northern Irish economy was falling behind that of its southern neighbour. During the decade which saw Lemass as Irish industry & commerce minister and then prime minister, exports to Northern Ireland saw a large increase in their value to the Irish economy. However, it was not in the traditional area of live animals that this expansion was realised, although that category did remain the preeminent Irish export throughout this decade. As was the case with the vast majority of its exports in this period, it was manufactured goods which saw the greatest increase in value and as a percentage share of exports, very nearly doubling in size, in fact. Meanwhile, Irish exports of food, drink & tobacco steadily grew; indeed, they very nearly surpassed its export of live animals in 1963. Nonetheless, it is relation to the import of goods from Northern Ireland these figures are perhaps most interesting. Not only was Ireland exporting goods to Northern Ireland at the advantageous average ratio of 2:1, but two-thirds of the imports it was taking were live animals. This product was being supplied to an already saturated market, of course, but, they could in turn then be processed for, or even redirected to, other markets. The fact that this category maintained its share of Northern Irish exports to Ireland throughout this period is a very interesting and perhaps unexpected revelation. However, it is surely in relation to the category food, drink & tobacco that this data is most fascinating because Ireland was exporting these products at the incredible average ratio of 19:1, clearly showing the underdeveloped nature of the Northern Irish economy; after all, it was in this category particularly that income from agriculture was becoming preeminent. Finally, the value and share that manufactured goods made up of its imports from its northern neighbour demonstrate the retarded nature of the latter's exports; Ireland was exporting twice as many manufactured goods to

Northern Ireland as it was importing. The southern economy was growing rapidly while that of the bordering state was contracting.

Such figures are indicative of reasonably high cross-border trade, although a noticeable decrease in line with the drop in the UK's importance to Ireland was a fairly consistent feature throughout this period. Lemass remarked, in relation to the effects of this new Anglo-Irish FTA agreement on the border between the two halves of the island, that it had a wider economic and political significance. The taoiseach said in an interview that:

> It does have the effect of diminishing the impact of the border on the North-South trade, and must also, of course, become a factor in our membership of the European Economic Community.[103]

Lemass felt that trade would thus increase as cooperation between the two parts of the island developed. Apart from the partition issue, if the taoiseach was prepared to use this argument in favour of Ireland's participation in the EEC, a further question is raised: where exactly did an FTA arrangement fit when the wider European dimension itself was considered?

The Irish government fully recognised that the UK itself desired the Anglo-Irish FTA agreement to work and that, despite the fact that there was some serious negotiating left to be done, they were acting in good faith. As Lemass recounted while in London: 'There was a genuine effort to recognise our problems and the will to seek an agreement'. Nevertheless, although the initiative had come from Dublin, it was acknowledged that there was a wider European aspect involved as well that might be beneficial. The taoiseach added:

> At some time after the agreement, and we have seen it in operation and there is no other danger in the European situation, we may begin to think again whether there is any advantage to us in joining the European Free Trade Association. It would have to be on a basis which would not involve for us any modification of the free trade area with Britain. Whether this is possible or not I do not know.

Once Ireland achieved its FTA with the UK, it no longer showed any real interest, beyond similar utterances, in EFTA, only ever a secondary consideration anyway; regardless of the inferences and implications that could be drawn from such statements, Ireland could now go about achieving its intermediate aim, an Anglo-Irish FTA agreement. Its long-term ambition remained the same, full EEC membership.[104] As Liam de Paor has written, 'Ireland, north and south, was to conform to the ideology of Common-Market Western Europe'.[105]

As the introduction to this chapter on *The 1965 Anglo-Irish FTA agreement* made apparent, one of Ireland's central aims in negotiating an accord with the UK was to facilitate the country's full accession to the EEC whenever that became possible. The Anglo-Irish FTA was therefore never envisaged as a weapon to be used against the EEC or EFTA, for instance, but was meant to compliment a concerted drive towards European free trade. Indeed, Lemass added that this new bilateral agreement opened the way for Ireland's membership of the GATT, which the *Cork Examiner* explained in the following terms:

> At present we were prohibited from [GATT] membership by reason of the terms of the existing trade agreements with Britain, which conflicted with the rules of G.A.T.T. because of the preferential clauses. But G.A.T.T. did provide for free trade area agreements, and it was hoped that this would pave the way for membership in the negotiations due to take place in the second half of this year.

An Anglo-Irish FTA agreement was rightly termed as a 'milestone' in bilateral relations, one which might conceivably have far-reaching consequences beyond the boundaries of the British Isles into Europe. Most of all though, it solved Ireland's immediate trade problems.[106]

Although immediate reactions to the agreement from influential quarters were mixed, it quickly became apparent that the government had pulled off quite a coup. In an address to Seanad Éireann on 29 July 1965 to explain the new arrangement, the Irish finance minister, Jack Lynch, told the assembly that it had become increasingly obvious to the government that Ireland's trade relations with the UK were no longer adequately guarded by a system based on preferential clauses and that the time had come for a radical change. Indeed, because of EFTA's advent, there were instances whereby Irish goods – the aforementioned man-made fibres included – were entering the UK market with an in-built handicap resulting from their lower tariffs and despite the Irish 'so-called preferential rate of duty'. In fact, Lynch told the assembled senators that not only had industry been affected in recent years, but that the UK's relations with Irish agriculture had also deteriorated. It was explained that:

> ... the forms of support given to U.K. producers and the restrictions applied to imports into the U.K. had resulted in the erosion of benefits ... once enjoyed in the U.K. market.

As the finance minister forcefully pointed out, the composition of exports was still dominated by agricultural goods which were as yet targeted at Ireland's only available market. In his considered opinion, an Anglo-Irish FTA which included agricultural and industrial provisions 'would not merely be consistent with, but would actually facilitate, future membership of both countries of the EEC'. Indeed, Lynch held that it would also 'represent substantial interim progress in the right direction'.[107] By marketing the Anglo-Irish FTA as the logical step before EEC membership, the government could of course deflect negative arguments which pointed out Ireland's increased economic dependence upon the UK. However, the truth of the matter is that the country was struggling to emerge as an separate entity, one which could manage without continuing to depend on the latter. In the eyes of the Six and the EEC, it was hard to make a case for Ireland as a truly independent consideration.

As previously stated, away from the Oireachtas there were mixed reactions initially to the Anglo-Irish FTA announcement from all sections of the economic community, but these soon shifted to a cautious welcome. Obviously, an organisation such as the NFA felt that this proposed agreement would only be acceptable once it was made clear that it fully catered for agriculture's requirements and that it would not close the door to improved future relations with the EEC. On the other hand, the Federation of Irish Industries realised that the deal had 'serious implications' for Ireland and quickly stressed that 'it is essential that the period over which trade is to be freed should be long enough to permit the work of preparing industry for freer trading conditions to be completed'. Indeed, the Irish Exporters' Association vouchsafed these legitimate fears, but felt that this bilateral FTA agreement appeared to be good in the long run for the country as a whole, echoing the government's feelings.[108] Clearly enough, the important responses from outside bodies were going to be those emanating from the EEC rather than from home, as it was clearly necessary that a bilateral FTA conformed with the concept of European economic integration as conceived in Brussels and beyond.

The government had been careful to make sure that they kept the EEC informed about the Anglo-Irish discussions as they progressed. Thus, on 26 July 1965, it notified them that:

> The Irish Government has been discussing with the British Government the possibility of improving the permanent trading arrangements between the two countries. One possibility which is being explored is the establishment of a free-trade area between Ireland and Great Britain in accordance with GATT, to which Ireland is in course of accession. The discussions have not yet reached finality. Membership of the European Economic Community still remains the Irish objective and any trade arrangements made with Britain will be consistent with eventual membership of the Community by both countries.

Ireland's ambassador in Brussels used the opportunity that this meeting to inform the EEC Commission of his government's intentions provided to give extra information about this new bilateral arrangement and to explain its implications for Irish tariffs and trade. As he pointed out to the senior EEC official present, the lowering of protective measures through an Anglo-Irish FTA agreement would help to prepare Irish agriculture and industry for the eventual entry of both countries into the EEC because it was held that, if Ireland could face up to the expected competition from the UK, then it would also be equally able to survive competition from its future partners in the EEC. The 'reasonableness of this line of argument' was acknowledged. Ireland's future intentions regarding EFTA were probed at this point in the meeting but, as the Irish diplomat tactfully replied, 'this was a possibility which could not, of course, be ruled out but ... only bilateral arrangements were at present under negotiation'. In addition, the governments of the Six were subsequently told of this development in Irish trade arrangements.[109] Ireland had finally taken the European integration question into its own hands by beginning to take serious political decisions and important economic initiatives. It was still preparing itself for full EEC entry, but realised that there were limits to what it could achieve in the immediate future. By working within these limits, it was still preparing itself to join the EEC. However, the exact terms of the Anglo-Irish FTA had not yet been worked out and the opinions emanating from the EEC were not always clear.

Back to the old reliable: the ramifications for EEC membership

The economic possibilities in an AIFTA notwithstanding, the Dublin government was adamant in making it clear to London that it attached great importance to the duty-free rights that Irish agricultural products entering the UK enjoyed; indeed, the cabinet concluded towards the end of 1965 that the 'prospects of an Agreement being concluded will be poor' otherwise.[110] In time, it was therefore decided that a delegation headed by the taoiseach would be sent to conclude an AIFTA agreement.[111] Any hint of a crisis was quickly averted, with London reasoning that, if the Irish were prepared to make the right kind of economic sacrifices, it should be prepared to facilitate them. The fact is that such an agreement also suited the UK; however, the first of the concessions would come from London. The FTA agreement that Wilson and Lemass signed mainly provided for two effects to come into force:

- the abolition of all remaining UK import duties on Irish goods;
- the gradual elimination of nearly all continuing Irish import duties on UK goods in ten equal annual stages.

On the agricultural side, the UK became a guaranteed market for Irish cattle and undertook to import more butter as well; the AIFTA also thus gave Irish industry tariff-free access to UK markets almost immediately. In return, Irish tariffs against most UK imports were to be reduced by 10% per annum over the next decade, so that by mid-1975 an FTA would be in operation between the two countries.[112] As the industry & commerce minister later said:

> ... [Ireland] needed the discipline of the challenge to our competitiveness ... if we could compete successfully against sophisticated British industrial imports we could become competitive in Europe.[113]

On 14 December 1965, the Anglo-Irish FTA agreement was thus signed in London and three weeks later it was debated in Dáil Éireann. It was not afforded easy passage.

Addressing parliament during a four-day debate in early January 1966, the taoiseach was at pains to point out that the AIFTA agreement represented a 'fair balance of advantages' to Ireland. Lemass stressed that it was not just a new bilateral arrangement, but that it would be 'absorbed in an agreement for our membership of a wider international trading group, whether the European Free Trade Agreement or the European Economic Community or ... a combination of both'. In spite of forwarding this reasonable argument, the reality of the situation was that Ireland was economically closer to the UK through this agreement than it had been for nearly half a century.[114] However, the taoiseach then stated that the idea to negotiate an Anglo-Irish FTA had initially come from the UK; it would only be a provisional arrangement until both countries could accede to the EEC. Accordingly, it was:

> ... not an arrangement which anybody asked or urged us to accept but one which we ourselves desired and which we proposed because we considered that it was necessary in this country's interests.

Emphasising that Ireland was making a free choice, Lemass recounted that his government, even before January 1963, but more so ever since, was adamant that the process of reducing industrial protection would continue 'in anticipation of, and as part of our preparation for, our [EEC] membership'. He related that there were three main factors which had contributed to this decision, which, according to Frances Nicholson and Roger East, can be listed as follows:

- protection was no longer effective in promoting industrial expansion in Ireland and was being replaced by a policy of 'capital grants, technical assistance, and tax inducements';
- in many cases, the government's outdated protectionist policies served only to support 'inefficiency and high costs';
- the country had to be readied – both in terms of economic

organisation and political willingness – to meet head-on the situation it would face when full EEC membership became possible, presumably before 1970.

Ireland thus embarked upon tariff reductions without reciprocal arrangements.[115]

Nevertheless, the AIFTA agreement had to be considered against imminent European developments as well. As Lemass recognised, most Western European nations – within either the context of the EEC or, of its 'competitor', EFTA – would have removed all tariffs and other restrictions against free trade with each other by the end of 1966. It was only a decade since the OEEC negotiations for an FTA had failed; paradoxically, Ireland's greatest hope and fear, therefore, was that the EEC and EFTA would in time join together in an enlarged free trade area or, perhaps, even a common market; it was not an outlandish conclusion to draw. Thus, plans for the reorganisation of agriculture and industry, especially in the context of external trade, would have to continue at full speed; these could be provided for within the context of an AIFTA. This agreement was an integral step in the general restructuring of its external trading arrangements. Beginning with the prerequisite of providing for agriculture's future, Ireland had to prepare its industries for free trade, some of which could not survive, so these would need to be replaced by adaptable and outward-looking enterprises. Of course, this was where the possibility of joining EFTA came back into the equation, a prospect that was still only referred to in the very vaguest of terms; there appeared to be no direction, just unending confusion.[116]

One thing which was clear, however, was that Ireland would be joining the EEC as soon as that was possible. In no uncertain terms, Lemass made it clear to industrialists on a continuous basis that, on acquiring full EEC membership, tariff reductions might have to be speeded up, perhaps at an even faster rate than that provided by the AIFTA; indeed, many, if not all, of the 'safeguards and escape clauses' negotiated through the Anglo-Irish agreement might not be upheld. Lemass stressed that there were 'no trading conditions negotiable with the EEC which would at the same time permit the preservation of our preferential access to the British market'. Indeed, he stressed that it would be:

> ... fatal ... [to] go on without making any changes either in respect of our own protective tariffs or in our trade arrangements with Britain until membership of the EEC became possible for us or until some ... unforeseeable development took place in the European trade situation.

The pragmatist in Lemass had emerged triumphant once again. The AIFTA arrangement was a 'trade agreement and nothing more', as he stressed that

Ireland had entered into this deal on its own initiative in order to further its own interests. Indeed, as some commentators testify, he believed 'no non-trade conditions or political implications' were inherent in the AIFTA, except that he saw it as 'facilitating our subsequent membership of the EEC on the basis of full equality of status and opportunity with other members'.[117] Not all of his fellow parliamentarians were so sure, especially on the opposition benches.

The leader of Fine Gael, Liam Cosgrave, noting these concerns, pointed to possible implications for Ireland in the short and medium term. In freeing up trade, he felt that rising unemployment and emigration figures might well follow; indeed, he expressed concern that the AIFTA was 'unbalanced' in favour of the UK, that the concessions Ireland received were 'small in the immediate future and limited and insecure thereafter'. Apart from parochial considerations such as scoring political points with the Irish public, there was also a need for Cosgrave to be critically constructive. He failed to do so on many fronts, but on others raised interesting ideas. Specifically, it was true that the AIFTA had no provisions for a stabilisation or social fund to cater for unemployment, such as those which he said were provided for by the EEC, but it is questionable whether he interpreted the activities of the latter correctly. He was unerring in relation to Austria's experience, however; Ireland might have thought more deeply about EEC association, because there was, as he said: 'surely ... some in-between arrangement that would have been possible for this country'.[118]

Within a fortnight of this debate, the taoiseach travelled to Strasbourg to address the Council of Europe, primarily in order to explain the significance of the AIFTA. At a press conference he gave before his speech, however, Lemass raised the EFTA issue in order to dismiss it as an obstacle to Ireland's ultimate goal; indeed, he was indicating that it might be a stepping-stone to full EEC membership. In holding that EFTA did not deal directly with the agriculture question, he was able to argue that it had not been in Ireland's interests to join that particular European trade organisation. Nevertheless, the advantages of it enroling into EFTA had now been 'enhanced' – by the creation of an Anglo-Irish FTA, the position of Irish agriculture in the UK marketplace had been secured and it was also in its interests to prepare industry for free trade – just as the disadvantages had been 'diminished'. The taoiseach held that, if the EEC was able to resolve its own difficulties and then come to an agreement with EFTA, Ireland would actively consider EFTA membership as an temporary step. There was an important proviso because, if this improvement in European trade relations did not take place, Ireland might wait a year or two before deciding to take action on EFTA membership. Lemass was quick in trying to reassure Europe that the AIFTA was a step towards European integration and not an attempt by Ireland to circumvent it; at the same time, he was signalling Ireland's desire for full EEC membership and its needs in that context.[119]

The taoiseach delivered his statement to the Consultative Assembly of the Council of Europe on 24 January 1966 in the course of which he basically claimed that although the new AIFTA would not affect his government's standing application to join the EEC, it would now have to consider joining EFTA as an interim step. Referring to the *Second programme for economic expansion* – the first part of which had been launched in August 1963, the second section following eleven months later – Lemass explained that it was due to run until 1970, by which time he assumed that Ireland would be a full EEC member. In the course of this seven year interval, unilateral tariff reductions were timetabled to continue along the lines of the two 'across-the-board' reductions already made. As the taoiseach then explained, it was extremely difficult for Ireland to develop links with the EEC and, at the same time, for it not to damage seriously its special trading relationship with the UK. Therefore, his government was understandably concentrating on improving Anglo-Irish ties in, as he put it, a 'way that would be consistent with the eventual participation of both countries in an enlarged European Community'. Lemass added his considered view that the positive conclusion of an Anglo-Irish FTA agreement was facilitated by two main factors; these were listed as follows:

- the bilateral free trade arrangements which already existed;
- his government's preparations to deal competently with European free trading conditions upon full EEC membership.

Firstly, therefore, he pointed to the high degree of free trade which in place already via an intricate process of various Anglo-Irish treaties and agreements. Indeed, as of February 1965, D.J.Maher put the statistics for existing free trade at 93% for Irish entry into the UK and at 66% for UK entry into Ireland, even if the UK surcharge was not part of this data. Secondly, there were what Lemass termed 'energetic measures we have been taking to prepare the Irish economy for the kind of trading conditions that will be encountered when the opportunity comes to join in an enlarged European Community'. Building on this point, he said that there was more to the AIFTA than immediate trading benefits; this was where the EEC, perhaps even EFTA, came into what was a potentially complicated, even unhelpful, equation.[120]

In fact, Lemass held that his new arrangement took Ireland a step closer towards the European norm, with concrete steps helping, as he put it, to 'dispel much of the uncertainty which in recent years has handicapped us in the taking of fundamental decisions affecting the future course of our economy'. It was at this point, however, that the taoiseach introduced an additional possibility, one which did not necessarily augur well for better short-term relations with the Six. What he actually said was that Ireland was prepared to consider all possibilities, including EFTA membership, in its drive to participate in a wider European free trading grouping; this would still only be an interim step to participating fully in a 'economically integrated Europe'. Indeed, according to Frances Nicholson and Roger East, whether Ireland's objective was reached through EFTA membership or via its participation in an enlarged EEC, its free trading arrangements with the UK – and the terms of economic transition provided for within – would need to be considered. In Lemass's opinion, the terms of the AIFTA 'afford us a reasonable opportunity of effecting, without undue disturbance to our economy, the change-over to free-trading conditions ... [and to] prepare ourselves for participation in a single European market'. Now that Ireland was in an FTA with the UK, Dublin appeared to be ready to discuss all options, including EFTA membership; however, it was most concerned about the prospect of renewed moves by London to join the EEC, at which stage it would have to be prepared to relaunch its dormant application.[121]

It was not so apparent though what Dublin should be doing. When it began to become apparent in early 1966 that a 'more liberal attitude' was slowly developing within the Six to UK membership and that of the other applicants, the taoiseach could only restate that:

> Our interest in acceding to the European Economic Community is ... constantly stressed in the capitals of the member-nations and has been re-emphasised by our embassies quite recently. It is the Government's firm intention to pursue actively our application for membership of the Common Market at the first appropriate moment ... it is obvious that the EEC is not at the moment considering new applications for membership and it is not likely that they will do so until they have determined their position on the British application.[122]

The positions of both the Six and the EEC on UK entry were not yet so defined that Ireland could afford to make concrete decisions; a much firmer basis for decision-making was needed before any preemptive action could be taken by Lemass, an important consideration to bear in mind as the fiftieth anniversary of the Easter Rising approached.

The OECD's 1967 annual report [123]

If an arbiter was needed to give credence to the view that Ireland had transformed itself, an organisation such as the OECD should surely suffice, contradictorily an independent judge and at the same time a body intimately involved in Ireland's European integration. Indeed, it is with that particular view that this examination of Anglo-Irish links in the context of the EEC concludes, symmetrically rounding off an analysis which was presented by that very same organisation back in the mid-1950s. In March 1967, the OECD issued its annual report on the state of the Irish economy; it painted an utterly different picture to the one depicted by the OEEC just over a decade earlier. However, despite presenting a more positive verdict, it must be said that there were still some very obvious problems.

The OECD report entitled 'Irlande 1967' provided rudimentary, but startling, statistics which showed the progress that had been made. While the country's population had stabilised at last, indeed there were increasing signs of its recovery, the total populace which was active in the workforce was continuing to fall. This particular finding was exculpated in many ways by the marked decrease in the those workers employed in agriculture but, even if industry and construction were beginning to take up most of the slack, it could not be said that the signs for the economy were so good if the country's dependents increased – with birth rates rising, death rates slowing, unemployment remaining steady, and emigration declining – just as the active population was falling. Although the percentage of the population directly involved in agriculture had dramatically fallen – causing problems of rising unemployment and underemployment, as well as exacerbating the continuing rural to urban shift – the numbers of those engaged in industry had in fact increased by a comparable inverse rate.[124] Whether it was statistics regarding production or related to living standards, there had definitely been an improvement in conditions. Compared to the late 1950s, the situation by the mid-1960s demonstrated a remarkable turnaround in fortunes; GNP per head was just over 62½% higher, the number of people owning cars and telephones had risen by 73¾% and nearly 47% respectively, more people owned radios and televisions.[125] Apart from presenting data to back such views, what was the OECD specifically saying about Ireland in 1967?

One of the problems most keenly noted by the OECD concerned Ireland's continuing, indeed spiralling, balance of payments difficulties, which continued at high levels throughout this time. Such a situation could hardly be dismissed for much longer, certainly not in the way that the Irish foreign minister did towards the end of 1964 when he said: 'During recent years our overall balance of trade has been reasonable. It has had its slight ups and downs and at the moment we are in one of our down periods'.[126] Taking things a little more seriously, the OECD's report remarked that the Irish government had instituted various restrictive measures in 1965 to remedy a deterioration in the commercial balance of payments deficit. By the start of the following year, it was noted that the situation had improved in relation to imports but, because exports also fell, these difficulties were still worsening; indeed, this is evidenced by the fact that the exports to imports ratio was widening. However, once invisible exports – investment revenue and tourism – were also included, the current balance of payments deficit did not seem to be so debilitating, even if it was eating into Ireland's meagre reserves. Another problem, however, facing the Dublin government was the fact that the ratio of goods and services that were being exported, viewed as a percentage of Ireland's GNP, continued to average a figure of around 36%, an extraordinarily high amount suggesting dependence and an underdeveloped economy. With around 50,000 people regularly unemployed, agricultural production in 1965 was only 11.8% higher than in 1953 – industrial production was more impressive at 171% of the earlier figure though – and inflation was running at around 4½%, it was clear that the OECD was suggesting that it was not an economic miracle over which Lemass was presiding, more like a passable economic recovery.[127]

Of course, the issue of most concern here boils down to answering the question: where did the OECD see the EEC fitting in for Ireland? Obviously, the UK came into that equation for various reasons, but the OECD's report was also able to state that the AIFTA agreement, augmented by the suppression of the UK's temporary import surcharge, had eased Ireland's economic position, while facilitating its transition from protection to free trade.[128] However, the reality of the situation was that the opportunities for Irish exporters to find markets abroad – that is, outside of the UK – were still limited, even if the demand for Irish products in the new markets that were available had increased relatively rapidly in preceding years.[129] The EEC was Ireland's second biggest market and, even if it shrank in financial terms in 1966, it was twice – perhaps even three – times the size of the US market and the remaining EFTA markets.[130] Nonetheless, the EEC market was dwarfed by that of the UK. Now that Anglo-Irish relations – economic and political – were improving at a rapid pace, a question remained as yet unanswered: where did Ireland really stand in relation to the EEC? Despite the fact that the OECD report did not offer much information on this matter, it was dealing with the reality of the situation after all, one conjecture that may be reached is that any future plans which the government may have had to join the EEC did not lessen the economic reality of Ireland's true position. The OECD was not particularly interested in any delusions that the Dublin government might have been entertaining; it just wanted to see even more substantial improvements appearing in the Irish economy.

Intermediate conclusions

Of course, Ireland's position on EEC entry remained in limbo throughout this whole period because, although its membership application remained a matter of record, any reactivation of its previous attempt to join could only occur as soon as a 'suitable opportunity' presented itself.[131] It was heading in the right direction, according to Roy Foster, as it belatedly moved towards the 'mainstream of European events'.[132] Indeed, as Richard Vaughan holds in his *Twentieth-century Europe*, the setting up of the bilateral FTA had important effects upon Ireland's growing adherence to the European integration concept, stating that: 'Although not a member of EFTA, Ireland became indirectly associated with it in 1965 when the Anglo-Irish Free Trade Area was set up, which abolished quotas and the remaining duties on imports of one partner from the other'.[133] Even if it was not in EFTA, it was still prepared to use this mechanism as a stepping-stone. Equally, the effects of the AIFTA and Ireland's continuing Europeanisation are clearly recognisable in figures contrasting markedly with totals from the previous decade, evidence of a change in orientation explored in more detail in the next chapter.[134]

Nonetheless, it is possible to make a couple of points here regarding these figures. For instance, although EFTA remained a minor consideration for Ireland when the UK totals were excluded, the combined figure as a destination for Irish exports was around 71% and, indeed, 56¾% of imports came from these countries. Ireland's links to EFTA had remained unformalised, but it was now interacting with the UK on basically the same premise as were Denmark or Norway. Clearly, the EEC and the US were taking care of a larger share of its internal and external needs and produce, but the UK retained its primordial position; Ireland stayed as a part of the sterling area, only of course because it was felt that therein lay the 'balance of advantage', and it can be argued that its inflation rate was basically 'imported' from the UK as well.[135] Manufacturing goods, both exported and imported, now made up the bulk of Irish economic interactivity, but in percentage terms food, drink and tobacco exports had been maintained, which was only good for the economy as a whole, while live animals still accounted for a large swathe of income with a monetary total that was basically unchanged. This did not mean that there was not agricultural and industrial unrest over prices and conditions – with the NFA, for instance, marching on the agriculture ministry in October 1966 demanding access to new markets or the CIO reports from the previous year making it clear that Irish industry was 'poorly equipped and managed' – after all, Ireland was making no apparent progress on EEC entry. However, the government stood firmly to its beliefs, even if only occasionally checked, and continued to work towards its integration.[136]

Seanad Éireann remained one of the few forums which provided for informed public debate and, at the same time, had the full attention of the government. This was particularly true when, in the summer of 1966, Garret FitzGerald was able to quiz the foreign minister about Ireland and the EEC but, while he made some very salient points, he only succeeded in discomfiting the latter.[137] The senator encouraged Aiken to initiate an 'active European policy to ensure the achievement of Irish membership' and even went on to suggest that he 'should reorganise his Department and our diplomatic missions abroad so that they contribute effectively to the achievement of this objective'. Asserting that it was not at all a personal reflection on Aiken's integrity, FitzGerald declared himself to be somewhat disquieted and concerned at the government's lack of progress, a view which was he said 'not confined to any particular Party but widespread among the political Parties, in the public service, among journalists and others interested in public affairs'. He also criticised Ireland's lack of actual preparedness for membership, although he did accept that the government had genuinely been interested in Europe and its free trading arrangements ever since 1957, especially when it was preparing for accession negotiations to begin. He was still unhappy though with the lack of recent developments, particularly citing Ireland's lack of contact with the institutions and the Six since 1963. The senator pointed out that a separate Irish diplomatic mission to the EEC had been cancelled at that time, as he berated the government for only having four members of staff at its Brussels mission – comprising an ambassador who was ill, a counsellor, and two other representatives, one each from industry & commerce and agriculture & fisheries – who were expected to cover Belgium, Luxembourg, the ECSC, the EEC, and Euratom. He also criticised the foreign minister himself for having visited the Belgian capital only once in the intervening three year period. The criticism did not stop there.[138]

FitzGerald held that Ireland's public relations efforts in Brussels could not justifiably be described as 'minimal' because that would be an over-exaggeration; indeed, he stated that this was only symptomatic of Aiken's own lack of robustness on the subject.[139] He strongly criticised the government's lack of communication, or at best its *ad hoc* nature, with European institutions and officials. His view was that partial blame lay in the fact that the Department of External Affairs had become a 'Department of United Nations affairs', partly on the fact that external relations were 'becoming increasingly economic' and that, using the good offices of Iveagh House as a conduit, Irish foreign policy was being made by the Departments of the Taoiseach, Industry & Commerce, and Agriculture & Fisheries. On a previous occasion, the senator had suggested to the taoiseach that he should either utilise the Department of External Affairs properly or, indeed, that he should go ahead and establish a Department of European Affairs – an idea that, however briefly, Lemass had himself formerly raised – but again this suggestion appears to have fallen on deaf ears. Basically, FitzGerald wanted:

- a reorientation of external affairs back to Europe;
- the government to set up an independent mission in Brussels to canvas the EEC and the Six to support its candidature;
- a stepping up of ministerial visits and positive public relations.

As he said: 'Foreign policy involves a compounding of principle and interest'. Ireland would need to be a little more adept is it really wanted to convince the EEC to let it join; this would certainly involve a more coordinated and fully thought out set of European policies. It was not the fact that Ireland was not considering new policies, never mind implementing them, which was worrying him, the senator said, but that Europe did not appear to be fully aware of the extent of the country's endeavours.[140]

As far as the foreign minister was concerned, Ireland's interests would be best served by following through with Lemass's idea to send a delegation to Brussels in the autumn of 1966. However, until the UK position was reconciled with the EEC, Aiken felt the European Commission to be accurate when it stated that, to all intents and purposes, 'there was nothing specific Ireland could do in the existing situation to further her interests under the heading of full membership, association or an item by item agreement'. The minister announced that, apart from recently beefing up Ireland's diplomatic staff in Brussels, despite the fact that the country had 'rather limited resources', the 'necessary steps' had in fact been 'put in train' to have a separate Irish mission accredited to the European Communities in order to promote trade and to foster competition. The 'whole Irish people' had to take responsibility though, in Aiken's opinion, to ready the country for entry. From his own point of view, he did admit:

> I myself think that it may be some time, even more years than we now expect, before the European Community will expand its membership. I hope I am right in thinking that it is inevitable that the countries of Europe will see that they have a definite interest in expanding the membership and I feel that when the matter of extending the membership is re-opened, Ireland's case will be considered, and considered not unsympathetically. I am constantly meeting the Foreign Ministers of all the Six countries and the Ministers of the seven EFTA countries and I have found no antagonism to the idea of Ireland becoming a member. The one doubt they expressed was whether Ireland could take the regime, whether we could suddenly dismantle our tariffs and accept goods freely from other countries.

The latter reference was precisely what FitzGerald had been saying. Ireland had made such a good job in the late 1950s of convincing the OEEC that it would have major difficulties in lowering its trade barriers in a seventeen nation FTA – indeed, that it might take up to thirty years for it to do so, though this figure was subsequently reduced to twenty years – that it was now difficult for Europe to be convinced only seven years later that the situation had changed so much that Ireland was now in a position to do exactly the opposite. Of course, through AIFTA's terms, Ireland was in many respects closer than ever to fulfilling those requirements for EEC entry, not the 'Council of Europe' as Aiken mistakenly referred to it.[141]

The government was reassessing its position in relation to Europe, an ever-changing and evolving situation in which the EEC of 1966 was no longer the same organisation that it had been even five years earlier. What Ireland was doing was to continue its process of harmonisation with the rest of Europe at home and abroad, whether it was establishing a body such An Chomhairle Oiliúna (AnCO) to undertake and to promote industrial training or the ratification of the European Convention on Extradition ten years after it had been signed.[142] Although the effective tariff rate in the mid-1960s was 79%, the AIFTA's ratification and the country's prospective EEC membership signalled that it was prepared to relinquish voluntarily unilateral control of its commercial policy.[143] Nonetheless, the reality was that the status of Ireland's outstanding application was as undefined as ever in 1966. It is with this in mind that the final chapter, entitled *Ireland's European integration, 1957 to 1966*, explores in a more generalised way the position in Europe pertaining to Ireland.

T.D.Williams has written that it was only towards the mid-1960s, that is at the end of what he calls the 'age of Lemass', that Irish diplomatic activity at the UN began to decline significantly, only to be replaced in turn by an 'intensification of interest in Europe'. Even if New York still remained the personal fiefdom of Aiken, where he played a 'very prominent role' in many controversial issues, Lemass's 'heart and his head were far more attached to the new conferences in Brussels', to rectifying relations with London and promoting dialogue with Belfast, to take notice of dissent; from time to time, de Valera did make 'some sceptical noises about Europe and the materialism for which, in his view, it partly stood', but he was no longer in a position to dictate government policy.[144] Lemass had long begun his drive to eliminate certain features – such as neutrality – as important policy considerations; in the latter case, he did so by making references in speeches that ran contrary to the neutralist positions being adopted by his Aiken at the UN. He restricted himself to this at first, but under his premiership – as distinct from de Valera's final administration – Aiken was slowly peripheralised away from the foreign policy mainstream or at least away from the wielding of real foreign policy power. In the five year period between April 1959 and April 1964, Aiken was out of the country on official business on 35 occasions – mostly to do with the UN and the active Irish foreign policy that was being exercised there – and was not even present in the Dáil chamber when it came to answering the question tabled regarding his extensive absences.[145] A complete change of tack had taken place in the decision-making process, that is in determining which issues were to be prioritised. This swing in Ireland's foreign policy orientation in the context of international organisations – away from the UN to the EEC – only compounded the changes in emphasis that were taking place away more generally from the political to the economic. The fact that it was 'hardly noticeable' until this period in time is only further evidence of the gradual nature of what was actually a profound change in character; this is where the last chapter leads.

Beginning with a quick review of the central years dealt with in this investigation, this final chapter reviews the evidence which strongly suggests Ireland's economic and political reorientation; moving on from an assessment of the evidence that is represented in the figures for exports and imports, it then concentrates on the part played by Northern Ireland in Irish-European affairs, before quickly reviewing and comparing what Ireland was in fact giving up, as opposed to what it was gaining, through European integration. The state of the Irish nation in 1966 demonstrates how far the country had come in the space of a decade and then leads into an investigation of the two characters who were at the centre of that transformation. This last chapter then concludes with an analysis of how Ireland was perceived by Brussels, before finishing with a brief assessment of the future that it faced following Lemass's retirement.

6 Ireland's European integration, 1957 to 1966

Perspectives on the past

In retrospect, some of Ireland's brushes with the reality, rather than the concept, of European integration may well be viewed as somewhat disappointing, especially when considering the first two decades of post-war history. However, a judgment which perceives this process in such a sceptical light still has to allow for opinions to be tempered by the many subsequent positive developments. Of course, initially negative results should not have been unexpected because, after all, this particular country remains a small, historically-hindered, semiperipheral power lacking in any major natural resources or strategic importance. Indeed, when Ireland's application for full EEC membership is examined through any reflective political prism – partition or emigration, neutrality or nationalism – it only leads to a conclusion that the government consciously and deliberately changed its foreign policy emphasis away from political considerations to economic ones between the years 1957 to 1966. Ireland embarked upon this economic odyssey primarily in order to emerge from a lesser-developed status, not necessarily in itself a disagreeable transition. Certainly, the country which Lemass left behind after his resignation was a totally different one to that which he had inherited. It is evident that by the mid-1960s Ireland enjoyed an enhanced liberal democracy with an open economy emphasising industrial development ahead of agriculture; it possessed a regenerated political elite which underscored a shift away from civil war politics to more modern preoccupations and it was experiencing a social reawakening that was being encouraged by both Anglo-American and European influences. Although in many respects structurally weak, it had modernised radically.

Obviously, the situation Ireland found itself in was not altogether of its own making. As a former colony, successive governments had interminable and understandable difficulties in developing an independent economy while trying to operate free of capitalist caprice in a hostile international environment. A Marxist analysis sees the recent past more in terms that the 'real turn' in 1958 was from 'British neo-colony to EEC/USA neo-colony'. According to Ronnie Munck, writing in *Ireland: nation, state, and class struggle*, the country was only a kind of 'small, subordinate cog' in an enormous capitalist wheel.[1] Clearly, changes in the European economy during the late 1950s – the creation of EFTA and the EEC – had indeed led logically to the AIFTA's development in 1965 and to Ireland's EEC entry in 1973, but what other choice did policy-makers have? Indeed, is it fair to perceive a foreign economic policy which advocated openness and market diversification – away from historic dependence on the UK to future interdependence with the EEC – as an ignoble enterprise? The results of reforms in policy direction resonated loudly throughout Ireland's economy and society, as traditionally-held political convictions were sacrificed for economic gain. As far as Lemass himself was concerned, it was a price that was well worth paying.

The fact is that developments in Europe up to 1966, in their own right usually more positive than negative, appealed to the government because of their modernising effects. This is not just commentators looking back with hindsight at, for example, Ireland's rather painful experiences during the FTA negotiations of the late 1950s or its exclusion from the EEC in 1963 as being beneficial in the long-term. The 'heady growth' experienced by the Six, the advantages of lowering internal tariffs, the evolution of CAP, access to a much larger market, and the political benefits accruing from economic accord, these were all attractive as well, especially as they would lead to a loosening of ties with the UK. De Gaulle's refutation of the latter's bid for accession and intransigence over issues such as supranationality aside, the potential of a beneficial outcome for Ireland in the medium-term remained very much alive. Therefore, the Irish government continued to prepare for eventual accession; indeed, a bid would be mounted at relatively little notice if the chances of success merited it. The EEC had shown a willingness to adapt to changing circumstances when and if necessitated, the Luxembourg compromise of 1966 – 'which purported to preserve the right of veto if a country had very important interests at stake' – was incontrovertible evidence of that.[2] It was clear that Lemass's policies would have to be continued by his successor, not just to attain accession, but for their own sake as well; yet, the UK remained the key.

Historically, Irish economic relations with the UK had been based on securing an outlet for agricultural produce. The various Anglo-Irish trade agreements provided for this. When the UK sought to join the EEC in 1961, it came as no surprise that Ireland reacted, even if it did so by promptly getting its application in first. In spite of this, as Brigid Laffan argues:

> ... the decision to apply for membership was not merely a passive reaction to a change in British policy but a decision that held out the beguiling prospect of placing Anglo-Irish relations in a wider multilateral setting.[3]

Paradoxically, in order for Ireland to extend its trading base outside of its existing restrictive economic reach, the AIFTA – an agreement which recognised economic realities, but which was diametrically opposed to Irish nationalist conventions – not only offered closer bilateral ties with the UK, but additionally gave it the chance to develop the range and quality of its products for expanded markets on a reasonably gradual basis. Of course, the AIFTA also had the benefit of preparing the country for the vigours of interaction with these other markets, particularly upon entry into the EEC. In turn, ameliorated economic relations with the UK enabled Ireland to face what might well have been a very uncertain future with some degree of self-confidence. Enhanced Anglo-Irish relations had political benefits as well.

It is quite apparent that Irish and UK ministers and officials meeting regularly in the context of both bilateral trade and European integration was 'immensely helpful' in developing an improved working relationship.[4] Bilateral concessions were both received and given. The remains of Roger Casement were, for instance, restored to Ireland on 23 February 1965 for reburial.[5] The return of a flag raised over the General Post Office during the Easter Rising followed one year later, just before the official commemorations.[6] Such episodes cannot be underestimated in terms of identity or, in truth, with regard to the tangibility of Anglo-Irish cooperation. This was very much a two-way process. A UK cabinet report from that period stated that there existed 'growing evidence of the Republican Government's desire to take a firm stand against ... IRA lawlessness and to co-operate with the Northern Ireland authorities', for example.[7] Thus, Dublin's interaction with London on economic matters extended into political collaboration as well, not only helping to reduce tensions, but also preparing Ireland for closer cooperation with the UK within the habitually envisioned context of the EEC.

In many respects, bilateral relations with the UK had never been better, but Ireland was looking further afield as well, even beyond the EEC. Additionally, domestic economic and political continuity, a material boom, and a more settled Western orientation, were considerable factors in the country's newly found self-assurance, allowing the Irish government to compare its achievements to those of Western Europe without embarrassment. All the same, nothing could be taken for granted, certainly not full EEC membership. Endeavours towards participation thus remained one of the more consistent and substantial aspects of the economy, alongside a revitalisation of domestic circumstances, a dependence upon the inflow of external capital to fuel rapid industrialisation, and periodically strengthened Anglo-Irish relations. It is with the evidence of this economic realignment that this final chapter – entitled *Ireland's European integration, 1957 to 1966* – proceeds, once evidence of change in the Irish political make-up has been revised and updated, prior to analyses of the roles that partition, emigration, neutrality and nationalism played in the Europeanisation of Irish affairs. Subsequently, this chapter explores the state of the Irish nation in 1966, before examining the substance of the Whitaker-Lemass dynamic. It concludes in two parts, surveying how Europe viewed Ireland, then exploring its future prospects as Lynch assumed control.

The political landscape and how it pertained to Europe: Part II [8]

Ireland's domestic political make-up was remarkably consistent throughout this period. This meant that Fianna Fáil stayed in power, while the opposition remained relatively divided. One of the principal problems that the opposition faced, of course, was that the policies being pursued by Fianna Fáil were obviously working. The latter's policies were benefitting large swathes of the Irish population and the 'feel good' factor that their forward looking policies engendered reflected in their relatively consistent high standing. What of the opposition? Why were they so ineffective? Were they so divided among and between themselves in this period that their lack of coherence handed Fianna Fáil a golden opportunity to stay in power or was there more to it than that? By briefly analysing the experiences of the other political parties in this decade, much of the political consensus that existed is evidenced, the lethargy of the opposition exposed, and the fact that the government carried its policies out relatively unhindered at home emphasised.

Like Fianna Fáil, Fine Gael had no clear class base for its support, but traditionally drew its voters from large farmers, manufacturers, conservatives, and liberals; both political groupings can justifiably be described as 'catch-all' parties. The leader of Fine Gael between 1959 and 1966 was James Dillon, latterly described by his party as having been distinguished for his 'intellectual ability and oratorical pugnacity'. In political terms Dillon was in fact a moderate, but he was also seen as a maverick, a status earned through his belief that 'Ireland should build on its historic links with Britain rather than deny them'.[9] Such beliefs were not politically advisable or pragmatic, especially when a nationalist, republican government was looking for a third way to economic independence. Indeed, views such as these were usually not advertised, even if they reflected the reality and fitted in with Fine Gael's own view that as a party it espouses opinions which are capable of 'realising the diversity of opinion and identity on the island of Ireland'. Nevertheless, even in the 1960s, it was the political party which advocated moderation and a centrist approach to politics. Undoubtedly, there was a remodelling of the party with Dillon's retirement as leader in April 1965, but this only came after the economic, political and social landscape had been utterly transformed. As a recent briefing paper on the history of Fine Gael remarks:

> In 1965 the publication of the 'Just Society' document signalled a new era for Fine Gael. It was to become a party of social reform complemented by its tradition of tolerance, openness and integrity. Younger, reformist minds ... [including Garret FitzGerald] came to dominate the party bringing innovation to the political arena.[10]

On the whole, Fine Gael was enthusiastic about European integration projects, but it was not in a position to influence the government unduly, even if it strengthened its position after the 1961 general election and reinforce its position as the major opposition party in Ireland. It certainly was not going to do so by espousing even greater dependence upon the UK.

A similar eagerness for all things European could not be said to have resided in the Labour party – Ireland's 'class-based' party which had rural and union support, as well as a more recent urban base – invariably Fine Gael's main coalition partner in any government when Fianna Fáil was voted out of office in 1948 and 1954. For nearly thirty years until he retired in March 1960, Norton was the leader of the Labour party, before being succeeded by Brendan Corish. Norton took an active part in the early days of the Council of Europe, but his party's attitude was generally ambivalent. In 1962, the Labour conference advocated that Ireland should basically do whatever the UK did.[11] One year later, with the admission of former Irish health minister, Noel Browne, into the parliamentary party, there were signs that the Labour party might begin to move back to the left, while the possibility of associate EEC membership – advocated by the two National Progressive Democrat parliamentarians who merged their forces with the Labour party that year – was considered more seriously. Indeed, within three years the latter was promoting a 'coherent, socialist philosophy'.[12] Although this development petered out, the question of EEC membership was hotly disputed internally as policy. By 1967, the Labour party had returned to a more traditional nationalist argument regarding Northern Ireland, in the process opposing Ireland's entry into the EEC partly, it was felt, because it would mean abandoning Dublin's right to demand unity. This bizarre logic increasingly tended to reflect Labour's opposition to European integration;[13] this was especially apparent during the referendum campaign for EEC membership in 1972 and merely reflected the convictions of a minority within the general Irish populace.[14]

However, it was the continuing inability of the Labour party to transcend Irish civil war politics, costing it dearly in terms of popular support and political representation. Unable to attract industrial workers in the same numbers as Fianna Fáil, Labour remained weak and divided. Socialist rhetoric has not been able to paper over changing opinions on the partition question, despite its attachment to popular policies such as social justice or military neutrality. Labour's parliamentary strength actually increased after the 1961 and 1965 general elections, but the divergence of views existing between the Labour party and Fine Gael on the European question did not aid the coherence of the opposition. As a consequence, the two parties were firmly out of power between 1957 and 1973; indeed, they were not even able to influence government policy unduly when it was in a minority position after 1961.

Additionally, there were also a number of smaller parties and independents represented in Dáil Éireann, including an innovative republican party, Clann na Poblachta, and what was effectively a small farmer's political pressure group, Clann na Talmhan. By the late 1950s, the influence of Clann na Poblachta as a political force had been on the wane for a decade, just as the other smaller parties and independents were doing. MacBride was its founder and most important member. According to Miriam Hederman, this Irish foreign minister 'had formulated a new foreign policy for the party, designed to reflect a radical, positive approach to external relations. Temperament and force of circumstances made him an "Irish European" in the context of his contemporaries'.[15] However, after the first Inter-Party government, this particular political party did not play an important role in the Europeanisation of Irish foreign policy. The other political party worth mentioning is Clann na Talmhan, who in many ways represented the interests of rural Ireland, but, having been successful in the mid-1940s, they were long declining by the end of the 1950s. The core support and policies of this party were by then represented by either Fine Gael or Fianna Fáil, before being slowly absorbed.

Fianna Fáil's 1957 election victory, although disappointingly followed by a reduction in seats four years later, proved to be a stabilising factor in economic and political terms. It campaigned in 1961 on a platform promoting its 'record of economic progress', while also advocating the prospect of further economic advancement once Ireland joined the EEC.[16] Although short of a majority, Fianna Fáil formed a minority government which proved to be surprisingly stable; partly due to divisions within the opposition, Lemass was able to govern with relative ease, while Ireland's proportional representation system – the single transferable vote – which slightly favours larger parties in terms of representation, helped to keep them in power. The electorate duly rewarded Fianna Fáil in 1965; in fact, in that general election, the incumbents won exactly half of the seats and enhanced its status as the 'natural' party of government. Working closely with trades unions and employers, farmers and workers, an era of revolutionary economic reform was advocated throughout, with preparations for entry into the EEC being a constituent part. In reviewing Fianna Fáil's position on Europe compared to that of Fine Gael, Martin Mansergh has written:

> Fianna Fáil for a party attached to national sovereignty had few doubts about the desirability of Ireland being part of Europe as a real extension of sovereignty, through we would be less instinctively federalist and more pragmatic in our approach than Fine Gael ...[17]

Once it had power, however, the most important point was that it was very difficult to shake Fianna Fáil off its chosen course, whether that was political, social or economic.

Changes in orientation: the evidence of exports and imports

It has already been intimated that the evidence of exports and imports backs up the assertion that Ireland had changed its economic and political orientation. Not only was it exporting a wider variety of products worth significantly more money to an ever more eclectic collection of countries, but it was also sourcing the goods that it imported from an array of different states, utilising the power that this gave for positive domestic progress and improved global relations. Ireland had entered the modern age twenty years after the rest of Western Europe, at first rather reluctantly, shaking off the stagnation of the previous decade, but quite quickly embracing such change. The numbers duly back up such assertions, because within the space of a decade the direction and make-up of the Irish economy was totally transformed, with industrialisation and agricultural reform at the heart of government planning, thus paving the way for political rebirth and social reformation.

In comparing where Irish goods went to in 1966 against where they went to in 1957, it is clear that the UK still dominated Irish economic thinking. The evidence is incontrovertible. Although Ireland's dependence upon the UK market decreased in real terms over the decade in which Lemass was a central character, it still prefigured all other considerations. In 1966, nearly 70% of total Irish goods went to the UK. That may have been a substantial decrease of nine percentage points on the earlier date, but it was irrefutable evidence that the UK was still a dominant and overbearing force. Only the EEC made any pretence at being anything resembling an alternative destination having nearly doubled its significance in the space of a decade, thus establishing itself as a prospective market. Throughout the intervening period, EFTA had remained unimportant in any meaningful terms; of course, the same applied to the remaining OEEC countries. That really only left the US in a position to make an impression on these figures, regularly accounting for 7-8% of the remaining exports as Ireland constantly searched for fresh markets. The fact of the matter was that, although it had succeeded up to a point in finding new destinations for its produce, the second and third placed markets – the EEC and the US respectively – paled into insignificance when compared to the UK. The years in which Lemass exercised control saw fundamental changes, but it was not the cultivation of new marketplaces which was the most interesting development; it was the shifting composition of Irish exports which was garnering the most noteworthy attention and support.[18]

Under Lemass, Ireland made the most of rather limited resources. Agriculture was the dominant sector in the economy, so the decision to change its orientation away from primary to processed products was an innovative move. The CAP incentive did not arrive until mid-1966, but then offered Ireland – once if acquired entry – an advantageous position of much increased agricultural subsidisation through central European funds.[19] Meanwhile, within the space of ten years, the make-up of Irish exports was transformed, rather dramatically at that. From an unhealthy reliance on sales of live animals – accounting for nearly 43% of all exports in 1957, a figure which in a decade halved percentage-wise while remaining much the same in monetary terms – Ireland was rapidly able to discover new markets for its processed goods, steadily increasing the foreign sales of its food, drink and tobacco products from around 31½% to nearly 36% of total export figures. Unquestionably, the most dramatic dissimilarity between the two dates came regarding the importance of manufactured goods, nearly doubling the magnitude of this sector in ten years, so that it suddenly became Ireland's largest export category.[20] The abandonment of protectionism as the 1960s progressed, coupled with the Irish government's strategy of promoting industrial growth – firstly through inward and then by means of foreign investment – accounted for this sharp rise in the sale of manufactured goods. By 1966, these came to symbolise the revolution that had taken place in the economy, even if an intrinsically unremunerative sector such as live animals was still a mainstay. There was also the promise that, once Ireland had implemented the full provisions of the AIFTA, full EEC membership would provide an even greater impulse towards increased foreign direct investment.[21] If these changes in Irish exports signalled a transformation in the orientation of the economy, upon what types of imports did Ireland stay dependent and from where did these products originate or had these figures dramatically altered as well?

On the face of it, the totals pertaining to the origin of Irish imports may not seem to be overly interesting at first glance. It is true that Ireland was sourcing many of its import needs from further afield than the UK but, as its nearest neighbour provided over half of its import requirements, this does suggest that this position of dependence was a mutually beneficial one. Indeed, the UK had an important market for its produce in these years, counterbalancing Ireland's need for access to the UK marketplace. Nevertheless, there is also clear evidence that the Irish government was also promoting a policy of using access to its internal market to enhance its relations with other countries. Both the EEC and the US benefitted from this policy, with the former regularly accounting for up to and over 15% of Irish imports, while the US was often making up the best part of 10% in total. During this time, the share for the rest of EFTA did not change in percentage terms, even if the volume did, while the remaining OEEC countries were a relatively trivial consideration once again. Overall, although it was proving to be a particularly slow process for Ireland to wean itself off the UK when sourcing its additional requisites and resources, the fact is that some progress was being made.

Of course, Ireland's major import needs were technological and concentrated on capital-intensive products and other highly valued manufactured goods. As industry and the general consumer had voracious appetites for durables of all kinds, disposable income and investment respectively came to be constituent parts of the economy. Obviously, a sector like live animals was well catered for by indigenous production, but it contrasts very well with the part this category played in total exports. The prevailing pattern over the ten year period showed no major changes, which not only goes to show that Ireland's dependence on certain goods endured, indeed that the country continued – with only the very slightest variations – to source them from essentially the same places, but that it further demonstrates that a plan had been made and followed. The only evident difference of note was that the importation of manufacturing goods went up by a significant 2½% percentage points, representing more than a doubling in monetary terms.

Ireland was modernising fast. It could cater for its own basic needs, but to compete in a free market it would also have to adapt to changing styles of trade, where the competition for newer export markets was far greater and dependent upon quality, price and innovation, where access to a huge free market made Ireland an attractive site for foreign investment, and where indigenous products would have to compete in the home market with imported goods. The economic present was a challenge and would become harder still, but it was not a threat unless inaction was mistaken for decisiveness. Lemass made several mistakes, but a lack of resolution or the fear to make decisions were not amongst them. This trait was again obvious in his attitude to Northern Ireland and the part that it played in Irish life, but it was evident in other conscious decisions that he took as well regarding such diverse issues as emigration, nationalism and neutrality. Interestingly, aside from his direct involvement in the country's reorientation away from the UK to Europe, it is in relation to Northern Ireland that he may well have had his most fundamental, if not necessarily wholly intentional, influence.

Northern Ireland's role in Irish-European affairs

In 1957, Ireland remained far behind its northern neighbour. Writing in *The dynamics of Irish politics*, Paul Bew *et al* have convincingly reinforced an argument regarding the importance of what they term the 'demonstration effect', which revealed, for instance, the considerably higher levels of social provision in the UK; this was accentuated by the decision to apply for EEC membership, only heightening an awareness in Ireland of the gap that had opened up between itself and other European countries.[22] In comparative terms, there had been some degree of convergence by 1961, with the Irish economy catching up just as Northern Ireland's began to slow down. Belinda Probert, writing in *Beyond orange and green*, notes that:[23]

> ... in the context of possible membership ... it was becoming apparent that the economic structure of Ireland had been transformed in such a way as to greatly reduce the significance of the barrier between North and South ...

Dating from 1965, improvements in north-south political relations were reflected in economic harmonisation, as the AIFTA foreshadowed prospective membership of the EEC. The 'policy of the sore thumb' –

Ireland's constant whinging about partition – had not worked at all with its European neighbours because the issue did not really interest them. Within an integrated Europe, there was some hope however of achieving understanding and cooperation between the two states sharing the island. In the process, Ireland was showing an ability to adapt to a new, post-war version of imperialism, that is neo-colonialism. It was intent on embracing 'multinational capitalism and the great transnational corporations' instead of rigidly sticking to protectionism as it had done in the first half of its decolonised existence.[24] Ireland in the mid-1960s was a radically different place to the country that it had been in the mid-1950s and was beginning the process of catching up with its neighbour and erstwhile adversary.

Despite Fianna Fáil's rhetoric, de Valera was at least partially responsible for the lack of urgency which became attached to solving the Northern Ireland question in his latter years as party leader and Irish premier. Indeed, upon victory in the 1957 general election, he called for '"one great and combined effort", not to end partition, but to end the country's economic ills'.[25] Thus, in pursuing policies of what was basically economic rapprochement with the UK in the late 1950s and early 1960s – just as he had done in the late 1930s – Lemass in turn did his utmost to soothe bilateral Anglo-Irish relations, while simultaneously not generating any national dissent by ruffling republican feathers. A symbolic extension into the political field, thereby improving relations with the Northern Ireland government and also relaxing the 'sore thumb' policy, was the natural step for a radical economic realist and patient political pragmatist to take. This new policy was first evidenced by the efforts of the governments to defeat the IRA – which between December 1956 and February 1962 together they essentially did – but it was the meetings between the two prime ministers which had the most impact. At the same time, however, this delicate change in policy alignment legitimised partition by recognising its existence, if not *de jure* in the written word through treaties, at least *de facto* through symbolic actions and deeds.[26] Of course, such interaction effectively ended a period of 'bitter hostility' marked not by conflict but by rhetoric; it could not have been achieved without similar thinking emanating from the corridors of power in Belfast.

The taoiseach maintained that more affable relations with Ireland's northern neighbour, inexorably linked to economic progress within the context of Europe, would eventually allow the peaceful ending of a partition which saw the island divided into two distinct jurisdictions. Indeed, he supposed that a redeveloped and invigorated Ireland – economically, politically and socially – would through time become more attractive to Northern Ireland. Nevertheless, in publicly speaking this way about weakening partition, Lemass sometimes abjured the realities of the division;

partition was very real, it could not be wished away and from that there was no escaping.[27] It was more customary for him to be placatory and understanding, as he was in an interview given to the *Belfast Telegraph* on becoming taoiseach. Indeed, this particular contribution to a developing debate on the relationship between Ireland and Northern Ireland was subsequently recognised as the 'most constructive attitude to the problem of partition that had yet emerged' from a politician of his standing. Gradually, increased cooperation followed between the Dublin and Belfast governments in matters of mutual interest such as electricity, tourism, and transport. It was undoubtedly true that Lemass's opinions were sometimes at variance with traditional anti-partitionist dogma, but he was able to employ such language when it suited him. On the whole, however, he was sensible and sensitive in his approach.[28] Indeed, there was some striking evidence emerging that a new and more realistic dimension to north-south relations was dawning. In July 1963, Lemass went even further along the path of detente in a speech which basically represented a complete *volte-face* in government policy, thus opening the way for what amounted to a recognition of the *status quo*.[29] The taoiseach was making all the right noises – explicitly dropping anti-partition as official policy – as he reached out to Ireland's northern neighbour.[30] Dublin keenly hoped that moderate politicians in Belfast were listening with interest.

A new and relatively liberal Northern Ireland prime minister, Terence O'Neill, came to power on 25 March 1963, having previously served as a home affairs and finance minister during which time he successfully endeavoured to attract industries and foreign investment. From the outset, with confidence in the ability of the state low, he made it clear that he aimed to revitalise the country's ailing economy which was convulsing from the collapse of the linen and shipbuilding industries. In order for Northern Ireland to compete in an ever-changing international environment, technological improvements – in areas such as agriculture, industry, and transport – were undeniably the way forward economically. Coupled with the adoption of economic planning to deal with its mounting problems – pressures such as a rural economy, the rises in underemployment and unemployment, and the beginnings of social unrest – the next step, although possibly the hardest, could not be put off any longer.

On three separate occasions, Harold Macmillan asked the Northern Ireland premier to see whether relations with Dublin might not be improved. This policy was also favoured by his successor as Conservative prime minister, Alec Douglas-Home, who expressed a hope to O'Neill on 22 November 1963 that he should meet with Lemass; this pressure on O'Neill was sustained under a relatively unsympathetic Labour government at Westminster one year later. For the new administration in London, it was not so much a symbolic meeting which was urged, rather that Stormont had to start facing stark facts and expediting change, including facing the detrimental effects of the island's intransigently distinct economies. At the same time, conciliatory signals were emerging. Although it might be argued that rhetoric is cheap – with Lemass declaring his ready 'willingness to meet the prime minister at any time to discuss practical problems of common interest and methods of co-operation to solve them' – there had been real changes in outlook. It was surely only a matter of time before a thaw in north-south relations came about and an invitation for the taoiseach to visit Belfast was extended. Then the matter would be in Dublin's hands.[31]

Planned with the utmost secrecy, the taoiseach's visit to Belfast on 14 January 1965, criticised wildly by fundamental Protestant tendencies, adds to a positive historical assessment of both leaders. Such a profound and symbolic decision to invite his southern counterpart to discuss matters of bilateral interest showed some foresight and was in many respects brave. Perhaps mistakenly taken without prior consultation with most members of his cabinet, this move was condemned by hardliners as the abandonment of traditional unionism. Although it was of course bound to arouse controversy and was by definition ill-prepared, this softening in relations did have genuinely beneficial results, both economic and political. For instance, Lemass's role in cajoling the National Party – a Northern nationalist political grouping seeking Irish unity – to act as the official opposition to those in Stormont favouring unionism was worthy of praise in the context of normalising northern politics. He was also the first major southern politician to make any effort to afford unionist traditions their rightful legitimacy. Indeed, even his entrance into the seat of power in Northern Ireland was an admission that the state itself existed at all. In relation to agriculture, for instance, it soon became apparent that there could be north-south cooperation on veterinary matters; for a variety of reasons, however, industrial development on a mutual basis was not included, so in many respects, the reality of cooperation did not quite match up with the symbolism.[32]

This successful invitation was reciprocated on 9 February 1965 when in turn O'Neill visited Ireland. The potential for cooperation was still tremendous. Nonetheless, it has to be admitted that the fact that these bilateral meetings attracted so much attention just goes to demonstrate the extent to which partitionist attitudes and actions had taken over the mind-set of politicians in both Dublin and Belfast in the four decades following the creation of the two states. The border was not just a political or physical barrier; it had become an economic and mental barrier as well.[33] Thus, it was a significant psychological step to take for the two prime ministers to meet in the first place, even if the practical effects of their interaction were somewhat limited. Still, a start had been made and the opportunity for change was very real and, although it was in some ways unpalatable, the obvious solution to the mounting and seemingly intractable problems facing both governments thus appeared to be cooperation.[34] Up to this, the two parts of the island had been ignoring each other for well over forty years, much to their mutual detriment. Such a situation could not possibly be allowed to continue, certainly not *ad infinitum*. Inertia in the Northern Ireland political system, however, which was partly engendered by nearly half a century of single partly rule, made it quite difficult to deal with the economic problems facing such a small and divided society. The launch in January 1965 of a programme entitled *Economic development in Northern Ireland*, although a positive step in the right direction, mirrored similar initiatives taken in Dublin. Nonetheless, because O'Neill did not enjoy the intrinsic domestic support in Northern Ireland that his Irish counterpart did, he was in a considerably weaker position to force the pace of accommodation and adjustment. It must be said that Lemass's agenda was not necessarily the same obviously as the Northern Ireland premier's, but they were interested in some similar ends.[35]

It was certainly clear that European integration was not going to be some kind of easy fix for partition. Alternatively cajoling or humouring Northern Ireland, the taoiseach helped to keep republicans satiated while creating the conditions necessary to break the impasse in north-south relations.[36] Northern Ireland was still determined to confront its own problems without compromising upon its identity. In the end, it was the economy which was attracting most attention in Dublin of course, not what was happening north of the border. Essentially, partition's existence was accepted, as the focus was turned to an economy that required much strengthening.[37] Ireland had its own problems, including the appeasement of wage demands and social deprivation; but, Lemass felt that there was not much that he could do in some respects other than to encourage responsible behaviour in workers and in employers.[38] By the mid-1960s, growth rates were an admirable 4½% on average, while Northern Ireland, with growth in the shape of 3¾%, was not particularly far behind.[39] The two economies were performing well ahead of the UK norm. There was no reason necessarily to anticipate the political or social crises yet to come. In truth, Ireland's expected economic amelioration within the EEC was an altogether distinct project from any aspirations towards political unity that membership in time might encourage, even if a shift to an open and progressive economy brought the south more into line with the practices more common to the north. Such progress notwithstanding, there were political and social storm-clouds on the horizon.[40]

On 8 March 1966, 'Nelson's Pillar' in Dublin city centre disappeared in an explosive cloud of debris and dust.[41] Ireland's revolutionary republican *élan* which, as Tom Garvin has written, had grown weak during the 1950s, was still capable of destruction.[42] As ever, the timing was supremely symbolic because, as Ireland was celebrating the golden anniversary of the Easter Rising, any 'triumphalist ceremonies' commemorating the occasion only served to sour the Lemass-O'Neill initiative. Writing in *Partition and the limits of Irish nationalism*, Clare O'Halloran therefore believes the meetings to have been 'significant only as a brief departure from the prevailing sterile political relationship between Belfast and Dublin'. Although he held them to be at least in part responsible, the northern premier felt the 1916 commemorations taking place in Ireland to have been a 'useful scapegoat' for opposition to an initiative which, along with various other factors, led to the rapid deterioration in cross-border cooperation. Although Lemass was himself careful not to antagonise unionists, de Valera had no such qualms it appears and spoke passionately of the country's reunification and the language's revival. Was it just the case that 'uncompromising irredentism' had been replaced by a 'softly softly' approach?[43] Criticism of rapprochement though as some kind of 'cunning stratagem' appears rather cynical, if not disingenuous.[44] The taoiseach supported a realistic reassessment of anti-partitionist dogma, even if it was his successor who would have to carry that policy out in the face of republican hawks within Fianna Fáil. There was a feeling that 1966 marked the end of a 'post-independence' period in Irish history, although it was not yet clear exactly where Ireland was going except in one chief respect.[45] It would join the EEC when it was precipitate to do so, that is when the UK did and once it could then follow. What would that mean for north-south relations?

It is clear that all along there were serious unionist concerns regarding the implications of the UK and Ireland being members of the EEC simply because of the open border that this development would bring. Obviously, Northern Ireland would benefit from EEC membership because of the increases in economic activity. A price would have to be paid, however, as the discrimination enshrined in Northern Ireland's 'Safeguarding of Employment Act' dating from 1947 – which were expressly designed to restrict migration from the south to the north through a complex system of permits – would probably have to be discontinued by law. The fear among unionists was that this would lead to a marked increase in the flow of Irish labour into Northern Ireland, especially to towns like Derry and Newry, on a temporary and even permanent basis. One of the constraints which was considered was to 'restrict the franchise to ... [Northern Ireland] nationals'.[46] The future of north-south relations was in the balance, even if other issues had already been decided in the context of EEC membership. Ireland had been undergoing fundamental change in the name of European integration, even if Lemass insisted that it was worth doing for its own sake.

A price worth paying?

With the objective of economic and political integration at the heart of its very being, it was little wonder that the EEC proved to be of enduring interest to the government. Undoubtedly, the country's prospective membership was seen as a means of escape from the twin evils of economic stagnation at home and dependency upon the UK market abroad. It has explicitly been pointed out that the two main political parties in Ireland had each reached a consensus regarding the EEC by the late 1950s. Both Fianna Fáil and Fine Gael wanted the country to join and were quite willing to do all that was necessary for economic betterment; for instance, both parties were happy to see a policy such as neutrality diminished in importance or even in substance in return for an end to emigration. After 1963, it was Paris which proved to be the main obstacle to membership, not deficiencies in economic or political policies which the Irish were evidently becoming ever keener to iron out of existence.

It was clear to all what the benefits the EEC would bring. The developing CAP would boost farming and slow down the rural to urban population shift by fixing higher prices for produce and by guaranteeing production subsidies. The diversification of markets would offer more opportunities for industry than it would pose problems, while allowing Irish agricultural produce free access to as many as ten countries instead of just one. Additionally, the various economic development and rehabilitation programmes for which the Treaty of Rome provided would help to finance the future, not mortgage it. In sum, although Ireland's application for EEC membership was linked to, indeed dictated by, its dependence upon the UK's economy, it was thought that the main effect of full participation would be to reduce such reliance.[47] Having dealt with Northern Ireland in the previous section, an obvious question to be asked in the light of Miriam Hederman discerning four features – partition, emigration, neutrality and nationalism – which differentiated Ireland from its European neighbours, comes down to posing the following: what effects did the Lemass years have on these policies?

As a concept and as the reality reinforces, emigration has been an emotionally loaded phenomenon for Ireland. Indeed, for well over fifty years after the Great Famine of the late 1840s, it psychologically overshadowed

Irish society and thinking, enduring as long as first-hand recollection existed and even for generations beyond. Although not alone in this period as a European country to experience emigration, abiding economic and social haemorrhaging effects of this tragedy were still felt well into the early 1960s. Indeed, in the previous decade, emigration figures were greater than at any other period since the turn of the century; thus, by 1961, the Irish population stood at an all-time low of 2,818,341 people.[48] Occupying the national psyche to an enormous extent, its solution understandably became a priority for the government, especially in the public sphere, even if emigration was privately welcomed as an economic escape valve which lessened the impact of unemployment. In return, of course, the value in financial terms of the diaspora was that it acted as a conduit for funding back into the economy – mainly in industry, but later in tourism, and in emigrants remittances – and as an example of possible attainment. Nevertheless, there was internal migration as well. Indeed, fundamental to the restructuring of agriculture was the consolidation of land holdings in number and size, as well as the utilisation of land. This led to rural depopulation and to increases in urbanisation and emigration. Thus, there is truth in the view that the effects of capitalist production – dating from the nineteenth century, away from labour intensive tillage to land extensive, but more profitable, cattle production – were being felt generations later.[49] With an additional 62,000 inhabitants by 1966, a mini-census revealed one of Ireland's few increases in population since the Great Famine.[50] The only way to reinforce the reverse of the emigration trend that was beginning to take hold in the mid-1960s, as the effects of the economic boom were being felt, was to mitigate against any sudden or long-term downturns. EEC membership offered such a hope, even if its fulfilment remained problematic.

Since the foundation of the Irish state in 1921, neutrality had been an intimate element – explicit or implicit – of foreign policy. Ostensibly, it reached its height during the Second World War when it became a watchword but, with partition enduring, it has lasted right up to the present day in one form or another. Non-belligerence, although benevolent towards the Allies in wartime, became military neutrality in the decades that followed, most prominently in regard to Ireland's rejection of NATO. When coupled with an ignominious departure from the British Commonwealth, it had the effect of sharply restricting diplomatic activity. This post-1945 international isolation did not ease for some considerable time to come because, even if it was positively pro-Western in its ideological orientation, the Irish government began to exercise both qualitative and quantitative independence in foreign policy – chiefly through ostentatious activism at the UN – which was especially bewildering to the US. Entwined with its abhorrence of partition – appropriately described as an 'introverted, brooding sense of grievance' which appeared to determine foreign policy – it was as yet no easier in the late 1950s for Western Europeans to understand Ireland's continued refusal to participate in defence or military alliances, especially in the light of its subsequent peacekeeping activities. Referring to such contradictions as a 'Jekyll and Hyde' approach to security policy, Patrick Keatinge has written that the decision to join the EEC in 1961 'in effect made neutrality conditional on the extent of European integration'.[51] By the mid-1960s, it was becoming more apparent that the government would not allow Ireland's neutral status to pose any great difficulties when it came to adhesion to an organisation such as the EEC. Although expressly economic, the EEC was also intrinsically political. 'Ireland's policy of neutrality has always been conditional upon the possibility of abandoning it for a political end', Bill McSweeney has declared.[52] Under Lemass, Irish foreign policy was thus redirected away from military neutrality to full membership of an economic organisation which represented the Western European mainstream.[53] As Dermot Keogh has written:

> ... [His] unambiguous response ... on neutrality finally convinced the Six that a non-member of NATO would not constitute a problem. Ireland ... was prepared to join any military defence arrangement organised by the member states of the EEC.[54]

By 1966, neutrality was no longer perceived as a block on Ireland's entry into the EEC; even this problem of a European defence mechanism was neutralised in many ways once France was withdrawn from NATO's institutional structure.[55]

Nationalism has characterised itself in Ireland through various means including race, religion and territorial integrity, but was usually defined in the context of otherness through comparisons with the UK, that is through a distinct historical experience and separate cultural definition.[56] With nationalism in mind, it is in fact possible to use the criteria advanced by Paul Bew and Henry Patterson when viewing its nineteenth century Irish antecedent; they examined nationalism in the context of agriculture and industry and put forward the following definitions, both of which echoed Ireland in the second half of the twentieth century as well:

- '... it meant the rejection of large scale cattle ranches in favour of smaller farms, more tillage and a larger agricultural workforce';
- '... it meant the project of an Irish industrial revolution probably assisted by the use of the weapon of tariff protection'.

What did this mean in the context of Lemass's tenure? Clearly, it can be said that although agrarian radicalism was high in the mid-1960s, virulently pushing for Ireland's inclusion in the EEC, it no longer played the same role in the country's economy that it had done up to only a decade earlier. Certainly, grassland production now predominated and would not be threatened by uneconomic or backward practices associated with small farms and a large rural labour force. Thus, the role of agriculture in defining Irish nationalism had changed. Indeed, the same could be said for industry. Again, by the mid-1960s, foreign capital and economic liberalism were beginning to drive the economy. The era of subsidised, home-grown industry had come and gone. The transition from quota and tariff-based protectionism to liberalisation was well under way, with dreams of self-sufficiency going unrealised. Irish nationalism was as yet basically unaffected by conflict in Northern Ireland – it had not yet become equated with the violent interpretation of republicanism – but its definition was open to reinterpretation having undergone a tremendous inversion in the post-war decades. In summing up, Paul Bew and Henry Patterson have thus written that: 'It is very clear that one politician, Seán Lemass, played a decisive role in this process'. Although they do not deny that the latter continued to employ nationalism in his rhetoric to legitimise some decisions, they nevertheless argue that his 'gradualism and disingenuousness' disarmed detractors of the course he had chosen. As Lemass applied political reality to Whitaker's economic liberalism, Ireland was preparing itself for EEC entry. In the meantime, nationalism became a very secondary consideration; the collective Irish psyche was weighing up the advantages of 'Europeanism'.[57]

Looking at the situation in Ireland through these various socio-economic, military and political prisms of emigration, neutrality and nationalism, it is possible to see something of what was sacrificed; but, what had been gained exactly? Where did Ireland stand in 1966 in comparison to a decade earlier back in 1957? The long-term effects of economic expansion were not as yet clear, but there had been many changes; domestic politics were not the same, indeed, the results of social innovations were evidently becoming more and more striking on a daily basis. What was the state of the nation some ten years after *Economic development* had been unveiled and the government's resulting *Programme for economic expansion* been launched? What did the future hold for a country that was so hindered geographically and historically that its impediments had become as much psychological as anything else, a state which had reluctantly realised that it was dependent upon external developments over which it exercised little control? What point had Ireland reached and where did it go to from here? Exactly where did the EEC fit into this equation and what could the government do to help itself in that context? These were the kind of questions that were being asked as Lemass's tenure came to a conclusion.

1966: the state of the nation

By 1966, certain choices had been made that had fundamental repercussions for the future of Ireland, especially in relation to its economy, politics and society. In turn, each of these areas of Irish life has to be examined to question the country's preparedness to exchange the UK's economic system for membership of an EEC in which Anglo-Irish economic relations would be subsumed. Thus, starting with the economy, the three main areas that are investigated are the agricultural, industrial and tertiary sectors. When it comes to politics, the situation that year in Ireland is clarified and then compared to its northern neighbour. Finally, in relation to Irish culture and society, a general outline is presented on the rapid changes in opinions and trends regarding religion, language and education as a representative sample of the wider reformation in opinions and views. At last, the government and the country was making an 'overdue rendezvous with the realities of the later twentieth-century', as Ireland began to feel both the benefits and the drawbacks of modernisation.[58]

Raymond Crotty, writing in *Irish agricultural production*, argued that the government's *Second programme for economic expansion*, while explicitly anticipating marked increases in agricultural production, did not appear to provide for the mechanisms which were necessary to accomplish this eventuality. Importantly, however, this document did at least explain the requirement upon which its plans for agriculture's future were based and depended; it cited:

> ... the assumption that, in the second half of the 1960's, international market arrangements for our agricultural products (which at present, due to reasons outside the control of the Government, are unsatisfactory) will be considerably improved, as a result, *inter alia*, of our being admitted to membership of the E.E.C.

A basic assumption was thus compromised as a repercussion of Ireland's exclusion in 1963. Nevertheless, it should be added that although the author argued that EEC membership would bring an increase to Irish farm product prices, this did not mean that by itself it would lead to any significant increase in terms of agricultural output. Indeed, even if the farming lobby was very consistent in seeking EEC entry and had considerable influence over government, he felt that the prices to be paid for agricultural produce would only see a 15% increase, on average, not the radical boost to the economy that they appeared to be predicting. Still, as Garret FitzGerald has written, it would at least have access to a market where prices were not depressed by the inflow of 'dumped international farm produce' which contributed to the UK marketplace becoming increasingly unrewarding. All assumptions about entry were open to review in 1966, particularly as Raymond Crotty argues that, despite all the rhetoric about an expansion in the importance of agriculture, the reality remained very different. After all, the volume of net agricultural production was basically the same at the end of the Lemass period as it had been in the beginning. In truth, despite the Irish government's rhetoric about joining the EEC before the end of the decade, full membership was still not as yet guaranteed.[59]

Nonetheless, the state of Irish industry in 1966 was very different again compared to agriculture, as was the situation regarding the services sector of the economy. Using similar criteria for industry to that used in assessing agriculture's readiness for Ireland's accession, Raymond Crotty convincingly demonstrated that the volume of net industrial production more than doubled in a decade; indeed, the respective figures for the third area of the economy were just as impressive.[60] John Bradley *et al* have written that while 'agricultural exports dominated trade up to the mid-1960s', manufactured goods soon became the preeminent part of Ireland's export total; additionally, the 'source of imports and, in particular, the destination of exports has broadened' since then.[61] Clearly, it was manufacturing industry – much of its growth due to the government's policy of attracting foreign investment, especially that of export-oriented multinationals – which was starting to account for a larger employment share, total Irish exports, and the economy's output. The contrast to Northern Ireland, which only enjoyed a brief surge in the 1960s that contradicted a generally unremitting economic decline, was palpable and of much propaganda value. 'The process of industrialisation, including its social ramifications, is central to an understanding of historical change in modern Ireland', as Liam Kennedy has eloquently stated.[62] This was the era that finally saw the modernisation and internationalisation of the Irish economy with employment, for instance, standing at around 4.8%; bare figures such as this demonstrated exactly where the country now stood in 1966 in relation to the previous position it had held back in 1957.[63]

The differences between Ireland and Northern Ireland were also visible in the tertiary sector. While the former was, for example, able to develop an increasingly significant tourist industry – aided by the setting up of Bord Fáilte in 1955 and the inauguration of transatlantic air travel in the early 1960s, thus facilitating outside contacts and attracting lucrative business, which by 1967 had passed the IR£80m mark, as earnings in this burgeoning sector grew by around 5% *per annum* – the latter stagnated in comparison. The mid-1960s saw an economic boom, reflected in societal changes, that in many ways Northern Ireland had already experienced. The former was planning for full employment, while the latter was combatting problems that had been suppressed or had not been experienced for a generation.[64] Indeed, Ireland was only just beginning to open up to exciting new ideas, possible developments and experiencing freedom when its neighbour was entering into a period of brooding reflection, consolidation and hazardous introspection.

It is also possible to see a parallel in the politics of the two countries, as this period saw a progressive renewal and invigoration in the south that was only matched by a reversal in the fortunes of a Northern Irish state steadily moving from moderation to destructive radicalism and entrenchent fundamentalism.[65] Politics in de Valera's Ireland were localised, parochial and clientelistic; his successor made some attempts to change that practice with limited success. When Lemass abruptly decided to retire from politics in October 1966, an era in contemporary Irish history came to a sudden end. As Dermot Keogh has written, it seems that he felt the time had come for a younger political generation – most of whom, having been elected in March 1957, he had himself gradually appointed – to take the reins of power. As Lemass had no designated successor, it was left to the Fianna Fáil parliamentary party to determine its new leader so that he could be put forward for election as taoiseach in Dáil Éireann. As a result though of various, rather disparate, candidates representing different tendencies and traditions within the party not being in a position to attract enough party support, a compromise solution was reached. The Irish finance minister, Jack Lynch, was put forward for election and took over the running of the country the following month. Having achieved so much in office in such a limited space of time, it is true that not securing EEC membership was one of Lemass's few regrets and was also evidence that his radicalism did not realise all of his stated aims and ambitions. Assessed as a 'taker of risks' – *vis-à-vis* his relations with Belfast, focusing Ireland on Europe, domestic policy – he certainly won more political arguments and battles than he lost. Dermot Keogh maintains that, having transcended the past, Lemass reformed Ireland's present and radically outlined its future, both economically and structurally, before handing power over to a new generation. Although he was not necessarily presented with a poisoned chalice, the new taoiseach would have a lot of work to do to keep rival factions united, while trying to realise what was now deemed as the indispensable goal of economic and political policy, full EEC membership.[66]

The political situation in Northern Ireland was much more complex, with the Belfast government at Stormont coming under a verbal siege. In making moves suggesting a thaw with Dublin, O'Neill's position as prime minister, although not necessarily under direct threat, was compromised. However, it was becoming more and more evident to the UK government that 'in the context of membership of the European Communities, Northern Ireland and the Republic will have certain common difficulties and opportunities which will differ in some respects from those which will face Great Britain'.[67] EEC membership would undoubtedly affect north-south relations rather markedly.[68] Therefore, as much as Westminster needed the Northern Irish government to deal with the problems it faced effectively and justly, it was beginning to appear that Stormont might not be equal to the task. The differences between Ireland and Northern Ireland were defined in diametrically opposed ways; just as the former was becoming a little more liberal and out-going, the latter was becoming increasingly conservative and inflexible. Economic and political rejuvenation, tied up in the concept of EEC membership, was reflected in Ireland as a whole.

By the mid-1960s, culture and society in Ireland had radically altered, a phenomenon reflected in changes in attitudes to the Catholic Church, a continuation in the decline of the language, and a reformation in education. The period when the government in Dublin regarded the Vatican as the epicentre of world power had long since passed away. The zenith of the Catholic Church's influence in domestic affairs had been marked in the early 1950s by the 'Mother and Child' controversy. From that point onwards, a slow but steady decline in the importance of religion in Ireland ensued, even if political visits to Rome were always of propaganda value. Successive popes – Pius XII, John XXIII and Paul VI – correctly viewed Ireland as a bastion, one of the world's most Catholic countries. Indeed, in reference to the fifteenth centenary celebrations of Saint Patrick in 1961, one pope was moved to remark on 'the harmonious relations existing between Church and State in Ireland which enabled you [Uachtarán na hÉireann (the Irish president)] and the highest officials of the Government to participate so fully in the splendid commemoration of Ireland's national patron and great apostle'.[69]

Nevertheless, the process begun by Lemass – 'somewhat cooler' in his attitude to the Catholic Church than de Valera, without being 'particularly anticlerical, or laic in political outlook' – was leading to a pluralist outlook and more tolerant society, one created in communion with a growing materialism and secularism, as a period of 'quiescence' descended on relations between Irish churchmen and statesmen. The Second Vatican

Council tended to reinforce this new vision of the relationship between church and state. Ever so slowly, film and literary censorship was relaxed and the Catholic Church's role in education and medicine lessened. Changes did not mean that the church was accepting policy with equanimity – indeed, it championed Christian charity and welfare reform in the shape of new housing – just that it no longer wielded the power to influence new practices unduly if the state was determined to see them enacted. Ireland's bucolic society was slowly contracting, with the nation gradually being enlivened by a growing spirit of ecumenism and by the modernisation of Irish attitudes.[70] Indeed, Garret FitzGerald has specifically written that the 'opening up [of] a much wider range of contacts between Ireland and the Continent has modified to some degree the impact of Anglo-American culture'.[71]

Of course, one of the rudimentary definitions of Irish individuality – its language – had also taken a battering. Constant exposure to English, whether in normal daily interaction or through newspaper readership, radio or television, meant that the days had died away when hopes of revitalising its wide usage were strong. In speaking so regularly of the vital role it played in realising and, indeed, in distinguishing nationality, de Valera frequently lamented its decline as the embodiment of Irishness, fearing a future in which the country would sink into 'amorphous cosmopolitanism'; it did not necessarily hold the same appeal for Lemass.[72] At the beginning of the nineteenth century, the language spoken by the mass population had been Irish. However, already within a couple of generations of the Great Famine, that decline had become so inexorable that as the twentieth century began this figure was 12% and falling. Well before the 1960s, despite a national reawakening earlier in the century, the language was seen as an integral part of the past, not as a symbol of what was to come. It was the UK, the US and the British Commonwealth which had traditionally been the destinations of emigrants, places where the Irish language had been of relatively little use. Now that Irish people were returning home to a booming national economy, it was Europe which was seen as the future. The traditional language – accounting for only 2½% of the population – had a negligible role to play in such a rapidly evolving environment.[73] Indeed, even when it came to the nation's name, it was apparent that the concept of progress would be enshrined.[74]

Interestingly, this was also reflected in changes in the structures and attitudes towards education in Ireland. This policy was initiated by Lemass on becoming taoiseach as funds were redirected towards an investment into one of the country's richest natural resources, its inhabitants. In 1962, the Irish section of the European Association of Teachers was founded as hopes of joining the EEC became buoyant. That same year, Patrick Hillery, the education minister, was able to write:

> Closer contact with the Continent should, as its first effect, redeem us from a certain provincialism which hangs heavily over the Irish mind. It is bad for us to have our intellectual, educational, artistic and other horizons confined to these islands, with only a very occasional glance over the hedge at what is going on in the rest of Europe.

It has been said that the movement towards a united Europe was an 'aim which was closely in line with the traditions both of Catholicism and of Irish scholarship on the Continent'. Although only a small section of society, the fact that the impact of European integration was being debated among educationalists at all was indicative of Ireland's evolving orientation and its openness to EEC membership. The government was already involved in education at the European and global level through the OECD and in 1962 also joined the UN Educational, Scientific and Cultural Organisation. Symptomatic of the necessity to break away from 'introspective practices', a decision on the need for a reconsideration and reorientation of the role in Ireland of education quickly led, for instance, to a reform of the secondary school system. Changes such as this resulted from plans published in September 1966 under the suggestive heading *Investment in education* by Donogh O'Malley, himself described as the 'most dynamic and imaginative in a series of energetic Ministers of Education'. The OECD had initiated this report in 1962; even in education, Europe was quite clearly the future direction in which Ireland was heading.[75]

It is quite obvious that the Ireland which Lemass left behind was rather a different country to the one which he had inherited. In all sectors of the economy, politics and society, there appeared to have been a fundamental revision, although it had not yet reached the stage that 'there is no longer any real poverty', as Richard Finnegan wrote.[76] By 1966, there was still a long way to go; by no means had Ireland attained all of the goals that Lemass had set out to achieve. Nonetheless, major steps had been taken to rectify the ills that affected the country and that had negatively effected its chances of entering the EEC in the first place. Politicians were more aware of these needs; perhaps more importantly, there was evidence that society as a whole – farmers, industrialists and workers included – were also coming to realise the relevance of European integration to their daily lives. If any one element was to be considered integral to the realisation of this process, to the centrality of the EEC in foreign economic thinking, it would have to be the energy and intelligence that were brought to bear on this subject by the two people who have become synonymous with this age.

The Whitaker-Lemass dynamic

Within the space of ten years, an economic orthodoxy which had in truth dominated Ireland's orientation since the early 1930s was suddenly turned on its head and speedily reversed. The recognition of Irish economic frailty and European vitality helped to reverse completely what was heretofore accepted as irrefutable, perhaps near infallible, teaching. Back in 1932, the Fianna Fáil election manifesto contained the following declaration that it pledged to introduce on agricultural and industrial development, as well as foreign trade:

> To organise systematically the establishment of the industries required to meet the needs of the community in manufactured goods ... to make ourselves as independent of foreign imports as possible and to provide for our people the employment that is at present denied them. Suitable fiscal laws would be passed to give the protection necessary against unfair foreign competition ... To preserve the home market for our farmers and to encourage the production by them of our food requirements to the greatest extent possible ... To negotiate trade agreements that would secure for our products preferences in foreign markets, always subject to the condition that the protection required for the maintenance and development of our own agricultural and manufacturing industries will not be lessened. The people of Britain and ourselves are each the other's best customer. Our geographical position and other factors make it unlikely that this close trade relationship will rapidly change. Machinery and other capital equipment for our industries will have to be purchased from abroad. We can in these purchases accord a preference to Britain in return for a preference in her markets for our agricultural produce.

A quarter of a century later, this policy had in effect still not changed very much. Fianna Fáil autarky and protectionist policies replaced the cautiously orthodox, but paradoxically open, economy favoured by the Cumann na nGaedheal governments of the 1920s. One of the last European states to introduce protectionism, the country was dominated by such thinking for thirty-five years, long after the rest of Europe had relinquished this practice.[77]

Between 1957 and 1966, two people in particular were responsible though for a radical remodelling of the government's economic policy and for spearheading reform. In the process, both ignorant provincialism and die-heart nationalism, two of the main obstacles to economic progress, were eroded from their positions of accepted conscious and subconscious orthodoxy.[78] Following a decade of seemingly aimless 'drift', it was progressive leadership and confidence that the country lacked most; indeed, these would become central elements in taking advantage of the 'rising tide lifting all boats'. However, the government would also have to be aware of an ever-present danger, as F.Scott Fitzgerald wrote, of being one of those 'boats against the current carried back ceaselessly into the past'.[79]

Seán Lemass was a perceptive politician and a receptive man. Having served in every de Valera administration between 1932 and 1959, basically as the senior economic minister, he was the most adept candidate to take over as taoiseach. Despite having to restrain his own radicalism for many years and having been responsible for implementing a strict protectionist policy that became synonymous with Fianna Fáil inspired economic nationalism, he was open to new ideas regarding Ireland's future economic direction. That was where T.K.Whitaker came into the equation. A retiring albeit resolute individual, the latter convinced Lemass to adapt a different approach to economic affairs.[80] Having served in the civil service for over two decades before he became the most senior civil servant in the finance ministry in 1956, he had his own ideas about how to run the economy and, by having recourse to the opinions of economists, intellectuals and other members of the civil service, he has become directly associated with the change in economic fortunes. Nevertheless, it was the fusion of these individuals' prescience which paved the way for real change. Although Lemass may not have been the economic 'superman' that adherents portrayed or Whitaker the financial equivalent of a soothsayer, it would be a grave mistake not to recognise fully the vibrant nature of their relationship or, fearing the creation of economic and political deities, not to give historical credit where it is due.[81] It is true that, 'without the courage of his political masters', much of Whitaker's initiatives would have been stillborn'; running contrary to de Valera's notion of Ireland – who exercised some 'considerable influence', even if it quickly diminished, in his early years as Irish president – Lemass accepted most of this senior civil servant's advice and vision, seeing to it that these ideas were implemented as policy.[82]

Ireland had already experienced economic cooperation in the European context with the enactment and distribution of Marshall Aid. D.George Boyce, writing in *Nationalism in Ireland*, presents his view of the changes during the late 1950s and early 1960s in the context of the Whitaker-Lemass dynamic. A dominant figure in cabinet, the taoiseach exercised full control over his administration, thus allowing him to give 'life and vigour' to the proposals of his finance secretary. In drawing attention to a quarter of a century of limited successes interspersed with the many continuing failures in policy, Whitaker cited a multifarious array of economic inhibitors, including the 'backwardness of agriculture, the stagnation of industry, the decline in population, emigration, the lack of public capital, and the lack of intelligent direction of public capital' as being particularly offensive. His exacting remedy was for the 'State to spend money on modernising agriculture and industry, to solicit for foreign capital by tax concessions and other facilities, and to abandon the old ... policy of protection for its own sake'.[83] In all probability, Ireland would soon be participating in a European free trading environment in one form or another, but would have to be ready economically and politically in order to do so. There were great risks involved in economic expansion and civil servants, employers, politicians, and workers took some convincing. Nonetheless, political stability allowed for an extensive economic programme to be followed through to a logical and fruitful conclusion and thus did not constantly face *ad hoc* determinants.

Of course, the finance secretary's role in bringing Lemass and O'Neill together was integral to creating this climate. It was through his working relationship with Jim Malley, the northern prime minister's private secretary, that an invitation to visit Belfast was extended by O'Neill to the Irish prime minister, an entreaty which after some hesitation was consequently accepted.[84] The fact of the matter was that Lemass and Whitaker complemented each other because they had the same basic goals in mind. Of course, it was the move to free trade and the concentration on economic considerations which distinguished this working relationship from most others.[85] That is why the partnership worked and that is one of the reasons why Europe began to become more convinced of Ireland's eligibility for the creation of a stronger link; the actual form of such ties was still somewhat open to debate, but that was the purpose of the accession negotiations, whenever they transpired.

The maintenance of a momentum towards free trade, characterised by the primarily symbolic 10% unilateral tariff cuts of 1963 and 1964, was inspired by an unshakable belief in the future well-being of the Irish economy within the EEC. However, practical steps were more important than aspirations. Thus, the domestic reviews of the readiness of agriculture and industry were crucial to creating the necessary atmosphere for the onslaught of free trade. Indeed, the AIFTA worked in the same way. Writing in his account of the *Irish Department of Finance*, Ronan Fanning has distinguished three principal interlinking components in the economic strategy which the finance department and in time the Whitaker-Lemass dynamic had promoted, listing them as:

- a requisite for the rapid enactment economic planning;
- the need for more diversity in external trade policy;
- the imperative of accession to the EEC.[86]

Arching over these considerations was Whitaker's firm belief that protectionism would have to be dismantled; otherwise Ireland faced economic impoverishment. Thus, in conjunction with the 'strength of the domestic developments set in train from the late 1950s' – Ireland's signing of the AIFTA, its participation in GATT, its eventual adhesion to the EEC – were all part of that process and evidence that the finance secretary won the argument.[87] Free trade was coming anyway, so he contended that it was better to have limited control – or at least the semblance of it – over the gradual enactment of adjustment policies, rather than having them painfully forced upon the country at some later stage, possibly by decree.[88]

Of all the elements that mattered, it was the EEC which remained of supreme import. In his efforts to convince the taoiseach of the legitimacy of his concept, the finance secretary argued from November 1960 that European developments would need to be watched closely and, once the UK began to make its position on EEC membership known from May 1961, Ireland had little choice but to follow the negotiations process wherever it led. Although the EEC was soon lost as a policy option in the near future, it was clear that a reorganisation of the economy for free trade was needed in its own right. Whitaker asserted that:

> ... [there] was a need to maintain a psychological impetus towards rapid adjustment to EEC conditions ... procrastination in making tariff reductions would merely result in a faster rate of reduction on joining the EEC ... [that unilateral reductions] would provide an earnest of our determination to adapt ourselves to EEC conditions ... [which] would be evidence not only of our realism but of our expectation that we would be admitted to membership.[89]

These tariff reductions led onto negotiations for the AIFTA because the UK was the realistic extent of Irish economic ambition in the short-term, whether in the context of GATT or the EEC, as their trading relations needed to be formalised from Dublin's perspective. The fact that Whitaker was able to convince Lemass of the legitimacy of his views over an extended period of time is testimony to his persuasive abilities and to the openness, strength and trust inherent in their professional relationship. The existence of a Whitaker-Lemass dynamic does not need eulogising, but that does not mean that it should not in fact be acknowledged; indeed, as one commentator has written, it is surely better to moderate 'traditional adulation' than just to debunk 'heroes'.[90]

Ireland viewed from Europe

It was becoming obvious to the Six and to the institutions in Brussels that Ireland no longer had rudimentary economic or political impediments to membership. The many dramatic improvements included an ever-expanding manufacturing base and an all-encompassing tariff revision, reassurances that the country was neither politically nor ideologically neutral, and improved Anglo-Irish relations in all areas of life. Dublin felt that it was ready to participate in the process of European integration – indeed, it continued to expect to be able to do so by the end of the decade at the very least – but what in turn did Europe think?

It was clear to Europeans that, although Ireland was paying 'lip-service' to the notion of political union, there was 'little intuitive understanding of the original motivations that led the countries of continental Europe to opt for integration'. Ireland was clearly only interested in accruing the economic benefits of membership. That being said, as Brigid Laffan makes clear in her *Integration and co-operation in Europe* in relation to contemporary Ireland:

> ... as a small state with a limited ability to influence its external environment, Ireland has a keen sense that the pooling of sovereignty is preferable to the maintenance of formal sovereignty without the power to exercise it.[91]

Even in the mid-1960s, Ireland was more than prepared to work towards economic integration and the material well-being of both itself and its partners; if in the process political integration resulted, the Irish attitude was so be it, the Lemass government could live with that. The time and energy expended in the abortive negotiations for a European FTA or the poor impression created at that stage by Irish demands for special treatment was not, in the long-term, time and energy wasted.[92] Ireland had worked at making a better impression in the intervening period, but it had also changed the actuality of its own position.

The second half of 1965 and the majority of 1966 had seen little interaction between Dublin and Brussels. Both had their own preoccupations, Ireland in securing the AIFTA, the EEC in surviving another de Gaulle inspired crisis. The question of enlargement receded into the background, but it was still there. Therefore, when the EEC found a formula through the Luxembourg compromise with which to proceed much as before and as London's interest in membership was rekindled, Ireland also began to pay close attention to events as they unfolded and prepared itself for any eventuality, including the resubmission of its candidature. As D.J.Maher has contended, the Irish government was not convinced of the perspicacity of resuming negotiations at that juncture, but it was not going to be caught unawares.[93]

Thus, Dublin set about making both major and minor adjustments to its relations with Europe, both inside and outside the Six. As an indication of its serious intent regarding full EEC membership, it decided to accredit a separate diplomatic mission to the three European Communities, while maintaining an ambassador in Brussels accredited to Belgium and, on a non-residential basis, to Luxembourg, a posting which itself had only been raised to embassy status a year previously.[94] In turn, on 13 September 1966, it was decided that Seán Morrissey would replace Francis Biggar as Head of the Mission of Ireland to the ECSC, EEC and Euratom; indeed, Biggar would be replaced by Gerard Woods as Irish ambassador to Belgium and Luxembourg, signifying the increased workload of its various representatives in Brussels.[95] Lemass's government also sought a meeting with the European Commission, the first such encounter at ministerial level for eighteen months; in addition, it decided to publish a further White Paper on the European Communities, due to come out in the early part of the following year. Its second round of negotiations to adhere to the EEC thus began in earnest, if not officially, one week later on 20 September 1966 when the finance minister, Jack Lynch, and Frank Aiken, the external affairs minister, met with various members of the European Commission in Brussels. The latter was represented by three commissioners: Sicco Mansholt at agriculture, Robert Marjolin at economic and financial affairs, and Jean Rey at external relations. For Dublin, this level of representation demonstrated overdue, if welcome, signs of the serious intent with which their case was now being viewed in Brussels.[96]

The main purpose of the delegation's visit was to express Ireland's continuing interest in the EEC; D.J.Maher has pointed out others, so that the reasons for this meeting were:

- to record the Irish government's abiding interest in membership;
- to explore the possibility of resuming negotiations;
- to discuss setting up an interim trading relationship;
- to allow for subsequent meetings at ministerial and senior official level.

Lynch and Aiken made it quite clear that EEC membership was at the forefront of the Irish government's foreign economic policy thinking. Indeed, Ireland's efforts at creating the right environment for entry were emphasised by Aiken along with its recent history of unilateral tariff cuts, unsuccessful efforts to negotiate interim agreements, and AIFTA's creation. Lynch supplemented this contribution by presenting a comprehensive analysis of the economic situation, supplying a detailed explanation as to how the AIFTA complemented the EEC and how it was 'providing a valuable means of preparing the Irish economy for the conditions it would encounter on accession to the EEC'. Further meetings were planned and the possibility of negotiations resuming towards the end of 1967, with accession coming two years later, was envisaged as being a reasonably likely scenario.[97]

This represented an innovation in the structure of Ireland's European integration policy as there was a new emphasis on who took the responsibility for handling negotiations. It was an understandable departure from the government's previous course, which had concentrated it in the hands of the taoiseach, demonstrating a new role for the external affairs and finance departments. Even if the Department of the Taoiseach still administered overall control, as Ronan Fanning explained, responsibility was apportioned so that the Department of Finance concerned itself with the internal aspects of the adhesion process, thus 'coordinating the preparation of detailed material, chairing interdepartmental committees' and so on, while the principal function of the Department of External Affairs was in its relation to the external features, that is 'leading discussions in Brussels'.[98] The structures for the negotiations were therefore back in place for when they would need to be reactivated. However, if the European Commission was thinking along the lines of such accession negotiations not being held for twelve months at least, what advice was coming from the Six?

Obviously, it was how the UK's candidature was played which was really of crucial importance. It was clear that France in the shape of de Gaulle was still the stumbling block and that London was being informed of that unchanging position on a regular basis. The French government portrayed a position amounting to it having 'no policy' on a possible UK application, but that was not the reality of de Gaulle's attitude filtering through from various sources.[99] As Northern Ireland's premier was told by Willi Brandt, West Germany's foreign minister in early 1967, there was no point in 'throwing oneself against a brick wall' on the membership issue, a message relayed back to Con O'Neill, the former's cousin, who himself felt that nothing had changed in relation to the French view on UK entry.[100] Three choices faced the London government, it appears; it could:

- decide to reapply for full EEC membership immediately;
- elect not to apply at all, certainly not while de Gaulle was in office;

- delay its application until it received further clarification and perhaps even settle on another deal altogether, intermediate or long-term.[101]

As 1966 came to a close and despite economic advantages existing in delaying a membership application, the outlook for Ireland was as yet only a matter of conjecture. Of course, it was desperately important that the country should not be perceived as a UK 'clone' or be seen as being too far away from the European heartland.[102] Only by actively pursuing economic and political policies favoured by the EEC and independent of the UK could Dublin secure a positive hearing from Brussels. Therein lay a contradiction; Ireland would not attempt any drastic economic change if the UK was not itself directly involved.

Prospects for the future

As things stood, Ireland's future prospects hinged on a lot of variables. The central unknown factor concerned economics – when would the country be able to join the EEC? – but there were many others. The country had a new leader, of course, but political stability down south was not reflected up north by anything approaching a similar situation, where a political and social precariousness pervaded. Socially, a period of changing attitudes in Ireland emerged towards previous constants such as the role of religion; it was also a time of reform in areas such as education; indeed, it was an era of technological development whether that concerned industry or the media. However, arching over all of these endeavours and hopes was one constant feature; this concerned future prosperity and that meant the EEC. There was another complication. It was assumed that both Ireland and the UK would be members by 1970, but of course there was an inherent risk in that dangerous assumption, as there was a very distinct threat that this particular eventuality would not necessarily pan out as planned.

On the same day, 10 November 1966, that Lemass formally announced his resignation as taoiseach, the UK prime minister reaffirmed London's wish to enter into 'exploratory talks' with the EEC.[103] Indeed, significant moves such as visits to the six capitals to explain the UK's needs and ascertain the various positions of the member states were also announced at that point in time. Thus, well ahead of schedule, it appeared as if the UK was readying itself to reopen accession negotiations. Promptly, Lynch made it known that he wanted a meeting with Wilson and this duly took place on 19 December 1966. The main issue of concern to Ireland was clearly the EEC, although Northern Ireland was a significant consideration as well. A new era in Ireland's European integration was obviously dawning, but there were no guarantees that success would be forthcoming in the short-term, whatever about the benefits that enhanced Anglo-Irish relations were clearly going to bring in the meantime. It is particularly vital to examine this meeting in detail because, although it moves slightly outside of the stated timeframe, it does provide a useful subject with which to conclude; in providing a detailed analysis of this Wilson-Lynch summit, it also shows exactly where Ireland stood in relation to Europe as the year came to a end.

Two subjects were of particular interest to the taoiseach as he arrived for his meeting at Downing Street, the EEC and Northern Ireland. When he arrived though, he was obviously surprised to be faced with a heavy-weight UK delegation, which not only comprised the prime minister, but also included George Brown, his foreign secretary, Douglas Jay, President of the Board of Trade, and Fred Peart, the agriculture minister, as well. What was billed as a *tête-à-tête* over lunch between the two prime ministers turned into a bilateral summit; indeed, it continued until 'all the business had been disposed of'.[104] Both subjects deserve attention here, the EEC for obvious reasons, the situation in the north because of how it was impacting on Ireland's internal and external policies.

In preparation for his encounter with Wilson, the taoiseach was intensively briefed on what were clearly only tentative attempts by Ireland and the UK to reestablish a rapport with the EEC. Dublin knew that, when London began to renegotiate, its accession negotiations would proceed at a lesser pace. However, it was imperative that both enter at the same time. Ireland evidently did not have the same problems with accession that the UK would have, because even on the supranational effects of membership, lessened somewhat following the Luxembourg compromise, it had 'no reservations'. It was the government's view that the:

> ... degree to which the institutions of the EEC are endowed with supranational powers is strictly limited and these have been substantially watered down by the Luxembourg decision ... which more of less ensures that a majority decision cannot be used to override the vital interest of a member country.

Of course, it was at Lynch's request that this meeting was taking place, primarily because he wanted to glean information from the UK government regarding its position within the EEC context.[105] The account that he received was not exactly what he was expecting to hear, but at least he now appreciated a little more precisely where the UK in fact stood and how they viewed their relative position.

The UK foreign minister gave an account of a recent meeting that he had conducted with his French counterpart, but he felt him to be 'aloof and uncommunicative'; he surmised that he was not talking to the person in charge. In a subsequent meeting with the French president, Brown got a better view of where the UK really stood, even if the former was not 'very helpful or oncoming'. The Irish external affairs secretary interpreted the Anglo-French meeting with these ominous words: 'Put crudely, the General's line was "What do you want? What is your problem? I have no problem, I am not trying to get into the Common Market"'. The UK prime minister added that although five of the Six were in favour of UK entry, partly as a result of the British Commonwealth no longer being a predominant issue, partly because objections regarding the supranational aspects of membership had receded, even if other issues, such as the Anglo-American relationship and the position of sterling, had not. It was clear that the UK was going to continue with its probings on the possibilities of adhesion and Wilson guaranteed that Dublin would be kept informed because of overlapping interests in the question. In fact, Brown had stated that, in the context of the EEC, he saw the UK and Ireland 'as one'. At that stage, however, Lynch was still not able to ascertain what kind of timetable that the UK had in mind, but it was apparent that the UK felt that developments could advance quickly. Indeed, it was readily apparent that the London government was not averse to precipitating the matter of full EEC membership by taking the initiative.[106]

Of course, Northern Ireland remained of particular concern to the Dublin government. The heady days back in the first couple of months 1965 were a part of the past, because it was obvious that tension was mounting. At their meeting in London, Lynch concentrated on the topical issue of institutionalised political and religious discrimination, especially in areas such as the equitable provision of educational, the flawed local electoral system, and housing allocations.[107] Wilson agreed that Northern Ireland was of considerable and understandable concern, but that O'Neill had to proceed slowly with his reforms in order not to antagonise further his party or cabinet, as his position was seen as 'none too secure', or indeed the wider constituency, inflamed by the virulence of Ian Paisley. As with the EEC question, the Irish delegation felt that substantive progress had been made because Ireland had communicated its concerns. However, the Northern Ireland problem was still festering unsolved.[108] Where the Irish government went from there was still open to question. In the context of full EEC membership, all that was clear was that it would be reacting to any new circumstances, not shaping them. Working out what the UK was going to decide to do next regarding the EEC was certainly not proving to be an easy task.[109] Nevertheless, in the space of a decade, at least Ireland had gone from perennial economic underachiever to an increasingly prosperous nation. Throughout this process, it was hoped that the EEC would shortly provide the country with a 'constructive external framework' within which to pursue its national interests and own self-advancement within the setting of European economic and political integration.[110] The future might have been bright, but it was also blindingly unknown.

Conclusions

Closed economy to open polity

Ireland's political independence, exercised assiduously during the Second World War, did not reap the results of a comparable economic experience until the mid-1960s and beyond, as its new-found affinity for the workings of the international political economy began to overtake more traditional concerns. With its fortunes – or as Patrick Keatinge and Brigid Laffan have labelled it Ireland's 'misfortunes' – tied so closely to those of the UK throughout its economic history, it is not until this later period that the effects of changes in orientation dating from the late 1950s really began to be felt. Ireland's emergence from the shelter of war-time neutrality into an interdependent, but polarised, world was a painfully slow and at times profoundly disappointing experience. As it observed the integration of its fellow Western Europeans nations, Irish peripherality – in both acts and ideas – was belatedly recognised as an as yet unconquered stumbling-block in the way of its economic habilitation. Its inhibitions with regard to the integration process, exacerbated by the UK's aloofness, were only stripped away as London began to recognise the dangers posed by the economic and political benefits that its European competitors stood to gain. The overall merits of striving towards, rather than against, Europe took considerably longer for the UK to recognise. A fundamental reappraisal of Ireland's economic and political outlook also took time to become convincing, both for its internal and external observers; France was still dubious about the UK, however, even if it realised that Dublin was not some London satrapy. Thus, Europe became the focal point of government policy despite, perhaps even as a consequence of, a traumatic phase of economic stagnation experienced by Ireland during the 1950s, disappointment regarding its utter rebuff by EFTA in the late 1950s, the EEC's outright indifference to its candidacy during the early 1960s, and the AIFTA's express implications for it from the mid-1960s.[1]

Ireland's sporadic internationalism during the first two post-war decades did not, and then of course could not, fully take the Paris treaty of 1950, the Rome treaties of 1957, or the European Communities Merger treaty of 1965 into account. Indeed, the country's adaptation to the perceived exigencies of European integration was slowed by its 'special relationship' with the UK and international developments that did not always necessitate rapid change, as well as domestic hesitancy due to economic retardation and a lack of political imagination. Almost imperceptibly – in counterbalancing negative relations with NATO or the British Commonwealth with the fact that, allied to its overdue but enthusiastic adherence to the UN, it had been a founder member of the Council of Europe and the OEEC – it proved that it was moving from a closed to a more open approach to the outside world. Patrick Keatinge and Brigid Laffan have stated: 'Ireland was gradually drawn into a broader, more stable and increasingly interdependent international system'; but, even as Europe assumed a more central position in its external affairs, Anglo-Irish ties retained their prominent placing.[2]

Ireland's application to enter the EEC was evidence of this change and reorientation, a belief reinforced by the arguments, data and documentary material presented throughout this thesis. Although he recognised that it was economically dependent, Lemass felt that Ireland could always exercise political autonomy by choosing the more preferred, or at least less abhorrent, commercial structure for its continued viability. It did so by imitating the policy direction taken by its nearest neighbour to a degree which Dublin might publicly eschew, but which Brussels recognised as fact.[3] Effectively, this meant that Ireland went where the UK led or was allowed to go; as Norman Davies has written regarding the reality of its economic dependence on the UK: 'Ireland had little alternative to following in Britain's contorted wake in negotiations with the EEC'.[4] Peter Sutherland has added his pertinent view that: 'Our positive orientation ... has in some senses been reactive to the British position'; implicitly, this statement says two other things as well:

- it backs up the thesis that Ireland often had to take the same decisions as the UK or else risk being left behind;
- even if within the scope of such decisions Ireland was still capable of doing things all on its own, it was as yet tied by default to the UK.[5]

According to Andrew Moravcsik's criteria, it is possible to assert that national self-interest meant that Ireland favoured EEC entry, indeed, it was quite prepared to sacrifice a degree of sovereignty to the European institutions – something which daunted other countries – in return for the benefits of membership. The problem was in realising that aim as entry was not going to be forthcoming without serious negotiations. With regard to the latter, Irish reluctance to accept the removal of industrial tariffs had, for instance, long been noted, even if its support for agricultural protection put it on a par with France or West Germany, but neither of those states were in a peripheral location or outside the EEC.[6]

All the same, credit is due for the policy initiated by the government which allocated state help for manufacturers to set up their factories or to extend them, as well as providing for access to new technology and training, continuing support for agriculture, and recognising the potential that tourism held; and furthermore, it gave income tax relief on any additional export earnings and basically set in place the required framework for promoting Irish goods abroad, whether that was through the diplomatic corps, semi-state bodies such as AnCO, Bord Fáilte, Córas Tráchtála Teoranta, and the IDA, or through financial incentives.[7] Unemployment was well below 5% throughout the first half of the 1960s, even as people returned to the country having previously emigrated.[8] All that time, the Irish government was preparing the nation for future European integration, though the UK was of course omnipresent in the practicalities and realities of its foreign economic policy. When de Gaulle vetoed the former, Ireland was left to kick its heels in frustration, even if it was true that the 'breakdown [in negotiations] provided a degree of breathing space to prepare the sluggish Irish economy for eventual participation in the Common Market'.[9] Additionally, it was becoming rather apparent that the organisation that Ireland was trying to join in 1966 had moved away from the free trading area concept of 1957; in truth, the EEC was no longer just some economic body, if it ever was that alone. With the advent of the EC in 1967, the Dublin government was now bent on attempting to join an organisation which was, according to Patrick Keatinge, 'more akin to a treaty-based association of more or less autonomous but interdependent states – in short, a *confederation*'.[10] The nature of the EEC had evolved and changed within a decade, just like Ireland itself had, although it is not necessarily the task of this analysis to expand upon the former's remodelling beyond its implications for the latter.

A confederal body has been defined by Patrick Keatinge as a group which is usually based on freely-negotiated treaties between separate political units, but that these agreements may go beyond normal inter-state arrangements. For instance, the international grouping that Ireland was still endeavouring to enter already had the ability to make laws for its members; indeed, if and when it acceded, it would thus be obliged to accept the *acquis communautaire*, the body of law that this organisation had built up. However, it was clear that the two major policy concerns facing this 'confederation' remained:

- evolving even more elaborate terms of economic union along the lines of setting up a customs union, enhancing the EEC's role in world trade negotiations, and the setting up of the CAP;
- developing a political partnership in Europe within the vague terms of 'ever closer union', even if this was along as yet undefined lines.

The attraction to Ireland of economic integration was self-evident. It was a 'particular incentive' for full membership because certain fiscal decisions would be made collectively in Brussels rather than in London; few influential people in Fianna Fáil were deluding themselves that any of the really important economic decisions would in the future be made in Dublin. As one Irish commentator has since written regarding its reasons for joining:

> ... it would have been absurd economically for Ireland to stay outside the EC once Britain went in. Elements of economic and political opportunism complemented this sense of determinism ... EC membership afforded Ireland the chance to break out of a suffocatingly close relationship with Britain and place Anglo-Irish relations in a broader, more equitable, multilateral context.

Although the political consequences of membership were not so clear, it seemed that the EC Commission was more adamant than its predecessors that prospective members were not just joining some economic body with a social undertaking; they would 'be required to participate fully in creating a continent which is economically and politically united' too.[11]

Obviously, one of the original and principal concepts behind economic and political cooperation was to maintain and promote peace in Western Europe; the EC had a security dimension that Ireland could not just ignore though, even if the issue was not fully or openly debated. Nevertheless, it was true that European integration meant more than a community of states working together in a confederal structure because, inherent in its conception, there also existed the desire to turn the EC into a federal union. Thus, this was the dynamic and continually developing body – even if the nature of integration and advancements made in its name were somewhat 'stop and go' – that Ireland was trying to join in the mid-1960s, five years after it had first applied for full EEC membership. Where this journey would ultimately bring the country was not as yet apparent because the path it had to follow was neither clearly defined nor staying its course easy; wherever it led though, there were lots of preparations on Ireland's part still left to be made.

Why did Ireland's first application fail?[12]

One concern at the heart of this thesis came down to answering: why did Ireland's application to join the EEC flounder? It failed, not necessarily just because the UK's bid was vetoed by the French president, even if that is the conventional basis proffered, not even as a result of its military neutrality or political convictions, but because it was not up the task economically. Ireland's first entreaty to enter the EEC miscarried – it was essentially ignored – for precisely the same reason that the Dublin government was unable to take up de Gaulle's benign and rather meaningless offer of membership in the spring of 1963. The simple truth of the matter, of course, was that the country was not yet ready to face the rigours implied in full adhesion to the Treaties of Paris and Rome, certainly not without the UK by its side.

Ireland's continued economic retardation throughout the opening post-war decade – and also for some considerable time beyond that – had many reasons it seemed, but little prospect of a quick fix. Amongst other concerns, the difficulties that the country faced included:

- its reliance upon the UK for export markets and technological imports;
- an agricultural orientation verging upon total economic dependence;
- the fragile, if innovative, state of its industrial base;
- a slumbering, haemorrhaging, and apparently apathetic population.

Problems such as these could not just be wished away, as no magic panacea existed; indeed, the resolution to this economic situation lay primarily in the hands of the Dublin government, not in London, Paris, or Brussels. The economy required a fundamental overhaul, that much was clear; but this would take time. Although Ireland's rehabilitation policy – immortalised in Whitaker's *Economic development* from late 1958 – made some remarkable progress during the first four years in which it was in operation, accordingly coinciding with the failure of the original application for membership, there was still a long way to go before the country would be ready to join the EEC as a fully-fledged participant. As the UK's own approach to Europe and the EEC changed, this was reflected in Irish attitudes. The problems that EFTA and the EEC posed in terms of trade or trade discrimination – mostly concerning bilateral Anglo-Irish links – led Dublin to look further than, but not exclusively beyond, the UK for the solutions to its economic needs.

Ireland's tardiness in confronting the realities posed by European integration – a totally different phenomenon to its affinity for the rhetorical and eloquent – is easily illustrated; the government was to discover that the tangible and the ethereal are not the same. It is true, for instance, that general incentives were introduced into the Irish economy during the 1950s to promote export industries and to attract foreign investment; for the first time in a generation, a relaxation in financial strictures began to be experienced and Ireland was the better for it. Nevertheless, the removal of protectionism did not really begin in earnest until the mid-1960s. Indeed, the comprehensive tariff cut of 10% – effective from January 1963 and announced in the light of agreement from the EEC in October 1962 to open membership negotiations with Dublin – was really only a veritable drop in the ocean of enshrined and established protectionism, a further 10% tariff cut in January 1964 having much the same effect. Thus, it is argued here that it was only with the emergence of the AIFTA agreement in mid-1966 that the Irish government began to face up to the economic realities presented by the EEC and freer trade in Europe. It should be emphasised again that agreement from Brussels to begin looking at Ireland's first EEC application only came some considerable time after accords had already been reached to do the same with Denmark and Norway, never mind the UK.

Indigenous agriculture and industry were not always competitive in these years. It has been remarked that planning was unquestionably less effective with regard to the former, net agricultural output barely being any higher in 1963 than it was six years earlier. Thus, even if net industrial output was well up by the end of the period under review, Irish agriculture was still having major trouble in adapting to the new circumstances in Europe, a situation made even graver by the prospect of the CAP emerging. For all of the government's talk, it was essentially no more ready to assume full EEC membership eighteen months after it had made its application than it had been when the latter organisation was formed. Ireland was much too slow in adapting to Europe's new trading realities, the import and export figures presenting clear evidence of that. Far too many exports still went to the UK, while half of total imports were consistently sourced from the same point; ¼ of all exports were made up of livestock, while ¾ of imports were manufactured goods. By any standard definition of the concept, Ireland was in a position of – near total – dependence upon its neighbour's economy. Creative attempts to convince the Six during the course of the application process that it was ready for full membership floundered in the face of the simple facts of its position.

At least, the government was more convincing politically. It is fair to say that Ireland had taken some giant political strides to come into line with the rest of Western Europe and, even it was not in NATO or the WEU, it was still fiercely anti-communist. The taoiseach thus regularly and enthusiastically told anyone in Europe prepared to listen that the country's neutrality would gladly be sacrificed in return for financial gain. Irish foreign policy began, in turn, to be determined more by economic factors than by political considerations, a score upon which Lemass even convinced de Gaulle. By their very nature, these 'convictions' are readily open to rapid and unprincipled modification. Thus, Dublin made it rather abundantly clear that political concerns such as these would by no means be permitted to come in the way of its accession to a major trade grouping; concurrently, Europe's potential for political development in the unforeseen future also went unquestioned however.

Of the three European Communities, it is obvious that Ireland was only interested in the EEC; the ECSC and Euratom hardly ever entered into the picture. The image of Irish representatives handing in a membership application for the latter organisation – diplomatic relations only being established the same day – on the very morning of the French president's infamous press conference is hard to shake off as anything other than inauspicious. Thus, the conclusion that these two European Communities were relatively immaterial, as far as Ireland was concerned, comes as no great surprise. In contrast, the EEC meant a huge new market for Irish agricultural products, with the prospect of industrial goods also becoming competitive within a relatively short transition period. Clearly, the Six were well aware of this situation; little wonder that they hesitated for some considerable time before allowing the Irish to begin the procedure of opening accession negotiations. By the spring of 1963, however, the latter's choice lay between waiting for something to happen or making it thus.

Of course, when it boiled down to it, Ireland could not have acceded to the EEC when the UK was not allowed to enter; neither would it have applied in the first place if London was not about to do the same thing. In the end, the period of time that spanned between the first application and the successful third attempt allowed the whole country 'breathing space' to ready itself for full membership and to convince itself that accession would turn out to be something very positive. The prospect of EEC membership – even further integration, perhaps – allowed it the opportunity to validate its individuality and economic vitality in its own eyes, as well as in those of Europe, even if emerging from the UK's shadow was not an easy task; the latter reality notwithstanding, joint construction of the AIFTA gave Ireland the means to effect this ambition. After that, it was always going to be a matter of patience, perseverance, and perspicacity in order to realise its wish of adhering to the EEC.

Bibliography

As was stated in the introduction, four main sources of primary archive material were utilised in writing *Protectionism to liberalisation: Ireland and the EEC, 1957 to 1966*. A deeper evaluation of this documentation is presented here, as these sources were not comprehensively assessed in that earlier section; a similar approach – a brief assessment in the introductory chapter and an indepth analysis plus bibliographical listing – has also been used for secondary materials. This bibliography is therefore divided into four sections in order to present an archival appraisal and a catalogue of primary materials, a literature survey and a list of secondary sources. Nonetheless, it might be worth pointing out that sources have worked in concert with each other throughout this investigation.

The section listing primary source materials that have been employed is divided under four principal headings, together with an additional miscellaneous grouping of primary sources; they reads as follows:

- **Irish sources**   National Archives, Bishop Street, Dublin
- **UK sources**   Public Record Office, Kew Gardens, London
- **US sources**   Harry S.Truman Library, Independence, Missouri
    Dwight D.Eisenhower Library, Abilene, Kansas
    John F.Kennedy Library, Boston, Massachusetts
    Lyndon B.Johnson Library, Austin, Texas
- **EU sources**   EC Archives, Villa Il Poggiolo, Florence
    European Parliament, Bâtiment Robert Schuman, Luxembourg
- **miscellaneous**   official Irish government publications
    newspapers, reviews and magazines
    other primary source materials

The section listing primary sources is preceded by the archival analysis, which explains why certain archives were used and also assesses the value of particular conferences or workshops that took place during the course of this investigation. In turn, an extensive list of secondary sources encompassing pertinent Irish and foreign materials is presented in the customary alphabetical form, following on from a brief essay reviewing and surveying the current state of the literature.

Archival appraisal *

As was previously made apparent, the archives utilised during this research were meant to concentrate on domestic political considerations, Anglo-Irish relations, the wider diaspora, and Ireland's process of European integration. Right from the outset, it should be made clear that internal factors played a pivotal role in this case study on Ireland and the EEC because, as was articulated, there was a real need for cabinet, departmental and intergovernmental debates on the subject to be more thoroughly assessed; other components, although secondary, completed the framework within which this singular element operated.

With the incorporation of debates and legislation enacted in Dáil and Seanad Éireann into this investigation – as well as an extensive evaluation of the relative importance of lobby groups (agricultural, federal, industrial) – a much more coherent picture of the role played by domestic political considerations in Ireland's European integration process emerged as a direct result. The National Archives in Dublin however provided the most abundant source of materials. The analytical approach adopted with regard to this documentation was one of assessment from the top of the bureaucratic ladder downwards, concentrating the research at the level where serious decisions were being made. The General Files (S Series), Cabinet Minutes and Government Minutes subsequently proved to be the most important source material available in the Department of the Taoiseach; in addition, the Department of Foreign Affairs also possessed a rich vein of material, with the Secretary's Office Files (P Series), Common Market Series and Confidential Reports being the most important deposits. Access to Department of Industry & Commerce, as well as Departments of Defence, Finance and Justice, materials proved to be more problematic. Furthermore, the possibility of

---

* Please note that a review of the NA, written for Richard Griffiths' 'European integration web site', may be found at *http://www.let.leidenuniv.nl/history/rtg/res 1/hitch.html#ire* (10 March 1999); a review of the ACE, written in conjunction with Richard Griffiths for his 'European integration web site', is also available at *http://www.let.leidenuniv.nl/history/rtg/res1/hitch.html#haec* (10 March 1999).

carrying out extensive oral history interviews with eye-witnesses was considered as a very real option and, of course, is doubtlessly a rewarding one in itself once care is taken to cross-reference material; however, this particular option was not taken up – except to confirm certain nuances – in part because of the abundance of archival materials accessible at the NA, but also as a result of similar testimonies already existing in the public domain through the publication of written memoirs and, indeed, interviews previously conducted in newspapers and for archives.

The materials that were readily available at the Public Record Office in London proved to be rather impressive, somewhat unexpectedly, with regard to this research. Relations with the UK were extremely pertinent to Dublin's policy regarding the EEC; at no time was this better illustrated than when Ireland's dependence upon the success or failure of the UK's first application for full EEC membership is considered. Looking at the question from the Irish perspective only – without fully assessing the material obtainable at the PRO – would have been to ignore what was shown to be a constituent element in the construction of this research's central argument. In reality, the repercussions of London's actions upon Ireland's own views of European integration proved to be irrefutable as a consequence; indeed, the fact that it was still dealt with by the Commonwealth Relations Office, not by the Foreign Office, amply demonstrates where Ireland stood. Dublin's problem was that a correlation on policy strategy did not apply, certainly not in the same terms, the other way round.

As was previously stated, the Irish diaspora was another area that has been assessed, at the level of diplomatic confidential reports and by integrating the views of the wider Anglicised world into the background study of Irish actions. In particular, the US acted as a 'godfather' figure to Europe throughout the post-war period. Indeed, it was 'American pragmatism' which actively pushed for the integration of Europe, a point made abundantly clear to Ireland by successive US presidents. It must be said that documentation originally found in the US as the archival basis for an MPhil thesis – centred on the subject of *Irish-American diplomatic relations, 1948 to 1963* – germinated promptings to investigate Ireland's first attempt at integration. In fact, a deep understanding of the specific importance of the US to the question of European integration and of its repercussions for Ireland has thus shown itself to be a principal aspiration of this research. John F.Kennedy evoked the dictum that 'there are no permanent enemies', citing it to reflect the development of better Anglo-Irish relations in the early 1960s. Indeed, as time progressed, the subject of partition played less of a role in government decision-making, at the national and international level, reflecting a change in foreign policy orientation away from the political to the economic. A central question remained: to what degree were such evaluations of Anglo-Irish relations true and what influence did this bilateral consideration have on Ireland's European policies? The resolution to this particular issue lay in much of the material already gathered, including oral histories such as those previously conducted with former Irish foreign ministers Frank Aiken and Liam Cosgrave, as well as in other US based archival materials extensively employed in the presentation of this research.

Lastly, in relation to the primary source materials, the question of Ireland and the EEC has been actively assessed and investigated directly from Europe's perspective; additionally, other questions were also posed:

- How important was Ireland's membership of the EEC to the Six?
- What were the views of the European institutions?
- How did Ireland react to the various developments in European trade in the late 1950s?

Part of the answer to the first two questions is indicated by the level of material available at the European Community Archives in Florence, although, to be perfectly honest, a review of the relevant sources available there did not prove to be as promising as would originally have been expected or hoped. The same thing could obviously be said about access to information at the European Parliament in Luxembourg, though to be fair this is also dictated by the lack of powers initially accorded to this institution and to the superior availability of material at national level. Indeed, the material available on Ireland from these sources is best described as scant. However, this in itself is both informative and illustrative, tending to demonstrate the lack of importance attached to Ireland by both the Six and the Seven. With regard to the initially envisaged possibility of fulfilling a significant proportion of the aims of this research through the wide use of material located at the ACE and the PE, the answer turned out to be rather negative. A sample of the available material was still utilised, demonstrating that these archives are relevant to some degree but, nonetheless, a personal assessment of their potential for further related research remains pessimistic.

In spite of this, conferences and workshops held at various stages during the course of this research proved to be excellent opportunities to talk to those most intimately involved from the past and the present – eyewitnesses and integration historians alike – allowing issues central to integration history to be raised. The transcript of one such conference – entitled *The creation of EFTA*, held at the University of Oslo from 14-17 May 1992 – provided the basis for the development of subsequent views on

EFTA's relevance to Ireland; another – entitled *The first attempt to enlarge the European Community, 1961-63*, held at the IUE from 17-19 February 1994 – explored the background to the various membership applications in political terms and initially proved to be a useful tool from which to view research on Ireland's first attempt to join the EEC. A further conference – entitled *Neutral states in Europe and European integration, 1945-1994*, held at the University of Innsbruck from 6-9 April 1995 – allowed the Irish integration experience to be compared and contrasted with those of other neutrals; in addition, another – entitled *The Europeanisation of domestic policy*, held at the IUE on 8 December 1995 – afforded historians and political scientists the opportunity to listen to and forge each others views, proving to be an important formative experience in the application of theory to Ireland's process of European integration. Workshops entitled *Research workshop on the failure of Community expansion, 1961-63*, and *EU enlargement and the myth of the 'awkward partner'* – held at the IUE on 14 December 1998 and 22 June 1999 respectively – were especially helpful in placing Ireland into its proper national, as well as European and wider international, context. It was ultimately primary source material, utilised comprehensively throughout this research, which was to be the most useful resource however; indeed, this was more likely to be from the Irish archives than from any other source.

Primary materials

- **Irish sources** National Archives, Bishop Street, Dublin

Department of Foreign Affairs
Secretary's Office (P Series)
Cultural Division Files (Series 305)
Confidential Reports (Series 313)
Trade Division Files (Series 314, 315 & 348)
Information – Publications (Series 316)
Consular Division Files (Series 317)
Protocol Division Files (Series 401)
Press & Information Section Files (Series 414)
Council of Europe: United Nations – Political and Legal Division Files (Series 417)
Visits to Ireland and Irish Visits Abroad (Series 434)
Protocol Division Series (Series 436)
Economic Division (EC Series)
European Communities Division (Common Market Series)
Embassy Canberra (Consular Files)

Embassy Holy See
Embassy Rome
Embassy Stockholm (Political Files D Series)
Embassy Washington (Economic Files E Series)
PMUN New York (miscellaneous)

Department of the Taoiseach
Cabinet Minutes
Government Cabinet Minutes
General Files (S Series)

- **UK sources** Public Record Office, Kew Gardens, London

European Free Trade Area: Steering Group (CAB 130)
Economic Steering Committee (CAB 134)

- **US sources** Harry S.Truman Library, Independence, Missouri

Acheson, Dean
Democratic National Committee
Ewing, Oscar R.
Hoffman, Paul G.
Matthews, Francis P.
Naval Aide Files
Oral History Interviews
President's Committee on Foreign Aid
President's Secretary's Files – Appointments
President's Secretary's Files – Intelligence
President's Secretary's Files – NSC Meetings
President's Secretary's Files – Subject
SMOF: Psychological Strategy Board
Snyder, John W.
Sweeney, Joseph
Tannenwald, Theodore
White House Central Files – Confidential
White House Central Files – General
White House Central Files – Official

- **US sources** Dwight D.Eisenhower Library, Abilene, Kansas

Dulles, John F. – General Correspondence
Dulles, John F. – Special Assistants – Chronological
Dulles, John F. – Subject
Dulles, John F. – Telephone Calls
Dulles, John F. – White House Memoranda

Herter, Christian A. – Chronological
Herter, Christian A. – Telephone
Lodge, Henry Cabot
Oral History Interviews
White House Central Files (Ann Whitman)
White House Central Files – Confidential
White House Central Files – Dulles-Herter
White House Central Files – General
White House Central Files – Official
White House Central Files – President's Personal Files
White House Office – Staff Secretary – International

- **US sources** John F.Kennedy Library, Boston, Massachusetts

National Security Files
Oral History Interviews
President's Office Files
White House Central Files

- **US sources** Lyndon B.Johnson Library, Austin, Texas

Confidential File
National Security File
President's Daily Diary
Vice-Presidential Security File

- **EU sources** EC Archives, Villa Il Poggiolo, Florence

Dossiers de la Haute Autorité de la Communauté Européenne du Charbon et de l'Acier

- **EU sources** European Parliament, Bâtiment Robert Schuman, Luxembourg

Irish government submission, 'The European Union and the new Europe' (Luxembourg: European Parliament document PE165.980, 1996)

- **miscellaneous** official Irish government publications

Bunreacht na hÉireann (Dublin: Stationery Office, 1937)
Texts concerning Ireland's position in relation to the North Atlantic Treaty (Dublin: Stationery Office, 1950)
Dáil debates (Dublin: Stationery Office, various)
Seanad debates (Dublin: Stationery Office, various)
Central Statistics Office, *Ireland: trade and shipping statistics* (Dublin: Stationery Office, various)

Economic development (Dublin: Stationery Office, 1958)
Programme for economic expansion (Dublin: Stationery Office, 1958)
European Economic Community Part I (Dublin: Stationery Office, 1961)
European Economic Community Part II (Dublin: Stationery Office, 1962)
Membership of the European Communities: implications for Ireland (Dublin: Stationery Office, 1970)
The accession of Ireland to the European Communities (Dublin: Stationery Office, 1972)

- **miscellaneous** newspapers, reviews and magazines

Books Ireland
Community report
Cork Examiner
Economist
Graduate
Irish Independent
Irish Press
Irish Times
London Review of Books
Observer
Sunday Independent
Sunday Press
Sunday Tribune
Times Literary Supplement
Working Group on European Integration *Newsletter*

- **miscellaneous** other primary source materials

Borchardt, K.-D., *European integration: the origins and growth of the European Union* (Luxembourg: Office for Official Publications of the European Communities, 1995)
Council of Europe report, 'Rélations Economiques Européennes: la position de certains pays Européens autres ques les Six en cas d'adhesion du Royaume-Uni à la Communauté Economique Européenne' (Strasbourg: Council of Europe, 1961)
Economic & Social Research Institute, various papers (Dublin: Economic & Social Research Institute, various)
European Communities official text, 'Treaty establishing the European Coal and Steel Community', in *Treaties establishing the European Communities* (Luxembourg: Office for Official Publications of the European Communities, 1973)
European Communities official text, 'Treaty establishing the European Economic Community', in *Treaties establishing the European Communities* (Luxembourg: Office for Official Publications of the European Communities, 1973)
European Communities official text, 'Treaty establishing the European Atomic Energy Community', in *Treaties establishing the European Communities*

(Luxembourg: Office for Official Publications of the European Communities, 1973)
European Communities report, 'Ireland', pp. 297-306, in *Portrait of the regions: France, United Kingdom, Ireland, vol. 2* (Luxembourg: Office for Official Publications of the European Communities, 1993)
European Communities report, *European Union: selected instruments taken from the treaties, book 1 vol. 1* (Luxembourg: Office for Official Publications of the European Communities, 1995)
De Gaulle, C., 'Conférence de press tenue au Palais de l'Élysée', pp. 61-79, in *Discours et messages: pour l'effort, août 1962-décembre 1965* (Paris: Librairie Pion, 1970)
Irish Council of Europe Movement publication, 'Opportunity: Ireland and Europe' (Dublin: Irish Council of Europe Movement, 1972)
IMF reports, *International financial statistics* (New York: International Monetary Fund, various)
Lenin, V.I., 'The Irish rebellion of 1916', pp. 353-8, in *V.I.Lenin: collected works, vol. 22 December 1915-July 1916* (London: Lawrence & Wishart, 1974)
Marx, K., *Karl Marx Friedrich Engels, vol. 31* (Berlin: Dietz Verlag, 1974)
OECD reports, 'Irlande' (Paris: OECD, various)
OEEC reports, 'Irlande' (Paris: OEEC, various)
Secretariat of the European Commission for Europe report, *Economic survey of Europe in 1959* (Geneva: United Nations, 1960)
US government publications, *Public papers of the Presidents of the United States* (Washington DC: Government Printing Office, various)
Weidenfeld, W., & W.Wessels (eds), *Europe from A to Z: guide to European integration* (Luxembourg: Office for Official Publications of the European Communities, 1997)
World Bank publications, *World development report* (Washington DC: World Bank, various)

Literature survey *

The availability of some secondary source materials has been of much benefit in constructing a framework within which to place this doctoral research. Despite the fact that very little of this particular material directly touched upon the subject of this text and despite the fact that access to the data on this subject in the archives has been very limited up until fairly recently because of the thirty year rule, secondary studies have in fact been extensively carried

---

* A bibliographical list on the subject of Ireland and European integration, supplied for Richard Griffiths' 'European integration web site', may be found at *http://www.let.leidenuniv.nl/history/rtg/res1/ire-bibl.html* (10 March 1999) and is based on the list of secondary sources given at the end of this thesis.

out on matters of relevance to this research on Ireland's integration into the EEC. There is, it must be said, a plethora of material available on the subject. The evaluation presented here of the most valuable secondary source material is essentially a list of suitable texts with informed comments. However, it gives indications of the gaps in the history of Irish integration policy, many of which have been filled by this piece of research, while also assessing the readings themselves critically. It thus takes the form of an extensive historiographical review.

Of the texts that have been closely examined, the best have included Paul Sharp's valuable study centred on the impact of interdependence on Ireland; however, because he did not have access to the material that has been released in the last few years, he has based his arguments on material in the public domain. Miriam Hederman was also limited in this way and concentrated on the role of domestic organisations and the media in Ireland. Susan Baker worked from documentation made available by Fianna Fáil, but her use of secondary source or publicly published papers concentrated on the performance of that political party as the government party rather than as the government *per se*; thus, the departmental documentation which has subsequently become available has thrown valuable light on this subject as well, putting her work into its appropriate setting as a result. Indeed, with the notable exception of D.J.Maher's study, most of these historians and political scientists have not had free access to the relevant archival material. In itself, his investigation is undoubtedly the single-most important into Ireland's early relationship with the EEC published to date. Though thorough and based on exhaustive research, its great strength is nevertheless its major weakness, because he has based his work almost totally on the Department of Finance records, to which he had unprecedented access; by necessity, his work is inherently 'limited' as a consequence and suffers from being too close to that department's specific perspective. A comprehensive analysis of this material through parallel techniques, coupled with an indepth investigation of other relevant documentation, has provided a much more rounded answer.

Generally speaking, it is only relatively recently that historians have begun to have access to the archival material dating from the early 1960s, the exact area where this research has concentrated; relevant archival material continued to be released throughout the duration of this research, enabling this PhD to examine chronologically the various proposed themes and to explore the question well into the mid-1960s. This reading has also revealed obvious gaps in our knowledge of an essential part of Irish history, indeed in the history of European integration, and thus one goal of this thesis has been to rectify, at least in part, this particular anomaly. Rather than repeating the bibliography, the most relevant texts are assessed here. John McCarthy's publication, *Planning Ireland's future: the legacy of T.K.Whitaker* is, for example, a collection of essays which puts the contribution of Whitaker, the aforementioned civil servant, into perspective. The editor's own essay is a rich source of information on the work of the latter, especially with his emphasis on the 'turnaround' aspect of Whitaker's contribution to Ireland's economy. Meanwhile, Ronan Fanning gives a concise history of the economic situation in the lead-up to this period; indeed, Joseph Lee's short contribution again deals with the years before this time, while John Bradley's account is based on developments in the economy from the 1960s. Finally, Bernard Share gives a cultural and social context in which the 1950s and the effects of Whitaker's programme are outlined. By its very nature, however, this collection only sketches aspects of Ireland's experience of European integration rather than giving an indepth appraisal of the precise subject at hand, that is Ireland's relations with the EEC between 1957 and 1966.

Other texts have concentrated on domestic economics rather than upon the shaping of a new foreign economic policy. Brian Farrell gives a concise, but detailed, view of Ireland's economic performance in the writing of his biopic on *Seán Lemass* and is particularly strong on the latter's pragmatism, indeed *volte-face*, in economic orientation. Elaborating on the subject of Ireland and Northern Ireland, Liam Kennedy gives a very well argued insight, in *The modern industrialisation of Ireland*, into economic policy at this time by comparing the two economies on the island. Indeed, it has to be said that this study is invaluable because it traces the evolution of what he calls 'the long-established distinction between a broadly industrial North and an agrarian South' to a time when Ireland became more industrialised and its northern neighbour steadily became deindustrialised. On the other hand, Joseph Lee and Gearóid Ó Tuathaigh, writing in *The age of de Valera*, give a succinct, although limited, view of the changes that Lemass wrought. This has in fact been done more thoroughly by Paul Bew and Henry Patterson, particularly in their book on *Seán Lemass and the making of modern Ireland, 1945 to 1966*, but one should remember that this argument comes from a distinctly Marxist perspective.

Some texts have concentrated on specific subject areas, as with Patrick Keatinge in his respected text *A singular stance: Irish neutrality in the 1980s*, a study that is clearly more interested in the implications of integration on neutrality rather than in anything else; indeed, Dermot Keogh has concentrated on the diplomatic elements involved in this relationship. Meanwhile, this PhD thesis contends that recent mainstream Irish history texts – excepting Dermot Keogh's *Twentieth-century Ireland: nation and state* or J.J.Lee's *Ireland, 1912-1985: politics and society*, which actually do deal with the question of Ireland and the EEC with a level of insight – suffer from the fact that such analyses cannot concentrate on the particular aspect that is central to this discussion. Ronan Fanning's *Independent Ireland* is clearly an example of this phenomenon, as is John A.Murphy's *Ireland in the twentieth century*. At the same time, Terence Brown's fascinating *Ireland: a social and cultural history* obviously deals with the issue from another historical perspective altogether. Therefore, a substantial gap exists in our knowledge of European integration. An extensive investigation into the history of Ireland's European integration, not only into the EEC, utilising the material that has been continually released, was badly needed; this text therefore forms the basis of one of the first documentary based investigations carried out to date.

Secondary sources

Acheson, D., *Power and diplomacy* (Cambridge: Harvard University Press, 1958)

Akenson, D.H., *Conor: a biography of Conor Cruise O'Brien, vols. 1 & 2* (Montreal: McGill-Queen's University, 1994)

Amin, S., *Unequal development: an essay on the social formation of peripheral capitalism* (Hassocks: Harvester, 1976)

Anderson, E., 'Towards a Baltic union, 1920-27', pp. 30-56, in *Lituanus* vol. 12 no. 2 1966

Apter, D.E., *Rethinking development: modernization, dependency and postmodern politics* (Newbury Park: Sage, 1987)

Archer, C., *Organizing Europe: the institutions of integration* (London: Edward Arnold, 1994)

Ardagh, J., *Ireland and the Irish: portrait of a changing society* (London: Hamish Hamilton, 1994)

Arter, D., *The politics of European integration in the twentieth century* (Aldershot: Dartmouth, 1993)

Asbeek Brusse, W., 'Alone within the Six: the Dutch cabinet and the British application for EEC membership, 1960-1963', pp. 1-29, paper presented at a conference entitled *The first attempt to enlarge the European Community, 1961-63*, held at the IUE from 17-19 February 1994

Atkinson, N., *Irish education: a history of educational institutions* (Dublin: Allen Figgis, 1969)

Baker, S., *Dependency, ideology and the industrial policy of Fianna Fáil in Ireland 1958-1972* (Florence: IUE PhD thesis, 1987)

Barker, E., *et al* (eds), *The European inheritance, vol. 3* (Oxford: Clarendon, 1954)

Barrington, R., & J.Cooney, *Inside the EEC: an Irish guide* (Dublin: O'Brien, 1984)

Barrington, R., *Health, medicine and politics in Ireland, 1900-1970* (Dublin: Institute of Public Administration, 1987)

Barry, F., 'Peripherality in economic geography and modern growth theory:

reflections from the Irish experience' (draft version)

Baxter-Moore, N.J., 'The impact of European Community membership on the Republic of Ireland', pp. 41-84, in N.Ørvik & C.Pentland (eds), *The European Community at the crossroads: the first twenty-five years* (Kingston: Queen's University Kingston, 1983)

Beckett, J.C., *A short history of Ireland* (London: Hutchinson, 1975)

Behan, B., *Hold your hour and have another* (Aylesbury: Corgi, 1970)

Bellò, C., *L'onesta democrazia di Piero Malvestiti: memorie e documenti* (Milan: Nuovo Edizioni Duomo, 1985)

Bew, P., & H.Patterson, *Seán Lemass and the making of modern Ireland, 1945-1966* (Dublin: Gill & Macmillan, 1982)

Bew, P., et al, *The dynamics of Irish politics* (London: Lawrence & Wishart, 1989)

Bew, P., & G.Gillespie, *Northern Ireland: a chronology of the troubles, 1968-1993* (Dublin: Gill & Macmillan, 1993)

Böll, H., *Irisches Tagesbuch* (Köln: Verlag Kiepenheuer & Witsch, 1957)

Bowman, J., *De Valera and the Ulster question, 1917-1973* (New York: Oxford University Press, 1983)

Boyce, D.G., *Nationalism in Ireland* (London: Routledge, 1991)

Bradley, J., et al, *Stabilization and growth in the EC periphery: a study of the Irish economy* (Aldershot: Avebury, 1993)

Breathnach, P., 'Uneven development and capitalist peripheralisation: the case of Ireland', pp. 122-41, in *Antipode* vol. 20 no. 2 1988

Brennan, P., et al (eds), *L'Irlande politique et sociale: l'Irlande, l'Europe et 1992* no. 4 (Paris: Le Centre d'Études Irlandaises de Paris Université de la Sorbonne Nouvelle Paris III, 1992)

Bristow, J.A., & A.A.Tait, (eds), *Economic policy in Ireland* (Dublin: Institute of Public Administration, 1968)

Brown, G., *In my way: the political memoirs of Lord George-Brown* (London: Victor Gollancz, 1971)

Brown, T., *Ireland: a social and cultural history, 1922-79* (Glasgow: Fontana, 1981)

Browne, N., *Against the tide* (Dublin: Gill & Macmillan, 1988)

Brunt, B., *The Republic of Ireland* (London: Paul Chapman, 1988)

Calvocoressi, P., 'Neutrality now', pp. 144-59, in S.Harden (ed.), *Neutral states and the European Community* (Oxford: Brassey's, 1994)

Camps, M., *Britain and the European Community, 1955-1963* (London: Oxford University Press, 1964)

Cardoso, F.H., & E.Faletto, *Dependency and development in Latin America* (Berkeley: University of California Press, 1978)

Carroll, J.T., 'General de Gaulle and Ireland's EEC application', pp. 81-97, in P.Joannon (ed.), *De Gaulle and Ireland* (Dublin: Institute of Public Administration, 1991)

Childs, D., *Britain since 1939: progress and decline* (London: Macmillan, 1995)

Chubb, B., & P.Lynch (eds), *Economic development and planning* (Dublin: Institute of Public Administration, 1969)

Chubb, B., *The government and politics of Ireland* (London: Longman, 1982)

Chubb, B., *The politics of the Irish constitution* (Dublin: Institute of Public Administration, 1991)
Collins, N., & F.McCann *Irish politics today* (Manchester: Manchester University Press, 1989)
Connolly, S.J., (ed.), *The Oxford companion to Irish history* (Oxford: Oxford University Press, 1998)
Coogan, T.P., *Ireland since the rising* (Westport: Greenwood, 1976)
Coogan, T.P., *De Valera: long fellow, long shadow* (London: Hutchinson, 1993)
Coolahan, J., *Irish education: its history and structure* (Dublin: Institute of Public Administration, 1981)
Coombes, D., (ed.), *Ireland and the European Communities: ten years of membership* (Dublin: Gill & Macmillan, 1983)
Craig, P., 'The nature of the Community: integration, democracy, and legitimacy', pp. 1-54, in P.Craig & G.de Búrca, *The evolution of EU law* (Oxford: Oxford University Press, 1999)
Cronin, S., *Washington's Irish policy, 1916-1986: independence, partition, neutrality* (Dublin: Anvil Press, 1987)
Crotty, R., *Irish agricultural production: its volume and share* (Cork: Cork University Press, 1966)
Crotty, R., 'Ireland: a case of peripheral underdevelopment or capitalist colonial undevelopment?', pp. 265-74, in G.Day & G.Rees (eds), *Regions, nations and European integration: remaking the Celtic periphery* (Cardiff: University of Wales, 1991)
Cullen, L.M., *An economic history of Ireland since 1660* (London: Batsford, 1978)
Deutsch, R., & V.Magowan, *Northern Ireland, 1968-73: a chronology of events, 1968-71* vol. 1 (Belfast: Blackstaff, 1973)
Dicken, P., *Global shift: the internationalization of economic activity* (London: Paul Chapman, 1992)
Dinan, D., 'After the "Emergency": Ireland in the post-war world', pp. 85-103, in *Éire-Ireland* vol. 24 no. 3 1989
Dinan, D., *Ever closer union?: an introduction to the European Community* (London: Macmillan, 1994)
Donaldson, L., *Development planning in Ireland* (New York: Praeger, 1966)
Driever, K., 'Probleme einer nachholender Integration: Irische Erfahrungen in der EG/EU', pp. 315-24, in *Aussenpolitik* vol. 45 no. 4 1994
Driscoll, D., 'Is Ireland really neutral?', pp. 55-61, in *Irish studies in international affairs* vol. 1 no. 3 1982
Drudy, P.J., & D.McAleese (eds), *Ireland and the European Community* (Cambridge: Cambridge University Press, 1984)
Duffy, T., 'Ireland and nuclear power', pp. 73-92, in *L'Irlande Politique et Sociale* no. 4
Dunphy, R., *Class, power and the Fianna Fáil party: a study of hegemony in Irish politics, 1923-1948* (Florence: IUE PhD thesis, 1988)
Dunphy, R., *The making of Fianna Fáil power in Ireland, 1923-1946* (Oxford: Clarendon Press, 1995)

Dwyer, T.R., *De Valera: the man and the myths* (Chester Springs: Poolbeg, 1981)
Edwards, O.D., & F.Pyle (eds), *1916: the Easter rising* (Dublin: Macgibbon & Kee, 1968)
Edwards, O.D., (ed.), *Conor Cruise O'Brien introduces Ireland* (London: Deutsch, 1969)
Edwards, O.D., *Eamon de Valera* (Cardiff: GPC, 1987)
Ellis, P.B., *A history of the Irish working class* (London: Pluto, 1985)
Eriksen, K.E., & H.Ø.Pharo, 'The Common Market issue in Norway 1961-63', pp. 1-31, paper presented at a conference entitled *The first attempt to enlarge the European Community, 1961-63*, held at the IUE from 17-19 February 1994
Fann, K.T., & D.C.Hodges (eds), *Readings in US Imperialism* (Boston: Porter Sargent, 1971)
Fanning, R., *The Irish Department of Finance, 1922-58* (Dublin: Institute of Public Administration, 1978)
Fanning, R., *Independent Ireland* (Dublin: Helicon, 1983)
Fanning, R., 'Irish neutrality: an historical review', pp. 27-38, in *Irish studies in international affairs* vol. 1 no. 3 1982
Fanning, R., et al (eds), *Documents on Irish foreign policy, vol.I 1919-22* (Dublin: Royal Irish Academy & Department of Foreign Affairs, 1998)
Farrell, B., *Gill's Irish lives: Seán Lemass* (Dublin: Gill & Macmillan, 1983)
FitzGerald, G., *Planning in Ireland: a PEP study* (Dublin: Institute of Public Administration, 1968)
FitzGerald, G., *Towards a new Ireland* (Dublin: Torc, 1973)
FitzGerald, G., *All in a life: an autobiography* (London: Macmillan, 1991)
FitzGerald, M., *Irish-American diplomatic relations, 1948 to 1963* (Cork: UCC MPhil thesis, 1997)
FitzGerald, M., 'Irish neutrality and European integration, 1960-1972', pp. 144-72, in M.Gehler & R.Steininger (eds), *Die Neutralen und die europäischen Integration, 1945-1994* (Vienna: Böhlau Verlag, 2000)
FitzGerald, M., 'Gli archivi della Comunità europea', pp. 1-9, in C.Pavone (ed.), *Storia d'Italia nel secolo ventesimo: strumenti e fonti* (forthcoming)
FitzGerald, M., 'Ireland's experience of European integration: from the "political" to the "economic"', pp. 1-15, unpublished paper presented at a conference entitled the *Europeanisation of domestic policy* held at the IUE on 8 December 1995
FitzGerald, M., 'Why did Ireland's first application fail?', pp. 1-8, unpublished paper presented at a workshop entitled *Research workshop on the failure of Community expansion, 1961-63*, held at the IUE on 14 December 1998
Fitzpatrick, D., 'Ireland since 1870', pp. 213-74, in R.F.Foster (ed.), *The Oxford illustrated history of Ireland* (London: BCA, 1991)
Foley, A., & M.Mulreany, *The Single European Market and the Irish economy* (Dublin: Institute of Public Administration, 1990)
Foot, P., *The politics of Harold Wilson* (Harmondsworth: Penguin, 1968)
Foster, R., *Modern Ireland, 1600-1972* (London: Allen Lane, 1989)
Foster, R.F., 'Varieties of Irishness: cultures and anarchy in Ireland', pp. 21-39, in R.F.Foster, *Paddy and Mr Punch: connections in Irish and English history*

(London: Allen Lane, 1993)

Franke, A., & J.Witte, 'Ökonomischer Strukturwandel und Stadtentwicklung in der Republik Irland seit 1945', pp. 195-312, in H.-D.von Frieling & J.Strassel (eds), *Stadtentwicklung, Weltmarkt, Nationales Wirtschaftwachstum: Studien zum Prozess der Stadtentwicklung in europäischen Zentrums- und Peripherie-ländern*, vol. *1* (Oldenburg: Bibliotheks- und Informationssystem der Universität Oldenburg, 1986)

Fulton, J., *The tragedy of belief: division, politics, and religion in Ireland* (Oxford: Clarendon, 1991)

Gallagher, M., *Political parties in the Republic of Ireland* (Dublin: Gill & Macmillan, 1985)

Gallagher, T., & J.O'Connell (eds), *Contemporary Irish studies* (Manchester: Manchester University Press, 1983)

Gallagher, T., 'The dimensions of Fianna Fail rule in Ireland', pp. 54-68, in *Western European politics* vol. 4 no. 1 1981

Garvin, T., *The evolution of Irish national politics* (Dublin: Gill & Macmillan, 1981)

Garvin, T., 'Wealth, poverty and development: reflections on current discontents', pp. 312-25, in *Studies* vol. 78 no. 311 1989

Geiger, T., 'Why Ireland needed the Marshall Plan but did not want it: Ireland, the Sterling Area and the European Recovery Program, 1947-1948', University of Manchester Department of History Working Paper no. 44

George, S., *An awkward partner: Britain in the European Community* (Oxford: Oxford University Press, 1998)

Gerbet, P., *La construction de l'Europe* (Paris: Imprimerie nationale, 1983)

Gerbet, P., 'French attitudes to the foreign policy and defence of Europe', pp. 150-9, in F.-G.Dreyfus *et al* (eds), *France and EEC membership evaluated* (London: Pinter, 1993)

Ginsborg, P., *A history of contemporary Italy* (London: Penguin, 1990)

Ginsborg, P., *L'Italia del tempo presente* (Turin: Einaudi, 1998)

Girvin, B., *Between two worlds: politics and economy in independent Ireland* (Dublin: Gill & Macmillan, 1989)

Girvin, B., 'Irish agricultural policy and the Green Pool: 1950-1955', pp. 239-59, in B.Girvin & R.T.Griffiths (eds), *The Green Pool and the origins of the Common Agricultural Policy* (London: Lothian, 1995)

Girvin, B., 'Nationalism, democracy, and Irish political culture', pp. 3-28, in B.Girvin & R.Sturm (eds), *Politics and society in contemporary Ireland* (Aldershot: Gower, 1986)

Girvin, B., 'Economic development and the politics of EC entry: Ireland 1956-63', pp. 1-35, paper presented at a conference entitled *The first attempt to enlarge the European Community, 1961-63*, held at the IUE from 17-19 February 1994

Girvin, B,, 'Irish economic development and the politics of EEC entry', in R.T.Griffiths & S.Ward (eds), *Courting the Common Market: the first attempt to enlarge the European Community, 1961-1963* (London: Lothian Foundation Press, 1996), pp. 247-62

Goldthorpe, J.H., & C.T.Whelan (eds), *The development of industrial society in*

Ireland (Oxford: Oxford University Press, 1992)

Gray, T., *The Irish answer* (London: Heinemann, 1966)

Greenwood, S., (ed.), *Britain and European integration since the Second World War: documents in contemporary history* (Manchester: Manchester University Press, 1996)

Griffiths, R.T., 'Ireland and EFTA' (unpublished article)

Griffiths, R.T., & S.Ward, 'United house or abandoned ship? EFTA and the EEC membership crisis, 1961-63', pp. 1-26, paper presented at a conference entitled *The first attempt to enlarge the European Community, 1961-63*, held at the IUE from 17-19 February 1994

Griffiths, R.T., 'The European integration experience, 1945-58', pp. 1-36, in K.Middlemas, *Orchestrating Europe: the informal politics of the European Union, 1973-95* (London: Fontana, 1995)

Griffiths, R.T., 'The European integration experience, 1958-73', pp. 37-70, in K.Middlemas, *Orchestrating Europe: the informal politics of the European Union, 1973-95* (London: Fontana, 1995)

Griffiths, R.T., & S.Ward (eds), *Courting the Common Market: the first attempt to enlarge the European Community, 1961-1963* (London: Lothian Foundation Press, 1996)

Groom, A.J.R., & M.Light (eds), *Contemporary international relations: a guide to theory* (London: Pinter, 1994)

Harkness, D., *Ireland in the twentieth century: divided island* (London: Macmillan, 1996)

Hagan, J.W., *The economy of Ireland: policy and performance* (Dublin: Irish Management Institute, 1975)

Handel, M., *Weak states in the international system* (London: Frank Cass, 1981)

Haughton, J., 'The historical background', pp. 1-48, in J.W.O'Hagan (ed.), *The economy of Ireland: policy and performance of a small European country* (London: Macmillan, 1995)

Hechter, M., *Internal colonialism: the Celtic fringe in British national development, 1536-1966* (London: Routledge & Kegan Paul, 1975)

Hederman, M., *The road to Europe: Irish attitudes, 1948-61* (Dublin: Institute of Public Administration, 1983)

Hederman, M., 'The beginning of the discussion on European Union in Ireland', pp. 763-800, in W.Lipgens & W.Loth (eds), *Documents on the history of European integration vol. 3* (Berlin: Walter de Gruyter, 1988)

Hennessey, T., *A history of Northern Ireland, 1920-1996* (Dublin: Gill & Macmillan, 1997)

Hickman, M.J., *Ireland and the European Community* (London: PNL, 1990)

Higgins, M.D., 'The limits of clientelism: towards an assessment of Irish politics', pp. 114-41, in C.Clapham (ed.), *Private patronage and public power: political clientelism in the modern state* (London: Frances Pinter, 1982)

Hill, R.J., & M.Marsh, *Modern Irish democracy: essays in honour of Basil Chubb* (Dublin: Irish Academic Press, 1993)

Hillery, P.J., 'Ireland and Britain in the European Community', pp. 1-11, in

Administration vol. 24 no. 1 1976

Hoffmann, S., *Contemporary theory in international relations* (Englewood Cliffs: Prentice-Hall, 1960)

Hussey, G., *Ireland today* (London: Penguin, 1995)

Hutchinson, G., *Edward Heath: a personal and political biography* (Edinburgh: Longman, 1970)

Jacobsen, J.K., *Chasing progress in the Irish Republic: ideology, democracy and dependent development* (Cambridge: Cambridge University Press, 1994)

Jackson, J.H., *World trade and the law of GATT* (New York: Bobbs-Merrill, 1969)

Jameson, F., 'Modernism and imperialism', pp. 43-66, in T.Eagleton *et al*, *Nationalism, colonialism and literature* (Minneapolis: University of Minnesota Press, 1990)

Joyce, J., & P.Murtagh, *The Boss: Charles J.Haughey in government* (Dublin: Poolbeg, 1983)

Kaiser, W., 'To join, or not to join: the "appeasement" policy of Britain's first EEC application', pp. 144-56, in B.Brivati & H.Jones (eds), *From reconstruction to integration: Britain and Europe since 1945* (Leicester: Leicester University Press, 1993)

Karsh, E., *Neutrality and small states* (London: Routledge, 1988)

Katzenstein, P.J., *Small states in world markets: industrial policy in Europe* (London: Cornell University Press, 1985)

Keatinge, P., *The formulation of Irish foreign policy* (Dublin: Institute of Public Administration, 1973)

Keatinge, P., *A singular stance: Irish neutrality in the 1980s* (Dublin: Institute of Public Administration, 1984)

Keatinge, P., 'Ireland and the world, 1957-82', pp. 225-40, in F.Litton (ed.), *Unequal achievement: the Irish experience, 1957-1982* (Dublin: Institute of Public Administration, 1982)

Keatinge, P., (ed.), *Ireland and EC membership evaluated* (London: Pinter, 1991)

Keatinge, P., & B.Laffan, 'Ireland in international affairs', pp. 200-21, in J.Coakley & M.Gallagher (eds), *Politics in the Republic of Ireland* (Galway: PSAI Press, 1992)

Keatinge, P., 'From community to union', pp. 2-9 & 160, in P.Keatinge (ed.), *Maastricht and Ireland: what the treaty means* (Dublin: Institute of European Affairs, 1992)

Kennedy, K.A., *et al*, *The economic development of Ireland in the twentieth century* (London: Routledge, 1988)

Kennedy, K.A., 'Irish economy transformed', pp. 33-42, in *Studies* vol. 87 no. 345 1998

Kennedy, L., *The modern industrialisation of Ireland, 1940-1988* (Dundalk: Dungalgan Press, 1989)

Kennedy, L., *Colonialism, religion and nationalism in Ireland* (Belfast: Institute of Irish Studies, 1996)

Kennedy, M., & J.M.Skelly (eds), *Irish diplomatic history, 1919-69: from independence to internationalism* (Dublin: Four Courts Press, 1999)

Kennedy, M., & E.O'Halpin, *Ireland and the Council of Europe: from isolation towards integration* (Strasbourg: Council of Europe, 2000)

Keogh, D., 'The Department of Foreign Affairs', pp. 275-96, in Z.Steiner (ed.), *The Times survey of foreign ministries of the world* (London: Times Books, 1982)

Keogh, D., *Ireland and Europe, 1919-1989: a diplomatic and political history* (Cork: Hibernian Press, 1990)

Keogh, D., *Twentieth-century Ireland: nation and state* (Dublin: Gill & Macmillan, 1994)

Keogh, D., *Ireland and the Vatican: the politics and diplomacy of church-state relations, 1922-1960* (Cork: Cork University Press, 1995)

Keogh, D., 'The diplomacy of "dignified calm": an analysis of Ireland's application for membership of the EEC, 1961-1963', pp. 81-101, in the *Journal of European integration history* vol. 3 no. 1 1997

Keohane, R.O., & S.Hoffman (eds), *The new European Community: decisionmaking and institutional change* (Boulder: Westview, 1991)

Kersten, J.W., *Policies for rural peripheral regions in the European Community* (Saarbrücken: Breitenbach, 1990)

Killeen, M.J., *Industrial development and full employment* (Dublin: IDA Ireland, 1976)

Kitzinger, U., *The second try: Labour and the EEC* (Oxford: Pergamon, 1968)

Laffan, B., 'Ireland and Denmark in the European Community: political and administrative aspects', pp. 43-62, in *Administration* vol. 29 no. 1 1981

Laffan, B., *Integration and co-operation in Europe* (London: Routledge, 1992)

Laffan, B., 'The European Union: a distinctive model of internationalization', pp. 235-53, in the *Journal of European Public Policy* vol. 5 no. 2 1998

Laursen, J., 'The great challenge: Denmark and the first attempt to enlarge the European Community, 1961-63', pp. 1-24, paper presented at a conference entitled *The first attempt to enlarge the European Community, 1961-63*, held at the IUE from 17-19 February 1994

Lawrence, R.J., *The Government of Northern Ireland: public finance and public services, 1921-1964* (Oxford: Clarendon Press, 1965)

Lee, J.J., (ed.), *Ireland, 1945-70* (Dublin: Gill & Macmillan, 1979)

Lee, J.J., & G.Ó Tuathaigh, *The age of de Valera* (Dublin: Ward River Press, 1982)

Lee, J.J., *Ireland, 1912-1985: politics and society* (Cambridge: Cambridge University Press, 1989)

Lee, S., 'Staying in the game? Coming into the game? Macmillan and European integration', pp. 123-47, in R.Aldous & S.Lee (eds), *Harold Macmillan and Britain's world role* (London: Macmillan, 1996)

Lewis, D.W.P., *The road to Europe: history, institutions and prospects of European integration, 1945-1993* (New York: Peter Lang, 1993)

Lindell, U., & S.Persson, 'The paradox of weak state power: a research and literature overview', pp. 79-97, in *Cooperation and conflict* vol. 21 no. 2 1986

Longford, Lord, & T.P.O'Neill, *Éamon de Valera* (Dublin: Gill & Macmillan, 1970)

Ludlow, N.P., 'Influence and vulnerability: the role of the EEC Commission in the enlargement negotiations', pp. 1-23, paper presented at a conference entitled *The first attempt to enlarge the European Community, 1961-63*, held at the IUE from 17-19 February 1994

Lyons, F.S.L., *Ireland since the Famine* (Glasgow: Fontana, 1976)

Mac Aogáin, E., 'Identità culturale e linguistica nella nuova Europa: prospettiva dall'Irlanda', pp. 59-66, in M.Pinna (ed.), *L'Europa delle diversità: identità e culture alle soglie del terzo millenio* (Milan: Francoangeli, 1993)

MacDonagh, O., *Ireland: the Union and its aftermath* (London: George Allen, 1977)

MacKernan, P., 'Irish foreign policy: context and concerns', pp. 172-89, in *Administration* vol. 35 no. 2 1987

Macmillan, H., *At the end of the day, 1961-1963* (London: Macmillan, 1973)

Magee, J., *Northern Ireland: crisis and conflict* (London: Routledge & Kegan Paul, 1974)

Maguire, M., 'Ireland', pp. 241-384, in P.Flora (ed.), *Growth to limits: the Western European welfare states since World War II, vol. 2* (Berlin: Walter de Gruyter, 1986)

Maher, D.J., *The tortuous path: the course of Ireland's entry into the EEC, 1948-73* (Dublin: Institute of Public Administration, 1986)

Mally, G., *Britain and European unity* (London: Hansard Society, 1966)

Manning, M., *Irish political parties* (Dublin: Gill & Macmillan, 1972)

Marwick, A., *British society since 1945* (London: Penguin, 1996)

Massoulié, F., et al, *La costruzione dell'Europa* (Florence: Giunti Casterman, 1997)

McAleese, D., 'Political independence, economic growth and the role of economic policy', pp. 271-95, in P.J.Drudy (ed.), *Irish studies 2 – Ireland: land, politics and people* (Cambridge: Cambridge University Press, 1982)

McAleese, D., 'European integration and the Irish economy', pp. 152-71, in *Administration* vol. 35 no. 2 1987

McAleese, D., & A.Matthews, 'The Single European Act and Ireland: implications for a small member state', pp. 39-60, in the *Journal of Common Market studies* vol. 26 no. 1 1987

McCarthy, C., *The decade of upheaval* (Dublin: Institute of Public Administration, 1973)

McCarthy, J.F., (ed.), *Planning Ireland's future: the legacy of T.K.Whitaker* (Dublin: Glendale, 1990)

McGilvray, J., *Social statistics in Ireland: a guide to their sources and uses* (Dublin: Institute of Public Administration, 1977)

McGilvray, J., & F.Kirwan, *Irish economic statistics* (Dublin: Institute of Public Administration, 1982)

McSweeney, B., 'Out of the ghetto: Irish foreign policy since the fifties', pp. 401-12, in *Studies* vol. 75 no. 300 1986

McSweeney, B., 'Ireland and European integration', pp. 187-93, in *Studies* vol. 79 no. 314 1990

Meenan, J., *The Irish economy since 1922* (Liverpool: Liverpool University Press, 1970)

Milward, A., *The European rescue of the nation-state* (London: Routledge, 1992)

Milward, A.S., et al (eds), *The frontier of national sovereignty: history and theory,*

1945-1992 (London: Routledge, 1993)

Milward, A., 'New Zealand, the United Kingdom and the EEC' (unpublished article)

Mjøset, L., *The Irish economy in a comparative institutional perspective* (Dublin: National Economic and Social Council, 1992)

Moody, T.W., & F.X.Martin (eds), *The course of Irish history* (Cork: Mercier, 1967)

Moody, T.W., et al (eds), 'A chronology of Irish history to 1976', in *A new history of Ireland* vol. 8 (Oxford: Clarendon Press, 1982)

Moravcsik, A., *The choice for Europe: social purpose and state power from Messina to Maastricht* (Ithaca: Cornell University Press, 1998)

Moravcsik, A., 'EU enlargement and the myth of the "awkward partner"', pp. 1-2, unpublished paper presented at a workshop entitled *EU enlargement and the myth of the 'awkward partner'* held at the IUE by the Working Group on European Integration on 22 June 1999

Moynihan, M., *Currency and central banking in Ireland, 1922-60* (Dublin: Central Bank of Ireland, 1975)

Moynihan, M., (ed.), *Speeches and statements by Eamon de Valera, 1917-73* (Dublin: Gill & Macmillan, 1980)

Munck, R., *Ireland: nation, state, and class struggle* (Boulder: Westview Press, 1985)

Murphy, A.E., (ed.), *Economists and the Irish economy from the eighteenth century to the present day* (Blackrock: Irish Academic Press, 1984)

Murphy, J.A., *Ireland in the twentieth century* (Dublin: Gill & Macmillan, 1989)

Murphy, S., 'The new Europe and Irish neutrality', pp. 377-88, in *Studies* vol. 79 no. 316 1990

Murphy, T., & P.Twomey (eds), *Ireland's evolving constitution, 1937-97: collected essays* (Oxford: Hart, 1998)

Neuhold, H. (ed.), *The European neutrals in the 1990s: new challenges and opportunities* (Boulder: Westview Press, 1992)

Nicholson, F., & R.East, *From the Six to the Twelve: the enlargement of the European Communities* (Harlow: Longman, 1987)

Nicoll, W., & T.Salmon, *Understanding the European Communities* (New York: Harvester Wheatsheaf, 1994)

Nolan, A., *Joseph Walshe and the management of Irish foreign policy, 1922-1946: a study in diplomatic and administrative history* (Cork: UCC PhD thesis, 1997)

Norton, D., 'Smuggling under the Common Agricultural Policy: Northern Ireland and the Republic of Ireland', pp. 297-312, in the *Journal of Common Market studies* vol. 24 no. 4 1986

O'Brien, C.C., (ed.), *The shaping of modern Ireland* (London: Routledge & Kegan Paul, 1960)

O'Brien, C.C., *To Katanga and back* (London: Hutchinson, 1962)

O'Brien, C.C., 'The embers of Easter, 1916-1966', pp. 225-40, in O.D.Edwards and F.Pyle (eds), *1916: the Easter rising* (London: MacGibbon & Kee, 1968)

O'Brien, C.C., 'Ireland in international affairs', pp. 13-20, in O.D.Edwards (ed.), *Conor Cruise O'Brien introduces Ireland* (London: Deutsch, 1969)

O'Brien, C.C., *States of Ireland* (London: Hutchinson, 1972)

O'Brien, F., *An béal bocht* (Dublin: Dolmen, 1941)
O'Brien, M., & C.C. O'Brien, *Ireland: a concise history* (London: BCA, 1992)
O'Carroll, J.P., & J.A.Murphy (eds), *De Valera and his times* (Cork: Cork University Press, 1983)
O'Day, A., & J.Stevenson, *Irish historical documents since 1800* (Dublin: Gill & Macmillan, 1992)
O'Donnell, R., (ed.), *Europe: the Irish experience* (Dublin: Institute of European Affairs, 2000)
O'Dowd, J., (ed.), *Ireland Europe and 1992* (Dublin: Tomar, 1989)
O'Farrell, P., *Ireland's English question: Anglo-Irish relations, 1534-1970* (London: B.T.Batsford, 1971)
O'Farrell, P.N., *Regional industrial development trends in Ireland, 1960-1973* (Dublin: IDA Ireland, 1975)
O'Halloran, C., *Partition and the limits of Irish nationalism: an ideology under stress* (Dublin: Gill & Macmillan, 1987)
O'Leary, C., *Irish elections, 1918-77: parties, voters and proportional representation* (Dublin: Gill & Macmillan, 1979)
O'Malley, E., *Industry and economic development: the challenge for the latecomer* (Dublin: Gill & Macmillan, 1989)
O'Malley, E., 'The problem of late industrialisation and the experience of the Republic of Ireland', pp. 141-54, in the *Cambridge journal of economics* vol. 9 no. 2 1985
Ó Muircheartaigh, F., (ed.), *Ireland in the coming times: essays to celebrate T.K.Whitaker's 80 years* (Dublin: Institute of Public Administration, 1998)
O'Neill, T., *The autobiography of Terence O'Neill* (London: Rupert Hart-Davis, 1972)
Orsello, G.P., *L'Unione europea* (Rome: Tascabili Economici Newton, 1996)
O'Sullivan, M., *Seán Lemass: a biography* (Dublin: Blackwater Press, 1994)
De Paor, L., *Divided Ulster* (Harmondsworth: Penguin, 1971)
Parker, G., 'Political geography and geopolitics', pp. 170-81, in A.J.R.Groom & M.Light (eds), *Contemporary international relations: a guide to theory* (London: Pinter, 1994)
Pierson, P., 'The path to European Union: an historical institutionalist perspective' (draft version)
Polach, J.G., *Euratom: its background, issues and economic implications* (New York: Oceana Publications, 1964)
Probert, B., *Beyond orange and green: the political economy of the Northern Ireland crisis* (London: Zen, 1979)
Rathkolb, O., 'The Austrian case: from the neutrals' association approach to a "special arrangement" with the EEC (1961-1963)', pp. 1-29, paper presented at a conference entitled *The first attempt to enlarge the European Community, 1961-63*, held at the IUE from 17-19 February 1994
Raymond, R.J., *The economics of neutrality: the United States, Great Britain and Ireland's war economy, 1937-1945* (Ann Arbor: University Microfilms International, 1981)

Raymond, R.J., 'Irish neutrality: ideology or pragmatism?', pp. 31-40, in *International affairs* vol. 60 no. 1 1983/4

Richards, C., *The new Italians* (London: Penguin, 1995)

Robertson, P., & J.Singleton, 'Britain, the Dominions and the EEC, 1961-1963' (draft article)

Rumpf, E., & A.C.Hepburn, *Nationalism and socialism in twentieth-century Ireland* (Liverpool: Liverpool University Press, 1977)

Salmon, T., 'Ireland: a neutral in the Community?', pp. 205-27, in the *Journal of Common Market studies* vol. 20 no. 3 1982

Salmon, T.C., *Unneutral Ireland: an ambivalent and unique security policy* (Oxford: Clarendon, 1989)

Schaad, M., 'Plan G – a "counterblast"? British policy towards the Messina countries, 1956', pp. 39-60, in *Contemporary European History* vol. 7 no. 1 1998

Schlesinger, P., 'On national identity: some conceptions and misconceptions criticized', pp. 219-64, in *Social science information sur les sciences sociales* vol. 26 no. 2 1987

Shivers, L., & D.Bowman, *More than the Troubles: a common sense view of the Northern Ireland conflict* (Philadelphia: New Society, 1984)

Shanks, M., & J.Lambert, *Britain and the new Europe: the future of the Common Market* (London: Chatto & Windus, 1962)

Sharp, P., *Irish foreign policy and the European Community: a study of the impact of interdependence in the foreign policy of a small state* (Aldershot: Dartmouth, 1990)

Skelly, J.M., *Irish diplomacy at the United Nations, 1945-1965: national interests and the national order* (Dublin: Irish Academic Press, 1997)

Smith, M., *Western Europe and the United States: the uncertain alliance* (London: George Allen & Unwin, 1984)

Sobiela-Caanitz, G., 'L'Irlande du Nord', pp. 113-20, in *Les régions d'Europe* (Paris: Presses d'Europe, 1973)

Spierenburg, D., & R.Poidevin, *Histoire de la Haute Authorité de la Communauté Européenne du Charbon et de l'Acier: une expérience supranationale* (Brussels: Bruylant, 1993)

Stallings, B., *Economic dependency in Africa and Latin America* (Beverly Hills: Sage, 1972)

Stefani, G., *et al*, *Meccanismi d'intervento pubblico nell'economia: le esperienze in Irlanda e Turchia* (Milan: Ciriec, 1977)

Steininger, R., '1961: Europe "at sixes and sevens" – the European Free Trade Association, the neutrals, and Great Britain's decision to join the E.E.C.', pp. 535-68, in the *Journal of European economic history* vol. 26 no. 3 1997

Steinnes, K., 'The European challenge: Britain's EEC application in 1961', pp. 61-79, in *Contemporary European History* vol. 7 no. 1 1998

Sutherland, P.D., 'Ireland: where do we really stand on European integration?', pp. 243-54, in *Studies* vol. 78 no. 311 1989

Swift, J., 'The changing role of ambassadors and embassies', pp. 3-13, in *Administration* vol. 46 no. 1 1998

Tait, A.A., & J.A.Bristow (eds), *Ireland: some problems of a developing economy* (Dublin: Gill & Macmillan, 1972)
Taylor, A.J.P., 'A patriot for one Ireland', pp. 253-9, in C.Wrigley (ed.), *From the Boer War to the Cold War: essays on twentieth-century Europe* (London: Hamish Hamilton, 1995)
Thomas, C., & A.Thomas, *Historical dictionary of Ireland* European Historical Dictionaries no. 20 (London: Scarecrow Press, 1997)
Tobin, F., *The best of decades: Ireland in the nineteen sixties* (Dublin: Gill & Macmillan, 1996)
Tratt, J., *The Macmillan government and Europe: a study in the process of policy development* (London: Macmillan, 1996)
Turner, J., *Macmillan* (London: Longman, 1994)
Vaïsse, M., 'De Gaulle and the British "application" to join the Common Market', pp. 51-69, in G.Wilkes (ed.), *Britain's failure to enter the European Community, 1961-63: the enlargement negotiations and crises in European, Atlantic and Commonwealth relations* (London: Frank Cass, 1997)
Vaughan, R., *Twentieth-century Europe: paths to unity* (London: Croom Helm, 1979)
Vaughan, W.E., & A.J.Fitzpatrick (eds), *Irish historical statistics: population, 1821-1971* (Dublin: Royal Irish Academy, 1978)
Vital, D., *The inequality of states: a study of the small power in international relations* (Oxford: Clarendon, 1967)
Wallace, W., 'The British approach to Europe', pp. 107-33, in W.J.Mommsen (ed.), *The long way to Europe: historical observations from a contemporary view* (Chicago: edition q, 1994)
Wallerstein, I., *The capitalist world economy: essays by Immanuel Wallerstein* (Cambridge: Cambridge University Press, 1979)
Whelan, B., *Europe: aspects of Irish foreign policy, 1945-51* (Cork: UCC MA thesis, 1984)
Whelan, B., 'The European Recovery Program (the Marshall Plan) and Ireland: summary and assessment', pp. 78-84, in *Éire-Ireland* vol. 24 no. 3 1989
Whitaker, T.K., 'From protection to free trade: the Irish experience', pp. 405-23, in *Administration* vol. 21 no. 4 1973
Whitaker, T.K., 'An ceangal le sterling: ar cheart é a bhriseadh?', pp. 82-90, in *Annual report: Central Bank of Ireland, 1976* (Dublin: Central Bank of Ireland, 1976)
Whitaker, T.K., 'Land of Change', pp. 4-18, in *Éire-Ireland* vol. 22 no. 1 1987
Whyte, J.H., *Church and state in modern Ireland, 1923-1979* (Dublin: Gill & Macmillan, 1980)
Wickham, J., 'Dependence and state structure: foreign firms and industrial policy in the Republic of Ireland', pp. 164-83, in O.Höll (ed.), *Small states in Europe and dependence* (Vienna: Wilhelm Braumüller, 1983)
Williams, T.D., 'Irish foreign policy, 1949-69', pp. 136-51, in J.J.Lee (ed.), *Ireland, 1945-70* (Dublin: Gill & Macmillan, 1979)
Wilson, H., *The Labour government, 1964-1970: a personal record* (London: Wiedenfeld & Nicolson, 1971)

Wilson, T., *Ulster: conflict and consent* (London: Basil Blackwell, 1989)

Witoszek, N., 'Nationalism, postmodernity and Ireland', pp. 101-21, in Ø.Sørensen (ed.), *Nationalism in small European nations* (Oslo: Research Council of Norway, 1996)

Wurm, C.A., 'Britain and European integration, 1945-63', pp. 249-61, in *Contemporary European History* vol. 7 no. 2 1998

Yachir, F., *The Mediterranean: between autonomy and dependency* (Tokyo: United Nations University, 1989)

Young, H., *The blessed plot: Britain and Europe from Churchill to Blair* (London: Macmillan, 1998)

Young, K., *Sir Alec Douglas-Home* (London: J.M.Dent, 1970)

Notes

Introduction

1. Throughout this text, the constitutionally-based term 'Ireland' is utilised to denote the Republic of Ireland; this terminology does not carry any political connotation as it expresses the country's name as used by the government in its relations with organisations such as the European Coal and Steel Community (ECSC), the European Atomic Energy Community (Euratom), the European Economic Community (EEC), the European Free Trade Association (EFTA), and beyond, including its relations with countries like the United Kingdom of Great Britain and Northern Ireland (UK), the United States of America (US), and the Union of Soviet Socialist Republics (USSR). Please note that abbreviations are extensively used throughout these footnotes and that the fullest form of each new reference is given when first utilised.
2. Among the dignitaries was Seán Lemass, the Irish prime minister. On many other occasions, John F.Kennedy (US president) made similar statements; for instance, on 28 June 1963, he declared in his famous oration Dáil Éireann (Irish lower parliamentary house): 'I sincerely believe that your future is as promising as your past is proud'; he quoted William Butler Yeats in making an oblique reference to the UK's unremitting links with Ireland: 'Let us not casually reduce the great past to a trouble of fools, for we need not feel the bitterness of the past to discover its meaning for the present and the future'. During his visit, he stated: '[In Ireland] the past [is] very real and has made the present very hopeful'. M.FitzGerald, *Irish-American diplomatic relations, 1948 to 1963* (Cork: unpublished University College Cork (UCC) MPhil thesis, 1997), pp. 194-6 & 205; Kennedy oration delivered in Dáil Éireann, 28 June 1963, *Public papers of the Presidents of the United States: John F.Kennedy 1963* (Washington DC: Government Printing Office, 1964), pp. 534-9; Kennedy speech given in Limerick, 29 June 1963, *John F.Kennedy 1963*, p. 541; Kennedy address delivered in Washington DC, 15 October 1963, *John F.Kennedy 1963*, p. 784.
3. Ireland's contribution to the 1996 Intergovernmental Conference entitled 'The European Union and the new Europe', European Parliament document PE165.980, European Parliament, Bâtiment Robert Schuman, Luxembourg (PE).
4. It is crucial to note in this context that European integration is taken to mean Ireland's attitude towards, membership of, and/or participation in post-Second World War Western European – and perhaps even wider international – institutions and organisations that had economic, political and/or social implications for the Irish government and nation.

5   J.J.Lee quoted in R.McDonnell (ed.), 'Senator Professor Joe Lee', pp. 22-4, in *Graduate* (UCC publication) Autumn 1993, *passim*.
6   Leader article, 'Ireland shines', *Economist*, 17 May 1997.
7   M.Hederman, *The road to Europe: Irish attitudes, 1948-61* (Dublin: Institute of Public Administration, 1983), p. 74.
8   Frank Aiken (foreign minister) speaking during a debate in Seanad Éireann (Irish upper parliamentary house), 14 July 1966, *Seanad Éireann parliamentary debates official report* (*Seanad debates*) vol. 61 col. 1916.
9   A.Moravcsik, *The choice for Europe: social purpose and state power from Messina to Maastricht* (Ithaca: Cornell University Press, 1998), p. 3; J.M.Skelly, *Irish diplomacy at the United Nations, 1945-1965: national interests and the national order* (Dublin: Irish Academic Press, 1997), p. 18. A review of the former appears in the Working Group on European Integration's *Newsletter*, no. 1 June 1999, produced in the Department of History & Civilisation at the European University Institute, Badia Fiesolana, Florence (IUE); it can also be found at *http://www.iue.it/HEC/wg-integ.html* (17 August 1999).
10   The theoretical question is dealt with in detail in Chapter 1 under the heading *Ireland's world position*.
11   P.Keatinge, *A singular stance: Irish neutrality in the 1980s* (Dublin: Institute of Public Administration, 1984), *passim*; L.Kennedy, *Colonialism, religion and nationalism in Ireland* (Belfast: Institute of Irish Studies, 1996), p. 217. This sub-heading comes from a term liberally employed by Patrick Keatinge to portray the country's approach to neutrality. However, its use in this context does not mean to suggest that Ireland's wider historical experience is necessarily any more unique than it is for any other nation, thus agreeing with Liam Kennedy's view that the Irish are not the 'most oppressed people ever'; his coinage of the acronym 'MOPE' is particularly apt when railing against any 'singular' sense of 'victimhood and exceptionalism'.
12   Ranging from Southern Italy's Mezzogiorno to Puerto Rico, Canada to the Netherlands, Greece to Portugal, Norway to Spain, all of these propositions failed to meet the necessary criteria because of a range of reasons, including, for example, strict relevance to the subject at hand. There was much more to this decision than practical considerations. In the context of the Western world, the Organisation for Economic Cooperation and Development (OECD) – the successor to the Organisation for European Economic Cooperation (OEEC) – generally placed Ireland near the bottom of its economic league. Two countries still stood out as offering some respite, Denmark and New Zealand; thus, both states are used to contextualise Ireland, as the latter's integration experience may be better understood by placing it in a comparative perspective, most especially in European terms. Nonetheless, the facts of its own peculiar position must be heard in all of their insular and parochial glory. As Liam Kennedy argues, it is obvious that, within a Western comparative framework and despite lagging behind the world's major players at the start of the twentieth century, Ireland was relatively comfortably placed economically. As a neo/post-colonialist ever since the 1920s, it was certainly not comparable to either African or Asian countries at their relative points of decolonisation. Kennedy, *Colonialism, religion and nationalism*, pp. xv & 170-1.
13   The comparative question is dealt with in even more detail under the heading *Ireland's world position* in Chapter 1. In Denmark's case, it was concluded that a thorough inspection of primary material was neither necessarily pertinent nor practical. A detailed review of corresponding and related secondary material was

obviously ascertained as essential and this is presented in the opening chapter; indeed, findings have been integrated throughout this research, but not in any conscious way as a comparative. At any rate, this study regarding Ireland's relationship with the EEC was carried out with Denmark in mind, but was ultimately dependent upon secondary sources only.

14 In New Zealand's case, simply because this 'singular' study centres on Ireland's relationship with the EEC, the issue of a 'shadow comparison' was once again concentrated on secondary sources and thus invoked the former's experiences only when it was deemed applicable in the light of the latter's EEC relations.

15 This issue is dealt with in some detail under the heading *Ireland's world position* in the next chapter.

16 P.Keatinge, *The formulation of Irish foreign policy* (Dublin: Institute of Public Administration, 1973), p. 307.

17 D.J.Maher, *The tortuous path: the course of Ireland's entry into the EEC, 1948-73* (Dublin: Institute of Public Administration, 1986).

18 Hederman, *The road to Europe*; D.Keogh, *Ireland and Europe, 1919-1989: a diplomatic history* (Cork: Hibernian Press, 1990). For an extensive assessment of related and relevant articles and texts, see the sections in the *Bibliography* headed *Literature survey* and *Secondary sources*.

19 P.Sharp, *Irish foreign policy and the European Community: a study of the impact of interdependence in the foreign policy of a small state* (Aldershot: Dartmouth, 1990), p. ix.

20 P.Gerbet, *La construction de l'Europe* (Paris: Imprimerie nationale, 1983), p. 294. In the original French, this quotation read: 'l'Irlande ... étant en union économique avec la Grande-Bretagne, elle ne pouvait s'en trouver séparée'.

21 Primary sources are examined in two sections – headed *Archival appraisal* and *Primary materials* – in the *Bibliography*; both precede secondary sources.

22 Éamon de Valera (parliamentary opposition leader) speech delivered in Dáil Éireann, 12 July 1955, entitled 'International co-operation and Irish unity', pp. 572-6, in M.Moynihan (ed.), *Speeches and statements by Eamon de Valera, 1917-73* (Dublin: Gill & Macmillan, 1980), p. 573.

23 Lemass speech delivered in Dáil Éireann, 5 July 1961, *Dáil Éireann parliamentary debates official report* (*Dáil debates*) vol. 191 col. 266.

24 See the sections entitled *Archival appraisal* and *Literature survey* in the *Bibliography*. The main purpose of an extended analysis at the end of the text, however, is clearly to list the primary and secondary source materials employed in the course of this extensive evaluation.

25 As previously stated, some of the ground covered in this text was presented in a different context in an MPhil dissertation – *Irish-American diplomatic relations, 1948 to 1963* – and has now been retraced in the light of Ireland's dealings with the European integration concept, as seen through the eyes of successive US governments. Additionally, four other papers have also been completed in the course of this research. One article – 'Irish neutrality and European integration, 1960 to 1972' – records an excellent example of the change in emphasis in Ireland's foreign policy away from political considerations to economic prerogatives, a central theme in this research. Another paper conceived for publication – 'Gli archivi della Comunità europea' – although not directly of much relevance to the text itself, has proven to be a useful way of trying to assess the value of the ACE, an archive which should have been a crucial resource, but was not. In turn, a third presentation – 'Ireland's experience of European integration: from the "political" to the "economic"'

- forms part of both the introductory first chapter and the sixth chapter survey of this investigation, giving a context in which the central subject sits, as well as a comprehensive overview, while a fourth paper – 'Why did Ireland's application fail?' – has helped in drawing some meaningful conclusions. M.FitzGerald, 'Irish neutrality and European integration, 1960-1972', pp. 144-72, in M.Gehler & R.Steininger (eds), *Die Neutralen und die europäische Integration, 1945-1995* (Vienna: Böhlau Verlag, 2000); M.FitzGerald, 'Gli archivi della Comunità europea', pp. 1-9, in C.Pavone (ed.), *Storia d'Italia nel secolo ventesimo: strumenti e fonti* (forthcoming); M.FitzGerald, 'Ireland's experience of European integration: from the "political" to the "economic"', pp. 1-15, unpublished paper presented at a conference – held on 8 December 1995 at the IUE – entitled the *Europeanisation of domestic policy*; M.FitzGerald, 'Why did Ireland's application fail?', 1-8, unpublished paper presented at a workshop – held on 14 December 1998 at the IUE – entitled *Research workshop on the failure of Community expansion, 1961-63*.

26   H.Young, 'The man who took us into Europe', *Observer*, 25 October 1998. This quotation was clearly written with the UK in mind, but it equally applies to Ireland. Its author, Con O'Neill, wrote it in the early 1970s as part of an official UK Foreign Office (FO) history of the latter's negotiations to enter the European Communities (EC). H.Young, *The blessed plot* (London: Macmillan, 1998).

Chapter 1

1   Ireland is a part of the geographical British Isles and on the Atlantic fringes of Western Europe. In the context of this text, Northern Ireland is regularly referred to as either a state or country, despite the shortcomings that such definitions present in this particular instance. Between 1922 and 1973, the Northern Irish government basically exercised 'Home Rule' in a kind of provincial self-rule. It controlled every aspect of governmental life that one would expect from an independent and sovereign state, except for jurisdiction over military and foreign affairs. Westminster did not directly control Northern Ireland, the administration at Stormont did. Nevertheless, if its position within the UK was constitutionally guaranteed from 1949, its actual status was different to that of Scotland, Wales or, for that matter, even England. This study regularly uses the terms 'north' or 'northern' in referring to Northern Ireland, much in the same way as it uses 'south' or 'southern' for Ireland. No significance should be attached to such titles and turns of phrase other than the linguistic variety that they offer the text.

2   Hederman, *The road to Europe*, pp. 11-4 & 16.

3   P.Ginsborg, *A history of contemporary Italy* (London: Penguin, 1990); P.Ginsborg, *L'Italia del tempo presente* (Turin: Einaudi, 1998); P.Ginsborg lecture (paper unavailable) entitled 'The complexities of the Italian Christian Democrats' delivered on 16 November 1998 at the IUE. Ireland's experiences in this period were by no means unique in European terms; indeed, comparisons can well be drawn with Italy.

4   Kennedy, *Colonialism, religion and nationalism*, pp. 177 & 179.

5   Moravcsik, *The choice for Europe*, p. 5. This question is answered in detail as the central chapters progress.

6   Hederman, *The road to Europe*, pp. 14-6. It is worth quoting some of Hederman's analysis at length, as she manages to portray Irish ignorance through typical self-

effacing humour. She has written:
> The prevailing Irish attitude to Europe was nostalgic, warm and idealised. (Europe here must be understood to exclude Great Britain and the USSR; the former because the relationship had been so prolonged and emotional that it was on quite a different footing; the USSR because it was, for the great majority of the Irish people a world apart: communist, vast, terrible and largely unknown). As far as 'greater Europe' was concerned popular views might be summed up as follows: Italy was a friendly country, the Italians sympathetic (though politically misguided perhaps) and Rome, as the seat of the Vatican, assumed to be an ally; France was admired for her culture and flair and commemorated in song and poetry for acts of friendship throughout the centuries that had long since been forgotten by the French (and which were inspired more by the political quarrels of the time than any great love of the wild Irish); Denmark, Holland and Belgium were regarded with some envy as small countries which had made their mark on the world (their strong co-operative movements and flourishing agriculture were constantly used as examples in the Irish countryside); Germany provoked more fear than affection but Austria retained its aura of music and glory and romance, mainly perhaps because so few Irish had managed to travel there; the Spanish civil war had had repercussions in Irish political life so the picture was probably a little closer to the reality than that of Portugal, for example, which was associated with Our Lady of Fatima, a somewhat unworldly image; Poland was always regarded with great sympathy, the analogy of repression and invasion acting as a bond; Turkey was looked on more as part of Asia Minor than of Europe but Greece floated in the after-glow of a smattering of classical education administered to most boys and a few girls in Irish secondary schools; the countries of Central Europe caused some confusion because of their changing fates but, again, as with Poland, were regarded with sympathy; Switzerland was a land apart, well-ordered, secure, prosperous and aloof.

7 P.Schlesinger, 'On national identity: some conceptions and misconceptions criticized', pp. 219-64, in *Social science information sur les sciences sociales* vol. 26 no. 2 1987, p. 222. This quotation originally comes from E.Barker *et al* (eds), *The European inheritance, vol. 3* (Oxford: Clarendon, 1954), p. 346.

8 Hederman, *The road to Europe*, p. 16.

9 Irish government internet publication, 'Statistical tables – population', *http://www.irlgov.ie/iveagh/foreignaffairs/facts/fai/populat1.html* (19 June 1997).

10 G.FitzGerald, 'When Ireland became divided', *London Review of Books*, 21 January 1999. This former foreign minister and taoiseach was reviewing R.Fanning *et al* (eds), *Documents on Irish foreign policy, vol.1 1919-22* (Dublin: Royal Irish Academy & Department of Foreign Affairs, 1998).

11 Unattributed article, 'Green is good', *Economist*, 17 May 1997.

12 Kennedy, *Colonialism, religion and nationalism*, p. 202.

13 K.A.Kennedy, 'Irish economy transformed', pp. 33-42, in *Studies* vol. 87 no. 345 1988, p. 33.

14 T.Garvin, 'Wealth, poverty and development: reflections on current discontents', pp. 312-25, in *Studies* vol. 78 no. 311 1989, *passim*. The Gross National Product (GNP) figures per capita are given as US$340, US$293, US$224 for Greece,

Spain and Portugal respectively in 1957, while the figure for the whole of Italy was US$516; in turn, Belgium, the Netherlands, France and West Germany (FRG) had totals of US$1,196, US$836, US$943, and US$927 respectively, while the figures US$1,057 and US$1,189 were given as the per capita totals for Denmark and the UK.

15   This section draws extensively from the views expressed in a couple of essays on core/periphery and dependency theories. I.Wallerstein, 'Dependence in an interdependent world: the limited possibilities of transformation within the capitalist world-economy', pp. 66-94, in I.Wallerstein, *The capitalist world-economy* (Cambridge: Cambridge University Press, 1979); Wallerstein, 'Semiperipheral countries and the contemporary world crisis', pp. 95-118, in Wallerstein, *The capitalist world-economy*.

16   Fianna Fáil internet publication, 'The history of Fianna Fáil by Dr.Martin Mansergh, Head of Research', *http://www.iol.ie/fiannafail/his.html* (8 July 1997). The texts that Martin Mansergh especially refers to are: R.Dunphy, *The making of Fianna Fáil power in Ireland, 1923-1946* (Oxford: Clarendon Press, 1995); and P.Bew & H.Patterson, *Seán Lemass and the making of modern Ireland, 1945-1966* (Dublin: Gill & Macmillan, 1982).

17   D.E.Apter, *Rethinking development: modernization, dependency and postmodern politics* (Newbury Park: Sage, 1987), p. 25.

18   T.dos Santos, 'The structure of dependence', pp. 225-36, in K.T.Fann & D.C.Hodges (eds), *Readings in US imperialism* (Boston: Porter Sargent, 1971); B.Stallings, *Economic dependency in Africa and Latin America* (Beverly Hills: Sage, 1972), p. 6. Note that the use of export and import figures are used extensively throughout this text to make exactly this point; at the end of this chapter, in the section headed *Irish foreign policy: from the political to the economic*, they help to demonstrate the change in trade orientation away from the UK to European markets and sources during the Lemass years, a process which is analysed in depth in Chapter 6, in the section headed *Changes in orientation: the evidence of exports and imports*.

19   N.Collins & F.McCann, *Irish politics today* (Manchester: Manchester University Press, 1989), pp. 6-7 (authors' italics); P.Dicken, *Global shift: the internationalization of economic activity* (London: Paul Chapman, 1992), pp. 4 & 11 (author's italics). This paragraph draws considerably from the latter's view of core/periphery theory; other authors might be chosen to enhance this opinion but, perhaps, it is best left to the former to expound upon Ireland's relative position in the world economy. They have written that:

> The world economy can usefully be divided into three areas: the *core*, the *periphery* and *semi-periphery* ... The semi-periphery group are intermediate in status. These countries are not as dependent as the periphery group. They have a much more diversified economic structure and in them industrialisation is well advanced. To a significant extent industry is locally owned and financed. Wage rates and living standards are higher than in the periphery. Countries often move into the intermediate group through strategies designed to increase their industrial sector substantially. But since these countries do not possess sufficient wealth for such development strategies, they obtain the finance from multinationals. These large international enterprises locate in the semi-periphery because of the relatively high levels of skill in the work-force, developed infrastructure, such as roads and

communications, lower wage rates than in the core and financial inducements from government ... This threefold model of the world economy will help us to understand Ireland's current position as a small semi-peripheral capitalist state with a large agricultural sector. The aim of the capitalist state is to provide the conditions for the functioning of an economy which is largely owned by private (non-state) organisations and individuals. In doing this it is constrained by the conditions operating in the international market system.

20 R.Crotty, *Irish agricultural production: its volume and share* (Cork: Cork University Press, 1966), pp. 68-83 & 166; B.Laffan, 'Ireland and Denmark in the European Community: political and administrative aspects', pp. 43-62, in *Administration* vol. 29 no. 1 1981, pp. 43-6. In the economic sector in which they had most in common – agriculture – Raymond Crotty is able to point to fundamental differences in their climate, historical development, social structure, and even their topography. Contemporary differences have been noted as well, adding weight to the argument that they are much too dissimilar to be constructively compared in the context of a specific study on Ireland and the EEC. Indeed, as Brigid Laffan has stated:

> Ireland and Denmark are 'small states' in terms of size, population and influence capability ... They have open economies, being heavily dependent on external trade and influenced by external economic forces. In 1961, both states applied for membership of the European Community and joined in 1973. This decision was without doubt one of the most important foreign policy decisions taken by either state in the post war period.

In many ways, it was here that the similarities ended because, apart from their relations with the UK, their experiences differed. In her brief comparison, Brigid Laffan has also recounted:

> British membership of the Community was the impetus to and precondition of Irish and Danish membership. British attitudes towards European integration and membership of the EEC played an important role in shaping the position adopted by Ireland and Denmark since the 1950s. When in 1956 it became apparent that the six founder member states of the European coal and steel community were preparing to establish an economic community, Britain in an attempt to prevent this proposed instead a west European free trade area under the auspices of the OEEC. Talks on the proposal (Maudling Talks) were held in 1958 ... During these negotiations, the Danes followed the British rather than the continental line favouring a free trade area. Ireland attended these talks but was not at all enthusiastic about membership of any free trade area feeling that high levels of protectionism were still necessary for her nascent industries. Economic dependence on Britain forced her to attend the talks and consider membership. After the failure of the 'Maudling Talks' the 'outer seven' of which Great Britain was the major state established ... EFTA ... Denmark joined EFTA with the other Scandinavian states. Ireland did not apply for membership. The British government informed the Irish ... that the Association would only include developed economies and that no transitional arrangements would be granted ... The fact that Portugal did join EFTA and was granted concessions did not go unnoticed in Dublin. As agriculture was

not to be included in EFTA, this lessened its appeal to the Irish. When British policy towards the EEC altered and she applied for membership in 1961, Ireland and Denmark followed suit. Britain was Denmark's major trading partner in agricultural goods and Ireland's in both agricultural and industrial goods. In 1960, 74 per cent of Ireland's total exports went to the United Kingdom. In Denmark's case, 46 per cent of her agricultural exports went to the UK in that year ... De Gaulle's veto of British membership in 1963 and again in 1967 led to the suspension of the other two applications. The issue of British membership of the Community had to be solved before the other two states could hope to join.

However, the central goal of this text is to record the 'singular' Irish experience in the European context. As a prospective EEC member in the 1960s, Ireland would need special treatment in many areas, including its steel industry, state aid for foreign investment, and its economic development policies. Denmark had political reasons why it wanted and needed the European project to work which were allied to political fears of what integration might ultimately mean; of course, it also needed to join for economic reasons. In Ireland's case, economics were the important consideration; politics did not really enter into the equation and were certainly not a core determinant.

21   A.Milward, 'New Zealand, the United Kingdom and the EEC', p. 1 (draft article). This quotation was originally conceived in regard to New Zealand's relations with the UK; it read: 'It is scarcely possible on this globe to be further away from the influence of Britain or the pull of its open markets than New Zealand, but the pattern of production and trade in that distant country was shaped almost entirely by Britain's own history and development'.

22   P.Robertson & J.Singleton, 'Britain, the Dominions and the EEC, 1961-1963', p. 1 (draft article).

23   Milward, 'New Zealand, the United Kingdom and the EEC', *passim*; Robertson & Singleton, 'Britain, the Dominions and the EEC, 1961-1963', *passim*.

24   F.Yachir, 'The future of Southern Europe: Canada or Puerto Rico?', pp. 25-37, in F.Yachir, *The Mediterranean: between autonomy and dependency* (Tokyo: United Nations University, 1989), pp. 36-7.

25   L.Kennedy, *The modern industrialisation of Ireland, 1940-1988* (Dundalk: Dungalgan Press, 1989), pp. 3-5.

26   This section has made liberal use of a previous dissertation, though mostly for structural purposes, with all quotations specifically referenced; see FitzGerald, *Irish-American diplomatic relations*, passim.

27   Hederman, *The road to Europe*, p. 16.

28   R.Vaughan, *Twentieth-century Europe: paths to unity* (London: Croom Helm, 1979), p. 62.

29   Irish government internet publication, 'Ireland in the world: the Irish abroad', *http://www.irlgov.ie/iveagh/foreignaffairs/facts/fai/chapter4/abroad/abroad.html* (19 June 1997).

30   J.A.Murphy, *Ireland in the twentieth century* (Dublin: Gill & Macmillan, 1989), p. 130.

31   An excellent example of how Dublin perceived this development in the postwar period is available in the Irish government publication, *European Economic Community* (Dublin: Stationery Office, 1961), D/T-S16877L/61, NA. It is fully, and necessarily, assessed in Chapter 3 under the section headed *European*

Economic Community: the government White Paper.
32 FitzGerald, Irish-American diplomatic relations, pp. 16-7. This view utilised Maher, The tortuous path, pp. 23-4. It is worth noting that by this stage Lemass also held the title tánaiste (deputy prime minister), which meant that he had emerged fully as de Valera's official heir apparent.
33 Hederman, The road to Europe, p. 19.
34 F.S.L.Lyons, Ireland since the Famine (Glasgow: Fontana, 1976), p. 589.
35 Maher, The tortuous path, p. 13.
36 T.D.Williams quoted in D.Keogh, 'The Department of Foreign Affairs', p. 290, in Z.Steiner (ed.), The Times survey of foreign ministries of the world (London: Times Books, 1982, pp. 275-96.
37 FitzGerald, Irish-American diplomatic relations, p. 19. This view utilised Hederman, The road to Europe, p. 19.
38 Irish government internet publication, 'Ireland in the world – international relations', http://www.irlgov.ie/iveagh/foreignaffairs/facts/fai/chapter4/internat/internat.html (19 June 1997).
39 Hederman, The road to Europe, pp. 19 & 24-5.
40 Hederman, The road to Europe, p. 25; Seán MacBride (foreign minister) speech delivered to Dáil Éireann, 21 July 1948, Dáil debates vol. 112 cols. 1022-3 (original in italics).
41 MacBride speaking in Dáil Éireann, 21 July 1948, Dáil debates vol. 112 col. 1023.
42 MacBride speaking in Dáil Éireann, 13 July 1949, Dáil debates vol. 117, cols. 742 & 744-6.
43 Hederman, The road to Europe, 28; MacBride speech delivered to Dáil Éireann, 13 July 1949, Dáil debates vol. 117 col. 748.
44 Hederman, The road to Europe, p. 37.
45 Hederman, The road to Europe, pp. 30-1 & 33.
46 Hederman, The road to Europe, p. 32; C.C.O'Brien, To Katanga and back (London: Hutchinson, 1962), p. 14.
47 FitzGerald, Irish-American diplomatic relations, p. 41. This view was based upon a Dean Acheson (US secretary of state) memorandum, 11 April 1949, 'Memoranda of Conversation', Box #64, Acheson Papers, Harry S.Truman Library, Independence, Missouri (HST).
48 FitzGerald, Irish-American diplomatic relations, p. 49. This view was based on a MacBride speech delivered to the National Press Club in Washington, 14 March 1951, Irish Information Bulletin #43, 'Foreign Affairs File', Box #151, Democratic National Committee, HST.
49 FitzGerald, Irish-American diplomatic relations, p. 99. This view was based on a Lemass speech given to the National Press Club in Washington, 1 October 1953, 'Foreign Affairs File', Box #151, Democratic National Committee, HST.
50 Bunreacht na hÉireann (1937 constitution) (Dublin: Stationery Office, 1937).
51 US government internet publication, 'US Department of State – background notes: European Community, January 1993', http://www.state.gov/www/background_notes/index.html European Community (1/93) (31 March 1998).
52 Hederman, The road to Europe, pp. 37-8.
53 Lyons, Ireland since the Famine, p. 591.
54 FitzGerald, Irish-American diplomatic relations, p. 77.
55 Lyons, Ireland since the Famine, p. 591; Hederman, The road to Europe, pp. 38-9.

56   P.D.Sutherland, 'Ireland: where do we really stand on European integration?', pp. 243-54, in *Studies* vol. 78 no. 311, pp. 243-4. This question is dealt with in detail in Chapter 4 under the heading *Ireland and the other two European Communities*.

57   S.Greenwood (ed.), *Britain and European cooperation since 1945* (Oxford: Blackwell, 1992), p. 75.

58   FitzGerald, 'When Ireland became divided', *London Review of Books*, 21 January 1999.

59   Hederman, *The road to Europe*, pp. 35 & 38; de Valera speech delivered to Dáil Éireann, 12 July 1950, *Dáil debates* vol. 122 col. 1608; de Valera's views reported in *Éire/Ireland* (Department of External Affairs bulletin) #136, 19 May 1952.

60   Sutherland, 'Ireland', p. 244.

61   De Valera speaking in Dáil Éireann, 21 July 1950, *Dáil debates* vol. 122 col. 1608.

62   Hederman, *The road to Europe*, p. 35; de Valera's views reported in *Éire/Ireland* #229, 12 April 1954. In the latter interview, it was reported that he preceded this by saying that:

> ... in his younger days, over thirty years ago, he had been an ardent supporter of the idea of a United States of Europe, but that, in recent years, he had become more aware of the magnitude of the difficulties involved. If, for example, Ireland entered into such a Federation her representation in the proposed legislature would probably be so small as to be ineffective, and matters vital to the Irish people could be easily ignored. Ireland's representation in the Council of Europe was now only 4 out of a total of 132 ... The idea of a complete political Federation of Europe was most attractive, but when one got down to the details it was not easy to find a workable scheme ... The larger states, such as France, Germany, Italy, might in the existing circumstances be willing to join such a Federation, each being confident that they were sufficiently powerful to ensure that matters vital to them would not be overlooked. But it was not so with the smaller States. They would of course have gained the security of the collective strength, but they would have lost the power to choose at will policies required to meet their individual political and economic exigencies. To this extent they would have lost their independence. Was the price too high? That was the critical question in regard to a close federal political union for Europe, such as that of the existing United States of America.

63   Hederman, *The road to Europe*, p. 36.

64   Hederman, *The road to Europe*, p. 36.

65   Hederman, *The road to Europe*, pp. 40-2. The government official in question was Gerald Boland making his maiden speech to the Council of Europe Assembly at its Third Ordinary Session in 1951.

66   Lyons, *Ireland since the* Famine, p. 590.

67   Hederman, *The road to Europe*, p. 38.

68   Lyons, *Ireland since the Famine*, p. 625.

69   Irish government internet publication, 'Facts about Ireland – the economy', http://www.irlgov.ie/iveagh/foreignaffairs/facts/fai/chapter5/home5.html (19 June 1997).

70   *Economist*, 21 September 1996. It is interesting to note – especially in the context of the main players who would affect Ireland's membership prospects – that Ludwig Erhard, the German economics minister, only advocated a wider customs

and trading union in the form of a 'Europe of the Sixteen'. The German chancellor, Konrad Adenauer, was interested in something more substantial for the Six initially but, at the same time, wanted a mechanism which would allow for an expansion in membership when the time was right.

71 *Economist*, 29 March 1997.
72 *Economist*, 17 May 1997.
73 Much of the basic information in this section has been drawn from M.Gallagher, *Electoral support for Irish political parties, 1927-1973* (London: Sage, 1976), *passim*. This brief review of the domestic positions of political parties and how that pertained to Europe concentrates on Fianna Fáil and acts as an introduction to the political scene; a review section on how this make-up evolved in subsequent years is presented in Chapter 6; it is headed *The political landscape and how it pertained to Europe: Part II*.
74 US government internet publication, 'US Department of State – 1996 human rights report: Ireland, January 1997', *http://www.state.gov/www/global/human_rig hts/1996_hrp_report/ireland.html* (31 March 1998).
75 US government internet publication, 'US Department of State – background notes: Ireland, November 1995', *http://www.state.gov/www/background_notes/eur bgnhb.html* Ireland (11/95) (31 March 1998).
76 Fianna Fáil internet publication, 'Fianna Fáil: the key dates', *http://www.iol.ie/fia nnafail/history.htm* (8 July 1997).
77 Sutherland, 'Ireland', p. 244.
78 Dunphy, *Class, power and the Fianna Fáil party*, pp. 406-7.
79 O'Leary, *Irish elections, 1918-1977*, pp. 103-4.
80 This assertion is based on a table that appears in FitzGerald, *Irish-American diplomatic relations*, p. 26. It was originally taken from M.Manning, *Irish political parties* (Dublin: Gill & Macmillan, 1972), *passim*; C.O'Leary, *Irish elections, 1918-77: parties, voters and proportional representation* (Dublin: Gill & Macmillan, 1979), pp. 103-4.
81 *Economist*, 17 May 1997; Kennedy, *Colonialism, religion and nationalism*, p. 174.
82 This quotation comes from a speech delivered by Mary McAleese, the Irish president, on the occasion of the 21st Jean Monnet Lecture, entitled 'Europe – the challenges of the new millennium', delivered at the IUE on 9 February 1999, *http://www.iue.it/general/jms.htm* (10 February 1999).
83 D.Arter, *The politics of European integration in the twentieth century* (Aldershot: Dartmouth, 1993), p. 265. This view utilised E.Anderson, 'Towards a Baltic union, 1920-27', pp. 30-56, in *Lituanus* vol. 12 no. 2 1966, pp. 31-2.
84 Arter, *The politics of European integration in the twentieth century*, p. 265. This view utilised B.Chubb, *The government and politics of Ireland* (London: Longman, 1971), p. 77 (author's italics).
85 Arter, *The politics of European integration in the twentieth century*, p. 265; de Valera radio broadcast delivered to the Irish nation, 17 March 1943, entitled 'The Ireland that we dreamed of', pp. 466-9, in Moynihan (ed.), *Speeches and statements*, p. 466.
86 Arter, *The politics of European integration in the twentieth century*, p. 265. This view utilised T.Gallagher, 'The dimensions of Fianna Fail rule in Ireland', pp. 54-68, in *Western European politics* vol. 4 no. 1.
87 N.Witoszek, 'Nationalism, postmodernity and Ireland', pp. 101-21, in Ø.Sørensen (ed.), *Nationalism in small European nations* (Oslo: Research Council of Norway,

1996), p. 102. This view utilised C.C.O'Brien, 'The embers of Easter, 1916-1966', pp. 225-40, in O.D.Edwards and F.Pyle (eds), *1916: the Easter rising* (London: MacGibbon and Kee, 1968), p. 237.

88 Witoszek, 'Nationalism, postmodernity and Ireland', pp. 102 & 105. This view utilised Schlesinger, 'On national identity', p. 253.

89 V.I.Lenin, 'The Irish rebellion of 1916', pp. 353-8, in *V.I.Lenin: collected works vol. 22 December 1915-July 1916* (London: Lawrence & Wishart, 1974), p. 357.

90 Witoszek, 'Nationalism, postmodernity and Ireland', p. 119. This view used J.Lee, *Ireland, 1912-1985* (Cambridge: Cambridge University Press, 1990); L.Mjøset, *The Irish economy in a comparative, institutional perspective: report* (Dublin: National Economic and Social Council, 1993).

91 J. Bradley, *et al*, *Stabilization and growth in the EC periphery: a study of the Irish economy* (Aldershot: Avebury, 1993), p. 10.

92 J.Swift, 'The changing role of ambassadors and embassies', pp. 3-13, in *Administration* vol. 46 no. 1 1998, p. 9.

93 S.Hoffmann, *Contemporary theory in international relations* (Englewood Cliffs: Prentice-Hall, 1960); A.Milward, *The European rescue of the nation-state* (London: Routledge, 1992), pp. 2-3.

94 S.Baker, *Dependency, ideology and the industrial policy of Fianna Fáil in Ireland, 1958-1972* (Florence: IUE PhD thesis, 1987), p. 25.

95 R.O.Keohane & S.Hoffmann, 'Institutional change in the 1980s', pp. 1-39, in R.O.Keohane & S.Hoffmann (eds), *The new European Community: decision-making and institutional change* (Boulder: Westview, 1991), p. 6.

96 Milward, *The European rescue of the nation-state*, p. 279. A useful set of documents is also available in the European Community Archives, Villa Il Poggiolo, Florence (ACE), that detail trade accords between Ireland and West Germany (FRG) in the early 1950s, specifically tracing the years leading up to the important trade agreement of 1955. 'Irlande/Accord/Commerce/République fédérale d'Allemagne' CEAB 3/193 0-56, *Commission des Communautés Européennes Dossiers de la Haute Autorité de la Communauté Européenne du Charbon et de l'Acier* vol. 1: 1952-1956, ACE. A more detailed analysis of trade relations between Ireland and the FRG in the years specifically under review is presented in Chapter 4 under the heading *Lemass prepares for EEC entry negotiations to begin*.

97 Baker, *Dependency, ideology and the industrial policy of Fianna Fáil in Ireland*, p. 9. The two texts that she refers to were T.K.Whitaker, *Economic development* (Dublin: Stationery Office, 1958), Department of the Taoiseach (D/T) file S16066B, National Archives, Dublin (NA); Irish government publication, *Programme for economic expansion* (Dublin: Stationery Office, 1958), D/T-S16066B, NA.

98 Greenwood (ed.), *Britain and European integration since the Second World War*, pp. 84-7; M.Schaad, 'Plan G – a "counterblast"? British policy towards the Messina countries, 1956', pp. 39-60, in *Contemporary European History* vol. 7 no. 1 1998.

99 N.J.Baxter-Moore, 'The impact of European Community membership on the Republic of Ireland', pp. 41-84, in N.Ørvik and C.Pentland (eds), *The European Community at the crossroads: the first twenty-five years* (Kingston: Queen's University Kingston, 1983), p. 44; Lemass speech delivered in Dáil Éireann, 5 July 1961, *Dáil debates* vol. 191 col. 266.

Chapter 2

1. The Six – also known as the 'Inner Six' – refers to the EEC, the original members of which were Belgium, France, the FRG, Italy, Luxembourg, and the Netherlands, while the Seven – the 'Outer Seven' – refers to EFTA, the original members of which were Austria, Denmark, Norway, Portugal, Sweden, Switzerland and the UK; the peripherals – the 'Forgotten Five' – refers to Greece, Iceland, Ireland, Turkey (all members of the OEEC in May 1959) and Spain. The latter is included as a peripheral despite the fact that it was outside the OEEC at that time, while Finland and Liechtenstein are usually incorporated with the Seven because of prompt developments in that direction. C.Archer, *Organizing Europe: the institutions of integration* (London: Edward Arnold, 1994), p. 177; M.Camps, *Britain and the European Community, 1955-1963* (Princeton: Princeton University Press, 1964), p. 211.
2. Hubert de Besche (Swedish foreign affairs deputy secretary) quoted in J.D.Brennan (Irish minister, Stockholm) to Con Cremin (Department of External Affairs (D/EA) secretary), 29 May 1959, Department of Foreign Affairs (D/FA) file D/2/3PtI, NA.
3. Greenwood (ed.), *Britain and European integration since the Second World War*, pp. 84-5.
4. The French government's view – as stated in OEEC Working Party no. 21 (WP#21) documentation – of Ireland, 15 October 1957, D/T-S16160E, NA. The original French refers to Ireland as being amongst '[les] autres pays moins développés'. R.T.Griffiths speaking at a conference entitled *The creation of EFTA* held at the University of Oslo in Norway from 14-17 May 1992 (transcript available from the IUE).
5. Whitaker, *Economic development*; Irish government publication, *Programme for economic expansion*; T.W.Moody & F.X.Martin (eds.), *The course of Irish history* (Cork: Mercier, 1967), p. 337.
6. Note that relevant events are detailed in T.W.Moody *et al* (eds), 'A chronology of Irish history to 1976', in *A new history of Ireland, vol. 8* (Oxford: Clarendon Press, 1982), pp. 436-47.
7. OEEC WP#13 report entitled 'Rapport Annuel 1956: Irlande – Deuxième Projet de Chapitre', 31 October 1956, CEAB 5/243/1, ACE; OEEC report, 'Irlande 1961' (Paris: OEEC, 1962), p. 2. It should be noted that the main aims of the OEEC and its participants, as outlined in French, were:

    ... à conjuger leurs forces économiques, à s'entendre sur l'utilisation la plus complète de leurs capacités et de leurs possibilités particulières, à augmenter leur production, développer et moderniser leur équipement industriel et agricole, accoître leurs échanges, réduire progressivement les entraves à leur commerce mutuel, favoriser le plein emploi de la main-d'oeuvre, restaurer ou maintenir la stabilité de leurs économies, ainsi que la confiance dans leurs devises nationales.

8. J.H.Whyte, *Church and state in modern Ireland, 1923-1979* (Dublin: Gill & Macmillan, 1980), p. 359.
9. T.P.Coogan, *Ireland since the rising* (Westport: Greenwood, 1976), p. 104.
10. Whyte, *Church and state*, pp. 356-8; Coogan, *Ireland since the rising*, pp. 104-5; G.FitzGerald, *Planning in Ireland: a PEP study* (Dublin: Institute of Public

Administration, 1968), p. 41; O.MacDonagh, *Ireland: the Union and its aftermath* (London: George Allen, 1977), pp. 137 & 141. J.H.Whyte has demonstrated that Tim Pat Coogan takes 1957 as the watershed year, Garret FitzGerald prefers 1958, while Oliver MacDonagh chooses 1959. All three authors, however, agree on the nature of the change. Tim Pat Coogan says: 'In the last few years an enormous psychological change has occurred in Ireland. The conviction that things could be improved has dawned on a people conditioned to believe that they could only get worse'. In turn, Garret FitzGerald talks of the *Programme for economic development* being an 'undoubtedly ... impressive economic achievement ... a transformation of the economy of the Republic and, most important of all perhaps, a transformation of the outlook of the Irish people'. Meanwhile, Oliver MacDonagh romantically feels that 1959 signalled the end of at least one Great Famine legacy, as it 'marked a decisive change in national power and attitude ... economically it stood for a change of heart and will ... To have maintained the courses set since 1945 would have been ... ruinous ... what was achieved in 1959- 72 was not merely the attainment of the first goal in a long economic race. It was also, in itself, a completed feat. For the first time in more than a century, the most powerful, that is, the retrogressive, trends in Irish social and economic life had been reversed'.

11 Maher, *The tortuous path*, p. 54.
12 OEEC WP#13, 'Rapport Annuel 1956'; *Irish Independent*, 25 January 1957, D/T-S16159A, NA. The OEEC, in its annual report from 1956, saw the UK market as the 'débouché essentiel de la production irlandaise'. Indeed, the UK was the essential outlet for Irish products. Thus, for example, whilst prices for cattle on the hoof exported to the UK were exceptionally favourable at the start of 1955, they were noted as sagging considerably in the second half of the year, primarily because of the effects of larger purchases of Argentine meat; this was noted as continuing into the first three quarters of 1956. Nevertheless, Ireland had, in many ways, maintained its own position by finding other markets. Under the provisions of certain trade arrangements dating from the 1920s, Irish cattle and sheep fattened during a minimal period in the UK benefitted from a system of price guarantees; these arrangements were extended, for a period of at least three years, in March 1956. However, the 'Pigs and Bacon Agreement', a long-term commitment by the UK to purchase all Irish pork exports, expired at the end of April 1956, leaving Irish exports to suffer the vagaries of world market prices, losing the protection offered by the guaranteed UK markets. Nonetheless, in the face of this new competition, the Irish government took positive action by instituting a price guarantee system for high quality pork products, which essentially meant bacon, to combat this economic development.
13 R.F.Foster, *Paddy and Mr Punch: connections in Irish and English history* (London: Allen Lane, 1993), pp. 31-2.
14 D/EA note included with Irish cabinet minute, 9 October 1956, D/T-S15281A, NA.
15 D/EA note included with Irish cabinet minute, 9 October 1956, D/T-S15281A, NA.
16 Maher, *The tortuous path*, pp. 55-6.
17 Irish delegation's report on a meeting of OEEC WP#22 held between 18-20 March 1957, *circa* late March 1957, D/T-S15281F, NA.
18 Maher, *The tortuous path*, pp. 55-6.
19 Irish commercial counsellor (embassy, London) memorandum on the UK

20 government's attitude to the proposed European common market, 9 October 1956, D/T-S15281A, NA.
20 Irish commercial counsellor (embassy, London) memorandum on the UK government's attitude to the proposed European common market, 9 October 1956, D/T-S15281A, NA; *Irish Independent*, 20 February 1957, D/T-S16159A, NA; *Irish Independent*, 21 February 1957, D/T-S16159A, NA.
21 Department of Industry & Commerce (D/I&C) note on the proposal for a Free Trade Area (FTA) embracing the OEEC countries wishing to join, October 1956, D/T-S15281A, NA.
22 D/I&C note on the proposal for an FTA embracing the OEEC countries wishing to join, October 1956, D/T-S15281A, NA.
23 The departmental secretaries present at this meeting held on 11 October 1956 included Maurice Moynihan (D/T secretary), T.K.Whitaker (Department of Finance (D/F) secretary), Seán Murphy (D/EA secretary), J.C.B.MacCarthy (D/I&C secretary), and J.Dempsey (Department of Agriculture (D/A) secretary).
24 Report of departmental secretaries meeting, 11 October 1956, D/T-S15281A, NA.
25 Report of departmental secretaries meeting, 11 October 1956, D/T-S15281A, NA.
26 Maher, *The tortuous path*, pp. 57-8.
27 Report of departmental secretaries meeting, 11 October 1956, D/T-S15281A, NA.
28 Maher, *The tortuous path*, pp. 57-8.
29 Report of departmental secretaries meeting, 11 October 1956, D/T-S15281A, NA.
30 Maher, *The tortuous path*, pp. 57-8.
31 William P.Fay (Irish embassy official, Paris) to J.J.Molloy (D/EA official), 25 September 1956, D/T-S15281A, NA; report of departmental secretaries meeting, 11 October 1956, D/T-S15281A, NA.
32 Maher, *The tortuous path*, pp. 57-8.
33 Irish government note on proposal for an FTA, *circa* mid-October 1956, D/T-S15281A, NA.
34 Draft report of departmental secretaries meeting, 8 November 1956, D/T-S15281B, NA (author's emphasis).
35 S.Lee, 'Staying in the game? Coming into the game? Macmillan and European integration', 123-147, in R.Aldous & S.Lee (eds), *Harold Macmillan and Britain's world role* (London: Macmillan, 1996), p. 124.
36 *Tipperary Star*, 26 January 1957, D/T-S16159A, NA; *Sunday Press*, 27 January 1957, D/T-S16159A, NA.
37 *Irish Press*, 9 January 1957, D/T-S16159A, NA; *Irish Press*, 10 January 1957, D/T-S16159A, NA.
38 *Irish Independent*, 14 January 1957, D/T-S16159A, NA; *Evening Mail*, 14 January 1957, D/T-S16159A, NA; *Irish Independent*, 17 January 1957, D/T-S16159A, NA.
39 Costello speech delivered at the Insurance Institute of Cork annual dinner, 12 January 1957, D/T-S16159A, NA.
40 Irish cabinet minute, 18 January 1957, CAB 2/17, NA.
41 *Irish Independent*, 21 January 1957, D/T-S16159A, NA; *Irish Independent*, 24 January 1957, D/T-S16159A, NA.
42 *Irish Times*, 23 January 1957, D/T-S16159A, NA.
43 Hederman, *The road to Europe*, backpage cover.
44 D/A progress report for January to March 1957, D/T-S15062C, NA.
45 This data comes from the following: Central Statistics Office, *Ireland: trade and shipping statistics*, *passim*. Please note that, due to unavailability, the category

'UK' does not include the relatively insignificant figures for the Channel Islands in 1963 and 1964. Indeed, due to a dearth in data for Norway in 1960 and 1961, the 'rest of EFTA' figures for these years only comprise of the other six EFTA countries; thus, these Norwegian figures have had to be included in the category 'others'. The figures for the latter category have been rounded off so that the total comes to 100% and includes, as the case may be, any remaining countries or products. The categories are broken down as follows:

- 'UK' encompasses Great Britain, Northern Ireland and the Channel Islands;
- 'EEC' obviously comprises Belgium, France, the FRG, Italy, Luxembourg, and the Netherlands;
- 'rest of EFTA' incorporates Austria, Denmark, Finland, Norway, Portugal, Sweden, and Switzerland (note that the UK is specifically not included);
- 'rest of OEEC' only includes those OEEC countries excluded by the EEC and EFTA, thus leaving Greece, Iceland and Turkey, as well as the addition of Spain (this category becomes 'rest of OECD' later;
- 'US' is fairly self-explanatory, comprising the United States;
- 'others' is composed of figures from those remaining countries.

In addition, note the following regarding the various categories that are utilised:

- 'live animals' is, as the title suggests, only made up of live animals;
- 'food, drink & tobacco' comprises foodstuffs of animal origin, fruit, nuts and vegetables, cereals and feeding stuffs, drink and tobacco, plus miscellaneous articles of food;
- 'manufactured goods' encompasses iron and steel, textiles, paper and cardboard, vehicles, chemicals, perfumery, dyes and colours;
- 'others' includes raw materials such as wood, timber and cork, hides, skins and leather, rubber, oils, fats, resins and gum, in addition to parcel post and some temporary transactions.

In Chapter 6, in the section headed *Changes in orientation: the evidence of exports and imports*, these sets of figures from 1957 are contrasted with the subsequent figures for 1966. Also note that these definitions are used throughout the text and the appendices unless specified otherwise.

Please note that the difference in percentages for Irish exports to the UK between 1955 and 1956, when this figure fell from 89.20% to 77.95%, is an interesting point in time to explain why the taking of figures from 1957 to 1966 is as arbitrary as any other set of figures. At a glance, this decrease of over 11% could be thought to be overly-significant. However, there are many instances in any such table of figures appearing as some sort of inexplicable phenomena. When, in this case, the size of Irish exports in that period is considered – just over IR£100 million – a fall of IR£13.75 million worth of exports to the vital UK market remains no 'mere bagatelle', especially in a year when exports themselves fell by nearly 2½%; nevertheless, the fact that Belgian figures rose by 17%, the French by 340%, the German by 60%, the Italian by 80%, and the Dutch by 195%, it can be appreciated that all such jumps have explanations, the general one being that Ireland was looking for new markets wherever it could find them, with the Irish government gradually seeing the benefits and necessity of accessing all European markets.

46   Costello speech delivered at the Irish Motor Trader's Association annual dinner,

47 *Irish Independent*, 1 February 1957, D/T-S16159A, NA.
  Irish Times, 1 February 1957, D/T-S16159A, NA.
48 Irish cabinet minute, 8 February 1957, CAB 2/17, NA.
49 Donnchadh Ó Briain (taoiseach's parliamentary secretary) reply in Dáil Éireann to a question tabled by Gerald Sweetman, 25 April 1957, *Dáil debates* Volume 161 Columns 279-280, D/T-S15281G, NA.
50 G.Mally, *Britain and European unity* (London: Hansard Society, 1966), p. 31.
51 Report of departmental secretaries meeting, 21 February 1957, D/T-S15281E, NA.
52 Farrell, *Seán Lemass*, pp. 117-8.
53 Lemass response to inquiries in Seanad Éireann, 28 March 1957, *Seanad debates* vol. 47 col. 332. Two senators had related the issue of the government imposing duties on certain imports with developments in Europe. John Douglas, a senator nominated by the previous government, had said:

> In a small market such as ours, it is necessary to have a certain amount of protection, but I believe Irish labour is just as competent as that in any other country to produce goods of first class quality at a price which should be able to compete with the markets of Europe. I hope the present Minister will give serious consideration to the protective tariffs which are at present enjoyed by many of our industries, to see whether it could not be possible to reduce that protection and still ensure that we can produce here goods for export which are up to the quality and the standard of similar goods produced in other parts of Europe ... This question must be considered in conjunction within that of a free trade area in Europe. If we in this country are to survive with that free trade area, it is essential we should produce goods which will compete with those produced by other countries within that area. I am convinced we can do it, but it is well that the situation would be reviewed if we are to join with those countries in free trade conditions and if we are to continue to be a prosperous nation.

Owen Sheehy Skeffington, a senator elected by the university electorate, in turn added his view that:

> If the cold wind of competition is kept entirely off our countries, they may wax fat, but they become unhealthy, and perhaps be quite unprepared to enter such an adventure as the European Common Market would provide ... [Thus] with the possibility at some future date – perhaps a not so very far distant one – of participating in the European Common Market, in order to do so, we shall have to have efficient industry. Some of our industries are extremely efficient, both the old and the new, but others are, shall we say, not so efficient. I attribute at least a measure of their failure to reach high efficiency, to the fact that we have been too prone to give them over-protection and not to examine afresh after a period of years whether an industry, which at the start required a protective tariff of 50 per cent., could not after five years do with a protective tariff of 30 per cent or 20 per cent.

John Douglas speaking in Seanad Éireann, 28 March 1957, *Seanad debates* vol. 47 cols. 325-6; Owen Sheehy Skeffington speaking in Seanad Éireann, 28 March 1957, *Seanad debates* vol. 47 cols. 328-9.

54 Lemass speaking in Seanad Éireann, 22 May 1957, *Seanad debates* vol. 48 col. 27.

378 *Protectionism to liberalisation*

55 Irish cabinet minute, 9 April 1957, Cabinet Minutes (CAB) 2/18, NA.
56 Irish government directive to the Irish delegation attending OEEC WP#23, *circa* early March 1957, D/T-S15281F, NA.
57 Report on Ireland's submission to OEEC WP#23, *circa* mid-May 1957, D/T-S15281H, NA; Fay to Murphy, *circa* mid-May 1957, D/T-S15281I, NA; MacCarthy report on the 'Consideration of Irish case' by OEEC WP#23, *circa* mid-May 1957, D/T-S15281J, NA; Maher, *The tortuous path*, pp. 76-8.
58 D/A memorandum for the government, 4 April 1957, D/T-S15281F, NA; Maher, *The tortuous path*, pp. 78-80.
59 Maher, *The tortuous path*, p. 80.
60 Report of departmental secretaries meeting, 12 June 1957, D/T-S15281I, NA.
61 Maher, *The tortuous path*, pp. 81-2.
62 Maher, *The tortuous path*, pp. 82-3. It should be pointed out that Iceland soon went its own way within this scenario, but the point is that these nations had partially peripheralised themselves and, therefore, contributed to their own later treatment as such.
63 Irish cabinet minute, 19 July 1957, CAB 2/18, NA.
64 Report of meeting discussing Anglo-Irish trade talks, 12 June 1957, D/T-S15281I, NA.
65 Irish cabinet minute, 1 November 1957, CAB 2/18, NA.
66 T.O'Carroll (D/I&C official) report of Irish government meeting on EFTA, 7 November 1957, D/FA-348/14/422PtI, NA.
67 O'Carroll report of Irish government meeting on EFTA, 7 November 1957, D/FA-348/14/422PtI, NA.
68 Whitaker, *Economic development, passim*.
69 Notes from three meetings between the Irish and UK governments on the implications of an FTA for Anglo-Irish trading arrangements, 12-13 November 1957, D/T-S15281L, NA.
70 Notes from three meetings between the Irish and UK governments on the implications of an FTA for Anglo-Irish trading arrangements, 12-13 November 1957, D/T-S15281L, NA.
71 Notes from three meetings between the Irish and UK governments on the implications of an FTA for Anglo-Irish trading arrangements, 12-13 November 1957, D/T-S15281L, NA.
72 D/I&C memorandum for the government on the visit of the UK Paymaster General, 28 December 1957, D/T-S15281N, NA.
73 Irish memorandum to OEEC WP#23 on special financial arrangements for countries in the process of economic development, 19 December 1957, D/T-S15281N, NA.
74 J.C.Nagle (D/A secretary) to Lewis Croome (UK agriculture official), 21 December 1957, D/T-S15281N, NA.
75 D/A memorandum on discussions with the UK government, 2 December 1957, D/T-S15281N, NA.
76 Lemass speech delivered to the National Agricultural and Industrial Development Association, 5 March 1958, quoted by Skeffington in Seanad Éireann, 27 March 1958, *Seanad debates* vol. 49 cols. 330-1; *Irish Times*, 6 March 1958. The *Irish Times* had prefaced this Lemass quote with the latter's view that 'if the other countries of Western Europe come together in a freer trade arrangement the implications of an Irish decision to maintain a position of isolation were not attractive to contemplate'.

77 Greek, Irish and Turkish submission to OEEC WP#23, 9 January 1958, D/T-S15281G, NA.
78 The government's practices were not universally acclaimed; one senator famously said of increases in duties in 1958 that:
> We are like people who are about to have a 'colossal sale' and who, in order to slash prices later, put them up well in advance. I wonder whether we are not putting on duties now simply for the purpose of cutting them in relation to the Free Trade Area, with a great flourish on the 1st January, 1959. Are we putting on new duties now for the cutting of which we will make an ostensible sacrifice if this Free Trade Area comes about?

It is clear that Ireland had made a very conscious decision because Lemass replied in some detail, essentially holding that:
> I do not think I ever, in any statement, even by implication suggested that no new tariffs were going to be imposed no matter what the circumstances.

Skeffington speaking in Seanad Éireann, 27 March 1958, *Seanad debates*, vol. 49 col. 333; Lemass speaking in Seanad Éireann, 27 March 1958, *Seanad debates* vol. 49 col. 337.

79 Lemass speaking in Seanad Éireann, 27 March 1958, *Seanad debates* vol. 49 col. 336. He added:
> Until these conditions exist, until Irish industry is given the opportunity of competing up on equal terms with the industries of other countries, then clearly we will have need to protect them, and the right to protect them, in circumstances where these conditions are not fulfilled, perhaps even under a free trade arrangement.

80 Aiken reply in Dáil Éireann to a question tabled by Noël Browne, 12 November 1958, D/T-S16159B, NA.
81 Maher, *The tortuous path*, pp. 84-5; John Turner, *Macmillan* (London: Longman, 1994), p. 216.
82 *Irish Press*, 15 November 1958, D/T-S16159B, NA.
83 'Irlande/Relation/Pays tiers/CECA', *1961* CEAB 5/953 1-3, ACE; 'Irlande/Relation/Pays tiers/CECA', *1961* CEAB 5/954 1-35, ACE. A particularly good example of this reticence is thoroughly dealt with in Chapter 6 in the section headed *Ireland and the other two European Communities*.
84 Draft letter from Lemass to David Eccles (UK Board of Trade (B/T) president), January 1958, D/T-S15281R, NA.
85 Lemass speech given to the Dublin Society of Chartered Accountants, 2 February 1959, D/T-S15281R, NA.
86 Lemass replies in Dáil Éireann to various questions, 20 May 1959, *Dáil debates* vol. 172 cols. 123-6, D/T-S16159B, NA.
87 Lemass replies in Dáil Éireann to various questions, 20 May 1959, *Dáil debates* vol. 172 cols. 123-6, D/T-S16159B, NA.
88 Lemass replies in Dáil Éireann to various questions, 20 May 1959, *Dáil debates* vol. 172 cols. 123-6, D/T-S16159B, NA.
89 Lemass replies in Dáil Éireann to various questions, 20 May 1959, *Dáil debates* vol. 172 cols. 123-6, D/T-S16159B, NA.
90 D/I&C memorandum, 26 May 1959, D/T-S15281R, NA.
91 Brennan to Cremin, 29 May 1959, D/FA-D/2/3PtI, NA.
92 R.T.Griffiths speaking at the conference entitled *EFTA at the creation* held at the

380 *Protectionism to liberalisation*

93 University of Oslo from 14-15 May 1992 (transcript available from the IUE).
Brennan to Cremin, 29 May 1959, D/FA-D/2/3PtI, NA. Interestingly, Brennan quoted the *New York Herald Tribune* of 27 May 1959 as having said that Switzerland was one of the prime movers in the revival of the FTA negotiations and that 'the Swiss see the new scheme not as a rival to the EEC but as a means of getting negotiations going again for a multilateral association of all Europe'. Thus, Sweden and the UK were not necessarily alone in wanting the peripherals to be excluded.

94 Brennan to Cremin, 29 May 1959, D/FA-D/2/3PtI, NA.

95 Irish foreign trade committee minutes, 6 September 1957, D/FA-348/14/422PtI, NA; Maher, *The tortuous path*, pp. 91-3.

96 Draft D/F memorandum on 'Economic Relations with Britain', 8 July 1959, D/T-S16674A/61, NA.

97 Draft D/F memorandum on 'Economic Relations with Britain', 8 July 1959, D/T-S16674A/61, NA.

98 A proposed memorandum on the implications of an EFTA on Anglo-Irish industrial trade showed that, in 1958, only £4,000 of Irish exports to the UK out of a total of £17,843,000 were subject to the full rates of duty, a 'valuable advantage' that Ireland obviously did not want to lose. The creation of EFTA had become a 'matter of most serious concern' to Dublin as its exports were suddenly in danger of rapidly contracting instead of steadily expanding; the added concern of agricultural products being included was that this would have of course meant potentially catastrophic effects. Lemass memorandum, 9 June 1959, D/T-S15281R, NA; Irish cabinet minute, 10 July 1959, D/T-S16674A/61, NA.

99 Report on the Anglo-Irish trade talks of 13 July 1959, D/T-S16674A/61, NA.

100 Note that the positions of Austria and Portugal within the Seven were unclear at this point in time, and that the Seven therefore comprised of only five nations at that stage.

101 UK Department of the Treasury note entitled 'The Relation of a UNISCAN Free Trade Area to Wider European Arrangements', 8 April 1959, GEN613/60 CAB130/136, Public Record Office, Kew Gardens, London (PRO); Treasury note entitled 'European Trading Association: draft statement of objectives', 14 April 1959, GEN613/61 (Revise) CAB130/136, PRO. Please note that no differentiation is made between the abbreviation CAB for Irish cabinet and UK cabinet minutes as the origins of the file are obvious from other information presented in the rest of the footnote.

102 It should not be forgotten that Ireland was no longer in the British Commonwealth – having left in 1948 – but it continued to maintain similar trade preferences dating from before that time and even subsequently.

103 Treasury note entitled 'European Trade Association', 27 April 1959, GEN613/76 CAB130/136, PRO.

104 UK departmental secretaries note entitled 'Visit of M.de Besche, 24th-25th April', 13 May 1959, ES(EI)(59)8 CAB134/1870, PRO.

105 UK departmental secretaries note entitled 'European Trade Association: Swedish Proposals', 14 May 1959, ES(EI)(59)13 CAB134/1870, PRO.

106 FO note entitled 'Problem of non-members of both the European Economic Community and the European Trading Association', 19 May 1959, ES(EI)(59)15 CAB134/1870, PRO.

107 FO note entitled 'Problem of non-members of both the European Economic Community and the European Trading Association', 19 May 1959, ES(EI)(59)15

108 CAB134/1870, PRO.
FO note entitled 'Problem of non-members of both the European Economic Community and the European Trading Association', 19 May 1959, ES(EI)(59)15 CAB134/1870, PRO.
109 FO note entitled 'Problem of non-members of both the European Economic Community and the European Trading Association', 19 May 1959, ES(EI)(59)15 CAB134/1870, PRO.
110 FO note entitled 'Problem of non-members of both the European Economic Community and the European Trading Association', 19 May 1959, ES(EI)(59)15 CAB134/1870, PRO.
111 UK departmental secretaries note entitled 'Commonwealth and European Trade Arrangements', 12 June 1959, ES(EI)(59)23 CAB134/1870, PRO; UK departmental secretaries note entitled 'European Economic Co-operation and Integration: a brief history', 26 June 1959, ES(EI)(59)31 CAB134/1870, PRO.
112 B/T note entitled 'Current Quotas between the Seven', 21 May 1959, ES(EI)(59)18 CAB134/1870, PRO.
113 UK departmental secretaries note entitled 'Brief for the use of Information Officers', 22 May 1959, ES(EI)(59)19 CAB134/1870, PRO.
114 UK departmental secretaries note entitled 'Stockholm Group: Information for the Commonwealth', 11 June 1959, GEN613/80 CAB130/136, PRO.
115 UK departmental secretaries note entitled 'Stockholm Group: Information for the Commonwealth', 11 June 1959, GEN613/80 CAB130/136, PRO.
116 UK departmental secretaries note entitled 'Stockholm Group: Information for the Commonwealth', 11 June 1959, GEN613/80 CAB130/136, PRO.
117 UK departmental secretaries note entitled 'Stockholm Group: Information for the Commonwealth', 11 June 1959, GEN613/80 CAB130/136, PRO.
118 UK departmental secretaries note entitled 'Record of Meetings of the Working Party in Stockholm', 17 June 1959, ES(EI)(59)27 CAB134/1870, PRO.
119 UK departmental secretaries note entitled 'Stockholm Group: Report to Ministers', 17 June 1959, ES(EI)(59)28 CAB134/1870, PRO.
120 UK cabinet steering committee on EFTA meeting notes, 25 June 1959, GEN613/97 CAB130/133, PRO. Among those present at the meeting were R.F.Bretherton (B/T official), John Coulson (UK Paymaster General official) and F.E.Figgures (UK Treasury official).
121 Treasury note entitled 'The Position of Portugal in the Stockholm Group', 30 June 1959, ES(EI)(59)34 CAB134/1870, PRO.
122 Treasury note entitled 'The Position of Portugal in the Stockholm Group', 30 June 1959, ES(EI)(59)34 CAB134/1870, PRO.
123 Treasury note entitled 'Stockholm Group: Ministerial Meeting, 20th July', 8 July 1959, ES(EI)(59)41 CAB134/1871, PRO; UK departmental secretaries note entitled 'Stockholm Group: Ministerial Meeting on 20th July: general brief', 15 July 1959, ES(EI)(59)45 CAB134/1871, PRO.
124 Irish government *aide-mémoire*, 26 June 1959, D/T-S15281R, NA; UK departmental secretaries note entitled 'Irish Republic's Trade with Europe', 7 July 1959, ES(EI)(59)39 CAB134/1870, PRO.
125 Irish government *aide-mémoire*, 26 June 1959, D/T-S15281R, NA; UK departmental secretaries note entitled 'Irish Republic's Trade with Europe', 7 July 1959, ES(EI)(59)39 CAB134/1870, PRO.
126 Bretherton to McCarthy, 25 June 1959, ES(EI)(59)39 (addendum) CAB134/1870, PRO; McCarthy to Bretherton, 6 July 1959, ES(EI)(59)39 (addendum)

	CAB134/1870, PRO; UK departmental secretaries note entitled 'Irish Republic's Trade with Europe', 9 July 1959, ES(EI)(59)39 (addendum) CAB134/1870, PRO; Richard T.Griffiths, 'Ireland and EFTA' (unpublished article).
127	UK departmental secretaries note entitled 'Meeting with Irish Ministers at the Board of Trade on Monday, 13th July, at 10.30a.m.', 20 July 1959, GEN613/93 CAB130/136, PRO.
128	UK departmental secretaries note entitled 'Meeting with Irish Ministers at the Board of Trade on Monday, 13th July, at 10.30a.m.', 20 July 1959, GEN613/93 CAB130/136, PRO.
129	UK departmental secretaries note entitled 'Meeting with Irish Ministers at the Board of Trade on Monday, 13th July, at 10.30a.m.', 20 July 1959, GEN613/93 CAB130/136, PRO.
130	UK departmental secretaries note entitled 'Meeting with Irish Ministers at the Board of Trade on Monday, 13th July, at 10.30a.m.', 20 July 1959, GEN613/93 CAB130/136, PRO.
131	UK departmental secretaries note entitled 'Meeting with Irish Ministers at the Board of Trade on Monday, 13th July, at 10.30a.m.', 20 July 1959, GEN613/93 CAB130/136, PRO.
132	UK departmental secretaries note entitled 'Meeting with Irish Ministers at the Board of Trade on Monday, 13th July, at 10.30a.m.', 20 July 1959, GEN613/93 CAB130/136, PRO.
133	A critical point has to be made here, concerning this research into *Ireland and the EEC, 1957 to 1966*, which is that the part played by partition in Anglo-Irish politics became decreasingly important as this period of time passed. Indeed, there was an incontrovertible transition in the handling of this subject by Irish governments from the de Valera years through to the Lemass tenure, culminating in the latter's meeting with Terence O'Neill, the Northern Ireland prime minister, in January 1965. A study of *Northern Ireland's role in Irish-European affairs* – regarding economic, political and social issues – is integrated into Chapter 6.
134	UK departmental secretaries note entitled 'Meeting with Irish Ministers at the Board of Trade on Monday, 13th July, at 10.30a.m.', 20 July 1959, GEN613/93 CAB130/136, PRO.
135	UK departmental secretaries note entitled 'Meeting with Irish Ministers at the Board of Trade on Monday, 13th July, at 10.30a.m.', 20 July 1959, GEN613/93 CAB130/136, PRO.
136	UK cabinet steering committee on EFTA meeting notes, 14 July 1959, GEN613/102 CAB130/133, PRO.
137	MacCarthy to Moynihan, 8 October 1959, D/T-S15281T, NA.
138	Whyte, *Church and state*, pp. 353-5 & 361.
139	Please note that a diagram depicting this relationship has appeared in FitzGerald, 'Irish neutrality and European integration', p. 8.
140	Note that from NATO intersection OEEC on would find: • the two North American members of NATO; • countries common to both organisations – that is with security and trade considerations (NATO ∩ OEEC) with Spain peripheral to both; • the four OEEC neutrals with Finland depicted outside the OEEC set. This would become a little more complex if EEC and EFTA sub-sets from 1957 and 1959 were added in; the position of the peripherals and neutrals, specifically Ireland, would mean that it is not only excluded from the major European trade

developments but is also outside the West's major security network. If another major trade organisation, such as the General Agreement on Tariffs and Trade (GATT) was integrated into this set-up, it would be found that Ireland was excluded even further still. Of the countries in question, Ireland was the penultimate member to accede to the GATT, doing so through Agreement N°106 on 22 December 1967. Note that Austria, Belgium, Canada, Denmark, Finland, France, the FRG, Greece, Italy, Luxembourg, the Netherlands, Norway, Sweden, Turkey, the UK, and the US were all members by 1951; Portugal was already affiliated through EFTA and later acceded in 1962. Subsequently, Switzerland signed a bilateral agreement with the US in the 'Dillon Round' of 1962 and acceded in 1966; Spain acceded in 1963 and Iceland acceded after Ireland in 1968. J.H.Jackson, *World Trade and the Law of GATT* (New York: Bobbs-Merrill, 1969), pp. 898-9.

141 Keatinge, *The formulation of Irish foreign policy*, p. 307. In October 1966, the Irish mission to the EEC in Brussels finally became a separate diplomatic and independently functioning entity.
142 G.David Anderson (UK embassy official, Dublin) to J.A.Belton (D/EA assistant secretary), 2 July 1959, D/T-S16671A, NA.
143 Moynihan to Belton, 6 July 1959, D/T-S16671A, NA.
144 Aidan Mulloy (embassy official, Brussels) to Sheila Murphy (D/EA official), 8 July 1959, D/T-S16671A, NA.
145 McDonald to Cremin, 26 June 1959, D/T-S15281R, NA.
146 Moynihan to Belton, 18 July 1959, D/T-S16671A, NA.
147 Aiken memorandum entitled 'Establishment of formal diplomatic relations with the EEC', 20 July 1959, D/T-S16671A, NA.
148 Molloy to Moynihan, 20 July 1959, D/T-S16671A, NA; Moynihan to Lemass, 20 July 1959, D/T-S16671A, NA.
149 Irish cabinet minute, 21 July 1959, CAB2/20, NA; Moynihan to Cremin, 21 July 1959, D/T-S16671A, NA; D/EA memorandum entitled 'Establishment of diplomatic relations between Ireland and the European Economic Community', 9 October 1959, D/T-S16671A, NA.
150 Lemass reply in Dáil Éireann to a question tabled by George Russell, 21 July 1959, D/T-S15281R, NA.
151 Lemass reply in Dáil Éireann to a question tabled by George Russell, 21 July 1959, D/T-S15281R, NA.
152 Lemass to K.Ticher (Director of Ticher Ltd., Dublin), 30 July 1959, D/T-S16671A, NA.
153 D/EA foreign trade committee discussion paper, *circa* late July 1959, D/FA-348/69/II, NA.
154 Lemass speech delivered in Dáil Éireann, 21 July 1959, *Dáil debates* vol. 176 cols. 1572-3, D/T-S16671A, NA.
155 A.Ó Coinneáin memorandum of a meeting between Lemass and the various ministers and secretaries at the Departments of Finance, External Affairs, Industry & Commerce, and Agriculture, 28 August 1959, D/T-S15281S, NA.
156 D/EA memorandum entitled 'Establishment of diplomatic relations between Ireland and the European Economic Community', 9 October 1959, D/T-S16671A, NA.
157 Moynihan memorandum, 6 October 1959, D/T-S16671A, NA; Moynihan memorandum, 7 October 1959, D/T-S16671A, NA.
158 D/EA memorandum entitled 'Establishment of diplomatic relations between

384 Protectionism to liberalisation

159   Ireland and the European Economic Community', 9 October 1959, D/T-S16671A, NA; Irish cabinet minute, 13 October 1959, CAB2/20, NA; Moynihan to Cremin, 13 October 1959, D/T-S16671A, NA.

159   Cremin to Moynihan, 3 December 1959, D/T-S16671A, NA; Moynihan to Cremin, 3 December 1959, D/T-S16671A, NA.

160   Lemass speech delivered to the Federation of Irish Industries, 21 September 1959, D/T-S16666B, NA; Lemass reply to a question posed in Dáil Éireann, 21 October 1959, D/T-S15281T, NA.

161   D/I&C memorandum, 14 October 1959, D/T-S15281T, NA; Mally, *Britain and European unity*, p. 42 (author's italics). The preamble to the convention – signed in Stockholm on 4 January 1960 – which established EFTA was quoted by the latter; this text read:
> Determined to facilitate the early establishment of a *multilateral association* for the removal of trade barriers and the *promotion of closer economic co-operation* between the members of the OEEC ...

162   Garret FitzGerald (Irish Council of Europe Movement executive committee chairman) article in the Irish Council of Europe movement newsletter, March 1960, D/T-S15279B/PtI, NA.

163   Lemass draft speech to an intergovernmental committee for the establishment of an FTA, *circa* October 1958, D/T-S15281Q, NA.

164   Baker, *Dependency, ideology and the industrial policy of Fianna Fáil in Ireland*, p. 25.

165   Lee, *Ireland, 1912-1985*, p. 352.

166   B.Girvin, 'Economic development and the politics of EC entry: Ireland 1956-63', pp. 1-35, paper presented at the conference entitled *The first attempt to enlarge the European Community, 1961-63*, held at the IUE from 17-19 February 1994, p. 25.

167   International Monetary Fund (IMF), *International financial statistics* vol. 16 no. 1, January 1963; Stallings, *Economic dependency in Africa and Latin America*, pp. 8 & 45. Barbara Stallings says that, though it does not represent dependency *per se*, 'exports and imports as a high percentage of GNP is a necessary precondition for the trade aspect of dependency to be relevant'. In fact, she shows that trade figures as a percentage of GNP for African and Latin American countries were 43% and 29% on average respectively in 1965, but that the figure was more likely to be in the region of 22% for developed countries such as the FRG or UK.

168   Draft *aide-mémoire*, 3 December 1959, D/T-S15281U, NA; Irish Council of Europe Movement newsletter, May 1960, D/T-S15279B/PtI, NA.

169   Irish foreign trade committee minutes, 9 September 1955, D/T-S15030B, NA.

170   MacCarthy to Whitaker, 6 April 1960, D/T-S15281W, NA.

171   Irish cabinet minutes, 9 August 1960, D/T-S15030D, NA; Irish government decision, 15 August 1960, D/T-15030D, NA; Jack Lynch (industry & commerce minister) speech to the Dublin Rotary Club, 31 October 1960, D/T-S16877F, NA.

172   McAleese, 'Political independence, economic growth and the role of economic policy', p. 286.

Chapter 3

1. Harold Macmillan (UK prime minister) to Lemass, 26 July 1961, D/T-S16877N/61, NA; Macmillan to Lemass, 29 July 1961, D/T-S16877O/61, NA; H.Macmillan, *At the end of the day, 1961-1963* (London: Macmillan, 1973), p. 11. Despite this courtesy, Lemass and Ireland were well down the UK's list of priorities; indeed, the former barely gets a mention in Macmillan's memoirs, except for a brief note on this episode:
   > Since the Prime Minister of Eire had made it clear that if Britain went into the Common Market his country would probably wish to do so, I invited him to come for personal consultations in July [1961]. This would be convenient because our talks would take place during the period that United Kingdom Ministers were making their Commonwealth visits. I found Seán Lemass particularly helpful, and enjoyed my meetings with him.
2. Note that the various articles of the *Treaty establishing the European Economic Community* (usually referred to as the Treaty of Rome despite the existence of two such treaties) are usually referred to in a shortened, bracketed form throughout this text; therefore, Article 237 of the *Treaty establishing the European Economic Community* is cited as follows in the text: (Article 237). Article 237 of the *Treaty establishing the European Economic Community* in the *Treaties establishing the European Communities* (Luxembourg, Luxembourg: Office for Official Publications of the European Communities, 1973), p. 336.
3. Working group of the Council of Europe secretariat report, 'Rélations Economiques Européennes: la position de certains pays Européens autres ques les Six en cas d'adhesion du Royaume-Uni à la Communauté Economique Européenne' (Strasbourg: Council of Europe, 1961), p. 54. In the original French, this document read: 'si, l'on considère l'ensemble de l'économie irlandaise, les intérêts industriels sont faibles en comparison des intérêts agricoles et il semble que l'Irlande doive nécessairement assumer un risque dans le domaine industriel si elle veut obtenir des arrangements satisfaisants pour son agriculture'.
4. Lemass to Ludwig Erhard (EEC Council president), 31 July 1961, D/T-S16877O/61, NA.
5. J.R.A.Bottomley (CRO official) to Christopher J.Audland (FO official), 14 July 1961, M6114/22, FO371/158220, PRO; Cremin to Whitaker, 31 July 1961, D/T-S16877O/61, NA.
6. D/T memorandum, 31 July 1961, D/T-S16877O/61, NA; *Europe* (unofficial daily EEC publication) viewpoint, 3 August 1961, D/T-S16877O/61, NA.
7. B.Gallagher (ambassador, The Hague) to Molloy (D/EA assistant secretary), 3 August 1961, D/T-S16877O/61, NA.
8. *Europe*, 3 August 1961, D/T-S16877O/61, NA.
9. Keogh, *Ireland and Europe*, pp. 232-3.
10. Hederman, *The road to Europe*, p. 65; Maher, *The tortuous path*, p. 112.
11. R.Fanning, 'Irish neutrality: an historical review', p. 31, *Irish studies in international affairs* vol. 1 no. 3 1982, pp. 27-38. Neutrality was a relatively secondary consideration in the process of Ireland's European integration and did not unduly interfere in its relationship with the EEC or its attempted entry. An enlargement upon this particular argument can be found in a previous research paper: FitzGerald, 'Irish neutrality and European integration', *passim*.

12 Lemass speech delivered in Dáil Éireann, 14 June 1961, *Dáil debates* vol. 190 col. 179. Originally quoted in Hederman, *The road to Europe*, pp. 68-9.
13 Keatinge, *The formulation of Irish foreign policy*, p. 45.
14 For the further development of this argument, another research paper goes into some detail: FitzGerald, 'Ireland's experience of European integration', *passim*.
15 Hederman, *The road to Europe*, pp. 69-71.
16 This supposition has, in fact, been drawn from a table originally used in an FO brief prepared for the UK government talks with a deputation of Irish government ministers held between 18-19 July 1961, *circa* early July 1961, M6114/15, FO371/158219, PRO.
17 Lemass speech delivered in Dáil Éireann, 5 July 1961, *Dáil debates* vol. 191 col. 266.
18 Girvin, 'Economic development and the politics of EC entry', pp. 11 & 34-5.
19 Lemass speech delivered in Dáil Éireann, 26 July 1961, *Dáil debates* vol. 191 cols. 1856-8.
20 Murphy, *Ireland in the twentieth century*, p. 148.
21 B.Lenihan, 'How Lemass threw his hat into the ring', *Irish Independent*, 10 December 1994. This article is a review of M.O'Sullivan, *Seán Lemass: a biography* (Dublin: Blackwater Press, 1994).
22 Lemass speech delivered in Dáil Éireann, 8 March 1961, as quoted in W.Durbin (CRO official) to J.A.Robinson (FO official), 17 March 1961, M6114/1, FO371/158219, PRO.
23 Lemass interview published in *Handelsblatt* and *Schweizerische Handelszeitung*, 18 May 1961, D/T-S16877J/61, NA.
24 Quinlan quoting the remarks of Walter Halstein and Maurice Fauré in Seanad Éireann, 26 July 1961, *Seanad debates* vol. 54 cols. 1360-1. Maurice Fauré had also added his opinion that:

> ... the people who signed the Treaty of Rome regarded it as a first step in the political integration of Europe towards a United States of Europe – I think myself, that this is exactly what it was; and I think, furthermore, that a political will and a political unity is essential. It is essential if we are going to maintain the position of Europe *vis-à-vis* the other continents, such as Africa, and it is vitally essential if we are going to do something about the problem of the reunification of Germany. A united Germany must be brought into the Western community, and in order to do that you have got to have a political will and not just a purely commercial and economic one ... Indeed, this political will which I talk about surpasses all the limited commercial aims, all the economic aims. You can well, perhaps, reproach me for being a dreamer; but to my mind it is this political will for unity, for political integration which will not alone bring about the unity of Europe but will also preserve what is left of liberty in the Western world.

The conference in question had been held in Dublin exactly two years previous to the senator's speech.
25 Frank Biggar (ambassador, Brussels) to Cremin, 18 May 1961, D/T-S16877J/61, NA.
26 Donal O'Sullivan (economic counsellor, London) to Hugh McCann (ambassador, London), 30 May 1961, on a conversation between O'Sullivan and Franke (Dutch agriculture ministry director general), D/T-S16877J/61, NA; McCann to Cremin,

31 May 1961, D/T-S16877J/61, NA.
27 Lemass to Lynch, 2 June 1961, D/T-S16877J/61, NA. The taoiseach specified certain considerations with which he wanted to deal; these were listed as:
   - the desirability of informing the Six of Ireland's intention to apply to join the EEC if any EFTA country also applied to do so;
   - the best means of subsequently communicating this decision;
   - the desirability of asking the EEC Commission to let Ireland attend discussions for a Common Agricultural Policy (CAP) if other non-EEC countries were also present.

   For chronological reasons, this meeting is detailed in the section *Determining factors – Part III: the UK*.
28 B.Gallagher to Cremin on a conversation with van Ittersum (Dutch foreign ministry official), 8 June 1961, D/T-S16877J/61, NA.
29 This could, for instance, be a reference to an interview given by the taoiseach in which he was reported to have said that: 'Anything which tends to emphasise the real community of interests between the people of both areas [that is Ireland and Northern Ireland] and the advantages of their reunification will ... contribute to the ending of Partition'. Lemass interview published in *Handelsblatt* and *Schweizerische Handelszeitung*, 18 May 1961, D/T-S16877J/61, NA.
30 Biggar to Cremin reporting on a conversation with Paul-Henri Spaak (Belgian deputy prime minister and foreign minister), 24 June 1961, D/T-S16877K/61, NA.
31 Preamble to the *Treaty establishing the European Economic Community*, p. 173.
32 Biggar to Cremin, 24 June 1961, D/T-S16877K/61, NA.
33 Lemass speech delivered in Dáil Éireann, 25 May 1961, *Dáil debates* vol. 189 cols. 958-9, D/T-S16877J/61, NA.
34 E.H.L.Albert (FO official) memorandum, 2 June 1961, on the reported remarks of Mr.Benirschke (Deutsche Presse Agentur London correspondent) relating to the Irish visit of Heinrich von Brentano (West German foreign minister), M6114/5, FO371/158219, PRO.
35 A.Meyer (FO official) note, 6 June 1961, M6114/5, FO371/158219, PRO.
36 Robinson note, 12 June 1961, M6114/5, FO371/158219, PRO.
37 Meyer note, 6 June 1961, M6114/5, FO371/158219, PRO. This official had continued his original remarks by saying that, as far as he was aware, the Irish government had:
   > ... not spoken in this sense either to us or in OEEC or in the Council of Europe. If the Irish want our help they should ask us. There seems to be no good reason for us to hang yet another millstone round our neck for the forthcoming negotiations. In fact the Irish should be able to associate with E.E.C. in much the same way as Portugal I imagine.
38 An FO note on the last point – that West Germany intended to keep potential members of the Six informed about the CAP and that they were prepared to discuss it with them – stated: 'X is interesting, & a further indication of German hopes that the prospect of new members will enable them to give less more slowly to the French on agriculture'; the 'X' is marked in ink in Rose's original. E.M.Rose (UK ambassador, Bonn) to F.G.K.Gallagher (FO official), 23 June 1961, M6114/8, FO371/158219, PRO; Robinson note, 29 June 1961, M6114/8, FO371/158219, PRO.
39 Cremin to Whitaker, 2 June 1961, D/T-S16877J/61, NA. The *Irish Times* journalist involved, who wrote the article for the edition dated 30 May 1961, was

named as Leo Muray.
40   *Irish Press*, 1 June 1961, D/T-S16877J/61, NA.
41   *Irish Times*, 6 June 1961, D/T-S16877J/61, NA.
42   McCann to Cremin, 7 July 1961, D/T-S16877M/61, NA.
43   Irish chargé d'affaires *ad interim* (Canberra) on a conversation with Philippe Monod (French ambassador, Canberra), 16 June 1961, D/T-S16877K/61, NA.
44   T.J.Horan (minister, Berne) to Cremin, 13 July 1961, D/T-S16877M/61, NA. The original French read: 'nous n'y pensons pas'.
45   D.R.McDonald (ambassador, Paris) to Cremin reporting on a conversation with Laloy (French foreign office official), 18 July 1961, D/T-S16877N/61, NA.
46   Thomas V.Commins (ambassador, Rome) to Cremin on a conversation with Attilio Cattani (Italian foreign ministry secretary general), 30 June 1961, D/T-S16877L/61, NA.
47   Unless clearly indicated otherwise, this section has been completed with the use of the following documents: Garret FitzGerald (Irish Council of the European Movement chairman) report on a visit to the EEC Commission, 11/12 April 1961, D/T-S16023C/61, NA; FitzGerald to Whitaker, 29 April 1961, D/T-S16023C/61, NA; Whitaker to Nicholas Nolan (D/T secretary), 2 May 1961, D/T-S16023C/61, NA.
48   Lemass speech delivered at the opening of a Comhlucht Siúicre Éireann Teoranta (the Irish sugar company) accelerated freeze drying plant located in Mallow, County Cork, 24 May 1961, D/T-S16877J/61, NA.
49   Robinson note, 19 July 1961, M6114/19, FO371/158219, PRO.
50   Article 238 of the *Treaty establishing the European Economic Community*, 336.
51   For three main reasons, Greece was viewed as a special case though by the EEC Commission, namely:
     • as a consequence of its membership of NATO;
     • because of the threat communism posed in South-Eastern Europe;
     • as a result of its historic trading relationship with Eastern Europe.
52   FitzGerald to Lemass, 18 May 1961, D/T-S16877J/61, NA.
53   Irish government publication, *European Economic Community* (Dublin: Stationery Office, 1961), D/T-S16877L/61, NA. This document is assessed later in this chapter in the section headed *European Economic Community: the government White Paper*.
54   Lemass speech delivered in Dáil Éireann, 2 March 1960, *Dáil debates* vol. 179 cols. 983-4. Originally quoted in Hederman, *The road to Europe*, p. 67.
55   Lemass speech delivered in Dáil Éireann, 16 May 1961, *Dáil debates* vol. 189 col. 298. Originally quoted in Hederman, *The road to Europe*, p. 68.
56   Lee, *Ireland, 1912-1985*, p. 608. Original quotation taken from the National Economic and Social Council, *Information for policy* (Dublin: Stationery Office, 1985).
57   Quinlan speech delivered in Seanad Éireann, 26 July 1961, *Seanad debates* vol. 54 cols. 1356-80; James Ryan (Irish finance minister) reply delivered in Seanad Éireann, 26 July 1961, *Seanad debates* vol. 54 col. 1368; Quinlan speaking in Seanad Éireann, 27 July 1961, *Seanad debates* vol. 54 cols. 1446-7; Ryan replies delivered in Seanad Éireann, 27 July 1961, *Seanad debates* vol. 54 cols. 1446-7.
58   National Farmers' Association (NFA) statement, 20 July 1960, D/T-S16877Y/62, NA; D/A report on Ireland and the EEC, August 1960, D/T-16877Y/62, NA. Originally quoted in Girvin, 'Economic development and the politics of EC entry', pp. 19-23.

59 Lemass to Juan Greene (NFA president), 13 July 1961, D/T-S16877M/61, NA.
60 Whitaker to Cremin, 7 July 1961, D/T-S16877M/61, NA.
61 Girvin, 'Economic development and the politics of EC entry', p. 20.
62 Unattributed article, 'Free Trade Bloc robs city men of jobs', *Sunday Review*, 16 April 1961, 'Patrician Year – 1961' 98/1/62 (formerly D/UhÉ-P5690), NA. This particular story recounted the fact that, because of the effects of EFTA, perhaps up to two hundred jobs had been lost the previous day in a wool-combing factory in Dublin. The plant's management had added that: 'Until we are able to secure other markets or until Ireland joins the EFTA, we have no alternative but to drastically reduce our production'.
63 D/T memorandum on a meeting held on 11 July 1961 between Lemass and a deputation from the Irish Congress of Trade Unions (ICTU), 14 July 1961, D/T-S16877N/61, NA.
64 Lemass speech delivered to the Irish Management Institute, 12 May 1961, quoted in *Bulletin from the European Community* vol. 4 no. 4, June 1961, D/T-S16877M/61, NA; Hederman, *The road to Europe*, p. 72.
65 Bottomley to Audland, 14 July 1961, M6114/22, FO371/158220, PRO.
66 McCann to Cremin regarding a conversation with Eric Roll (UK agriculture ministry deputy secretary), 26 May 1961, D/T-S16877J/61, NA; H.Lintott (CRO official) to Roderick E.Barclay (FO official), 2 June 1961, M6114/4, FO371/158219, PRO.
67 Biggar to Cremin regarding a meeting with A.H.Tandy (UK chef de mission at the EEC), 23 May 1961, D/T-S16877J/61, NA.
68 McCann to Cremin, 18 May 1961, D/T-S16877J/61, NA.
69 W.R.Bickford (CRO official) to F.G.K.Gallagher, 6 April 1961, M6114/2, FO371/158219, PRO. This comment was prompted by an *Irish Independent* editorial, from 30 March 1961, on Finnish association with EFTA; indeed, Bickford felt that: 'The Finnish precedent is interesting from Ireland's viewpoint'.
70 Lemass speech delivered at the Irish National Convention of Junior Chambers of Commerce held at Shannon Airport, County Clare, 4 June 1961, D/T-S16877J/61, NA.
71 Barclay minute, 9 May 1961, M6114/3, FO371/158219, PRO.
72 F.G.K.Gallagher note, 9 May 1961, M6114/3, FO371/158219, PRO; Robinson note, 12 May 1961, M6114/3, FO371/158219, PRO.
73 F.Mills (CRO secretary of state) to Philip F.de Zulueta (UK prime minister's office official), 15 June 1961, M6114/6, FO371/158219, PRO.
74 Whitaker memorandum on a meeting held on 6 June 1961 of departmental secretaries and Irish ambassadors, 7 June 1961, D/T-S16877J/61, NA.
75 Lemass to Macmillan, 10 June 1961, D/T-S16877J/61, NA.
76 Whitaker memorandum on a meeting held on 6 June 1961 of departmental secretaries and Irish ambassadors, 7 June 1961, D/T-S16877J/61, NA; O'Carroll note on a meeting held on 8 June 1961 of Irish government ministers and departmental secretaries, 9 June 1961, D/T-S16877J/61, NA.
77 Unless otherwise stated, this section has been completed using the Irish government White Paper entitled the *European Economic Community*.
78 Whitaker to Cremin, 19 June 1961, D/T-S16877J/61, NA.
79 Whitaker memorandum on a meeting held on 6 June 1961 of departmental secretaries and Irish ambassadors, 7 June 1961, D/T-S16877J/61, NA. Aiken later revealed that, apart from pushing Ireland's candidacy, these meetings also provided the opportunity to promote both Irish trade and foreign exchange

earning activities, as well as economic cooperation generally. The Minister for External Affairs said:
> In 1961, in order to emphasise that much was required of our diplomatic service in this regard, I summoned every ambassador and every diplomatic representative home to Ireland. We gave them a full week of discussions, talks and lectures on the various opportunities that existed and told them that they should be followed up to increase our foreign earnings. They were addressed, not only by the Taoiseach, myself, the Minister for Industry and Commerce and the secretaries of the various economic departments but they had discussions with organisations like the Irish Exporters, Córas Tráchtála, Bord Fáilte and the Industrial Development Authority. All the people concerned, who wanted to sell and promote trade, felt it was a very useful thing to have those kind of discussions.

Aiken speaking in Seanad Éireann, 18 November 1964, *Seanad debates* vol. 58 col. 53.

80 O'Carroll note on a meeting held on 8 June 1961 of Irish government ministers and departmental secretaries, 9 June 1961, D/T-S16877J/61, NA.
81 Lemass minute, 22 June 1961, D/T-S16877K/61, NA.
82 Exchanges between Brendan Corish (Labour party leader) and Lemass in Dáil Éireann, 29 June 1961, *Dáil debates* vol. 190 col. 1340, D/T-S16877L/61, NA.
83 Oireachtas is a generic term for Dáil Éireann, Seanad Éireann, and Uachtarán na hÉireann (Irish president). White Papers and bills must be approved at all three stages and be in accordance with the Irish constitution before they reach the next stage of their debate or before they can come into law.
84 Cremin note of a conversation with Edward G.Stockdale (US ambassador, Dublin) and Burdett (US State Department official heading British and Northern European affairs), 6 July 1961, D/T-S16877M/61, NA. This aspect of the publication is, in itself, worth taking a closer look as this document demonstrates that the Irish government's opinions on the history of European integration had developed to the point where accession to the EEC had become an official foreign policy goal.
85 The data has partly been compiled using a table originally published in the White Paper *European Economic Community* and from figures that come from the following publications: Central Statistics Office, *Ireland: trade and shipping statistics, passim.*
86 In the middle of May 1961, de Besche (Swedish foreign affairs affairs secretary general) told the other members of EFTA that an enlarged EEC, along the lines that the UK probably favoured – the UK entering, along with some other EFTA countries, although probably only those in NATO, Denmark and Norway, with the other EFTA countries negotiating association – would mean that a country such as Ireland would then find it difficult even to associate itself with the EEC; no consideration was given to a country like Ireland entering the EEC as a full member. R.Steininger, '1961: Europe "at sixes and sevens" – the European Free Trade Association, the neutrals, and Great Britain's decision to join the E.E.C.', pp. 535-68, in *The journal of European economic history* vol. 26 no. 3 1997, p. 553.
87 Unless clearly indicated otherwise, this section has been completed with the use of the following documents: D/T memorandum for the government, 27 June 1961, D/T-S16877K/61, NA; Irish government *aide-mémoire* to the Luxembourg

88 government, 5 July 1961, D/T-S16877M/61, NA.
88 A.E.Furness (CRO private secretary) to K.M.Wilford (UK Lord Privy Seal private secretary) on a meeting held on 30 June 1961 between the Irish ambassador and the UK Lord Chancellor, 30 June 1961, M6114/11, FO371/158219, PRO.
89 Robinson note #1, 3 July 1961, M6114/11, FO371/158219, PRO.
90 Robinson note #1, 3 July 1961, M6114/11, FO371/158219, PRO.
91 Robinson note #2, 3 July 1961, M6114/11, FO371/158219, PRO.
92 Lemass speech delivered in Dáil Éireann, 5 July 1961, *Dáil Debates* vol. 191 cols. 206-71.
93 Maher, *The tortuous path*, p. 126.
94 In the original French, the *aide-mémoire* read: 'l'état de la situation commerciale et économique de l'Irlande est tel qu'elle ne peut envisager de devenir membre de la Communauté que dans le cas où la Grande Bretagne aurait décidé de poser sa candidature comme membre'.
95 In French, the *aide-mémoire* had held that: 'L'Irlande serait prête à accepter en principe, les dispositions du Traité de Rome comme on l'exige des membres, mais, au stade actuel de son évolution, elle ne serait pas à même de se conformer entièrement à certaines clauses de ce traité dans le laps de temps prévu'.
96 In the original French, the *aide-mémoire* stated that the aims of the *Programme for economic expansion* 'sont conformes à ceux de la Communaunté Economique Européenne et leur réalisation sera dans l'intérêt commun'.
97 F.O'Brien, *An béal bocht* (Dublin: Dolmen, 1941), *passim*.
98 Cremin note of a telephone conversation with Biggar regarding the latter's meetings with Hallstein, Spaak and Hommel (Luxembourg ambassador to the EEC), 6 July 1961, D/T-S16877M/61, NA.
99 Biggar to Cremin, 7 July 1961, D/T-S16877M/61, NA.
100 Biggar to Cremin on a conversation with Forthomme (Belgian foreign office director-general for special affairs), 10 July 1961, D/T-S16877M/61, NA.
101 B.Gallagher to Cremin, 5 July 1961, D/T-S16877M/61, NA.
102 Brian Ó Ceallaigh (chargé d'affaires *ad interim*, Bonn), 12 July 1961, D/T-S16877M/61, NA.
103 Commins to Cremin, 6 July 1961, D/T-S16877M/61, NA.
104 Cremin to Whitaker, 26 July 1961, D/T-S16877N/61, NA.
105 *Europe*, 11 July 1961, D/T-S16877N/61, NA.
106 Cremin note on a conversation with Stockdale and Burdett, 6 July 1961, D/T-S16877M/61, NA; FitzGerald, *Irish-American diplomatic relations*, *passim*.
107 Cremin to MacCarthy, 7 July 1961, D/T-S16877M/61, NA; Bottomley to Audland, 14 July 1961, M6114/22, FO371/158220, PRO. It is very always interesting to note what the officials of one government thought of their counterparts in another. According to informed UK government opinion, Cremin was viewed as being 'markedly friendly and agreeable', but without having shown 'evidence of independence of thought or a readiness to assume undue responsibility'; Whitaker, meanwhile, was seen as follows: 'Brilliantly able, but with a quiet and unassuming but pleasant manner'. Nagle was perceived as having 'a sharp intellect and a considerable flair for patient and astute negotiation'; in addition, it was felt that MacCarthy had 'done very well' and that relations with him were 'excellent'. These views were for the most part positive and, because of their inherent secrecy, fairly reliable as a consequence.
108 H.A.F.Rumbold (FO official) memorandum, 1 June 1961, M6114/4, FO371/158219, PRO.

109 Macmillan to Lemass, 16 June 1961, D/T-S16877K/61, NA; Macmillan to Lemass, 3 July 1961, D/T-S16877L/61, NA; Lemass to Macmillan, 5 July 1961, D/T-S16877L/61, NA.
110 McCann to Cremin, 21 June 1961, D/T-S16877K/61, NA; Cremin memorandum, 21 June 1961, D/T-S16877K/61, NA.
111 *Irish Press*, 24 June 1961, D/T-S16877K/61, NA.
112 Lemass to Macmillan, 24 June 1961, D/T-S16877K/61, NA.
113 Draft agenda for the Anglo-Irish meetings, 28 June 1961, D/T-S16877K/61, NA.
114 UK Lord Chancellor's view as quoted in McCann to Cremin, 30 June 1961, D/T-S16877L/61, NA.
115 Cremin to Whitaker, 1 July 1961, D/T-S16877L/61, NA.
116 Whitaker to Nolan, 4 July 1961, D/T-S16877L/61, NA; draft agenda for the Anglo-Irish meetings, mid-July 1961, D/T-S16877N/61, NA.
117 Draft agenda for the Anglo-Irish meetings, mid-July 1961, D/T-S16877N/61, NA.
118 Reginald Maudling (B/T president) quoted in McCann to Cremin, 12 July 1961, D/T-S16877M/61, NA.
119 Draft agenda for the Anglo-Irish meetings, mid-July 1961, D/T-S16877N/61, NA.
120 FO note, *circa* end of June 1961, M6114/9, FO371/158219, PRO; CRO note, *circa* end of June 1961, M6114/9, FO371/158219, PRO.
121 De Zulueta to A.W.France (Treasury official), 30 June 1961, M6114/9, FO371/158219, PRO.
122 France to de Zulueta, 30 June 1961, M6114/9, FO371/158219, PRO. Cledwyn Hughes (UK Labour party Member of Parliament for Anglesey) question to Braine (CRO secretary of state) on contacts between the UK government and Ireland on the EEC question, 5 July 1961, M6114/14, FO371/158219, PRO.
123 Lemass speech reported in the *Irish Press*, 18 July 1961, D/T-S16877N/61, NA.
124 Lemass speech reported in the *Irish Press*, 19 July 1961, D/T-S16877N/61, NA.
125 Lemass interview with the British Broadcasting Corporation (BBC), 18 July 1961, D/T-S16877N/61, NA.
126 Lemass interview with the BBC, 18 July 1961, D/T-S16877N/61, NA.
127 Lemass speech reported in the *Irish Press*, 20 July 1961, D/T-S16877N/61, NA.
128 Lemass speech delivered to Macra na Feirme (an Irish farming organisation) in Wexford, 22 July 1961, D/T-S16877N/61, NA.
129 Keating, *A singular stance*, p. 25.
130 Preamble to the Bonn Declaration of the Six, 18 July 1961, which is quoted in Maher, *The tortuous path*, p. 133; Mally, *Britain and European unity*, pp. 48-9.
131 Quinlan speaking in Seanad Éireann, 26 July 1961, *Seanad debates* vol. 54 cols. 1356-80.
132 Nagle note, 20 July 1961, D/T-S16877N/61, NA.
133 UK Foreign Office minute, 18 July 1961, M6114/24, FO371/158220, PRO.
134 In many respects, of course, it suited London that Ireland was trying to enter the EEC as a full member; the latter would not only help to forestall further French hegemony, but it would also probably help to lessen the future federal shape of Europe by diluting it, whether that was in terms of exhausting economic aims by its agricultural demands or political integration through its neutrality.
135 Barclay minute, 18 July 1961, M6114/24, FO371/158220, PRO. The West German official in question was Harkort (FRG foreign ministry deputy secretary for economic affairs).
136 Bottomley to F.G.K.Gallagher, 20 July 1961, M6114/25, FO371/158220, PRO.
137 Cremin memorandum, 26 July 1961, D/T-S16877N/61, NA; Cremin to Whitaker,

	26 July 1961, D/T-S16877N/61, NA.
138	M.Shanks & J.Lambert, *Britain and the new Europe: the future of the Common Market* (London: Chatto & Windus, 1962), pp. 187 & 233. At least the authors noted that 'there is quite a chance that Eire may get full membership', even if it was one of 'those [states] whose economies are not strong enough to meet the full competition of the Common Market ... [and if] associate status will presumably only be temporary; in the course of time, it is to be hoped that the economies of the associates will be strong enough to stand the pressures of full membership'. Barclay minute, 21 July 1961, M6114/26, FO371/158220, PRO.
139	Cremin memorandum, 26 July 1961, D/T-S16877N/61, NA; Cremin to Whitaker, 26 July 1961, D/T-S16877N/61, NA.
140	Maclennan to Lintott, 25 July 1961, M6114/26, FO371/158220, PRO.
141	Cremin memorandum, 26 July 1961, D/T-S16877N/61, NA; Cremin to Whitaker, 26 July 1961, D/T-S16877N/61, NA.
142	Hallstein as quoted in a Molloy memorandum, 29 July 1961, D/T-S16877N/61, NA; Mansholt as quoted in N.Piers Ludlow, 'Influence and vulnerability: the role of the EEC Commission in the enlargement negotiations', 1-23, paper presented at the conference entitled *The first attempt to enlarge the European Community, 1961-63*, held from 17-19 February 1994 at the IUE, 1; *Irish Times*, 26 July 1961, D/T-S16877N/61, NA; *Gazette de Lausanne* as quoted in A.O'Rourke (chargé d'affaires *ad interim*, Berne) to Cremin, 26 July 1961, D/T-S16877O/61, NA.
143	Tandy telegram to the FO, 3 August 1961, M6114/31, FO371/158220, PRO; Tandy to the FO, 4 August 1961, M6114/31, FO371/158220, PRO; J.R.Rich (FO official) note, early August 1961, M6114/31, FO371/158220, PRO.
144	B.Gallagher to Molloy, 3 August 1961, D/T-S16877O/61, NA. The EEC official in question was Pierre Lucion (Jean Rey's chef de cabinet).
145	B.Gallagher to Molloy, 5 August 1961, D/T-S16877O/61, NA.
146	Ludlow, 'Influence and vulnerability', pp. 21-2.
147	Florence O'Riordan (chargé d'affaires *ad interim*, The Hague) to Molloy, 3 August 1961, D/T-S16877O/61, NA.
148	O'Riordan to Molloy, 11 August 1961, D/T-S16877O/61, NA.
149	O'Riordan report, 11 August 1961, D/T-S16877O/61, NA. The Dutch official in question was Kymmell (Dutch foreign ministry official heading up the European integration division).
150	W.Asbeek Brusse, 'Alone within the Six: the Dutch cabinet and the British application for EEC membership, 1960-1963', p. 22, paper presented at the conference entitled *The first attempt to enlarge the European Community, 1961-63*, held from 17-19 February 1994 at the IUE.
151	O'Carroll note, 12 August 1961, D/T-S16877O/61, NA (emphasis added).
152	Vaughan, *Twentieth-century Europe*, p. 152.
153	O'Carroll note, 12 August 1961, D/T-S16877O/61, NA.
154	Audland minute, 14 August 1961, M6114/33, FO371/158220, PRO.
155	O'Carroll note, 14 August 1961, D/T-S16877O/61, NA.
156	Erhard to Lemass, 14 August 1961, D/T-S16877O/61, NA. In the original German, this statement read: 'Zur Unterrichtung des Rates wäre ich Eurer Exzellenz für eine Mitteilung dankbar, inwieweit der Rat bei seinen Ueberlegungen auch das Aide-mémoire in Betracht ziehen soll, das den Mitgliedstaaten der Europäischen Wirtschafts-gemeinschaft am 4. Juli 1961 von der Regierung Irlands überreicht worden ist'.
157	Lemass to Erhard, 18 August 1961, D/T-S16877O/61, NA.

158 D.P.Reilly (FO official) minute, 17 August 1961, M6114/33, FO371/158220, PRO.
159 Lemass interview conducted with the BBC in Belfast on 4 August 1961 as reported in the *Irish Press*, 5 August 1961, D/T-S16877O/61, NA.
160 B.McSweeney, 'Out of the ghetto: Irish foreign policy since the fifties', pp. 401-2, *Studies* vol. 75 no. 300 1986, *passim*.
161 Heath reference made in O'Sullivan and Slevin (Irish embassy official, London) 'Note of discussions between Irish and British Ministers in London on Tuesday, 18th July, 1961', D/T-S16877N/61, NA.
162 Nagle to O'Carroll, 5 August 1961, D/T-S16877O/61, NA.
163 Nagle to Molloy, 14 August 1961, D/T-S16877O/61, NA. O'Sullivan became Ireland's economic counsellor to the EEC.
164 O'Carroll to Nagle, 10 August 1961, D/T-S16877O/61, NA.
165 Biggar to Molloy, 12 August 1961, D/T-S16877O/61, NA.
166 Council of Europe report, 'Rélations Economiques Européennes', pp. 52-3. In the original French, this document read: 'il est peu probable que la République d'Irlande éprouverait de grandes difficultés à adopter le niveau du tarif extérieur commun de la C.E.E. à l'égard des pays tiers ... il lui serait difficile d'accepter la démobilisation des barrières douanières appliquées aux importations en provenance de ses partenaires sur la base du calendrier prévu par le Traité de Rome'.
167 Council of Europe report, 'Rélations Economiques Européennes', pp. 52-3. In the original French, this document declared: 'La République d'Irlande suit une politique de neutralité que le Gouvernement a proclamé sa volonté de maintenir aussi longtemps que subsisterait le partage de l'Ile ... En outre, l'Irlande partage avec le Royaume-Uni les traditions du droit coutumier et un grande nombre d'institutions qui diffèrent considérablement de celles du continent européen'.
168 Maher, *The tortuous path*, p. 138.
169 Maher, *The tortuous path*, p. 141.
170 Mally, *Britain and European unity*, pp. 60-83. The latter quoted Heath's speech to the representatives of the Six, delivered in Paris on 10 October 1961.
171 Council of Europe report, 'Rélations Economiques Européennes', p. 55. In the original French, this document read: 'le Conseil des Ministres, à l'unanimité, m'a chargé de vous suggérer de tenir au début de janvier 1962, à Bruxelles, une réunion pour permettre aux Etats membres de la Communauté d'avoir avec le Gouvernement irlandais un échange de vues sur les problèmes particuliers que pose la demande du Gouvernement irlandais et les conséquences qu'il convient d'en tirer ainsi que sur certaines questions de procédure'.
172 Lemass speech to the Cork Chamber of Commerce, 11 November 1961. Originally quoted in Maher, *The tortuous path*, p. 143.
173 Lemass speaking in Dáil Éireann, 11 October 1961, *Dáil debates* vol. 192 col. 43.
174 C.C.O'Brien, 'The embers of Easter' (originally published in the *Irish Times*, 7 April 1966), in D.H.Akenson, *Conor: a biography of Conor Cruise O'Brien, vol. 2* (Montreal, Canada: McGill-Queen's University Press, 1994); Karl Marx to Friedrich Engels, 2 November 1867, *Karl Marx Friedrich Engels, vol. 31* (Berlin, Germany: Dietz Verlag, 1974), p. 376. In the original German, this statement from Karl Marx read: 'Ich habe früher Trennung Irlands von England für unmöglich gehalten. Ich halte sie jetzt für unvermeidlich, obgleich nach der Trennung Federation kommen mag'.
175 David Bell (Dublin solicitor) to P.Berry (Department of Justice (D/J) secretary),

Notes 395

	30 January 1960, 'Proposed establishment of a factory for the production of hand grenades for sale to the Venezuelan Government' D/FA-315/59/343/26, NA; MacDonagh (D/J official) memorandum, 13 February 1960, D/FA-315/59/343/26, NA; D/J memorandum, 9 March 1960, D/FA-315/59/343/26, NA.
176	Cremin to Berry, 21 March 1960, D/FA-315/59/343/26, NA.
177	Moravcsik, *The choice for Europe*, pp. 5 & 162-3.
178	T.C.Salmon, *Unneutral Ireland: an ambivalent and unique security policy* (Oxford: Clarendon, 1989), p. 215; T.Salmon, 'Ireland: a neutral in the Community?', pp. 205-27, *Journal of Common Market studies* vol. 20 no. 3 1982, p. 215.

Chapter 4

1	As Richard Griffiths has written in summarising Ireland's experience of European integration in this period: >Ireland's membership application was perhaps even more closely linked [than Denmark's or Norway's applications were] with that of the United Kingdom. Ireland had not taken part in the EEC/EFTA split of the late 1950s, but had special trading arrangements with Britain dating back to the time when it formed part of the United Kingdom. [Appointed in July 1960 as Lord Privy Seal with special responsibility for Europe] Edward Heath specifically mentioned Ireland in his opening speech to the EEC governments in October 1961, expressing the hope that their trading relationship would be 'subsumed in the wider arrangements of the enlarged Community'. The EEC Council of Ministers signalled the start of negotiations with Ireland in October 1962 but, as in the case of Norway, substantial negotiations never actually opened. R.T.Griffiths, 'The European integration experience, 1958-73', pp. 37-70, in K.Middlemas, *Orchestrat-ing Europe: the informal politics of the European Union, 1973-95* (London: Fontana, 1995), pp. 40-3.
2	W.Nicoll & T.C.Salmon, *Understanding the new European Community* (New York: Harvester Wheatsheaf, 1994), pp. 214 & 233.
3	W.Wallace, 'The British approach to Europe', pp. 107-33, in W.J.Mommsen (ed.), *The long way to Europe: historical observations from a contemporary view* (Chicago: edition q, 1994).
4	Girvin, 'Economic development and the politics of EC entry', pp. 34-5.
5	P.Calvocoressi, 'Neutrality now', pp. 144-59, in S.Harden (ed.), *Neutral states and the European Community* (Oxford: Brassey's, 1994), p. 152.
6	E.O'Malley, *Industry and economic development: the challenge for the latecomer* (Dublin: Gill & Macmillan, 1989), p. 74.
7	E.O'Malley, 'The problem of late industrialisation and the experience of the Republic of Ireland', pp. 141-54, in *Cambridge journal of economics* vol. 9 no. 2, p. 144.
8	These figures come from a chart originally used in B.Moore *et al*, 'Industrial policy and economic development: the experience of Northern Ireland and the Republic of Ireland', pp. 99-114, in *Cambridge journal of economics* vol. 2 no. 1 1978, p. 108. The data for Ireland in the period 1945 to 1951 does not appear to be available; presumably, however, this figure was relatively low.
9	L.de Paor, *Divided Ulster* (Harmondsworth: Penguin, 1971), p. 133.

10 J.Wickham, 'Dependence and state structure: foreign firms and industrial policy in the Republic of Ireland', pp. 164-83, in O.Höll (ed.), *Small states in Europe and dependence* (Vienna: Wilhelm Braumüller, 1983), pp. 168-9.
11 Moore et al, 'Industrial policy and economic development', *passim*.
12 Wickham, 'Dependence and state structure', p. 181.
13 Maher, *The tortuous path*, pp. 129 & 175-6.
14 G.Cunningham (CRO official) to P.A.R.Brown (B/T official), *circa* mid-November 1962, M6314/19, FO371/164771, PRO; G.L.Pearson (British Trade Commission official in Dublin) to Cunningham, 14 November 1962, M6314/19, FO371/164771, PRO.
15 Bradley et al, *Stabilization and growth on the EC periphery*, p. 10.
16 P.Gerbet, *La construction de l'Europe* (Paris: Imprimerie national, 1983), p. 294. In the original French, the author said: 'l'Irlande ... étant en union économique avec la Grande-Bretagne, elle ne pouvait s'en trouver séparée'.
17 Unless otherwise specified, this section – *The Dublin government presents its case in Brussels* – has been completed using the following two documents: *Treaty establishing the European Economic Community, passim*; Lemass statement to the EEC Council, 18 January 1962. The full text of this speech given by the taoiseach is available in Maher, *The tortuous path*, pp. 375-85.
18 Whitaker to Lynch, 5 January 1962, D/T-S16877X/62, NA. Originally quoted in Girvin, 'Economic development and the politics of EC entry', p. 12.
19 Biggar to Sheila Murphy (D/EA official), 30 December 1961, D/T-S16877X/62, NA. Originally quoted in Girvin, 'Economic development and the politics of EC entry', pp. 12-3.
20 Whitaker to Lynch, 5 January 1962, D/T-S16877X/62, NA. Originally quoted in Girvin, 'Economic development and the politics of EC entry', pp. 14-6.
21 Girvin, 'Economic development and the politics of EC entry', pp. 18-9.
22 D/T memorandum on a meeting held on 9 January 1962 between Lemass, Haughey and representatives from various agricultural organisations, 9 January 1962, D/T-S16877Y/62, NA; D/T memorandum on a meeting held on 11 January 1962 between Lemass, Lynch and a delegation from the ICTU, 11 January 1962, D/T-S17120A/62, NA. Originally quoted in Girvin, 'Economic development and the politics of EC entry', pp. 22-5.
23 Lemass speech delivered to the Árd-Fheis (party conference) of Fianna Fáil held on 16 January 1962 in Dublin, 16 January 1962, D/T-S16877Y/62, NA. Originally quoted in Girvin, 'Economic development and the politics of EC entry', pp. 25-7.
24 Maher, *The tortuous path*, p. 145.
25 Report on an article in the *Statist*, 26 January 1962, D/T-S17246A/62, NA; O'Sullivan to Cremin, 29 January 1962, D/T-S17246A/62, NA. Originally quoted in Girvin, 'Economic development and the politics of EC entry', p. 27.
26 Unless otherwise specified, this section – entitled *Second time around* – has been completed using the document: *Treaty establishing the European Economic Community, passim*.
27 Nolan memorandum of a telephone conversation with Whitaker, 10 February 1962, D/T-S17246A/62, NA; Nolan to Lemass, 10 February 1962, D/T-S17246A/62, NA. Originally quoted in Girvin, 'Economic development and the politics of EC entry', pp. 27-8.
28 Lemass speech delivered in Dáil Éireann, 14 February 1962, *Dáil debates* vol. 193 col. 19.

29	Spaak speech reported in the *Irish Independent*, 26 January 1962, D/T-S17246A/62, NA. Originally quoted in Girvin, 'Economic development and the politics of EC entry', p. 28.
30	Lemass interview with the *Economist*, 9 February 1962, D/T-S17246A/62, NA. Originally quoted in Girvin, 'Economic development and the politics of EC entry', p. 28.
31	Aiken speech delivered in Dáil Éireann, 14 February 1962, *Dáil debates* vol. 193 col. 75.
32	Keatinge, *A place among the nations*, p. 76.
33	O'Brien, 'Ireland in international affairs', *passim*.
34	D.Driscoll, 'Is Ireland really "neutral"?', *Irish Studies in International Affairs* vol. 1 no. 3 1982, pp. 55-61.
35	Maher, *The tortuous path*, p. 148.
36	Irish embassy (London) to D/EA secretary, 7 February 1962, D/T-S17246A/62, NA. Originally quoted in Girvin, 'Economic development and the politics of EC entry', pp. 28-9.
37	FitzGerald, *Irish-American diplomatic relations, 1948 to 1963*, pp. 148-66.
38	Irish embassy (Brussels) to D/EA secretary, 19 February 1962, D/T-S17246C/62, NA; Irish embassy (Brussels) to D/EA secretary, 23 February 1962, D/T-S17246C/62, NA. Originally quoted in Girvin, 'Economic development and the politics of EC entry', pp. 29-30.
39	Whitaker to Cremin, 1 March 1962, D/T-S17246D/62, NA. Originally quoted in Girvin, 'Economic development and the politics of EC entry', pp. 30-1.
40	Report of departmental secretaries meeting, 1 March 1962, D/T-S17246D/62, NA. Originally quoted in Girvin, 'Economic development and the politics of EC entry', pp. 30-1.
41	Lemass interview conducted with Radio Telefís Éireann (RTÉ), 15 March 1962, D/T-S17246D/62, NA. Originally quoted in Girvin, 'Economic development and the politics of EC entry', pp. 31-2.
42	Cremin memorandum, 3 April 1962, D/T-S17246F/62, NA. Originally quoted in Girvin, 'Economic development and the politics of EC entry', pp. 32-3 (author's own emphasis).
43	Mally, *Britain and European unity*, pp. 83-91. The latter referred to a speech delivered to the Western European Union (WEU) Council, 10 April 1962, in which the UK Lord Privy Seal added: 'unlike you, we have had to take account of the problems of countries which would be called upon to accept the political and the economic implications of this experiment at one and the same time'.
44	*New York Times*, 18 July 1962. Originally quoted in Maher, *The tortuous path*, p. 152. It is interesting to note that Harold Wilson, the UK Labour party leader and parliamentary opposition at Westminster, had only just said the previous month that he hoped de Gaulle would not look upon Irish neutrality as a block to full EEC membership, that European defence – and as he termed it the 'cold war' – was catered for by NATO. The UK Labour party, which was itself badly split over the future direction of the EEC, was not helping Ireland in its candidacy by raising such issues, even if at the same time it made the Macmillan government distinctly uncomfortable. Wilson speech delivered in the House of Commons, 7 June 1962, entitled 'A no with nuances', pp. 83-99, in U.Kitzinger, *The second try: Labour and the EEC* (Oxford: Pergamon, 1968), p. 98.
45	Salmon, 'Ireland', *passim*; Salmon, *Unneutral Ireland*, p. 239.

46	The term 'active neutrality' refers to Ireland's independent foreign policy that included the initiation of a global non-proliferation treaty, a commitment to peacekeeping, and support for consideration of the position to be played by China in global politics; in many respects, Ireland's views at the UN accorded with positions consistently taken by Sweden. The term 'military neutrality' essentially boiled down to considering how best could the Irish government further the state's improving, though inherently weak, economic performance while not making any unnecessary military alliance or defence commitment – joining NATO or WEU – although being prepared to do so if required. FitzGerald, 'Irish neutrality and European integration', p. 4.
47	T.D.Williams, 'Irish foreign policy, 1949-69', pp. 136-51, in J.J.Lee (ed.), *Ireland, 1945-70* (Dublin: Gill & Macmillan, 1979), *passim*.
48	Girvin, 'Economic development and the politics of EC entry', pp. 28 & 33.
49	Girvin, 'Economic development and the politics of EC entry', pp. 28-9; Maher, *The tortuous path*, p. 148.
50	Thus, an aspect of the statement delivered by Lemass on 18 January 1962 in Brussels which interested the EEC related to Dublin's interpretation of the 'dumping' provision (Article 91); this particular subject is dealt with in detail in a section entitled *Lemass prepares for EEC entry negotiations to begin*.
51	Maher, *The tortuous path*, pp. 146-8.
52	Irish government publication, *European Economic Community* Part II (Dublin: Stationery Office, 1962).
53	Maher, *The tortuous path*, pp. 153-5.
54	Biggar to Murphy, 25 July 1962, D/T-S17246L/62, NA; report on departmental secretaries meeting, 7 September 1962, D/T-S17246N/62, NA. Originally quoted in Girvin, 'Economic development and the politics of EC entry', p. 34.
55	Maher, *The tortuous path*, pp. 155-8.
56	Maher, *The tortuous path*, pp. 155-8.
57	Matthew McCloskey (US ambassador to Ireland) to Kennedy, 14 September 1962, 'National Security Files', Box #118, Kennedy Papers, JFK. Most of this material previously appeared in FitzGerald, *Irish-American diplomatic relations, passim*.
58	Maher, *The tortuous path*, p. 159.
59	Pierson Dixon (UK ambassador, Paris) telegram to the FO, 17 October 1962, M6314/21, FO371/164772, PRO; Dixon to the FO, 19 October 1962, M6314/21, FO371/164772, PRO.
60	J.T.Carroll, 'General de Gaulle and Ireland's EEC application', pp. 81-97, in P.Joannon (ed.), *De Gaulle and Ireland* (Dublin: Institute of Public Administration, 1991), p. 89.
61	M.Vaïsse, 'De Gaulle and the British "application" to join the Common Market', pp. 51-69, in G.Wilkes (ed.), *Britain's failure to enter the European Community, 1961-63: the enlargement negotiations and crises in European, Atlantic and Commonwealth relations* (London: Frank Cass, 1997), *passim*.
62	Lintott note, 23 October 1962, M6314/24, FO371/164772, PRO.
63	Maher, *The tortuous path*, pp. 158-60.
64	Emilio Colombo (EEC Council president) to Lemass, 23 October 1962, D/T-S17339/62, NA. In the original Italian, this document read: 'mi prego comunicarLe che il Consiglio dei Ministri della Comunità Economica Europea ... si è pronunciato sulla domanda del Governo irlandese di aprire negoziati per aderire al Trattato di Roma ... Sono lieto d'informarLa che il Consiglio dei Ministri ha dato all'unanimità il suo accordo a questa domanda di apertura di negoziati'.

Notes 399

65	Lemass to Colombo, 9 November 1962, D/T-S17339/62, NA.
66	Spaak view referred to in O.Rathkolb, 'The Austrian case: from the neutrals' association approach to a "special arrangement" with the EEC (1961-1963)', pp. 1-29, paper presented at the conference entitled *The first attempt to enlarge the European Community, 1961-63*, held from 17-19 February 1994 at the IUE, p. 25.
67	Ray Colegate (EFTA official, Brussels) quoted in R.T.Griffiths & S.Ward, 'United house or abandoned ship? EFTA and the EEC membership crisis, 1961-63', pp. 1-26, paper presented at the conference entitled *The first attempt to enlarge the European Community, 1961-63*, held from 17-19 February 1994 at the IUE, pp. 20-1.
68	Lemass statement reported in the *Irish Press*, 24 October 1962. Originally quoted in P.B.Ellis, *A history of the Irish working class* (London: Pluto, 1985), p. 301.
69	Lemass speech delivered in Dáil Éireann, 30 October 1962, *Dáil debates* vol. 197 cols. 7-8.
70	Lemass speech delivered in Dáil Éireann, 22 November 1962, *Dáil debates* vol. 197 cols. 1688-9.
71	Barclay minute, 19 October 1962, M6314/25, FO371/164772, PRO.
72	Report of departmental secretaries meeting, 13 December 1962, D/T-S17337/62, NA.
73	J.Laursen, 'The great challenge: Denmark and the first attempt to enlarge the European Community, 1961-63', pp. 1-24, paper presented at the conference entitled *The first attempt to enlarge the European Community, 1961-63*, held from 17-19 February 1994 at the IUE, p. 1.
74	These subjects respectively form the basis of the next two sections entitled *Lemass prepares for entry negotiations with the EEC to begin* and *Ireland and the other two European Communities*.
75	Unless otherwise specified, this section – entitled *Lemass prepares for EEC entry negotiations to begin* – has been completed using the following: *Treaty establishing the European Economic Community, passim*; draft brief for negotiations with the EEC, circa December 1962, D/T-S17339/62Annex, NA.
76	T.K.Whitaker, 'An ceangal le sterling: ar cheart é a bhriseadh?', pp. 82-90, in *Annual report: Central Bank of Ireland, 1976*, p. 86. In Irish, it read: 'nuair a bhí muide ag bisiú an tsaol bhí Sasana ag dul ar gcúl'.
77	H.Böll, *Irisches Tagesbuch* (Köln: Verlag Kiepenheuer & Witsch, 1957), pp. 36-8. The author recounts a story where, upon arriving in Westport, County Mayo, without anything except West German marks, his efforts to exchange some of his currency proves to be difficult. The bank manager there told the writer that he would have to send the notes on to Dublin for verification and, eventually, the transaction was conducted successfully in that way. Meanwhile, the author continued his travels in Ireland on credit. It is interesting to note that tourism was quickly recognised in Ireland as an important sectoral employer, as well as a foreign currency earner, and that such accounts soon became things of the past. Lemass, the new industry & commerce minister, remarked upon the potential that tourism held soon after returning to office in 1957, noting that this type of trade was expected to grow at the rate of 10% *per annum* within Europe, in addition to increased transatlantic trade. In turn, the foreign minister was able to report that over the next six years, Ireland's total income from tourism increased by IR£21 million, that is by 63%, and was very happy to add that 'tourism is becoming a rapidly increasing element in our external earnings'. Lemass speaking in Seanad

Éireann, 11 December 1957, *Seanad debates* vol. 48 cols. 1152-3; Aiken speaking in Seanad Éireann, 18 November 1964, *Seanad debates* vol. 58 col. 45.

As Richard Vaughan subsequently wrote: 'In 1970, in Ireland, tourism was the largest single export and the greatest national industry, providing 15 per cent of employment and an income of £101 million'; it should be noted that Sean Barrett, a lecturer in economics at University College, Dublin, has noted that: 'Tourism into the Republic did not grow at all between 1966 and 1986'. However, in the period under review, there is no doubt but that tourism became both a very important source of employment and income, even if its full potential was not realised for another two decades. S.Barrett, 'Time to reap the benefits from open skies', *Irish Times*, 8 January 1999; Vaughan, *Twentieth-century Europe*, pp. 194-5.

78 Especially when looked at in retrospect, the figures do not mask the reality. Towards the end of 1964, Aiken tried his best to dress up the improvements in Irish export figures, but failed to hide the truth of the situation. He said:

> In 1963 alone, our exports to every single country of the EEC increased and the over-all increase for the Common Market area was 40 per cent in value terms as compared with 1962. To the EFTA area, including Great Britain, our exports increased from £125 million to £140 million, an increase of 12 per cent in the same period. The same level of expansion, namely 12 per cent, is apparent in our export trade to the dollar area for 1963 as against 1962.

No matter how hard he tried to cover up the fact, the UK remained the first among unequals. Aiken speaking in Seanad Éireann, 18 November 1964, *Seanad debates* vol. 58 cols. 44-5.

79 The fears that Dublin held regarding dumping are easily explained, but one of the few effective tools that it previously had at its disposal was the right to introduce a customs duty. As the taoiseach had himself said on more than one occasion, duties such as these were 'increased and extended to protect the output of the Irish manufacturers against imports from the Continent which appeared to be of the character of dumping'. In accepting the Treaty of Rome, Ireland would have to operate by different rules that might not offer such security. Lemass speaking in Seanad Éireann, 27 March 1958, *Seanad debates* vol. 49 col. 328.

80 In the light of subsequent developments, this opinion is particularly interesting, especially in relation to Article 119. After its economic effects, it is arguable that the area in which Ireland has been affected most by European integration has been social policy, particularly with regard to the concept of men and women being treated equally, expressly with regard to equal pay for equal work, before the law. It is worth noting that Ireland's civil service bar on married women was revoked during the 1960s, but that societal attitudes were fairly slow to change; it should be mentioned that, of all the civil servants who dealt with the first application for full EEC membership, the only Irish government department that was headed by a woman was the newly formed Department of Transport & Power (D/T&P).

81 Lemass to Nolan, 25 September 1962, D/T-S17389/62, NA; Lemass speech delivered in Dáil Éireann, 13 December 1962, *Dáil debates* vol. 198 col. 1477, D/T-S17389/62, NA.

82 *Irish Independent*, 14 December 1962, D/T-S17389/62, NA.

83 Lemass to Nolan, 12 December 1962, D/T-S17389/62, NA; *Irish Independent*, 14 December 1962, D/T-S17389/62, NA; Cremin to Whitaker, 18 December 1962, D/T-S17389/62, NA; report of departmental secretaries meeting, 10 January 1963, D/T-S17337/63, NA.

84	Lemass speech delivered to the Cork Chamber of Commerce, 15 November 1962, D/T-S17389/62Annex, NA.
85	Lemass speech delivered to the Fianna Fáil Árd-Fheis in Dublin, 20 November 1962, D/T-S17389/62, NA.
86	Lee, 'Staying in the game?', p. 124.
87	Lemass speech delivered at the opening of a new factory in Ennis, County Clare, 3 December 1962, D/T-S17389/62, NA.
88	European Communities is a generic term for the three organisations that operated collectively at the forefront of European integration, that is the ECSC, the EEC and Euratom. However, as this particular section makes it perfectly clear, the Irish government was only really interested in membership of one of these.
89	Keatinge, *The formulation of Irish foreign policy*, p. 307.
90	Lemass speech delivered in Brussels on 18 January 1962 quoted in D/F memorandum on Euratom, *circa* December 1962, D/T-S17337/62, NA.
91	D/F memorandum on Euratom, *circa* December 1962, D/T-S17337/62, NA.
92	Interdepartmental Committee report on Ireland's membership of the ECSC, *circa* December 1962, D/T-S17170/62, NA.
93	Francis Biggar (ambassador to Belgium, minister to Luxembourg and chef de mission to the EEC) to Cremin, 8 November 1962, D/T-S17337/62, NA. It was Arthur Tandy, the UK chef de mission to the EEC, who had telephoned Biggar.
94	Lemass to Nolan, 13 November 1962, D/T-S17170/62, NA; Nolan to Whitaker, 13 November 1962, D/T-S17337/62, NA.
95	Heath speech to the ministers of the ECSC member states, 17 July 1962, D/T-S17170/62, NA; Biggar to Cremin, 8 November 1962, D/T-S17337/62, NA.
96	Whitaker to Nolan, 14 November 1962, D/T-S17337/62, NA.
97	Keatinge, *The formulation of Irish foreign policy*, p. 31.
98	Greenwood (ed.), *Britain and European integration since the Second World War*, pp. 70-1; Mally, *Britain and European unity*, p. 39. The latter refers to the association agreement signed between the ECSC and the UK in London on 21 December 1954.
99	Keogh, *Twentieth-century Ireland*, p. 229.
100	Cremin's view as stated in the report from the departmental secretaries meeting, 13 December 1962, D/T-S17337/62, NA.
101	Lemass to Nolan, 19 October 1961, D/T-S17170/61, NA.
102	Lemass to Lynch, 1 November 1961, D/T-S17170/61, NA.
103	Interdepartmental Committee report on Ireland's membership of the ECSC, *circa* December 1962, D/T-S17170/62, NA; D/F note on the Irish coal and steel industries, early January 1963, D/T-S17170/63, NA.
104	'Irlande/Relation/Pays tiers/CECA', *1961* CEAB 5/953 1-3, ACE; 'Irlande/Relation/Pays tiers/CECA', *1961* CEAB 5/954 1-35, ACE (author's emphasis). In the original French, the document read: Dans le case de l'IRLANDE, la Commission s'est abstenue de préciser les demandes de concessions étant donné qu'il ne s'agit que de pourparlers préalables en vue d'une adhésion de l'IRLANDE au GATT. La CECA ferait donc bien de renoncer, elle aussi, à une précision de ses demandes présentées dans la liste commune.
105	D/F note on the Irish coal and steel industries, early January 1963, D/T-S17170/63, NA.

106 Interdepartmental Committee report on Ireland's membership of the ECSC, *circa* December 1962, D/T-S17170/62, NA; D/F note on the Irish coal and steel industries, early January 1963, D/T-S17170/63, NA.
107 Interdepartmental Committee report on Ireland's membership of the ECSC, *circa* December 1962, D/T-S17170/62, NA; D/F note on the Irish coal and steel industries, early January 1963, D/T-S17170/63, NA; Government Information Bureau press release, 14 January 1963, D/T-S17170/63, NA.
108 Seán Murray (D/F assistant secretary) to J.Connor (D/T&P assistant secretary), 19 December 1962, D/T-S17170/62, NA; report of departmental secretaries meeting, 13 December 1962, D/T-S17337/62, NA.
109 Whitaker memorandum on the implications of Euratom membership for Ireland, *circa* September 1962, D/T-S17337/62, NA; T.J.Beere (D/T&P secretary) to Whitaker, 23 November 1962, D/T-S17337/62, NA; D/F memorandum on Euratom, *circa* December 1962, D/T-S17337/62, NA.
110 Whitaker memorandum on the implications of Euratom membership for Ireland, *circa* September 1962, D/T-S17337/62, NA; D/F memorandum on Euratom, *circa* December 1962, D/T-S17337/62, NA.
111 MacCarthy to Murray, 19 September 1962, D/T-S17337/62, NA.
112 Nagle to Murray, 20 September 1962, D/T-S17337/62, NA; D/F memorandum on Euratom, *circa* December 1962, D/T-S17337/62, NA.
113 Beere to Whitaker, 23 November 1962, D/T-S17337/62, NA.
114 D/EA memorandum, 17 November 1962, D/T-S17337/62, NA; Irish cabinet minutes, 23 November 1962, CAB2/22, NA; Nolan to Cremin, 23 November 1962, D/T-S17337/62, NA; Carroll, 'General de Gaulle and Ireland's EEC application', p. 90.
115 Report of departmental secretaries meeting, 13 December 1962, D/T-S17337/62, NA.
116 Report of departmental secretaries meeting, 10 January 1963, D/T-S17337/63, NA.
117 Cremin to Whitaker, 15 December 1962, D/T-S17337/62, NA.
118 Note of telephone conversation between the D/EA and Biggar, 20 December 1962, D/T-S17170/62, NA; Whitaker to MacCarthy, 2 January 1963, D/T-S17170/63, NA.
119 Murray to Beere, 21 December 1962, D/T-S17170/62, NA.
120 Biggar to Cremin, 22 January 1963, D/T-S17170/63, NA.
121 Article 98 of the *Treaty establishing the European Coal and Steel Community* in *Treaties establishing the European Communities* (Luxembourg: Office for Official Publications of the European Communities, 1973), p. 99.
122 Lemass to J.W.de Pous (ECSC Council president), 7 January 1963, D/T-S17170/63, NA.
123 E.Rumpf & A.C.Hepburn, *Nationalism and socialism in twentieth-century Ireland* (Liverpool: Liverpool University Press, 1977), p. 118; C.Bellò, *L'onesta democrazia di Piero Malvestiti: memorie e documenti* (Milan: Nuove Edizioni Duomo, 1985), p. 259; Biggar to Cremin, 22 January 1963, D/T-S17170/63, NA.
124 J.P.Slavin (embassy official, London) to Sheila Murphy (D/EA assistant secretary), 29 January 1963, D/T-S17170/63, NA. The senior official in question was J.R.A.Bottomley, assistant secretary at the CRO.
125 Slavin to Murphy, 31 January 1963, D/T-S17170/63, NA.
126 Lemass to Carroll, 4 February 1963, D/T-S17170/63, NA.
127 D/F note on the Irish coal and steel industries, early January 1963, D/T-S17170/63, NA.
128 Cremin to Whitaker, 15 December 1962, D/T-S17337/62, NA.

129 Whitaker to Cremin, 20 December 1962, D/T-S17337/62, NA.
130 Article 205 of the *Treaty establishing the European Atomic Energy Community* in *Treaties establishing the European Communities* (Luxembourg: Office for Official Publications of the European Communities, 1983), p. 624.
131 Biggar telephone call to D/EA, 28 February 1963, D/T-S17337/63, NA; Biggar to D/EA, 28 March 1963, D/T-S17337/63, NA.
132 Biggar to Cremin, 3 April 1963, D/T-S17337/63, NA.
133 D/F note on the Irish coal and steel industries, early January 1963, D/T-S17170/63, NA.
134 Whitaker to O'Carroll, 4 February 1963, D/T-S17170/63, NA.
135 D/F memorandum on Euratom, *circa* December 1962, D/T-S17337/62, NA; Biggar to Cremin, 3 April 1963, D/T-S17337/63, NA.
136 C.de Gaulle, 'Conférence de press tenue au Palais de l'Élysée', 14 January 1963, in *Discours et messages: pour l'effort, août 1962-décembre 1965* (Paris: Librairie Pion, 1970), pp. 61-79; D.J.Maher, *The tortuous path*, p. 161. In the original French, de Gaulle declared:

L'Angleterre ... est insulaire, maritime, liée par ses échanges, ses marchés, son ravitaillement, aux pays les plus divers et souvent les plus lointains. Elle exerce une activité essentiellement industrielle et commerciale et très peu agricole. Elle a, dans tout son travail, des habitudes et des traditions très marquées, très originales. Bref, la nature, la structure, la conjecture, qui sont propres à l'Angleterre, différent profondément de celles des Continentaux.

In addition, the French president had also been moved to ask whether the UK government was prepared to accept what he termed:

... un tarif qui soit véritablement commun, de renoncer à toute préférence à l'égard du Commonwealth, de cesser de prétendre que son agriculture soit privilégiée et encore de tenir pour caducs les engagements qu'elle a pris avec les pays qui font partie de sa zone de libre-échange.

137 Report of departmental secretaries meeting, 10 January 1963, D/T-S17337/63, NA.
138 W.Kaiser, 'To join, or not to join: the "appeasement" policy of Britain's first EEC application', pp. 144-56, in B.Brivati & H.Jones (eds), *From reconstruction to integration: Britain and Europe since 1945* (Leicester: Leicester University Press, 1993), p. 148.
139 P.Gerbet, 'French attitudes to the foreign policy and defence of Europe', pp. 150-9, in F.-G.Dreyfus *et al* (eds), *France and EEC membership evaluated* (London: Pinter, 1993), pp. 150-2.
140 Kaiser, 'To join, or not to join', p. 151.
141 Carroll, 'General de Gaulle and Ireland's EEC application', pp. 82 & 96.
142 CRO note, 31 January 1963, M10811/5, FO371/171401, PRO.
143 French agriculture minister in conversation with Christopher Soames in January 1963, quoted in Arter, *The politics of European integration in the twentieth century*, p. 145 (not my emphasis). Originally cited in Macmillan, *At the end of the day*, p. 365. In the original French, this statement read: 'C'est très simple. Maintenant, avec les six, il y a cinq poules et un coq. Si vous joignez (avec des autres pays), il y aura peut-être sept ou huit poules. Mais, il y aura *deux* coqs'. Brown, *In my way*, p. 220.
144 R.T.Griffiths speaking at the conference entitled *EFTA at its creation* held at the University of Oslo from 14-15 May 1992.
145 Lemass speech delivered on 16 January 1963 at the opening of the new Potez Industries of Ireland, Ltd., plant in Galway, GIS1/217, NA.

146	Lemass speech delivered on 16 January 1963 at the opening of the new Potez Industries of Ireland, Ltd., plant in Galway, GIS1/217, NA.
147	Lemass speech delivered to a Fianna Fáil party Comhairle Dáil-Cheantair (constituency committee) in Dublin, 24 January 1963, GIS1/217, NA.
148	Carroll, 'General de Gaulle and Ireland's EEC application', p. 90.
149	Lemass speech delivered at the Catholic Workers' College in Dublin, 29 January 1963, GIS1/217, NA.
150	Lemass speech delivered at the Catholic Workers' College in Dublin, 29 January 1963, GIS1/217, NA.
151	T.K.Whitaker, 'From protection to free trade: the Irish experience', pp. 405-23, in *Administration* vol. 21 no. 4 1973, *passim*.
152	Lemass speech delivered in Dáil Éireann, 5 February 1963, *Dáil debates* vol. 199 cols. 932-8.
153	Lemass speech delivered in Dáil Éireann, 5 February 1963, *Dáil debates* vol. 199 cols. 939-40. Originally quoted in Bew & Patterson, *Seán Lemass*, pp. 141-2 & 174.
154	Arter, *The politics of European integration in the twentieth century*, p. 153.
155	Mally, *Britain and European unity*, pp. 101-36. The latter quoted from statements delivered by the Belgian, German, Luxembourg, Dutch and UK foreign ministers, as well as the Italian industry minister, in Brussels, 29 January 1963, and from a speech delivered by Hallstein on 5 February 1963 to the European Parliament in Strasbourg.
156	CRO memorandum, 31 January 1963, M10811/5, FO371/171401, PRO; M.E.MacGlashan note, early February 1963, M10811/5, FO371/171401, PRO; F.G.K.Gallagher minute, 1 February 1963, M10811/5, FO371/171401, PRO; Gallagher minute, 4 February 1963, M10811/5, FO371/171401, PRO.
157	CRO memorandum, 31 January 1963, M10811/5, FO371/171401, PRO; MacGlashan note, early February 1963, M10811/5, FO371/171401, PRO; Gallagher minute, 1 February 1963, M10811/5, FO371/171401, PRO; Gallagher minute, 4 February 1963, M10811/5, FO371/171401, PRO.
158	Maher, *The tortuous path*, pp. 166-9 & 185-91.
159	Maher, *The tortuous path*, pp. 166-9 & 185-91.
160	K.Young, *Sir Alec Douglas-Home* (London: J.M.Dent, 1970), p. 152.
161	Maher, *The tortuous path*, pp. 166-9 & 185-91.
162	Lemass reply to a question in Dáil Éireann, 10 June 1965, *Dáil debates* vol. 216 col. 722; Lemass reply to a question in Dáil Éireann, 3 March 1966, *Dáil debates* vol. 221 col. 922.
163	Moore *et al*, 'Industrial policy and economic development', p. 110.
164	Lyons, *Ireland since the Famine*, p. 630.
165	P.J.Hillery (former president and foreign minister) lecture (paper unavailable) entitled 'Ireland's accession to the European Community' presented on 5 March 1998 at the IUE; Whitaker, 'From protection to free trade', pp. 422-3. The latter was originally quoted in Baxter-Moore, 'The impact', pp. 45 & 71.
166	T.K.Whitaker speaking at the conference entitled *The first attempt to enlarge the European Community, 1961-63* held from 17-19 February 1994 at the IUE.
167	M.Freedman, 'Irish neutrality doesn't forsake the rule of law', *Chicago Daily News*, 16 May 1964, D/FA-96/40 Washington (formerly P150/1), NA.
168	Obviously, this particular text is not the place to go into questions such as the complexities of evolving social policy; still, Peter Sutherland has pointed out a couple of important developments regarding the 'doctrines of the supremacy of Community Law and Direct Effect' that deserve a mention, issues which apparently attracted little enough attention in Ireland. Indeed, he added: 'The former of these is

Chapter 5

1. Lemass interview conducted with the *Cork Examiner*, 29 July 1965, 'European Economic Community, 23.6.1965-15.10.1965' D/T-S17427S, NA.
2. Williams, 'Irish foreign policy, 1949-69', pp. 144 & 146. It is the opinion of T.D.Williams that 'political collaboration' was a more important result of the Anglo-Irish Free Trade Area agreement (AIFTA), and other developments in Anglo-Irish relations, than economic cooperation; however, he freely acknowledges that Lemass himself was 'more concerned with issues such as economic growth and development', thus diverging from the more traditional Fianna Fáil views held by the likes of de Valera and Aiken.
3. Maher, *The tortuous path*, pp. 167-8.
4. F.Nicholson & R.East, *From the Six to the Twelve: the enlargement of the European Communities* (Harlow: Longman, 1987), p. 84. This text referred to an official Franco-Irish joint communiqué dating from 13 June 1964. Evidence which backs up this opinion regarding the enduring good nature of Franco-Irish economic ties, as well as other links with Europe, are as many as they are varied. Perhaps the fact that it was remarked upon in the writings of authors such as Brendan Behan is proof enough of their positive impact; indeed, in the mid-1950s – possibly in relation to the Italian investors referred to in the section in this chapter entitled *The taoiseach's visit to Rome for the papal consistory* – he wrote that 'the motor assembly people should be as welcome as the flowers of May; they bring Continental technique and a width of ideas as wide as Europe to our shores'. However, flowers wither not long after they bloom; the car assembly industry was one of the manufacturing enterprises which was expected to suffer the most from the onset of free trading conditions. B.Behan, 'On the road to Kilkenny', pp. 155-8, in B.Behan, *Hold your hour and have another* (Aylesbury: Corgi, 1970), p. 155. This article was originally written for the *Irish Press* sometime between 1954 and 1956.
5. Nicholson & East, *From the Six*, pp. 84-5; Franco-Irish joint communiqué, 13 June 1964. The former text made reference to an official French cabinet communiqué from 17 June 1964, and also made reference to an official Franco-Irish statement which dated from *circa* 9 July 1964. Again, Brendan Behan recounts some of his own experiences in this regard, especially on the subject of his travels on the 'Continong' in the 1950s. B.Behan, 'I'm back from the "Continong"', pp. 122-5, in Behan, *Hold your hour*, p. 122.
6. Nicholson & East, *From the Six*, pp. 84-5; official Franco-Irish joint communiqué, 13 June 1964. Other than economic relations, the other main references were made in regard to their historical ties and close cultural links. In relation to the former, Aiken and de Murville noted 'with satisfaction that no difficulties exist in Franco-Irish relations, which are characterized by a friendship deeply rooted in history and by a mutual and profound sympathy between the two peoples'; regarding the latter,

strong reference was made to a future cultural agreement that was going to be negotiated, which would include:
- developing a programme for more cultural interchange;
- increasing the number of exchange programmes and scholarships;
- encouraging the teaching of French in Irish schools.

7   Aiken speaking in Seanad Éireann, 18 November 1964, *Seanad debates* vol. 58 cols. 41-2 & 45. The foreign minister added his view that:
> Our missions are directly concerned with a wide range of commercial problems involving Governments abroad. These arise principally in connection with the negotiation and operation of trade agreements and other similar arrangements and involve frequent representations to Governments in regard to the modification of official import restrictions. Our missions are called upon to deal with a sizeable volume of inquiries from State-sponsored organisations and from private trade, and to arrange contacts in the commercial and foreign earnings fields for visiting Irish interests. In addition, the missions have to keep in touch with market developments generally in the countries of their accreditation and to explore market opportunities of interest to Ireland. Our missions are as a matter of course required to report on the economic policies of the Governments to which they are accredited and on reactions in their countries of accreditation to developments in the main international economic organisations whose activities are of particular interest to our own economy. It will, I am sure, be appreciated that the duties I have outlined represent a heavy and varied volume of responsibility, especially in view of the size of missions and the other demands on the time of the staff.

8   D/F publication of 'Monthly digest of E.E.C. developments and related matters, December, 1964', *circa* late January 1965, 'European Economic Community, 1.1.1965-30.4.1965' D/T-S17427Q, NA.
9   Lemass speech delivered in Dáil Éireann, 11 November 1964, *Dáil debates* vol. 212 col. 667, D/T-S17427Q, NA.
10 Lemass speech to the NFA in Dublin, 6 January 1965, D/T-S17427Q, NA.
11 Lemass speech to the NFA in Dublin, 6 January 1965, D/T-S17427Q, NA.
12 Maher, *The tortuous path*, p. 178.
13 Maher, *The tortuous path*, p. 178.
14 Lemass speech to the NFA in Dublin, 6 January 1965, D/T-S17427Q, NA.
15 Charles Haughey took over as Irish agriculture minister from Paddy Smith when the latter resigned alleging that the taoiseach was sacrificing rural interests for urban advancement.
16 *Irish Press*, 27 January 1965, D/T-S17427Q, NA; Gallagher, 'Electoral support', p. 27.
17 Irish embassy (Brussels) report of a meeting held on 26 January 1965 between Haughey and Jean Rey (Executive Commissioner for Foreign Relations at the EEC), 26 January 1965, D/T-S17427Q, NA.
18 Irish embassy (Brussels) report on the meeting held between Haughey and Rey, 26 January 1965, D/T-S17427Q, NA.
19 Irish embassy (Brussels) report on the meeting held between Haughey and Rey, 26 January 1965, D/T-S17427Q, NA. The EEC Commission official in question was Robert Touleman, Head of Section concerned with relations between the Community and third countries. In fact, as a result of the arguments regarding its candidacy, it was ascertained that the 'Austrians could never be full members of the

Notes 407

Community', more for political reasons obviously than for anything else. Ireland was still conscious of not falling into the same trap as before because of its military neutrality, but mostly as a result of its economic retardation.

20 Irish embassy (Brussels) report on the meeting held between Haughey and Rey, 26 January 1965, D/T-S17427Q, NA.
21 Irish embassy (Brussels) report on the meeting held between Haughey and Rey, 26 January 1965, D/T-S17427Q, NA; D/F publication of 'Monthly digest of E.E.C. developments and related matters, February, 1965', circa late March 1965, D/T-S17427Q, NA.
22 Irish embassy (Brussels) report of a meeting held on 27 January 1965 between Haughey and Sicco Mansholt (Vice President of the Commission of the EEC and Executive Commissioner for Agriculture at the EEC), 27 January 1965, D/T-S17427Q, NA; D/T report entitled 'Possibility of interim arrangement with the EEC and Britain', 24 March 1965, D/T-S17427Q, NA. It was later said of Mansholt's proposition that:

> His speculation in this regard was in the direction of quantitative access arrangements between Britain and a Community of which Ireland was a member. Britain ... might be willing to accord such an enlarged Community quantitative access on a scale equal to that enjoyed in Britain by Ireland. This access might not necessarily be reserved for Ireland. In return the Community would give a reciprocal tariff quota arrangement to Britain.

23 Irish embassy (Brussels) report on the meeting held between Haughey and Mansholt, 27 January 1965, D/T-S17427Q, NA; D/T report entitled 'Possibility of interim arrangement with the EEC and Britain', 24 March 1965, D/T-S17427Q, NA.
24 Irish embassy (Brussels) report on the meeting held between Haughey and Mansholt, 27 January 1965, D/T-S17427Q, NA.
25 *Irish Press*, 28 January 1965, D/T-S17427Q, NA. The official in question was Rolf Lahr, the West German secretary of state for foreign affairs.
26 Note on a meeting held on 31 January 1965 between Haughey and Schwarz (FRG agriculture, forestry & food minister) in Berlin, 31 January 1965, D/T-S17427Q, NA.
27 *Irish Press*, 3 February 1965, D/T-S17427Q, NA.
28 *Irish Independent*, 4 February 1965, D/T-S17427Q, NA.
29 Lemass speech delivered in Dáil Éireann, 11 November 1964, *Dáil debates* vol. 212 col. 667, D/T-S17427Q, NA; *Irish Independent*, 28 January 1965, D/T-S17427Q, NA; *Irish Press*, 28 January 1965, D/T-S17427Q, NA; *Irish Times*, 28 January 1965, D/T-S17427Q, NA; Lemass memorandum, 1 February 1965, D/T-S17427Q, NA; Eamonn Kennedy (ambassador, Bonn) to D/EA secretary, 5 February 1965, D/T-S17427Q, NA.
30 Haughey speech delivered in Dáil Éireann, 11 February 1965, *Dáil debates* vol. 214 cols. 343-4, D/T-S17427Q, NA.
31 Lemass speech delivered to the Chamber of Commerce in Cork, 4 February 1965, D/T-S17427Q, NA.
32 Lemass speech delivered to the Chamber of Commerce in Cork, 4 February 1965, D/T-S17427Q, NA.
33 J.W.Lennon (ambassador, The Hague) to D/EA secretary, 10 February 1965, D/T-S17427Q, NA; Lennon to D/EA secretary, 23 February 1965, D/T-S17427Q, NA; Lennon to D/EA secretary, 3 March 1965, D/T-S17427Q, NA; Lennon to D/EA secretary, 15 March 1965, D/T-S17427Q, NA.

34   Lemass speech delivered to the Chamber of Commerce in Cork, 4 February 1965, D/T-S17427Q, NA.
35   McCann to Whitaker, 12 February 1965, D/T-S17427Q, NA; McCann note, 12 February 1965, D/T-S17427Q, NA.
36   This section, entitled *The taoiseach's visit to Rome for the papal consistory*, makes fairly liberal use of Dermot Keogh's *Ireland and the Vatican*, although all specific references are noted. D.Keogh, *Ireland and the Vatican: the politics and diplomacy of church-state relations, 1922-1960* (Cork: Cork University Press, 1995), *passim*.
37   Keogh, *Ireland and the Vatican*, pp. 318-20. By way of illustration, many episodes might be chosen. Rather than repeating those that have already been published, however, it is more profitable to concentrate on a couple of less well-known, although interlinked, events. Firstly, there was the Irish president's trip to Italy in 1950 and, secondly, a later president's inability and reluctance to do the same. The first official trip by an Irish head of state to Italy came in May 1950, when Seán T.O'Kelly paid a visit to the post-war republic. Ostensibly, he went to Rome for a papal audience – soon after causing considerable controversy because of his indiscretion in revealing its contents – and then to Bobbio – in order to commemorate the fourteenth centenary of Saint Columbanus' founding of a basilica there. To enthusiastic greetings from the inhabitants, he noted that it was a great privilege for him to be in Bobbio to venerate an Irish and Italian saint; he addressed his audience in Italian, saying: 'È un gran privilegio per me come capo dello stato d'Irlanda di venire qui per venerare ... nostro santo, adesso vostro santo'. He also used the occasion of his trip to remark that Italy was a progressive and prosperous nation, with a population possessing many qualities, who he encouraged to strive to maintain peace. In Italian, his rather presumptuous and pretentious, never mind to say offensive and patronising, speech read:
> L'Italia ... mi è sembrata un paese molto progredito e prospero. Dovunque una popol-azione molto intensa, sana gente, intelligente, colta, educata: uomini e donne; molti figli; in genere ben vestiti e ben nutriti; le quali cose vogliono indicare un futuro prosperoso per il vostro popolo, che spero lo raggiunga e mantenga, nella pace, per molti anni.

Whatever the Italians made of O'Kelly, his successor was invited back in August 1965 on the occasion of the 27th bi-centenary of the death of Saint Columbanus. De Valera declined the invitation, noting that Joseph Shields, the ambassador to Italy, would be there; he regretted not being able to be present, saying that he had 'most happy memories of my former visit'. It is not that so much should be read into the Irish president declining this particular invitation though, just that the Irish view of Italy was for so long coloured by religion alone that Lemass's visit in early 1965 seems to have been all the more incongruous. Seán T.O'Kelly (Irish president) speech delivered in Bobbio (Italy), *circa* 13 May 1950, quoted in *Liberta*, 14 May 1950, 'Bobbio' 98/1/40 (formerly D/UhÉ-P4510), NA; Monsignor Pietro Zuccarino (Bishop of Bobbio) to de Valera, 1 August 1965, 98/1/40, NA; de Valera to Zuccarino, 26 August 1965, 98/1/40, NA.

38   Article 44.1.2°, *Bunreacht na hÉireann*, quoted in Kelly, *Irish constitution*, p. 537. This article of Bunreacht na hÉireann granted the Catholic Church its 'special position' in Irish society; it read:
> The State recognises the special position of the Holy Catholic Apostolic and Roman Church as the guardian of the Faith professed by the great majority of the citizens.

This clause was subsequently revoked in the early 1970s by an overwhelming

	majority in what was the fifth amendment to the Irish constitution; that referendum also deleted a further clause which recognised the other churches operating in Ireland, leaving the constitution to profess the freedom of religious conscience and practice enshrined in law on a general basis.
39	Whyte, *Church and state*, pp. 331 & 362-3. It is quite obvious that the Holy See was a particularly important posting in diplomatic terms considering the calibre of its office holders, who included Thomas J.Kiernan (who would serve as the ambassador to the US), Joseph P.Walshe (who had served as external affairs secretary), and Con C.Cremin (who would go on to serve in that position). In later years, it does not appear as if the Vatican continued to have such import. Moynihan to the D/UhÉ secretary, 11 November 1958, 'Holy See: Appt. of Irish Rep. ' 98/1/54 (formerly D/UhÉ-U5111), NA.
40	*Irish Press*, 1 March 1965, D/T-S17427Q, NA.
41	McCann to Thomas V.Commins (ambassador, Holy See), 10 February 1965, 'Visit to Rome of Taoiseach, Public Consistory, Vatican, 25 February 1965', D/FA-96/2/13 (formerly D/FA-P387), NA.
42	*Irish Press*, 1 March 1965, D/T-S17427Q, NA.
43	'Audience with Holy Father of Taoiseach on occasion of Public Consistory, 27 February 1965', D/FA-96/2/14 (formerly D/FA-P387/1), NA.
44	Irish ambassador (Holy See) to D/EA secretary, 11 March 1955, 'European Unity', D/FA-96/14/19 (formerly D/FA-14/89 Vatican), NA; Keogh, *Ireland and the Vatican, passim*.
45	Irish ambassador (Holy See) to D/EA secretary, 21 January 1955, D/FA-96/14/19, NA; Irish ambassador (Holy See) to D/EA secretary, 8 March 1955, D/FA-96/14/19, NA.
46	Irish ambassador (Holy See) to D/EA secretary, 3 August 1962, D/FA-96/14/19, NA.
47	Nicholas Nolan (D/T secretary) to McCann, 15 February 1965, D/FA-96/2/13, NA.
48	C.Richards, *The new Italians* (London: Penguin, 1995), p. 5.
49	D/FA report entitled 'Trade and Commercial Relations with Italy' prepared for the Lemass visit to Rome, *circa* mid-February 1965, D/FA-96/2/13, NA.
50	D/FA report, *circa* mid-February 1965, D/FA-96/2/13, NA.
51	D/FA report, *circa* mid-February 1965, D/FA-96/2/13, NA.
52	D/FA report entitled 'Italian Plan for European Political Union' prepared for the Lemass visit to Rome, *circa* mid-February 1965, D/FA-96/2/13, NA; D/FA report entitled 'Analysis of Italian Plan for European Political Union' prepared for the Lemass visit to Rome, *circa* mid-February 1965, D/FA-96/2/13, NA.
53	Michael Flynn (Irish embassy first secretary, Rome) note, 28 February 1965, D/FA-96/2/13, NA; D/F publication of 'Monthly digest of E.E.C. developments and related matters, March, 1965', *circa* late April 1965, D/T-S17427Q, NA.
54	Flynn note, 1 March 1965, D/FA-96/2/13, NA.
55	D/T report, 24 March 1965, D/T-S17427Q, NA; D/EA appendix entitled 'Alternative arrangement suggested by the Department of External Affairs', 24 March 1965, D/T-S17427Q, NA; Seán F.Murray (D/F official) to Nolan, 24 March 1965, D/T-S17427Q, NA. Murray wrote to say that the report was agreed upon by the departmental secretaries.
56	Irish embassy (Brussels) report on the meeting held between Haughey and Mansholt, 27 January 1965, D/T-S17427Q, NA.
57	D/T report, 24 March 1965, D/T-S17427Q, NA.
58	D/T report, 24 March 1965, D/T-S17427Q, NA.

59   Irish embassy (Brussels) report on the meeting held between Haughey and Mansholt, 27 January 1965, D/T-S17427Q, NA; D/T report, 24 March 1965, D/T-S17427Q, NA.
60   D/T report, 24 March 1965, D/T-S17427Q, NA; D/EA appendix, 24 March 1965, D/T-S17427Q, NA.
61   D/F memorandum on 'European Political Integration', *circa* mid-April 1965, D/T-S17427Q, NA; D.J.Maher (D/F official) to D.O'Sullivan (D/EA assistant secretary), 21 April 1965, D/T-S17427Q, NA. Quoted in the report 'European Political Integration', Lemass's speech was delivered to the Fianna Fáil Árd Fheis (annual party conference) on 16 January 1962. Some other notable elements were presented in this document which are worth mentioning in passing. Obviously enough, however, there was nothing new. In the section of the report which dealt with the various efforts that were made to develop the idea of European integration, even before the decision was taken to establish the EEC, little new insight or indeed information was put forward which was not already publicly available. In fact, the same might be said of the part dealing with the establishment of the EEC and the subsequent moves taken in the following five years towards achieving the goal of political integration. Indeed, this also applied to the sections centred on renewed efforts that were subsequently made in 1964 towards this end, as well as to some additional special aspects of European integration. On levels such as these, this Department of Finance presentation did not have very much to offer except as a recapitulation of how Ireland viewed the European political integration process.
62   D/F memorandum on 'European Political Integration', *circa* mid-April 1965, D/T-S17427Q, NA; Maher to O'Sullivan, 21 April 1965, D/T-S17427Q, NA.
63   D/F publication of 'Monthly digest of E.E.C. developments and related matters, March, 1965', *circa* late April 1965, D/T-S17427Q, NA.
64   Lemass speech, 6 January 1965, D/T-S17427Q, NA; D/F publication of 'Monthly digest of E.E.C. developments and related matters, February, 1965', *circa* late March 1965, D/T-S17427Q, NA; Maher, *The tortuous path*, pp. 178-81.
65   Biggar to D/EA secretary, 7 April 1965, D/T-S17427Q, NA. The official in question here was Mr.Boegner (French permanent representative to the EEC).
66   Irish government cabinet minute GC11/1, 27 April 1965, 'Eleventh Government Cabinet Minutes GC11/1-GC11/83 27/4/65-4/8/66' 97/5/1, NA; Nolan to Whitaker, 27 April 1965, D/T-S17427Q, NA.
67   Unpublished Lemass interview, 25 March 1965, D/T-S17427Q, NA.
68   Lemass interview conducted with the *Irish Independent*, 23 April 1965, D/T-S17427Q, NA; Lemass interview conducted with the *Irish Independent*, 24 April 1965, D/T-S17427Q, NA.
69   Haughey speech delivered in Dáil Éireann, 29 April 1965, *Dáil debates* vol. 215 cols. 442-3, D/T-S17427Q, NA.
70   Lemass note, 3 May 1965, 'European Economic Community, 1.5.1965-22.6.1965' D/T-S17427R/65, NA.
71   Lemass reply to a parliamentary question in Dáil Éireann, 4 May 1965, *Dáil debates* vol. 215 col. 269, D/T-S17427R, NA.
72   J.G.Molloy (ambassador, London) to D/EA secretary, 4 May 1965, D/T-S17427Q, NA; Biggar to O'Sullivan, 7 May 1965, D/T-S17427R, NA.
73   Biggar to D/EA secretary, 7 May 1965, D/T-S17427R, NA. Biggar reported on the views of André Rossi (General Rapporteur of the European Parliament).
74   Lemass speech delivered to the National Convention of Junior Chambers of Commerce of Ireland at the International Hotel in Bray, 1 May 1965, D/T-S17427R,

Notes 411

	NA.
75	Williams, 'Irish foreign policy', p. 143.
76	Lemass speech, 1 May 1965, D/T-S17427R, NA.
77	D/F publication 'Monthly digest of E.E.C. developments and related matters, April, 1965', late May 1965, D/T-S17427R, NA.
78	Nicholson & East, *From the Six*, p. 85.
79	Lemass speech delivered in Dáil Éireann, 13 May 1965, *Dáil debates* vol. 215 cols. 1315-20, D/T-S17427R, NA.
80	Lemass speech delivered in Dáil Éireann, 13 May 1965, *Dáil debates* vol. 215 cols. 1315-20, D/T-S17427R, NA.
81	Lemass speaking in Dáil Éireann, 25 May 1965, *Dáil debates* vol. 215 col. 1909, D/T-S17427R, NA.
82	Irish government cabinet minute, GC11/60, 29 March 1966, 'Eleventh Government Cabinet Minutes GC11/1-GC11/84: 27/4/65-4/8/66', 97/5/1, NA.
83	Lemass speech delivered in Dáil Éireann, 13 May 1965, *Dáil debates* vol. 215 cols. 1315-20, D/T-S17427R, NA.
84	Lemass speech delivered in Dáil Éireann, 13 May 1965, *Dáil debates* vol. 215 cols. 1315-20, D/T-S17427R, NA; Irish government cabinet minute GC12/66, 24 October 1967, 'Twelfth Government Cabinet Minutes GC12/8-GC12/76 3/1/67-19/12/67' 98/5/1, NA. It was only on 24 October 1967 that the finance minister, Charles Haughey, obtained cabinet approval for Ireland to join the GATT.
85	Lemass speech delivered in Dáil Éireann, 13 May 1965, *Dáil debates* vol. 215 cols. 1315-20, D/T-S17427R, NA.
86	Whitaker to McCarthy, 19 July 1965, D/T-S17427S, NA.
87	Brendan Dillon (embassy official, Brussels) to O'Sullivan, 17 August 1965, D/T-S17427S, NA; Robert McDonagh (chargé d'affaires *ad interim*, Copenhagen) to D/EA secretary, 18 August 1965, D/T-S17427S, NA; Kennedy to D/EA secretary, 20 August 1965, D/T-S17427S, NA; Lennon to O'Sullivan, 20 August 1965, D/T-S17427S, NA; Dillon to O'Sullivan, 20 August 1965, D/T-S17427S, NA; Dillon to O'Sullivan, 23 August 1965, D/T-S17427S, NA; Shields to O'Sullivan, 24 August 1965, D/T-S17427S, NA.
88	In response to this latest in a series of EEC emergencies, it was noted in Irish diplomatic reports from Italy, for instance, that: 'It is considered that France cannot afford to let the EEC die'; indeed, similar reports from Luxembourg asserted that: 'The feeling is that the present crisis is not very different from previous crises and that, like those, will blow over'. D/F publication 'Monthly digest of E.E.C. developments and related matters, July, 1965', 26 August 1965, D/T-S17427S, NA.
89	Lemass response to a parliamentary question in Dáil Éireann, 21 July 1965, *Dáil debates* vol. 217 col. 1856, D/T-S17427S, NA.
90	Lemass speech delivered in Dáil Éireann, 13 May 1965, *Dáil debates* vol. 215 col. 1315-20, D/T-S17427R, NA.
91	De Paor, *Divided Ulster*, p. 138.
92	*Irish Times*, 26 May 1965, D/T-S17427R, NA.
93	Biggar to O'Sullivan, 27 May 1965, D/T-S17427R, NA; Lemass speaking in Dáil Éireann, 9 June 1965, *Dáil debates* vol. 216 col. 473, D/T-S17427R, NA.
94	Lemass speaking in Dáil Éireann, 10 June 1965, *Dáil debates* vol. 216 cols. 721-2, D/T-S17427R, NA.
95	Seán Flanagan (junior industry & commerce minister) speaking in Seanad Éireann, 7 July 1965, *Seanad debates* vol. 59 col. 339.
96	J.F.Shields (ambassador, Rome), 15 July 1965, D/T-S17427S, NA.

97	D/F publication 'Monthly digest of E.E.C. developments and related matters, July, 1965', 26 August 1965, D/T-S17427S, NA.
98	D/F publication 'Monthly digest of E.E.C. developments and related matters, June, 1965', 28 July 1965, D/T-S17427S, NA.
99	D/F publication 'Monthly digest of E.E.C. developments and related matters, July, 1965', 26 August 1965, D/T-S17427S, NA.
100	Lemass interview conducted with the *Cork Examiner*, 29 July 1965, D/T-S17427S, NA.
101	Lemass interview conducted with the *Cork Examiner*, 29 July 1965, D/T-S17427S, NA; D/F publication 'Monthly digest of E.E.C. developments and related matters, July, 1965', 26 August 1965, D/T-S17427S, NA.
102	Lemass interview conducted with the *Cork Examiner*, 29 July 1965, D/T-S17427S, NA; D/F publication 'Monthly digest of E.E.C. developments and related matters, July, 1965', 26 August 1965, D/T-S17427S, NA.
103	Lemass interview conducted with the *Cork Examiner*, 29 July 1965, D/T-S17427S, NA; D/F publication 'Monthly digest of E.E.C. developments and related matters, July, 1965', 26 August 1965, D/T-S17427S, NA.
104	Lemass interview conducted with the *Cork Examiner*, 29 July 1965, D/T-S17427S, NA.
105	De Paor, *Divided Ulster*, p. 172.
106	Lemass interview conducted with the *Cork Examiner*, 29 July 1965, D/T-S17427S, NA.
107	D/F publication 'Monthly digest of E.E.C. developments and related matters, July, 1965', 26 August 1965, D/T-S17427S, NA.
108	D/F publication 'Monthly digest of E.E.C. developments and related matters, July, 1965', 26 August 1965, D/T-S17427S, NA.
109	Biggar to O'Sullivan, 27 July 1965, D/T-S17427S, NA. Biggar had been in conversation with Mr.Lucion.
110	Irish government cabinet minute GC11/36, 29 November 1965, 97/5/1, NA.
111	Irish cabinet minute GC11/40, 10 December 1965, 97/5/1, NA.
112	Nicholson & East, *From the Six*, p. 85.
113	Lee, *Ireland*, 353. This quotation originally came from the following: J.Lynch, 'Why Ireland joined', in *Community report* vol. 3 no. 1 January 1983, p. 5.
114	Nicholson & East, *From the Six*, p. 85; Lemass speech delivered in Dáil Éireann, 4 January 1966, *Dáil debates*, vol. 219 cols. 1139-40. Lemass actually went on to review the background to the AIFTA, but it is enough to comment on that here, rather than in the main text. In revealing how this new bilateral arrangement had come about, Frances Nicholson and Roger East have explained that the taoiseach mentioned the unsuccessful OEEC-sponsored FTA negotiations during the second half of the 1950s. In Dáil Éireann, they reveal that he now aired the view that Ireland had decided not to participate in EFTA at that point 'because of our expectations at that time that pressures to open up the EEC to include Britain and other West European countries were likely to build up', an interesting case of history seen in retrospect. At least he had the grace to admit that the Anglo-Irish negotiations which immediately followed EFTA's rejection of Ireland were 'largely unsuccessful'. A quick recap of de Gaulle's veto of the UK, with little or no emphasis on the EEC overlooking Ireland, was followed by him recounting a meeting with Macmillan, and then others with Wilson, in order to remedy the perilous situation in which his government found itself.
115	Nicholson & East, *From the Six*, pp. 85-6; Lemass speech delivered in Dáil Éireann,

4 January 1966, *Dáil debates*, vol. 219 cols. 1140-41.
116 Nicholson & East, *From the Six*, p. 86; Lemass speech delivered in Dáil Éireann, 4 January 1966, *Dáil debates*, vol. 219 cols. 1139-61.
117 Nicholson & East, *From the Six*, p. 86; Lemass speech delivered in Dáil Éireann, 4 January 1966, *Dáil debates*, vol. 219 cols. 1139-61.
118 Nicholson & East, *From the Six*, p. 86; Cosgrave's reply delivered in Dáil Éireann, 4 January 1966, *Dáil debates*, vol. 219 cols. 1162-75.
119 Nicholson & East, *From the Six*, p. 87.
120 Maher, *Tortuous path*, p. 179; Nicholson & East, *From the Six*, pp. 83 & 86-7.
121 Nicholson & East, *From the Six*, pp. 86-7.
122 Lemass reply to a parliamentary question in Dáil Éireann, 30 March 1966, *Dáil debates* vol. 222 cols. 266-9.
123 The OECD, instituted on 14 December 1960 and taking effect on 30 September 1961, originally included the OEEC states, Canada and the US. It listed its main objectives as follows:
- 'à réaliser la plus forte expansion possible de l'économie et de l'emploi et une progression du niveau de vie dans les pays Membres, tout en maintenant la stabilité financière, et contribuer ... au développement de l'économie mondiale';
- 'à contribuer à une saine expansion économique dans les pays Membres, ainsi que non membres, en voie de développement économique';
- 'à contribuer à l'expansion du commerce mondial sur une base multilatérale et non discriminatoire, conformément aux obligations internationales'.

OECD report, 'Irlande 1967', p. 2. This document is freely used in this section, but is noted if referred to specifically; see Chapter 2 for an analysis of *The OEEC's 1956 annual report*.
124 D.McAleese, 'Political independence, economic growth and the role of economic policy', pp. 271-95, in P.J.Drudy (ed.), *Irish studies 2 – Ireland: land, politics and people* (Cambridge: Cambridge University Press, 1982), pp. 275-6. As Dermot McAleese has subsequently written:
> Associated with ... growth in absolute living standards, and explaining much of it, was a sharp decline in the percentage of the labour force working in agriculture ... and a commensurate increase in the percentage working in industry ...
125 Statistics, upon which these opinions are based, were compiled using the following documents: OEEC report, 'Irlande 1961'; OECD report, 'Irlande 1962'; OECD report from March 1963 entitled 'Irlande 1963' (Paris: OCDE, 1963); OECD report from March 1964 entitled 'Irlande 1964' (Paris: OCDE, 1964); OECD report from March 1965 entitled 'Irlande 1965' (Paris: OCDE, 1965); OECD report from February 1966 entitled 'Irlande 1966' (Paris: OCDE, 1966); OECD report, 'Irlande 1967'.
126 Aiken speaking in Seanad Éireann, 18 November 1964, *Seanad debates* vol. 58 col. 46.
127 OECD report, 'Irlande 1967', *passim*. Statistics, upon which these opinions are based, were compiled using the following documents: OEEC report, 'Irlande 1961'; OECD report, 'Irlande 1962'; OECD report, 'Irlande 1963'; OECD report, 'Irlande 1964'; OECD report, 'Irlande 1965'; OECD report, 'Irlande 1966'; OECD report, 'Irlande 1967'; Central Statistics Office, *Ireland: trade and shipping statistics*, *passim*.
128 OECD report, 'Irlande 1967', p. 26.
129 OECD report, 'Irlande 1967', p. 28.

130 OECD report, 'Irlande 1967', p. 17.
131 Lemass reply to a parliamentary question in Dáil Éireann, 18 May 1966, *Dáil debates* vol. 222 col. 1962.
132 R.Foster, 'Orangemen backed by Pope', *Observer*, 12 July 1998. However, in writing that this move by Ireland to the European mainstream was the first instance of this phenonmenon in nearly three hundred years, Roy Foster may be stretching the point. He was making an historical comparison, and in so doing taking a giant leap, between the Battle of the Boyne in 1690 and the 'Republic's enthusiastic adoption of Community membership over the past 20 years'. This modern version of 'Europeanisation' was equated to a war in which a 'grand coalition representing Spain, the Holy Roman Empire, the Netherlands, Sweden, Denmark, Bavaria and Brandenburg as well as Williamite England', at the very least implicitly blessed in their endeavours by the pope, faced up to the 'French-backed Jacobites'. This, Roy Foster holds, marked the previous instance in which Ireland was located in the 'mainstream of European events'.
133 Vaughan, *Twentieth-century Europe*, p. 178.
134 This data originally comes from the following publications: Central Statistics Office, *Ireland: trade and shipping statistics, passim*. It should be noted that the same categories were previously utilised in Chapter 2 under the section headed *1957: Ireland and the European integration question*.
135 The position Ireland faced was not all bad though; Dermot McAleese has added:
> One could conclude that Ireland's diminished dependence on the U.K. as an export market has been replaced by an increased dependence on overseas subsidiaries' capacity to find market outlets in the U.S.A. and continental Europe.

McAleese, 'Political independence', pp. 277 & 281.
136 J.Haughton, 'The historical background', pp. 1-48, in J.W.O'Hagan (ed.), *The economy of Ireland: policy and performance of a small European country* (London: Macmillan, 1995), p. 37; Keogh, *Twentieth-century Ireland*, pp. 290-1.
137 Of course, the Seanad provided other opportunities between the years 1957 to 1966 for Ireland's European integration to be debated, but it appears that this platform was usually neglected. One of the few exceptions arose in the summer of 1961, when one of the senators elected by the university electorate, Patrick Quinlan, endeavoured to draw information from the Irish finance minister, James Ryan, an exchange referred to in Chapter 3 under the heading *Determining factors – Part II: domestic considerations*. Patrick Quinlan speech delivered in Seanad Éireann, 26 July 1961, *Seanad debates* vol. 54 cols. 1329-30 & 1356-80; Quinlan speaking in Seanad Éireann, 27 July 1961, *Seanad debates* vol. 54 cols. 1446-7.
138 Garret FitzGerald speech delivered in Seanad Éireann, 14 July 1966, *Seanad debates* vol. 61 cols. 1833-920.
139 FitzGerald speech delivered in Seanad Éireann, 14 July 1966, *Seanad debates* vol. 61 col. 1852. FitzGerald was referring to an Aiken speech delivered in Dáil Éireann, 11 February 1965, *Dáil debates* vol. 214 col. 205. Referring to a speech that the minister had made in the Dáil the previous year, FitzGerald chided Aiken for saying so little about the EEC with the words: 'not exactly a dynamic utterance, that speech'. The former had a point, because all that the latter had been prepared to say on the EEC was:
> We continue to follow closely the various developments in the European Economic Community through the Embassy in Brussels and by occasional visits by Ministers and officials to the Headquarters of the Organisation.

Ireland's application for membership of the Community still stands and it is the intention of the Government to proceed with it at the earliest appropriate moment.

140 At this time, the taoiseach established a Department of Labour instead of a Department of European Affairs and, in so doing, devolved some responsibilities away from the Department of Industry & Commerce, thus stressing the emphasis of government policy. FitzGerald speech delivered in Seanad Éireann, 6 July 1966, *Seanad debates* vol. 61 col. 1537; FitzGerald speech delivered in Seanad Éireann, 14 July 1966, *Seanad debates* vol. 61 cols. 1833-920.

141 FitzGerald speech delivered in Seanad Éireann, 14 July 1966, *Seanad debates* vol. 61 cols. 1833-920; Aiken reply delivered in Seanad Éireann, 14 July 1966, *Seanad debates* vol. 61 cols. 1873-84. Reference is also made to an Aiken speech delivered in Seanad Éireann, 18 November 1964, *Seanad debates* vol. 58 cols. 47 & 53.

142 Haughton, 'Historical background', p. 37; Irish government cabinet minute GC11/60, 29 March 1966, 97/5/1, NA. In domestic terms, the setting up of An Chomhairle Oiliúna (AnCO) in 1966 was only part of the government's strategy to ready the population – in this case through the provision of industrial training – for the onset of free trade; through the latter decision, Aiken was given cabinet permission to ratify the European Convention on Extradition – which had been signed in Paris back in December 1957 – furnishing another instance of the government's adoption of Europeanising influences as a basis for external policy.

143 McAleese, 'Political independence', pp. 285-6; Williams, 'Irish foreign policy', p. 141. As T.D.Williams has written, this was the period that marked the 'beginning of the negotiations for a voluntary commitment to European integration'.

144 Williams, 'Irish foreign policy', *passim*. T.D.Williams has written that:
> Aiken ... was not much interested in Europe. At one point he had advocated the reduction of Irish diplomatic representation in Western Europe to one single embassy. Lemass and Whitaker went to Europe ... in their effort to seek admission to the EEC; Aiken said little or nothing ... preference for the UN represented his conception of the respective importance of the UN historical role versus that of the European.

In his defence, however, Aiken is on record as having said: 'I am sure that no one who considers the matter carefully would suggest that any of the country's embassies should be closed'. Aiken speaking in Seanad Éireann, 18 November 1964, *Seanad debates* vol. 58 col. 46.

145 Notice of Aiken's absence, 2 June 1964, *Dáil debates* vol. 210 col. 298; FitzGerald, 'Irish neutrality and European integration', p. 4.

Chapter 6

1 R.Munck, *Ireland: nation, state, and class struggle* (Boulder: Westview Press, 1985), pp. 32-4. Paul Bew and Henry Patterson use similar terminology when assessing Ireland's 'position in the international economy as a small, weak and dependent capitalist economy'. Bew & Patterson, *Seán Lemass*, p. 195.

2 Unattributed article, 'Around Europe in 40 years', *Economist*, 31 May 1997. The Luxembourg compromise arose in the first place because de Gaulle viewed the growing influence and power of European institutions as a burgeoning supranational development to the detriment of national independence. He had withdrawn his

	ministers from EEC meetings in 1965 as a consequence, paralysing the process of European integration.
3	B.Laffan, *Integration and co-operation in Europe* (London: Routledge, 1992), p. 195.
4	G.FitzGerald, 'Joining EEC brought heads and incomes up', *Irish Times*, 29 December 1997.
5	Having been found guilty of inciting rebellion, a charge complicated by him being revealed a homosexual, Roger Casement was hanged as a traitor on 3 August 1916. Within a week of the reinstatement to Ireland of his remains, he was reinterred on 1 March 1965. The Irish president delivered an unpretentious oration at a funeral service accorded the status of a full state occasion; but, it had only been made possible by Wilson's acquiescence in releasing the body. In praising Casement, firstly as a native of Ulster, then as a humanitarian and also as a supporter of nationalism, the symbolism of the occasion was not lost on the domestic or international audience. De Valera speech delivered at Glasnevin Cemetery in Dublin, 1 March 1965, entitled 'At Casement's grave', pp. 603-5, in Moynihan (ed.), *Speeches and statements, passim*; A.J.P.Taylor, 'A patriot for one Ireland', pp. 253-9, in C.Wrigley (ed.), *From the Boer War to the Cold War: essays on twentieth-century Europe* (London: Hamish Hamilton, 1995), p. 253; P.Ziegler, *Wilson: the authorised life of Lord Wilson of Rievaulx* (London: Weidenfeld & Nicolson, 1993), pp. 242-3.
6	Upon the flag's reinstatement, the taoiseach wrote to Wilson about the 'gratitude ... and deep appreciation of the Irish Government and people ... The return of the flag can be welcomed as yet another step towards the building of goodwill and the most friendly relations between our two countries'. Lemass concluded by thanking the UK prime minister for the 'speed and the generosity with which your government responded favourably to our representations for the return of the green flag bearing the words "Irish Republic"'. Symbolic gestures sometimes had tangible effects. R.Donnelly, '1916 flag return praised', *Irish Times*, 1/2 January 1997; B.Purcell, 'Lemass praised Wilson for return of 1916 flag', *Irish Independent*, 1/2 January 1997. Both newspaper articles cited a letter from Lemass to Wilson, dated *circa* mid-April 1966.
7	R.Donnelly & R.Borrill, 'British feared IRA violence on anniversary', *Irish Times*, 1/2 January 1997. This newspaper article cited a UK cabinet report from Roy Jenkins (UK home secretary) to the UK government, dated *circa* 6 April 1966.
8	Much of the basic information in this section has been drawn from Gallagher, *Electoral support, passim*. It concentrates on the domestic positions of political parties and how that pertained to Europe, especially on how this situation evolved once Fianna Fáil came back to power in 1957; an introduction to this area was presented in Chapter 1; it is headed *The political landscape and how it pertained to Europe: Part I*.
9	Fine Gael internet publication, 'James Dillon', *http://www.finegael.com/jdillon.ht m* (8 July 1997).
10	Fine Gael internet publication, 'Briefing paper on the history of Fine Gael 1933-1995, including comments on the place of Fine Gael in Irish political life', *http://www.finegael.com/hist.htm* (8 July 1997). It is also very interesting to note that this document concludes by stating that:

> Fine Gael is a party of Europe. In taking our place in a united Europe we will broaden our national identity and partake in a new arrangement where national conflicts will lose their significance. Fine Gael is the only party consistent with the view that Ireland's future is safe within a prosperous

and united Europe. Europe will open new possibilities for the advancement of Ireland, a future where every person has a place.
11 M.Gallagher, *The Irish Labour party in transition, 1957-82* (Manchester: Manchester University Press, 1982), p. 50.
12 Lyons, *Ireland since the Famine*, p. 586.
13 Gallagher, *The Irish Labour party in transition*, p. 130.
14 Labour internet publication, 'Labour: history', *http://www.labour.ie/party/history.htm* (9 July 1997).
15 Hederman, *The road to Europe*, p. 22.
16 Gallagher, *The Irish Labour party in transition*, p. 47.
17 Fianna Fáil internet publication, 'The history of Fianna Fáil', *http://www.iol.ie/fiannafail/his.html* (8 July 1997).
18 Bradley et al, *Stabilization and growth on the European periphery*, p. 10. It is clear that the destination of exports began to alter in the early 1950s, but it was only at the end of the decade that this process began to gather pace; by the mid-1960s, though there was still room for progress, especially in attracting new markets on a consistent and viable basis, it was readily apparent that very real changes were taking place.
19 M.Davenport, 'The economic impact of the EEC', pp. 275-308, in R.T.Griffiths (ed.), *The economic development of the EEC,* vol. 12 of 'The economic development of Europe since 1870' (Cheltenham: Edgar Reference Collection, 1997), p. 280. Originally published as M.Davenport, 'The economic impact of the EEC', pp. 225-8, in A.Boltho (ed.), *The European economy: growth and crisis* (Oxford: Oxford University Press, 1982), p. 230.
20 Bradley et al, *Stabilization and growth on the EC periphery*, p. 10. Thus, this changing composition of Irish exports has been depicted before, although it was to be some years yet until goods other than animals and food were surpassed by non-agricultural goods as the largest percentage of total exports.
21 Davenport, 'The economic impact of the EEC', p. 283 (originally p. 233).
22 P.Bew et al, *The dynamics of Irish politics* (London: Lawrence & Wishart, 1989), p. 96. This view utilised M.Maguire, 'Ireland', pp. 241-384, in P.Flora (ed.), *Growth to limits: the Western European welfare states since World War II*, vol. 2 (Berlin: Walter de Gruyter, 1986), p. 342.
23 Munck, *Ireland*, p. 34. This view utilised B.Probert, *Beyond orange and green: the political economy of the Northern Ireland crisis* (London: Zen, 1979), p. 90.
24 F.Jameson, 'Modernism and imperialism', pp. 43-66, in T.Eagleton et al, *Nationalism, colonialism and literature* (Minneapolis: University of Minnesota Press, 1990), p. 47.
25 D.G.Boyce, *Nationalism in Ireland* (London: Routledge, 1991), pp. 355-6.
26 J.Coakley, 'Fianna Fáil', pp. 191-2, in S.J.Connolly (ed.), *The Oxford companion to Irish history* (Oxford: Oxford University Press, 1998), p. 192; R.J.Lawrence, *The Government of Northern Ireland: public finance and public services, 1921-1964* (Oxford: Clarendon Press, 1965), p. 102; T.Wilson, *Ulster: conflict and consent* (London: Basil Blackwell, 1989), pp. 151-2. By the end of 1966, it should be noted that although the IRA remained in existence, it appears to have been well-monitored and to have had much of its activities curtailed, although the threat remained; it also seems that it was consciously concentrating on political rather than military means to pursue its aims. C.Keena, 'Garda document details IRA/Sinn Fein links', *Irish Times*, 2 January 1998. This newspaper article cited a document from the Irish police commissioner to Lynch, dated *circa* end November 1966; it also utilised a Peter Berry (Irish Department of Justice secretary) *aide-mémoire* to Lynch, dated *circa*

        end November 1966.

27   In 1959, Lemass related his view to a UK audience, subsequently published in a Fianna Fáil pamphlet, that:

> It is, indeed, the simple truth that Ireland is one nation, in its history, in its geography and in its people, entitled to have its essential unity expressed in its political institutions ... Ireland is, by every test, one nation. It is on that essential unity that we found our case for political integration.

However, he followed this assertion up, recognising that there was room for manoeuvre within his image of north-south relations when he asked: 'is it not plain common sense that the two existing political communities in our small island should seek every opportunity of working together in practical matters for their mutual and common good?' Wilson, *Ulster*, p. 4; Farrell, *Seán Lemass*, p. 115. Both quotations were originally taken from S.Lemass, *One nation* (Dublin: Fianna Fáil, 1959), pp. 4-14.

28   J.Magee, *Northern Ireland: crisis and conflict* (London: Routledge & Kegan Paul, 1974), p. 20. This view utilised a Lemass interview with the *Belfast Telegraph*, 23 June 1959 & 9 July 1959. The taoiseach said:

> I have no illusions about the strength of the barriers of prejudice and suspicion which now divide the people, but given good will nothing is impossible. Meanwhile better relations can be fostered by practical co-operation for mutual benefit in the economic sphere ... Even at present, and without reference to any wider issue, we would be prepared to consider and discuss proposals as to how policy might be directed so as to ensure that the economic progress of both parts of the country will be impaired as little as possible by the existing political division.

The previous year, when he ostensibly spoke in Belfast about Ireland's future in a European FTA, he had then advocated his beliefs regarding 'breaking down the barriers of suspicion, antagonism, prejudice and misunderstanding', adding that:

> Anything which tends to break or lower these barriers is good; anything which tends to raise or strengthen them is bad. I think it is as simple as that, and certainly that outlook will continue to settle our policy and determine our actions.

Farrell, *Seán Lemass*, p. 114. This speech was originally delivered by the tánaiste to the Irish Association for Cultural, Social and Economic Relations in Belfast on the subject of a European FTA, 10 February 1958.

29   Magee, *Northern Ireland*, p. 109. This view utilised a Lemass speech delivered in Tralee in July 1963. On this occasion, the taoiseach stated:

> We recognise that the Government and Parliament there [Northern Ireland] exist with the support of the majority of the Six County area – artificial though that area is ... We believe that it is foolish in the extreme that in this island and amongst people of the same race there should persist a desire to avoid contacts, even in respect of matters where concerted action is seen to be beneficial. We would hope that from the extension of useful contacts at every level of activity, a new situation would develop which would permit of wider responsibilities in accord with our desires ...

30   C.C.O'Brien, 'The embers of Easter', pp. 98-111, in Akenson (ed.), *Conor*, p. 102. This article had originally appeared in the *Irish Times*, 7 April 1966.

31   Farrell, *Seán Lemass*, p. 116; T.O'Neill, *The autobiography of Terence O'Neill* (London: Rupert Hart-Davis, 1972), pp. 53 & 83; E.Phoenix, 'O'Neill-Lemass meeting caused unease', *Irish Times*, 3 January 1996; E.Phoenix, 'Files show Labour

32 tried to force O'Neill to introduce radical reforms in north', *Irish Times*, 1/2 January 1997. Brian Farrell's view utilised Lemass speaking in Dáil Éireann, 4 April 1963, *Dáil debates* vol. 201 col. 113.

32 Boyce, *Nationalism in Ireland*, p. 363: Farrell, *Seán Lemass*, p. 114; O'Neill, *The autobiography*, pp. 72-3; Phoenix, *Irish Times*, 3 January 1996; unattributed article, 'Files reveal IRA was stepping up plans for campaign in 1966', *Irish Times*, 1/2 January 1997. Symbolic change was relatively easy to achieve; more and more, for example, Lemass referred to the country as Northern Ireland rather than as the pejorative 'Six Counties'. Substance was a far more difficult task to accomplish.

33 In the previous chapter, the poor state of trade within the island was outlined. On only one occasion in these years did more than 5% of Irish imports come from Northern Ireland; simultaneously, trade figures in the other direction, while not as startling, still demonstrated that the economic barrier was very real.

34 C.O'Halloran, *Partition and the limits of Irish nationalism: an ideology under stress* (Dublin: Gill & Macmillan, 1987), p. xviii; Phoenix, *Irish Times*, 3 January 1996.

35 P.Bew & G.Gillespie, *Northern Ireland: a chronology of the troubles, 1968-1993* (Dublin: Gill & Macmillan, 1993), pp. 1 & 4; Lawrence, *Government of Northern Ireland*, p. 102; Northern Ireland government publication, *Economic development in Northern Ireland* (Belfast: Northern Ireland Command Paper no. 479, 1965); Terence O'Neill (Northern Ireland prime minister) address to the Commonwealth Parliamentary Association at Westminster, 4 November 1968. The latter quotation was taken from Magee, *Northern Ireland*, p. 113. Speaking in 1968 of the meetings held three years previously, O'Neill said:

> ... I decided to take the initiative of meeting ... Lemass. I knew he was a hard-headed realist, prepared to recognize the realities of the situation, and I regarded our meeting as a *de facto*, if not *de jure* recognition of Northern Ireland. We agreed from the start to set political and constitutional issues on one side, and concentrate instead upon promoting economic and other forms of practical co-operation – in tourism, in power supply and so on. This was the basis – the sensible, realistic basis – of my two meetings with Mr Lemass ... What I must emphasize is that, from my point of view, the object of such talks was to promote a decent, sane neighbourly relationship ... But if such a relationship is to flourish, it demands sensible restraint and ... prudence ...

36 Lemass cajoled Northern Ireland's leaders by stating that there were much better ways of dealing with its problems than just by dispatching deputations to London to plead for help, that the 'bread of charity is never very filling', for example, or humoured them by declaring that 'unity means first that – bringing the people together', that it was not a matter of territorial acquisition. Farrell, *Seán Lemass*, p. 115; Bew & Patterson, *Lemass*, p. 11. The former comes from an interview with the *Scotsman* reported in the *Irish Press*, 13 February 1961; the latter quote comes from a retrospective interview with the *Irish Press*, 28 January 1969.

37 O'Brien, 'The embers of Easter', p. 101.

38 Lemass certainly did not agree with one industrialist, for example, who accused Irish trade unions of having 'communistic influence'. The taoiseach's views regarding the economic effects of European integration were regularly vocalised; the government could create a framework, but the attraction of foreign investment and the readaption of indigenous industry had to be effected by the investors, employers and workers. P.O'Morain, 'Lemass warned of union power', *Irish Times*, 1/2 January 1997. This newspaper article cited various communications between Lemass and the W & R

	Jacob chairman during 1966.
39	Wilson, *Ulster*, p. 88.
40	Somewhat presciently, Seamus Heaney wrote of the Northern Ireland situation at that point in time: 'Life goes on, yet people are reluctant to dismiss the possibility of an explosion'. Foster, *Modern Ireland*, p. 585. This Seamus Heaney quotation originally appeared in the *New Statesman*, 1 July 1966.
41	P.O'Morain, 'Nelson Pillar blast created problem', *Irish Times*, 1/2 January 1997.
42	Garvin, 'Wealth, poverty and development', p. 320.
43	De Valera statement delivered on 1916's fiftieth anniversary, 10 April 1966, entitled 'Easter Rising', pp. 605-7, in Moynihan (ed.), *Speeches and statements*, pp. 605-6; O'Halloran, *Partition and the limits*, pp. 186-8. Clare O'Halloran has written that: 'The inflated rhetoric of de Valera and others sat uneasily with the previous year's pragmatism and showed how little Lemass's so-called realism had challenged received wisdom on partition. Uncompromising irredentism had not been officially rejected by Lemass, but merely laid aside in favour of a "softly softly" approach'.
44	Phoenix, *Irish Times*, 3 January 1996. In writing his article reviewing the archival releases on the O'Neill-Lemass meetings, Eamon Phoenix recorded the views of some Unionist MPs, including James Kilfedder. However, summing up the Northern Ireland prime minister's views, he wrote that: 'The main plank of the unionist platform would remain the maintenance of the constitutional position ... this did not mean that it was wrong to discuss matters of common interest with their nearest neighbours on the same island'. Clearly, Lemass was thinking on a different wavelength. John Bowman wrote that the taoiseach suggested to Aiken on 21 January 1966 that, in the future, an Irish unity policy pursued by the Northern nationalists might be better off to recognise the prevailing position, but to espouse its future achievement on a 'federal basis'. J.Bowman, 'Ahern warned Lemass about federal formula', *Irish Times*, 2 January 1998. This newspaper article was based on an exchange of memoranda between Lemass and Aiken, *circa* late January 1966.
45	C.C.O'Brien, 'Two-faced Cathleen', pp. 131-6, in Akenson (ed.), *Conor*, p. 136. This article had originally appeared in the *New York Review of Books*, 29 June 1967.
46	Unattributed article, 'Open borders feared', *Irish Times*, 2 January 1998. This newspaper article cited a Northern Ireland cabinet memorandum, dated 8 June 1967.
47	N.MacQueen, 'European Union', p. 180, in Connolly (ed.), *The Oxford companion*, p. 180.
48	R.B.Finnegan, *Ireland: the challenge of conflict and change* (Boulder: Westview Press, 1983), p. 47. OEEC and OECD estimates put the average rate *per annum* of Irish emigration at 39,400 people in the period from 1951 to 1956, at 43,100 people between 1956 and 1961, and at 16,800 people from 1961 to 1966. OEEC report, 'Irlande 1961'; OECD report, 'Irlande 1962'; OECD report, 'Irlande 1967'.
49	A.Matthews, *The common agricultural policy and the less developed countries* (Dublin: Gill & Macmillan, 1985), p. 198. This view originally utilised Crotty, *Irish agricultural production, passim*. The former writes of the 'consequences of capitalist production relations in nineteenth century Irish agriculture when labour made surplus by the move to land-extensive more profitable cattle production was forced to emigrate'; the latter gets straight to the heart of the matter, unequivocally stating that: 'Historically, the expansion of cattle production in Ireland has not been attended by happy results ... socially or economically'.
50	Foster, *Modern Ireland*, p. 579.
51	P.Keatinge, *European security: Ireland's choices* (Dublin: Institute of European Affairs, 1996), p. 111. Elsewhere, he has written: 'Official political commitments to

subscribe to a hypothetical EC defence policy started with the government of Seán Lemass'. P.Keatinge, 'Ireland and European neutrality after the Cold War', pp. 157-75, in R.J.Hill & M.Marsh (eds), *Modern Irish democracy: essays in honour of Basil Chubb* (Dublin: Irish Academic Press, 1993), p. 172.

52 B.McSweeney, 'Ireland and European integration', pp. 187-93, in *Studies* vol. 79 no. 314 1990, p. 191. He added his view that:

> For most of our history, the principal end in view was reunification. Our neutrality was never absolute or permanent and we negotiated entry into the EC on that condition. Since our first application to join ... neutrality has been conditional upon our readiness to join an integrated defence in the future ... Our non-membership of a military alliance was a policy followed by successive governments because domestic public opinion seemed to favour it and, in the delicate balance of power in the Dail [sic], no party could afford to tamper with it. Neither could they afford to affirm it unconditionally, because it was clear to every government that such an affirmation would have serious consequences for our capacity to negotiate economic benefits in the EC.

53 Unattributed article, 'New order forces Irish "rethink" on security', *Irish Times*, 27 May 1996; P.Cullen, 'Congo recalled as Irish watch battle for Zaire', *Irish Times*, 19 April 1997; T.Farrell, 'An Irishman's diary', *Irish Times*, 5 June 1997; P.Keatinge, 'Visitors may marvel at "Jekyll and Hyde" approach to European security', *Irish Times*, 2 July 1996; N.MacQueen, 'Foreign policy', pp. 203-4, in Connolly (ed.), *The Oxford companion*, p. 204; N.MacQueen, 'Neutrality', pp. 385-6, in Connolly (ed.), *The Oxford companion*, p. 386. Patrick Keatinge was using this 'Jekyll and Hyde' analogy in a contemporary context, but it equally applies historically to Lemass's policy – reality versus the symbolic. Under the aegis of the UN, Ireland's neutrality was progressive throughout the late 1950s and immediately beyond. According to Norrie MacQueen, 'neutrality found a more comprehensible diplomatic expression' by that time, a 'reassertion of the international activism of the 1930s'. She added that the country:

> ... emerged as a considerable 'middle power' player in UN diplomacy. Positions were taken which were frequently at odds with 'western' interests on issues such as the representation of China ... and nuclear disengagement ... The question of neutrality featured prominently in the national debates over entry to Europe in the 1960s ...

Neutrality did not hinder Ireland's peace-keeping activities either, but appeared to encourage them; this was most apparent in the Congo during the early 1960s when Irish troops were sent there under the UN banner.

54 D.Keogh, 'The diplomacy of "dignified calm": an analysis of Ireland's application for membership of the EEC, 1961-1963', pp. 81-101, in the *Journal of European integration history* vol. 3 no. 1 1997, p. 82.

55 Greenwood (ed.), *Britain and European integration since the Second World War*, 147. This French government move occurred in March 1966.

56 Boyce, *Nationalism in Ireland*, p. 19.

57 Bew & Patterson, *Seán Lemass*, pp. 191-7; T.Garvin, *The evolution of Irish nationalist politics* (Dublin: Gill & Macmillan, 1981); J.Lee, 'Searching for lost European civilisation amid the free market', *Irish Times*, 2 July 1996. The latter argues that in the 1950s the 'founding fathers sought to transcend nationalism by Europeanism'; under Lemass, Ireland also made this transition, but he was certainly less convinced about it than he was about the possibilities of economic advancement

422 Protectionism to liberalisation

58   within the context of European free trade and integration.
     Farrell, *Seán Lemass*, p. 109.
59   Crotty, *Irish agricultural production, passim*; Irish government publication, *Second programme for economic expansion*, p. 22. Raymond Crotty states, for example, that in 1963 the volume of net agricultural production was IR£143m as opposed to IR£130.7m in 1957. Even considering that inflation was relatively low, this performance does not suggest any radical economic advancement in terms of yield. Seamus Sheehy, an agricultural economics professor, wrote subsequently about the various attractions in EEC membership of the CAP, but did not neglect to mention the UK becoming increasingly self-sufficient because of the same reason. FitzGerald, *Irish Times*, 29 December 1997; S.Sheehy, 'CAP may finally ensure viable rural economy', *Irish Times*, 30 December 1997.
60   Crotty, *Irish agricultural production, passim*. Raymond Crotty states that the volume of net industrial production in 1963 was IR£211m as opposed to IR£124.2m in 1957; for the tertiary sector these figures read IR£284m and IR£182.7 respectively. In contrast to agriculture, this was the kind of achievement in terms of yield that does suggest radical economic advancement.
61   Bradley *et al*, *Stabilization and growth on the EC periphery*, p. 10.
62   Kennedy, *Modern industrialisation*, p. 5.
63   Foster, *Modern Ireland*, p. 569.
64   In 1957, unemployment in Ireland stood at 78,000 but, by 1966, with unemployment continuing to fall and confidence high, the National Industrial and Economic Council (NIEC) was outlining the possible choices that might credibly lead to full employment. In contrast, the employment rate that O'Neill faced upon taking office was 11.2% for Northern Ireland; his country had not faced such serious economic problems since the Great Depression of the early 1930s. Obviously, the two countries sharing the island were going in totally different directions in economic terms. R.Deutsch & V.Magowan, *Northern Ireland, 1968-73: a chronology of events, 1968-71, vol. 1* (Belfast: Blackstaff, 1973), p. 3; Kennedy, *Economic development*, pp. 71-2; Keogh, 'Diplomacy of "dignified calm"', p. 83.
65   Foster, *Modern Ireland*, p. 582.
66   Farrell, *Seán Lemass*, pp. 98-124; Keogh, *Twentieth-century Ireland*, pp. 291-5.
67   Magee, *Northern Ireland*, p. 162; UK government publication, *The future of Northern Ireland: a paper for discussion* (London: Her Majesty's Stationery Office, 1972).
68   J.C.Beckett, *A short history of Ireland* (London: Hutchinson, 1975), p. 185.
69   Cardinal Agagianian to de Valera, 8 July 1961, 98/1/62, NA. Obviously, de Valera's main hope was that Ireland's celebrations of Saint Patrick would reflect well on the country in the Vatican's eyes; in this he was not disappointed. He was also keen that Ireland's renown as a Catholic country would be reinforced by such symbols as the number of cardinals present at the celebrations; in turn, of course, this occasion presented an excellent opportunity for the Irish people to show their spiritual devotion. D/UhÉ secretary to Cardinal John D'Alton's secretary, 24 December 1960, 98/1/62, NA.
70   Keogh, *Ireland and the Vatican, passim*; Whyte, *Church and state, passim*. Cooperation between Ireland and Northern Ireland was aided in many ways by Cardinal William Conway, the Archbishop of Armagh and Primate of All-Ireland between September 1963 and April 1977. Dermot Keogh has written:
> Both Dublin and London had been quite happy with the firm leadership offered the nationalist community by the late cardinal. He had been

unequivocal in his condemnation of physical force, nationalism and the murderous campaign of the ... IRA ...
In his article, John Bowman paid particular attention to the work of Brian Lenihan, Irish justice minister, who introduced some modest reforms in regard to the censorship of films and literary works. J.Bowman, 'Lenihan saw laws as an embarrassment', *Irish Times*, 2 January 1997. This article referred to a Lenihan memorandum for the cabinet, undated *circa* 1965.

71 FitzGerald, *Irish Times*, 29 December 1997.
72 De Valera, 'Easter Rising', p. 606.
73 E.Mac Aogáin, 'Identità culturale e linguistica nella nuova Europa: prospettiva dall'Irlanda', pp. 59-66, in M.Pinna (ed.), *L'Europa delle diversità: identità e culture alle soglie del terzo millenio* (Milan: Francoangeli, 1993), *passim*.
74 Ireland – not Éire – remains the official name of the country in English, both in everyday language usage and in the context of international organisations. Article N°4 of Bunreacht na hÉireann provides for this specific naming; it reads: 'The name of the State is Éire, or in the English language, Ireland'. Of course, by Article N°25.4.6, the Irish language version of the constitution prevails in the case of conflict; but, as the name of the state in English is 'Ireland', it is listed alphabetically in agreements and treaties according to the formula furnished in the constitution and through international practice. This was not necessarily the case in Ireland's earliest dealings with Europe. For instance, in the statute which provided the basis for the Council of Europe, it was referred to as the 'Irish Republic', although in much the same way as France was termed the 'French Republic' and Italy as the 'Italian Republic'. However, this practice was to change. Indeed, the Irish foreign minister, David Andrews, reasserted that fact in a written reply to a question from Trevor Sargent (Green Party) in Dáil Éireann, remarking that it was 'longstanding practice to use the English-language version of the name of the State in international organisations. This practice was followed on entry to the European Communities in 1973 and Ireland is listed accordingly'. MacBride speaking in Dáil Éireann, 13 July 1949, *Dáil debates* vol. 117 col. 746; unattributed *Irish Times* article, 'Cá háit sin?', http:// www.irish-times.com/irish-times/paper/teangabeo/beo4.html (3 June 1998); J.M.Kelly, *The Irish constitution* (Dublin: Jurist Publishing, 1980), *passim*.
75 N.Atkinson, *Irish education: a history of educational institutions* (Dublin: Allen Figgis, 1969), pp. 172 & 200; J.Coolahan, *Irish education: its history and structure* (Dublin: Institute of Public Administration, 1981), pp. 132 & 165. The former view utilised a Patrick Hillery (education minister) article published in the *European teacher* no. 1 1962, pp. 7-9. Seminal documents from this era included: Irish government publication, *Investment in education: report of the survey team* (Dublin: Stationery Office, 1966); Irish government publication, *Investment in education: annexes and appendices* (Dublin: Stationery Office, 1966).
76 Finnegan, *Ireland*, p. 63. This view utilised T.Gray, *The Irish answer* (London: Heinemann, 1966), p. 340.
77 Fianna Fáil party publication, 'Fianna Fáil manifesto 1932', reproduced in Dunphy, *Class, power and the Fianna Fail party*, p. ii; Fianna Fáil party publication, 'Fianna Fáil manifesto, 9 February 1932', pp. 188-9, in A.O'Day & J.Stevenson, *Irish historical documents since 1800* (Dublin: Gill & Macmillan, 1992); P.Murtagh, 'He let down party and country, blame is his alone', *Irish Times*, 12 July 1997. Note that J.J.Lee used the word 'malaise' to describe the post-war decade, applying 'drift' to the 1970s and beyond. Lee, *Ireland*, *passim*.
78 S.O'Faoláin, *The Irish: a character study* (Old Greenwich: Devin-Adair, 1949), pp.

	173-80. Both characteristics were picked out as being responsible for holding Irish people – in this case, writers specifically – back in the past. Lemass and Whitaker were part of the process which broke this mould.
79	This F.Scott Fitzgerald quotation comes from McAleese, 'Europe – the challenges of the new millennium', http://www.iue.it/general/jms.htm (10 February 1999).
80	Keogh, 'Diplomacy of "dignified calm"', p. 86. Dermot Keogh suggests that Lemass was actually 'not an easy or enthusiastic convert to a free trade policy' but, once convinced, that he became a devotee.
81	Foster, *Modern Ireland*, pp. 540 & 577-8.
82	J.Hanna, 'Always with us', pp. 101-2, in *Books Ireland* no. 212 April 1998; G.Hussey, *Ireland today* (London: Penguin, 1995), p. 12. The former appeared as a book review of F.Ó Muircheartaigh (ed.), *Ireland in the coming times: essays to celebrate T.K.Whitaker's 80 years* (Dublin: Institute of Public Administration, 1998).
83	Boyce, *Nationalism in Ireland*, pp. 356-7; J.Tratt, *The Macmillan government and Europe: a study in the process of policy development* (London: Macmillan, 1996), p. 8. According to D.George Boyce, 'Lemass took up the Whitaker report, and used his power and skills to hurry along the civil servants, dispel gloom and defeatism, and convince workers and employers of the need for planning'. He subsequently added the opinion that he 'was helped by the general economic climate of the 1960s; and the return in 1965 of ... an adverse balance of payments, together with inflation and disappointing agricultural performance showed that the "economic miracle" was by no means accomplished for all time ... Lemass showed that he could not only replace de Valera in 1959, but keep the party in office in 1961 and then lead it to an impressive victory in 1965'.
	Writing on the Macmillan cabinet and government, Jacqueline Tratt's views might equally apply to the Lemass-Whitaker axis; she has written:

> The prime minister, although notionally first among equals, traditionally enjoys the facility of gathering about him ... like-minded ministers and advisers for the purpose first, of developing a policy, and secondly, of deciding how best to present that policy to the rest of the cabinet. Many of the prime minister's closest advisers are senior civil servants who have usually had many years' experience of government and often know, better than their political masters, what is and is not politically, socially and economically possible. Serving at the heart of the government, the work of senior officials in developing government policy, particularly in this case, should not be underestimated.

This does not take much adaption to see how the taoiseach and a senior finance civil servant could have worked so well together. Firstly, although the cabinet had to reflect the different views in Fianna Fáil, there is no doubt but that Lemass was in charge. By 1959, his leadership was no longer a questioned inheritance. With Lynch at the taoiseach's old post in industry & commerce and Aiken safely tucked away in New York, Lemass was able to develop Ireland's European policy and to win over or marginalise any detractors, such as his finance minister. Aided by the latter's secretary, Lemass was able to develop a credible policy which, if questioned because of a lack of progress or too rapid a development, was ignored or passed over.

84	Farrell, *Seán Lemass*, pp. 116-7; O'Neill, *The autobiography*, pp. 68-73.
85	Other examples existed. See, for instance, the relationship between de Valera and the pre-war and war-time Irish external affairs secretary, Joseph P.Walshe, in Keogh, *Twentieth-century Ireland, passim*; A.Nolan, *Joseph Walshe and the management of Irish foreign policy, 1922-1946: a study in diplomatic and administrative history*

	(Cork: unpublished UCC PhD, 1998), *passim*.
86	R.Fanning, *The Irish Department of Finance, 1922-58* (Dublin: Institute of Public Administration, 1978), p. 606.
87	Kennedy, 'Irish economy transformed', p. 41.
88	Fanning, *Irish Department of Finance*, p. 608.
89	Fanning, *Irish Department of Finance*, pp. 609-10; Keogh, 'Diplomacy of "dignified calm"', *passim*. Whitaker references come from a file of official and semi-official correspondence to which both Ronan Fanning and Dermot Keogh had access in compiling their separate analyses.
90	T.Barnard, 'Pigs, bogs and baileys', *Times Literary Supplement*, 5 June 1998. This article originally appeared as a book review of Connelly (ed.), *The Oxford companion*.
91	Laffan, *Integration and co-operation*, pp. 195-6.
92	Farrell, *Seán Lemass*, p. 110.
93	Maher, *The tortuous path*, pp. 195 & 199.
94	Irish government minute G11/21, 7 September 1965, 'Minutes of Governmental Meetings G11/1-G11/84 Minutes: Eleventh Government 21 April 1965 – 15 November 1966', 97/4/1, NA.
95	Gerard Woods took over from Biggar as ambassador to Luxembourg after a government decision on 4 October 1966. In the meantime, as part of a diplomatic reshuffle, Thomas Commins was moved from the Holy See to Paris, Denis McDonald from Paris to Rome (and Ankara), and Joseph Shields from Rome to the Holy See; in turn, Biggar took over as Ireland's new ambassador to Austria and Switzerland. Irish government minute G11/75, 13 September 1966, 97/4/1, NA; Irish government minute G11/78, 4 October 1966, 97/4/1, NA.
96	Maher, *The tortuous path*, p. 199; P.Smyth, 'Dublin seeks Euratom treaty amendments', *Irish Times*, 1 October 1996. It is interesting to note in the context of the European Communities, which in 1966 were well on their way to being merged one year later, that the term EEC was used in Ireland for many years to come to mean this new expanded and inclusive entity.
97	Maher, *The tortuous path*, p. 200.
98	Fanning, *Irish Department*, p. 611; Irish government publication, *The accession of Ireland to the European Communities* (Dublin: Stationery Office, 1972). This view was based on a memorandum prepared in 1975 for Ronan Fanning by the Department of Finance entitled 'Principal developments since 1960'.
99	R.Donnelly, 'French veto induced British threats', *Irish Times*, 2 January 1998. This newspaper article cited various George Brown (UK foreign minister) memoranda, dated *circa* 30 April 1967.
100	O'Neill, *The autobiography*, pp. 90-1. O'Neill met with Willi Brandt towards the end of March 1967.
101	Donnelly, *Irish Times*, 2 January 1998.
102	FitzGerald, *Irish Times*, 29 December 1997.
103	P.Foot, *The politics of Harold Wilson* (Harmondsworth: Penguin, 1968), pp. 233-5. It is also interesting to note that, after Lemass's resignation from office, the tánaiste and external affairs minister, Frank Aiken, was no longer listed as a member of the government at the front of the *Dáil debates* due to what might be generously termed as a 'typographical error', although he did make it into the index; perhaps the compilers of these parliamentary reports mistook his absences from the chamber as evidence of the fact that the more important aspects of Irish foreign relations – bilateral relations with the UK and European integration – were mostly being dealt

with through the new taoiseach's office, as they had been with his predecessor. General elections were held on 5 March 1957, 4 October 1961, and 7 April 1965 respectively. As a consequence, four governments were formed during the period under review, the first led by Éamon de Valera, the others by Seán Lemass, who took over as taoiseach on 23 June 1959 upon the former's resignation from office; when the latter resigned, Jack Lynch took over to form a new government on 10 November 1966. Note that by Article 28.1° of Bunreacht na hÉireann, the government should comprise of no more than fifteen members and, thus, the amalgamation of ministries or the doubling up of departments under a minister was one way of juggling these figures. Article 28.11.1° of the constitution declares that all the other members of the government are also deemed to have resigned from office upon the taoiseach's resignation, even if they still continue to carry out their duties until their successors have been appointed; effectively, most of the ministers held onto to their posts when Lynch became taoiseach, although there were some changes.

104   J.Bowman, 'Lynch went to London to ascertain Britain's policy and progress on EEC', *Irish Times*, 1/2 January 1997. This newspaper article cited a Hugh McCann (Irish external affairs secretary) memorandum compiled after the summit, *circa* 19 December 1966.
105   Bowman, 'Lynch went to London', *Irish Times*, 1/2 January 1997.
106   Bowman, 'Lynch went to London', *Irish Times*, 1/2 January 1997.
107   According to the Irish government, these were the principal grievances of the Catholic community and the nationalist population in Northern Ireland. Using the example of the additional funding being provided on the basis of 'positive discrimination' for the education of minority traditions in Ireland, as well as Ireland's endeavours to promote assimilated schooling, the taoiseach urged the UK prime minister to push O'Neill to introduce a similar programme. He stated that: 'Anything that can be done to reduce political and religious discrimination in Northern Ireland would considerably help to achieve a relaxation in tension'. However, the new taoiseach acknowledged that the UK prime minister had taken various concrete steps to help to improve north-south relations, as well as Anglo-Irish relations, and that he favoured the policy of 'functional co-operation' established by his predecessor. It also should be noted that one of his briefing documents for the bilateral meeting had listed:
  • the negotiation, conclusion and enactment of the AIFTA;
  • the return of Casement's remains for reburial in Ireland;
  • the reinstatement of the 1916 flag;
  • 'the pressure, public and private, brought to bear on the Stormont regime'.
Information on this last item was hazy, so Lynch was advised not to cite this listing, just to be aware of its significance. Bowman, 'Lynch went to London', *Irish Times*, 1/2 January 1997.
108   Bowman, 'Lynch went to London', *Irish Times*, 1/2 January 1997; E.Phoenix, 'O'Neill's policy begins to go badly wrong', *Irish Times*, 1/2 January 1997; unattributed article, 'Irish concerns raised in Lynch-Wilson meeting', *Irish Times*, 1/2 January 1997.
109   J.Downey, 'Second-guessing UK over Europe proved difficult', *Irish Independent*, 1/2 January 1997. In the spring of 1967, the UK foreign secretary, George Brown, embarked with Wilson upon a tour of the European capitals. It soon became apparent that, under Labour, the UK was becoming very serious about reattempting to join the

EEC. G.Brown, *In my way: the political memoirs of Lord George-Brown* (London: Victor Gollancz, 1971), pp. 205-6.
110 R.Burke, 'Treaty strengthens EU in important areas', *Irish Times*, 2 October 1997. During his tenure as foreign minister, Ray Burke wrote this article in favour of the Amsterdam Treaty.

Conclusions

1 P.Keatinge & B.Laffan, 'Ireland in international affairs', pp. 200-21, in J.Coakley & M.Gallagher (eds), *Politics in the Republic of Ireland* (Galway: PSAI Press, 1992), pp. 200-5.
2 Keatinge & Laffan, 'Ireland in international affairs', pp. 202-5 & 219.
3 McAleese, 'Political independence, economic growth and the growth of economic policy', pp. 289-90.
4 N.Davies, *Europe: a history* (Oxford: Oxford University Press, 1996), p. 1088.
5 Sutherland, 'Ireland', p. 243.
6 Moravcsik, *The choice for Europe*, pp. 5 & 162-3.
7 Aiken speech delivered in Seanad Éireann, 18 November 1964, *Seanad debates* vol. 58 cols. 51-4.
8 Bradley et al, *Stabilization and growth on the EC periphery*, p. 12.
9 R.T.Griffiths & S.Ward (eds), *Courting the Common Market: the first attempt to enlarge the European Community, 1961-1963* (London: Lothian Foundation Press, 1996), p. 4.
10 P.Keatinge, 'From community to union', pp. 2-9 & 160, in P.Keatinge (ed.), *Maastricht and Ireland: what the treaty means* (Dublin: Institute of European Affairs, 1992), p. 3 (author's italics).
11 D.Dinan, *Historical dictionary of the European Community* (Metuchen: Scarecrow Press, 1993), pp. 137-8; Keatinge, 'From community to union', pp. 3-4; McAleese, 'Political independence, economic growth and the growth of economic policy', p. 278. According to Desmond Dinan, the economic determinants 'had to do with the expected windfall for Irish farmers of participation in the ... CAP'. Additionally, there were a 'host of other benefits, mostly in the form of grants and loans, that would accrue to Ireland'. However, he has also written that the 'element of political opportunism, by contrast, consisted of the anticipated impact of Community membership on Anglo-Irish relations'. Other than those dubious grounds for hope, the political price remained unknown; it was nonetheless clear that Ireland was happy to pay whatever that turned out to be, once the economic gain proved worthwhile.
12 This section is based on the presentation entitled 'Why did Ireland's first application fail?' given at the *Research workshop on the failure of Community expansion, 1961-63*.